α

031BBCP

KLEN

Rem 91 160 —
(B. O, O,)

45 —
——
RO

HANDBOOK of CRIMINAL JUSTICE EVALUATION

HANDBOOK of CRIMINAL JUSTICE EVALUATION

edited by
Malcolm W. Klein and Katherine S. Teilmann

SAGE PUBLICATIONS   Beverly Hills   London

For information address:

SAGE Publications, Inc.
275 South Beverly Drive
Beverly Hills, California 90212

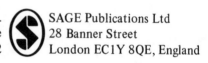

SAGE Publications Ltd
28 Banner Street
London EC1Y 8QE, England

Printed in the United States of America

Library of Congress Cataloging in Publication Data

Main entry under title:

Handbook of criminal justice evaluation.

    Bibliography: p.
    Includes index.
    1. Criminal justice, Administration of—
Evaluation—Addresses, essays, lectures.
2. Evaluation research (Social action programs)—
Addresses, essays, lectures.   I. Klein, Malcolm W.
II. Teilmann, Katherine S.
HV7921.H33   364'.072   80-16909

ISBN 0-8039-1052-5

FIRST PRINTING

CONTENTS

INTRODUCTION

It is not common practice for an editors' introduction to constitute a personal statement. However, the format and content of this handbook are a direct reflection of the editors' views, so it is best that we describe these at the outset.

We were alerted to the need for this statement by the very first response to the publisher's announcement of the *Handbook.* We received a phone call from a surprisingly incensed researcher who wanted to know (1) how on earth the announced contributors were selected, (2) why the contributors were not "representative" of the work currently being done in criminal justice evaluation, and (3) why he or his particular colleagues had not been invited to contribute, given their very substantial level of funding from the Law Enforcement Assistance Administration.

The answers stem from our view of what is currently needed in a major statement on criminal justice evaluation. We believe an overview of what is now being done is less important than a careful consideration of major *issues* to be faced. Thus, no attempt at "representativeness" has been undertaken. Further, we feel that these issues provide a more useful framework than would a set of substantive categories such as police/prosecution/courts/corrections or prevention/enforcement/prosecution/rehabilitation. Finally, we have been very concerned with the audiences for this handbook, and have oriented our efforts less toward displaying evaluations and more toward explaining issues and reviewing trends. In this sense, we have tried to develop a "teaching handbook."

Given this concern for issues rather than for representation of work done or traditional content areas, and given our sensitivity to the need to present these issues to a variety of evaluation audiences, the selection of contributing authors became an admittedly personal enterprise. The editors sought the counsel of a small group of advisors in whom they had personal confidence. The advisors gave generously of their time in suggesting both content and contributors.[1] The outline for the *Handbook* was then developed and reactions again obtained from the advisors and from the initial group of invited contributors.

Our aim in this process, and in the selection of contributors, was to seek not only demonstrated competence in *doing* evaluation, but also to seek those with experience and wisdom in *explaining issues* in evaluation. The editors made the selections on these bases, and not to represent disciplines or particular facets of the criminal justice system. In this sense, it is almost happenstance that disciplines represented by the contributors include sociology, political science, psychology, economics, operations research, criminology, and the law. By contrast, there is no happenstance that sociologists are the predominant group among the contributors.

In selecting and organizing the chapters of this handbook, we have been guided by two major foci: concern with conceptualizing criminal justice evaluation and concern for the divergent and sometimes opposed audiences of evaluation.

As to the first concern, conceptualization, there are several points to be made. First, we are firmly of the opinion that the most valuable evaluations are those that can draw conclusions about *idea systems,* be these theories, paradigms, or conceptual frameworks. This opinion also means that we have been dissatisfied with a major portion of the evaluation literature, for much of this literature is insufficiently concerned with conceptual issues. It is not surprising that the reader will find many of the chapters in this handbook to mirror this fundamental interest in the conceptual or theoretical basis of evaluation research.

Likewise, we are interested in the relationship between evaluation research and more traditional forms of social science research, both basic and applied. It is clear that evaluation research is to some extent different—otherwise, why a handbook? But it is equally clear to us that much of evaluation research has suffered by inattention to the basic logics associated with more traditional endeavors. Evaluation research is a development, not a new phenomenon. Accordingly, many of our contributors were selected because of their background in both evaluation and traditional research and because of their appreciation for the contribution of the one to the other.

Also, we have found a number of evaluation proposals and projects in the criminal justice field attempt to divorce content from method. Evaluation paradigms and methods cannot be divorced from the substantive content of the field; there is an interplay between content and method which requires the evaluator to be conversant with issues of criminal justice. Methods cannot be overlays. Thus, the reader will find that a number of the *Handbook's* chapters reflect this content/method connection.

Finally, under this heading we admit to a genuine concern that a technological imbalance is developing in criminal justice evaluation. New developments within the field, along with importations of advancing technologies from other disciplines, threaten to stamp what is not new as of lesser value. Some of the chapters solicited for the *Handbook* are intended to present what is new, but we have chosen the writers of those chapters specifically because of their understanding of the place of the "new" within the constraints of the "old" as the latter is reflected in issues, content, and method. Again, our aim is to stress the conceptual component of the evaluation enterprise so that developing technologies derive their value not from their novelty or abstruseness, but from their capacity to illuminate idea systems.

Much of the above can be summarized operationally by applying a simple test to every evaluation research proposal and project. The test is to ask of each decision made, *why* it was made. If there is a coherent idea system underlying the evaluation, then the answer to each *why* should derive from that idea system, or be explainable as an exception thereto. Decisions on geographic areas, sampling procedures, data collection procedures, time periods, practitioner/research feedback mechanisms, and projected statistical models are all examples of decisions relatable to the underlying idea system. If readers of a proposal or site-visitors of a project can be shown how each decision is related to (preferably, determined by) the idea system leading to the project, then they can have some genuine faith that the project will pay off, that its conclusions will have both short-range and long-range value. Where the test has consistently been failed, worthwhile projects are hard to find. Good evaluation emanates from good ideas and, one hopes, permits their modification and improvement.

Our second major focus, beyond this fundamental concern with conceptualizing evaluations, is an interest in the audiences of evaluation efforts. Perhaps the greatest divergence of opinions concerning evaluation research is a function of this one aspect of its intrinsic nature, namely that it has divergent audiences. In the past, research tended to be carried out by scientists *for* scientists or by agency personnel *for* agency personnel. The first stressed discipline-building while the second stressed short-term agency needs and accountability. In between were occasional one-way contracts (scientists consult in terms of agency goals) analogous to engineering. In all three paradigms, action and research were typically well separated.

But when action and research meld, then values face off against values and one's audiences are forced out into the open. Scientists worry about being "seduced" by agency concerns; agencies complain of the impractical concerns of scientists. The chapter by Ward Edwards (and the implicit confrontation with companion chapters in Part II) is based, conceptually, upon this very fact of conflicting audiences and values and the conclusion that evaluation must somehow involve recognition of all relevant audiences.

Indeed, Edwards's approach might well appear to be an appropriate solution. Yet the other paradigm illustrators in Part II stop short of this, in a sense allow *their* values to direct their selection of pertinent audiences. And so the issue is joined and the problem of multiple audiences highlighted.

If there is no general consensus on values and audiences, then perhaps more time must be spent in making explicit the audience dimension in the evaluation enterprise. We hope the *Handbook* will serve this function by itself being responsive to several diverse audiences. Specifically, we intend the *Handbook* to speak to six of *our* audiences.

First among these, and in the current state of criminal justice evaluation perhaps the most important, are the funders of evaluation. At the federal, state, and local levels, funders sometimes do and almost always can establish the criteria by which evaluation proposals, projects, and reports are to be judged. So far, the funders deserve more blame than praise, because short-range, often politically determined, criteria have permitted the design and completion of conceptually limited criminal justice evaluations. There is a base on which to build; the *Handbook* is in part designed to encourage the broadening of that base.

The second audience consists of the policy makers in the legislatures and executive offices of our political structure who are increasingly calling for accountability in criminal justice operations. We hope they will become more sensitive to the complexities of achieving worthwhile evaluation results and more insistent that those who fund and monitor evaluation efforts will demand competent efforts (in our terms, of course). Many chapters in the *Handbook* contribute to the demonstration that competency can be achieved.

The third audience, who along with policy makers are the usual "consumers" of evaluation, are the practitioners who make the system work. At both the line and command levels, police, prosecutors, defense lawyers, judges, correctional officials, and various community agents and leaders have evidenced their sincere desire to achieve more than has yet been achieved. They share the frustration of high hopes and disappointing results. They resent our crime rates and our seeming inability to effect significant change. And with most competent evaluations consistently demonstrating the ineffectiveness of their target programs, practitioners are understandably suspicious of the evaluation enterprise. Effective action/research collaboration is severely damaged by such suspicions; and better understanding of the evaluation process may be a first step in overcoming practitioner reticence to be evaluated and to contribute substantially to the process.

Fourth among our audiences—and here we betray a slight bias—are the nonacademic evaluators who currently comprise a substantial portion of the evaluation community. They are part of a rapidly growing industry which understandably tends to be responsive to the market (i.e., the funders, our first audience). In our view, they have sometimes been overly responsive, settling for funder-established goals ("deliverables" is a common term for limited final reports) when more conceptually oriented products would be in their own long-range interests. Evaluation research, as a prideful profession, will develop in direct proportion to the extent that evaluators serve their funding masters and the development of their disciplines at one and the same time.

The fifth audience consists of our academic colleagues, some of whom have and some of whom have not as yet seen the value of evaluation research opportunities for building the knowledge base of their disciplines. There is, among some, a disdain for research smacking of an applied or a policy nature. Among others, there is simply not enough familiarity with the issues and opportunities of evaluation research. For both groups, we hope the *Handbook* will serve to enlist their talents and to alert them to both the problems and the procedures for building their professions through participation in evaluation programs.

And finally there is our favorite audience, the students, formal and informal, of evaluation research. It rests upon them to determine the future of the field. We have tried very hard to bring together in this handbook a great deal of the experience of others upon which students can build their own incursions into the evaluation arena. Whether theirs is a problem focus or a discipline focus, we urge them to search these pages for the excitement and challenge to their interests that we find intrinsic to criminal justice evaluation.

NOTE

1. We acknowledge with pleasure and gratitude the counsel of Albert Reiss, Rita James Simon, Sheldon Messinger, Lloyd Ohlin, Maynard Erickson, Ilene Nagel, Alfred Blumstein, Richard Berk, Saleem Shah, James F. Short, Jr., Marvin Wolfgang, Solomon Kobrin, Ward Edwards, LaMar T. Empey, Daniel Glaser, and the late Robert Martinson.

PART I

ON THE STATE OF THE ART

Malcolm W. Klein and Katherine S. Teilmann

The old joke describes the meeting of two friends: "How's your wife?" asks the first. "Compared to what?" responds the second. Assessing the state of the art in criminal justice evaluation raises the same question: Compared to what?

The current standard of criminal justice evaluation could be compared with the past; we have come a long way. But it could be compared with the future; it is commonplace to hear that our technology is barely in its infancy. It could be compared to other areas with strong evaluation interests; it seems we must now more a borrower than a lender be. And it could be compared to where various pertinent audiences would like it to be; for some it is insufficiently useful and for others, already incomprehensible.

In the broadest sense, evaluation research as we now know it can be traced back to the interests of social and other scientists in "applied" science. Applied psychology, for instance, has a long history as an acknowledged subdiscipline. However, it seems more appropriate to assign to Kurt Lewin and his students the principal role in building the foundation for modern evaluation research. Lewin's field theory was applied to a series of practical interpersonal, group, and organizational problems in which the "intrusion" of practical goals into the rigors of the research process became legitimated through the conception of "action research." It was the essence of action research that there was an interplay between research process and social action, that the research served the goals of the action while drawing from it refinements of theoretical propositions. Action researchers "got their hands dirty" in the practical problems of social service. They found havens in public health and education, in "group dynamics" and "human relations" and "sensitivity groups."

Perhaps the most striking aspect of the development of evaluation research out of this action research background is the greater focus now on the policy level rather than the direct practice level of social service. Social programming in America has inexorably led to a greater concern for accountability. The failure of the 1960s War on Poverty programs to be able to demonstrate their effectiveness has increased the salience of accountability at the policy level, so that today both social planners and politicians are coming to expect tangible proof of "results."

In response, evaluation researchers have developed a rather full armament of logics and techniques to suit all occasions. But in this development, they may have moved past their policy-making audience. Is it likely that program administrators, program monitors, and members of legislatures can be very familiar with time-series analysis, with the distinction between cost-benefit and benefit-cost, and with Bayes's Theorem? When is a field at a "cutting edge," and when merely esoteric?

The chapters in Part I are concerned with such questions. For both the policy maker and the student of research, the technical advances in evaluation research must be made available and, one hopes, understandable. Clearly, we can become seduced by new technologies. Clearly, we can become too dependent upon available data sources. Clearly, we can become defensive in the face of technologies imported from other fields and applied by "outsiders" to our own field of criminal justice.

The rational response to such "dangers" is to become more familiar with the developing state of the art and the directions it seems to be taking. If audiences other than the technologists of the art can be brought closer to the cutting edge, the value of the product of research cannot help but be reinforced. The four chapters of Part I were solicited with this in mind; they report on past styles of criminological research, current trends in methodology, recently available statistical procedures, and broadly available sources of data for evaluation purposes.

For students interested in the form of criminological research in the past, the chapter by Wolfgang provides a very detailed review of who we have been and what we have done. For researchers concerned with contributing to the *quality* of research in the field, Wolfgang has provided valuable historical data and made it abundantly clear that there is room for growth in quality. We are invited to enter the arena; and in particular, the weak but important areas are suggested by Wolfgang so that evaluators and policy makers alike may combine to concentrate their efforts where they may be most readily felt.

The Silberman chapter follows this directly with descriptions and specific examples of methodologies being developed in response to an assessment of needs in the field. For researchers seeking the cutting edge and for students preparing to meet the evaluation challenges of the immediate future, this compendium of promising methodologies provides a quick primer. It also reflects the views of one government agency, and readers would do well to keep this potential limitation in mind while considering the value of the methodologies described by Silberman.

Similarly, the chapter by Berk provides an overview of a deliberately selected set of approaches to *statistical* analysis. Written for those already versed in graduate-level statistics, this chapter brings together a series of approaches to analysis with emphasis on their functions for evaluation researchers. Beyond the review of fundamental and advanced techniques already accepted in the field, some innovative approaches to old problems are introduced. Evaluators less familiar with these approaches can now gauge their utility for varied evaluation purposes, and refer to the cited texts and original sources for greater detail.

Finally, the chapter by the Gottfredsons spells out in one place the variety of available data sources to which criminology evaluators may turn. Many policy makers, evaluators, and students are familiar with some of these, but few will be knowledgeable about all. The advantages and, more important, the limitations of major data sources are elucidated by the Gottfredsons. For funders and policy makers, familiarity with the data sources and their pitfalls may increase tolerance for the complexity and duration of many evaluation endeavors. They and other evaluation consumers can refer to these materials for better questioning and interpretation of evaluation results. And of course, knowledge of the wide range of available data sources should serve to broaden the repertoire and therefore the utility of evaluations by experts and students alike.

As we said to many contributors to this volume when queried about our goals, the chapters should stand as information benchmarks, so that no reader can afterwards say, "But if only I had known—." Now they can know, and higher-quality evaluations should be facilitated, as called for by Wolfgang.

1

On an Evaluation of Criminology

Marvin E. Wolfgang

INTRODUCTION

An attempt to evaluate the quality of the scientific literature in criminology should be useful in providing some guidelines for future research and theory. Several strategies for performing that task are included in the assessment described here, and it is an abiding hope that these alternate methods will help to make scholars more sensitive generally to the quality of evaluation research in criminology.

Evaluating the research and theory in criminological literature is not the same as assessing the impact of that knowledge on criminal codes, judicial sentencing, or penal philosophy. To perform this latter task would require a set of criteria and tools of measurement quite different from those used in the evaluative research reported in this chapter.

Our purpose is to describe and evaluate the character, the quality of criminological literature in the United States from 1945 to 1972. Because the term *criminology* refers to the scientific study of crime, criminals, and society's reactions to both, it would be redundant to say that the literature examined for this purpose falls within the domain and rubrics of the scientific method of research and analysis. But it should be stressed that purely polemical, political,

AUTHOR'S NOTE: This summary is based on research suggested by the National Science Foundation, Research Applied to National Needs, Grant GI-34810. In no way is the National Science Foundation responsible for this publication except through funding. The full report of this project appears in Marvin E. Wolfgang, Robert M. Figlio, and Terence P. Thornberry, *Evaluating Criminology* (New York: Elsevier, 1978). Permission to quote from *Evaluating Criminology* has been granted by Elsevier, for which I acknowledge my gratitude. The original publication is © 1978 by Elsevier, and all material reprinted here is by permission of the publisher.

rhetorical writings are excluded. Works that involve experiments, hypothesis-testing, that are empirical—either quantitative or qualitative—or that are theoretical, are included so long as they contain the ingredients of a scientific pursuit of knowledge.

The dates selected require some explanation. With the end of the war coming in 1945, there was an upsurge in university life and development of the behavioral sciences, including criminology. Many new students, new publications, new research began to flourish. The historical moment seems to be a natural boundary for this analysis. The terminal year, 1972, has no such justification; the research began in 1973 and simply used the last completed year available.

The task of sifting the published material over these twenty-eight years was not simple. Because our resources and time were limited, the decision was made to limit the field of reference rather than years covered. We had originally intended to analyze all works during the last ten years of the period, but decided instead to do a longer time-series study to capture any changes in focus. Consequently, we stopped short of works on the police, criminal justice, probation, parole, and corrections. Any topic dealing with etiology, crime types, delinquency, and the like, that focused on the offense and the offender rather than on police-court-correction response, was a candidate for inclusion. Textbooks were excluded.

Using indexes from related areas, covering well over 1000 journals, using the *Cumulative Book Index,* the *Library of Congress Union Catalogue, Dissertation Abstracts,* and several other sources, we located 6500 documents. After applying the criteria of scientificity, the list was reduced: Of the 4700 articles examined, 3134 were retained, and of the 1600 books, dissertations, and reports examined, 556 were included in the study—439 books and 117 dissertations and reports. Thus, 3690 works published in the United States between 1945 and 1972 constitute the basis for the evaluation of criminology.

What follows is *not* an evaluation of scholars in criminology but of some of their works. More than a few of the authors of the 3690 works have written extensively on the police, the judiciary, or corrections, and those writings are not included here. Hence, neither imputative nor invidious comparisons of persons should be made. I repeat: We are evaluating the literature, the orientations in criminology over time, and the offense foci relative to the quality of research studies.

The methods used to evaluate criminology include (1) citation index, (2) peer nomination, (3) content analysis. The citation index refers to the number of times any of the 3690 works was cited over the twenty-eight-year period. The history of citation frequency counts is relatively recent but firmly established. Peer nomination refers to the sample of authors from the original source documents who were asked to nominate the best books and articles over that same period. Content analysis means that each book, article, dissertation, or report was read, described in a schedule of items selected to characterize the work, and includes a global rating by the reviewer.

This tripartite process of evaluation is meant to discern the best works and their orientations. There may be other methods, but these three have a sufficient degree of concordance to make the systematic analysis reasonable.

THE CITATION INDEX

There is a considerable literature in the philosophy and sociology of science which suggests that the sheer number of citations alone, with or without self-citations, with or without negative citations, is a valid measure of the quality of a work.[1] Based upon this history, we have used frequency of citation as the operational definition of quality. Thus, we assume that the quality of a work is a direct and positive function of the number of citations it has received since publication.

An amazing aspect of this analysis is the skewness of the distribution. There were over 220,000 citations found in the 3,690 source documents; 20,202 were to works exclusively in the subject areas and time boundaries of this study. But there is a most uneven distribution: 82 works received 50 percent of all citations, 17 received 25 percent of the citations. The 82 works with half of the citations appear in Table 1.1.

Another way of expressing this finding is to point out that only 2.2 percent of all the works in criminology received one-half, and one-half of 1 percent (0.5 percent) received one-quarter of the citations. This is a fascinating clustering of quality in a very small number of publications.

Perhaps the compression of citations around a small number of works is more understandable when we note that 2113, or 57.3 percent, of all works published between 1945 and 1972 were *never* cited in other books, articles, dissertations, or reports. From one point of view, this finding can be said to be a major condemnation of the quality and impact of publications in criminology. Thus, among the 3134 articles, only 45 had 25 percent of the citations to articles, and 165 received 50 percent. One percent of the books and 1.4 percent of articles accounted for 25 percent of the citations; and 3.6 percent of the books and 5.3 percent of the articles had 50 percent of the citations. For most publications, being cited is a rare event. If there is cumulativity in criminological research and theory, it is based on a very small proportion of what is published.

The total life of a work is important in this analysis. That is, a work published twenty years ago obviously has a longer time-span over which to be cited than one published five years ago. Our analysis controlled for this variable of time space. The data indicate that citation rates peak two or three years after publication, hold constant until nine years after publication, decline at the tenth year, hold constant until the fourteenth year, and then decay around twenty-three years after publication. In short, once cited, works continued to be cited

TABLE 1.1   Books and Articles Receiving 44 or More Citations (50 percent
            of total citations)

	Number of Citations
H. S. Becker, *The Outsiders: Studies in the Sociology of Deviance*, 1963	648
S. and E. Glueck, *Unraveling Juvenile Delinquency*, 1950	648
A. K. Cohen, *Delinquent Boys: The Culture of the Gang*, 1955	611
R. A. Cloward and L.E. Ohlin, *Delinquency and Opportunity: A Theory of Delinquent Gangs*, 1960	535
R. K. Merton, *Social Theory and Social Structure*, 1957	472
J. F. Short and F. L. Strodtbeck, *Group Process and Gang Delinquency*, 1965	263
M. E. Wolfgang, *Patterns in Criminal Homicide*, 1958	257
W. B. Miller, "Lower-Class Culture as a Generating Milieu of Gang Delinquency," 1958	229
D. Abrahamsen, *The Psychology of Crime*, 1960	216
T. Sellin and M. E. Wolfgang, *The Measurement of Delinquency*, 1964	205
D. Matza, *Delinquency and Drift*, 1964	199
M. E. Wolfgang and F. Ferracuti, *The Subculture of Violence: Towards an Integrated Theory in Criminology*, 1967	172
K. R. Eissler, ed., *Searchlights on Delinquency; New Psychoanalytic Studies*, 1949	155
I. Chein et al., *Road to H: Narcotics, Delinquency and Social Policy*, 1964	142
B. Lander, *Towards an Understanding of Juvenile Delinquency*, 1954	141
D. R. Cressey, *Theft of the Nation: The Structure and Operations of Organized Crime in America*, 1969	137
M. L. Barron, *The Juvenile in Delinquent Society*, 1954	132
G. B. Vold, *Theoretical Criminology*, 1958	129
G. M. Sykes and D. Matza, "Techniques of Neutralization: a Theory of Delinquency," 1957	127
W. McCord, J. McCord, and I. K. Zola, *Origins of Crime; A New Evaluation of the Cambridge-Somerville Youth Study*, 1959	124
A. D. Biderman et al., *Report on a Pilot Study in the District of Columbia on Victimization and Attitudes toward Law Enforcement*, 1967	122
W. C. Kvaraceus, ed., *Delinquent Behavior: Culture and the Individual*, 1959	120
M. B. Clinard, ed., *Anomie and Deviant Behavior: A Discussion and Critique*, 1964	114
S. and E. Glueck, *Predicting Delinquency and Crime*, 1959	113
D. R. Cressey, *Other People's Money: A Study in the Social Psychology of Embezzlement*, 1953	111
H. A. Bloch and A. Niederhoffer, *The Gangs: A Study in Adolescent Behavior*, 1958	110
A. R. Lindesmith, *The Addict and the Law*, 1965	106
S. and E. Glueck, *Physique and Delinquency*, 1956	105
D. P. Ausubel, *Drug Addiction: Physiological, Psychological, and Sociological Aspects*, 1958	104

TABLE 1.1   (Cont)

	Number of Citations
D. Abrahamsen, *Who are the Guilty? A Study of Education and Crime*, 1952	102
W. H. Sheldon, E. M. Hartl, and E. McDermott, *Varieties of Delinquent Youth; an Introduction to Constitutional Psychiatry*, 1949	101
A. Cohen, K. Schuessler, and A. Lindesmith, eds., *The Sutherland Papers*, 1956	101
H. J. Anslinger and W. F. Tompkins, *The Traffic in Narcotics*, 1953	100
E. H. Sutherland, ed., *The Professional Thief, by a Professional Thief*, 1937	99
A. L. Porterfield, *Youth in Trouble; Studies in Delinquency and Despair with Plans for Prevention*, 1946	97
W. C. Kvaraceus, *Juvenile Delinquency and the School*, 1945	96
A. K. Cohen and J. F. Short, "Research in Delinquent Subcultures," 1958	95
S. Kobrin, "The Conflict of Values in Delinquency Areas," 1951	94
E. Goffman, *Stigma; Notes on the Management of Spoiled Identity*, 1963	91
E. M. Lemert, *Human Deviance, Social Problems and Social Control*, 1967	84
M. A. Merrill, *Problems of Child Delinquency*, 1947	84
D. J. Pittman, ed., *Society, Culture and Drinking Patterns*, 1962	84
A. R. Lindesmith, *Opiate Addiction*, 1947	79
R. A. Cloward, "Illegitimate Means, Anomie and Deviant Behavior," 1959	77
A. F Henry and J. F. Short, *Suicide and Homicide; Some Economic, Sociological and Psychological Aspects of Aggression*, 1954	76
A. J. Reiss and A. L. Rhodes, "The Distribution of Juvenile Delinquency in the Social Class Structure," 1961	75
H. C. Quay, ed., *Juvenile Delinquency: Research and Theory*, 1965	73
F. Redl and D. Wineman, *Children Who Hate: The Disorganization and Breakdown of Behavior Controls*, 1951	73
S. R. Hathaway, ed., *Analyzing and Predicting Juvenile Delinquency with the MMPI*, 1953	72
W. C. Kvaraceus, *The Community and the Delinquent; Co-operative Approaches to Preventing and Controlling Delinquency*, 1954	70
F. J. Murphy, M. M. Shirley, and H. L. Witmer, "The Incidence of Hidden Delinquency," 1946	70
L. Yablonsky, *The Violent Gang*, 1962	69
W. C. Reckless, S. Dinitz, and E. Murray, "Self-Concept as an Insulator Against Delinquency," 1956	67
K. T. Erikson, *The Wayward Puritans; a Study in the Sociology of Deviance*, 1966	66
F. I. Nye and J. F. Short, "Scaling Delinquent Behavior," 1957	63
W. C. Reckless, S. Dinitz, and B. Kay, "The Self-Component in Potential Delinquency and Potential Non-Delinquency," 1957	61
S. and E. Glueck, *Delinquents in the Making; Paths to Prevention*, 1952	60
I. Spergel, *Racketville, Slumtown and Haulburg*, 1964	60

TABLE 1.1 (Cont)

	Number of Citations
M. O. Cameron, *The Booster and the Snitch; Department Store Shoplifting*, 1964	59
A. K. Cohen, *Deviance and Control*, 1966	59
M. Gold, *Status Forces in Delinquent Boys*, 1963	58
R. L. Akers, "Socio-economic Status and Delinquent Behavior; a Retest," 1964	57
C. F. Schmid, "Urban Crime Areas," 1960	57
V. Aubert, "White-Collar Crime and Social Structure," 1952	56
H. S. Becker, "Becoming a Marihuana User," 1953	56
J. I. Kitsuse, "Societal Reaction to Deviant Behavior; Problems of Theory and Method," 1962	56
R. A. Dentler and L. J. Monroe, "Social Correlates of Early Adolescent Theft," 1961	53
H. Finestone, "Cats, Kicks and Color," 1957	52
T. Hirschi, *Causes of Delinquency*, 1969	51
A. J. Reiss, "Social Correlates of Psychological Types of Delinquency," 1952	50
P. W. Tappan, "Who is the Criminal?" 1947	50
M. W. Klein and B. G. Myerhoff, eds., *Juvenile Gangs in Context: Theory, Research and Action*, 1967	49
L. E. Ohlin, *Selection for Parole; A Manual of Parole Prediction*, 1951	49
O. Pollack, *The Criminality of Women*, 1950	49
P. H. Gebhard et al., *Sex Offenders: An Analysis of Types*, 1965	48
K. F. Schuessler and D. R. Cressey, "Personality Characteristics of Criminals," 1950	48
D. Matza, "Juvenile Delinquency and Subterranean Values," 1961	47
M. S. Guttmacher, *Sex Offenses: The Problem, Causes and Prevention*, 1951	46
R. J. Chilton, "Continuity in Delinquency Area Research; a Comparison of Studies for Baltimore, Detroit and Indianapolis," 1964	45
J. H. Skolnick, *The Politics of Protest: Violent Aspects of Protest and Confrontation*, 1969	45
J. P. Clark, "Socio-economic Class and Areas as Correlates of Illegal Behavior among Juveniles," 1962	44
A. K. Cohen, "The Sociology of the Deviant Act: Anomie Theory and Beyond," 1965	44

for a fairly substantial period—the rate of citations, on the average, does not drop to half its peak value until sixteen years after publication.

Works may be classified by type of orientation (Table 1.2) and by offense type (Table 1.3). In general, it may be said that by orientation, the best work has been performed in the areas of labeling, differential association, peer group studies, anomie, follow-up or replication studies, and subcultural studies.

The lowest-quality work, and therefore that in need of more developed attention, has been in the areas of psychological studies; biological studies, including genetics, chemical or hormonal; attitudes toward punishment, recidivism, deterrence; and in historical studies of individuals. Low citation frequencies (but as we shall see, high global ratings) occur in the areas of prediction, measurement, demography, modeling, and operations research.

Examination of Table 1.3, citations by offense type, shows no area of superior quality. However, studies of misdemeanors, deviance, and juvenile delinquency are among the best, while studies of alcohol, sex crimes, consensual crimes, political and military crime are at the opposite end. Only 15 percent of offense-related studies can be considered above average, none having achieved enough citations proportionately to be called superior.

PEER NOMINATIONS

Previous research[2] in the physical sciences encouraged our use of peer nominations as a basis of quality in criminology. The sample of authors employed consisted of the 100 authors most frequently cited in the *Criminology Index* and the 100 authors who most frequently appeared in the Source Document Index (the 3690 works). Because of an overlap, there were 161 members in the peer nomination sample. Respondents were asked to nominate the twenty best books and the twenty best articles from the lists provided. They were also asked to select the five best in each category and to check from a list the characteristics of these works that caused the respondents to nominate them.

A total of 287 books and 791 articles were nominated by the peer respondents, or 51.6 percent of the books and 24.7 percent of the articles. The most frequently nominated book was selected by 62 of the 107 judges, thus indicating that 58 percent of the respondents agreed that this was one of the twenty best books in the field. Similarly, the tenth-ranked book was nominated by slightly more than one-third of the judges, and the twentieth book by over one-fifth of the sample. Tables 1.4 and 1.5 show these distributions.

The relationship between citation index and peer nomination may be noted. Pearsonian correlations between peer nomination and citation frequencies for both books and articles are high: .69 for books and .68 for articles. Both

TABLE 1.2   Average Number of Citations, Percentage, and Number of Cities and Documents by Orientation

Orientation	Average No. of Cites	$\bar{X}$ Cites/ Yr.[a]	Cities N	Cities Percent	Documents N	Documents Percent	Ratio of Percentage of Citations to Percentage of Works in Category	$\bar{X}$ Global Rating
Definition of discipline	6.14	0.57	976	1.1	159	1.3	0.85	4.05
Statistics:	7.86	0.84	1,344	1.5	171	1.4	1.07	3.97
Official	7.20	0.64	1,152	1.2	160	1.3	0.92	3.84
Self-report	11.36	0.92	784	0.8	69	0.5	1.60	4.19
Victimization	10.70	1.56	246	0.3	23	0.2	1.50	4.00
Measurement	7.42	0.77	1,344	1.5	181	1.4	1.07	4.19
Historical	3.93	0.43	640	0.7	163	1.3	0.54	3.64
Individuals	3.02	0.34	368	0.4	122	1.0	0.40	3.10
Schools	6.65	1.18	153	0.2	23	0.2	1.00	4.13
Phenomena	7.00	0.60	1,904	2.1	272	2.2	0.95	3.69
Demographic	5.67	0.61	1,264	1.4	223	1.8	0.78	4.02
Psychological	4.51	0.36	3,248	3.5	720	5.8	0.60	3.49
Clinical	4.71	0.32	1,280	1.4	272	2.2	.064	3.06
Testing	2.59	0.19	1,200	1.3	464	3.7	0.35	3.72
Learning Theory	4.27	0.41	256	0.3	60	0.5	0.60	3.57
Psychiatric	4.89	0.24	2,896	3.1	592	4.7	0.66	3.11
Sociopsychological	8.00	0.66	5,888	6.4	736	5.9	1.08	3.87
Labeling	16.12	1.15	2,064	2.2	128	1.0	2.20	4.24
Differential association	16.53	0.86	1,488	1.6	90	0.7	2.29	4.43
Family and home life	6.87	0.38	3,408	3.7	496	4.0	0.92	3.22
Control theories	11.46	1.21	928	1.0	81	0.6	1.67	4.11
Peer groups	19.15	0.18	3,984	4.3	208	1.7	2.53	3.89
Biological	3.45	0.32	656	0.7	190	1.5	0.47	3.15
Genetic	2.26	0.48	188	0.2	83	0.7	0.29	3.45
Chemical or hormonal	3.31	0.47	202	0.2	61	0.5	0.40	3.00
Testing	2.50	0.37	150	0.2	60	0.5	0.40	3.42
Sociocultural	11.43	0.79	7,680	8.4	672	5.4	1.56	4.06
Anomie	25.41	0.55	3,024	3.3	119	0.9	3.67	4.02
Culture conflict	9.23	0.95	720	0.8	78	0.6	1.33	4.06
Ecological	9.63	0.64	896	1.0	93	0.7	1.43	3.97
Social disorganization	8.54	0.73	1,008	1.1	118	0.9	1.22	3.75
Crime as a normal phenomenon	9.18	1.37	496	0.5	54	0.4	1.25	4.16
Multifactor	12.95	1.05	4,352	4.7	336	2.7	1.74	3.65
Typological studies	9.23	0.93	1,920	2.1	208	2.7	1.23	3.93
Offenders	10.82	0.71	3,808	4.1	352	2.8	1.46	3.76
Offenses	8.87	0.89	816	0.9	92	0.7	1.29	4.07
Prediction	3.64	0.32	608	0.7	167	1.3	0.54	3.69
Crime	8.35	0.61	1,696	1.8	203	1.6	1.12	3.63
Recidivism	2.62	0.23	304	0.3	116	0.9	0.33	3.46
Victimology	9.23	1.00	720	0.8	78	0.6	1.33	4.07
Replications	6.08	0.54	432	0.5	71	0.6	0.83	4.05
Attitudes towards	4.74	0.63	1,440	1.6	304	2.4	0.67	3.45
Crime	5.48	0.63	1,168	1.3	213	1.7	0.76	3.77
Criminals	5.07	0.45	832	0.9	164	1.3	0.69	3.34
Punishment	2.54	0.24	244	0.3	96	0.8	0.38	3.87
Law	4.62	0.55	656	0.7	142	1.1	0.64	3.62
Economic	3.74	0.36	576	0.6	154	1.2	0.50	3.82
Deterrence	2.94	0.43	288	0.3	98	0.8	0.38	3.65
Prevention	3.75	0.34	1,440	1.6	384	3.1	0.52	2.86
Modeling or operations research	5.13	0.44	190	0.2	37	0.3	0.67	4.63
Treatment	3.64	0.29	1,920	2.1	528	4.2	0.50	3.24
Critiques	8.00	0.71	2,432	2.6	304	2.4	1.08	4.17
Test of a major theory	13.88	1.06	2,304	2.5	166	1.3	1.92	4.45
Case study	4.90	0.40	1,568	1.7	320	2.6	0.65	3.04
Follow-up or replication	13.85	0.95	1,440	1.6	104	0.8	2.00	4.07
Longitudinal study	6.04	0.46	544	0.6	90	0.7	0.86	3.83
Legal	6.95	0.49	2,112	2.3	304	2.4	0.96	3.61
Evaluation study	8.39	0.81	1,536	1.7	183	1.5	1.13	3.80
Recidivism	3.08	0.22	222	0.2	72	0.6	0.33	3.72
Organizational theory	4.23	0.47	288	0.3	68	0.5	0.60	3.62
Subcultural	30.29	0.38	3,968	4.3	131	1.0	4.30	4.20
Other	4.67	0.90	322	0.4	69	0.5	0.80	3.42

a. Mean number of citations per year since publication.
b. Because documents can appear in up to five different orientation categories, the number of documents listed is in excess of the total number of documents in the study. The same comment applies to our citation counts associated with these documents. Also, a work could be counted more than once or appear in more than one category if it made both a methodological and a theoretical contribution.
$\bar{X}$ documents per category = 202
$\bar{X}$ citations per work = 7.35
$\bar{X}$ global rating = 3.63

Offense Type	Average No. of Cites	$\bar{X}$ Cites/Yr.[a]	Cites		Documents		Ratio of Percentage of Citations to Percentage of Works in Category	$\bar{X}$ Global Rating
			N	Percent	N	Percent		
General	6.28	0.53	7,071	13.6	1,126	14.4	0.94	3.66
Violent	5.86	0.57	6,519	12.5	1,113	14.3	0.87	3.67
Political	4.68	0.65	317	0.6	317	4.1	0.15	3.91
Drugs	8.02	0.89	4,544	8.7	566	7.3	1.19	3.37
Alcohol	4.60	0.56	1,058	2.0	230	2.9	0.69	3.53
White collar	7.26	0.62	1,975	3.8	272	3.5	1.09	3.75
Sex	4.11	0.33	1,566	3.0	381	4.9	0.61	3.41
Consensual	4.02	0.36	876	1.7	218	2.8	0.61	3.50
Property	5.78	0.55	5,400	10.4	934	12.0	0.87	3.64
Juvenile status	6.24	0.39	4,286	8.2	687	8.8	0.93	3.42
Organized crime	5.71	0.29	725	1.4	127	1.6	0.88	3.61
Felony	5.86	0.49	258	0.5	44	0.6	0.83	3.65
Misdemeanor	13.43	1.12	188	0.4	14	0.2	2.00	4.15
Military	0.28	0.02	4	0	14	0.2	0	3.25
Ordinance	8.21	0.59	616	1.2	75	1.0	1.20	3.57
Suicide	6.10	0.54	250	0.5	41	0.5	1.00	4.00
Deviance	12.36	1.07	2,708	5.2	219	2.8	1.86	3.97
Juvenile delinquency	9.82	0.46	13,173	25.3	1,341	17.2	1.47	3.56
Crimes against family	6.12	0.44	98	0.2	16	0.2	1.00	3.62
Index crimes	8.17	1.11	433	0.8	53	0.7	1.14	4.28

a. Mean number of cites per year since publication.
$\bar{X}$ documents per category = 389
$\bar{X}$ citations per work = 6.68
$\bar{X}$ global rating = 3.60

TABLE 1.4   Most Frequently Nominated Books

	Number of Nominations
1. A.K. Cohen, *Delinquent Boys*, 1955	62
2. R. A. Cloward and L. E. Ohlin, *Delinquency and Opportunity*, 1960	59
3. E. H. Sutherland, *White Collar Crime*, 1961	54
4.5. R. K. Merton, *Social Theory and Social Structure*, 1957	44
4.5. T. Sellin and M. E. Wolfgang, *The Measurement of Delinquency*, 1964	44
6. S. and E. Glueck, *Unraveling Juvenile Delinquency*, 1950	42
7. D. Matza, *Delinquency and Drift*, 1964	40
8.5. H. S. Becker, *The Outsiders*, 1963	39
8.5. J. F. Short and F. Strodtbeck, *Group Process and Gang Delinquency*, 1965	39
10. M. E. Wolfgang, R. M. Figlio, and T. Sellin, *Delinquency in a Birth Cohort*, 1972	38
11. T. Hirschi and H. C. Selvin, *Delinquency Research*, 1967	37
12. M. E. Wolfgang, *Patterns in Criminal Homicide*, 1958	35
13. K. T. Erikson, *Wayward Puritans*, 1966	32
14. E. M. Lemert, *Human Deviance, Social Problems and Social Control*, 1967	31
15. N. Katzenbach et al., *The Challenge of Crime in a Free Society*, 1967	29
16. D. R. Cressey, *Other People's Money*, 1953	28
17. T. Hirschi, *Causes of Delinquency*, 1969	27
18. E. Schur, *Crimes Without Victims*, 1965	26
19. E. M. Goffman, *Stigma*, 1963	25
20. E. H. Sutherland, *The Professional Thief*, 1937	24
21.5. T. S. Szasz, *Law, Liberty and Psychiatry*, 1963	22
21.5 G. B. Vold, *Theoretical Criminology*, 1958	22
24. L. T. Empey and S. G. Lubeck, *The Silverlake Experiment*, 1971	21
24. L. N. Robins, *Deviant Children Grown Up*, 1966	21
24. M. E. Wolfgang and F. Ferracuti, *The Subculture of Violence*, 1967	21
26.5 A. Bandura and R. H. Walters, *Adolescent Aggression*, 1959	19
26.5 L. Yablonsky, *The Violent Gang*, 1962	19
27. A. R. Lindesmith, *Opiate Addiction*, 1947	18
28.5 D. Matza, *Becoming Deviant*, 1969	16
28.5 J. Skolnick, *The Politics of Protest*, 1969	16
31.5 I. Chein et al., *The Road to H*, 1964	15
31.5 J. Lofland, *Deviance and Identity*, 1969	15
31.5 F. Redl and D. Wineman, *Children Who Hate*, 1951	15
31.5 P. H. Ennis, *Criminal Victimization in the United States*, 1967	15
35.5 M. B. Clinard, ed., *Anomie and Deviant Behavior*, 1964	14
35.5 N. N. Kittrie, *The Right to Be Different*, 1971	14
35.5 A. M. Platt, *The Child Savers*, 1969	14
35.5 E. Powers and H. Wtimer, *An Experiment in the Prevention of Delinquency*, 1972	14
39. N. Morris and G. Hawkins, *Honest Politician's Guide to Crime Control*, 1969	13
39. H. Von Hentig, *The Criminal and His Victim*, 1948	13
39. L. T. Wilkins, *Social Deviance*, 1964	13

TABLE 1.5 Most Frequently Nominated Articles

	Number of Nominations
1. G. M. Sykes and D. Matza, "Techniques of Neutralization," 1957	43
2. W. B. Miller, "Lower Class Culture as a Generating Milieu of Gang Delinquency," 1958	35
3. R. A. Cloward, "Illegitimate Means, Anomic and Deviant Behavior," 1959	31
4. H. S. Becker, "Becoming a Marihuana User," 1953	27
5.5. S. Kobrin, "The Conflict of Values in Delinquency Areas," 1951	23
5.5. E. H. Sutherland, "Is White Collar Crime, Crime?" 1945	23
8. D. Matza and G. M. Sykes, "Juvenile Delinquency and Subterranean Values," 1961	20
8. W. C. Reckless, S. Dinitz, and E. Murray, "Self-Concept as an Insulator against Delinquency," 1956	20
8. M. E. Wolfgang, "Victim-Precipitated Criminal Homicide," 1957	20
10. A. K. Cohen, "The Sociology of the Deviant Act," 1965	17
11.5. J. P. Gibbs, "Concepts of Deviant Behavior," 1966	14
11.5. T. Hirschi and H. C. Selvin, "False Criteria of Causality in Developing Research," 1966	14
14. K. T. Erikson, "Notes on the Sociology of Deviance," 1962	13
14. H. Finestone, "Cats, Kicks and Color," 1967	13
14. A. J. Reiss, "The Social Integration of Queers and Peers," 1961	13
18. D. Bell, "Crime as an American Way of Life," 1953	12
18. A. K. Cohen and J. F. Short, "Research in Delinquent Subcultures," 1958	12
18. R. A. Gordon, "Issues in the Ecological Study of Delinquency," 1967	12
18. J. F. Short and F. I. Nye, "Reported Behavior as a Criterion of Deviant Behavior," 1958	12
18. A. T. Turk, "Conflict and Criminality," 1966	12
21. L. Yablonsky, "The Delinquent Gang as a Near Group," 1959	11
24.5. D. J. Black and A. J. Reiss, "Police Control of Juveniles," 1970	10
24.5. R. L. Burgess and R. L. Akers, "A Differential Association-Reinforcement Theory of Criminal Behavior," 1966	10
24.5. J. P. Clark and E. P. Wenninger, "Socio-Economic Class and Area as Correlates of Illegal Behavior among Juveniles," 1962	10
24.5. D. R. Cressey, "Changing Criminals: The Application of the Theory of Differential Association," 1955	10
24.5. D. Glaser, "Criminality Theories and Behavioral Images," 1956	10
24.5. E. M. Lemert, "The Behavior of the Systematic Check Forger," 1958	10
24.5. F. I. Nye, J. F. Short, and V. J. Olson, "Socioeconomic Status and Delinquent Behavior," 1958	10
24.5. A. J. Reiss and A. L. Rhodes, "The Distribution of Juvenile Delinquency in the Social Class Structure," 1961	10
24.5. J. F. Short, R. Rivera, and R. A. Tennyson, "Perceived Opportunity, Gang Membership and Delinquency," 1965	10

TABLE 1.5 (Cont)

	Number of Nominations
34.5. J. Andenaes, "The General Preventive Effects of Punishment," 1966	9
34.5. H. S. Becker, "Whose Side are We on?" 1967	9
34.5. D. J. Bordua, "Delinquent Subcultures: Sociological Interpretations of Gang Delinquency," 1961	9
34.5. M. Gold, "Undetected Delinquent Behavior," 1966	9
34.5. R. A. Gordon, "Social Level, Social Disability and Gang Interaction," 1967	9
34.5. J. F. Short, R. A. Tennyson, and K. I. Howard, "Behavior Dimensions of Gang Delinquency," 1963	9
34.5. J. F. Short and F. I. Nye, "Extent of Unrecorded Juvenile Delinquency," 1958	9
34.5. M. E. Wolfgang, "Uniform Crime Reports: A Critical Appraisal," 1963	9
34.5. M. E. Wolfgang and F. Ferracuti, "The Subculture of Violence," 1962	9

coefficients are significant well beyond the .001 level, as might be expected, given the large Ns–287 for books and 791 for articles.

In short, the association between the frequency of peer nominations and the number of citations that the nominated documents received is positive, high, and statistically significant.

The two approaches to measuring the quality of scientific work provide comparable and consistent information. The rankings of the ten most frequently nominated articles and books are similar to the citation frequencies. Table 1.6 shows these similarities.

Eight of the ten most frequently nominated books and six of the ten most frequently nominated articles are among the ten most cited works. Although two of the books and four of the articles are not among the most frequently cited works, they nonetheless are all highly cited, especially in view of the fact that, overall, over half of the documents in the bibliography were never cited. Results from these two methods of measuring quality are quite similar.

CONTENT ANALYSIS

The collection of elements that we have used for examining the methodological and theoretical components of criminological research is based on the set of attributes that, according to general consensus, appear best able to characterize and describe research. In general, we view these components as descriptors that, in themselves and collectively, provide a syndrome that diagnoses the subject.

TABLE 1.6   Ten Most Frequently Nominated Books and Articles and
             Citation Frequencies

	Frequency		Rank	
	Nominations	Citations	Nominations	Citations
Authors and Books[a]				
Cohen	62	611	1	3
Cloward and Ohlin	59	535	2	4
Sutherland	54	28	3	–
Merton	44	472	4.5	5
Sellin and Wolfgang	44	205	4.5	9
Glueck and Glueck	42	648	6	1
Matza	40	199	7	10
Becker	39	648	8.5	1
Short and Strodtbeck	39	263	8.5	6
Wolfgang, Figlio and Sellin	38	7	10	–
Articles				
Sykes and Matza	43	127	1	2
Miller	35	229	2	1
Cloward	31	77	3	5
Becker	27	56	4	9
Kobrin	23	94	5.5	4
Sutherland	23	20	5.5	–
Matza and Sykes	20	47	8	–
Reckless, Dinitz, and Murray	20	67	8	8
Wolfgang	20	16	8	–
Cohen	17	44	10	–

a. For more complete bibliographic information see Tables 1.4 and 1.5.

Our intention with these components is not to place value judgments of our own on the works, but to use them as a basis for displaying the characteristics of research efforts. This is not to say that the descriptors are value-free; the judgmental elements are based upon the values assumed under the rubric of scientific inquiry. Hence, we have sought to remove, as much as we could, the subjective judgmental perceptions of individual recorders of the components. Only at the end of the methodological and theoretical component schedules have we applied a global rating of each work, and consequently of each subfield of research in criminology included within our substantive frame.

Detailed below are the contents of the schedule of the various components or attributes of strategy and technique with which we have chosen to dissect the books, articles, dissertations, and reports examined in this study.

For purposes of analyzing the contents of the documents, a major dichotomy was exercised between (a) those published works that involved quantitative expressions and included methodological research elements, and (b) those items that were classified principally as theoretical research. The classification of all articles and books could not be mutually exclusive, because some had quantitative, empirical, and, therefore, methodological aspects while at the same time they possessed elements of logical inquiry that sought to make contributions to criminological theory. About 13 percent of the works were classified as having addressed both of these concerns to the extent that neither orientation could be excluded. The remaining works (87 percent) were coded as either essentially methodological or theoretical.

METHODOLOGICAL COMPONENTS OF RESEARCH

After the initial methodological-theoretical determination had been made by our staff, each item in the appropriate schedule was marked "yes," "no," or "not appropriate." The items are not always mutually exclusive: A given work may have been both descriptive and analytical, may have included questionnaires and interviews, may have had different sample units, and may have used different kinds of variables. Most of the attributes are self-explanatory:

I. Study orientation
   1. descriptive (simple description of percentage tables, and so on)
   2. analytical (discusses interrelationships among variables)
   3. modeling (attempts at mathematizing phenomenon studied)
   4. predictive

II. Data-gathering process
   1. survey
   2. field observation
   3. questionnaire or schedule
   4. interviews
   5. laboratory observation
   6. simulation (computer-generated data)
   7. psychological and/or physiological testing
   8. official records
   9. self-report (crime or victimization) schedule
   10. other published sources

III. Sampling technique
   1. nonprobability
   2. probability

IV. Scope
1. individual
2. census tract
3. city
4. state
5. region
6. nation

V. Sample size (number of enumeration units)

VI. Estimate of standard error (parametric estimates and standard errors)

VII. Method
1. bivariate
2. multivariate
3. hypothesis-testing
4. parametric estimation
5. simulation

VIII. Statistical techniques
1. t, z tests (tests of differences between two groups)
2. f test, analysis of variance techniques (more than two groups)
3. other parametric tests
4. correlation, linear
5. correlation, nonlinear
6. regression techniques, linear
7. regression techniques, nonlinear
8. factor analysis
9. path analysis
10. chi-square tests
11. other nonparametric tests
12. confidence intervals
13. percentages, proportions, rates, and so on
14. graph analysis
15. case study
16. content analysis

IX. Assumptions underlying the study
1. expressed symbolically (at least partially, using mathematical or logical symbols)
2. expressed linguistically (at least partially, verbally)

X. Operational definitions
1. expressed symbolically
2. expressed linguistically

XI. Hypotheses
1. expressed symbolically
2. expressed linguistically

   XII. Variables
      1. hard (demographic)
      2. soft (personality, attitudes, preferences, and so on)

  XIII. Major theme of work
      1. supported
      2. partially supported

   XIV. Type of interpretations and conclusions
      1. methodological
      2. theoretical
      3. policy-oriented

    XV. Rigor
      1. interpretations of data are congruent with the data studied
      2. interpretations depart from study data
      3. interpretations are purely assumptive implications
      4. remaining problems identified in study area

   XVI. Global rating (circle appropriate number)
      Poor   Excellent
         1 2 3 4 5 6 7

COMPONENTS OF THEORETICAL RESEARCH

Although it is difficult to describe or discuss a theoretical work in nonsubjective terms, we have attempted to isolate those characteristics that are relatively objective in their interpretation and application. Early in the process of determining how to proceed in this content analysis of the criminological literature, we reluctantly abandoned the search for unidimensionality of components that would describe both empirical and theoretical works. Part of that abandonment was a function of our having spent some time reviewing the literature in the history, philosophy, and sociology of science, as well as studying literary criticism and critiques in art and music. Just as in music there are separate studies of theory and composition, so we have found an operational clarity and facility in examining the components of empirical and theoretical works separately.

It is possible that components and linguistically fixed terms designating these components of theoretical research might be different if examined by another study group. We are neither defensive nor aggressive about the items selected by our research team, but we are satisfied that we have captured a set of components that depict the character of theoretical research in criminology in the substantive and temporal domains of our inquiry.

In a manner similar to that employed in empirical studies, predominantly theoretical works were classified by the various attributes they exhibited according to the following set of evaluative items. Most of the entries are self-explanatory:

  I. Theoretical scope
     1. universally applicable
     2. culturally specific
     3. historically specific
     4. specific to a social group
     5. specific to a type of individual
     6. specific to a phenomenon

  II. Units of analysis
     1. individual
     2. society
     3. culture
     4. institution
     5. group
     6. organization
     7. social role
     8. interaction
     9. process
     10. phenomena
     11. method

  III. Hypotheses stated linguistically or symbolically

  IV. Assumptions (statements assumed to be true) expressed

  V. Logic of inquiry
     1. theoretical propositions *not* emphatically derived but logically derived according to a theoretical structure
     2. theoretical propositions *not* emphatically derived and *not* logically derived (e.g., based on author's opinion)
     3. theoretical propositions partially empirically derived
     4. theoretical propositions based on empirical evidence

  VI. Empirical support offered from
     1. author's own experience (clinical, law enforcement, teaching, and so on)
     2. official data (Bureau of the Census, FBI, institutional records, and so on)
     3. nonofficial data (surveys, field observations, interviews, and so on)
     4. other published sources (theoretical works, and so on)

VII. Definitions and concepts expressed

VIII. Dependent variables expressed

IX. Independent variables expressed

X. Type of conclusions and interpretations
  1. theoretical
  2. methodological
  3. policy-oriented

XI. Internal consistency
  1. interpretations logically follow from assumptions and definitions
  2. interpretations logically follow from empirical evidence

XII. Testability
  1. demonstrated (tested)
  2. suggested
  3. problem not referred to

XIII. Contribution to conceptualization
  1. construction of
    a. theory
    b. methodology
    c. concept

XIV. Extent to which theory can be generalized
  1. universally applicable
  2. specific to a culture
  3. historically specific
  4. specific to a society
  5. specific to a social group
  6. specific to a type of individual
  7. to a specific issue

Although it is common to refer to different "levels" of theory—grand, middle, and minor—we have chosen to use the notion of theoretical scope, that is, the degree or extent of applicability of theory from the specific to the general. We describe the units of analysis; the logic of inquiry; the extent to which empirical support is provided; the most important sources of official and nonofficial data, if any; the extent to which other published theoretical works are employed; whether definitions and concepts, dependent and independent variables are expressed; and, finally, the character of the interpretations and whether there is internal consistency of those interpretations logically derived from the assumptions and definitions, as well as from empirical evidence. The content analysis of the components of theoretical contribution to conceptualization is made toward construction, modification, critique or review of theory, methodology, or concepts.

EMPIRICAL STUDIES

Approximately two-thirds of these works are descriptive (68.6 percent) and analytical (65.7 percent), employing interviews and psychological tests and surveys as the predominant modes of data-gathering from official records, but using probability sampling techniques in only one out of ten studies (9.7 percent). Purposive or fortuitous nonprobability sampling is the most common technique, and individuals overwhelmingly constitute the enumerative unit of analysis. Percentages, proportions, and rates are the statistical techniques presented in two-thirds of the works studied, followed by t, z, or f tests and simple linear correlations.

The most common nonparametric technique is chi-square, which exceeds in proportion the number of studies utilizing appropriate probability sampling techniques. Most assumptions in these researches are expressed linguistically, as are the operational definitions and hypotheses, although hypotheses are expressed in only slightly over half (53.2 percent) of the works.

Demographic variables and officially recorded data are quite common, although soft personality variables and attitudes and preferences appear in six out of ten works. The major theme of each of these studies is generally or partially supported, and interpretations are congruent with the data analysis in about three out of four works. Interpretations and conclusions are most likely to be theoretical and heuristic, as they are in almost three-quarters (73.3 percent) of the works, but there is a sizable portion, nearly two-fifths (39.5 percent), that has policy-oriented implications.

Part of the process of analyzing the contents of these works has been to produce a global rating of each work. The staff engaged in a careful reading of each of these several thousand articles and books, and had employed a seven-point rating scale, ranging from 1, poor, to 7, excellent. Considering for the moment only the empirical works analyzed for their methodological components, the mean rating given was 3.639. The mode is 4.0 and the median 3.617, thus indicating a clear convergence of these three styles of measuring central tendency ($S = 1.574$). Thus, it must be said that, in general, the quality of this collection of empirical works in criminological research stands somewhat below the midpoint between poor and excellent. There were 220 works rated as poor (7.8 percent), while only 21 were rated as excellent (0.7 percent); 475, or 16.7 percent, were given a score of 2, while as few as 205 were scored 6 (7.2 percent). The bulk of the works are distributed between the three mid-scoring points, namely at 3 (23.3 percent, or 661); 4 (27.2 percent, or 771), and 5 (17.1 percent, or 485).

COMPONENTS OF THEORETICAL RESEARCH

Because we wish to consider theoretical aspects of the works in this section, we describe only the components of theoretical research as indicated (N = 1732). There is an overlap, particularly in those works that are predominantly empirical, with some theory (19.4 percent, or 563, of the methodological documents) and in those works that are apparently devoted to theory but have some empirical observations (23.2 percent, or 401, of the theory documents).

THEORETICAL STUDIES

Of the theoretical works in criminology, nearly half (49.2 percent) are polemical, without much structure, and with little capacity for generating hypotheses. About one-fourth (26.4 percent) may be designated as formal theory, and one out of four of the works contains some empirical referents.

Most of the theoretical research is of limited scope, either with regard to a specific phenomenon or to a type of individual. Only about one in eight (12 percent) of the works could be viewed as having universal applicability. It is therefore no surprise that the major unit for analysis is the individual in about half (52.8 percent) of the works, although nearly two-thirds (65.5 percent) also contain a specific phenomenon, like drugs or gangs, as the unit of analysis. Hypotheses are stated linguistically or symbolically in 56.8 percent of the works, and assumptions are expressed in three-quarters. But the theoretical propositions found in these writings are only infrequently based on empirical evidence and are infrequently logically derived, according to a theoretical structure. Empirical evidence to buttress theoretical propositions is commonly lacking, from either the author's own experience, official or nonofficial data, or other public sources. Empirical support ranges from less than 50 percent, as in the case of the theorist's own experience, to less than 20 percent from nonofficial data.

Definition of terms and articulation of concepts, as well as clearly expressed dependent and independent variables, appear rather regularly in these writings. Conclusions and interpretations are, as might be expected, mostly theoretical themselves, but about half of the conclusions and interpretations contain social policy relevance. In only about 30 percent of the writings do interpretations logically follow from any empirical evidence, and in slightly over half are the interpretations a logical follow-up from the assumptions and definitions.

Very few of the theoretical propositions within the framework of theoretical writings have been demonstrated; over one-quarter present suggestions for testability, but in three-fifths of the cases testability is not even referred to as a problem. The construction of novel and innovative theory, conceptualization, or methodologies, appears infrequently in these theoretical works.

GLOBAL RATINGS

As in the case of analyzing the methodological components from empirical research, with the mean at 3.648, the mode at 4.0, and the median at 3.675, research team. The scoring system also ranged from 1, for poor, to 7, for excellent. Scaling distributions are very similar to those registered for empirical research, with the mean at 3.648, the mode at 4.0, and the median at 3.675, indicating a high degree of concordance among these three measures of central tendency (S = 1.536). The distribution of the global rating is biased to the lower or poor end of the scale, with 147, or 8.5 percent, recorded as poor, and only 24, or 1.4 percent, as excellent. Theoretical works given the score of 2 (14.3 percent, or 247) were nearly twice as high as works given a score of 6 at the other end of the scale (7.6 percent, or 131). The middle scores show a distribution of 22.7 percent at score 3, 25.9 percent at score 4, and 19.5 percent at score 5, indicating again a general skewness to the lower end of the scale. In short, it appears that theoretical criminology stands at about the same posture and distance from excellence as empirical criminology, so far as these global ratings of quality indicate.

OFFENSE CLASSIFICATION

In examining the literature and taking note of the heavy preponderance of references to or analyses of specific criminological phenomena, a listing of eighty different kinds of offenses was included for purposes of classifying the empirical and theoretical works separately.

Although it is possible to examine each one of the eighty offenses through cross-tabulation with any of the existing variables in the methodological and theoretical components of the literature, for more manageable utility in promoting generalizations we have collapsed the offense classification into twenty-four groupings, as follows:

- alcohol
- consensual crimes
- conspiracy
- crimes against family
- deviance
- drugs
- euthanasia
- felony

- general
- index crimes
- juvenile delinquency
- juvenile status offenses
- military offenses
- misdemeanor
- ordinance offenses
- organized crime

- perjury and libel
- political crime
- property
- resisting arrest and prison break

- sex crimes
- suicide
- violent crimes
- white-collar crimes

For purposes of the present analysis we have selected eight categories of offenses for illustrative review of scientific content. These eight are: (1) general crime, (2) violent offenses, (3) political offenses, (4) drugs, (5) white-collar crimes, (6) sex crimes, (7) property offenses, and (8) juvenile delinquency. Table 1.7 shows the distribution of empirical and theoretical works in these categories.

There is a similarity in the frequency distributions of the criminological literature according to the empirical and theoretical classifications. In both cases the preponderance of the literature has been devoted to juvenile delinquency and a general category of problems of crime and crime control.

This present discussion is concerned only with what is known as the *primary* code. That is, in recording the ingredients of these works, the staff designated up to five types of offenses covered by any of the articles or books from the list in the code book, and ordered these types from the most to the least important in terms of the extent of treatment they received from the authors. For present purposes we are briefly analyzing only the first type of offense, or the most important listed.

These eight offense categories accounted for nearly nine out of ten of the works of both empirical (86 percent) and theoretical (82.8 percent) character. There are only two striking differences in the distributions. Among descriptions of political crime, there is almost an equal absolute number of empirical (159) and of theoretical (161) works. However, proportionately, political crime is represented nearly twice as often among all works in theory (9.3 percent) as among empirical works (5.5 percent). In white-collar crime, again with similar numbers (52 and 42), the proportionate distribution in theory is somewhat higher (2.4 percent) compared to empirical studies (1.8 percent).

RESEARCH QUALITY AND POLICY IMPLICATIONS

We draw special attention to the extent to which, by offense classification, criminology has made policy-oriented expressions. In general, and in absolute numerical terms, there are more empirical studies carrying policy-oriented implications (1147) than may be found in the theoretical works (858); but among theoretical works, proportionately more attention is given to social policy (49.5 percent) than among quantitative empirical works (39.6 percent).

TABLE 1.7   Distribution of Eight Offense Categories
by Empirical and Theoretical Works

Offense Category	Empirical (N = 2897) Percentage	Theoretical (N = 1732) Percentage
Drugs	10.4	8.2
General	18.6	20.5
Juvenile delinquency	25.4	22.3
Political	5.5	9.3
Property	6.9	4.7
Sex	4.3	3.2
Violent	13.1	12.3
White-collar	1.8	2.4
Remaining categories	14.0	17.1
	100.0	100.0

The highest proportion of policy references among the theoretical works is related to drug offenses (67 percent), the smallest to crimes of violence (39 percent). Policy statements also appear in relatively substantial proportions in theory concerning sex crimes (56 percent), juvenile delinquency (53 percent), and white-collar crime (45 percent). Among empirical works, policy-oriented assertions and implications are most common for sex crimes (53 percent) and least likely for property and violent crimes.

The users of scientific research results may be other scientific researchers or they may be nonresearch administrators of institutions and agencies in the public or private sector. If scientists, they can be expected to replicate previous research, criticize it, or build upon it by using the results to formulate new syntheses of theory or to test new hypotheses emerging from the prior research, and hence help to develop science in the incremental way history has demonstrated.

But if the user is an administrator—of legislation, of an agency, or of the judiciary—he or she needs policy statements that are rooted in tested theory, through descriptions of policy interpretations that are consistent with the data of the research, before becoming able, comfortably and rationally, to take action.

Relative to these assertions, criminological research and theory present a poor posture and appear to offer more policy orientations than they should, if science is to be the guide and determinant of rational policy. For example, in only 7 percent of the works has theory been tested, yet almost one-half of the theoretical studies make explicit or implicit policy statements. In 56 percent of theory and 53 percent of empirical works, social policy statements are made about sex crimes. But the lowest proportion of studies that contain material with tested theory is found in discussions of sex crimes (3.8 percent). Drug offenses represent another case of striking disparity between policy assertions (67 percent theoretical, 40 percent empirical) and studies with tested theory (4 percent). Even juvenile delinquency, the offense category with the highest number of works containing policy orientations (267 empirical, 180 theoretical), shows only 7 percent with tested theories.

It may also be surprising to some observers that crimes of violence have the lowest proportion of policy statements, whether among empirical (32 percent) or theoretical (39 percent) works, especially in view of the long-standing public concern about violent crime. But only 6.6 percent of the studies present evidence of having tested theories in this area.

Property crimes and white-collar crimes enjoy the most theory-testing (18 percent, 17 percent), although the proportion of empirical writers making policy statements on these offense categories is the lowest.

Before basing action on research, another element of concern is consistency between theory or data and their interpretations. *For these eight offense categories, interpretive commentary—often policy-oriented—is generally not consistent with the research, is not derived from the data discovered or directly from the theory used.* In only 31.8 percent of the studies can it be said that the interpretations presented rest solidly on, or are linked to, the research performed.

The greatest disparity is found among drug offenses: policy-oriented statements, 67 percent; tested theory, 4.3 percent; consistency between research and interpretations, 25.6 percent, the lowest of any offense category. It appears that with respect to drug offenses, writers in criminology are much more willing to make policy statements that they can buttress with theory-testing or reliable interpretations of their research material.

The highest frequency of consistency between interpretations and data linkage (48 percent) is in the offense category of white-collar crime. This category has relatively few studies and a high policy-oriented count. But at least white-collar crime studies also have the second highest proportion of studies with tested theory as well as firmly based interpretations that rely intimately on the data or theory of research.

How do the eight offense categories fare in the global ratings from poor (score 1) to excellent (score 7)? There is considerable convergence around the mean, both for theoretical and for empirical studies.

The lowest mean rating is for theoretical literature concerning the drug offense (1.18), which may be related to the observation that this has the poorest showing of any offense category for the testing of theory and for consistency between research and interpretations. The highest theory scores are shared by the general crime category and political crimes (3.76). Among empirical studies, political crime is lowest (3.0) and white-collar crime highest (3.78), the latter of which may be a reflection of highest frequency of theory-testing and data interpretation consistency.

CONTENT ANALYSIS–PREDICTING QUALITY

We shall look at the three measures of research quality—citation frequency, peer nomination frequency, and global ratings—in relation to each other and to the methodological and theoretical content variables discussed previously. Two major concerns form the substance of this treatment: (a) an examination of the concordances among these three quality measures, and (b) the determination of the strength of the content variables in predicting quality as measured by the three indexes.

In relation to global ratings, we see that 46 percent of the works received ratings below the modal value of 4 which includes 26.1 percent, and that only 27.9 percent received ratings above the average (Table 1.8). Indeed, only about 10 percent of the works were judged 6 or 7 in quality, while about 23 percent were designated by only a 1 or 2. The distribution is biased toward the low end of the rating scale, with a mean of 3.62, somewhat below the perceived average quality level of 4.

The conclusions that one must draw from these distributions are that being cited or nominated is an uncommon event, with multiple citations or nominations being especially rare, and that, generally speaking, most works are of low quality in terms of global rating. What, then, are the relationships among these measures, and can we predict the quality of a work from a knowledge of its research techniques and strategies? If we can, then the implications for evaluation research can be drawn.

The scatterplot of Figure 1.1 for nominated books and articles versus citation frequency indicates a strong positive correlation (0.72 for books, 0.68 for articles) between these two quality measures. It should be mentioned again that the respondents to the peer nomination survey chose from the list of works published between 1945 and 1972, according to their own judgments, the twenty best books and the twenty best articles. The citation frequency derived from the *Criminology Index*[3] is a completely independent measure computed by counting the number of citations of a work made by the universe of authors whose publications constitute the Source Document Index for the *Criminology*

TABLE 1.8   Percentage Distribution of
Global Ratings

	Global Rating	Percentage
(Poor)	1	7.9
	2	15.4
	3	22.7
(Average)	4	26.1
	5	17.6
	6	9.3
(Excellent)	7	1.0

Index. The *Criminology Index* was not available to the participants in the peer nomination survey because at the time of the survey it had not yet been published.

We find it remarkable that these two measures exhibit such strong agreement. Of course, well-known works are likely to be highly cited, and a high citation rate certainly contributes toward making a work well known. These measures could be said to reflect one another. However, the peer nominators were asked to choose the *best* works. The fact that a work was well known to an individual was only one characteristic we offered the respondents as a reason for choice among the characteristics of quality. Such attributes as germinal, innovative, well-designed and well-executed, of practical value, policy-relevant, research stimulant, influential, and timeless were also included in the list of characteristics.

As a result of these concordances, then, we suggest that the citation index has received validation support in addition to that described previously in our comments on the Citation Index.

The raw data relationship between citation frequency and global rating for cited books and articles together is displayed in Figure 1.2. The relationship (0.27, total), while not as strong as that observed between citation and nomination frequencies, is nonetheless positive and significant ($r = 0.29$ for books, and 0.26 for articles).

In Figure 1.3 we see that the positive relationship between global rating and peer nomination frequency is clearly visible. The overall correlation is 0.34; for books, it is $r = 0.41$, and for articles, $r = 0.30$.[4]

These graphs and correlations, when considered together with the Global Ratings by Nominated and Not Nominated Works for Methodological, Theoretical, and Total Documents (presented by Wolfgang et al., 1978: 101), further support the hypothesis that these quality measures are strongly concordant. A

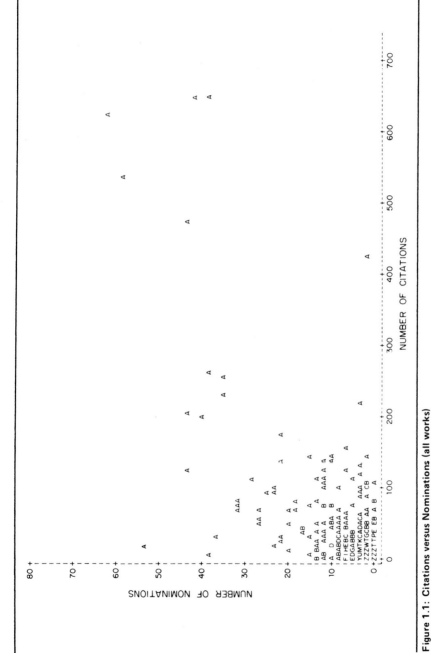

Figure 1.1: Citations versus Nominations (all works)

NOTE: Number of entries is designated by letters: A = 1, B = 2, C = 3 . . . Z = 26 or more.

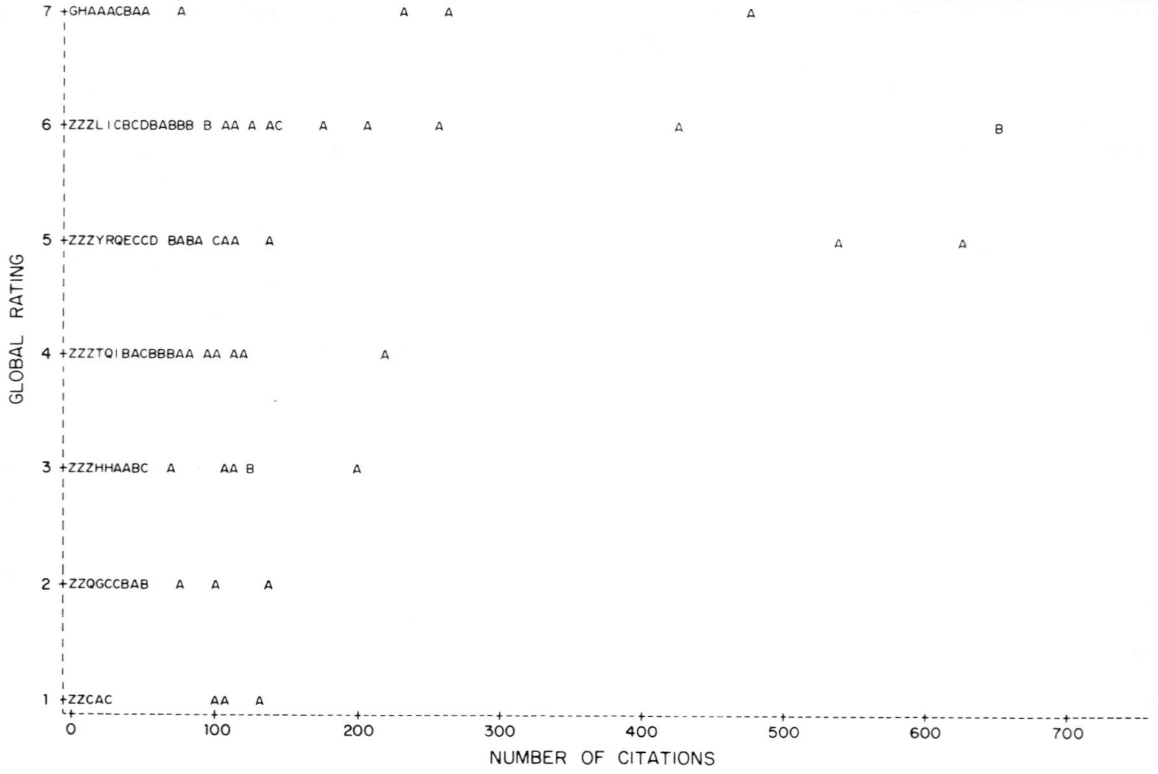

Figure 1.2: Global Rating versus Citation Frequency

NOTE: Number of entries is designated by letters: A = 1, B = 2, C = 3 . . . Z = 26 or more.

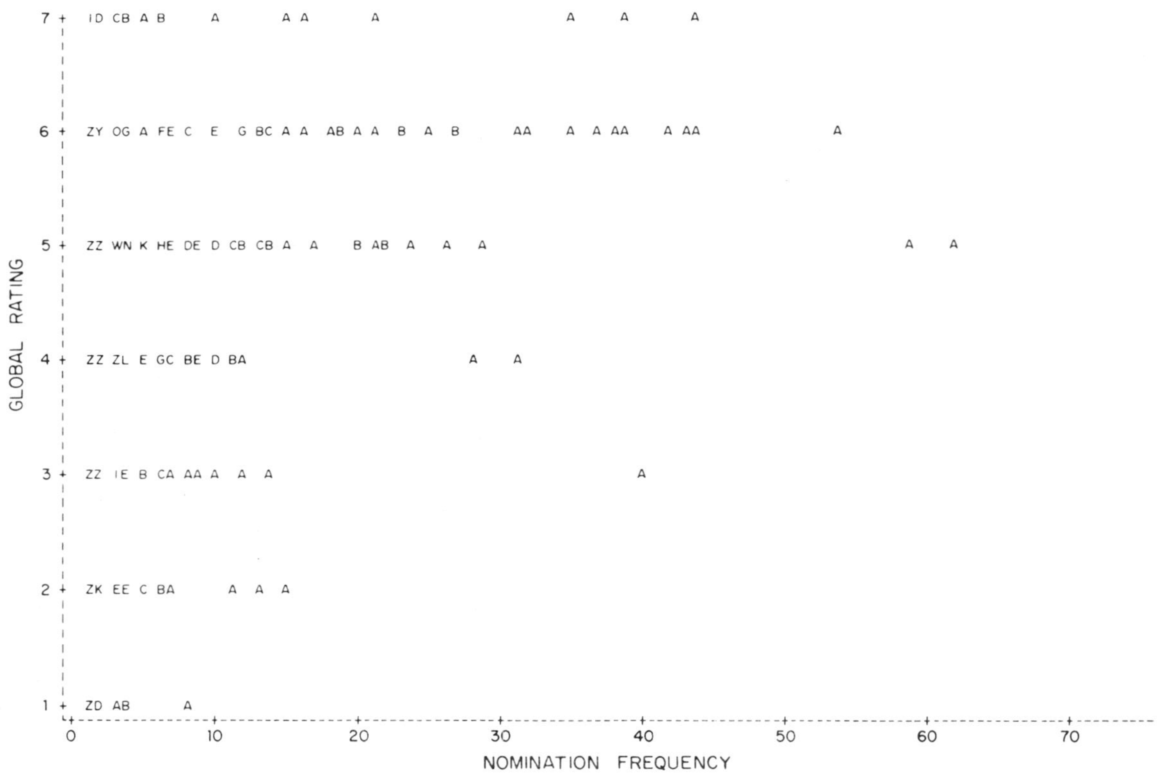

Figure 1.3: Global Rating versus Nomination Frequency

NOTE: Number of entries is designated by letters: A = 1, B = 2, C = 3 . . . Z = 26 or more.

47

strong relationship exists between the proportion of books and articles nominated and the global rating. Of course, the several sources of variability in these
data tend to obscure this relationship on a work-by-work basis. Many works that
received high global ratings from our readers were not nominated by the peer
survey respondents. Because each respondent was allowed to choose only 20
articles from a list of almost 4000, it is reasonable to assume that quite a few
works of high quality would not be nominated by them. On the other hand, it is
possible that some works of low global rating would also be nominated as among
the "best" by outside judges for reasons other than those deemed appropriate by
our evaluators. That is, the interrater reliability across these different judging
populations is unknown, and therefore, it is remarkable that the data do exhibit
the observed level of agreement among these independent measures.

Variables such as assumptions, linguistic; operational definitions, symbolic
and linguistic; interpretations congruent; and analytical are predictive in a
positive manner; while the variable, interpretations depart, is negatively predictive of global quality. These variables, for the most part, are associated with the
first and most important factor structure of "rigor." Thus, it is primarily on the
rigor of a work that our readers judged global quality. Other technical qualities,
such as the use of correlational analysis and bivariate analysis (under the
structure of "techniques") and methodological or theoretical interpretations and
conclusions (under "aim" or "orientation") are also related to the quality
judgment. The factor structure of the methodological content variable clearly is
related to global quality group membership.

The expected percentages for Table 1.9 show that the classification of global
rating groups by content variables is substantially better than that expected by
chance. We would expect that 28 percent of the works would fall into the low
group if chance were operating. In fact, 72 percent of the actual low group
works are predicted by the discriminant functions to be in that group. Similarly,
21 percent of the works would be expected to fall into the high group while, in
fact, 67 percent were actually predicted to lie at that level. It is very difficult to
classify group 2 (average), which has a large number of works (1589) and a wide
range of characteristics, with these variables, as evidenced by the relatively small
departure from chance (51 percent expected, 62 percent actual). As a result of
the size of the average group, the inordinately large number of misclassifications
caused by the diversity of group 2 overwhelms the success experienced in
accurately predicting the group membership of the low- and high-quality works.
Even though 67 percent of the high-quality works are correctly classified as part
of that category when we expect only 21 percent by chance, 68 percent of the
predicted group 3s actually belong to group 2. Somewhat better results obtain in
the prediction of the low group where 47 percent of the predicted low-category

TABLE 1.9   Predicted Global Rating Group Membership by Actual Group
Membership: Methodological Content, All Works Having a
Global Rating

		Group, Predicted (percentage)						
Actual	N	Low		Average		High		
Low	446	72.4	(51)	24.0	(9)	3.6	(3)	100.0
Average	1,589	18.8	(47)	61.5	(86)	19.7	(68)	100.0
High	192	4.2	(1)	28.6	(5)	67.2	(28)	100.0

Overall: 64.2 percent of cases correctly classified by functions 1 and 2

group actually belong in group 2, even though 72 percent of the actual low
works are being predicted to lie in group 1.

Stated in a different way, if we were going to throw out those works that are
of low quality, using the methodological content variables as a guide, we would
correctly dispose of 72 percent of the actual poor works, 19 percent of the
average, and only 4 percent of the high-quality works. On the other hand, if we
were interested in identifying the "good" works, using these variables as predictors, we would encompass 67 percent of the actual good works, 20 percent of
the average, and only 4 percent of the poor works in this "good" category by
applying the content schedule to the publications. Our ability to identify the
end points on the discriminate function is fairly impressive; the ability to isolate
the good from the poor within the average group is not so apparent. The
problem lies in the generous scatter of the average group in discriminate space.

CONCLUSION

Each mode of analysis—the citation frequency count, the peer nomination,
the content analysis global ratings—as well as the combination of them, has been
described and analyzed. We have shown statistically significant relationships
between and among these three methods. We have recognized that negative
citations can increase the frequency count used as a basis of judging quality,
although previous research has generally negated the importance of them. We
have indicated that some works in the criminological literature, despite the
excellent quality attributed to them by our raters, for various reasons have had
little impact, were infrequently cited, or had few nominations from peers.

Criminology is still sufficiently young to be viewed as a growing discipline
approaching maturity. Its growth rate is still relatively high, about 7.14 percent
per annum since 1945. We are pleased to report that the quality of research and

theory has also increased. Based on this apparently secure development, criminology may be entering a stage in which the lessons learned produce not only descriptions of what is, but prescriptions about what kind of research to do—even, perhaps, what kinds of social action, based on research, are indicated.

One sign of the recognition and growing maturity of a discipline of organizing knowledge, such as criminology, is the extent to which groups outside the discipline seek its advice. From physics and genetics to psychiatry, this proposition has some credence. From criminology, an increasing number of important questions are being asked by Congress, state legislatures, community programs, and agencies accustomed to applying research findings to decisions that affect large organizations and many people.

It may be arguable that the best decisions, whatever that may mean, can and should be based on the highest-quality research and theory. When the major aspect of a policy decision is ethical rather than researchable in a scientific process, the quality of research that is ancillary to the ethical issue may be of little importance in making a decision. Moreover, an innovative idea that is unresearched or inadequately researched may still prove useful for taking action in the absence of firmly established high-quality research.

When there is research and carefully developed theory supported by research, then information is available, ignorance is denied its power to permit any kind of decision, and the principle of the best available evidence can be invoked. Competing claims for the efficacy or efficiency of some decisions over others may not always be readily resolvable. Rival hypotheses may stand in a similar posture of scientific acceptability. These problems are part of the dark figures of certainty which make for the continual searching and researching that characterize a science in all fields. Criminology should be neither condemned nor excessively praised for whatever deficiencies or abundance of claims the field may make. It is probably proper, however, to say that more correct decisions will be made from use of the highest-quality research.

Criminology represents an area in which the demarcation between pure or basic research and applied research is amorphous, for much basic research may later have unanticipated social applications. Moreover, this same area, for this reason, is a clear representative of a traditional yet increasingly visible problem in the relationship between science and society. As prescriptive requests of the criminological community of scholars from funding and decision-making organizations increase, so do the dangers of responding with inadequate, incomplete research findings, and so does the likelihood of answering the calls for research where funds and power reside. Scholars should avoid being seduced by the imminent needs of such agencies. The precious commodity of intellectual and scientific integrity should not be vulgarized by the temptation of getting funds to do that which is requested, unless what is requested has interest to the scholars and properly permits cumulation of research. On the other side of that coin of integrity, it is also the case that scholars in criminology have an obligation to be attuned to what are viewed as important research issues by those outside the traditional scholarly community. A response to these inquiries need not compromise the canons of scientific inquiry.

The analyses we have offered are meant to convey the message that very careful scrutiny should be given to any requests for research in all areas of criminology. This surely is not a new admonition. But we are also saying that some subareas of criminology require more latitude, more flexibility of research experience, because they have been relatively and inadequately explored. Race and crime, violent crime, corporate and white-collar crime are among these.

Areas of high-quality and relatively many studies may be viewed as firmly entrenched and require less funding in the future. Areas of high-quality and few studies require more funding. If certain typical areas of crime and criminality are deemed important but have been represented by few studies or even many studies, and with low-quality research, funding agencies should encourage more high-quality research designs, and so forth. High-quality, important areas, low-quality, unimportant areas—these variables can be juggled in a complex matrix by using the evaluations from the research we have described.

We seek to follow the logical lines of our own inquiry by not making implications that leap far beyond the territory of our own data and the analyses we have offered. We hope our study provides many implications, but we prefer that they be inferred by our readers. Our allegiance to the rational rubrics of what is known as the scientific method of obtaining empirical approximations of reality should by now be clear. Our research has been firmly rooted in this belief system but contains no other ideological positions. The issues of positivism, critical, radical, or new criminology, reductionism, abstractionism, existentialism, and phenomenology, are not relevant to this research about quality of research.

Evaluation of what is good, middling, or poor, will continue. We welcome it and expect variations on our own versions of evaluation. Replications in all areas are needed, and we anticipate that future efforts at evaluation will improve our own analysis.

NOTES

1. See de Solla Price (1963, 1970), Myers (1970), Cole and Cole (1967, 1973: ch. 2). For a warning of the bias in the use of the *Social Science Citation Index* (*SSCI*), see Chubin (1973). For a time-series analysis of the rise in collaborative research in sociology, see Patel (1972).

2. See Zuckerman and Merton (1961) and Persell (1971).
3. See Wolfgang et al. (1975).
4. We investigated various data transformations (log, inverse, inverse square) when computing the correlation coefficients. The relationship between citation frequency and nomination frequency is simple and linear. The relationship between global rating has a best fit with a log transformation of either citation or nomination frequency.

REFERENCES

de Solla Price, D. T. (1970) "Citation Measures of Hard Science, Soft Science, Technology, and Non-Science," pp. 3-22 in C. E. Nelson and D. K. Pollack, *Communication amongst Scientists and Engineers.* Lexington, MA: D. C. Heath.
——— (1963) *Little Science, Big Science.* New York: Columbia University Press.
Myers, C. R. (1970) "Journal Citations and Scientific Eminence in Contemporary Psychology." *American Psychologist* 25: 1041-1048.
Chubin, D. (1973) "On the Use of the *SCI* in Sociology." *American Sociologist* 8 (November): 187-191.
Cole, J. R. and S. Cole (1973) *Social Stratification in Science.* Chicago: University of Chicago Press.
Cole, S. and J. R. Cole (1967) "Scientific Output and Recognition: A Study in the Operation of the Reward System in Science." *American Sociological Review* 32 (June): 377-390.
Patel, N. (1972) "Quantitative and Collaborative Trends in American Sociological Research." *American Sociologist* 7 (November): 5-6.
Persell, C. H. (1971) *The Quality of Research on Education: An Empirical Study on Researchers and Their Work.* New York: Columbia University Press.
Wolfgang, M. E., R. M. Figlio, and T. P. Thornberry (1978) *Evaluating Criminology.* New York: Elsevier.
——— (1975) *Criminology Index.* New York: Elsevier.
Zuckerman, H. and R. K. Merton (1961) "Patterns of Evaluation in Science: Institutionalization, Structure, and Functions of the Referee System." *Minerva*: 2: 66-100.

2

Recent Advances in Evaluation Methods

George Silberman

Ever since the major thrust for social program accountability in the early 1960s, a good deal of tension has existed between evaluators and those who consume their work (i.e., administrators, community groups, legislators, and so on). No doubt much of the negative reaction to evaluative efforts is a function of the natural antagonisms that exist between performer and critic. As many evaluators will readily admit, however, the questions raised regarding the relevance, timeliness, and validity of evaluations point to legitimate shortcomings in our ability to evaluate.

Recognizing the need to increase this ability, or in other words to improve the methodology of evaluations, the Law Enforcement Assistance Administration (LEAA), in 1977, partitioned its Office of Evaluation into two distinct entities. One was the Office of Program Evaluation, which retained the responsibility for funding evaluations of criminal justice programs and initiatives. The second, the Office of Research and Evaluation Methods (OREM), was created in order to support efforts to develop and test new methodologies, i.e., techniques that would allow evaluators to do something they cannot do now, do it more efficiently, and do it with greater confidence in their findings. Offered below are brief descriptions of some of the projects currently being supported by OREM under its Methodology Development Program (MDP). The chapter concludes with some personal observations on the implications these efforts have for the future of criminal justice evaluation.

ONGOING RESEARCH

Given the ultimate objective of many criminal justice programs, to reduce crime, it is understandable that crime rate is a key variable in a large number of evaluations. The appropriateness of crime rate as it is currently measured, however, has recently been questioned by a number of researchers. One criticism is that it does not take into account the opportunities for crime. In other words, a truly meaningful auto theft rate should include not only population and number of incidents, but also number of vehicles; the rate for commercial robberies should include number of retail establishments; rape rates, the number of women; and so on. Although the concept of incorporating opportunities for crime in the calculation of crime rates is a simple one, the task quickly increases in complexity as one attempts to refine the measures. In the case of rape, for instance, the argument can be made that single women, more frequently unescorted, and women between the ages of 15 and 23, more socially active, are at greater risk than other women. The optimal rate measure should therèfore include a weighting system that would take these factors into account. An attempt to construct appropriate "population at risk" measures for Part I offenses is currently under way at Oklahoma State University (see Harries). It is hoped that the research will provide evaluators with measures that more realistically model the true rate of any particular crime.

Some programs which do not have as their direct goal the reduction of the crime rate are those which fall under the general heading, "rehabilitation." Here the immediate objective is to reduce the size of the offender population. In the case of such programs, therefore, the more legitimate outcome variable is the number of criminals rather than the number of crimes. The problems involved in estimating the size of the criminal population are both obvious and seemingly insurmountable. They are not, however, unique. To some extent, the same set of problems (how to define the population, how to observe action that is, by its nature, secretive, and so forth) confront doctors trying to determine how many undetected cancer victims there are, therapists who wish to know how many alcoholics exist, and analysts concerned with size of the heroin-addicted population, to name but a few examples. There has been a good deal of effort in each of these areas to develop models that provide better estimates of the population in question. One project funded under the MDP is trying to adapt these models for use in estimating the size of the offender populations (see Stollmack and Green). Although the models are too complex to allow detailed discussion of them here, the logic underlying one of the techniques frequently employed will help illustrate the general approach to the problem.

I am sure that the reader has seen the wildlife documentaries in which a zoologist goes through great pains to tag an animal. Typically, tagging is done in order to study longevity and migration patterns. The procedure also allows one to estimate the size of the animal population. If we assume that all animals, both previously tagged and untagged, have the same probability of being caught, the frequency with which tagged animals are encountered is simply a function of the area in which they are found and the total size of the population. Since we can measure both the area and the number of animals "recaptured," we can estimate the third variable, population size. If one now considers arrest as the tagging step, it becomes apparent how this model can be employed for estimating the number of criminals.

Armed with the ability to measure accurately both the crime rate and the size of the offender population, the evaluator can certainly present more useful products. However, policy makers in criminal justice, as in all service-delivery areas, are ultimately political and may therefore be more concerned with the perceived effectiveness of a program than with its actual impact. Faced with the need to supply information on such issues as fear of crime and degree of satisfaction with the criminal justice system, evaluators have relied heavily on surveys as a means of data collection.

The two basic problems that continue to plague survey researchers are validity and comparability. The former can be restated simply in the form of the question, "How can we be sure that the respondent is telling us the truth?" The fact of the matter is that we can never be absolutely sure. Faced with this dilemma, we continue to consider the answers valid in those situations where there is no reason to assume that the individual would benefit from lying. The problem with this perspective is that it ignores the situation where the individual is, in fact, honest; nevertheless the individual's responses are misleading. Consider the following example. A victim of a crime is asked to indicate how satisfied he is with police services immediately following his victimization, and offers a very negative assessment. The same individual is then resurveyed following the capture and conviction of his assailant. Once again he indicates that he is dissatisfied with the police. Our natural conclusion is that the police solving the crime did not make any difference to him. In reality however, what happened was that our victim emerged from the court to find that his car had been towed, and although very happy with the police in general, was particularly dissatisfied at the moment that the interviewer approached him.

This example may seem extreme, but the extent to which short-term, unaccounted-for events bias survey results is a fundamental problem which questions the validity of the responses given. The magnitude of the problem is attested to by the preliminary results from a study at the University of California—Santa Barbara (Berk and Bielby) which found that the variation observed (changes in level of satisfaction) was more a function of short-term, supposedly orthogonal factors, than of true substantive change in the way people felt about the criminal justice system. Fortunately, the methodology employed by the researchers holds some promise for the future, in that it allows the analyst to disassemble the results into change influenced by short-term factors, change insensitive to short-term influences, systematic measurement error, and stochastic measurement error.

The second problem with the surveys mentioned above concerns comparability. At various times this problem has been referred to as one of anchoring or standardization. Regardless of the terminology employed, the issue remains: How does one assure that two survey items attempting to tap the same dimension are doing so and, if not, how do they differ from each other (e.g., is one more susceptible to short-term influences, is one more likely to induce falsification)? One way to circumvent this problem is to construct questions (or items, scales, and the like) that are universally accepted as legitimate and therefore employed by most of the analysts trying to collect information in the area. If two studies use exactly the same questions to measure satisfaction, for instance, we can feel more at ease in comparing their findings.

This solution, albeit obvious, raises the strategic issue of how to construct these universally accepted measures. The approach selected by the MDP was to allow researchers to focus their attention on construction and testing of a particular measure, rather than hope for such an effort in the course of a substantive study. The single project funded in this area to date is attempting to develop a scale with which we can measure fear of crime (see Baumer and Rosenbaum). If successful, i.e., if evaluators begin consistently to use the measure, one could envision similar efforts focusing on citizen satisfaction, sanction severity, and other attitudinal dimensions frequently used in criminal justice.

The attempt to standardize the measures employed by the evaluation community extends beyond the range of attitudinal measures. The MDP is now supporting one effort to develop a standard measure of recidivism, another study which it is hoped will lead to greater comparability in the way we construct offender categories, and a project investigating the possibility of developing a scale with which we can measure the environment in correctional institutions.

In the case of recidivism, two issues must be resolved before a definition can be provided which gains widespread acceptance. One is the question of the time frame. If one reviews the evaluations which use recidivism in their analyses, it quickly becomes apparent that some look for "failure" within the six-month period following release, others extend the period to a year, and some employ two-year follow-ups. Given this disparity in the length of time the released offender is observed, what is called failure in one study may well be defined as success in another. The second question that must be answered is raised by the fact that an individual can recidivate for a wide variety of reasons. In the case of released violent offenders, therefore, should we consider them to recidivate if they commit misdemeanors, if they violate the conditions of their parole, or only if they commit the same crimes for which they were initially incarcerated?

A research team at the University of Illinois—Chicago Circle is examining both these issues as well as presenting the programmatic implications of the use of the various definitions of *success* and *failure* (see Maltz).

The project on classification (Brennan), by reviewing all the methods currently in use for categorizing offenders, hopes to provide us with a better understanding of the implications that correspond with the statistical properties of each technique. In addition, the researcher will indicate the most appropriate algorithm (cluster analysis, multidimensional scaling, or the like) for meeting the varying objectives of classification (risk assessment, treatment, prediction, and so forth). If widely accepted, these prescriptions should increase the consistency in the way both criminal justice personnel and researchers build offender taxonomies.

The third study (Srivastava) focused on measuring environment, attacks a problem that has long plagued criminal justice. In assessing the effectiveness of various modes of incarceration, evaluators have typically adopted what might best be described as a "black-box" approach. What this means is that the intervention, a prison sentence, is treated as a dummy (discrete) variable. Hence, the analysis involves simply comparing the offender's behavior prior to incarceration with his postrelease behavior. Excluded from the analysis are a host of factors affecting the experiences of the individual while institutionalized, including environmental considerations. This omission of environment is understandable, given the difficulties and costs involved in measuring that particular dimension of a prison, jail, or halfway house. Based on previous research which has constructed scales to measure environment in such diverse entities as mental hospitals, supermarkets, and army bases, this project attempts to do the same for juvenile residential treatment homes. The intent is that the measurement technique developed will capture the significant features of the environment, yet will not be so costly as to preclude its use in a standard evaluative effort. Moreover, the technique is expected to be adaptable, with only slight modification, for use in other correctional settings, e.g., prisons and jails.

Although the ability to quantify environment will certainly shed some light on our "black box," the perspective of a correctional facility as an independent entity, or alternatively a "closed system," is somewhat unrealistic. In corrections, as in other areas of the criminal justice system, the trend is toward increasingly complex service-delivery systems. The introduction of community group participation in securing neighborhoods, efforts which involve cooperation between the police and prosecutors, coordination between parole boards and job placement centers, are but a few examples of the growing popularity of multi-group participation in criminal justice programs. For someone evaluating any one of these programs, this trend presents the difficult problem of trying to measure the interaction between the various groups involved. What is really needed is the ability to measure the social dynamics of the relationships that grow out of such programs. A logical place to turn for a solution to the problem, therefore, would be to that literature which has examined group interaction. Two sociologists whose backgrounds are in this area have received funds under the MDP to investigate the utility of a technique known as "network analysis" for solving the problem (Miller and Lincoln). The specific focus of the research is on a program to deinstitutionalize juvenile status offenders which involved police, juvenile courts, counseling agencies, community groups, and a program administrative unit. The three objectives of the project are (1) to indicate the type of data needed to discern the quantity and quality of interaction, (2) to determine the most efficient means for collecting those data, and (3) to present the most appropriate methods for analysis.

A project closely related to this effort is being conducted at the University of Minnesota (see Arabie). The technique being refined under the grant, "block-modeling," also derives from the general class of methodologies referred to as sociometrics. The typical unit of analysis in blockmodels is the individual rather than the organization. The method holds a great deal more promise for measuring interaction than such earlier versions as "clique analysis," for a number of reasons. One is that it allows one to identify "floaters" or individuals who frequently move from one group affiliation to another. A second advantage of blockmodels is that they can indicate "bridges" or individuals who link two or more groups. The two major tasks of the research are to refine the statistical underpinnings of blockmodels and to develop computer software that will make the technique available to interested analysts.

In the discussion of the "network analysis" project above, the idea of criminal justice agencies as constituting a service-delivery system was introduced. Using the methodologies discussed to this point, as well as those that have already gained wide acceptance, the evaluator is well equipped to determine the effectiveness of a particular program or system (i.e., the extent to which services are delivered) and, one hopes, the determinants of effectiveness (i.e., why things worked or did not work). But the evaluator frequently has another mandate, to determine the efficiency of the service-delivery mechanism. Efficiency can be loosely defined as the ratio between outputs and inputs, the most efficient system being the one that maximizes the product (output) while minimizing the resources expended (input). The issue of efficiency is basic to the field of economics and it is not surprising that the best developmental work in the area has been done by economists.

The problem with much of that previous work, however, is that it relies heavily on two assumptions. One is that the firm's major objective is profit maximization, and the second is that the output is a definable product. In the case of public agencies in general, the former does not hold, and in the case of criminal justice in particular, one would have great difficulty with the latter. Because of these problems a group of economists have arisen who are rebuilding traditional economic theory to make it applicable to the public sector. One analyst who has focused most of her attention on the economics of the criminal justice system, in particular corrections, received funds under the MDP (see Witte). The objective of her research is to estimate cost and production functions for correctional institutions, using both traditional estimation procedures and a new technique called "frontier cost analysis."

Once again, the mathematics of the procedure are too complex to allow details to be given in this context, but the conceptual difference between frontier analysis and previous techniques is quite simple. Imagine a situation in which 100 correctional institutions are placed on a graph which has cost as one axis and production as the other. Traditional estimation procedures for determining the pattern presented by the resultant scattergram try to determine a line or curve (functional form) which comes close to as many points as possible. The problem with this approach is that it does not differentiate between efficient and inefficient prisons. In effect, if most of your prisons are inefficient, the production function estimated will depict an inefficient mode of operation. Frontier analysis, alternatively, determines the most efficient institutions before estimating the functional form, and then weights them heavily. The result is that the functional form selected depicts an efficient universe. The implication for evaluation is that comparisons need not be made to a possibly inefficient standard, and better understanding can therefore be gained of how truly "efficient" any particular system is.

The final MDP grant I would like to discuss touches on a problem that has been faced by almost everyone who has ever performed evaluation in the criminal justice area (see Fox and Tracey). That the behavior of the criminal is difficult to observe is obvious. Less obvious, but no less a problem, is the fact that the various subsystems within criminal justice have a long tradition of secrecy and mistrust for outsiders. In any evaluative effort, therefore, it is not uncommon that the analysts will not only have to guess about what the criminals are doing but also about what police, prosecutors, judges, and wardens are doing in response. What is obviously needed is some method for increasing our ability to elicit sensitive information in a valid manner. Such a technique was developed by statisticians approximately fifteen years ago. Known as "randomized response," it can be illustrated by the following example. Assembled in a room are 50 corrections guards. If they were asked to raise their hands if they had ever transported narcotics to inmates, it is doubtful whether any would respond in the affirmative. Under randomized response, the question is posed in the following manner. Each guard is asked to take out a coin, flip it, and raise a hand if the coin has come up heads *or* if the guard has ever trafficked in drugs while on duty. Under these circumstances, the observer can never tell which question the guard is responding to, and the assumption, therefore, is that the individuals will be less hesitant to tell the truth. Let us say that with the coin flip, 31 hands are raised. Since we expect 25 heads to come up, we can assume that 6 of the guards are raising their hands only because they are guilty. In addition, since what side of the coin came up is independent of guilt or innocence, we assume that there are an equal number of guards among the 25 who received heads who are also guilty. The aggregate number of offenders within our sample is therefore estimated to be 12.

The possible applications of randomized response for the criminal justice evaluator are too numerous to list. In effect, anytime that the design calls for aggregate estimates of behavior along a sensitive dimension (e.g., crime, corruption, inefficiency) the technique is appropriate. One additional benefit both the evaluator and respondent enjoy is that, since we can never be sure which question is being answered, the respondent cannot be held responsible should there be any attempt to prosecute on the basis of the research findings.

FUTURE DIRECTIONS

In the introductory remarks I promised some personal reflections on the future of criminal justice evaluation. To a large extent these observations derive from the trends exhibited by the grants awarded under the MDP. In order to illustrate why I believe the projects described above to be truly representative of what the future holds in store, it is necessary to offer a brief description of the actual framework of the program, i.e., the manner in which research is solicited and selected under the MDP.

In deciding how to structure the request for submissions two distinct strategies were considered. One was for us to identify the specific issues we wished to see addressed. That is, the solicitation would list all the areas we considered legitimate for funding (e.g., how to quantify the severity of sanctions, better techniques for collecting data on victimization, statistical refinements of time-series models, and so on). The alternative approach, and the one selected, was simply to indicate that any attempt to make an advance in evaluation methodology would constitute an appropriate submission. Although this "open" approach detracted from the degree of control we would exercise over the direction of the MDP, it was chosen because of two perceived benefits. One was that researchers could propose subjects that they were truly interested in, rather than modifying their designs in order to meet rigidly established boundaries for acceptability. Second, by allowing the submitters this freedom, we did not restrict the universe of funding opportunities to those methodological problems of which staff within LEAA are aware.

The assumption that internal staff were not all-knowing also played a key role when it came to structuring the selection process. Although the expertise existed internally to ascertain the technical soundness of the proposals submitted, we felt that the most appropriate raters of the significance of the issue areas proposed were individuals with extensive "hands-on" experience in criminal justice evaluations. Therefore, the selection of which projects to fund relied heavily on a peer review panel, consisting of representatives of each of the social science disciplines, as well as statistics and operations research.

The projects selected, therefore, represent the methodological advances that evaluators perceive as the most needed at this point in time.

What trends, then, are manifest in this select group of projects? One obvious one is the increasing statistical sophistication being brought to bear on evaluation questions. This observation is equally true for all areas of social research and should come as no surprise to anyone. The growing number of young evaluators who feel as comfortable with statistical models as their predecessors felt with conceptual ones may make some of us feel ill at ease, but certainly bodes well for the future legitimacy of evaluation as a discipline.

A second trend that emerges is that the universe of variables viewed as legitimate for inclusion in evaluation is rapidly expanding. Whereas fifteen years ago one typically measured the crime rate before a program was implemented and compared that with the postimplementation rate, today we are presented with the possibility of including in the evaluation design number of criminals, environment, efficiency, and subsystem interactions, to name but a few.

The final trend that I see as significant is that toward standardization. If the time is near when evaluators begin to employ the same instruments when looking for similar answers, then the future of evaluation as a knowledge-building endeavor is indeed rosy.

Where, then, do these trends leave us? Certainly far ahead of where we used to be. The improved statistical methods increase the validity of our empirical studies; the addition of new operational variables expands our coverage, allowing us to write reports less full of apologies for all the things we could not measure; and finally, by standardizing the measures we use, we can make significant contributions to criminological research and criminal justice administration. But there is another side to the coin. Unless there is among policy makers a growth in familiarity with statistics to correspond with that in the evaluation community, evaluators may be providing their clients with products that are of no use. Collecting information on more variables is expensive, as are such techniques as randomized response, and in the upcoming era of fiscal austerity the money simply may not exist to do all we have the capability of doing. Finally, are we sure that by moving toward standard measures we do not sacrifice at least some of the creativity essential to a fledgling discipline?

Having presented some arguments for both sides of the issue, let me close by indicating where I think we must go from here. Throughout history a curious race has been run between theory and technology. For some period of time, be it a decade or a century, one will sprint furiously to outdistance the other. Then, the leader seems to run out of breath, and waits until its opponent catches up.

The process is repeated endlessly, with who does the sprinting a seemingly random phenomenon. Although progress is being made throughout this process, it is latent until the time when the two coexist. It is then that progress is realized.

At this point, criminal justice evaluation and evaluative research in general find themselves in a situation where theory lags far behind technology. As a result, the technical breakthroughs being made advance the quality of evaluations to a limited extent. The area where developmental work is sorely needed is in theory-building. When advances begin to be made along this dimension, i.e., when theory catches up with technology, evaluators will have a potential that far exceeds that of the present.

REFERENCES

The following studies, conducted under National Institute of Justice grants, are available through the Office of Research and Evaluation Methods, National Institute of Justice, Department of Justice, 633 Indiana Avenue, N.W. Washington, D.C. 20531.

Arabie, P., "Blockmodel Techniques for Criminal Justice Research," NIJ Grant 78-NI-AX-0142.
Baumer, T. and D. Rosenbaum, "Measuring Fear of Crime," NIJ Grant 79-NI-AX-0124.
Berk, R. and W. Bielby, "Sources of Error in Criminal Justice Surveys," NIJ Grant 78-NI-AX-0143.
Brennan, T., "Multivariate Taxonomic Techniques," NIJ Grant 78-NI-AX-0065.
Fox, J. and P. Tracey, "A Comparative Validation of Randomized Response and Direct Question Methods," NIJ Grant 78-NI-AX-0123.
Harries, K., "Specification and Test of Populations at Risk," NIJ Grant 78-NI-AX-0064.
Maltz, M., "Developing Improved Techniques for Evaluating Correctional Programs," NIJ Grant 79-NI-AX-0068.
Miller, J. and J. Lincoln, "Analysis of Interorganizational Networks for the Delivery of Criminal Justice Services," NIJ Grant 78-NI-AX-0135.
Srivastava, R. K., "An Ecological Approach to Environmental Evaluation," NIJ Grant 78-NI-AX-0078.
Stollmack, S. and M. Green "Development of Criminal Incidence and Prevalence Models," NIJ Grant 78-NI-AX-0154.
Witte, A., "An Empirical Investigation of Short and Long Run Cost Functions Characterizing Correctional Institutions," NIJ Grant 78-NI-AX-0059.

3

Recent Statistical Developments: Implications for Criminal Justice Evaluation

Richard A. Berk

INTRODUCTION

The rapidly expanding literature on evaluation research methods is becoming more of a problem than a solution. Hardly a month goes by without some new development, often written in highly technical language and sometimes coupled with self-serving claims that are difficult to verify. Moreover, such innovations rarely surface in a vacuum, but speak to past practices and sectarian issues that are typically unimportant for outsiders. Hence, it is almost impossible to keep up with evolving research methods and easy to confuse cute gimmicks with genuine breakthroughs and real advances with reinventions. One significant consequence is a substantial lag between state-of-the-art and current practice.

Recent statistical developments have contributed enormously to this situation. According to a recent article in the *American Statistician* (Minton and Freund, 1977: 114),

> a comprehensive outline of statistics today includes an astonishing array of branches and sub-branches of theory, special methodologies applied to various disciplines, and even competing theories and practices based on differing philosophies. There now exist more than 50 professional journals on statistics, and several hundred other journals publish special statistical methodologies or adaptations to subfields covering almost all of the world's activities.

AUTHOR'S NOTE: Thanks go to William Bielby and Ann Witte for helpful suggestions on a draft of this chapter. In addition, support from the National Institute of Justice, Office of Research and Evaluation Methods, is gratefully acknowledged.

Faced with these complexities, there is no doubt that the evaluation research community would benefit substantially from a series of didactic reviews of recent statistical developments having important implications for empirical research. This chapter is a step in that direction; some statistical developments with special relevance to criminal justice evaluations will be briefly described. Before proceeding however, several essential caveats should be noted.

First, the review will focus on statistical procedures for analysis of the kinds of data common in criminal justice evaluations. This means that some substantive areas will be slighted, and statistical procedures applied to other ends will be neglected. In particular, no effort will be made to review some rather exciting developments in research design and data collection. Topics such as optimally efficient sampling procedures and randomized response techniques will be ignored.

Second, some rather difficult choices had to be made about which data-analytic procedures to include. In the eyes of some readers, important procedures will be given insufficient attention or, worse, will be ignored altogether. There is really no response to such charges, and it is essential to keep in mind that the review is meant to be eclectic, but not exhaustive.

Third, the chapter is written for individuals with a working knowledge of elementary statistics up through the general linear model (multiple regression, analysis of variance, and analysis of covariance). Readers without this background may find the review a bit frustrating. On the other hand, the statistical procedures will not be described in a highly technical manner. The goal is to provide a preliminary understanding of recent developments, not a thorough exegesis. Readers who find themselves intrigued by the material should consult primary sources.

Finally, the review will emphasize perspectives that attempt to build models of the phenomena in question. There is some debate about what one means by the term "model" (Bielby and Hauser, 1977: 141-142), but in this review a model is simply a formal statement of the underlying causal processes a researcher believes generated the observed data. Statistical procedures whose parameters have ambiguous links to causal processes will not be covered, in part because their relevance for evaluation research is unclear.

MODELS WITH LIMITED DEPENDENT VARIABLES

Standard applications of the general linear model (i.e., multiple regression, analysis of variance, analysis of covariance) assume that one's endogenous (dependent) variable is equal-interval. Examples abound: the length of prison sentences, the time police take to respond to a call for assistance, expenditures on criminal justice services, and the like. Note, however, that these variables are clearly bounded at the lower end, since one cannot observe values that are less than zero. It is also possible (though less common) to find equal-interval endogenous variables that are bounded as well at the upper end. For example, one might undertake a study of prison sentences given to individuals convicted of misdemeanors and find no sentences that exceed one year. Finally, many studies employ nominal outcome variables that can be considered a special case of an endogenous variable with an upper and lower bound. Individuals are either arrested or not, police officers either make an arrest or not, a prisoner is either given parole or not. If such variables are coded as "1" for one of the outcomes (a "success") and "0" for the other outcome (a "failure"), observations less than zero or greater than 1 cannot be obtained.

Endogenous variables that have upper and/or lower bounds are often called "limited dependent variables," and they present the data analyst with a variety of statistical difficulties. Fortunately, solutions to these difficulties are usually available.

Nominal Endogenous Variables

Consider an experiment in which prisoners are randomly assigned to a vocational training program for different periods of time. Some prisoners might receive two weeks of training, some four weeks, some six weeks, and so on. In addition, some prisoners are randomly assigned to zero weeks of training. (The use of a randomized experiment simplifies the discussion and does not fundamentally limit its generality.) Finally, of the wide variety of outcomes that might be of concern, assume that prisoners obtaining jobs within some reasonable time is of special interest. An ex-prisoner is *defined* as a "failure"; for example, he or she remains unemployed for two years.[1] The problem then, is to estimate the impact of the vocational training program on ex-prisoners' success in the job market.

One option builds on the general linear model, and an appropriate equation in the population[2] can be represented as follows:

$$Y_i = \alpha + \beta X_i + \epsilon_i, \qquad\qquad [1]$$

where Y_i equals 1 if an ex-prisoner finds a job and 0 if an ex-prisoner does not find a job. X_i is treated as an equal-interval measure of the amount of time in the program,[3] and ϵ_i is an independently distributed random error (a random "shock") with an expected value of zero. Equation 1 is called a "linear probability model," and it can be estimated with ordinary least squares much as in other applications of regression analysis. The regression coefficient β is then interpreted as the change in the *probability* of finding a job for every unit change in X_i (in this case, one week). The intercept α represents the probability of finding a job among those ex-prisoners who received no vocational training (i.e., the mean of Y_i when X_i is zero). This model can be easily extended to include many exogenous variables, some equal-interval and some nominal, and is therefore analogous to the usual applications of multiple regression.

Figure 3.1 shows the scatterplot and fitted regression line for equation 1. The observations on Y_i and X_i are shown by x's, where each x represents many observations. That is, the observations necessarily pile up on the two boundaries. The straight line labeled "LP" (for the linear probability model) is determined by the estimated values of α and β and provides predicted probabilities of finding a job for various values of X_i. For example, the predicted probability (i.e., the mean of Y_i) for people with six weeks of training is about .50. Finally, if the estimate of the slope is .15, it means that for every additional week of vocational training, the probability of finding a job increases .15.

While in practice the linear probability model is often perfectly adequate, it is nevertheless subject to several technical problems. First, since the variance of each random error ϵ_i is equal to the product of the expected value of Y_i and the expected value of $1 - Y_i$ (a probability times 1 minus that probability), the errors are heteroskedastic (i.e., the variance is larger in the middle of the scatterplot, where Y_i approximates $1 - Y_i$). This, in turn, leads to inefficiency and biased[4] standard errors, although estimates of the slope and intercept remain unbiased. In other words, the variance of the sampling distributions of α and β will be "unnecessarily" large, and then when one attempts to estimate this "inflated" variance from data, one's estimates will biased (and inconsistent).[5] In short, significance tests may well be misleading.[6]

Second, if one is interested in using the predicted values of the linear probability model (e.g., the predicted probability of finding a job), one may find predicted probabilities outside of the 1-0 range. Figure 3.1 shows this with dotted extensions of the regression line. For example, the predicted probability of finding a job for ex-prisoners with ten weeks of vocational training is about 1.2. Clearly, this leads to serious problems of interpretation.

The heteroskedasticity can be handled within a generalized least squares framework (e.g., Pindyck and Rubinfeld, 1976: 240-241) in which observations are "reweighted" by the inverse of the estimated standard deviations of the errors. (Sometimes this is called "weighted least squares.") Since the estimated variances will be larger in the middle ranges of the predicted probabilities than at the extremes, the former are given less weight than the latter. The result is homoskedastic errors, and asymptotically (i.e., in large samples) one's difficulties with significance tests disappear. The resulting estimates of the slope and intercept can be interpreted just as in ordinary least squares, and significance tests have their usual meaning.

However, predicted probabilities outside of the 1-0 range are not so easily addressed. One solution that is often adequate if the "outlaw" predictions are

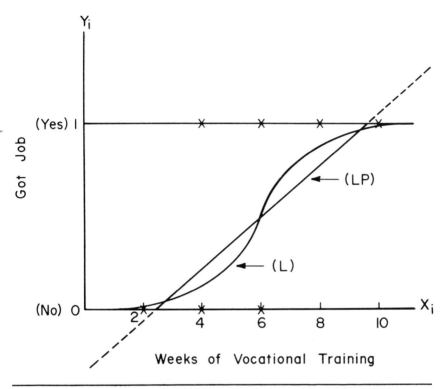

Figure 3.1: The Linear Probability Model (LP) versus the Logit Model (L)

not too common and not too large, is simply to "recode" them back to reasonable values. A predicted probability of 1.3, for example, might be coded at .99, and a predicted probability of −.3 might be recoded back to .01. Yet, this is hardly elegant and, especially in smaller samples, may prevent one from fully capitalizing on the properties of generalized least squares.

In response to such problems, alternative estimation procedures have been developed that in essence fit an S-shaped curve through the scatterplot. All of these have the convenient property of not exceeding the 1-0 range, which in turn eliminates the problem of outlaws. Perhaps the most popular option relies on the logistic curve; it is called the logit model. One form of the logistic model can be represented as:

$$P_i = 1/1 + e^{-(\alpha + \beta X_i)} \qquad [2]$$

where P_i is the probability that an individual will (in this case) get a job, and e is the base of natural logarithms (2.7183).

A logistic curve is shown in Figure 3.1, and it can be seen that it approaches but does not exceed the upper and lower bounds of the 1-0 endogenous variable. In addition, it is steepest where P_i equals .50 and tapers off on either side of .50. One important consequence is that the slope varies, depending on what part of the lⁱ ʒistic curve one considers, and this necessarily produces some complications in interpretation.

Basically, one has two options. First, one can rewrite equation 2 in the following equivalent manner:

$$\text{Log } [P_i/(1 - P_i)] = \alpha + \beta X_i \qquad [3]$$

In this form, one can see that the logarithm of the odds of, say, an ex-prisoner getting a job is "regressed" on the usual linear combination of exogenous variables.[7] Then, the slope indicates the change in the log of the odds of an ex-prisoner finding a job for every additional week of vocational training. Yet, this is often not fully satisfactory, since the log of the odds is not an especially convenient unit of measurement for an endogenous variable (see, for example, Bloom and Singer, 1979). Alternatively, one can return to the logistic curve and the probability metric and consider the slope of the curve at different points. It is common to evaluate (i.e., differentiate) the curve at the mean of X_i (and simultaneously at the means of all other exogenous variables), and that generates an estimate of the change in the probability for a unit change in X_i for "average" cases. Of course, since the slope is not constant, evaluating the curve at other values of X_i will yield different values for the slope. Thus, the slope may be .30 for cases at the mean of X_i and .10 for cases one standard deviation above the mean. Also, it is important to emphasize that these slopes (i.e., derivatives) are not the same as the slopes estimated in equation 2. The former reflect changes in the probabilities, while the latter reflect changes in the logarithm of the odds. One is a nonlinear transformation of the other.

Logistic models may be estimated through maximum likelihood procedures (e.g., Nerlove and Press, 1973; McFadden, 1974)[8] and as such, the estimated standard errors and significance tests are asymptotically valid (i.e., in large samples). However, impressionistic evidence also suggests that they perform well in small samples. Perhaps the major difficulty with the maximum likelihood approach is the cost of running the requisite computer programs. All rely on iterative procedures that can rapidly generate large bills. Many have used this fact to argue for the use of the linear probability models (with adjustments for heteroskedasticity), despite some superior statistical qualities of the logit formulation. Their position is further strengthened by the common observation that the substantive conclusions from the two approaches are usually much the same.[9]

The logistic model can be elaborated in a number of ways. First, one is not limited to a single exogenous variable, and both nominal and equal-interval variables may be employed (Witte and Schmidt, 1979). Second, one may use an endogenous variable with more than two categories—with "acquitted," "dismissed," "pled guilty," and "found guilty," for example. Under such circumstances, one basically estimates a single logit equation for all possible pairs of binary outcomes (e.g., acquitted versus dismissed, dismissed versus found guilty, and so forth), with redundant comparisons excluded (Nerlove and Press, 1973). Then, one interprets each of the equations much as in the single-equation case. Third, when all of one's exogenous variables are categorical, one may resort to alternative estimation techniques that can markedly cut one's computational costs. The techniques rely either on maximum likelihood procedures (e.g., Goodman, 1972) or generalized least squares (e.g., Grizzle et al., 1969).[10] In large samples, both yield virtually identical results.

To this point we have been comparing the linear probability model with the logit model. However, the logistic curve is not the only relevant S-shaped curve, and one alternative relies on the cumulative normal (i.e., the S-shaped cumulative version of the more familiar "bell-shaped" normal distribution). Techniques using the cumulative normal are called probit models, and they have found occasional applications in criminal justice evaluations (e.g., Mallar and Thornton, 1978). Probit models have many characteristics in common with logit approaches, although the coefficients that emerge have very different interpretations. The slopes reflect the change in a random normal variant (like a "z score") related to the probability of a given outcome for every unit change in the exogenous variable (Hanushek and Jackson, 1977: 204-207). Since the substantive implications of such coefficients are ambiguous, it is common to take the derivative of the predicted cumulative normal curve for "interesting" values of the X_i (much as in the case of the logit model). In any case, the logit and probit approaches yield very similar substantive conclusions, and a choice between them may often rest on available software.

Finally, discriminant (function) analysis may also have been used in situations where the endogenous variable is nominal. However, discriminant procedures can be formultated in logistic terms (Effron, 1971) so that on *theoretical* grounds either technique may suffice. Differences between logit and discriminant approaches stem from the assumptions one is prepared to make about the nature of the *exogenous* variables. In particular, discriminant analysis requires that the exogenous variables be drawn from a multivariate normal distribution. When this assumption is violated (e.g., when one or more of the predictors are nominal), one can be seriously misled (Halperin et al., 1971). Logit techniques chart a more conservative course by making no assumptions about the underlying distributions of the exogenous variables. The estimates that result are treated as *conditional* on the given exogenous observations (i.e., the data on hand). Readers interested more generally in the tradeoffs between conditional and unconditional estimation procedures should consult any reasonably thorough econometrics text (e.g., Kmenta, 1971: 297-304), but in most criminal justice applications the advantages of discriminant analysis do not outweigh the disadvantages.

Truncated and Censored Endogenous Variables.

The complications produced when an endogenous variable is limited on one side only are even more serious than the nominal case. Moreover, the full implications are only now coming to the attention of empirical researchers. Since so many endogenous variables in criminal justice research are bounded on one side, a great deal of future work will no doubt be affected.

Consider the following example. Instead of using whether or not an ex-prisoner finds employment as an outcome variable, suppose that one is interested in the hourly wages earned by ex-prisoners. Ex-prisoners who do not find work are coded as earning zero wages. The exogenous variable is the same as before: the weeks of vocational training obtained in prison.

Figure 3.2 provides an initial sense of the kinds of difficulties that can result. While one normally expects the bivariate scatterplot to be shaped roughly like an ellipse, the bivariate scatterplot in Figure 3.2 is truncated from below; its lower-left portion is flattened. This, in turn, means that the residuals are constrained for values of X_i below 6. There is less room for them to vary beneath the regression line than above it. For example, the distance from a to b in Figure 3.2 is smaller than the distance from b to c. More precisely stated, *all* of the residuals are, in principle, constrained from below, but the constraint is more serious at lower values of X_i.

Such truncations have at least two important implications. First, one's errors (ϵ_i) will not have equal variances over the full range of X_i. The resulting heteroskedasticity leads to inefficiency in one's estimates of the slope and intercept, and biased estimates of their standard errors. Second, and more important, one's estimates of the slope and intercept will be biased and inconsistent. In particular, the slope will be attenuated (whether the truncation is from below or above, in the bivariate case). In Figure 3.2 one can see that the estimated regression line is flatter than the true regression line.[11]

Much of the current interest in truncated endogenous variables stems from a classic paper by James Tobin (1958). In that paper, he observes that the bias in one's estimate of the slope is greater to the degree that a large number of observations on the endogenous variable fall at the boundary.[12] In essence, when a large number of observations cluster on the boundary, the scatterplot is shifted

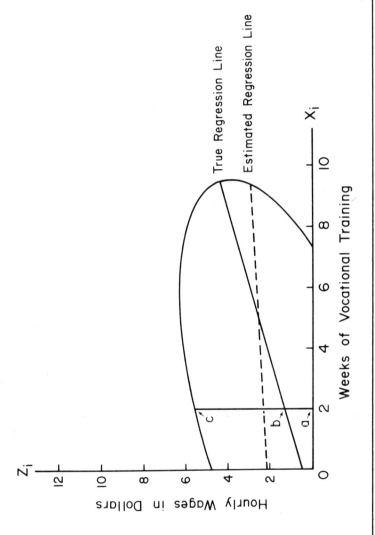

Figure 3.2: An Instance of a Truncated Endogenous Variable

toward the boundary. Then, the plot is more severely flattened, and the attenuation in the slope is increased. Moreover, serious truncation implies that characterizing the entire causal process with only a single functional form (e.g., a linear relationship) is incorrect. Rather, one may well need one functional form for observations clustering at the boundary and another functional form for observations above the boundary. That is, by using a single functional form, one has committed a specification error.[13]

Tobin's solution is to estimate simultaneously a probit model for observations on or below the boundary (for truncation from below) and a linear model for the other observations (called a Tobit model). In our example, one would simultaneously estimate a probit model for whether or not an ex-prisoner found a job (coded 1-0) and a linear regression model based on the wages of those who found jobs. In other words, one would estimate two functional forms at once for different parts of the distribution of the endogenous variable, and maximum likelihood procedures exist for such models.

Recently, Tobin's early work has been recast and extended by a number of talented econometricians (e.g., Amemyia, 1974; Nelson, 1973; Heckman, 1974, 1976, 1979).[14] Heckman's efforts are particularly instructive because of the substantive fallout under the alternative rubrics of "censoring" or "sample selection bias."

In this context, suppose one tried to circumvent the truncation problems described above by focusing exclusively on *employed* ex-prisoners. For this subset of ex-prisoners, one would, in principle, be able to obtain nonzero observations of their wages. This sort of "sampling" strategy is common in a wide variety of criminal justice studies, despite sample size reduction. For example, one might examine the sentences, given a subset of offenders found guilty of felonies. Offenders tried for felonies but acquitted with no sentence (perhaps coded zero) would be excluded from the analysis; a sentence length would be observed for the others. Unfortunately, the biases described by Tobin remain, although under a different guise.

Consider Figure 3.3, in which hourly wages (Z_i) is regressed on weeks of vocational training (X_i). Note that the regression line can be extended below the boundary of zero wages (i.e., unemployment), even though negative wages cannot actually be observed.

What determines whether a real wage will be observed? That is, what determines whether the ex-prisoner finds a job? Observations A_1, A_2, and A_3 represent the wages of ex-prisoners whose hours of job training alone would have placed them below the threshold of zero wages (i.e., unemployment). Yet, through forces captured in the error term (ϵ_i), wages are in fact observed. In essence, random "luck" led to a job and consequently to wages.

Observations B_1, B_2, and B_3 represent wages of ex-prisoners whose hours of vocational training were sufficient by themselves to land the ex-prisoners jobs.

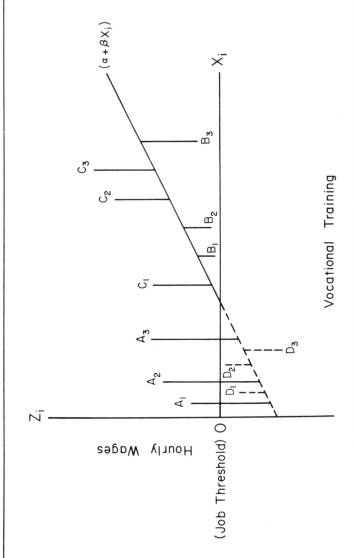

Figure 3.3: An Illustration of Heckman's Censoring Model

These individuals did not need luck to pass the threshold; indeed, their luck was bad luck (i.e., the residuals are negative). That is, their bad luck lowered their wages from what they should have received based on their vocational training, but the impact of the training was large enough to at least allow them to enter the labor force.

Observations C_1, C_2, and C_3 represent the wages of employed ex-prisoners who have found work solely as a function of their vocational training, but who have also benefitted from good luck. For these individuals, higher wages were received than one would have expected from their vocational training alone.

Finally, "observations" D_1, D_2, and D_3 represent ex-prisoners who did not pass the job threshold either because of vocational training *or* good luck. (There is also the case, not shown, in which *bad* luck outweighs vocational training, so no job is found.) These individuals have no wages that can be observed, and consequently their wage observations are "censored." That is, they have wage-earning potential not realized in the form of wages. Note also that in our illustration, these individuals are dropped from the analysis (in the Tobin framework, the Ds are coded as zero).

What, then, are the consequences of dropping observations D_1, D_2, and D_3? Consider the A observations and the fact that coupled with the large positive residuals are relatively low values for weeks of vocational training. This means that the residuals and weeks of training are *inversely* related. For the B observations, there are large negative residuals coupled with relatively many weeks of training. Hence, again there is an *inverse* relationship between the residuals and weeks of training. For the C observations, large positive residuals are coupled with relatively many weeks of training, leading to a *positive* relationship between the residuals and training. Finally, the D observations are censored and hence neglected altogether.

Now, note that the inverse (negative) relationships between the residuals and vocational training created by the B observations is approximately cancelled out by the positive relationships between the residuals and training for the C observations. That is, there are three observations with positive associations and three observations with negative associations. However, since the D observations are excluded (and could not be observed in any case), there are no observations to counterbalance the negative associations for the A observations. Consequently, *overall*, one is left with a tendency for the residuals and weeks of vocational training to be negatively correlated.

Generalizing from Figure 3.3, whenever one capitalizes on a subset of observations reflecting some naturally occurring selection process (e.g., one must find a job before wages can be observed), one risks building in correlations between the residuals and the exogenous variable(s). This, in turn, means that one's regression estimates will be biased and inconsistent. In short, Tobin's conclusions may well follow, even if one tries to circumvent the truncation difficulties by excluding the problematic observations.

Fortunately, there are several ways in which the inconsistency problems caused by truncation (or censoring) can be eliminated. First, if one is *really* concerned solely with the subset of cases for which observations are obtained, one can define the problem away. That is, one can proceed with regression analyses for the subset as usual, as long as one is clear that any conclusions are relevant *only for that subset.* However, this is often trickier than it might first appear. In our example, it would be all too easy to estimate a model explaining for ex-prisoners who find jobs the impact of vocational training on "earning potential," and then slip into talking about the more general impact of vocational training on the "earning potential" for ex-prisoners. Part of the temptation derives from the common tendency to treat a measured variable as an indicator of some more fundamental, underlying attribute such as "earning potential" (or "criminality," "crime seriousness," and so forth) which presumably characterizes not just the subset of cases for which real observations are obtained, but also the subset for which real observations are not obtained. In addition, evaluators are often mandated to study program effects for a population of cases, including both the uncensored and censored observations. In our example, one could well imagine a policy maker wanting to know about the impact of vocational training on all ex-prisoners, not just those who managed to find jobs.

A second approach is to turn to the Tobit model described earlier. Then one works with the full set of cases, not just the subset for which real observations are obtained. Perhaps the major difficulty is the computational costs of the maximum likelihood procedures.

A third strategy is to employ estimation procedures for the subset of cases with real observations, after making a number of adjustments that produce consistent estimates (Amemiya, 1973). The natures of these procedures are well beyond the scope of this discussion, but they are within the data transformation capabilities of many routinely available statistical packages, such as SAS and SPSS. Perhaps the major problem is that such estimators are inefficient and, in addition, there is some debate about how best to generate estimates of the standard errors (Sickles and Schmidt, 1978). Consequently, it is common to use the estimates of the causal parameters solely as start values for Tobin's maximum likelihood approach.

Finally, one can break up Tobin's dual likelihood function into its constituent parts and proceed with two separate equations (Heckman, 1978). In the first equation, one applies a probit model to estimate the probability that a case (e.g., an ex-prisoner) will exceed the threshold (e.g., get a job). All of the cases are used in this equation, and once *predicted* probabilities are generated for each case (e.g., the predicted probability of finding a job), a new variable called a "hazard rate" is constructed. Then, a second equation is estimated with least squares procedures for the subset of cases having real observations on the endogenous variable of interest (e.g., wages). However, the hazard rate is introduced as a new variable that basically controls for the sample selection bias. Perhaps the major advantage of this two-equation procedure is that valid expressions for the standard errors have been derived. When the Tobit model is not computationally feasible, the two-equation approach is perhaps the best alternative.

It is important to stress that the practical importance of the problems produced by truncation and censoring have yet to be demonstrated in criminal justice studies. So far, the proper statistical adjustments have not led to markedly different results (e.g., Witte and Schmidt, 1977). Yet, the biases are in principle very significant, and may help to explain the abundance of null findings in program evaluations.

MULTIPLE-EQUATION MODELS

Suppose one were interested in the impact of different police patrolling practices and, in particular, the effect of police officers walking a beat rather than riding in patrol cars. Imagine, then, a research design in which one examines variation across a large number of cities in the percentage of their police personnel walking a beat, and how this variation corresponds to city clearance rates.[15] Such relationships can be represented with a pair of equations: one that characterizes the causes of differential personnel allocations across cities, and one that characterizes the causes of differential clearance rates. These two equations could take the following form:

$$Y_1 = \alpha_0 + \alpha_1 X_1 + \alpha_2 X_2 + \ldots + \alpha_K X_K + \epsilon_1; \qquad [4a]$$

$$Y_2 = \beta_0 + \beta_1 Y_1 + \beta_2 Z_1 + \beta_2 Z_2 + \ldots + \beta_L Z_L + \epsilon_2. \qquad [4b]$$

Y_1 is the percentage of police personnel walking a beat; X_1 through X_K form a set of K exogenous variables in the first equation; Y_2 is the clearance rate; and Z_1 through Z_L are a set of L exogenous variables in the second equation.[16] In practice, the exogenous variables represented by the Xs and Zs may overlap to varying degrees; at the extremes, each equation may have its own unique set of exogenous variables or the same exogenous variables may be present in both equations. The a's are the regression coefficients for the first equation and the βs are the regression coefficients for the second equation (a_0 and β_0 represent the intercepts). The error terms, for their respective equations, are ϵ_1 and ϵ_2, and we shall assume that these error terms are uncorrelated. That is, random perturbations affecting the first equation are uncorrelated with random perturbations affecting the second equation. We shall also assume that for each equation itself, the errors fulfill the standard ordinary least squares assumptions.

The first equation indicates that the percentage of police personnel walking a beat in different cities is a linear function of such things as the police budget, population density (e.g., patrolling on foot in many parts of Los Angeles may not be feasible), the number of patrol cars standardized by the number of patrol officers, and the like. The second equation indicates that clearance rates across different cities are a linear function of such things as percentage of detectives on the police force and the quality of the crime laboratory (perhaps indexed by its budget). However, the second equation also includes the endogenous variable from the first equation: the percentage of police officers on foot patrol.

Equations 4a and 4b might be simply treated as separate regression equations, were it not for the presence of Y_1 as a predictor in equation 4b. In other words, if Y_1 were not a predictor in equation 4b, one could proceed by considering each equation completely in isolation with the usual least squares procedures. However, since Y_1 is a predictor in the second equation, what happens in the first equation has implications for the second. Cities with larger budgets might have more police officers on patrol (equation 4a), and then these cities may have higher clearance rates (equation 4b). Since these equations are linked, one really needs to consider both equations as a single model.

Equations such as 4a and 4b are called recursive models, and recursive models may be extended to include many equations. Recursive models are characterized by uncorrelated errors across equations and by the absence of reciprocal causation. That is, besides the assumption that the errors are uncorrelated across equations, one assumes that there is no "feedback" between the endogenous variables. For example, Y_1 may cause Y_2, but Y_2 is not permitted to cause Y_1. It is important to stress that such assumptions should be justified by theory and/or previous research, since by and large they cannot be extracted inductively from the data alone (Duncan, 1975).[17]

Recursive models are easily estimated. One may resort to ordinary least squares to obtain unbiased and efficient estimates of the model's parameters, and the slopes and intercepts are then interpreted just as in single-equation models. In addition, however, it is also common (especially for sociologists) to represent such models with diagrams (see, for example, Duncan, 1975) and to employ standardized rather than metric (unstandardized) coefficients. In this form, recursive models are translated in "path diagrams" and the standardized regression coefficients are called "path coefficients." Path coefficients then indicate the change in standard deviations in the endogenous variable for a change of one standard deviation in any given exogenous variable (or an endogenous variable used as a predictor). There is no particular advantage to using the standardized coefficients, and indeed, they may often suggest rather misleading conclusions about the causal importance of different variables (see, for example, Hanushek and Jackson, 1977: 76-79).[18] In contrast, the choice between diagrams and equations as a way to represent the model makes no difference except in terms of packaging. Some researchers find equations easier to understand, while others prefer diagrams.

In recursive models, each equation by itself may be interpreted just as in single-equation models, and it is also possible to characterize formally causal effects across equations. "Direct effects" refers to causal relationships for which there are no intermediate variables. Each of the regression coefficients in equations 4a and 4b represents direct effects. "Shared effects" refer to causal impacts generated by two or more variables that cannot be partitioned into components uniquely attributable to a single variable. Thus, population density and police budgets may both have direct effects on the percentage of officers on foot patrol and, in addition, there may be a shared effect that cannot be partitioned between them. Shared effects are *not* interaction effects.[19]

Finally, "indirect effects" refers to relationships for which there are one or more intermediate variables. The impact of X_1, for example, on Y_2 *through* Y_1 is an instance of an indirect effect. Cities with greater population densities may have a higher percentage of their police on foot patrol, and cities with more police officers on foot patrol may have higher clearance rates. The impact of population density on clearance rates is an indirect effect. (A single coefficient for an indirect effect can be calculated.)

When the relationships between exogenous variables and endogenous variables are separated into direct, indirect, and shared effects, and when standardized coefficients are used, the process is called "path analysis." However, one can undertake the same sort of partitioning with unstandardized coefficients, and, especially in policy-relevant research, the latter is usually preferable. One's results will typically be more easily translated into practical recommendations and the ambiguities of standardized coefficients are avoided.

Multiple-equation models are not restricted to the recursive format. Suppose that one were to alter equation 4a so that Y_2 becomes a predictor of Y_1. The Y_1 and Y_2 are then reciprocally related: Y_2 causes Y_1 in equation 4a, and Y_1 causes Y_2 in equation 4b. One might argue that not only does the percentage of officers on foot patrol affect clearance rates, but clearance rates "feedback" on patrolling practices. If the use of foot patrols increases the clearance rate, cities will use more foot patrols. Such models are called nonrecursive, in part to denote this two-way causation.

Nonrecursive models lead to a number of statistical complications.[20] In particular, endogenous variables used as predictors are necessarily correlated with the error terms in their respective equations (e.g., Y_2 would be correlated with ϵ_1), which means that ordinary least squares estimates are biased and inconsistent. Worse, it may be impossible to obtain distinct estimates of all the regression coefficients in the model. The first complication requires the use of alternative estimation procedures, and the second requires that one consider the issue of "identification."

In nonrecursive models, identification must be addressed first. In brief, the input information available from the data set is contained within the first and second moments of the data set (i.e., the means, the variances, and the covariances). All of the regression parameters are functions of these moments, and there must be a sufficient number to yield distinct estimates of each regression parameter. When there are not enough moments, one or more of the equations will be "underidentified," and it will be impossible to obtain distinct estimates for the underidentified equation(s).[21] When there are precisely the number of moments required, the equations are "just identified," and distinct estimates may be obtained. When there is a surplus of moments, more than one distinct estimate for each coefficient may be obtained, and some sort of "averaging" procedure must be implemented. Techniques for determining whether each equation is identified can be found in a variety of texts (e.g., Kmenta, 1971) and for relatively simple nonrecursive models, at least, these are easy to apply. Regardless, it is the underidentified case that is problematic, since without alterations in one's model or the imposition of additional assumptions, interpretable estimates for the regression parameters cannot be obtained.[22]

Assuming that one has equations that are just identified or overidentified, the next problem is how best to estimate the regression coefficients from the data. Fortunately, there are a number of viable procedures, with two-stage least squares perhaps the most popular. Recall that ordinary least squares estimates are biased and inconsistent because endogenous variables used as predictors (e.g., Y_1 and Y_2) are correlated with the errors (e.g., ϵ_1 and ϵ_2). One requires, therefore, some means to eliminate these correlations, and two-stage least squares accomplishes this in two steps.

First, each endogenous variable is regressed on *all* of the exogenous variables (e.g., the Xs *and* the Zs in equations 4a and 4b), using ordinary least squares. The equations with each endogenous variable regressed on all of the exogenous variables are called the "reduced-form" equations. Then, the predicted values are calculated for each of the endogenous variables, based on the regression results. Note that since by assumption (i.e., specification) each of the exogenous variables is asymptotically uncorrelated with the errors in the original equations, and since the predicted values for the endogenous variables are a linear combination of these, the predicted values are also asymptotically uncorrelated with those errors. In other words, the predicted values are "purged" of their correlations with the errors.

Second, the purged endogenous variables are inserted back into the original equations (called the "structural-form" equations) as replacements for the original endogenous variables. Then, one can proceed with ordinary least squares to obtain consistent estimates of the regression coefficients. Since the endogenous variables are now asymptotically uncorrelated with the errors (as a result of the first stage of the process), the inconsistency disappears.

In practice, two-stage least squares is accomplished in one pass through the data, although both the reduced-form and structural-form results may be obtained. The reduced-form results provide coefficients for the impact of all exogenous variables, ignoring how the endogenous variables are related to one another. They often have important policy implications as representations of the causal impact factors that are external to a system of reciprocal relations, and thus can be interpreted as single-equation models (i.e., fully in isolation from one another). The structural forms have to be handled a bit more carefully. One can interpret the regression coefficients as usual (along with significance tests), but measures of the error variances (and the R^2s) capture the effects of stochastic factors across all the equations in the model. Hence, they do not have their usual meaning and are often difficult to use in a substantive manner. Readers interested in some recent applications in criminal justice evaluations should consult the growing literature on economic approaches to crime (e.g., Becker and Landes, 1974; Blumstein et al., 1978).

Two-stage least squares has become popular because it is robust to specification errors and computationally inexpensive. Basically, each structural equation in the second stage is estimated one at a time. Yet it is possible to obtain more efficient estimates with procedures that use the entire set of structural equations at once. Three-stage least squares is one example and, in addition, maximum likelihood procedures exist (Kmenta, 1971: 573-581).[23]

UNOBSERVED VARIABLES

Since the data bases used in empirical work contain variables for which one has observations, the idea of an unobserved variable may not seem particularly relevant to criminal justice evaluations. At best, unobserved variables may serve to make researchers cautious about specifications resting only on the data at hand; neglected causal variables may be flagged. However, unobserved variables actually play a critical empirical role in the kinds of statistical procedures we have been addressing, and have recently become the subject of great interest.

Consider the bivariate least squares model represented in equation 1. Besides Y_i and X_i, the equation includes an error term represented by ϵ_i. These random perturbations are not directly observed, and yet their variance (at least) is routinely estimated. Recall that in ordinary least squares the errors are assumed to explain the difference between the values of Y_i and the values of Y_i predicted from exogenous variables. We assume that each error has an expected value of zero, the same variance, and is uncorrelated with all other errors. Building on these premises, residuals obtained from a given data set can be used to estimate the errors and their common variance. In other words, one poses a causal model including unobserved random perturbations, and then, with the help of some additional assumptions, the unobserved errors become observable.

Similar processes may be employed in a range of other circumstances. A model is proposed, some additional assumptions are made, and then it is often possible to estimate certain characteristics of variables that cannot be directly observed. Perhaps the most widely known applications involve exogenous variables that are measured imperfectly.

Suppose that in equation 1, X_i is measured imperfectly. X_i is, in fact, a linear combination of some "true" value X_i' and some random measurement error W_i. Using the classic "errors in variables" model (Kmenta, 1971: 307-309),

$$X_i = X_i' + W_i. \qquad [5]$$

In equation 5, one typically assumes that as random measurement error, W_i, has an expected value of zero and a constant variance, it is not serially correlated with itself and is not correlated with the true score X_i'. In other words, W_i fulfills the standard OLS assumptions. Note that while one can observe X_i in equation 5, both the true scores and the errors are unobservable.

Even though the measurement error in equation 5 is random, the measurement error leads to biased and inconsistent estimates when X_i is used as an *exogenous* variable in a regression equation. (If X_i is endogenous, the random measurement error inflates the variance of the error term but the metric regression parameter estimates remain unbiased.) Too often such problems are ignored, which means that many researchers report results that are biased to some unknown degree. Alternatively, arguments are sometimes made that discount the bias; the variance in the measurement error is said to be small, relative to the variance in the true scores. In other words, the amount of random measurement error is claimed to be trivial.

However, there are sometimes better ways to proceed, and our ability to address formally the causes and consequences of measurement error has improved dramatically over the past decade. Continuing with the classic errors in variables perspective, suppose that one were able to obtain a second round of measures on X_i under approximately the same conditions that held when the first round of measures on X_i were collected. One could then represent the second set of measures in an equation identical to equation 5, except that the observations on X_i would be different. If one treats the second round as a replication of the first round,

$$X_i^* = X_i' + V_i. \qquad [6]$$

The X_i^* are the second round measures of X_i; V_i is a new error term having the same properties as W_i; and the X_i' are the same true scores as before. One also assumes that V_i is uncorrelated with W_i (sometimes a heroic assumption).

Equations 5 and 6 imply that the true scores are the same in both instances, but another set of random measurement errors alter the observed values in the second round.

Using equations 5 and 6 in concert with the two sets of observations, it is possible to estimate the variance of the true scores and the variances of W_i and V_i, even though these variables are unobserved. And while the variances may be of general interest themselves, they may also be used to obtain a consistent estimate of the formerly inconsistent regression coefficient for the observed X values (Duncan, 1975: 199-222).[24]

Of late, it has become popular to represent models with errors in variables not only with sets of equations, but with figures much like earlier path diagrams. Thus:

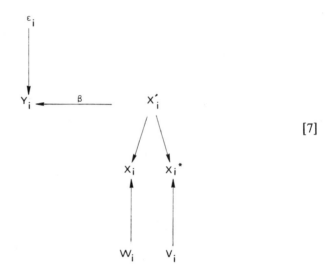

[7]

Y_i is now seen as a linear function of its stochastic term and the *true* value of X. This is the substantive part of the model and is identical to equation 1 except that now true rather than observed values of the exogenous variable are inserted. Equations 5 and 6, which captured the measurement process, are also depicted; both sets of observations on the single exogenous variable are a linear function of the same underlying (unobserved) true scores and two unobserved random perturbations. In such formulations, the true scores are often called latent or unmeasured variables, and they have the same basic status as factors in factor analytic techniques (Bielby and Hauser, 1977). Indeed, taken as a whole, the appropriate maximum likelihood procedures are often called confirmatory factor analysis. (As such, they are attributed to the work of Karl Joreskog and his colleagues.)[25]

Models with unobserved variables may be elaborated in a wide variety of interesting ways (Bielby and Hauser, 1977; Aigner and Goldberger, 1977). Both exogenous and endogenous variables may be unobserved. Far more complicated measurement structures may be modeled (e.g., one can have correlated measurement errors). Panel data or cross-sectional data may be analyzed using multiple recursive or nonrecursive equations. For our purposes here, however, the most important point is that unobserved variables can become part of one's causal model.

The author is unaware of any published criminal justice evaluations in which confirmatory factor analytic models have been used. However, there are at least three possible applications which may well be in process somewhere and for which such models are ideally suited. First, confirmatory factor analysis can be used to address the classic underadjustment problem in nonequivalent control group designs (e.g., Magidson, 1977). For example, important differences between the experimental and control groups can be treated as an unobserved variable that becomes part of one's substantive model. If the model's specification is correct, experimental and control groups become statistically equivalent prior to the treatment. Second, when one has multiple indicators of some underlying variable of interest, that underlying variable rather than each of the indicators may be used in one's substantive model. For example, one may be studying the rearrest rates of individuals on parole and believe that past proclivity to crime is a critical underlying causal variable. In addition, one may have a variety of observed indicators of that past proclivity: the age at first arrest, the number of prior arrests, the number of years spent in prison, the number of previous convictions, and so on. A common strategy is to include all of these indicators in a causal model, but besides likely multicollinearity, one's *theory* claims that past criminal proclivity, not the proxies for it, is the relevant causal variable. Hence, a proper specification would include the single latent variable as the cause of rearrest, not the indicators. Such a model would look much like our earlier diagram, with X_i' the past proclivity causing both Y_i (the number of rearrests) and many observed indicators. Finally, confirmatory factor analysis can be used to study measurement error itself in criminal justice evaluations. Here, the equations representing the measurement process are no longer just means to consistent estimates, but themselves a subject of study. In collaboration with William Bielby, the author is employing such models to explore the measurement error in survey items commonly used in criminal justice evaluations.[26]

TIME-SERIES MODELS

Longitudinal data are widely available for criminal justice evaluations: arrests per month, homicides per year, convictions per month, and the like. Until recently it was common to analyze such data almost exclusively with single- or multiple-equation least squares procedures, much as with cross-sectional data. With longitudinal data, however, a number of complications often develop. First, serially correlated residuals are likely, which in turn requires the use of generalized least squares. Second, a given endogenous variable is often taken to be a function of one or more exogenous variables with delayed causal effects. Thus, a police department's budget could be estimated as a function of the crime rate not only of the immediately preceding year, but of a large number of earlier years. Among other problems, serious multicollinearity usually results, and distributed lag approaches become necessary (Kmenta, 1971: 473-495). In brief, distributed lag techniques propose a simplifying set of mechanisms (a theory) by which the regression coefficients of the lagged exogenous variables are related to the endogenous variable, and these simplifications make estimation feasible.[27] However, these approaches usually imply that a given endogenous variable is also a function of itself at some earlier point in time (e.g., Y_t is a function Y_{t-1}) and when coupled with serially correlated errors, regression coefficients become inconsistent. Consequently, procedures much like two-stage least squares are required (Johnson, 1972: 300-321).

Third, the use of lagged endogenous variables for any reason makes the model dynamic. While this in turn opens up the possibility for over-time simulations of the behavior of endogenous variables, additional statistical technology is required (Pindyck and Rubinfeld, 1976: 308-369). One has to worry, for example, about whether the endogenous variables evidence reasonably stable patterns over time or if they oscillate with increasingly large deviations from their mean.

Finally, one sometimes has data with both cross-sectional and time-series variation. One might, for instance, have data on the relationship between crime rates and police expenditures by month for five years and over a large number of cities. Months are the over-time units and cities are the cross-sectional units. Such data typically have enormous potential, but raise still more complications. For example, one may have to deal with cross-sectional serial correlation as well as longitudinal serial correlation (Kmenta, 1971: 508-517).[28]

Despite these and other difficulties, structural-equation models for longitudinal data will no doubt be productively used in the future. Indeed, if one wants to represent formally and test an elaborate theory about a social program or social process, one really has little choice. Yet, deriving from the initial work of Box and Jenkins (1970), viable alternatives for longitudinal data are evolving that do not require such thorough substantive grounding.

Recall the logic of randomized experiments. The world is assumed (often explicitly) to be too complex for formal modeling, so one designs experiments to simplify it. After experimental and control subjects are randomly assigned, any preexisting differences between experimentals and controls are, on the average, eliminated. That is, by the time the treatment is introduced, external factors that might be confounded with experimental and control group comparisons have been randomized away. One does not really care what these confounding influences might be; they are treated as an unfortunate annoyance (for that experiment). The strategy, in brief, is to focus on a relatively simple causal process and eliminate confounding variables.

Time-series techniques used in evaluation settings build on a similar strategy. Rather than trying formally to model a set of complicated longitudinal processes, one attempts to eliminate from the data a wide variety of confounding influences in order to focus on relatively simple causal mechanisms of interest. In evaluation contexts, that is typically the impact of some intervention.

Suppose one were concerned with the impact of a new law allowing state police to use radar to detect speeding.[29] The premise is that wide knowledge that police are using radar will act as a deterrent. As an outcome measure, one might include data on the number of automobile fatalities by month, and attempt to determine if the time series shows a reduction in fatalities after the passage of the legislation.

A moment's thought will quickly suggest a number of causal variables that may be confounded with the introduction of radar: seasonal patterns in the number of drivers on the road, variation by month in weather conditions, responses to rising gasoline prices, and the like. In addition, a time series of fatalities will vary as a function of stochastic forces over and above what might be formally modeled with substantive variables. This means that chance patterns confounded with the introduction of radar must also be addressed.

A structural equation analysis might attempt to model formally these processes and also to include one or more variables to tap the impact of the intervention. In its simplest form, the intervention might be captured with a single dummy variable coded as zero before the legislation, and 1 thereafter. Then, one could, in principle, determine if the intercept of the time series dropped when the radar was introduced. Yet, any conclusions about the intervention rest fundamentally on the model's specification. In particular, if important casual variables have been overlooked or if data on these variables are not available, misspecification will undermine the analysis.

Time-series techniques proceed somewhat differently (Box and Tiao, 1975). To begin, certain kinds of deterministic or stochastic confounding influences are removed through differencing. Differencing simply involves subtracting earlier observations from later observations. If, for example, the time series evidences changes in level over time, subtracting each Y_{t-1} from the following Y_t will remove the pattern. Changes in slope can be removed by taking the difference of these differences. Thus, if drivers speed less because of increases in the price of gasoline and if this in turn reduces the number of fatalities, differencing will remove the shifting levels from the data. (One can then work directly with these differences as the "new" data.) Similarly, perhaps automobile fatalities rise and fall as a function of the time of the year. Fatalities may increase in summer months when people do more driving; months with more rainfall may also be months with more accidents. Such cyclical patterns can be removed with appropriate differencing. In the case of monthly patterns, one subtracts Y_{t-12} from Y_t; the number of accidents in January in a year is subtracted from the number of January accidents in the next year, and this is done for each month and for all years (except the earliest year for which no earlier observations exist). Before such patterns are removed, the time series is called nonstationary; after they are removed the time series is called stationary (if some other assumptions are met). Yet, the really essential point is that the impact of certain confounding causal variables is not modeled; the impact is removed.[30]

It is also necessary to develop a model for the stochastic processes in the (now) stationary time series. Such models are not specified in response to substantive theory, but are derived *inductively* from the data. Again, one does not really care about the substantive meaning of the proposed processes; one simply wants to adjust for them. In brief, one tries a range of possible stochastic models, evaluates a number of diagnostic statistics for each, and then selects the model that best fits the data. In simple models, at least, various kinds of serial correlation in the stationary time series are the main concern, and the goal is to provide appropriate models for these.[31]

Some models for the serial correlation are called "autoregressive," and they come in various orders (conventionally designated by "p"). An autoregressive model of order 1 (i.e., an AR1) can be diagramed as follows:

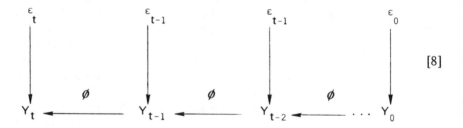

$$[8]$$

In the form of an equation an AR1 can be represented as:

$$Y_t = \phi Y_{t-1} + \epsilon_t. \qquad [9]$$

Y_t are the time-series observations, ϵ_t is an error term meeting OLS assumptions, and ϕ is a coefficient, much like a regression coefficient, but in stationary time series ranges between +1 and −1. Among the most important implications of AR1 models is that each time-series observation is directly dependent on the previous observation and a random perturbation. In addition, the impact of earlier observations on later observations dissipates exponentially with longer lags, and ultimately each observation is a function only of current and earlier perturbations. Higher-order autoregressive models permit Y_t to be directly affected not only by the immediately preceding Y_{t-1}, but also directly by earlier observations (e.g., Y_{t-2} and Y_{t-3}), a kind of multiple autoregressive model.

A second set of models accounting for serial correlation in a stationary time series is called "moving average models." These also come in various orders (conventionally designated by "q"), but the simplest comes in order 1 (i.e., an MA1):

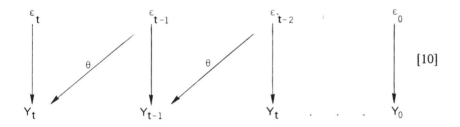

$$[10]$$

Alternatively, in equation form:

$$Y_t = \theta \epsilon_{t-1} + \epsilon_t. \qquad [11]$$

Y_t and ϵ_t are the same as before, while θ is a new coefficient which in a stationary time series necessarily ranges between +1 and −1.[32] Perhaps the most important consequence for the MA1 model (and all moving average models) is that adjacent time-series observations are made to correspond (i.e., correlate) because they are affected by the same random perturbation. This implies that moving average models have no "memory" in the sense that autoregressive models do. For example, the values of Y_{t-2} are unrelated to the values of Y_t. Yet, like autoregressive models, moving average models can come in higher orders so that, for example, ϵ_{t-2} as well as ϵ_{t-1} can directly influence Y_t (an MA2 model).

Autoregressive models and moving average models have very specific implications for the pattern of correlations observed in the time series Y_t, and the goal is to use these models to account for that pattern. With this accomplished, one has a model for the stochastic patterns in the stationary time series.

In practice, one uses differencing, autoregressive models, and moving average models in concert to characterize the time series. In this form, they are called ARIMA models and are meant to capture ongoing properties of the time series.[33] However, in the usual evaluation applications, one also must capture the impact of the intervention. In simple models, one employs a dummy variable (coded 1 before the intervention and zero thereafter) whose impact on the time series can take a number of forms (Box and Tiao, 1975). One may, for example, try to capture the impact of the intervention with a change in the level of the time series after the intervention (i.e., a shift in the mean); or one may allow for a more gradual shift to a new level; or it is possible to model changes in the slope of the time series (much like an interaction effect). These alterations are contained in what are called "transfer functions," and maximum likelihood estimation procedures are readily available.

The Box-Jenkins intervention model can be formally represented in a more familiar manner. Borrowing from Box and Tiao (1975) and keeping the generalized linear model in mind,

$$Y_t = f(X_t, \beta_k, t) + N_t \qquad [12]$$

where Y_t is the time series of interest, N_t is a noise model for the stochastic residuals, and $f(X_t, \beta_k, t)$ can allow for the deterministic effects of time, t, the effects of exogenous variables (e.g., the program), X_t, and a *set* of K causal parameters, β_k, much like regression coefficients. For example, a simple shift in the level of a series coupled with an MA1 model for the residuals can be summarized as follows:

$$Y_t = \beta X_t + N_t \qquad [13]$$
$$N_t = \theta \epsilon_{t-1} + \epsilon_t.$$

Viewed in these terms, Box-Jenkins intervention models used in evaluation settings rest on the conventional linear model to capture program effects

equation models are nonrecursive if, in the absence of reciprocal causation, the errors are correlated across equations.

21. In an underidentified equation, at least one regression coefficient is a function of another coefficient and hence, one cannot obtain a unique estimate for either. Then, without these estimates, a unique least squares solution for the equation as a whole is impossible. Yet, one can proceed with *other* equations in the model that are not underidentified.

22. For example, one might assume that one coefficient is a particular linear function of another, or fix a given regression coefficient to some a priori value.

23. These are called "full information" maximum likelihood procedures.

In other words, W_i fulfills the standard OLS assumptions.

24. When the data are in standard deviation units, this is called "correcting for attenuation" (McNemar, 1962: 145-154). Alternatively, instrumental variable techniques may be employed (Kmenta, 1971: 309-314).

25. An excellent introduction to these procedures can be found in Duncan (1975), while a somewhat more advanced treatment can be found in Hanushek and Jackson (1977). It may also be worth noting that the more usual structural-equation models (without errors in variables) are a special case of the confirmatory factor analytic model.

26. This research is funded by the National Institute for Law Enforcement and Criminal Justice.

27. For example, $\beta_0(X_t + \delta X_{t-1} + \delta^2 X_{t-1} + \ldots)$, where $0 \leqslant \delta < 1$. This is called a geometric lag distribution (Kmenta 1971: 474). For an interesting application in criminal justice, see Fox (1979).

28. An introductory overview of more recent technique for pooled cross-sectional and time-series data can be found in Berk et al. (1979) or Maddala (1977: 322-331).

29. California is the only state which does not have such a law, although legislation has been introduced several times.

30. Introductory discussion of nonstationary and differencing can be found in Pindyck and Rubinfeld (1976: 435-449).

31. In particular, one is concerned with the pattern of correlations between observations at increasing lags: Y_t versus Y_{t-1}, Y_t versus Y_{t-2}, Y_t versus Y_{t-3}, and so on.

32. For purposes of exposition, some liberty has been taken here. In fact, moving average models require that the sign before the θ be negative. This follows from the relationship between moving average models and the serial correlations they are supposed to explain.

33. Excellent introductory discussions of ARIMA models can be found in Pindyck and Rubinfeld (1976) and Nelson (1973). "AR" stands for autoregressive. "MA" stands for moving average "I" stands for integrated, which in turn refers to the differencing process.

34. The poisson distribution is used to characterize the event of failure, and therefore the distribution of the proportion who fail over time is distributed exponentially. Such models can be complicated in a number of ways. For example, it is possible to model the experiences of two populations: good risks and bad risks.

35. See Tuma et al. (1979) for a somewhat more general perspective.

REFERENCES

Aigner, D. S. and A. S. Goldberger [eds.] (1977) *Latent Variables in Socio-Economic Models.* New York: Elsevier.

Amemiya, T. (1974) "Multivariate Regression and Simultaneous Equation Models When the Dependent Variables Are Truncated Normal." *Econometrica* 42, 6.

――― (9173) "Regression Analysis When the Dependent Variable is Truncated Normal." *Econometrica* 41: 997-1017.

Barnett, V. and T. Lewis (1978) *Outliers in Statistical Data.* New York: John Wiley.

Becker, G. S. and W. M. Landes [eds.] (1974) *Essays in the Economics of Crime and Punishment.* New York: Columbia University Press.

Berk, R. A. and M. Brewer (1978) "Feet of Clay in Hobnail Boots: An Evaluation of the Use of Statistical Inference in Applied Research," in T. Cook (ed.) *Evaluation Studies Review Annual.* Beverly Hills, CA: Sage Publications.

Berk, R. A., S. F. Berk, B. R. Loseke, D. Rauma (1980) "Bringing the Cops Back in: A Study of Efforts To Make the Criminal Justice System More Responsible to Incidents of Family Violence." *Social Science Research* (June).

Berk, R. A., D. M. Hoffman, J. E. Maki, D. Rauma, and H. Wong (1979) "An Introduction to Estimation Procedures for Pooled Cross-Sectional and Time Series Data." *Evaluation Quarterly* 3, 3.

Bielby, W. T. and R. M. Hauser (1977) "Structural Equation Models," in A. Inkeles et. al. (eds.) *Annual Review of Sociology* 3. Palo Alto, CA: Annual Reviews.

Bloom, H. S. and N. M. Singer (1979) "Determining the Cost-Effectiveness of Correctional Programs: The Case of the Patuxent Institution." *Evaluation Quarterly* 4: 609-628.

Blumstein, A., J. Cohen, and D. Nagin [eds.] (1978) *Deterrence and Incapacitation: Estimating the Effects of Criminal Sanctions on Crime Rates.* Washington, DC: National Academy of Sciences.

Box G.E.P. and G. M. Jenkins (1970) *Time Series Analysis: Forecasting and Control.* San Francisco: Holden-Day.

――― and G. C. Tiao (1975) "Intervention Analysis with Applications in Economic and Environmental Problems." *Journal of the American Statistical Association* 70, 1.

Deutsch, S. S. and F. B. Alt (1977) "The Effect of Massachusetts' Gun Control Law on Gun-Related Crimes in the City of Boston." *Evaluation Quarterly* 1, 4.

Duncan, O. D. (1975) *Introduction to Structural Equation Models.* New York: Academic Press.

Effron, B. (1971) "The Efficiency of Logistic Regression Compared to Normal Discriminant Analysis." *Journal of the American Statistical Association* 70: 892-901.

Evers, M. and N. K. Namboodiri (1978) "On the Design Matrix Strategy in the Analysis of Categorical Data," in K. F. Schuessler (ed.) *Sociological Methodology, 1979..* San Francisco: Jossey-Bass.

Fienberg, S. E. (1978) "A Note on Fitting and Interpreting Parameters in Models for Categorical Data," in K. F. Schuessler (ed.) *Sociological Methodology, 1979.* San Francisco: Jossey-Bass.

Fox J. A. (1979) "Crime Trends and Police Expenditures: An Investigation of Lag Structure." *Evaluation Quarterly* 3, 1.

Goodman, L. (1972) "A General Model for the Analysis of Surveys." *American Journal of Sociology* 77, 6.

Granger, C.W.J. and P. Newbold (1977) *Forecasting Economic Time Series.* New York: Academic Press.

Grizzle, J. E., F. F. Starmer, and G. G. Koch (1969) "Analysis of Categorical Data by Linear Models." *Biometrics* 23 (September).

Halperin, P. A., W. C. Blackwelder, and J. I. Verter (1971) 'Estimation of the Multivariate Logistic Risk Function: A Comparison of Discriminant Function and Maximum Likelihood Approaches." *Journal of Chronic Diseases* 24: 125-142.

Hanushek, E. A. and J. E. Jackson (1977) *Statistical Methods for Social Scientists.* New York: Academic Press.

Hausman, J. A. (1978) "Specification Tests in Econometrics." *Econometrica* 46, 6.

Heckman, J. J. (1979) "Sample Selection Bias as a Specification Error." *Econometrica* 47, 1.

——— (1978) "Dummy Endogenous Variables in a Simultaneous Equation System." *Econometrica* 46: 931-961.

——— (1976) "The Common Problem of Statistical Models of Truncation, Sample Selection and Limited Dependent Variables, and a Simple Estimation for Such Models." *Annuals of Economic and Social Measurement* 5, 2.

——— (1974) "Shadow Press, Market Wages, and Labor Supply." *Econometrica* 42, 3.

Johnson, J. (1972) *Econometric Methods.* New York: McGraw-Hill.

Kmenta, J. (1971) *Elements of Econometrics.* New York: MacMillan.

Leamer, E. E. (1978) *Specification Searches: Ad Hoc Inference with Non-Experimental Data.* New York: John Wiley.

Lee, L. (1979) "Indentification and Estimation in Binary Choice Models with Limited (Censored) Dependent Variables." *Econometrica* 47: 977-996.

Lloyd, M. R. and G. W. Joe (1979) "Recidivism Comparisons Across Groups: Methods of Estimation and Tests of Significance for Recidivism Rates and Asymptotes." *Evaluation Quarterly* 3, 1.

Maddala, G. S. (1977) *Econometrics.* New York: McGraw-Hill.

Magidson, J. (1977) "Toward A Causal Model Approach for Adjusting for Preexisting Differences in the Non-equivalent Control Group Situation: A General Alternative to ANCOVA." *Evaluation Quarterly* 1, 3.

Mallar, C. D. and C.V.D. Thornton (1978) "Transitional Aid Among Released Prisoners: Evidence from the LIFE Experiment." *Journal of Human Resources* 13, 2: 208-236.

Maltz, M. D. and R. McCleary (1977) "The Mathematics of Behavioral Change: Recidivism and Construct Validity." *Evaluation Quarterly* 1, 2.

——— and S. P. Pollock (1979) "Recidivism and Likelihood Functions: A Reply to Stollmack." *Evaluation Quarterly* 3, 1.

McFadden D. (1974) "Conditional Logit Analysis of Qualitative Choice Behavior," in P. Zarenbka (ed.) *Frontiers in Econometrics.* New York: Academic Press.

McNemar, Q. (1962) *Psychological Statistics.* New York: John Wiley.

Minton, P. D. and R. J. Freund (1977) "Organization for the Conduct of Statistical Activities in Colleges and Universities." *American Statistician* 31, 3.

Morimune, K. (1979) "Comparisons of Normal and Logistic Models in the Bivariate Dichotomous Analysis." *Econometrica* 47: 957-975.

Nelson, C. R. (1973) *Applied Time Series Analysis for Managerial Forecasting.* San Francisco: Holden-Day.

Nelson, F. D. (1974) "Censored Regression Models with Unobserved Stochastic Censoring Thresholds." Working Paper 63, National Bureau of Economic Research Computing Center, Cambridge, Massachusetts, December.

Nerlove, M. and S. J. Press (1973) *Univariate and Multivariate Log-Linear and Logistic Models.* Santa Monica, CA: Rand Corporation.

Pindyck, R. S. and D. L. Rubinfeld (1976) *Econometric Models and Econometric Models and Economic Forecasts.* New York: McGraw-Hill.

Ross, H. L. (1973) "Law, Science, and Accidents: The British Road Safety Act of 1967." *Journal of Legal Studies* 2, 1.

Rossi, P. H., R. A. Berk, and K. J. Lenihan (1980) *Money, Work and Crime: A Summary of Findings from the Transitional Aid Research Project.* New York: Academic Press.

Sickles, R. C. and P. Schmidt (1978) "Simultaneous Equations Models with Truncated Dependent Variables: A Simultaneous Tobit Model." *Journal of Economics and Business* 31, 1.

Stollmack, S. (1971) "Comments on 'the Mathematics of Behavioral Change.' " *Evaluation Quarterly* 3 1.

Stollmack, S. and C. M. Harris (1974) "Failure Rate Analysis Applied to Recidivism Data." *Operations Research* 22: 1192-1205.

Tobin, J. (1958) "Estimation of Relationships for Limited Dependent Variables." *Econometrica* 26, 1.

Tuma, N. D., M. T. Hannan, and L. P. Groenveld (1979) "Dynamic Analysis of Event Histories." *American Journal of Sociology* 84, 4.

Wang, M., M. R. Novick, G. L. Isaacs, and D. Ozenne (1977) "A Bayesian Data Analysis System for the Evaluation of Social Programs." *Journal of the American Statistical Association* 72, 360.

Witte, A. D. and P. Schmidt (1979) "An Analysis of the Type of Criminal Activity Using the Logit Model." *Journal of Research in Crime and Delinquency* 16: 164-179.

––– (1977) "An Analysis of Recidivism, Using the Truncated Lognormal Distribution." *Journal of the Royal Statistical Society Series C* (Applied Statistics) 26, 3.

Witte, A. D., R. Sickles, and P. Schmidt (1979) "An Application of the Simultaneous Tobit Model: A Study of the Determinants of Criminal Recidivism." *Journal of Economics and Business* 31: 124-139.

Zellner, A. (1971) *An Introduction to Bayesian Inferences in Econometrics.* New York: John Wiley.

4

Data for Criminal Justice Evaluation: Some Resources and Pitfalls

Don M. Gottfredson and Michael R. Gottfredson

The aim of this chapter is to identify some sources of data often used in criminal justice evaluations, noting briefly some commonly overlooked shortcomings of these nevertheless useful resources. Particular data needs, of course, will vary with evaluation problems. It is hoped, however, that some indication of the nature of available data will alert the evaluator to where he or she may turn for help, and that this will be useful if a few warning signs are posted along the way. As a prelude, a cursory examination of what data are is in order as a reminder of the sorts of concerns properly worried about.

Unless the meaning of individual data elements is quite clear, it is very easy to be misled. In a certain prison, the captain's clerk was assigned to interview all incoming inmates and to complete a 5 x 8 "data card." The following conversation was frequent:

Captain's clerk: Religion?

Inmate: None

Captain's clerk: Doesn't look good. Besides, Catholics have more holidays. How about Catholic?

Inmate: O.K.

Data are, of course, recorded observations of a wide variety of types. These range from naturalistic observations through interviews, questionnaires, various "unobtrusive" measures, official records (and, particularly, coded extractions therefrom) to tests or measures of abilities, aptitudes, interests, opinions or beliefs, or measures of personality. All of these may be represented in criminal justice evaluation study data. Thus, the area of "criminal justice data" is wide; and this discussion will be limited to some observations about a few commonly used data sources.

Data are also classifications or measurements. The first, a prerequisite to the second, often is as far as we get in criminal justice data. Examples include offense classifications, offender "types," "prior record" classifications, or probation or parole violation or recidivism categories. A main requirement of classification is that the classes be inclusive of all elements of the population of interest; a second is that the categories established be mutually exclusive. If the requirement of inclusivity is not met, as is typical in measures of "crime," then generalizations about the extent of crime will be flawed. The requirement of exclusivity often means that some information is lost, in classification, as, for example, when the offense of a person convicted of both robbery and burglary is classified into the robbery category. Differing types of measurement, such as nominal, ordinal, interval, and ratio scales, have differing characteristics which affect the choice of appropriate analytic methods,[1] and these issues also must be borne in mind in assessing the utility of available criminal justice data. Much of it is nominal only, various measures may at least be ordered, and some may qualify as interval scales. Ratio scales will be rare indeed.

Data are affected by the "personal equation." Errors in data may be partitioned at least into two parts: There is variable error, as in all measurement; but there is also the possibility, perhaps the probability, of constant error associated with the observer, the method of observation and recording, or both. Data are merely *relatively* accurate, *relatively* reliable, and *relatively* valid. Thus, the investigator must seek data sufficiently accurate, reliable, and valid for the purpose; and evidence as to these characteristics of data is thus critically important. Often it is lacking.

Data are, for the present discussion, best viewed as indicants of concepts, concepts which are defined by the set of procedures used in arriving at the concepts, that is, operationally defined.[2] The concept of operational definition goes much further than Humpty-Dumpty's assertion, "When I use a word . . . it means exactly what I choose it to mean—neither more nor less."[3] If the operational meanings of terms such as *arrest, offense, crime,* or *parole violation* are explicit, and remembered, then the data sources to be discussed can be extremely useful. If "surplus" meanings are added, and if the basis for the original recording is forgotten, generalizations therefrom are quite apt to be misleading or incorrect.

Data are, finally, fundamental to the scientific attitude, hard-earned, expensive, and deserving of respect.

SOME DATA RESOURCES AND PITFALLS[4]

Measures of Crime

Measures of the amount and characteristics of crime rely fundamentally upon three methods: asking officials (such as police) about crimes known to them, asking people about their victimizations, and asking people about offenses they have committed. The first has led to the Uniform Crime Reports (UCR) system, the second to victimization surveys, and the third to studies of self-reported delinquency and crime. Each may be useful for different purposes; and each has some limitations.

Uniform Crime Reports. Each year the Federal Bureau of Investigation, in its *Crime in the United States,* publishes data it receives voluntarily from law enforcement agencies throughout the country on the number of offenses known to them, the number of reported crimes that have been cleared by arrest, the number of law enforcement officers killed, and the value of property stolen and recovered. The amount, trends, rates, and descriptions of selected offenses are also reported. Offenses known to the police and arrests are tabulated by state, region, size of place, and degree of urbanization. Each volume also includes data about the number of law enforcement personnel.

The most extensive data are presented for a group of offenses known as the Crime Index. Data on four categories of crimes against persons (willful homicide, forcible rape, aggravated assault, and robbery) and three property crimes (burglary, larceny-theft, and motor vehicle theft) comprise the Index.[5] The Crime Index is the simple sum of these offenses. Both completed and attempted offenses are included.[6]

Data about persons arrested (including some demographic characteristics) are also reported in the UCR program. In addition to the Index crimes, arrest data are presented for what are called Part I offenses (which include the Index crimes and manslaughter by negligence) and Part II offenses (all offenses not included as Part I crimes, such as forgery, fraud, vandalism, and narcotics). Since 1932, a Standard Classification of Offenses has been used to aid in the compilation of these data.

Perhaps the most detailed data in the UCR is about murder, for which a special data collection form is solicited by the FBI. Thus, murders are also tabulated by characteristics of the victim, the circumstances surrounding the death, and the type of weapon used. Various detailed data are also available concerning law enforcement officers killed and bombing incidents.

Data about offenses known to the police or about arrests of persons accused of crime such as those available through the UCR program may be extremely useful for many criminal justice evaluation problems. But their utility, like all data, depends on the purpose they are to serve, and it depends as well on a clear understanding of the operational meanings of the data.

The UCR (and like) data represent events reported to the police (or discovered by them), recorded by the police, and transmitted to the FBI as crimes. Thus, in order to enter this data set, an event must be noticed by someone, defined by that person as a crime, reported to the police (if it has not been discovered by them), recorded as a crime by the police, and submitted to the collection agency.

The main limitations of this obviously useful resource must be stressed, but they are readily apparent from the operational meanings of the data.[7] Much of the concern surrounding the use of "official records" for evaluations, such as the data reported in the UCR, derives from two sources. The first is that individual behavior is such that not all events that may be considered as crimes are included in the tabulations. For example, much crime probably goes unnoticed, much is never reported to the police[8] and, if it is reported, the police may decide not to record it as crime.[9] Thus, the evaluator must be aware of the potential impact that the changes in the proclivity to notice, report, or record events as crimes may have, and to ensure that program effects may be disentangled from any changes in these proclivities.

The second is that the behavior of groups is such that reporting and recording practices may change over time. The 1967 President's Commission on Law Enforcement and Administration of Justice concluded, for example, that

> one change of importance in the amount of crime that is reported in our society is the change in expectations of the poor and members of minority groups about civil rights and social protection. Not long ago there was a tendency to dismiss reports of all but the most serious offenses in slum areas and segregated minority group districts. . . . Crimes that were once unknown to the police, or ignored when complaints were received, are now much more likely to be reported and recorded.[10]

Various other changes in police practices may offset the recording and reporting of crime. If police are more inclined toward formal than informal dispositions of cases, reported crime will tend to increase. If police are more proactive and efficient in discovery of offenses, reported crime will tend to increase. If clerical and statistical staff increase or are more efficient, reported crime may go up. If the FBI is successful in encouraging more complete and accurate reporting, then reported crime may go up. If there is a political pressure for reported crime to go down, it may; and if the pressure is on to demonstrate a rising crime rate, that too might occur.[11]

Since reporting by police agencies is voluntary, the reporting rate is pertinent also. For the 1978 UCR, for example, this varied by urban, suburban, and rural areas and by whether "offenses known to the police" or arrests were the focus of concern. In the standard metropolitan statistical areas (generally, central-city areas and environs with populations of 50,000 persons or more, which includes 73 percent of the U.S. population), 69 percent of the agencies, representing 92 percent of the relevant urban population, reported. In other cities, 75 percent of the agencies, representing 92 percent of the small cities population, reported; and in rural areas 53 percent of the agencies, representing 79 percent of the rural population, reported. It should be noted that some of the tables presented in the UCR are national estimates, based on the reporting agencies.[12]

These limitations do not so much fault the system of reporting and recording of crimes known to the police as they call attention to the obligation of the investigator to recall the operational meanings of the data when using them for evaluations or making generalizations. Other concerns, of course, might include such variable factors as perceived requirements of insurance to report crimes, the changing age composition of the population, increasing urbanization, changing opportunities (as with cars available to be stolen), and inflation.

A few additional cautions may be in order. For example, if the crime index is regarded as a measure of "serious crime," the simple unit weighting of all offenses included must be noted; it may be noted also that many offenses that may be thought quite serious are not included—for example, arson, kidnapping, child molestation, simple assault, extortion, combination in restraint of trade, trusts, monopolies; or weapons offenses. Similarly, some nonindex crimes, such as fraud or embezzlement, may be quite significant in dollar loss to victims; and consumer frauds may be another case in point, along with other "white-collar" offenses. Further, it must be remembered that the counts possible from this resource are of events (of known offenses, of arrests, or of charges) and not of offenders; and the reporting is not by individual cases but by summary data. Most evaluations of programs or treatments require the follow-up of cohorts of individual offenders, and for this objective an additional program of the FBI provides an invaluable resource if the operational meanings of concepts are heeded.

Arrest Records. When an adult is arrested (for a felony or some misdemeanors), and sometimes when juveniles are arrested, fingerprints usually are taken by local police agencies. They usually are also taken when a person is jailed or imprisoned. Often they are taken when people are committed to state hospitals or addict treatment facilities, or placed on probation or parole. They are often taken for various applications for employment or licensing, and they are taken when a person enters or leaves the armed services. These are sent by the police agencies to the FBI with identifying information such as name, "aliases," date of birth, sex, and race. (In many states, fingerprints are sent also to state identification bureaus and sometimes to regional centers.)[13] Changes in the status of the person within the criminal justice system also are reported often—notably, arrest warrants and, sometimes, discharges from sentences. From these submissions, summary records of all fingerprint reports ever submitted on an individual are prepared; these are usually called arrest records (although they are more than that) colloquially known as "rap sheets." Given the FBI number, the FBI can retrieve this record easily. Even without that number, from the name and birthdate the FBI usually can identify the individual (although this is more difficult). The advantage to the evaluator in obtaining such records from the FBI, if possible, rather than from states or regions, is that data are received from all states so that the records will be more complete. If, for example, follow-up data are obtained from a state identification bureau, the records may not reflect arrests or convictions in other states. The phrase "if possible" in the statement above is quite necessary, however. Traditionally, since 1950, the FBI has rarely provided current arrest records for evaluations, citing economy or staff time as obstacles.[14] More recently the Bureau has provided access for research purposes more often. A needed system, such as that advocated by Glaser (see note 13) for FBI assistance to "state and local agencies in policy evaluation research through procuring follow-up statistics on cohorts of their past releases," is not yet offered by the Bureau; but one may, with Glaser, maintain a cautious optimism.

If arrest records cannot be obtained from the FBI, they may be sought from state or regional identification centers. These records, similar or identical to the FBI records, may, as noted, lack entries made in other jurisdictions since the last FBI update; nevertheless, they are extremely valuable for follow-up studies. This value noted, it must be said also that extracting data from them for evaluation purposes is fraught with difficulties. Again, remembering the origin of the record in the fingerprinting system—the operational definition—will guide the evaluator to appropriate caution and avoidance of surplus meanings.

In many evaluation studies, data coded from these arrest records provide not only the basic source of outcome measures such as arrests, convictions, or new offense classifications; they are also used widely to provide data concerning the offender's prior record of such arrests and convictions (as well as data on such variables as age, age at first arrest, age at first conviction or sentence, race, or number of "aliases"). Even when such data are coded from other case files, such as presentence reports or social histories in correctional agency files, it is likely that the origin of the data, if traced, would be found in the arrest record. That is, the arrest record was apt to be used as one resource for preparation of such narrative reports.

The need for careful definition of terms, explicit instructions for extracting data from these records, coder training, and coder reliability assessment, often is overlooked. The need is readily apparent, however, when a serious effort is made to extract such data reliably. What, for example, is meant by an "arrest"? Are traffic violation citations to be included? Perhaps not. What about "Driving while intoxicated? Manslaughter by vehicle? Three entires, in the same jurisdiction, with dates very close in time, may show charges of murder 1, murder 2, and manslaughter, in that order. Is this one arrest or three? What if the charges are listed as in different jurisdictions? What if there is a three-week gap between charges two and three? Four months? Are all convictions to be counted? What about convictions by courts-martial in the military services? Excluded? Perhaps insubordination, an offense peculiar to the military services should be. How about an assault?

Variables such as age ordinarily seem straightforward. Can coder reliability be expected without instructions and training? Age at last birthday? At nearest birthday? At time of arrest? At conviction? Sentence? Admission to prison?

In coding such data from arrest records, some items will be capable of quite objective coding; others will require some subjective judgment by the person doing the extracting. Reliability of extraction of data must be expected to vary among the items.[15] In the absence of explicit coding instructions, the operational meanings of concepts used will be unclear and reliability may be expected to decrease; and in the absence of the measurement of reliability, reliability itself must be questioned.

Victimization Survey Data. It is well known that police statistics on crimes known to them do not reflect the total extent of crime. Even if all citizens reported all events they defined as crimes to some element of the criminal justice system (for example, not only to police but to prosecutors), all would not be included in police statistics. Even if all were reported to police, not all could be expected to be reported further to the FBI. What is more critical, it is well known that many crimes are not reported to *any* authorities, and that the tendency to report varies, among other things, with types of offenses. Thus, the second major basis available for counting crimes—asking potential victims about their victimizations—has been pursued vigorously in the last decade.

For the 1967 President's Commission on Law Enforcement and Administration of Justice, the National Opinion Research Center of the University of Chicago completed a national survey by sampling 10,000 households to ask "whether the person questioned, or any member of his or her household, had been a victim of crime during the past year, whether the crime had been reported, and, if not, the reasons for not reporting."[16] The Commission concluded from the results that "the actual amount of crime . . . is several times that reported in the UCR," with the disparity between reported and unreported crime varying over crime categories. According to the Commission, for example, the proportions of victimizations reported to the survey staff and not reported to the police were highest for consumer fraud (90 percent) and lowest for auto theft (11 percent). Reasons given by victims for not reporting also varied over offense classifications. Overall, the most frequent reason given for not notifying police was that "police could not be effective or would not want to be bothered."

Since July 1972, the Law Enforcement Assistance Administration, through its National Criminal Justice Information and Statistics Service in collaboration with the Bureau of the Census, has continued this line of investigation, and a very substantial data set from the National Crime Panel (NCP) victimization surveys is now available. These extensive surveys, aimed at regularly providing data on the nature and incidence of common crime, seek data also on the costs and consequences of crime and on characteristics of victims and of criminal events.

There are two parts to the National Crime Panel program: a continuing (repeated) survey of probability samples selected as representative of households and businesses in the nation, and a similar survey of one-time, independent probability samples of households and businesses in twenty-six of America's largest cities.

As in the case of the Uniform Crime Reports, the advantages and limitations of these data may best be realized from an understanding of the operational meanings of the concepts used. These meanings are given by the methods of sample selection and interview and questionnaire procedures, as well as by the definitions used to guide the classifications of variables employed.[17]

In the nationwide sample of the National Crime Panel, households and businesses are surveyed to measure the extent and nature of the "common crimes" of theft and violence. The same samples of households and businesses are taken twice a year for three years, with persons interviewed about their experiences with crime in the preceding six months. (Note that the households or businesses selected may be the same, but that the persons interviewed may or may not be.)

After an initial letter to each household, a personal visit is made in the attempt to collect data on all household members aged 12 or over. Subsequently, telephone interviews are sometimes used. In the household survey, there are three types of respondents: household respondents, self-respondents, and proxy respondents.

The household respondent is chosen to answer questions which pertain to the entire household. Questions asked of the household respondent include such items as whether the residence is owned or rented and total family income. In addition, the household respondent is asked a series of household "screen" questions, designed to elicit information concerning crimes against the household, such as burglary and auto theft. The interviewer is instructed to interview as the household respondent only the most knowledgeable household member— that is, the one who appears to know, or who could reasonably be expected to know, the answers to the household questions. Usually this is the head of the household or the spouse of the head of the household. If it becomes apparent that the particular household member being interviewed is unable to answer these questions, a more knowledgeable respondent is sought, or arrangements are made to call back when a knowledgeable respondent is available.

Questions that pertain to individual victimization are asked as many times as there are household members 12 years of age or older. Information about each household member 14 and over is obtained by self-response. Information concerning those household members 12 to 13 years old is asked by proxy. The questions asked of individual members concern personal characteristics and whether they were victimized in some way during the preceding six months.

Information about each household member aged 12 to 13 is obtained by a proxy; that is, the questions for these persons are asked of the household respondent or some other knowledgeable household member. Proxy respondents are also utilized for those household members who are physically or mentally unable to answer the individual questions, as well as for those household members who are temporarily absent and not expected to return within the enumeration period.

In the commercial survey, which is no longer in operation, interviews were sought from the owners or managers. If that was not feasible, then others believed knowledgeable about the business were interviewed, such as the assistant manager, an accountant, or other employees.

Generally, the survey appears to have been well accepted by respondents, and the reported response rates were high. Recently, Renshaw reported:

> The average annual response rate for the national sample in 1973, 1974 and 1975 has been about 96 percent for the household survey and was 97 percent in the commercial survey for 1973, 99 percent in 1974 and 1975. The household survey response rates for the 26 cities ranged from 92 percent to 98 percent; and from 93 to 99.9 percent in the commercial survey.[18]

For the household and commercial portions of the survey, the questionnaires used were roughly similar.[19] The four parts of the household questionnaires were designed to obtain (1) basic demographic data and data on persons not interviewed, (2) data on household members 12 years old or older and data on crimes against the household as a whole during the reference period (from the household respondents), (3) data from each household member 12 years old or older, or a proxy, and (4) detailed data about crimes reported in either the second or third portion, that is, in response to "screen questions." (An example of a screen question for the third portion is: "Did anyone take something directly from you by using force, such as by means of a stickup, mugging, or threat?") In this fourth part, one crime incident report was completed for each incident reported in response to a screen question. The three parts of the commercial questionnaire were aimed at (1) classifying and describing the business and obtaining data on noninterviews, (2) "screening" questions to identify incidents of burglaries and robberies (and to obtain data on insurance and security measures), and (3) creating burglary and robbery incident reports, one being completed for each incident identified by a screen question. In both questionnaires, confidentiality was assured.

Because probability samples of households were taken, estimated standard errors of estimate of victimization rates may be calculated. For example, from the 1974 survey, the personal victimization rate for rape and attempted rape (for persons 12 years old or older, male and female, living in cities and country, of any ethnic group, and so forth) may be calculated as an estimated 99 per 100,000 persons, with an approximate standard error of estimate of 10.[20] It must be noted, of course, that as the samples are partitioned on other variables, numbers of cases tend to decrease rapidly and the size of the standard error relative to the size of the estimate will increase.

In the city surveys, about 10,000 households (or 21,000 persons 12 or older) and 2,000 businesses have been sampled. Generally, procedures and definitions are the same as in the national sample, but the probability samples selected have not been studied repeatedly (as in the national sample). The reference period used has been twelve months (rather than six). In a random half of city households, additional data were collected from persons 16 years old or older on perceptions of the crime problem.

Some of the advantages of these survey data for evaluation may be noted briefly. First, with this method it is possible to measure both crimes reported to the police and crimes not reported to them. A common criticism of evaluations in criminal justice is that by relying solely on police records it is difficult to judge whether a program had an effect on crime or whether it altered the proportion of events reported to the police. Because reporting rates may be monitored, victimization surveys may help the investigator make less ambiguous inferences about crime.[21] Second, the method permits the collection of crime data independent of police agencies. To the extent that the program being evaluated may be affected by police practices, this may be important. Third, surveys such as these used in the NCP program—because they are based on samples—permit the collection of much more detailed data about crime incidents and victims than is feasible with enumerations. Fourth, because victimization experiences are appended to individual records, these data permit the use of alternative bases for rates (i.e., different "exposures to risk"). Thus, for example, age-, sex-, race-, income-, household-, and automobile-based rates may be computed, perhaps facilitating more sophisticated evaluative designs.

Again, some limitations of this obviously useful method should be noted. Since they are based on retrospective surveys, these data may be influenced by memory effects, both in the form of underinclusion (forgetting) and overinclusion (telescoping).[22] They also depend on the respondent's willingness and truthfulness in responding to survey questions. For some crimes (for example, rape) or some situations (for example, intrafamilial events), the victim may be reluctant to report victimizations to interviewers. Some evidence suggests that the method is prone toward less accurate measurement of assault and rape victimizations, particularly those among nonstrangers.[23]

Perhaps the single largest impediment to the widespread use of victimization survey methods for evaluations is their cost. Conducting a sample survey, including sample selection, interview schedule preparation, interview training, fieldwork, and data preparation requires a sizable evaluation budget, particularly with sample sizes large enough to estimate adequately phenomena as statistically rare as criminal victimization. If the rarest crimes are of interest (for example, crimes of violence), the size of the sample necessary to uncover sufficiently large numbers of victimizations to permit multivariate analyses may be beyond the range of typical evaluation budgets. Techniques that may diminish the importance of this impediment, such as telephone sampling and interviewing, are being investigated.[24]

Perhaps a more fundamental limitation of these survey data is related (as in the UCR reports) to the classification requirement of inclusivity. Since the objective of the surveys has been to measure victimizations of the common crimes of theft and violence, no data are collected on various other offenses. These include, for example "white-collar" offenses, consumer fraud, gambling, abortion, illegal drug use, and various crimes by and against corporations.

Self-Reported Crime. The third general method for measuring the extent of crime, besides counting crimes known to the police or reported by victims, is to ask people about the offenses they themselves have committed. There is a wealth of literature on this complex topic, including studies of self-reported delinquency as well as adult crime; and a separate chapter in this volume is devoted to it (see Chapter 10).

Other Criminal Justice Data Systems

Other sources of crime data independent of law enforcement agencies are found in agencies interested in the extent of crime as related to the agency's fundamental role. The National Center for Health Statistics, for example, of the Department of Health, Education, and Welfare, collects data on mortality by cause of death, including homicide and suicide. (Again, there may be differences in definitions and other aspects of the operational meanings of terms such as homicide.) The U.S. Department of Justice publishes annual data about the enforcement of immigration and naturalization laws, including statistics on aliens deported (by reason) and prosecutions and convictions for immigration law violations.[25] The United States Department of Commerce Small Business

Administration publishes data from both industrial and governmental reports.[26] The Interstate Commerce Commission publishes data on loss and damage claims paid to common carriers of freight, analyzed by cause (including theft, hijacking, or shortage for unknown reasons).[27]

At the time of the President's Commission on Law Enforcement and Administration of Justice, only a little over a decade ago, Lejins described the national state of criminal justice information system affairs.[28] Then, as now, fully adequate procedures in every area of the enterprise—police, prosecution, courts, jails, prisons, probation, and parole—were lacking. He found that little progress had been made in the proceeding 35 years—since the 1932 report of the famous predecessor of the commission for which he was writing—the National Commission on Law Observance and Enforcement, known as the Wickersham Commission.

It now can be said that there has been a great deal of progress since that time toward planning and implementing information systems in all these areas; but it must be said also that the systems desired still are in the process of development.

Persons under Correctional Supervision. There are several potentially useful data series that pertain to people under custody, both in institutions and on community supervision. For the most part these data are collected and tabulated separately for juveniles and adults.

Since 1971 the Department of Justice has presented, in its *Children in Custody* series, results from censuses of state and local juvenile facilities. The censuses aim to include all residential facilities operated by state and local governments for delinquent juveniles that have a resident population of at least 50 percent juveniles. Excluded are juvenile detention centers operated as parts of jails, and privately operated facilities. Data are collected on the number of facilities, inmates, staff, and expenditures. Some characteristics of inmate populations are also presented. The methodology for the censuses, including the definitions of the key concepts and the scope of coverage, is reported by the Department of Justice and should be studied carefully since it impacts significantly on the ways in which the data may be used.[29]

For adults, several data systems exist that may be pertinent to many evaluation efforts. First, there is a special study of jails undertaken by the Bureau of the Census for the Law Enforcement Assistance Administration. The study had two parts: a jail census and a sample survey. The census, undertaken in 1972, was designed to identify and gather data on characteristics of all locally operated jails (defined as locally administered adult institutions with authority to hold for more than forty-eight hours persons suspected or convicted of a crime).[30] Each jail identified was surveyed about the number and characteristics of facilities, inmates, and programs. The survey of the inmates of local jails was designed to collect information on the characteristics of the inmates (socioeconomic, offense, bail, pretrial delay, and geographic distribution characteristics). These data are based on a sample survey rather than a complete enumeration.[31]

Some data about persons incarcerated in state and federal correctional institutions are also available. The series, *Prisoners in State and Federal Institutions*, is published annually by the National Prisoner Statistics program of the Department of Justice. The Bureau of the Census also collects the data for this program, and the aim is an enumeration of adult and youthful offenders held in custody, whose maximum sentences are one year and one day or longer. The data are tabulated by sex and state and rates per 100,000 of the civilian population.[32] More detailed data about prisoners in these institutions are provided in a special sample survey conducted by the Bureau of the Census.[33] Included is information on such items as socioeconomic status, correctional history, and drug use.

No nationwide data with standard collection procedures are available for persons under probation supervision. Data for the federal system have been published.[34] Major difficulties—e.g., with the compatibility of definitions and eligibility—complicate efforts to collect uniform probation data. Perhaps this emphasizes the need to consider the operational meaning of probation experience data carefully.

On the other hand, a national system of data collection for parole does exist—the Uniform Parole Reports. This series was designed as a system for follow-up on persons paroled from prison and, as a result, may have a special utility for program evaluation efforts.[35] Voluntarily, paroling authorities report all persons released from prison by a discretionary act of parole. (All U.S. paroling authorities have at one time contributed to the program, but the regularity of reporting is somewhat variable.) Further data are collected thereafter on all parolees (for most states) or on randomly drawn samples (depending on the wishes and resources of participating agencies). Thus, it must be understood that the UPR data are limited to parolees (unconditional releases or discharges are not included) and that, while in some states entire parolee populations are included, some states are sampled. Data on parolees then are collected by agency staff by coding from agency case files that concern some offense and offender attributes (such as offense, some prior record items, type of admission to prison) and items of parole outcome after one year (and for some cohorts, two and three years) after parole. Note also that the person may have been discharged from parole before the end of the follow-up period (which is, however, discernible from the individual records in the system). Some efforts have been made to assess the reliability of coding these data from the case files.[36] As with other, similar data collection efforts, the need to review the procedural descriptions of the data collection mechanisms and to be familiar with the coding instructions is imperative. Given that by now oft-repeated admonition, this reporting system has obvious utility to the evaluator whose study requires the follow-up of cohorts of prisoners subsequently paroled.

Many state correctional agencies now have carefully designed statistical systems including provisions for follow-up studies of persons subsequently released (by the various modes of release). A hundred years of effort, since Congress (wishing to determine the nature and extent of the nation's criminal population) ordered a census of paupers and prisoners as part of the census of 1850,[37] have seen much progress, especially recently. The U.S. marshals who then set out on horseback across the thirty-one states and Indian territories to count prisoners, are reported to have failed, as they did again in 1870. Only after a former president of what is now the American Correctional Association, Rutherford B. Hayes, became President of the United States and ordered such a census in 1880, was the effort successful.[38] A number of state correctional agencies—including the California Department of Corrections, the California Youth Authority, the Federal Bureau of Prisons, and the correctional systems of the states of Washington, Wisconsin, and Minnesota, to name a few notable examples—have a lengthy experience, and much data, on offenders, offenses, offender attributes, time served, and various program elements; and they maintain systems of follow-up to determine outcomes. When such systems are in place, data are collected on populations, not samples, at least for core elements of the systems. Data usually are collected with care, but reliability evidence ordinarily is lacking. Definitions and procedures vary, and it must be repeated that the operational meanings of variables must be ascertained.

Another aspect of progress in correctional statistics systems is the OBSCIS effort, (Offender-Based System of Correctional Information and Statistics).[39] The OBSCIS program is an outgrowth of Project SEARCH (System for Electronic Analysis and Retrieval of Criminal Histories). SEARCH has been aimed at the development of systems in each state to support statistical information needs of both state and national programs. It is conceptually distinguished from the Prisoners in State and Federal Institutions reports of the National Prisoner Statistics program, mainly because its concept is that of an "offender-based tracking system" (OBTS). Thus, the National Prisoner Statistics program, initiated in 1923 and in annual operation since 1928 (first under the Bureau of the Census, and from 1950 under the Bureau of Prisons) has been aimed at the basic task of the 1850 U.S. Marshal: enumeration. The tracking of offenders, so essential to many evaluation efforts, is a principle aim of the Project SEARCH endeavors.[41] The idea of offender tracking is not new,[42] but the implementation of it has seen a long, complex, and arduous road; and still the evaluator may discover, in respect to data needs for a particular problem, that the concept is there but the data not yet available.

The recent burgeoning of criminal justice data system development is reflected in the 1976 *Directory of Automated Criminal Justice Information*

System published by the Law Enforcement Assistance Administration from a 1975 survey.[43] Volume I lists and indexes automated systems used by police, courts, corrections, and other agencies; 540 such systems are described briefly (from 278 jurisdictions), providing another useful resource for evaluation planning. (Volume II deals with privacy and security controls for these systems.)

Generally, regardless of the source of data for follow-up studies of offenders, the investigator is well advised to be alert to possible sources of bias in the comparison of outcome data for various groups. If, for example, more intensive supervision and surveillance is afforded one group, compared with others about whom less is known (such as those in "regular" caseloads or discharged without supervision), then this differential opportunity to obtain information should be taken into account in any comparison of outcomes.

Similarly, care must be taken that any group compared have a similar exposure to the risk of criterion behaviors or events. If, for example, one group is more subject than another to confinement for rules violations (rather than new crimes) and the dependent variable of interest is new convictions, the comparison may be biased.

The issue of duration of the follow-up study is another relevant data collection question. Even if subjects of groups to be compared are equally exposed to risk of "failure," however defined, and even if there is no bias in the source of data on the groups, the length of the follow-up data collection effort is a critical aspect of definition of the outcome variables.[44]

SOME COMMON PITFALLS NOT PREVIOUSLY NOTED

The resources discussed (all too briefly to convey adequately the complexities involved and varieties of meanings that may be associated with data elements and procedures for collecting them) offer potentials for assistance to evaluators in a wide variety of assessment efforts. Woe to the person, however, who seeks to fit the problem to the data rather than the other way around. A further hint of the complexity of "tracking" systems so often required for cohort analysis was offered aptly by Beattie in a 1972 caveat derived from many years of criminal justice data experience:

It is unfortunate that we have assumed that existing record systems can systematically supply a complete history of how each arrested defendant is handled. There are all kinds of unresolved complications to be found in tracing defendants through the criminal justice system. A defendant may be arrested or booked on certain charges and later be rebooked on other charges; complaints may have been filed on a portion of the arrest charges and not on others; a defendant may appear in different courts to answer the portions of these charges at different times, some of which may be final dispositions and others [of] which are left dangling; defendants may be convicted and sentenced on charges which are not even listed in the original booking or complaint and defendants may receive sentences in court on cases where a formal arrest was never recorded. An attempt to follow each offense in an offender-based transactional system to the bitter end usually generates nothing but frustration and defeats the real purpose of an offender-base transactional system, which is to determine what is done with individual defendants to the point of either conviction and sentence, or of no conviction and release.[45]

It may be added that dispositions frequently are not discernable from arrest records, some dispositions are ambiguous as to the actual sanction applied (for example, "30 days or 30 dollars"), and the actual time of sentence served (for example, in jail, in prison, on parole) often cannot be discovered.

Certainly, the issues of accuracy and reliability (including coder reliability) cannot be ignored. Often, validity must be assumed; attempts to measure it are rare.

A particular pitfall, often ignored in evaluations, is that of forgetting that the dependent variable in an "outcome" evaluation is, like the independent variables considered, subject to varying degrees of unreliability. It is of little use to have a fairly dependable ruler made of wood if we wish to measure a table of rubber that continually expands and contracts. Consider the related hazards, for example, of "parole violation" criteria in this respect. If, as is the case in commonly used definitions of that concept, the measure reflects variability in agency response (for example, parole officer or parole board actions) as well as in known parolee behavior, then shifts in agency policy (implicit or explicit) may of course affect the reliability of that outcome measure.

Forgetting the operational meaning of the concepts employed is perhaps the greatest hazard. "Robbery" means one thing in one data set, something else in another. Many elements, when counted, undoubtedly provide underestimates; and the elements properly, if tiresomely, should be preceded by "known number of"—for example, known number of arrests, convictions, sentences, or instances of drug abuse.

An understanding of specific operational meanings is also required if the evaluator is to choose statistical methods appropriate to the data at hand; and if assumptions underlying the statistics to be used are to be violated, the investigator will at least be aware of that.

STATE OF THE ART

In the last century and increasingly in recent decades, progress has been made toward the development and implementation of record-keeping procedures in juvenile and adult criminal justice. Yet, much remains to be done, and the information systems envisioned and seen as necessary by criminal justice leaders and several national commissions on crime are not yet in place. A unified system, with common elements across criminal justice jurisdictional boundaries, and with the facility for follow-up studies so often needed for program evaluations, is easily imagined but may not be expected in the near future. Meanwhile, a wide variety of data resources has become available to assist in evaluations. All can be useful for some purposes; all have limitations. If the strengths and limitations of the systems noted in this chapter are understood, the evaluator may find them helpful. If not, the data required for specific evaluation problems, even if they must be collected de novo, are apt to be similar in kind to those discussed. Attention to the fundamental requirements of reliability and validity and to clear operational definitions of terms thus continues to be required as a sine qua non of evaluation research.

NOTES

1. See Stevens (1951).
2. See Bridgman (1927).
3. See Dodgson (1941).
4. The data resources to be described here are among the best known and most widely used sources for a variety of criminal justice evaluation problems. They also tend to be national in scope. Many evaluation problems are, of course, concerned with issues of more limited jurisdiction or with specialized programs. In such instances the evaluator is typically confronted with the task of collecting from local agencies data that are specific to the problem. The data discussed in this chapter are, however, likely to be similar to the kinds of data useful to many evaluations and, consequently, the strengths and limitations of the data discussed are likely to be generalizable to data issues in evaluation (e.g., arrest records). It should be noted that no effort has been made in this chapter to be comprehensive; that is, to cover all of the commonly used sources of data relevant to criminal justice evaluations. The field of crime statistics is a rapidly growing one indeed. Those interested in the variety of data available should consult Gottfredson et al. (1978) and Parisi (1977).
5. According to the President's Commission on Law Enforcement and Administration of Justice (1967: 20), "the seven crimes for which all offenses known are reported were selected in 1927 and modified in 1958 by a special advisory committee of the International Association of Chiefs of Police on the basis of their serious nature, their frequency, and the reliability of reporting from citizens to police."

Until 1973, larceny was counted as an index offense only if the property taken was valued at $50 or more. Beginning with the 1973 Uniform Crime Reports, the classification "larceny-theft" included larceny under $50 as well. Note that the total property offenses and the crime index are affected by this change. In 1974, the classification "auto theft" was renamed "motor vehicle theft."
6. See Federal Bureau of Investigation (annual). Especially useful for understanding the definitions of terms used and the operational meanings of the concepts employed in this data series is the *Uniform Crime Reporting Handbook* (Federal Bureau of Investigation, 1978).

7. The limitations of the Uniform Crime Reports, for various purposes, have been discussed widely in the literature. For general discussions, see Nettler (1978: especially chs. 3-4); Sutherland and Cressey (1970); President's Commission on Law Enforcement and the Administration of Justice (1967); Blumstein (1975); Doleschal and Wilkins (1972); Hindelang (1974); and Wolfgang (1963).

8. See, for example, Hindelang and Gottfredson (1976).

9. See, for example, Black (1970); Black and Reiss (1967); Lundman et al. (1978).

10. See President's Commission on Law Enforcement and Administration of Justice (1967: 25).

11. For a discussion of police practice factors potentially affecting reporting, with examples, see President's Commission on Law Enforcement and Administration of Justice (1967: 25-27) and Seidman and Couzens (1974).

12. The data collection estimation procedures and response rates by table for the Uniform Crime Reports are reported each year as appendices to *Crime in the United States*.

13. See Glaser (1973: 89-95), on which this description relies, for an excellent and useful discussion of the utility in evaluation of arrest reports from fingerprint submissions.

14. Since January, 1973, a computerized system available to the Bureau of Prisons for unrestricted procurement of records on past federal prisoners arrested after January 1, 1970, or released after February 1, 1973, has been in operation (see Glaser (1973: 92-93). In 1966, the FBI established a National Crime Information Center (NCIC) aimed at instant response to law enforcement inquiries about wanted persons, stolen cars or guns, and the like. Since 1970, a national Computerized Criminal History (CCH) system has been under development as part of the NCIC. According to the National Advisory Commission on Criminal Justice Standards and Goals (1973: 35), "when fully implemented, the CCH system will be able to supply criminal histories to any requesting agency anywhere in the country."

15. See, for example of coding instructions and further discussion of the sorts of difficulties involved, Singer and Gottfredson (1973); Gottfredson and Singer (1973); and National Council on Crime and Delinquency Research Center (1966). For examples of reliability assessments with such data, see Venezia et al. (1967) and Venezia and Gottfredson (1969).

16. See Ennis (1967). Other, more detailed surveys were made also in various cities by the Bureau of Social Science Research and by the Survey Research Center of the University of Michigan. For a general discussion of the history and methodology of victimization surveys, see Hindelang (1976).

17. Information about sampling and interview procedures is given in Garofalo and Hindelang (1977). Detailed information is found in Bureau of the Census (n.d.). Critical for a clear understanding of the operational meanings of the concepts used is Bureau of the Census (1972, n.d.). General discussions of the uses and limitations of these victimization data may be found in Hindelang et al. (1978); National Academy of Sciences (1976); and Sparks (forthcoming). The data are made available by the Law Enforcement Assistance Administration through a grant to DUALabs of Arlington, Virginia.

18. See Renshaw (1976: 179).

19. A concise description is given in Gottfredson et al. (1978) note 4, supra.

20. See Gottfredson et al. (1978) note 4, supra.

21. For one such use of the method, see Schnieder (1976). A general discussion of the use of these surveys for planning is provided in Skogan (1975).

22. For a general discussion, see Hindelang et al. (1978: ch. 10). For a discussion of the procedures used in the NCS to minimize memory effects, see Garofalo and Hindelang (1977).

23. See Law Enforcement Assistance Administration (1972).
24. See, for example, Tuchfarber and Klecka (1976).
25. See Department of Justice (n.d.).
26. See Kingsbury (quarterly).
27. See Interstate Commerce Commission, Bureau of Accounts (quarterly).
28. See Lejins (1967: 178-206).
29. Those interested in the complete definition of the universe, and definitions of terms, should consult Department of Justice (n.d.). A related program, although not a "tracking" system, is the series on juvenile court statistics begun in 1926 by the Children's Bureau of the U.S. Department of Labor, and continued until 1975 by the Department of Health, Education and Welfare. With the passage in 1974 of the Juvenile Justice and Delinquency Prevention Act, responsibility was passed to the Office of Juvenile Justice and Delinquency Prevention in the Law Enforcement Assistance Administration. The program is now conducted under a grant to the National Center for Juvenile Justice (of the National Council of Juvenile and Family Court Judges). See Corbett and Vereb (n.d.).
30. Specifically excluded were federal and state correctional institutions, juvenile detention centers, drunk tanks, lockups, and state-operated jails.
31. Documentation and results of the census may be found in Department of Justice (1975). For the survey, see Department of Justice (1974).
32. See Department of Justice (annual).
33. See Department of Justice (1976).
34. See Administrative Office of the U.S. Courts (1969, 1974).
35. See Gottfredson et al. (1970).
36. See note 15, supra.
37. See Friel (1976).
38. See Friel (1976) note 37, supra, at page 24.
39. See SEARCH Group, Inc. (1975)
40. See, for example, SEARCH Group, Inc. (1970).
41. A tracking system particularly relevant to prosecution is PROMIS. For general discussions, see Brounstein and Hamilton (1975) and Hamilton and Work (1973). A development especially relevant to juvenile court and other juvenile justice concerns is the project JISRA (see Boxerman, 1977).
42. Friel (1976: note 38, supra, at page 26), for example, credits Charles E. Gilke with a substantial propagation of the concept, beginning with the Cleveland Survey in 1919.
43. See Department of Justice (1976).
44. See Glaser (1973: note 14, supra, at pages 95-102) for further discussion of these issues. In the same work, see also pages 103 to 136 for discussion of deficiencies of operational records for both operational and research purposes, of problems in data collection outside operational systems, and proposals for integrating these.
45. See Beattie (1972: 59).

REFERENCES

Administrative Office of the U.S. Courts (1969, 1974) *Census of Persons Under Supervision of the Federal Probation System.* Washington, DC: Author.
Beattie, R. H. (1972) "Data Utilization," p. 59 in *Proceedings of the International Symposium on Criminal Justice Information and Statistics Systems.* Sacramento, CA: California Crime Technological Research Foundation.

Black, D. (1970) "Production of Crime Rates." *American Sociological Review* 35: 733-748.

——— and A. Reiss (1967) "Patterns of Behavior in Police and Citizen Transactions," in *Studies of Crime and Law Enforcement in Major Metropolitan Areas, Volume II.* Washington, DC: Government Printing Office.

Blumstein, A. (1975) "Seriousness Weights in an Index of Crime." *American Sociological Review* 39: 854-864.

Boxerman, L. (1977) *Juvenile Justice Information Systems [Volumes 1, 2, and 3].* Reno, NV: National Council of Juvenile and Family Court Judges.

Bridgman, P. W. (1927) *The Logic of Modern Physics.* New York: Macmillan.

Brounstein, S. and W. Hamilton (1975) "Analysis of the Criminal Justice System with the Prosecutors Management Information System (PROMIS)," in L. Oberlander (ed.) *Quantitative Tools for Criminal Justice Planning.* Washington, DC: Law Enforcement Assistance Administration.

Bureau of the Census (1975) *Interviewer's Manual: National Crime Survey.* Washington, DC: Department of Commerce.

——— (1972) *Interviewer's Manual: Commercial Victimization Survey.* Washington, DC: Department of Commerce.

——— (n.d.) *Survey Documentation: National Crime Survey, National Sample.* Washington, DC: Department of Commerce.

Corbett, J. and T. S. Vereb (n.d.) *Juvenile Court Statistics, 1974.* Washington, DC: Department of Justice.

Department of Justice (annual) *Children in Custody.* Washington, DC: Government Printing Office.

Department of Justice (annual) "Prisoners in State and Federal Institutions," in *National Prisoner Statistics Bulletin.* Washington, DC: Government Printing Office.

Department of Justice (1976) *1976 Directory of Automated Criminal Justice Information Systems [Volumes 1 and 2].* Washington, DC: Author.

Department of Justice (1975) *The Nation's Jails: A Report on the Census of Jails from the 1972 Survey of Inmates of Local Jails.* Washington, DC: Government Printing Office.

Department of Justice (1974) *Survey of Inmates of Local Jails—Advance Report.* Washington, DC: Government Printing Office.

Dodgson, C. L. (1941) *Through the Looking Glass and What Alice Found There.* New York: Heritage.

Doleschal, E. and L. Wilkins (1972) *Criminal Statistics.* Rockville, MD: National Institute of Mental Health.

Ennis, P. (1967) "Criminal Victimization in the United States: A Report of a National Survey. Field Surveys II," Washington, DC: President's Commission on Law Enforcement and Administration of Justice.

Federal Bureau of Investigation (annual) *Uniform Crime Reports.* Washington, DC: Government Printing Office.

——— (1978) *Uniform Crime Reporting Handbook.* Washington, DC: Government Printing Office.

Friel, C. M. (1976) "Zeitgeist: A Perspective on Criminal Justice Information and Statistical Systems," pp. 23-29 in SEARCH Group, Inc., Third International Symposium. Sacramento, CA: SEARCH Group, Inc.

Garofalo, J. and M. Hindelang (1977) *An Introduction to the National Crime Survey.* Washington, DC: Government Printing Office.

Glaser, D. (1973) *Routinizing Evaluation: Getting Feedback on Effectiveness of Crime and Delinquency Programs.* Washington, DC: Government Printing Office.

Gottfredson, D. M. and S. M. Singer (1973) "Parole Decision-Making Coding Manual," Parole Decision-Making Project Report 2, National Council on Crime and Delinquency Research Center, Davis, California, June.

Gottfredson, D. M. et al. (1970) "A National Uniform Parole Reporting System," National Council on Crime and Delinquency Research Center, Davis, California.

Gottfredson, M. R., M. J. Hindelang, and N. Parisi [eds.] (1978) *Sourcebook of Criminal Justice Statistics, 1977.* Washington, DC: Government Printing Office.

Hamilton, W. and C. Work (1973) "The Prosecutor's Role in the Urban Court System: The Case for Management Consciousness." *Journal of Criminal Law and Criminology* 64: 183-189.

Hindelang, M. (1976) *Criminal Victimization in Eight American Cities.* Cambridge, MA: Ballinger.

——— (1974) "The Uniform Crime Reports Revisited." *Journal of Criminal Justice* 2: 1-7.

——— and M. R. Gottfredson (1976) "The Victim's Decision Not To Invoke the Criminal Process," in McDonald (ed.) *The Victim and the Criminal Justice System.* Beverly Hills, CA: Sage Publications.

——— and J. Garofalo (1978) *Victims of Personal Crime.* Cambridge, MA: Ballinger.

Interstate Commerce Commission, Bureau of Accounts (quarterly) *Quarterly Freight Loss and Damage Claims.* Washington, DC: Government Prining Office.

Kingsbury, J. (quarterly) *The Cost of Crimes Against Businesses.* Washington, DC: Government Printing Office.

Law Enforcement Assistance Administration (1972) *San Jose Methods Test of Known Crime Victims, Statistics Technical Report No. 1.* Washington, DC: Government Printing Office.

Lejins, P. P. (1967) "National Crime Data Reporting System: Proposal for a Model," pp. 178-206 in President's Commission on Law Enforcement and Administration of Justice, *Crime and Its Impact—An Assessment.* Washington, DC: Government Printing Office.

Lundman, R., R. Sykes, and J. Clark (1978) "Police Control of Juveniles: A Replication." *Journal of Research in Crime and Delinquency* 15: 74-91.

National Academy of Sciences (1976) *Surveying Crime: A Report of the Panel for the Evaluation of Crime Surveys.* Washington, DC: National Research Council.

National Advisory Commission on Criminal Justice Standards and Goals (1973) *Criminal Justice System.* Washington, DC: Government Printing Office.

National Council on Crime and Delinquency Research Center (1966) *Uniform Parole Reports Coding Manual.* Davis, CA: Author.

Nettler, G. (1978) *Explaining Crime.* New York: McGraw-Hill.

Parisi, N. (1977) *Sources of National Criminal Justice Statistics: An Annotated Bibliography.* Washington, DC: Government Printing Office.

President's Commission on Law Enforcement and Administration of Justice (1967) *The Challenge of Crime in a Free Society.* Washington, DC: Government Printing Office.

Renshaw, B. II. (1976) "The Evolution and Direction of the Law Enforcement Administration's National Victimization Statistics," in *SEARCH Group, Inc., Third International Symposium.* Sacramento, CA: SEARCH Group, Inc.

Schneider, A. (1976) "Victimization Surveys and Criminal Justice System Evaluation," in W. Skogan (ed.) *Sample Surveys of the Victims of Crime.* Cambridge, MA: Ballinger.

SEARCH Group, Inc. (1975) *OBSCIS—Offender-Based State Corrections Information System, Volume 1: The OBSCIS Approach.* Sacramento, CA: Author.

——— (1970) *Designing Statewide Criminal Justice Systems: The Demonstration of a Prototype.* Sacramento, CA: Author.

Seidman, D. and M. Couzens (1974) "Getting the Crime Rate Down: Political Pressure and Crime Reporting." *Law and Society Review* 8: 457-493.

Singer, S. M. and D. M. Gottfredson (1973) "Development of a Data Base for Parole Decision-Making," Parole Decision-Making Project Report 1, National Council on Crime and Delinquency Research Center, Davis, California, June.

Skogan, W. (1975) "The Use of Victimization Surveys in Criminal Justice Planning," in L. Oberlander (ed.) *Quantitative Tools for Criminal Justice Plannings.* Washington, DC: Law Enforcement Assistance Administration.

Sparks, R. F. (forthcoming) *Surveying Victims: A Study of the Measurement of Criminal Victimization, Perceptions of Crime and Attitudes to Criminal Justice.* Washington, DC: Government Printing Office.

Stevens, S. S. (1951) "Mathematics, Measurement and Psychophysics," in S. S. Stevens (ed.) *Handbook of Experimental Psychology.* New York: John Wiley.

Sutherland, E. and D. Cressey (1970) *Criminology.* Philadelphia: J. B. Lippincott.

Tuchfarber, A. and W. Klecka (1976) *Random Digit Dialing: Lowering the Cost of Victimization Surveys.* Washington, DC: Police Foundation.

Venezia, P. S. and D. M. Gottfredson (1969) "Uniform Parole Reporting: Inter-State Reliability," National Council on Crime and Delinquency Research Center, Davis, California.

Venezia, P. S. et al. (1967) "Uniform Parole Reports: Intra-Agency Reliability," National Council on Crime and Delinquency Research Center, Davis, California.

Wolfgang, M. (1963) "Uniform Crime Reports: A Critical Appraisal." *University of Pennsylvania Law Review* 111: 708.

PART II

ON ALTERNATIVE PARADIGMS

Malcolm W. Klein and Katherine S. Teilmann

Is there some single, comprehensive enterprise properly labeled "evaluation research"? Signs of its existence certainly abound; there are texts on evaluation research, journals and annual reviews devoted to it, even handbooks in several areas in addition to the massive two-volume set published by Sage Publications. There is even an evaluation of evaluations.[1] There is a national professional organization, the Evaluation Research Society. There are graduate training programs in evaluation research and postdoctoral training programs as well. It must be out there, with so many adherents telling others what it is, and so many providing illustrations through the evaluation of a very broad range of social programs.

But we are skeptical. A few decades ago, when the Lewinian "action research" was so prominent, perhaps there was a relatively denotable entity. Then the major issue posed by different perspectives was that of "research seduction," alluded to in the chapter by Short. With the controlled experiment as the dominant research paradigm, seduction of the researcher by the interests and needs of the practitioner did indeed seem to capture the heart of evaluation concerns.

Now, however, the term *evaluation* has taken on not only varying *shades* of meaning but different *core* meanings as well. Evaluators can now come together, using much of the same jargon, and yet talk right past each other. For their consumers and their students, this can understandably be very confusing.

In Part II of the *Handbook,* we have attempted to provide some order to the developing chaos by providing descriptions of several predominant approaches to the process of evaluation. We refer to these as *paradigms* of evaluation research because they are not merely alternative methodologies; they are patterned, organized perspectives which tend to subsume goal, value, and method alike. They are integrated viewpoints on evaluation research and, as such, they are both contrasting and to some extent antagonistic to each other.

Policy makers and funders of evaluations must understand that there are these different paradigms and, further, that each will yield a different evaluation in both form and substance. The consumers of evaluation thus should not merely ask for an evaluation, but for a *particular form* of evaluation (or, at least, for a justification of the particular form recommended to them). They should know beforehand which paradigm is most appropriate to their problems, and appreciate the form of the answers that will emanate from that paradigm. It is no longer acceptable or wise to write evaluation contracts in ignorance of the available paradigms; it is probably of questionable wisdom as well to seek eclectic evaluation packages unless (as is unusual) the paradigmatic "mix" is clearly articulated at the outset.

In soliciting chapters for Part II, we have deliberately selected "proponents" of the viewpoints and paradigms to be presented. We did not ask for balanced presentations, but for something approaching advocacy. Six of the chapters provide just that, with a delightful touch of polemicism here and there. The chapter by Grizzle and Witte, by way of contrast, is a very deliberate attempt to take an overview of contrasting paradigms and suggest the kind of accommodations which can be made between them. The remarkable thing about this summary chapter is that it was written without its authors' exposure to the others, and even without their knowledge that the others were being written.

If we are correct in suggesting that the six paradigmatic statements incorporate somewhat contrasting goals and values, then it seems likely that they would appeal to different audiences. We would expect the chapters by Edwards on his decision theory approach and by Krisberg on process evaluation to be embraced principally by practitioner-oriented audiences, Krisberg more by those in the trenches and Edwards by those at the command post. Often, process evaluation uses its data on program process to modify and improve programming even as the evaluation is proceeding. It is thus directly and immediately responsive to program directors and field agents. Edwards's approach, while similar in intent, places even more emphasis on *prior* planning at the initiation and subsequent stages of programming. In addition, it explicitly solicits the values and intentions of all the relevant audiences of the evaluation.

Blumstein's chapter is more principally concerned with an operations research or engineering approach to planning and evaluation. Although it describes a particular prototype of this general paradigm, the prototype has clearly generalizable features which should make it particularly appealing to program planners.

By contrast, Empey's chapter on field experimentation should prove most compatible to most traditionally oriented program evaluators. It stresses the need for employing the logic of the experimental model, even where its practice is precluded, and argues as well for the amalgamation of process and outcome data collection. Students in the traditional social science disciplines should also feel particularly comfortable with the characteristics of the experimental paradigm.

Finally, while they speak directly to the utility of evaluation projects, both the Glaser and Short chapters are most explicitly concerned with the theoretical underpinnings and contributions of all evaluation research. To the extent that theoretical frameworks are absent as guide and product of program evaluation— and in the overwhelming number of instances they are—to that extent, these writers question the ultimate value of the evaluation enterprise as a whole. The argument is persuasive. As noted earlier, we selected our authors with some personal care, and we would add our editors' voices to those of Glaser and Short.

One word of warning about all of the above: In suggesting the more likely compatible audiences for the various paradigm chapters, we do not wish to suggest selective reading. Our entire purpose would be lost if planners read Edwards only, if program directors read Krisberg only, and so on. We urge all audiences to review all paradigms so that they might appreciate and make use of the broad spectrum of available perspectives. We asked at the beginning of this introduction if there is a single enterprise properly labeled "evaluation research." Our answer is no, and with that answer we must suggest that evaluation research comprises a veritable cafeteria of goals, values, styles, and technologies. The competent evaluator, the effective evaluation consumer, and the wise evaluation student will learn to recognize and know when to partake of each offering in that cafeteria.

NOTE

1. We refer in these last instances to the Streuning and Guttentag (eds.) *Handbook of Evaluation Research* (Sage, 1975) and the critical volume by Bernstein and Freeman, *Academic and Entrepreneurial Research* (Russell Sage Foundation, 1975).

5

The Interplay of Theory, Issues,
Policy, and Data

Daniel Glaser

What does theory do for an evaluation? How does it help? Why should explanations for crime be reflected in the design and the data analysis of criminal justice program assessments?

This essay tries to answer these questions by elaborating three theses:

(1) One cannot generalize with confidence from the findings of evaluations that are not explicitly grounded in scientific theory.

(2) Theory increases the prospects of useful findings from evaluation research because it fosters and guides monitoring of the programs that are evaluated.

(3) Theory is the bridge between applied and pure science, permitting each to enhance the other; there is relatively little contribution to enduring knowledge from evaluation research unless that research is nested in the principles of a more abstract science.

Evaluation refers here to investigation of whether a particular agency, policy, or program "works," that is, how much it contributes to the achievement of some measurable objective, such as the reduction of recidivism rates. *Theory* answers "why" questions; it explains puzzling or problematic aspects of events, conditions, or processes. Theory is scientific when hypotheses deduced from it are conceivably falsifiable by empirical evidence (Popper, 1959).

THEORY AND GENERALIZATION

The typical criminal justice evaluation that is the concern of this chapter assesses the effects of a specified intervention into the activities or experiences of a particular set of persons at a definite time and place. All application of conclusions from it is made at a later time, almost always with a different set of subjects, and often at another location, perhaps hundreds or thousands of miles away. Nevertheless, the sampling issue that seems to concern the evaluators most is that of *selection bias,* the question of how representative their research sample is of all possible subjects in the setting and period in which their study occurs. The evaluators' worry is that, for the particular time and place they study, the persons in their sample may differ from the rest of the persons in the administrative category studied (e.g., juvenile arrestees, convicted male sex offenders, misdemeanant probationers). Of course, this selection bias is always worth knowing about and taking into account, but application bias and theory focus are neglected issues that are much more important.

Application bias is any difference between the sample or population in a particular category of subjects (e.g., parolees, arrestees, female prisoners) selected for an evaluation, and the other populations in this category to whom the particular evaluation's conclusions will be applied at a later time and possibly at a different location. The intake and output of police, courts, and correctional institutions vary too much to assume that subjects in the same administrative category, but at different times and places, are actually identical.

The characteristics of arrestees, probationers, or persons in other offense categories depend upon the demography of the jurisdiction, its laws, criminal justice budgets, policy changes with the turnover of top officials, and the intake and output of the other agencies in the area that deal with deviant conduct, including mental health facilities and schools. Thus, the intake of criminal justice organizations varies with the fluctuating tolerance of deviance by the community and by other people-processing establishments, as well as with economic conditions, media campaigns for "crackdowns" on particular types of conduct, and many other variables. Therefore, a *selection* bias that makes a research sample differ by as little as 20 percent in ethnic or offense composition from the population of persons in the same administrative category at its time and place, may often not be as large as the *application* bias that makes the sample differ from the groups to which its conclusions are applied, differences not only in ethnicity and offense but also in age, criminal record, and many other factors that can greatly affect the results of most evaluations.

Nevertheless, the most important sampling issue in generalizing from evaluation research is *theory focus,* which refers to the extent to which subjects are selected for study on the basis of a theory as to why the program or policy being assessed should have a particular effect on them. This focus is important because it is potentially the main source of utility and validity in generalizing from the evaluation's findings. Theory often is set forth to justify research, but it is neglected in the sample design because of the custom or convenience of using administrative rather than theory-derived categories. Theory-focused sampling can diminish handicaps from application bias or selection bias in generalizing from evaluative research, because it fosters comparison of outcomes for persons in a set of rubrics with theoretically contrasting implications, regardless of the location of these persons in time, place, or administrative category. If the theory is sound, similar—hence, robust—findings in many studies are more probable, using theory-derived rather than administrative categories. This contention is most readily justified by illustration. The evaluation of individual and group psychotherapy and counseling programs for offenders will be discussed in detail to illuminate each of this chapter's three theses, and other types of examples will also be discussed briefly.

When research first became firmly established as a component of large-scale correctional administrations in the early 1960s, the persons most frequently recruited to direct it were clinical psychologists with prior employment in prisons. This was especially evident in the two largest penal systems, the California Department of Corrections and the Federal Bureau of Prisons. Psychologists, of course, are trained in research and frequently aspire to do it. Prison administrators were more comfortable with researchers who already had worked satisfactorily in the prisons than with newcomers to the institutions, from academia or elsewhere.

Traditionally, prison psychologists provide therapy for only a small fraction of the offenders received by their institution, concentrating primarily on those inmates who, in comparison with others, show unusual emotional or behavioral problems. Typical clinical treatment encourages clients to talk to the psychologist, either separately or in groups, in the hope that talking about the events or ideas and expressing the emotions that underlie their behavioral problems will lead to insight and to improved conduct.

Research money procured by clinicians in the 1960s, especially in California (to which most of this illustration will be confined), tended to be focused primarily on evaluation of various types of clinical psychology. There were controlled experiments and quasi-experiments to assess individual psychotherapy, group psychotherapy, and therapeutic community for prisoners. There was also group counseling, an extensive program in which psychologists trained other prison staff of all types to supervise groups of inmates assembled at regular intervals (e.g., once a week) to talk out their problems with each other. In the therapeutic communities, as many as five mornings a week were devoted to large group counseling sessions with line staff, and often with a psychologist also present, while on most afternoons there were smaller group therapy sessions, each with a psychologist or a psychiatric social worker.

In traditional prison psychological services and in these special sessions, the talk tends to be mostly on the immediate aggravations of the clients' daily lives, but it can wander to family relationships, past criminal activities, or anything else, with clinicians or other staff differing greatly in the extent, purpose, or style of their intrusions into or direction of the talk. At any rate, no explicit theory was set forth to justify this research by indicating exactly how and why these diverse conversations were to reduce recidivism. The evaluations of the California studies were directed by the Sacramento or other research offices which procured from the separate prisons the lists of inmates who participated in the various programs, and later determined from state records whether such participation correlated inversely with recidivism rates. On the whole, it did not (Harrison and Mueller, 1964; Kassebaum et al., 1971).

If a theory on crime causation underlies the California research cited above and the tremendous number of similar evaluations elsewhere (reported in Akman et al., 1968, and Lipton et al., 1975), it is only the theory that offenses are produced by emotional disturbances, conflicting self-concepts, and inability to get along with others, all of which might be alleviated through discussion in a setting where speaking freely is encouraged. Yet, the clinical psychology literature as well as everyday observations suggest that such feelings, personality variations, and predominantly noncriminal thoughts or experiences, which usually preoccupy the various types of talk sessions, are about as common in law-abiding as in criminal circles. Not only does a close relationship between these psychological problems and recidivism seem unlikely, but the only personality tests that have had appreciable accuracy in identifying delinquents or criminals are those that ask directly about offensive behavior (e.g., psychopathy and socialization scales, see Waldo and Dinitz, 1967). Prison psychotherapy and counseling seem to be provided mainly to help administrators adjust emotionally disturbed inmates to institutional life, although findings on their effectiveness for this purpose have been mixed (Lipton et al., 1975: 301-302, 307-330). Still, the relevance of these treatments to recidivism reduction in certain cases and circumstances might be predicted by some types of widely promulgated sociological theories of crime causation.

Sutherland's *differential association theory,* especially influential in criminology in the 1960s, when the California research was in progress, has four main ideas concerning relevance to evaluation of the recidivism-reducing effects of individual or group psychotherapy or counseling (see Sutherland and Cressey, 1978: 80-81).

(1) People commit crimes because they learn definitions of their situations that are favorable to law violation more than they learn definitions that are unfavorable to law violation.

(2) Most of this learning occurs in communication with others, in intimate groups.

(3) The learning that affects definitions of situations includes techniques, motives, rationalizations, and attitudes about crime.

(4) The relative strength of the learned criminal and anticriminal definitions is a function of the frequency, duration, priority, and intensity of the learning.

A more recently influential explanation for delinquency, Hirschi's (1969) *control theory,* can be summarized as follows:

(1) All persons learn how to be delinquent, either from others or alone, and would be delinquent if they "dared."

(2) People dare not be delinquent, however, if they develop bonds with conventional society that they value sufficiently to fear jeopardizing them.

(3) These bonds that make people control themselves include:
   (a) attachments to conventional persons;
   (b) valued conventional pursuits and statuses (e.g., a job or a college enrollment) from which they would be ejected if found delinquent;
   (c) sheer time required for conventional pursuits; and
   (d) anticriminal beliefs.

If evaluation of the recidivism reduction capacity of individual or group psychotherapy or counseling were guided by differential association theory, two principal working hypotheses derived from it might be phrased as follows:

Hypothesis 1. The recidivism reduction achieved by these talk programs will vary directly with the extent that they produce intimate personal relationships between anticriminal staff and criminal clients, thus fostering the offender's learning anticriminal definitions.

Hypothesis 2. The recidivism reduction achieved by these talk programs will vary inversely with the prior criminal learning of the offenders.

Control theory supports the hypothesis 1 as concerned with an aspect of the development of bonds with conventional society; it also suggests hypotheses on other sources of conventional bonds in correctional programs (e.g., education or paid work). However, it does not support hypothesis 2. Therefore, distinctly more useful than control theory, especially when applied to advanced offenders, would be a *differential* control theory that takes into account the variance in bonds to delinquent or criminal, as well as to conventional, society. (A differential framework would similarly improve the Elliott et al. [1979] "integrated" theory on delinquency.)

Testing of hypothesis 1 requires sampling talk programs that differ in the extent and intensity of personal contact between presumably anticriminal staff and ostensibly criminal clients. Thus, hypothesis 1 implies that

(1) individual therapy or counseling will generally reduce recidivism rates more than group programs; and
(2) recidivism rates will vary inversely with the duration of the clients' participation in the programs with the same staff persons.

These deduced hypotheses, closer to the operational level than the more abstract hypothesis 1, use individuality of treatment as an index of intimacy, but low turnover of staff as an index of both duration, and intimacy of differential association with sources of anticriminal definitions. From a control theory standpoint, they are also indexes of bonds fostered with conventional society.

Testing of hypothesis 2 would sample clients differing on indexes of the frequency, duration, priority, and intensity of their criminal learning. This hypothesis implies that

(1) first offenders will have their recidivism rates reduced by talk programs more readily than will offenders with prior criminal records;
(2) probationers will have their recidivism rates reduced by talk programs more readily than prisoners or ex-prisoners such as parolees;
(3) recidivism rate reduction will vary inversely with the age of first involvement in delinquency or crime; and
(4) for offenders with delinquency or criminal records that *began* at about the same age, the posttreatment recidivism rates will vary directly with age.

If the theory from which the above hypotheses are derived is valid, both selection and application bias should not be nearly the problems that they are with evaluations in which sampling is done by administrative categories unguided by theory. Atheoretical evaluations only hypothesize that the various types of talk programs will reduce recidivism rates for most offenders. Yet if the above theory is valid, the effectiveness of these programs will vary greatly with the attributes of the persons in the research sample and in the populations to which the research conclusions are generalized. While it is appropriate with theory-focused research that the samples be fairly representative of the categories to which the theory refers—such as young compared to old offenders, or first offense probationers compared to recidivist prisoners—the main requirement is only that the samples have these types of contrast and variance in the persons studied. If these differences within samples are appreciable, the findings should be much more robust than those of atheoretical evaluations. Indeed, this entire discussion on theory guidance of correctional evaluations suggests by now that

Martinson's (1974) widely cited and extremely influential conclusion that "nothing works" is erroneous, because it comes from analysis not guided by theory. Furthermore, his conclusion can be invalidated by a theory-focused analysis of the very data on which his conclusion is based—the data in the survey of evaluations that he conducted with Lipton and Wilks (Lipton et al., 1975).

Of course, the value of theory guidance in assessing counseling and therapy programs is most clearly determined if studies are initially designed to test it, but none was planned to test the above theories. Nevertheless, assessment is possible, because some studies inadvertently employed some of the sampling or, in analyzing their data, made some of the client differentiations that are suggested by the two hypotheses above. As predicted from Hypothesis 1, evaluations surveyed by Lipton et al. usually found little or no recidivism reduction with group programs and found individual programs somewhat more often effective, but observed that group methods were most effective for participants who had at least one year with the same group leader; consistent with hypothesis 2, the group methods also were more often effective with young and unadvanced than with older or advanced offenders (Lipton et al., 1975: 223-229).

Also, as implied by differential association theory, individual counseling and psychotherapy most often reduced recidivism for criminally unadvanced young adults, particularly when these types of treatment focused on fostering anticriminal definitions by intensive vocational guidance (Lipton et al., 1975: 172-179, 207-214). As predicted from hypothesis 2, counseling lowered recidivism rates more for probationers than for similar offenders given prison terms and then paroled (Lipton et al., 1975: 52-55).

One can also infer that the intensity of probation officers' interaction with their clients varies inversely with the size of caseloads. If so, then hypothesis 1 is supported by the findings that recidivism rates varied directly with size of caseload for young probationers; but, as hypothesis 2 predicts, this finding was much lower or nonexistent with older probationers or with parolees of any age except (per hypothesis 1) for those parolees who were in the same small caseload for over a year (Lipton et al., 1975: 27, 45-50, 102-150).

Of interest also are the findings of the Community Treatment Program of the California Youth Authority, in which the experimental group had intensive supervision on immediate parole and the control group had an average of about eight months of incarceration followed by parole to traditional high caseloads. Supporting hypothesis 2 is the finding that only that half of those in the experimental group who were least advanced in crime—categorized as neurotics— had distinctly lower recidivism rates during and after supervision than did neurotics in the control group (Palmer, 1974).

In summary, both differential association and control theory predict that recidivism reduction by counseling and psychotherapy programs will vary directly with the extent that they produce intimate personal bonds between staff and clients. The validity of this hypothesis is supported by the finding of more recidivism reduction with individual than with group programs, with low turnover of staff and with low caseloads. Differential association theory also predicts more recidivism reduction through these talk programs with lawbreakers who have had little criminal learning, and this is supported by findings of greater effectiveness with unadvanced than with advanced offenders. Of course, theory-focused research should be more complex for an optimum test of differential association theory; it should go beyond considering criminal and noncriminal association separately, as was done here, and take into account their interaction, as well as the interactions among the frequency, duration, priority, and intensity of each. Thus, instead of studying zero-order relationships only, tests for interaction, path diagrams, or other techniques of multivariate analysis should be employed.

It has been argued that theory-focused sampling would increase the fruit-fulness of evaluations of talk programs and reduce the problems from selection or application bias. However, use of theory in evaluation may be impeded if researchers regard programs only as boxes for which input and output are to be compared; the second thesis of this chapter is, essentially, that theory leads researchers to crawl into the boxes to look around.

THEORY AND MONITORING

Evaluations guided by theory as to why an activity should have a particular effect may be severely limited if they unquestioningly accept official prescriptions, administrative descriptions, or traditional conceptions of what occurs in treatment endeavors. Administrators of programs have multiple goals and diverse pressures or constraints that make their practices diverge from their ideals, their plans, and even their statements about their activities. Whenever this divergence occurs, ignoring it may attenuate the findings of the theory-guided evaluations. Thus, a key issue in evaluation should be that of *the reality of theory relevance:* Does the program to be evaluated have, in fact, the characteristics that are assumed in a theory on why the program should be effective and for whom?

There has not been much integration of theory-guided monitoring (sometimes called "process evaluation") into the effectiveness assessments (sometimes called "outcome evaluations") with which this chapter is concerned. The need for even simple monitoring is dramatically illustrated by an anecdote related by Charles Silberman (at an American Justice Institute conference on May 18, 1979)—that in preparing *Criminal Violence, Criminal Justice* (1978), he wanted to visit what were regarded as the most effective programs for delinquency prevention. The head of a state agency told him that a center located in a high-drug-use neighborhood of a large city, and providing twenty-four-hour service as well as a "crash pad" for immediate aid for youths in trouble, would be the model for a whole series of new centers in that state. Impressed because such a program fitted his theories on what should be effective, Silberman went to visit this center late one afternoon. As he approached it he saw young people in the neighborhood who seemed to be in desperate straits and "spaced out" from drugs. When he asked to see the "crash pad," however, the center's director told him that the "pad" was just a room with beds that were empty at present. When Silberman asked what activities would be occurring that evening and which ones he could observe, he was told that none were scheduled. When he asked about the possibility of visiting on some other night, he learned that this center was open only from 9 a.m. to 5 p.m., as these were the only hours in which the staff, who came from elsewhere in the city, felt safe coming and going in that neighborhood. Thus, reliance on the description of a center by the state director would be utterly misleading in a theory-guided evaluation of this project, which was to be the model for many more.

A method of monitoring must usually be more complex than that described in Silberman's visit. This is evident in the psychotherapy and counseling programs already discussed. Because the prisoners who participate in these talk programs usually serve indeterminate sentences, their length of incarceration depends largely on whether their institution record indicates to the parole board that they are seeking rehabilitation. This impression may be conveyed merely by their enrollment in treatment programs as well as by what they say when personally interviewed by board members. Inmates are thus often motivated toward insincere participation and "game-playing" in therapy and counseling, to convince the staff that they have gained insight, as well as to learn psychological jargon with which to impress the parole board. All of these facts have been illustrated in many "I was in prison" books and in some research reports (notably Kassebaum et al., 1971). Yet the extent of sincerity and the bonds between inmates and therapists with which differential association or control theory should be concerned have not, to my knowledge, been systematically assessed in evaluations.

Complicating the problem of monitoring psychotherapy and counseling is the fact that there are diverse schools of thought on how these activities should be pursued—for example, the Freudian, Rogerian, Adlerian, and reality methods. In addition, research has indicated that one of the most crucial variables in the effectiveness of any of these treatments is the personality of the therapist or counselor. Furthermore, staff differ greatly in their goals for these programs: For example, some only try to increase adjustment to institutional life, others try to correct what they believe are basic personality problems stemming from early traumas, and still others concentrate on what are presumed to be the immediate precipitants to recidivism in adult life. Finally, some staff who volunteer to lead group counseling may do so to impress their supervisors favorably in order to improve their prospects for promotion; thus, they may sometimes be as insincere in their participation in these programs as are the prisoners who enroll in them to impress the parole board.

It should be borne in mind that offenders supplement the talk programs that are formally organized by staff with informal talk there and elsewhere. Certainly the "offstage" reactions of inmates to the formal sessions should be learned. Besides, even the formal sessions often are dominated (just as are the informal ones) by the most articulate and aggressive spokespersons for procriminal ideologies, especially when staff are nondirective and passive. Thus, some formal sessions may well contribute more to learning procriminal than anticriminal perspectives.

At about this point in thinking about evaluation, some timid souls give up. Many psychotherapeutic clinicians and other correctional workers simply despair of the possibility of getting more precise assessments of their work, and merely contend that one must have faith that their treatment efforts do some good. Also, some social scientists adopt a rhetoric that denigrates all statistical evaluations as "positivism," and which they caricature as necessarily requiring conclusions in mathematical form in order to simulate the physical sciences. Yet physical and biological as well as social sciences vary their research methods with the requirements of the problem that is under study, seeking qualitative rather than quantitative data when appropriate. Furthermore, a criminologist can maintain the canons of scientific method by trying to maximize objectivity so that his or her research procedures can be replicated and yield similar results for different investigators, even when the research task is to identify and interpret subjective thoughts and feelings of the persons studied. Thus, the best feasible monitoring of programs to be evaluated is desirable even when it is difficult, for it is likely to yield more widely acceptable and replicable conclusions than blind faith alone.

There are many ways to incorporate necessarily subjective impressions of inmate and staff roles into a theory-guided analysis of talk programs. One can have staff, participant observers, detached observers (e.g., those watching sessions through a one-way glass), or posttreatment interviewers of the subjects describe the qualities of staff and offender behavior in the program. A variety of questionnaires, rating forms, or other procedures can be developed to make these tasks systematic and to increase the reliability of their findings. From the standpoint of differential association or control theory, such efforts would seek to assess the extent to which each client learned anticriminal definitions or built bonds with conventional persons in the psychotherapy or counseling activity. The external validity and utility of the ratings would be suggested by their correlation with recidivism reduction, especially for those offenders deemed theoretically most likely to benefit from such talk programs (e.g., the unadvanced offenders, especially those with some prior success in work, school, and other legitimate alternatives to crime). As far as I know, this type of rating and analysis has not been reported in the research literature.

A few studies classified clients before treatment (e.g., by interviews, records, and tests) concerning the probable sincerity or other qualities of their participation in a program. Thus, in the PICO project (Adams, 1961) and in the Community Treatment Program (Warren, 1967; Palmer, 1974) clients were differentiated before entering the programs, on the basis of a theory regarding types of persons who would benefit most from particular kinds of rehabilitative services. Indeed, pretreatment predictions on amenability to their methods of counseling were checked by continual monitoring of participation in the Community Treatment Program, leading to reclassification of a few clients after they had been part of the experimental groups for several months.

From the standpoint of differential association and other criminological theory, a number of well-known, large research projects, although very rigorously designed and conducted, were poorly conceived from the start and have had highly misleading results because they lacked theoretical focus in their sampling, monitoring, or interpretation. For example, in the California Men's Colony East, the prison in which an exceptionally well-controlled experiment in group counseling was directed by Kassebaum et al. (1971), most of the subjects were offenders who theoretically had the fewest prospects for reformation through mere talk sessions. Over half of them had served prior prison or reformatory sentences, and most of the remainder had prior jail or training-school terms. Hence, they were much above average in their enculturation in crime and in groups that are manipulative of custodial and counseling personnel.

Kassebaum et al. randomly assigned these prisoners to separate housing units that differed in the hours per week, staff training, and group size of the counseling provided for the residents. In one unit, inmates were given only one hour of counseling per week, had minimally trained staff, and were permitted to volunteer to participate; their parole outcomes were compared to those of the nonvolunteers in their unit. All other units in the experiment participated mandatorily, and the parole outcomes of random assignees to the units given counseling were compared to the parole outcomes of the inmates randomly assigned to units without it. Monitoring indicated that participation in the counseling groups was highly insincere, hostile, and associated with criminal rather than anticriminal values. Indeed, in the large groups there were often long periods of total silence and complaints of utter boredom. None of the variations in this experiment was associated with lower rates of parole failure in the counseled than in the noncounseled units.

Had this project been designed on the basis of a theory on why counseling should have an impact on recidivism and for whom, its sampling and the random assignment of prisoners to alternative types of service would have been much different. For example, a design based on differential association theory would have sought inmates conceived as most amenable to counseling, such as young persons with little prior criminal record. To test this assumption on amenability, inmates of the types assigned to the study by Kassebaum et al. might also have been randomly assigned to counseling, as was done in the PICO project (Adams, 1961), but housed in units separate from those of the amenables. Differential association theory would also make the researchers prefer individual to group counseling, with as much intensity and frequency as possible, and oriented toward augmenting the anticriminal and diminishing the criminal perspectives of its clients. Control groups of similar amenables, and nonamenables in separate control groups, would have no counseling and a minimum of personal intimacy with staff or, at most, only that which is traditional in prisons. (In addition, a separate experiment could randomly select some criminally enculturated and manipulative inmates—nonamenables for counseling—for programs of tightly disciplined work simulating outside employment, with tangible rewards for clearly satisfactory individual performances. This would be guided by a hypothesis that such offenders are much more readily influenced by rewarded experience than by talk.)

All units in this theory-guided experiment in counseling would have to be monitored, to check that contrasting patterns of differential association would prevail in the experimental and control settings. If the monitoring revealed that the reverse of expected staff-inmate relationships characterized a group, results contrasting those originally predicted would be forecast, just as a medical researcher would revise the expectations in an experiment if it became known that subjects given a new medicine to swallow were retaining it in their mouths and then spitting it out.

If the theory of differential association is valid for explaining much criminal behavior, a controlled experiment in counseling with the theory-guided design described above would be much more likely than that of Kassebaum et al. to find the correlates of recidivism reduction by counseling, or to suggest, on the basis of monitoring, a more fruitful research design. Even more important, any positive contribution to knowledge that it produced would consist of widely applicable general principles or guidelines on methods of counseling for various theoretically distinct types of subjects, rather than the sweeping generalizations on all prisoner counseling that most of the California research sought in vain.

In any part of the criminal justice system, monitoring is needed to understand both favorable and unfavorable evaluations. Thus, Wilson and Boland (1978: 383) complain: "Though there have been experiments on policing, most have attempted to measure the effect of a greater or lesser police *presence* on crime, as in the Kansas City patrol experiment and various quasi-experiments in New York City. . . . None of these made a significant effort to monitor what the police actually did." Accordingly, the authors indicate, most studies lack evidence on how aggressively officers probe for possible offenses and suspects in their patrolling, which may be a major factor in the failure to find a consistent relationship between frequency of patrol and crime rates.

Studies of the criminal courts have found labeling theory inadequate to account for the correlates of case disposition (Bernstein et al., 1977a, 1977b), implying that system characteristics rather than reactions to particular types of offenders must be comprehended to account for variations in court practices. However, research based upon theory derived from studies of other types of organizations suggests that the "loose coupling" among court subsystems (e.g., prosecution offices, judges, probation staff, and defense counsels) makes it impossible to explain variations in court decision patterns by focus on any single subsystem alone (Hagan et al., 1979). In addition, total system attributes, such as case pressure, have been shown unpredictive of plea bargaining rates or other court statistics to which they are customarily presumed to be linked (Heumann, 1975). An analysis of a sudden cessation of charge bargaining in one court system revealed an intricate array of methods by which persons in each court role manipulated almost every type of legal procedure to make the ultimate consequences of this policy change much less drastic than its sponsors expected (Church, 1976). These and other studies suggest a crying need in the courts for further monitoring that is both grounded in available theory and oriented toward developing new and more adequate perspectives, so that the incentives and exchanges among all role incumbents will be better understood (a good beginning was provided by Sudnow, 1965).

In summary, it has been suggested: (1) that monitoring is needed to assure that programs or policies evaluated actually conform to the assumptions made in the theory on which the research design is based; (2) that where evaluation results do not seem to confirm this theory, monitoring becomes necessary to try to improve the theory and thereby to generate a revised evaluation design. The creation of new theory is seldom independent of older theory, however. According to the third thesis of this chapter, any explanations that guide applied science, such as evaluation research, should be based upon theory from more firmly established and abstract pure science.

THE NESTING OF SCIENTIFIC THEORY

Zetterberg (1963) observes that very young children learn physics from books or chapters entitled "automobiles," "airplanes," or "guns," but that by the time they are in high school or college they learn from physics books whose chapters have such titles as "mechanics," "optics," and "thermodynamics." Automobiles, airplanes, or guns are only referred to in physics books to illustrate the application of more abstract scientific principles.

Zetterberg (1963) also points out that scientific principles can be differentiated by what he calls their "informative value." This concept refers to the variety of phenomena for which a theoretical statement provides useful explanations. Because the first law of thermodynamics, on the conservation of energy, explains a vast array of chemical processes and the source of power in engines and guns, it has much more informative value than a less abstract principle, such as that of the differential gear that transmits the engine's power to the back wheels of a car. Similarly, Darwin's principle of species differentiation by the survival of the fittest in competition for existence, has much more informative value than an application of that principle, such as the explanation for the predominance of white animals in arctic regions.

It is a defect of criminal justice evaluation that its conclusions are not usually viewed as applications or derivations of more informative abstract theoretical principles. For example, the customary rationale for a particular correctional program is usually some more or less tested assertion that it often helps to reform offenders, rather than the application of general principles of human behavior which might explain why the programs should be reformative and for whom.

Theories may usefully be thought of as nested, like a set of graduated boxes in which each fits into the next larger one. The most informative theory can be conceived as the largest container, holding a series of narrower derived theories. Perhaps the most informative abstract ideas for guidance of sentencing, corrections, and crime prevention—the "largest" containers—are provided by psychology's learning theory. Two of its useful principles can be expressed in simplified form as follows:

(1) Behavior that is rewarded in given types of circumstances tends to be repeated in such circumstances, but to cease when no longer rewarded.

(2) The behavior that is repeated in circumstances where it previously was rewarded may often cease when it evokes punishment, but will recur if the punishment ends (or can be avoided or endured), unless alternative behavior is comparably rewarded.

Many more principles could be added that are also of wide applicability, such as those concerned with the effects on behavior of immediacy, intensity, and scheduling of rewards and punishments, but the above two will suffice for illustration of the importance of nesting.

These generalizations on learning are highly informative because they have been applied and found valid in a large range of research, and on many species of animals. They apply to rats in mazes that get rewards from food pellets and punishments from electric shocks, to pigeons in Skinner boxes, to children raising their educational attainment rapidly by means of teaching machines, to catatonic patients restored to fairly normal conduct in mental hospital "token economy" programs, and many more situations (Verhave, 1966; Ayllon and Azrin, 1968; Ullmann and Krasner, 1975). For guidance of sentencing, corrections, and crime prevention policies, some more specialized (and hence less informative) criminological propositions can be derived from these principles, such as the following:

(1a) If crime has been rewarding in certain types of circumstances, it is likely to be repeated there.

(2a) If crime is punished after it has been rewarding, the punishment is not likely to be effective in preventing recidivism if the offender returns to the types of circumstances where it was rewarding, unless noncriminal alternative behavior becomes at least as rewarding as the crime.

If the above two criminological principles are taken together, two even narrower propositions to guide sentencing and corrections can be derived from them, as follows:

1b(2). Severe fines alone, or fines plus prison terms, suffice to prevent recidivism of persons who have had rewarding noncriminal careers to which they can return.

2b(1). Punishments for offenders who have had little or no successful experience in work or school tend to reduce recidivism only if they are supplemented by educational and vocational training plus realistic work experience that are adequate to enable these persons to procure and hold jobs.

The major advantage of nesting such applied science propositions in more abstract, pure psychology is that confidence in their validity is increased by the fact that they are implied by theory that has been widely validated. Furthermore, if evaluation research finds the above propositions correct, it augments confidence not only in them, but also in the more abstract principles, 1b, 2b, and 2, from which they are derived. But if either of these applied propositions, 1b(2) or 2b(1), is not found valid—if the fines or the education and job aid do not reduce recidivism—and theory-guided monitoring confirms that the programs evaluated fit the descriptions in these propositions—then the negative results stimulate improvement of the abstract theory to account for these findings. Thus, applied and pure science may contribute to each other if both are guided by the same informative general theory.

Because no creatures have a capacity for use of language comparable to that of humans, abstract laws of learning that explain findings in research on nonhuman species, such as propositions 1 and 2, with which this discussion began, may require qualification if they are to be more fruitful when applied to humans. These qualifications could include the following four principles from social psychology:

(A) The rewards that most influence the conduct of humans are favorable self-conceptions.

(B) Favorable self-conceptions come mainly from the responses that a person's conduct elicits from other people.

(C) People may also reward or punish themselves by covert communication to themselves about their own conduct.

(D) Humans can learn new types of conduct through written and oral communication from others, through vicariously experiencing the conduct and its rewards when observing others do it, or by devising it themselves; but vicarious experience—or modeling—is probably the most influential of these modes of learning.

The above principles have been very diversely formulated and tested in social psychology (e.g., contrast Mead, 1934 with Bandura, 1967), but are widely asserted or implied. They can be highly informative in guiding criminal justice policies because nested in them is Sutherland's differential association theory of crime causation, summarized in the first section of this essay, which states that social learning, especially in intimate personal groups, explains the acquisition of both criminal and anticriminal ideas, attitudes, skills, and rationalizations.

The term *differential* and Sutherland's focus on pro- and anticriminal sources of learning implies that his theory is also nested in the most informative of all principles in sociology and anthropology—what I have called "the law of sociocultural relativity"—that "social separation fosters cultural differentiation" (Glaser, 1976: 257). This law is the basis for the major implication of differential association theory for correctional policy (which was repeatedly illustrated in the preceding sections of this essay): Both crime prevention and reformation of offenders require an *increase* of the frequency, duration, priority, and intensity of association with anticriminal influences, and/or a *decrease* in these aspects of association with criminal influences. A policy maker or researcher who thinks with this sociocultural relativity perspective is sensitized to the procriminal subcultures in offender groups, to the counterproductivity of mass treatment programs that isolate lawbreakers from conventional persons, and to fostering as much collaborative and mutually rewarding interactions between these types of persons as is safely feasible.

An additional pure science source of theoretical guidance for criminal justice evaluation research has been provided by economics, which views illegal gain as "an alternative to income gained honestly," so that "a rational individual . . . will consider all of the opportunities open to him in terms of a benefit-cost analysis" (Votey and Phillips, 1974: 1062). This perspective justifies punishments of lawbreakers, to increase the cost of committing crimes, but also trade training and job placement, to increase their potential benefits from lawful conduct. An economic viewpoint was integrated with differential association in the "opportunity theory" of Cloward and Ohlin (1960), which stressed that youths' perceptions of probable benefits from illegitimate or legitimate pursuits are largely determined by the older youths and adults through whom they are socialized. These approaches also have been integrated with control theory by Glaser (1978, 1979) as "differential anticipation" theory (perhaps preferably called "differential expectation"), which asserts that a person refrains from or commits crime because of his or her expectations as to its consequences, but these expectations are determined by:

(1) the person's total conventional and criminal social bonds;
(2) the person's prior learning experiences that have provided skills, tastes, and ideas conducive to gratification in criminal or in alternative pursuits; and
(3) the person's perceptions of needs, opportunities, and risks when interpreting momentary circumstances.

Such a theory's strength lies in its nesting in more abstract and firmly established principles of learning psychology, social psychology, sociology, and economics. These more general theories are highly informative in explaining most problematic human conduct other than innate reflexes. Because of the utility of the theories in which it is nested, differential expectation is especially informative as a basis for explaining most crimes that the law calls "willful," that is, not due to negligence or to ignorance of the law. Its merit for criminal justice evaluation is that a researcher whose thinking is well grounded in such general principles will design sampling and data analysis to focus on theoretically probable contrasts in the effects of programs on the life expectations of the subjects, will monitor the programs to assure that the theoretically presumed contrasts exist, will probe for explanations for any unanticipated results, and will be guided in this probing by the basic principles of psychology, sociology, and economics.

It should be emphasized in conclusion, however, that only a smattering of all the relevant and informative theory for criminal justice evaluation could be presented in this brief essay. As already indicated, much that is pertinent in learning psychology has been omitted, and much more could certainly be derived from sociology and economics. For instance, the theory that guides fruitful sociological research on organizations can enrich the evaluation of most criminal justice agencies. Political science also has much to offer, for example, in understanding the resistance of some officials to guidance by evaluation research, and in many other problems that develop in the effort to reform the criminal justice system. Lloyd E. Ohlin and his associates have brilliantly illustrated the possibilities of integrating sociological and political science perspectives in evaluating correctional change in Massachusetts (Coates et al., 1978; Miller et al., 1978).

Theory that is nested in more abstract and established principles of the pure sciences is especially useful when some evaluation findings are negative. Persons whose thinking is well grounded in explanatory theory do not evaluate a practice simply by counting the number of settings or studies in which it was found to "work" and the number in which it was not. Instead, they intensively probe for theoretically relevant differences in the circumstances or research methods that may account for contrasting results. The public expects such a search for theory-guided explanation when engineers try to explain the crash of one out of thousands of airplanes; it is presumed that application of the principles of physics to interpret the evidence will make the deviant case more understandable and perhaps avoidable in the future. Yet a comparable analysis of diversity in results is not so readily feasible for criminal justice researchers who are not guided by abstract theory but rely instead on ad hoc explanations to design their evaluation procedures and present their findings.

It follows that evaluators usually are revealing the theoretical inadequacy of their work if they proclaim that a particular criminal justice practice is ineffective only because the number of experiments or quasi-experiments in which it was found superior did not exceed the number in which it was no better or worse than the alternative practices in control or comparison groups. If researchers are well guided by theory in their sampling, monitoring, and data analyses, they should usually be able to provide tested or testable explanations for marked variations in effectiveness in different comparisons, explanations nested in highly informative principles of the behavioral or social sciences.

SUMMARY AND CONCLUSION

Three themes were set forth at the beginning of this essay, and each was then elaborated and illustrated. Their collective implication is that evaluations of criminal justice policies and practices tend to be of very deficient utility if inadequately guided by theory, because:

(1) Theory-focused sampling reduces invalidity of findings due to selection and application biases.

(2) Theory-focused sampling and data analysis increases capacity to show the relative effectiveness of various programs for different types of subjects or settings.

(3) Theory fosters monitoring of programs under evaluation
   (a) to assure their fit with the theory's implications on why, where, and for whom the programs should work;
   (b) to revise theory to fit the programs more adequately.

(4) Theory facilitates the accumulation from evaluation studies of highly informative guiding principles for criminal justice policy and practice, especially if the theory is nested in well-established principles of the behavioral and social sciences.

(5) Theory increases the ability to learn from diversity in evaluation outcomes.

REFERENCES

Adams, S. (1961 "Interaction between Individual Interview Therapy and Treatment Amenability in Older Youth Authority Wards," pp. 27-44 in *Inquiries Concerning Kinds of Treatments for Kinds of Delinquents*. Sacramento, CA: California Department of Corrections. (Reprinted as pages 548-561 of "The PICO Project" in N. Johnston et al., The Sociology of Punishment and Corrections. New York: John Wiley, 1970.

Akman, D. D., A. Normandeau, and M. W. Wolfgang (1968) "The Group Treatment Literature in Correctional Institutions: An International Bibliography, 1945-1967." *Journal of Criminal Law, Criminology and Police Science* 59: 41-56.

Ayllon, T., and N. Azrin (1968) *The Token Economy*. Englewood Cliffs, NJ: Prentice-Hall.

Bandura, A. (1967) *Principles of Behavior Modification*. New York: Holt, Rinehart & Winston.

Bernstein, I. N., W. R. Kelly, and P. A. Doyle (1977a) "Societal Reaction to Deviants: The Case of Criminal Defendants." American Sociological Review 42: 743-755.

Bernstein, I. N., E. Kick, J. T. Leung, and B. Schulz (1977b) "Charge Reduction: An Intermediary Stage in the Process of Labeling Criminal Defendants." *Social Forces* 56: 362-384.

Church, T. W., Jr. (1976) "Plea Bargains, Concessions and the Courts: Analysis of a Quasi-Experiment." *Law and Society Review* 10: 377-401.

Cloward, R. A., and L. E. Ohlin (1960) *Delinquency and Opportunity*. New York: Free Press.

Coates, R. B., A. D. Miller, and L. E. Ohlin (1978) *Diversity in a Youth Correctional System: Handling Delinquents in Massachusetts*. Cambridge, MA: Ballinger.

Elliott, D. E., S. S. Ageton, and R. J. Canter (1979) "An Integrated Theoretical Perspective on Delinquent Behavior." *Journal of Research on Crime and Delinquency* 16: 3-27.

Glaser, D. (1979) "Crime Causation Theories and Their Implications for Public Policies," in N. Morris and M. Tonry (eds.) *Crime and Justice—1978*. Chicago: University of Chicago Press.

——— (1978) *Crime in Our Changing Society*. New York: Holt, Rinehart & Winston.

——— (1976) "Marginal workers," pp. 254-266 in J. F. Short, Jr. (ed.) *Delinquency, Crime and Society*. Chicago: University of Chicago Press.

Hagan, J., J. Hewitt, and D. Alwin (1979) "Ceremonial Justice: Crime and Punishment in a Loosely Coupled System." *Social Forces* 58: 506-527.

Harrison, R. M., and P.F.C. Mueller (1964) *Clue-Hunting about Group Counseling and Parole Outcome*. Sacramento, CA: California Department of Corrections.

Heumann, M. (1975) "A Note on Plea Bargaining and Case Pressure." *Law and Society Review* 9: 515-528.

Hirschi, T. (1969) *Causes of Delinquency*. Berkeley: University of California Press.

Kassebaum, G., D. A. Ward, and D. M. Wilner (1971) *Prison Treatment and Parole Survival*. New York: John Wiley.

Lipton, D., R. Martinson, and J. Wilks (1975) *The Effectiveness of Correctional Treatment: A Survey of Treatment Evaluation Studies*. New York: Praeger.

Martinson, R. (1974) "What works? Questions and Answers about Prison Reform." *The Public Interest*. 35: 22-54.

Mead, G. H. (1934) *Mind, Self and Society*. Chicago: University of Chicago Press.

Miller, A. D., L. E. Ohlin, and R. B. Coates (1978) *A Theory of Social Reform: Correctional Change Processes in Two States*. Cambridge, MA: Ballinger.

Palmer, T. (1974) "The Youth Authority's Community Treatment Project." *Federal Proba-tion* 38: 3-20.

Popper, K. R. (1959) *The Logic of Scientific Discovery*. New York: Basic Books.

Silberman, C. E. (1978) *Criminal Violence, Criminal Justice*. New York: Basic Books.

Sudnow, D. (1965) "Normal Crimes: Sociological Features of the Penal Code in a Public Defender's Office." *Social Problems* 12: 255-276.

Sutherland, E. H., and D. R. Cressey (1978) *Criminology*. Philadelphia: J. B. Lippincott.

Ulmann, L. P., and L. Krasner (1975) *A Psychological Approach to Abnormal Behavior*. Englewood Cliffs, NJ: Prentice-Hall.

Verhave, T. [ed.] (1966) *The Experimental Analysis of Behavior*. Englewood Cliffs, NJ: Prentice-Hall.

Votey, H. L., Jr., and L. Phillips (1974) "The Control of Criminal Activity: An Economic Analysis," in D. Glaser (ed.) *Handbook of Criminology*. Skolie, IL: Rand McNally.

Waldo, G. P., and S. Dinitz (1967) "Personality Attributes of the Criminal: An Analysis of Research Studies 1950-65." *Journal of Research in Crime and Delinquency* 4: 185-202.

Warren, M. Q. (1967) *The Community Treatment Project After Five Years*. Sacramento, CA: California Department of the Youth Authority.

Wilson, J. Q., and B. Boland (1978) "The Effect of the Police on Crime." *Law and Society Review*. 12: 367-390.

Zetterberg, H. L. (1963) *On Theory and Verification in Sociology*. Totawa, NJ: Bedminster Press.

6

Field Experimentation in Criminal Justice: Rationale and Design

LaMar T. Empey

The traditional importance of the experiment in science can scarcely be exaggerated. The experiment, says Poincare (1953: 31), "is the sole source of truth; it alone can teach us anything new." "The cardinal principle of experimentation," adds Kaplan (1964: 45), "is that we must accept the outcome whether or not it is to our liking." And with reference to experimental evaluation in criminal justice, Bernstein (1975: 56) says,

> The use of rigorous procedures is particularly important in evaluation research as long as it seeks to demonstrate causality. If one is interested in knowing whether the action program is directly responsible for producing the desired outcomes, one must be able to rule out alternative explanations.

Such forceful statements notwithstanding, other scientists disagree. One group maintains that rigorous methods of experimentation are impractical, if not irrelevant (see Adams, 1975; Edwards et al., 1975; and summaries by Boruch, 1976: 160-174, Rossi, 1972: 32). Not only are randomized experiments almost impossible to implement in the real world, and are excessively costly and time-consuming, but they have little payoff for administrators and policy makers. Useful evaluations are those which are devoted to improving decisions about programs and their competitors, not to testing their relative merits. What administrators seek, and what evaluations should provide, is information which will help them to make day-to-day decisions within the value contexts of their own choosing.

A second group of dissenters argue that what is needed is process-oriented, qualitative research (see Rossi, 1972: 33-34; Weiss and Rein, 1970). In programs involving real people, experimental designs may be not only inappropriate but harmful. The reason is that they reinforce the belief that the problems for which corrections are sought lie not within the larger institutional structures of society but within the beliefs, personalities, and characters of aberrant individuals (Deutscher, 1973). In order to avoid reinforcing this inherent bias, therefore, evaluation research should concentrate on the problems of institutional change, and should track inevitable shifts in program implementation. The most justifiable and informative kind of research, therefore, would be that which takes into account the way social institutions, not individuals, adapt to, or resist, remedial programs.

SOURCES OF CONFLICT

Since these polar positions continue to confuse important decision makers, as well as to divide the research community, an examination of their sources is important.

Pursuing Answers to Different Questions

The first source of conflict is the most obvious. It has to do with the fact that different approaches to research ask different questions and, as a result, provide different answers. More often than not, experimental studies have sought answers to only two principal questions: (1) Is the *impact* on clients of some innovation demonstrably different (superior?) to one or more alternatives? and (2) Is it legitimate to assume that the innovation was the *cause* of these differences?

As a result, critics of experimentation are quite right in suggesting that this method of investigation usually leaves important questions unanswered: What kinds of interaction between clients and significant others produced the outcomes that were observed? How were important decisions made, and by whom? Were any changes actually introduced into the institutional structures that are central to the lives of clients—homes, schools, places of employment, or legal systems?

When the primary method for evaluation has been the randomized experiment, the innovative program itself has too often remained an unstudied, mysterious, black box. Even if it had proven more successful than one or more control programs, as measured by some quantitative assessment of outcome, one would remain uncertain as to what elements of the innovation had produced the desirable outcome. Hence, if one wanted to know what factors have contributed to some observed outcome, one must conduct process research on it.

Yet, even if the limitations of experimental studies are acknowledged, it is also clear that the need for process research by no means invalidates the need for a rigorous assessment of outcome. Since the goal of any innovation should be to provide some payoff for clients, as well as for administrators, it would be a peculiar argument indeed which suggested that findings should be ignored which indicate that, while some innovation has altered traditional decision-making processes and institutional structures, it has produced no better outcome for the people it was supposed to help. *Thus, an optimal approach to evaluation would be that which provides for a rigorous assessment of both process and outcome.* Indeed, once this fact is recognized, it is quite clear that there is no lasting and inherent incompatibility between experimental and process designs. Both might be fruitfully employed in the same study.

Vested Interests

A second source of conflict is less easily resolved. It is inherent in the ideologies and vested interests of different political, professional, and scientific groups. As each pursues its own unique concerns, impediments to experimentation are created.

1. Political and Bureaucratic Impediments. Perhaps the most noteworthy impediments are political and bureaucratic in character. Campbell (1975: 71-72) points out that, while it would seem that the United States and other modern countries should be ready for an experimental approach to social reform, such is not the case.

It is one of the most characteristic aspects of the present situation that *specific reforms are advocated as though they were certain to be successful.* For this reason, knowing outcomes has immediate political implications. Given the inherent difficulty of making significant improvements by the means usually provided, and given the discrepancy between promise and possibility, most administrators wisely prefer to limit the evaluations to those the outcomes of which they can control, particularly insofar as published outcomes or press releases are concerned. Ambiguity, lack of truly comparable comparison bases, and lack of concrete evidence all work to increase the administrator's control over what gets said, or at least to reduce the bite of criticism in the case of actual failure. There is safety in the cloak of ignorance.

Given the extent to which consumer, as well as legislative, groups are now beginning to demand greater accountability from administrators and politicians, Campbell's conclusion may be somewhat overstated. Nonetheless, since it is generally true that there has been safety in ignorance, some resistance to experimentation will continue.

2. Professional versus Scientific Interests. In a similar way, but for different reasons, resistance to evaluation can be anticipated among working professionals within any organization. This resistance can be illustrated by contrasting the ideology which gives meaning to their work with that of the scientist.

Experimental scientists are trained skeptics. In theory, at least, their primary commitment is to knowledge, not to the success of some program. However desirable that program may appear in theory, therefore, they are inclined to be leery of its utility until its effects are shown to be demonstrably superior.

By contrast, those professionals who are motivated or are hired to help people can ill afford to be skeptical about what they are doing. Persons who do not believe in the efficacy of their work are poor workers indeed. Furthermore, professionals are particularly susceptible to the changing, but doctrinal, ideologies and proposals for reform. For example, the belief is widespread that institutionalization in any form is harmful to juveniles. Therefore, it seems patently obvious to many professionals that almost any community alternative would be better.

Given this "obvious" conclusion, why evaluate new programs? Even more to the point, why set up experimental designs which might deny to the members of some control group a new and highly desirable form of treatment? Why utilize the random assignment of clients to alternative treatments when clinicians already know what is best for them? Since assignment is best left to persons trained for that task, it should not be left to the vagaries of chance.

In short, working professionals often feel they have as much to lose as high-level administrators, if evaluation experiments are conducted. Not only may it be a threat to their jobs, but it tends to demean their professional skills and integrity.

3. Situational Impediments. Experience also highlights many situational impediments to randomized experimentation. For example, consider the problems that were encountered when efforts were made to test the Head Start program experimentally:

> It would seem at first glance to be quite easy to divide preschool children into experimental and control groups, admitting the former into Head Start programs and withholding admission from the latter. However, Head Start was instituted in such haste that, at least during the first year, institutions had all they could do to fill the Head Start classes that were authorized. In short, initially there was no surplus of potential clients which could have been diverted into control groups [Rossi, 1972: 31].

Similar problems were encountered in the Provo Experiment (Empey and Erickson, 1972), where the population of very serious delinquents in a small court was not large enough to permit its division into experimental and control groups and still to maintain sufficient clients for the experimental program. Even though authorities were willing to permit the random placement of delinquents, unanticipated problems made such placement difficult.

Another situational problem has to do with the fact that many broad spectrum programs, supposedly uniform in different jurisdictions, are anything but uniform. "Because of this variability, dividing clients among control and experimental groups would be fatuous, since the treatment to be administered to the experimental groups would not be uniform" (Rossi, 1972: 31).

In a similar way, innovative programs rarely remain the same throughout their life-spans: clear-cut goals are not defined; staff members either lack, or are not trained to follow, well-established guidelines; and the programs themselves are subjected to a trial-and-error existence (Weiss and Rein, 1969: 34). Again, therefore, it would be foolish to divide clients into experimental and control groups on the assumption that a uniform "stimulus" would be administered to the experimentals.

Finally, some legal impediments to randomized experimentation have been enacted in recent years. Laws have been passed which contain specific injunctions against its use. Sometimes these laws are designed to insure that all persons in need of some new service will receive it, which would not be the case if randomized assignment were used (Rossi, 1972: 31). In other cases, they are overarching provisions which are intended to protect human subjects from unscrupulous investigators and unethical or harmful research. But while this goal is laudable, such laws may also have the effect of denying the appropriate use of experimental methods for ethically justifiable purposes. Furthermore, they may have the unintended effect of denying the use of means by which officials can be held accountable for the services they are supposed to render, or for discovering the unanticipated, but dysfunctional, results of some innovation. But whether this is true or not, it is clear that in addition to administrative and professional resistance to evaluation, there are also many situational factors which make it difficult.

Value Differences among Scientists

The last major source of conflict, though highly important, is rarely discussed. It has to do with the fact that disputations over the relative merits of contrasting approaches to evaluation among scientists themselves often reflect fundamental differences over social values and the most appropriate way for resolving social or political problems. While some scientists avow social neutrality, others either identify with those in power or with some reform movement. Thus, it would not be entirely inaccurate to suggest that scientists can be divided roughly into three different ideological camps:

1. The Positivists. Proponents of rigorous experimentation probably hue most closely to the traditional values of the positivistic faith. These values suggest that, in their roles as scientists, program evaluators should remain neutral with respect to popular reforms, at least in the conduct of their research. As scientists, they may become involved with social policy, but their role is that of helping others to understand and to test the implications of various courses of action, not with suggesting which course of action is preferable (see Boruch, 1976; Bernstein and Freeman, 1975; Campbell and Stanley, 1963; Houston, 1972).

Yet, this avowal of neutrality is not entirely convincing, because positivists retain an idealistic bias—namely, that evidence, not political or bureaucratic considerations, should dictate policy choices among competing alternatives. That is why, in clinging to the values of experimentation, they may find themselves opposed by political conservatives in one instance, and by social reformers in another. Yet, because they believe that experimentation is the most valid method for determining the ultimate impact of an innovation, and of assessing causal relations between intervention and outcome, it provides the most certain means by which to choose among competing alternatives. "By submitting to the judgment of the experiment," as Kaplan (1964: 145) suggests, "we correct the presumption of the demand that the world conform to our expectations."

2. *The Pragmatists.* A second group of investigators, by contrast, are considerably more pragmatic (see Adams, 1975; Edwards et al., 1975; Guttentag, 1973). Certainty and proof occupy a much lower position in their hierarchy of values. Indeed, they would not necessarily consider it unwise to suggest that the world should conform, if not to their expectations, at least to the expectations of policy and decision makers.

> For example, an educatonal program which, on the evidence, in fact educates no one may nevertheless be desirable. Perhaps it is addressed to a disadvantaged group and contributes to the feeling of members or leaders that the group's needs are being felt and responded. Or perhaps some officeholder needs to be able to point to the program's existence to prove that he kept his campaign promises. Or both. As citizens, we may question whether these are proper reasons for continuing an educationally useless program. As evaluation researchers, however, we clearly fail in understanding the decision problem unless we recognize that these value dimensions are relevant to it [Edwards et al., 1975: 141].

In short, pragmatists are committed far more than positivists to the problems of the moment. To them, that research is most desirable which helps policy makers to thread their way through the tangled web of competing demands and alternative policies. Furthermore, it is the policy maker's own set of values and constraints, not those which stress the validity of research findings, which should dictate the uses to which research is put. That is why the demands of the positivist for rigorous proof of cause and effect seem not only irrelevant much of the time, but downright dysfunctional. The pragmatist would agree with the policy maker that, where circumstance dictates, the results of research should be ignored.

3. The Reformers. The third group of scientists tend to be reformers. As a result, they are interested in promoting change, and are inclined to use research to that end. Their commitment to change, in fact, would probably be greater than their commitment to evaluation research in general, or to the acquisition of knowledge for the sake of knowledge.

Perhaps the best example of a reform group today would be radical criminologists (see Edwards et al., 1974; Platt, 1974; Quinney, 1970, 1974; Schwendinger and Schwendinger, 1975). Indeed, it might be more accurate to describe them as revolutionary in perspective rather than reformist. Their position is that nothing can be done to lessen the crime problem by conducting experimental research within the framework of capitalist society, or by using that research to alter the current system of criminal justice. They contend that "only with the collapse of capitalist society and the creation of a new society, based on socialist principles, will there be a solution to the crime problem" (Quinney, 1974: 24).

Given this belief, radical scholars are inclined to indict positivists as well as pragmatists as handmaidens of the capitalist elite. The emphasis of positivists upon value neutrality, for example, has caused them to be a cynical and passionless lot who are more concerned with trivia than with the central issues of our age (Platt, 1974: 359). "In the name of developing knowledge about crime, most criminologists support current institutions at the expense of human freedoms and social revolution" (Quinney, 1974: 13). What scientists should be doing, instead, is documenting the need for revolution and helping to encourage it.

Other scientists are less radical in their prescriptions for change but they are reform-minded nonetheless. With respect to the problem of delinquency, for instance, labeling theorists enjoin us to "leave kids alone whenever possible" (Schur, 1973: 155). We should develop a policy of "radical nonintervention" which would "accommodate society to the widest possible diversity of behavior and attitudes, rather than forcing as many individuals as possible to 'adjust' to supposedly common societal standards" (Schur, 1973: 154). Thus, such reforms as decriminalization or diversion have been strongly advocated by this group.

What all of this means is that, whether they are of a radical or a more moderate stripe, the interest of reformers in promoting change is likely to have a distinct impact on the research they conduct. To the degree that they are committed to change, they will be inclined to use research to justify conclusions that they have already reached rather than to weigh carefully the pros and cons of their reform proposals. This approach to research is an old and honorable one, but it is closer to the kind used by lawyers and debaters than it is to the kind used by the classical positivists. That is, the object of any investigation is to win a case or to further a cause, not to examine the relative merits of either, since the cause itself is not subject to question.

But while it is clear that positivists and reformers differ greatly over this approach to research, it is far less clear that there are wide differences between reformers and pragmatists over it. To be sure, their social objectives may differ—reformers favoring change, while pragmatists are willing to defer to the needs of the policy maker. But to the extent that pragmatists actually conduct their research within the value context of the policy maker, they are like reformers in their willingness to see research directed toward some predetermined end, or put to some expedient use. Furthermore, since both pragmatists and reformers tend to disavow the utility of the randomized experiment, their research is not likely to conform to the highest standards of validity and objectivity. Thus, the only real value difference between pragmatists and reformers is in the nature of the goals being sought.

What can be said, then, about this bewildering array of value conflicts and impediments to experimental evaluation? Does this kind of research have any redeeming social value? More specifically, does a disinterested evaluation of programs in criminal justice have anything to contribute?

Any attempt to answer these questions must pay heed to the social context in which they are posed. In response to a mounting wave of cynicism and disillusionment during the past decade or two, the administration of justice in this country, no less than the traditional philosophy of science, has been subjected to a great deal of questioning, if not scorn. Both social institutions have been under attack. Hence, by considering the remarkable reforms that are now being advocated in justice, we can better determine whether a rigorous assessment of them makes any sense. Experimentation may, or may not, be relevant.

NATURE OF CURRENT REFORMS

What is striking about current justice reforms is that they are every bit as revolutionary as those which led to the construction of the first prisons and asylums following the War of Independence, to the stress that was placed upon rehabilitation following the Cincinnati Prison Congress of 1870, or to the creation of the juvenile court at the turn of the twentieth century. Yet, while these reforms reflect a pervasive disillusionment with the way our systems now operate, many are inherently contradictory and are based upon competing ideologies.

On the one hand, one set of reforms is liberal in character and is based upon the assumption that juvenile and adult systems have overcriminalized offenders, have labeled and stigmatized them unnecessarily, have been overly centralized, and have discriminated against the young, racial minorities, females, and lower-class people (Miller, 1973: 456). Hence, the following reforms should be implemented: *decriminalization* of status and victimless offenses, *diversion* of lesser offenders from legal processing, *due process* for all, and *deinstitutionalization* of correctional programs (Bayh, 1971; Law Enforcement Assistance Administration, 1974; Lemert, 1967; National Advisory Commission on Criminal Justice Standards and Goals, 1973a, 1973b; National Task Force to Develop Standards and Goals for Juvenile Justice and Delinquency Prevention, 1977).

On the other hand, a second set of reforms is conservative in nature and suggests that our systems of justice may have been excessively lenient, have denied the rights of victims, have eroded discipline and respect for authority, and now threatens to destroy social order (Miller, 1973: 454-455). In this instance, therefore, a strikingly different set of reforms is advocated: *just deserts* for criminal acts, *determinate sentences* based upon prior history and current offense, *incapacitation* of chronic offenders, and *deterrence* of others. Since the concept of rehabilitation is bankrupt, efforts to reform offenders should be secondary to the goals of protecting the community, of deterring further crime, and of ensuring that justice is uniform for all (Morris, 1974; Van Den Haag, 1975; Wilks and Martinson, 1976; Wilson, 1975).

Liberal reforms were first advocated during the 1960s and, since then, have been applied primarily to juveniles. Meanwhile, conservative reforms gained increasing credence during the 1970s, and are ostensibly designed to control adult crime. Hence, one might conclude that liberal and conservative reforms are not necessarily incompatible, since they would be applied to different populations. But this is not proving to be the case, particularly since juveniles commit about half of all serious, traditional crime. Instead, conservative reforms are being reflected in a more punitive response not only to adults, but to juveniles as well.

Historically, the philosophy of the juvenile court has suggested that sharp distinctions between status offenders and youthful criminals should not be drawn. Instead, the court should attend to the needs of all children, not to the acts they have committed. But because of the assumption that crime is getting out of control, that point of view is being reversed; the tendency now is to pay much more attention to the acts of juveniles, and to draw distinctions among offenders based upon them. Hence, while we are witnesses to growing sentiments favoring decriminalization, diversion, and deinstitutionalization for status offenders, the opposite is true for juvenile criminals.

In 1976, for example, California joined several other states by passing a law which made serious juvenile felons, 16 and older, subject to legal processing in criminal court and to adult sanctions (California Welfare and Institutions Code, 1976). Even more striking were legislative changes in other states.

In Arizona, a completely new criminal and juvenile code was implemented in October of 1978. This code explicitly *denies* rehabilitation as one of its goals. Similarly, the new juvenile justice code of Washington lists "treatment" sixth in a list of ten purposes of the new code [Revised Criminal Code of Washington, 1977: 80]. It lists "protection of the community" first; and "making the juvenile accountable for his acts" third. The fourth purpose . . . is "to provide punishment commensurate with the age, crime, and criminal history of the juvenile offender" [Erickson, 1979].

In short, significant steps have been taken to eliminate the rehabilitative philosophy which has dominated our thinking, if not all of our practices, and to return to a more classical model of justice. This has had the effect of loosening legal controls over young status offenders, and perhaps of ensuring greater due process for all, but it has also led to a repopularization of certain hoary principles: reducing distinctions based on age, limiting official discretion, and reasserting a more retributive stance toward criminals, whether young or old.

These trends should give us pause. As David Rothman (1971: iv-xv) has so cogently pointed out, there is a prevailing tendency to regard major societal innovations as "reforms," as improvements over that which existed before. Solitary confinement in prison, for example, was once considered to be an enlightened and humane response to criminals. Later, the principles and techniques of rehabilitation became ascendant. Yet, in light of current debates, it would be difficult to maintain that any of these were unadulterated and unmistakable steps forward in the progress of humanity. To do so, Rothman suggests, would not only be bad logic but bad history.

If that is the case, how should today's innovations be regarded? Are they progressive steps in the treatment of offenders? Do they merit the unqualified support of wise and well-meaning citizens? Let me paraphrase Rothman's answer (1971: xv): If we are to describe any, or all, of today's innovations as "reforms," we will be taking for granted precisely what should be the focus of investigation. Our innovations should be carefully evaluated rather than accepted outright as improvements over existing practices. Otherwise, we will fall into the same trap as all the reformers who have preceded us—namely, the tendency to equate change with effectiveness, and to assume that good intentions or persuasive arguments are the same as correcting offenders or protecting society.

In short, Rothman's critique suggests that, if this generation of Americans is to be a bit more farsighted than those which have preceded it, to say nothing of being more responsible, skepticism and experimental evaluation are warranted. Since we are on one of those watersheds in history when potentially irrevocable changes are being introduced into some of our most cherished institutions, the goal toward which evaluation should be directed should not be some predetermined set of reforms, but the acquisition of objective evidence regarding the most humane methods for correcting offenders and for protecting society. Thus, certain principles for the conduct of evaluation research are implied. And while these principles draw heavily upon the tenets of the positivistic faith, they tap some of the tenets of the pragmatic and reformist faiths as well:

1. There is social value in research which requires those who participate in it to submit their official judgments to the quality of the evidence they can provide. Historically, the only people who have paid much attention to the results of rigorously controlled field experiments, particularly in the short run, are a small number of academics. Published largely in scientific journals, these results are read by scientists and ignored by others. It is hoped that this pattern might begin to change, since expedience and immediate applicability cannot be the only criteria for judging the utility of research. Indeed, even though the path has been long and devious by which objective evidence has eventually found its way into the deliberations of the body politic, it has tended in the physical and natural sciences to be a more reliable source for policy decisions than has research whose quality is so questionable that it has been readily dismissed by an increasingly skeptical public. The value of such evidence, in fact, is further illustrated by the second principle, which follows.

2. Where attempts will inevitably be made to attribute causality to the effects of some innovation, that innovation should be submitted to experimental analysis. More than scientific curiosity is at stake when attempts are made to attribute causality to some social innovation; the lives of people are also deeply affected. Hence, in planning for and conducting research, steps must be taken to guard against its misuse and misinterpretation. No less important, however, are the admonitions of pragmatist and reformist investigators regarding the political and administrative aspects of change. At the very least, as the next principle suggests, information is required which bears not only upon the eventual outcome of any innovation, but upon the institutional and social alterations that it either induces or fails to induce. No less than the subjects of any innovation, staff and policy makers need to be informed on its operational qualities and problems.

3. Experimental analysis is most valuable if it provides for a rigorous assessment of both process and outcome. Too often, the unanticipated consequences of "doing good" are ignored. Changes are introduced into the institutional structures of society, and into the lives of its people, which have negative as well as positive consequences. Conversely, positive changes sometimes occur which remain undocumented. Thus, in order to assess more fully the implications of any "reform," and in order to avoid making the cure worse than the disease, process as well as outcome research is required.

Finally, as the last principle suggests, the actual conduct of evaluation research must be organized in such a way that it provides relevant information for all of its potential audiences, not merely for the scientific community.

4. The study of process and outcome should be designed to address three needs: (a) the needs of science for contributions to basic theory and knowledge;

(b) the needs of policy makers and practitioners for setting and implementing policy; and (c) the needs of all three groups for the conduct of further innovation—innovation which builds upon that which has been learned in the past. This principle, along with those that preceded it, makes it all too clear that new models for collaboration among policy makers, scientists, and professionals are required if field experimentation is to be a useful social tool. New organizational arrangements are required by which the needs of all three groups can be anticipated and research addressed to them. In the pages that follow, therefore, the elements of a possible model are outlined.

A MODEL FOR FIELD EXPERIMENTATION

Kurt Lewin (1968: 441) has indicated why the need for model is so pressing. "Reforms," he points out, "usually emerge from a more or less vague idea. An objective appears in the cloudy form of a dream or wish, which can hardly be called a goal. To become real, to be able to steer action, something has to be developed which might be called a 'plan.' "

Ironically, the administrators and program people who must give form and substance to any "plan" are not usually trained in the kinds of theory-building that are useful in conceptualizing some new approach to justice problems. Meanwhile, social scientists who do have such training are seldom involved in the planning process. Their ideas as to what will work may be little better than anyone else's, but they can be of use in helping their potential colleagues to state their assumptions in ways that will make them more amenable to systematic implementation and test. Furthermore, they be able to better explain the need for careful study, and the way it might be linked to the planning process. In lieu of such procedures, however, research people are usually called in after a "plan," often a haphazard one, has been created, and then asked to evaluate it. Consequently, anger and misunderstanding, rather than some successful reform or new contributions to knowledge, have been the result.

Criteria for Model Construction

In order to avoid these difficulties, any effort to construct a model for field experimentation should take into account the three principal criteria for judging effective research: (1) *control,* (2) *representativeness,* and (3) *naturalness* (Golden, 1976: 13-15).

1. Control. When the goal of any study is to establish relationships between the methods used in some experiment (the independent variable) and a reduction in the recidivism rate (the dependent variable), control is the most important criterion for judging the adequacy of the overall strategy. In a field experiment, a new form of intervention or treatment is imposed on a group of offenders who have been randomly selected from some known and carefully delimited population of offenders. "The idea is to minimize the number of elements, both within the subjects and within the environment, that can vary in the research situation, so that the important relationships between the independent and dependent variables can be highlighted and established without ambiguity" (Golden, 1976: 13).

2. Representativeness. The representativeness of any experiment can be judged in terms of two criteria: (a) *external validity*—the extent to which the findings of the experiment can be generalized to other offenders, programs, or settings, and (b) *internal validity*—the extent to which the control exercised by the investigator is able to minimize the amount of error due to extraneous variables, "so that it is possible to conclude that differences in the dependent variable are attributable to differences in the independent variable" (Golden, 1976: 14).

3. Naturalness. Ordinarily, the primary goal of recent correctional experiments has been to contrast the relative effects of some new community program with those of more traditional programs. In many cases, however, these experiments have concentrated less upon using the natural, ongoing processes of the community to reintegrate the offender than upon creating some new form of institutional control. To the degree this has occurred, therefore, *naturalness* has been sacrificed. Little has been learned about the way existing structures might be used to facilitate new forms of adjustment. By contrast, future experiments might do more to facilitate *naturalness*—that is, to exercise some control over interaction without blocking entirely the ordinary relationships and processes of the community.

In summary, then, field experiments represent an attempt to wed some of the advantages of both field and laboratory studies. The goal is to increase control without sacrificing the naturalness of the environment. Yet, it is obvious that neither objective can be fully realized. It is impossible, for example, to manipulate the elements of any innovation (the independent variable) in such a way that complete control is exercised over them. Extraneous influences—outside pressures on offenders, institutional impediments, and other such factors—will inevitably lessen attempts at control. Likewise, it would be a rare experiment indeed which was able to maximize the external validity of the study by selecting experimental and control groups from a criminal population that included all types, ages, and classes of offenders; some compromise is required. Finally, any innovation must to some extent be contrived and artificial. By its very nature, it cannot be completely natural, since it introduces new experiences and structures into the community.

With these inherent limitations in mind, then, the elements that follow might be included in any field experimental model.

Project Goals

Much more can be done to facilitate the definition of project goals, and thus to improve the quality of any experiment. These goals would be of two types: (1) goals that pay heed to the importance of research in generating knowledge, and (2) goals that define the objectives of a program innovation.

Steps must be taken at the outset to ensure that the pursuit of knowledge will rank high in priority. The task of planning for, and financing, good research is no less demanding than planning for, and financing, good programs. Research must be acknowledged as an acceptable social goal; it must be legitimated in terms of workable organizational structure; and it must be supported by an appropriate budget. It must become something more than an afterthought. Otherwise, further talk about collaboration between research and action people will be empty.

The need for productive negotiations over program goals is no less important. In contrast to the past, however, research people might be recruited to work with program people in defining and clarifying the substance of such goals, and in setting up what appears to be a sensible method for realizing them. The reason is that the task of planning good research is not greatly different from that of planning sound programs: Basic assumptions must be clarified, the range of methods outlined for addressing them, and some choices made among the alternatives. In that way, all three criteria for judging the quality of an experiment might be improved.

It is common today, for example, to hear program people say that their objectives are to "divert offenders" or to "reduce recidivism." Yet, when stated in these terms, program goals say everything and nothing. The reason is that they are not expressed in substantive terms. "Diversion" in a police-operated program, for instance, may have a far different meaning from "diversion" in a program run by youth advocates or by a crisis intervention unit. Unless program goals are given substance in theoretical and operational terms, therefore, it is not possible to assess their implications either for research or action.

Ordinarily, substance is best gained when it is recognized that there are two types of goals that will inevitably be pursued in the running of any program: (1) *final* goals such as a reduction in recidivism; and (2) *intermediate* goals which are in the service of final goals. The intermediate goals of a police diversion unit, for example, may be to organize the families of first-time offenders into neighborhood units. The assumption would be that, by increasing the informal controls of families and communities, the delinquent acts of their children might be reduced (the final goal). By contrast, the members of a crisis intervention unit might seek to achieve the same final objective by selecting immediate and intensive intervention with the families of offenders as their intermediate goal. By reducing intrafamily tension and difficulty, they would hope to reduce recidivism.

Much more than final goals, intermediate goals require a great deal of specification, since they come close to defining the "independent variable" of the study. How are the informal controls of families and communities increased? What guidance is needed by parents and neighborhoods to accomplish this task?

What are the limits of crisis intervention? How long is it administered? Upon what principles should it operate? Why would increases in informal controls, or the use of a crisis intervention unit, actually achieve the final goal of reducing crime?

Any tendency to ignore questions such as these is as much a detriment to sound research as it is to program effectiveness. Furthermore, as soon as program and research people begin to consider such questions jointly, they soon discover that reasonable answers cannot be pursued until additional issues relative to their collaboration are examined. For example, they soon discover that intermediate program goals—increased neighborhood controls or crisis intervention—cannot really be defined with much precision until other elements of a collaborative working model are considered. These elements, in fact, are an interlocking web in which one element cannot really be fully completed until others are considered. That is why a joint effort by program and research people might be desirable, and why a prolonged dialogue between them is necessary prior to program inception, not afterward.

Definition of Target Population

The nature of the interlocking web is illustrated by the fact that one cannot finalize program goals, or meet the criterion of good research for effective control, until one is explicit about the target population for any new program. Just as program goals may change, depending upon the interests of the people who are to run the program, so they will change depending upon the target population involved. For example, the police are more likely to divert 12-year-olds from legal processing than they are to divert 16- and 17-year-olds. Yet, what if these 12-year-olds are potential recruits for, or are neophyte members of, a tough street gang—a gang in which 16- and 17-year-olds are core members. What should be the target population of the police-neighborhood program?

On the one hand, it is likely that the efforts required to control the 12-year-olds will be different from those required for the older boys. On the other hand, it might be difficult to work with the younger group without doing something about the older one. Furthermore, a decision to work with both groups, while it might increase the generalizability of the study, could easily lessen the control of the program over experimental variables. What, then, should be the target population of the program, the neophytes or both groups?

Once one begins to ask questions like these, two things happen. First, program planners are faced immediately with the tremendous complexity of any intervention task. Then, they begin to recognize the need for greater specificity. If the innovation is to have any chance for success, and if its efforts are to be studied and assessed, some parameters in terms both of objectives and of target population will have to be set.

It may turn out, in cases like the one above, that a decision will be made to work with a highly heterogeneous population, including both older and younger boys. Such a decision, however, will in no way change the need to be specific. Indeed, the task will now become even more complex. In lieu of a single set of goals for a relatively narrow population, one will have to set, and to measure, the pursuit of different goals for different subpopulations. And while the external validity of the study may be increased, experimental controls and internal validity may be threatened. There is no totally happy compromise.

Theoretical Statement of the Problem

One way out of this dilemma is to devote considerable effort to defining program assumptions in theoretical terms, so that one can put some flesh on the skeleton of program goals. It is not very helpful, for example, to tell program people that they are supposed to "build strong informal controls in the community" or to "reduce intrafamily tensions." They need to know why this is important, and how to do it. Indeed, only by making a careful statement of theoretical assumptions and guidelines can one begin to be explicit about the substance of some new program.

Any effort to use theory in this way, however, would represent a radical departure from tradition. Attempts by program people to construct and to use theory, in any formal sense, have been negligible—first, because of a general distrust of theory, and second, because the task of theory construction is profoundly difficult. Yet, it is because theoretical assumptions and guidelines are not spelled out that so many action programs are disorganized and so difficult to evaluate.

With all these problems, however it is an error to assume that program people do not use theory. Any time a program is set up, or any time one technique is chosen over another, someone has an idea in the back of his or her mind that it will make a difference—that it is somehow preferable to other programs and techniques. That person, in other words, does have a theory—however ill-stated—about what leads to illegal behavior and how best it can be controlled. What is needed, therefore, is to make that theory explicit rather than to leave it vague and amorphous. If this were done, both the action and research components of the innovation would be improved. Furthermore, the common tendency for staff members to employ contradictory theories, and therefore contradictory methods, in the same program would be avoided.

The first step in making assumptions explicit is to develop a theoretical statement of the problem to be addressed, how it comes about, and what its roots are. What are the assumptions that the program will make about the sources of crime or conformity? Is it being assumed that crime is the result of poverty, a delinquent subculture, a psychological disease, a relatively normal expression of common, but subterranean, values, or is it due to the lack of effective social control by the agencies of law enforcement, to labeling and stigma, or to some combination of these? All are possible, and all have been employed in programs at one time or another. Yet, since it is obvious that each implies a different course of action, some choice among them must be made.

In order to illustrate how this might be accomplished, consider the problems associated with the task of deinstitutionalizing correctional programs. Suppose that, in lieu of confining young ghetto criminals in training schools or prisons, a policy decision is made to rest the effectiveness of a nonresidential, community program for them. What facts about youth crime in ghetto areas might be considered? What kind of a theory might be constructed to explain these facts? With regard to "facts," several findings might be cited:

(1) For three quarters of a century, official measures of crime, now supplemented by victimization studies, indicate that the highest rates of traditional crime are concentrated in the overcrowded and deteriorated areas of the city—particularly violent crimes. The prototypical official offender or victim of personal crime is a young, poor, minority, ghetto dweller (Shaw and McKay, 1942; 1969; Federal Bureau of Investigation, 1976; National Criminal Justice Information and Statistics Service, 1975, 1976).

(2) In addition to crime, ghetto areas are also characterized by a high incidence of other problems: illegitimacy and single parenthood, infant mortality, school failure and dropout, physical and mental disease, and unemployment (Moynihan, 1965; Shaw and McKay, 1969).

(3) The incidence of street gangs is also high in ghetto areas. Many, perhaps the majority, of all criminal acts are committed in groups (Cohen, 1955; Cloward and Ohlin, 1961; Erickson and Jensen, 1977; Miller, 1958; Shaw and McKay, 1969: 173).

Since several theories have been constructed to explain these "facts," the choice of any single theory for the purposes of organizing a program will necessarily be arbitrary. For the purposes of illustration, however, a combination of control theory (Hirschi, 1969) and the subcultural theories of Cohen (1955) and Shaw and McKay (1931; 1969) might be used. Taken in concert, these theories suggest that high rates of poverty, disease, and illegitimacy, and low rates of education and employment, tend to demoralize and to disrupt the families of lower-class people. Not only do they lack adequate access to the cultural heritage and resources of the larger society, according to which they might socialize their children, but their control over their children is greatly weakened. The basic attachment of the young to conventional role models and activities, therefore, is weak or broken.

This state of affairs carries over into the world of middle-class institutions, particularly the school. Because slum children suffer from a lack of ability to compete successfully, and because their ties to parents are weak, success in school, and later in work, is unlikely. Over time, as a result, a sense of strain and alienation develops. Unable to establish effective ties with teachers and conventional friends, their bonds to the moral norms and conventional tracks of society are further weakened. Lacking any stake in conformity, they are free to deviate. But rather than pursuing dangerous and deviant acts by themselves, these children adjust to their marginality by identifying with the values and carriers of delinquent subculture. The gangs and deviant groups of the ghetto become substitute societies for them. Conformity to the norms and status systems of these groups, rather than to those of conventional groups, becomes a rule.

The statement of this theory in narrative terms, while helpful, is not sufficient. If it is to guide either action or research, its basic concepts must be isolated and related to one another in propositional form. Hence, the following are the kinds of statements that are needed:

(1) Poor attachment to conventional institutions leads to a decreased stake in conformity.
(2) A decreased stake in conformity leads to identification with nonconventional peers.
(3) Identification with nonconventional peers leads to criminal behavior.

There are two major benefits to be gained from stating one's theoretical assumptions in this way. First, program planners have an explicit foundation upon which to build an *intervention strategy*. The conceptual foundation for the proposed innovation is no longer quite so cloudy as it once was. Second, those who are charged with evaluating the program also have the origins of a base upon which to build their *research strategy*. Rather than designing research whose links to the conceptual foundations of the innovation are weak or nonexistent, evaluators now have some explicit guidelines for defining the variables they might be expected to measure.

The Intervention Strategy

Once the problem to be addressed has been clarified, an operational strategy for intervention is required. Further, any such strategy is likely to require specific statements of two types: (1) a set of *intervention principles*, and (2) a set of *operational guidelines*.

Intervention principles would be comprised of a second set of propositions, derived from the theoretical statement of the problem, and would indicate how that problem might be addressed. In other words, the experimental controls and the actions of staff would be guided by the following:

1. Improve attachment to home, school, and world of work. The linkage of young criminals with these conventional institutions must be reestablished and strengthened.

2. Increase stake in conformity. Find ways for making conventional institutions and activities more attractive for offenders.

3. Decrease identification with delinquent groups and subculture(s). Find ways for reducing the attractiveness of these sources of youth crime and of enhancing the values of those which contribute to constructive conventional behavior.

Such principles, once stated, would be of use both to the action and the research components of the study. Notice, first, that when intervention principles are clearly stated, they become virtually synonymous with the *intermediate* program goals mentioned earlier—i.e., those goals which, in theoretical terms, must be realized if the final goal of reducing recidivism is to be achieved. In this instance, they would be to improve attachment, to increase stake in conformity, and to decrease identification with delinquent groups and subcultures. In short, by working through one's basic assumptions, it is possible to be increasingly explicit about the kinds of goals which program people will be charged with achieving, and the program "variables" they will be expected to manipulate.

In much the same way, intervention principles provide the invaluable function of clarifying the nature of the research task; that is, while action is concerned with implementing the basic principles, research will be devoted to assessing the success and consequences of that implementation. Rather than divergent, therefore, their two roles would be complementary. The theoretical principles that give meaning to action would also give meaning to research.

The *operational guidelines* of the intervention strategy, by contrast, are detailed statements of the ways by which the intervention principles will be translated into action. Any new intervention strategy requires answers to a host of organizational as well as client-related questions: What is the nature of the organization's social structure and activities? What are the consequences of this kind of organization within the network of organizations that already exist in the community—deviant as well as conventional? Significantly, these questions must be answered so as to effect the best possible compromise between the need for effective experimental controls and the need for the program to be as natural as possible.

In terms of working with clients, some of the same kinds of statements are needed: What new staff roles are required? How does one improve the attachment of convicted offenders to conventional institutions, give them a stake in conformity, and decrease their ties to delinquent groups? To what degree will it be necessary to alter the "natural" practices and structures of schools, places of employment, and other neighborhood institutions? How are clients to be treated who continue to violate the law? Should any act, no matter how deviant, be tolerated? What kinds of new and ongoing training are required by staff to think through, and to deal with, issues like these?

The operational guidelines should either be designed to answer such questions, at the outset, or to provide ongoing mechanisms by which they might be addressed as they arise. In either event, the intervention principles, not some ad hoc process, should dictate the answers that are given. Indeed, this is the means by which the expedient wandering of innovative programs can be reduced and some consistency introduced into them.

In addition, it must be recognized that operational guidelines will differ, depending upon the nature of the target population. For example, if the intervention principles stated above were applied to a group of adolescent criminals, one might want to pay far greater attention to their attachment to their homes and schools than if one were working with a group of young adults. By contrast, if the target group were young adults, opportunities for vocational training, a decent job, and some autonomy from weak parental controls might be more salient. In short, even if one had only one set of program principles, those principles might be operationalized in far different ways, depending upon the target population(s) in question, and upon the need for some reasonable compromise among the research criteria of *control, representativeness,* and *naturalness.*

In summary, through this attention to the explicit definition of intervention principles and guidelines one would hope to overcome the historical inclination of action and research people to go their divergent ways. Ordinarily, action people are left to their own devices in setting up a program, while research people come in after all that is done. All too often, the results are disastrous. To action people, the research that is finally produced often seems unrelated to their central concerns; indeed, it usually is. But, by working from a common framework, it might be hoped that research would reflect more directly on the accuracy of original assumptions, the extent to which intermediate goals were defined and then successfully implemented, and, finally, what the results of these efforts were in terms of reducing crime.

The Research Strategy

The next major component in the model would be a research strategy. This strategy might be more or less elaborate, depending upon the nature of the negotiations with the program administrator and the availability of research funds. In contrast to negotiations in the past, however, the participation of research with action people in the entire planning process now enables the investigator to outline more fully the need for, and the types of, research that might be conducted. Indeed, given an ideal set of conditions, research might be used to realize four major objectives:

1. Test of Basic Assumptions. Research could be used to test the theoretical assumptions upon which the new program was constructed. How accurate were these assumptions for the target population in question? Were the problems of young criminals anything akin to the way they were defined by the theoretical statement? Were their attachments to home, school, and world of work broken? Did they, in fact, exhibit a decreased stake in conformity? To what degree did they identify with delinquent values and friends, as contrasted with conventional norms and role models?

If any research tests are needed, they are tests of program assumptions like these. While various professional and practitioner groups are inclined to question the *methods* they use, or how well they run their programs, they are strikingly disinclined to question, or even to state clearly, the *assumptions* upon which they operate. Yet, no matter how well any program is run, it can be no better than the assumptions upon which it is predicated.

One reason that we witness so many program failures, in fact, may be due to the incorrectness of program assumptions rather than to inadequacies of program operation. Because assumptions are incorrect, programs are irrelevant or destructive. It is for this reason that research could make vital contributions to future programming and revision if steps were taken to examine the accuracy and utility of the theoretical assumptions that are made. Findings might help others not only to assess the generalizability of the study, but also to assess the relevance of the experimental controls that were applied.

In order to make a reasonable test of program assumptions, it will be necessary to obtain data from a random sample of less criminal or noncriminal subjects from the same population from which the experimental subjects are drawn. An effort would then be made to determine the extent to which their bond to conventional people and institutions is broken, whether they possess a stake in conformity, and whether they identify with prosocial or nonconventional values and groups. If the theoretical assumptions are accurate, there should be demonstrable differences between the criminal and noncriminal samples along the lines suggested by the theory.

When this kind of research was conducted in the Silverlake Experiment (Empey and Lubeck, 1971: 119-137), it was found that, while there were differences between criminal and noncriminal adolescents, they were not always in the direction postulated by the theory. First, it was discovered that attachment to family and school (or lack of it) was more predictive of delinquent behavior than was identification with delinquent values and peers. While peer identification was important, it was less predictive of criminal behavior than was family disruption, lack of family control, and poor performance in school. Hence, the implication was that even more should have been done in the experimental program to repair these disruptions and to reattach clients to these institutions, particularly for the younger offenders.

Second, when these kinds of findings were tied to process research on the adjustments of different delinquents to the experimental program, it was found that the closer individuals conformed to the theoretical description of the causes of delinquency, the better they did in the experimental program. To the degree that they departed from that model, they did less well. Those individuals who still possessed some stake in conformity and who were not strongly identified with delinquent values and groups might have done better had they been placed in a different type of program.

In short, the examination of theoretical assumptions revealed weaknesses in the foundation of the experimental program and implied the need to revise those assumptions if they were to be applied in future programming for the target population in question.

2. Examination of Program Process. The second way that research can be useful is to provide information on the intervention strategy—to test the accuracy and implementation of its principles and guidelines. Did the program actually operate according to design, according to the way it was described on paper? Were important "variables"—within community structures as well as within offenders—effectively manipulated? What changes might be required to make the operation more consistent with the ideals stated in the principles?

As was pointed out earlier, this is an area about which amazingly little is known. Sound, qualitatively oriented process research has rarely been conducted. In most cases, research people described the offenders in any program in demographic, usually theoretically nonrelevant, terms, and measure what happens to them after they leave it; but interaction within and around the program itself remains unstudied and undescribed. This is analogous to a steel manufacturer who feeds a number of raw materials into an assembly line, proceeds to ignore what happens to those ingredients and how they are combined while on the line, and then wonders why he gets brass as a final product rather than steel. It is no wonder that we have so much difficulty in trying to replicate any program or experiment. Neither are we explicit about how it was constructed, nor do we study and describe what happens to it while it is in process.

Information is desperately needed concerning not only what occurs within the confines of any program, but also what happens when that program, and its people, interact with other organizations and people in the community. We rarely determine whether significant institutional structures and key decision-making, as well as clients, are changed. For example, the program guidelines outlined above suggested that the attachment of young criminals to home, school, and work should be improved. To what degree was this actually accomplished? To what degree were regular or vocational schools changed so that linkage could be reestablished? To what degree were linkages established with places of employment or with conventional associates who had a stake in conformity? What lessons were learned when efforts were made to accomplish these program goals?

The task of answering these kinds of questions requires the type of *field* research used by anthropologists and phenomenologists; indeed, it aptly describes the "field" part of "field experimentation." Field research is usually exploratory and descriptive in nature, strong on naturalness and weak on control and representativeness. The investigator tries to interfere as little as possible with ongoing behavior in any program, so that he or she can accurately describe the interaction which occurs in the natural setting of the experiment.

This work, however, need not be totally unfocused, nor is it totally irrelevant to the importance of control as a criterion of experimental research. Instead, in seeking to analyze process, the investigator will want to be fully cognizant of the intervention strategy, so that he or she can act as a kind of monitor whose job it is to observe the extent to which program operation faithfully adheres to the prescriptions of the intervention strategy, and to observe what the unanticipated, as well as anticipated, consequences of their implementation are.

In pursuing this task, the investigator may also ask staff members or clients to keep logs or diaries on their experiences in the program, to interview parents or gatekeepers in the community, or to observe how critical incidents, such as new criminal offenses or community conflicts, are handled and resolved. In short, the field investigator may resort to a variety of devices in order to provide as full a description as possible of the consequences of trying to conduct an innovative program in the natural setting of the community. Future experimentation, as a result, is likely to benefit from that which is learned.

At present, our justice systems are pursuing a host of new diversion and deinstitutionalization programs. In the face of considerable opposition, the prevailing assumption is that such programs will enhance the linkage of offenders to nonlegal, noncoercive organizations, and thereby prevent the escalation of early delinquent behaviors into criminal careers. Based on a mounting body of process research, however, one could argue just as well that, rather than decreasing the effects of coercive supervision and labeling, or successfully changing a significant number of criminal offenders, the locus of control has merely been transferred from legal to nonlegal bureaucracies (see summaries by Empey, 1978: 541-542; Klein, 1979). Furthermore, with increased resources, these bureaucracies have increased, not decreased, the number of nonserious offenders under their supervision. Meanwhile, the needs of more serious offenders for help, or the needs of the community for greater protection, have gone unaddressed by these reforms.

These early outcomes illustrate the point made earlier—namely, that "reforms" should not be taken for granted. Rather, they should be examined to determine whether the purposes for which they were created are actually being realized. If, in future years, we are to avoid lamenting today's "reforms" the way we now lament prisons and reform schools, care should be taken to examine what is actually occurring, not simply what we hope will occur.

3. *Assessment of Outcome.* A third, highly important, contribution that experimental research can provide is a defensible assessment of outcome. That is why the random selection of experimental and control groups from some carefully defined target population is so important. By ruling out the possibility that any observed differences in outcome are due to systematic variations among offenders, the internal validity of the experiment is enhanced. Greater confidence can be placed in the idea that, if differences between groups do appear, they are due to variations in programming, not to variations in offenders.

In seeking to maximize the measurement of impact, several cautions should be observed. First, if at all possible, steps should be taken to select an untreated control group, as well as other control groups, for comparison with the experimental group. If this were done, a mistake that is commonly made in interpreting the results of experimental studies could be avoided.

This common misinterpretation can be illustrated by Hackler's (1972: 346) description of the findings of the Silverlake Experiment (Empey and Lubeck, 1971). These findings, said Hackler, "support the well known 'law of delinquency . . . program research': the more carefully you evaluate the program, the greater the probability that it will show little effect on the boys."

What Hackler was referring to was the fact that no differences in outcome were observed in this study between an experimental community group and a control group which had been placed in a private institution. But such a finding *does not* demonstrate that one or both programs *had no effect.* The only way that conclusion could be demonstrated would be to employ the use of a control group that was left entirely untreated. Then, if there were no differences between this group and the other two, one might conclude that correctional programs have no effect. Otherwise, with only two treated groups for comparison, one can only indicate whether there were any differences between the two.

The task of gaining administrative support for the selection of a nontreated control group is a difficult one, but it has been done. In their study of police diversion programs, Klein (1975) joined with a large metropolitan police department in randomly assigning a pool of several hundred offenders to one of four dispositions at time of arrest: (a) counsel and release with no service (the untreated group); (b) nondetained petition and appearance in court (traditional treatment); (c) referral to a nonjustice agency with purchase of service (experimental treatment); and (d) referral to a nonjustice agency without purchase of service (experimental treatment). By making these alternative assignments, they were able to determine not only whether alternative programs had differential effects but whether they were at all preferable to merely counseling offenders at arrest and releasing them.

A second caution has to do with the need to provide a fail-safe method for ensuring that truly random selection is carried out. Two steps are important in accomplishing this task. First, selection procedures should be centralized at some key point in the processing of offenders. For example, suppose administrative and judicial support has been gained for the evaluation of the ghetto community program described earlier, and that the random assignment of offenders to three dispositions is to be allowed: (a) to an experimental group in the community; (b) to a control group in a traditional institution; and (c) to an untreated control group on suspended sentence. Where should random assignment be located?

The most functional place to locate it would be at that point in time when sentence is passed during the dispositional phase of any trial. The procedures of due process would have been carried out and the offender's guilt established. The only remaining task would be that of passing sentence. Hence, if court authorities were willing to employ a procedure used in the Provo Experiment (Empey and Erickson, 1972), the judge would merely announce a sentence which was dictated, not by the recommendations of a probation officer or defense and prosecuting attorneys, but by random selection. This method is diagramed in Figure 6.1.

Even if this procedure is agreed upon, random selection per se cannot be left to probation or court personnel. Instead, it must involve direction and monitoring by members of the research team. The reason is that court people are inclined to tamper with the selection process. Since they are used to imposing their own criteria in making dispositions, they are often tempted to use clinical or judicial, rather than scientific, judgment. But here, their only role is to announce, and to support the results of, random selection, not to make the selection themselves.

Where they do have a role to play is in negotiating the constraints that must inevitably be placed upon the eligibility of offenders for random selection. Normally, these constraints are of two types. First, all offenders, no matter how heinous their crimes, could not be defined as potential candidates of some experimental community program; the definition of the target population would have to eliminate some offenders. Second, if the experimental program is to be an alternative to incarceration, then all members of the target population would have to be eligible for confinement under normal circumstances. One could not include minor offenders in it. But once these criteria were agreed upon, fail-safe procedures would go into effect. Otherwise, the randomness of the selection procedure would be destroyed (Klein, 1975).

A third caution is related. It has to do with the necessity to implement measurements of outcome that are also free from direct, even if well-inten-

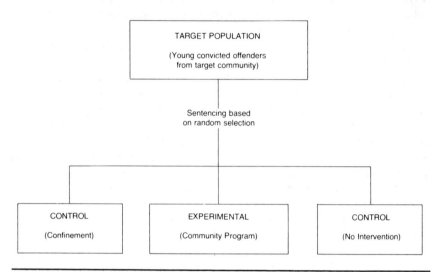

Figure 6.1: Selection of Experimental and Control Groups

tioned, manipulation by program people. For example, outcome in the Community Treatment Program of the California Youth Authority was measured in terms of parole revocation. After follow-up, moreover, this particular measure tended to favor experimentals over controls (Palmer, 1971). Yet, careful analysis revealed that these differing rates of success may have been due more to the way experimental and control agents handled their clients than to the way the clients actually behaved (Lerman, 1975: ch. 4).

Because the parole agents for the control group were more inclined to revoke parole for new offenses than were experimental agents (68 versus 29 percent), the members of the experimental group appeared to be the more successful (Warren and Palmer, 1966). But when the actual number of new offenses was considered, differences tended to disappear; if not more delinquent than controls, experimentals were equally delinquent. Hence, it is clear that other measures of outcome—such things as self-reported offenses or arrest statistics, which are free from direct manipulation by program staff—should be employed and should be gathered by research personnel.

A fourth caution has to do with the well-known threats to internal validity: *history, maturation, regression,* and *mortality.* While random selection helps to minimize their effects as no other design can, complex problems remain, particularly in field experiments (Campbell and Stanley, 1963: 13-16). For example, one of the most flagrant violations in criminal justice evaluations has been the tendency to drop from the experimental group any individuals who fail to participate in, or to complete, the experimental program. As a result, *mortality* becomes a threat to validity: Wayward or noncooperative subjects are eliminated from the analysis, which selectively biases the results in favor of the experimentals. Hence, any study must incorporate means by which such threats to internal validity can be minimized in both the collection and analysis of data.

Fifth, the measurement of outcome, to be most definitive, should be concerned not merely with recidivism. Indeed, if the experimental strategy is to receive a complete test, outcome should be measured in terms of intermediate as well as final goals—whether, in the example cited above, attachment for clients to home, school, or employment is enhanced, whether their stake in conformity is increased, or whether their identification with nondelinquent groups and activities is improved. Since these goals are derived from theoretically important variables, some before-and-after assessments of them are implied, so that any changes can be documented. If they are observed, moreover, one would want to see whether variations in them are associated with variations in recidivism rates—whether, in this program or any other, the pursuit of theoretically relevant, intermediate goals always assumes that their realization will somehow reduce recidivism and improve adjustment. That assumption should be carefully tested.

A sixth caution has to do with the finding that one program rarely proves to be more successful, overall, than another. Yet, few studies have used their measurements of offender characteristics to establish different offender types, and then have attempted to determine whether, under varying conditions, these types were affected differentially. In those few instances in which this has been done, there have been indications that different outcomes might have been observed, even if overall comparisons were not changed (Glaser, 1979). And since it strains the imagination to believe that all programs affect all offenders in exactly the same way, attention to this matter is desperately needed.

Finally, since experimental comparisons of outcome have been equivocal, corollary comparisons in terms of cost and even humaneness are often desirable. For example, several studies have shown that, *with no loss in effectiveness,* community programs not only disrupt the lives of clients for much shorter periods of time than total incarceration, but are usually far less costly (Empey and Erickson, 1972: 201; Empey and Lubeck, 1971: 309; Ohlin et al., 1977: 30; Vinter et al., 1975: 53). In light of the growing belief that total incapacitation of more offenders is warranted, some consideration of these matters in experimental studies is advised, since they bear directly on policy issues of great importance.

4. The Effectiveness of Collaboration. The fourth kind of research has to do with the need of policy makers, professionals, and scientists for more information on the nature and problems of collaborative field experimentation itself. Hence, systematic process data might well be collected on efforts to implement a model like the one being described here. How well does it work? Were the activities of action and research people effectively linked? How could they be improved? A study of the collaborative endeavor, itself, could be of inestimable value for others who may wish to follow and to improve upon it.

Assessment of Implications

The final element of the working model would be an assessment of research findings for basic theory, for the practical concerns of the policy maker and practitioner, and for the future of collaborative endeavors in which action and research people join together in the conduct of field experiments.

In terms of basic theory, this assessment might involve a reformulation of the basic theory and intervention principles upon which the program was based. Although it is conceivable that findings might confirm the conceptual structure of the study, that eventuality is unlikely. It would be extremely important, therefore, to indicate where basic assumptions may have been inaccurate and to suggest new lines for inquiry based upon the empirical findings of the study. Such information could be extremely useful to people engaged in basic research as well as to those who set policy and run intervention programs.

Second, study findings could be assessed in terms of their implications for public policy—the relative utility of the experimental program versus other alternatives, the comparative costs of these programs, the implications of the experiment for the sponsoring organization, or the unanticipated and perhaps negative consequences of the reform effort.

Finally, the assessment of implications would be concerned with the philosophy and methodology of field experimentation—the problems of gathering action, theory, and research together in a common endeavor, the ethical and philosophical issues that are encountered, and the potential of the field experiment for future research and criminal justice programs. If the people involved in this endeavor could adhere, even roughly, to the working model sketched above, they might contribute substantially to the understanding of crucial problems that have plagued social scientists, practitioners, and policy makers for a long time.

ADMINISTERING THE MODEL

This chapter has suggested that, in addition to all of the usual impediments to rigorous evaluation, scientists themselves are divided over the merits of this kind of research. However, in light of the strong possibility that this generation of reformers will repeat the age-old error of assuming that their reforms will succeed where others have failed, it has been argued that rigorous evaluation in the form of field experimentation has redeeming social value.

If this kind of evaluation is to be conducted, however, much more attention will have to be devoted to the creation of models by which the roles of administrative, professional, and research people can be functionally integrated. In order to conform to the highest criteria governing research, a working model should incorporate several elements: (1) mutual research and project goals; (2) a carefully defined target population; (3) a formal theoretical statement of the problem; (4) an intervention strategy, (5) a research strategy; and (6) an assessment of study findings for theory, policy, and future experimentation. Yet, with all the attention that was paid to the reasons for, and characteristics of, the model, one fundamental question was not addressed: Who should administer the model?

Agreement on the answer to that question will not be easily achieved, given the many vested interests that will be affected by it. Nonetheless, an answer seems quite obvious: The model would be best administered by a mature and experienced research person. In their review of federally funded evaluation research, Bernstein and Freeman (1975) found that the highest-quality research was conducted by university-affiliated investigators who, as in the model suggested here, effected interdependent relations between action and research staffs, who utilized theory to set the context for their research, and who applied rigorous methods. In short, the most effective studies were those which utilized directors who conformed more closely to the traditions of science than to the traditions of the helping professions.

This is not to say that any research-oriented administrator would be unconstrained to act as he or she wished. Instead, the administrator would be constrained by two sets of rules or obligations. The first would be the details of the working agreement, or even contract, that could be set up with the appropriate policy maker, and between the administrator and policy maker, and the working professionals and research people under them. This agreement however, would conform more closely to the kind of contract that governs research work than that which governs work in clinics or welfare or service agencies. Hence, rather than evaluating the work of either professional or research people in terms of their capacity to conform to the traditional rules of a particular service agency or bureaucracy, one would evaluate their work in terms of their capacity to implement the intervention and research strategies of the innovative program.

In that way, the services of professional practitioners, in particular, would not be jeopardized if the program did not prove to be a success. Instead, practitioners would be rewarded for their commitment to, and skill in, implementing the experimental program. Indeed, as experience with research indicates, people trained in experimentation would be extremely valuable in taking what was learned from prior studies and applying it to new ones. They could become an important new source of skilled people for a prolonged research strategy.

Second, the research administrator would be constrained by the rules that govern good research, and, in particular, by the intervention research strategy of the experiment itself. This means that, in addition to supervising the research staff, he or she would have to work with program people in the day-to-day task of ensuring that the intervention strategy would be faithfully followed. The research administrator's role would be analagous to, but much more complicated than, the role of the laboratory experimenter who must ensure that the controls of the experiment are maximized and the effects of extraneous variables are minimized. But in this instance, this task would require an unusual devotion to the problems of the program staff. Since operational problems that are unanticipated inevitably arise, the administrator would have to be prepared to unite both program and research people in examining those problems, seeing how they might be addressed so that responses would conform as closely as possible to theoretical principles, and then making certain that they would be considered in during the research.

Finally, the research administrator would have to be prepared to help design the various components of the research so that they would interfere as little as possible with the ongoing interaction and naturalness of the program. This means that he or she would have to take steps to ensure that the gathering of research data is legitimated by the clients of the program as well as by its staff. They would have to understand its purpose, and why research people were there.

At the same time, it is imperative that everyone—staff, clients and investigators—understand that research itself plays a neutral role. Not only must the findings speak for themselves, but information that is honestly and freely shared by staff or clients with research people could never be used in a punitive way against them. On those rare occasions in which some particularly dangerous information might be revealed, the informer would be approached by the administrator regarding his or her willingness to participate with program staff in trying to resolve the problem. Otherwise, research information would be utilized only for long run purposes, or for the purposes of ensuring that the program might operate as consistently as possible with its original design.

The plans for administration just described, along with the experimental model, are diagramed in Figure 6.2. The research administrator works with the policy maker initially in outlining the original conception of the proposed experiment. Assuming that their negotiations were successful, program and research directors are then chosen so that they might participate in the development of the experimental model. Following that, program and research staff members are also added and jointly trained, adding to, as well as learning from, the outlines of the experiment. The idea is that, before clients are ever added to the picture, a great deal of preparation has taken place. Furthermore, as the enterprise progresses, its various units continue to be guided by, and responsive to, the elements of the working model. One hopes, then, that the various persons

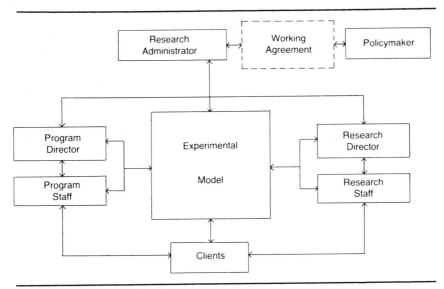

Figure 6.2: Plan for Administration

in the enterprise are therefore more committed to seeking knowledge from the experimental effort.

REFERENCES

Adams, S. (1975) *Evaluative Research in Corrections: A Practical Guide.* Washington, DC: Government Printing Office.

Bayh, B. (1971) Statement to the U.S. Senate Committee on the Judiciary, Subcommittee to Investigate Juvenile Delinquency, 92nd Congress, First Session, May 3-18.

Bernstein, I. N. (1975) "Evaluations Research in Corrections: Status and Prospects Revisited." *Federal Probation* 29 (March): 56-57.

——— and H. E. Freeman (1975) *Academic and Entrepreneurial Research.* New York: Russell Sage.

Boruch, R. F. (1976) "On Common Contentions about Randomized Field Experiments," pp. 158-194 in Gene V Glass (ed.) *Evaluation Studies Review Annual, Volume 1.* Beverly Hills, CA: Sage Publications.

California Welfare and Institutions Code (1976) "Assembly Bill 3121." Chapter 1071: 1-24.

Campbell, D. T. (1975) "Reforms as Experiments," pp. 71-100 in E. L. Struening and M. Guttentag (eds.) *Handbook of Evaluation Research.* Beverly Hills, CA: Sage Publications.

——— and J. C. Stanley (1963) *Experimental and Quasi-Experimental Designs for Research.* Skokie, IL: Rand McNally.

Cloward, R. A. and L. E. Ohlin (1961) *Delinquency and Opportunity: A Theory of Delinquent Gangs*. New York: Free Press.

Cohen, A. K. (1955) *Delinquent Boys: The Culture of the Gang*. New York: Free Press.

Deutscher, I. (1973) "Public Issues or Private Troubles: Is Evaluation Research Sociological?" *Sociological Focus* 9 (August): 231-237.

Edwards, R. C., M. Reich, and T. E. Weisskopf (1974) "Toward a Socialist Alternative," pp. 429-434 in R. Quinney (ed.) *Criminal Justice in America*. Boston: Little, Brown.

Edwards, W., M. Guttentag, and K. Snapper (1975) "A Decision-Theoretic Approach to Evaluation Research," pp. 139-182 in E. L. Struening and M. Guttentag (eds.) *Handbook of Evaluation Research, Volume 1*. Beverly Hills, CA: Sage Publications.

Empey, L. T. (1978) *American Delinquency: Its Meaning and Construction*. Homewood, IL: Irwin.

——— and M. Erickson (1972) *The Provo Experiment: Evaluating Community Control of Delinquency*. Lexington, MA: D. C. Heath.

Empey, L. T. and Steven G. Lubeck (1971) *The Silverlake Experiment: Testing Delinquency Theory and Community Intervention*. Chicago: AVC.

Erickson, M. L. (1979) "Some Empirical Questions Concerning the Current Revolution in Juvenile Justice," in L. T. Empey [ed.] *The Future of Childhood and Juvenile Justice*. Charlottesville, VA: University of Virginia Press.

——— and G. F. Jensen (1977) "Delinquency Is Still Group Behavior!: Toward Revitalizing the Group Premise in the Sociology of Deviance." *Journal of Criminal Law and Criminology* 68: 262-273.

Federal Bureau of Investigation (1976) *Uniform Crime Reports, 1975*. Washington, DC: Government Printing Office.

Golden, M. P. (1976) *The Research Experience*. Itasca, IL: Peacock.

Glaser, D. (1979) "Disillusion with Rehabilitation: Theoretical and Empirical Questions," in L. T. Empey (ed.) *The Future of Childhood and Juvenile Justice*. Charlottesville, VA: University of Virginia Press.

Guttentag, M. (1973) "Evaluation of Social Intervention Programs." *Annals of the New York Academy of Sciences* 218: 3-15.

Hackler, J. C. (1972) "Review of the Silverlake Experiment." *Contemporary Sociology* 1 (July): 346.

Hirschi, T. (1969) *Causes of Delinquency*. Berkeley, CA: University of California Press.

Houston, T. R., Jr. (1972) "The Behavioral Sciences Impact—Effectiveness Model," pp. 59-66 in P. H. Rossi and W. Williams (eds.) *Evaluating Social Programs*. New York: Seminar.

Kaplan, A. (1964) *The Conduct of Inquiry*. New York: ITT.

Klein, M. W. (1979) "Deinstitutionalization and Diversion of Juvenile Offenders: A Litany of Impediments," pp. 145-201 in N. Morris and M. Tonry (eds.) *Crime and Justice: An Annual Review, Volume I*. Chicago: University of Chicago Press.

——— (1975) *Alternative Dispositions for Juvenile Offenders: An Assessment of the Juvenile Referral and Resource Development Program*. Los Angeles: Social Science Research Institute, University of Southern California.

Law Enforcement Assistance Administration (1974) *Indexed Legislative History of the "Juvenile Justice and Delinquency Prevention Act of 1974."* Washington, DC: Author.

Lemert, E. M. (1967) "The Juvenile Court—Quest and Realities," pp. 91-106 in *The President's Commission on Law Enforcement and Administration of Justice, Task Force Report: Juvenile Delinquency and Youth Crime. Washington, DC: Government Printing Office*.

Lerman, P. (1975) *Community Treatment and Social Control.* Chicago: University of Chicago Press.

Lewin, K. (1968) "Feedback problems of Social Diagnosis and Action," in W. Buckley (ed.) *Modern Systems Research for the Behavioral Scientist.* Chicago: AVC.

Miller, W. B. (1973) "Ideology and Criminal Justice Policy: Some Current Issues,' pp. 453-473 in S. L. Messinger et al. (eds.) *The Aldine Crime and Justice Annual, 1973.* Chicago: AVC.

——— (1958) "Lower-Class Culture as a Generating Milieu of Gang Delinquency." *Journal of Social Issues* 14 (Summer): 5-19.

Morris, N. (1974) "The Future of Imprisonment: Toward a Punitive Philosophy." *Michigan Law Review* 72: 1161-1180.

Moynihan, D. P. (1965) *The Negro Family: The Case for National Action.* Washington, DC: Department of Labor.

National Advisory Commission on Criminal Justice Standards and Goals (1973a) A National Strategy To Reduce Crime. Washington, DC: Government Printing Office.

——— (1973b) *Report on Courts.* Washington, DC: Government Printing Office.

National Criminal Justice Information and Statistics Service (1976) *Criminal Victimization in the United States: A Comparison of 1973 and 1974 Findings.* Washington, DC: Government Printng Office.

——— (1975) *Criminal Victimization in the United States: 1973. Advance Report.* Washington, DC: Government Printing Office.

National Task Force to Develop Standards and Goals for Juvenile Justice and Delinquency prevention (1977) *Jurisdiction—Status Offense.* Washington, DC: National Institute for Juvenile Justice and Delinquency Prevention.

Ohlin, L. E., A. D. Miller, and R. B. Coates (1977) *Juvenile Correctional Reform in Massachusetts.* Washington, DC: Government Printing Office.

Palmer, T. B. (1971) "California's Treatment Program for Delinquent Adolescents." *Journal of Research in Crime and Delinquency* 8 (January): 74-92.

Platt, A. M. (1974) "The Triumph of Benevolence: The Origins of the Juvenile Justice System in the United States," pp. 356-389 in R. Quinney (ed.) *Criminal Justice in America.* Boston: Little, Brown.

Poincare, H. (1953) "Hypotheses in Physics," pp. 31-40 in P. P. Wiener (ed.) *Readings in the Philosophy of Science.* New York: Scribners.

Quinney, R. (1974) *Criminal Justice in America.* Boston: Little, Brown.

——— (1970) *The Social Reality of Crime.* Boston: Little, Brown.

Revised Criminal Code of Washington (1977) "Title 13. Juvenile Courts and Juvenile Delinquents." Pages 66-90.

Rossi, P. H. (1972) "Testing for Success and Failure in Social Action," pp. 15-58 in P. H. Rossi and W. Williams (eds.) *Evaluating Social Programs: Theory, Practice and Politics.* New York: Seminar Press.

Rothman, D. J. (1971) *The Discovery of the Asylum.* Boston: Little, Brown.

Schur, E. M. (1973) *Radical Nonintervention: Rethinking the Delinquency Problem.* Englewood Cliffs, NJ: Prentice-Hall.

Schwendinger, H. and J. Schwendinger (1975) "Defenders of Order or Guardians of Human Rights," pp. 113-138 in I. Taylor et al. (eds.) *Critical Criminology.* Boston: Routledge & Kegan Paul.

Shaw, C. R. and H. D. McKay (1969) *Juvenile Delinquency and Urban Areas.* Chicago: University of Chicago Press.

——— (1942) *Juvenile Delinquency and Urban Areas.* Chicago: University of Chicago Press.

——— (1931) "Social Factors in Juvenile Delinquency." *Report of the National Commission on Law Observance and Enforcement* 2, 13.

Van Den Haag, E. (1975) *Punishing Criminals.* New York: Basic Books.

Vinter, R. D., G. Downs, and J. Hall (1975) *Juvenile Corrections in the United States: Residential Programs and Deinstitutionalization. National Assessment of Juvenile Corrections. Ann Arbor: University of Michigan.*

Warren, M. Q. and T. B. Palmer *(1966) The Community Treatment Project After Five Years.* Sacramento: California Youth Authority.

Weiss, R. S. and M. Rein (1969) "The Evaluation of Broad-Aim Programs: Difficulties in Experimental Design and an Alternative." *Administrative Science Quarterly* 15: 97-109.

Wilks, J. and R. Martinson (1976) "Is the Treatment of Criminal Offenders Really Necessary?" *Federal Probation* 40 (March): 3-8.

Wilson, J. Q. (1975) *Thinking About Crime.* New York: Basic Books.

7

Multiattribute Utility for Evaluation: Structures, Uses, and Problems

Ward Edwards

In 1975, Edwards, Guttentag, and Snapper published a somewhat polemical chapter in the *Handbook of Evaluation Research* (Guttentag and Streuning, 1975), arguing for the application of multiattribute utility evaluation to "social" programs. In 1975, Edwards and Guttentag published a considerably more careful but essentially similar argument for the same idea.

Recently, I have had two shocks; this chapter serves primarily the purpose of responding to them. The first came when I presented to a seminar on evaluation research a report of my recent use of multiattribute utility methods to evaluate desegregation plans for the Los Angeles Unified School District (see below). After that meeting, one of its organizers told me that a list of questions had been prepared for me, of which the most important was, "Why did the multiattribute utility approach to program evaluation die?" That was quite a shock, since the approach is not only alive and well, but flourishing mightily and spreading fast. The second came when I discussed with the editors of this handbook what the contents of this chapter should be. They informed me that the Edwards et al. (1975) and Edwards and Guttentag chapters were regarded by many as antiexperimental. Since I was trained as an experimental psychologist, have been doing and publishing experiments all of my professional life, and am currently engaged in a substantial experimental program designed to evaluate alternative methods of eliciting multiattribute utilities, the idea that good friends and close colleagues could think of me as antiexperimental was also shocking. It is perfectly true that I regard the experimental evaluation of major social programs as impossible, except for very special kinds of programs (e.g., drug trials). It is also true that I agree with Campbell and Boruch (1975: 276) that the various biases inherent in quasi-experiments "cumulate as powerful arguments for randomized assignment to treatments—that is, experiments rather than quasi-experiments." If randomized assignment is impossible and quasi-experiments are biased and unsatisfactory, I do not believe that the would-be evaluator should conclude that all he or she can do is to turn into what Edwards et al. (1975) called a baseball statistician, collecting whatever numbers about the program happen to be obtainable as a mode of evaluating it. Nor is it useful to wail about the obtuseness of a world that rejects the idea that control cities or control countries are meaningful, and thereafter sit on one's hands. I do not consider such a view antiexperimental; it only addresses the question of what experiments can, and what experiments cannot, reasonably be done.

Since many readers will not be familiar with the two works cited above, this chapter must inevitably recapitulate their content to some extent. It begins with the obvious but seldom asked question, "Why evaluate?" Next, it examines a careful definition of what an evaluation is. Next it presents my 1979 version of the technology of multiattribute utility measurement—a version different in detail from that used by other inventors and advocates of the approach, but identical in spirit and very similar in result. The difference, incidentally, is caused mostly by my eagerness to make the technology readily useful to those with little or no mathematics or other technical training. For those familiar with prior expositions, some new technical wrinkles, of recent and unpublished vintage, are included; they lead to a considerably simpler method than I had proposed before. Finally, the chapter looks at examples. Unfortunately, those who take seriously the idea that this chapter, by reason of its inclusion in a handbook of criminal justice evaluation, should be about criminal justice evaluations alone, will find this section weak, since only one incomplete example from criminal justice-related evaluations is available. Three other completed and effective examples from other subject areas may help.

WHY EVALUATE?

Most evaluators would agree that an evaluation should be both accurate and useful. To know that information will be useful, an evaluator must know its probable uses. Typically, those will be to guide decisions about the program. That is why this chapter advocates methods for evaluation that originate in decision analysis.

Decision-analytic experience argues that a client, confronted with a difficult decision problem, typically will have only somewhat vague ideas about what information is needed—and sometimes will not even know what action options are available. The most creative and often the most time-consuming part of decision analysis is to formulate options, and the evaluative structure relevant to choosing from among them. Such formulation tasks require that the evaluator get close to the client, preferably at relatively high and powerful levels when the client is an organization, learn in detail what the problem is, and design an evaluative procedure in collaboration with the client to help solve it. All this must be done before it is appropriate to begin to think about data collection.

One evaluative stance is that the role of evaluation is to provide objective information about program characteristics and effects—information that someone else has asked for and may or may not ultimately use. From this stance, the formulation of the problem, identification of options, and specification of the ways in which information will be used are not the evaluator's concern.

I believe that the most serious danger an evaluation faces is not inaccuracy, but irrelevance. The arm's-length evaluator unconcerned with the client's real decision or other problems may be mythical; if not, he or she is virtually certain to produce unread documents full of irrelevant information.

The question, "Why was this program evaluated?" is always appropriate. The answers, "Because it was there" and "Because I was funded to do so," are always unsatisfactory, though too often applicable. I see four possible reasons to evaluate a social program. The first is to satisfy simple curiosity. The question, "How are we doing?" is natural and human, especially if the doing consumes resources that could have alternative uses. A slightly more formal version of simple curiosity is legal mandate, which I interpret to mean that legislators, as well as program people, may want an answer to the question of how well a program is doing. Moreover, for public programs it is an entirely legitimate public concern.

This reason for evaluation is congruous with a detached academic stance. For that reason, academics often espouse it.

But curiosity gives inadequate guidance about what should be evaluated or how the evaluation should be conducted. Evaluators can be, and often are, curious about far too many aspects of a complex program. The question, "What are we doing?" is logically prior to the question "How well are we doing it?" Most social programs have multiple objectives—and some of these may be unacknowledged by legislators, program people, or both. Moreover, they usually also have unexpected effects, relevant to answering the question "What are we doing?"—but effects not necessarily obvious enough to be issues at program-planning time, or even when the evaluation is being designed.

This rather unstructured reason for evaluation typically leads to what Edwards et al. (1975) have called the baseball statistician's approach to evaluation. If the evaluator has an unclear understanding of what purpose the evaluation should serve, he or she may well try to make it serve as many purposes as seem feasible. This leads to collecting compendia of information about program processes and effects—usually unreadable, but probably capable of providing numerical answers to almost any thinkable objective question. As a boy, I was exposed to a book called *What Every Young Boy Wants to Know About Sex* (a very misleading title). Allowing for a change of subject matter, the spirit of such evaluations is much the same.

Another reason for evaluating a program is to guide programmatic choices intended to fine-tune the program. This is a better reason than sheer curiosity, since it restricts the field of relevant information. The set of knobs and dials that can, in fact, be manipulated to fine-tune a social program is usually limited, not only by budget constraints, personnel constraints, and legal mandates, but also by the ethos and expectations of program people and of those served. Program administrators, for example, typically need far more process information than outcome information for this purpose. This kind of evaluation bears a close relationship to development of a management information system. The main difference is that a MIS usually attempts only to track what is happening, while an evaluation effort almost always makes at least some attempt to conclude something about whether what is happening is good or bad.

A third reason for evaluating a program is to guide choice among major programmatic options. This is a typical decision-analysis problem, probably the most natural setting for the methods to be discussed in this chapter. (I claim that these methods apply to all four of the purposes evaluation can serve. I elaborate on this claim later.)

A fourth reason for evaluating a program is to guide life-or-death decisions about the program—the guns-versus-butter kind of choice. This is distinct from the third reason because the third assumes that a program of some sort will continue, and attempts to choose from among major alternatives the kind of program. This purpose, by contrast, makes no such assumption, and typically does not offer a specific alternative use for program resources if the program is killed. This, too, is a typical decision-analysis problem.

While these last two purposes should lead to evaluations that consider processes, their focus should be, and usually is, on program outcomes. Thus, this four-element taxonomy of reasons for evaluation collapses reasonably well into Scriven's distinction between process and outcome evaluation, and into Sussman's distinction between formative (fine-tuning) and summative (life-or-death choice) evaluation.

Since this chapter appears in the *Handbook of Criminal Justice Evaluation*, I had better note that the term "social program" is far broader than the person-oriented social service-delivery programs that are of greatest interest to its most likely readers. At least as I use the term, any program characterized by (a) significant impact on public interests and welfare, and (b) significant opportunity for public inputs into major program-relevant decision processes, is a social program. Thus, in these days of environmental concerns, plant site location is usually a social problem, and construction and operation of the plant is a social program. Public health programs are social programs. Programs affecting U.S. military and diplomatic postures and capabilities vis-à-vis the rest of the world are social programs—almost certainly the most important ones our country undertakes. I do not see important or useful distinctions between evaluation of person-oriented social service-delivery programs and evaluation of other social programs, other than in the identity and expertise of the typical evaluators. That view, which some readers will surely characterize as myopic, underlies much of my skepticism about experimental approaches to evaluation. It might be difficult to persuade an electric utility to construct both an experimental and a control plant.

WHAT IS AN EVALUATION?

The key idea behind the multiattribute utility approach to evaluation is simple: *Evaluation means measurement of how well the thing being evaluated serves the values relevant to evaluating it.*

Many words in the preceding definition seem to need further definition.

Measurement was defined long ago by S. S. Stevens as "assignment of numbers to objects according to rules." Note that the definition specifies numbers, but says nothing about their source. From any decision-theoretical point of view, relevant numbers often come from human judgment rather than some more objective source. While people, even if expert, are sometimes reluctant to express their judgments in numerical form, the evidence abundantly indicates that judgments so expressed are far more accurate and far more useful than human judgments expressed in the more familiar vague, qualitative, verbal forms. I do not mean that all judgments should be numerical. Some judgments have to do with structure and relevance, and are not conveniently thought of as scalar quantities. But any judgment to which such verbal labels as "good" or "bad" or "more" or "less" can be applied should be thought of as having scalar properties, and so should be made in numerical form. The discomfort associated with the imprecision of such numbers is more than compensated for by two advantages. First, they are far more precise than the verbal alternatives. Second, they lend themselves to convenient manipulations; arithmetic is a useful language, since its syntax is completely explicit and consistent.

How well means just what it says. The implication is that most evaluations should be comparative. The comparison may be between one program and a (real or imagined) alternative to it—but it should be a comparison. The question, "How are we doing?" is not very meaningful. An example of this same argument in a statistical context is contained in Edwards (1965). *Thing being evaluated* often needs definition also. It is sometimes quite difficult to draw the boundaries around a program. But that is not a major point of this chapter.

Values relevant to evaluating it is surely the most important idea in the definition. A value is simply some characteristic of a program that some relevant person, group, or organization cares about. Decision analysts call these "attributes," or "dimensions of value"; I shall use these labels interchangeably. Identification of attributes is an early step in multiattribute utility measurement. Different people with stakes in a program (e.g., program managers, funders, clients) may well have different relevant attributes; usually all should be at least considered. Fortunately, such consideration may often lead to the conclusion that some attribute is sufficiently unimportant, or important to few enough people, that it can safely be neglected. But the list of attributes relevant to any evaluation is normally distressingly large. I cannot recall a case in which fewer than four attributes were relevant; and the largest number of attributes used in a multiattribute utility evaluation of a service-delivery program, so far as I know, is 144 (see Edwards, 1979; at least one military application uses about 1300 attributes).

This multiplicity of relevant attributes poses serious instrumentation and design problems. Many attributes cannot be other than judgmentally measured; often, these are the most important ones. Experts should make such judgments; their selection is an important task. The cost of measuring performance on so many attributes may well be high. And the task of including the appropriate attributes in an experimental design is in some cases difficult or impossible— which is another reason for my frequent rejection of experimental approaches. Experimentation can usefully provide performance measures with respect to one or more attributes for the program. This role makes experimental data useful as inputs into multiattribute utility evaluations. But experiments cannot provide performance measures for all attributes, except in very unusual cases. They cannot provide performance measures for alternatives to the existing program, unless those alternatives are already in place and operating. Hence, no multiattribute utility evaluation can depend exclusively on experimental methods for its data inputs.

Finally, the multiplicity of relevant values requires the only important technical device that multiattribute utility measurement has to offer: aggregation. If many values are relevant, and two programs or programmatic options are to be compared, the typical result will be that one does well on attribute A and poorly on attribute B, while for the other option the opposite is true. How, then, can we decide which option is better? Obviously, we can do so only if we know how to combine these two measures of performance. Arithmetic makes this easy, if and only if we can assess the relative importance of the attributes, as well as how well each option serves each attribute.

In addition to the multiplicity of values that results from program complexity and from individual differences, another reason lists of values are typically long is because the relevance of values changes over time. The values relevant to planning a program may differ from those relevant to starting its execution; these may differ from those relevant to established and secure programs; and these may differ from those relevant to assessment of how well some program, whether terminating or well-established, has done its job. The distinction between process evaluation and impact evaluation captures this idea. For the moment I shall ignore the fact that both programs and the values relevant to their evaluation change over time, and write as though both programs and evaluation of them were static affairs.

Virtually the entire structure of multiattribute utility measurement flows from the one-sentence definition with which I started this section. I suppose that makes the definition important. If evaluation is not about how well the object of evaluation performs with respect to the relevant values, what is it about?

SMART: A TECHNOLOGY FOR MULTIATTRIBUTE UTILITY MEASUREMENT

In 1971 I proposed a Simple Multiattribute Rating Technique (SMART). My purpose was to devise the simplest possible method of implementing the basic ideas about evaluation implicit in the definition discussed above. The definition was not new; it had previously been proposed by Howard Raiffa (1968), and others had been using various implementations of it. But without exception, the kinds of judgments required seemed to me extremely difficult to make and likely to be unreliable. Some involved choices among hypothetical gambles; others required rather sophisticated indifference or preference judgments. For a rather modern discussion of the techniques I am referring to, along with several instances of their application to real evaluative problems, see Keeney and Raiffa (1976), which is by far the best exposition of the mathematical logic underlying multiattribute utility.

The motto of decision analysis is "divide and conquer"; in my view, this means not only that decision problems should be divided into appropriate elements and then recombined by means of appropriate formal aggregation rules, but also that the judgmental tasks should be partitioned to fit the expertise of available judges. The same is true of evaluations.

The tradition of decision analysis is that a single person makes decisions. This is an obvious myth, for important decisions. The myth is important, because the goal of a decision is to maximize utility or expected utility. Utility means subjective value; that is, it lies inside the decision maker's head.

But in virtually all real-world decision contexts, many individuals contribute to decisions. Major decisions are normally organizational, not individual. Before the boss signs off, the staff has performed a great deal of data collection and interpretation, option generation, evaluative thinking, advice-giving, and other forms of assistance and kibitzing. I claim that, at least for decisions of less than major political importance made within administrative organizations, the organization itself is the decision maker. Moreover, I believe that organizations have values, just as individuals do. While these organizational values reflect individual inputs, they should be some kind of coherent combination of individual values, not the values of any single person.

Political decisions are more complicated. In a recent attempt to report a large political application of multiattribute utility measurement (Edwards, 1979), I identified eleven different, fairly autonomous, organizations or individuals, each with a major say in the final decision. Conceptually, even such a diffusion of evaluation and decision responsibilities can fit the multiattribute utility framework. The relevant technology requires only the extension of the idea of organizational values to many organizations, rather than just one.

The idea that organizations have values makes a crucial difference to the technology of decision-making. The formal theory requires that all judgments bearing on the decision be made by one person. But the number of such judgments can be far too large and too complex for any single individual. Organizations have and use experts; it is natural to allocate the many different judgments embodied in a multiattribute utility analysis to many heads, partitioning them so that each person works in the area of his or her own expertise and/or responsibility.

SMART divides decision problems into appropriate elements and also fits the partition to the skills of available judges. It has been presented in a number of places (e.g., Edwards, 1971, 1977; Edwards et al., 1975). This version discusses new problems and presents a few new technological wrinkles.

AN EXAMPLE

SMART consists of ten steps. Before discussing them in detail, I want to present a very simple illustration of its structure, both so that the whole procedure will be clear as I review issues concerned with its parts, and because in so doing I will be able to introduce both the relevant technical terms and most of the relevant arithmetic in a very simplified and straightforward way. I will refer to each step of SMART as I come to it in the example, so that as I review those steps in detail later in the chapter, the reader can refer back to the example and see where each takes place.

Scenario

My son Page and I (step 1) both use an old, not very good, bicycle. We agree to get rid of this one and buy a new one. But (step 2 and a beginning of step 3) which?

We are both interested in two aspects of any bicycle: performance and comfort. Under performance, two questions are important: "How many gears does it have?" and "How heavy is it?" The more gears it has, the better; the lighter, the better. Under comfort, two questions are important: "How comfortable is the seat?" and "Is the size of the bike appropriate?" Thus, we agree on the value tree presented in Figure 7.1 (step 4).

Value Trees

Value trees are convenient structures in which to array values, starting with abstract ones at the top of the tree and working down to quite specific and measurable ones at the bottom. Unique points in a value tree (or any other tree structure) are called *nodes*. Each point at which several lines come together is a node; the ends of lines at the bottom of the tree are also nodes. Each line descending from a node is called a *branch*. Branches that have no nodes below them are called *twigs*. Since each branch and each twig ends in a node, it makes no difference whether the label is taken to describe the branch or twig or the node below it.

A tree structure has levels; to find the level of a node, one simply counts the number of nodes on the unique path between it and the top of the tree, including in the count both the node in question and the node that is the top of the tree.

This application uses two kinds of weights. Both are normalized; that is, they sum to 1 over some appropriate set of nodes. *Normalized weights* sum to 1 only over the set of nodes immediately below some higher-level node. *Final weights* sum to 1 over all twigs in the tree. For the first two levels of the tree, these will be identical; below that, they will not. (The weight of the top-level node is 1.) When, in discussing weights later, I write of multiplying weights downward through the tree, I mean multiplying all normalized weights on the path between a twig and the top of the tree together; this produces the final weight of that twig.

I obtain final weights by multiplying down through the tree rather than by direct judgment of weights, simply because most value trees are far too complex and have too many twigs to permit direct comparisons of their importance.

Importance Weighting

Page and I disagree about the relative degrees of importance of the four performance measures. I am more interested in comfort than in performance by a three-to-two ratio. Under performance, I regard gears and weight as equally important. Under comfort, I regard the comfort of the seat as being four times as important as correct size. Page is primarily interested in performance; he considers it four times as important as comfort. Under performance, he considers number of gears to be one and one-half times as important as weight; under comfort, he regards size as three times as important as comfort of the seat.

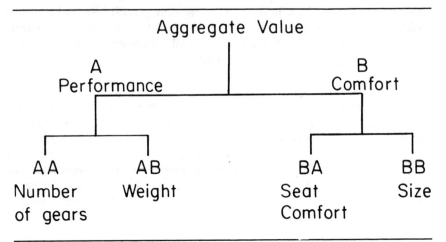

Figure 7.1: A Value Tree for Bicycles

In order to generate a compromise set of weights, we agree to average our normalized weights over the various dimensions of value (steps 5 and 6).

Table 1 presents my weights, Page's weights, and the compromise weights. The calculations in Table 7.1 follow directly from the ratio judgments described in the preceding paragraph. For example, I consider the ratio of the weight of comfort to that of performance to be 3:2, so my normalized weight for comfort is 3/5 = .60, and my normalized weight for performance is 2/5 = .40. This calculation carries out step 7 for that branch of the value tree. Similarly, I consider the ratio of seat comfort to correct size to be 4:1, so the normalized weights for those two dimensions are 4/5 = .80 and 1/5 = .20. My final weight for seat comfort is .60 × .80 = .48. Final weights sum to 1 over all twigs in the tree. Calculations for Page's weights are parallel, but based on his ratio judgments. Calculations of compromise weights consist of averaging normalized weights and then multiplying downward through the tree. Ratio judgments are not the only way of obtaining normalized weights. I originally proposed them (Edwards, 1971, 1977), and still regard them as the best way of obtaining weights in simple situations. But sometimes a simpler, less time-consuming elicitation process is acceptable. This chapter describes such a process in its extended discussion of step 6, below.

Note that this evaluative structure has one example of each of four kinds of values. More gears are preferable to less. Less weight is preferable to more. Seat comfort is a judgmental dimension having no easily identifiable physical characteristic. And size has an intermediate optimum point; a bike can be too small,

TABLE 7.1   Weights

	Ward		Page		Compromise	
	Normalized Weight	Final Weight	Normalized Weight	Final Weight	Normalized Weight	Final Weight
A						
Performance	.4		.8		.6	
B						
Comfort	.6		.2		.4	
AA						
Number of gears	.5	.20	.6	.48	.55	.33
AB						
Weight	.5	.20	.4	.32	.45	.27
BA						
Seat comfort	.8	.48	.25	.05	.575	.265
BB						
Size	.2	.12	.75	.15	.425	.135

NOTE: Final weight for AA is the normalized weight for A times the normalized weight for AA. Final weights sum to 1 over all twigs in the tree.

too large, or just right. Incidentally, Page and I are the same size, so the same-sized bike will be best for both of us. Little is lost by treating utility (subjective value) for gears as linear, increasing from 1 to 10, utility for weight as linear, decreasing from its largest to its smallest plausible values, and utility for size as bilinear, increasing from its smallest plausible value to its optimum and then decreasing to its largest plausible value. Figure 7.2 shows how to translate these physical properties of bikes into numbers called, in the technical jargon of multiattribute utility, single-attribute utilities.

Bikes

Now, armed with our evaluative mechanism, we travel to the bicycle shop. There we quickly narrow our options to three bicycles, which we will label X, Y, and Z (step 3, refined). Table 7.2 (see p. 189) shows the characteristics, measured in utility units, of each bicycle. Table 7.2 is the output of step 8. Utilities for gears, weight, and size come from Figure 7.2. Page and I simply rated seat comfort on a 0-100 scale and averaged the ratings. Bike X can be interpreted as a three-gear bike with a relatively heavy weight, a very comfortable seat, and of the right size. Bikes Y and Z are both high-performance bikes, also the right size, and both having ten speeds; they differ in seat comfort and in weight, with the heavier one having the more comfortable seat. Since, as it happens, all three bikes are of the right size, that particular dimension of evaluation obviously will make no difference to the final outcome. Nevertheless, it could have been relevant, and was therefore appropriate to include in the analysis.

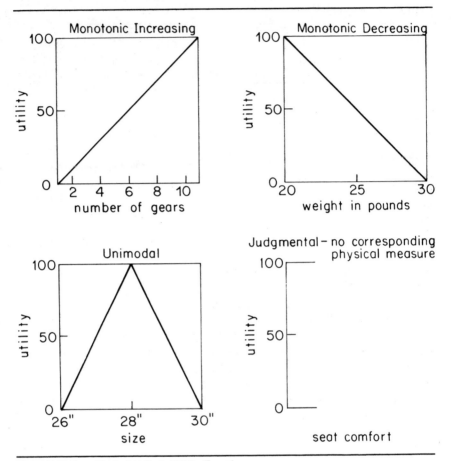

Figure 7.2: Four Single-Attribute Utility Functions

Analysis

Table 7.3 (see p. 190) shows the details of the computations for each set of weights and each bike (step 9). The calculation takes the single-dimension value or utility for the bike, multiplies it by the appropriate final weight, and adds those products up over the various values that enter into the decision. Thus, for my weights and bike X, 30 x .2 is 6, 10 x .2 is 2, 100 x .48 is 48, and 100 x .12 is 12. The sum of these numbers is 68, which is my aggregate utility for bike X. All of the other single-dimension utilities for bikes and all of the other weights are used in exactly the same way.

At this point, we can observe some interesting properties of the results. First of all, my favorite is bike X, which scores very well on seat comfort, although

TABLE 7.2   Single-Dimension Utilities of Bikes

	Bike X	Bike Y	Bike Z
Gears	30	100	100
Weight	10	80	100
Seat comfort	100	40	10
Size	100	100	100

not so well on performance. On the other hand, Page likes bike X least of all. Page's favorite is bike Z, which scores excellently on performance, but not so well on comfort. On the other hand, the compromise weights show that the best compromise is neither X nor Z but rather bike Y, which gives me a lot more comfort than bike Z, while taking away from Page only a little bit of performance that bike Z has. Thus, depending upon whose weights are used, SMART may come up with one solution, or with another, and if weights averaged over people are used, it may come up with a compromise that is in some sense intermediate, compared with the optimal solutions for the people whose weights were averaged (step 10).

Now, after that overview of the whole process, it is time to examine its ten steps in detail.

SMART, 1979 MODEL

Step 1

Identify the person, persons, organization, or organizations whose values are to be maximized. In the bicycle example, this was Page and I. In criminal justice contexts, both persons and organizations will usually be relevant. The generic name for such individuals or groups is stakeholders. In a parole policy context, for example, stakeholders might include prisoners and parolees, administrators in the parole system, judges, police, prison officials, and representatives of public interest groups concerned with parole. For some such groups (e.g., prisoners and parolees), finding an appropriate judge of stakeholder values may be difficult. For others, relevant individuals should be easy to identify. In any case, the idea of a stakeholder is nothing like the idea of a random sample of the public. A stakeholder is one who has a personal interest in and knowledge of the question at hand, and who can be expected to have thought enough about it to have meaningful values with respect to it.

Since judgments must be made by individuals, those individuals must be carefully identified as spokesmen or spokeswomen for the relevant stakeholder groups. If the groups are organized, that identification is usually already done. If

TABLE 7.3 Computations of Aggregate Utilities

Dimensions of Value	Bike X			Bike Y			Bike Z		
	W. wt.	P. wt.	C. wt.	W. wt.	P. wt.	C. wt.	W. wt.	P. wt.	C. wt.
AA (gears)	6	14.4	9.9	20	48	33	20	.28	33
AB (weight)	2	3.2	2.7	16	25.6	23.6	20	.32	27
BA (seat)	48	5	26.5	19.2	2	10.6	4.8	.5	2.65
BB (size)	12	15	13.5	12	15	13.5	12	15	13.5
Sum	68	37.6	52.6	67.2	90.6	80.7	56.8	95.5	76.15

NOTE: W. wt. stands for computations using Ward's weights; P. wt. stands for computations using Page's weights; and C. wt. stands for computations using the compromise or average weights.

not, the evaluator must be able to identify and obtain the cooperation of appropriate people. Typically, the technology requires significant amounts of face-to-face contact with each such person.

Step 2

Identify the issue or issues for which the values being solicited are relevant. This will often depend on which of the four purposes discussed earlier is, in fact, the purpose of the evaluation; it may also depend on the age of the program being evaluated. This would ordinarily be done by the evaluator in collaboration with people from the organization funding the evaluation, and also in collaboration with representatives of the program being evaluated. In the bicycle example, the issue was to choose which bike to buy; in the Community Anti-Crime Program evaluation I review below, an issue is what level of future funding the program should receive.

Step 3

Identify the entities to be evaluated. This will depend on the purpose of the evaluation. If the purpose is curiosity or fine-tuning, the entity to be evaluated is simply the program now in place. If the purpose is programmatic choice, not only the current program but also the options alternative to it should be evaluated. If the purpose is to decide whether a program should live or die, it is certainly desirable, if possible, to consider what will happen if the program is killed, and to evaluate that state of affairs.

It will often be useful also to evaluate a preprogram state, so that changes produced by a program can be identified and evaluated. And, for planning purposes, it may be useful to evaluate plausible future states of the program, as well as its present state. Formulation of believable future states presents major technical problems. For a discussion of possible solutions, see Edwards and O'Connor (1975).

Step 4

Identify the relevant dimensions of value. This value-structuring task is probably the most important, difficult, and creative aspect of multiattribute utility measurement.

It can be approached in at least two ways. The simplest is to prepare a list of values that are relevant to the evaluation. Such a list is the necessary end product of step 4 in any case, and for relatively simple evaluations it may be easy to go directly to it. But for any but the simplest cases, it will not be feasible. Too many values are relevant, and relevant values are not all at the same level of generality or abstraction. For example, deinstitutionalization of status offenders may be a program goal. But it is far too general a goal to be evaluated directly. It can be subdivided in various ways. For example, it might be subdivided by categories of status offenses, by diversion and decriminalization methods, by administrative or organizational levels at which the program is implemented, or, most likely, by some combination of these.

Thus, most evaluations perform step 4 by developing a value tree—a hierarchical structure of values, with abstract and unmeasurable values at the top and well-defined and measurable ones at the bottom. (The bicycle example used one, though in that simple case it was unnecessary.)

The values of all stakeholders should be represented in the value tree. The best way I know to accomplish this is to develop a trial tree, using the expertise of program people and evaluators, and then to propose it to stakeholder representatives. If the proposed tree is carefully thought through, its structure will usually be accepted. Experience seems to show that stakeholders agree about value structures, but disagree about weights. But most stakeholder representatives will wish to add values (twigs) not appearing on the originally proposed tree. Seldom, if ever, will any stakeholder wish to eliminate a twig or branch.

This fact presents the evaluator with a dilemma: too many twigs. Ideally, 4 or 5 attributes are enough. Since many more attributes than that must usually be considered, I committed myself in print to the view that 8 attributes are enough, and 15 are too many (Edwards, 1971, 1977). Yet, my own most recent multiattribute utility measurement effort used 144 twigs.

Why should the number of attributes be kept small? First, because large numbers of attributes dilute the impact of measures of the importance of one attribute relative to another. In addition, the larger the number of attributes, the more work it is to obtain performance measures for each, for each program or other object of evaluation. Finally, problems of value independence among attributes (see Keeney and Raiffa, 1976: 109) are more complex, though also far less important, if the number of attributes is large than if it is small.

But stakeholders do care about many attributes—the more stakeholders, and the more divergence of view and values among them, the more attributes. Hence, a significant part of the art of multiattribute utility evaluation consists of trying to reduce the number of attributes—and accepting with resignation and good grace a remaining number larger than one would wish.

If all or most of the relevant stakeholder representatives can be assembled in a face-to-face group, reducing the number of attributes may be relatively easy. The first step is for the evaluator to look for attributes that are simply verbal relabelings of other attributes. If the stakeholders agree, then the wording of one attribute description can be changed and the other can be eliminated. Similarly, if two attributes can be expected to be very highly positively correlated, then it may be possible to use one as a proxy for the other, and thus reduce the list.

The next step is to ask the stakeholders to assess the importance of the remaining attributes, using the techniques described below. It may be and usually is the case that stakeholders will disagree about which attributes are very important, but they will agree that certain ones are unimportant. These unimportant attributes are candidates for elimination, if the stakeholders agree. This tactic should not ordinarily be allowed to deprive some unfortunately idiosyncratic stakeholder of his or her favorite attribute, unless the cooperation of that stakeholder in the evaluative process or his or her acceptance of the evaluative result is unimportant. But social facilitation, such as that which face-to-face interaction can provide, may help to promote agreement.

If it is impractical to assemble the stakeholder representatives into a face-to-face group, eliminating attributes is far more difficult. No one has yet tried written procedures for this purpose, so I do not know whether or not they would work well enough to be worthwhile. The alternative is to accept a list of values long enough to please everyone, no matter how preposterously long a list that requires.

One could think of yet other approaches. For example, stakeholders might be limited in the number of attributes they are allowed to propose. A plausible limit would be five. Then the union of all such lists, after combining the duplicated ones, might turn out to be shorter than one elicited from a face-to-face group. But I think the advantages of using a trial tree prepared by program people and evaluators far exceed the advantages of using a purely stakeholder-generated list. Logical structure, coherence, and avoidance of redundancy take thought, time, and expertise; stakeholder representatives may not have enough of any of these.

Selfishness is an important issue for most lists of values. Evaluators and senior program people tend to be distressingly idealistic; they too often suppose that the values relevant to a program have to do only with its impact on its targets.

This might conceivably be true for a program in its early planning stage, when few people are directly involved. But people implement programs and have legitimate personal values that bear on program evaluation. Every organization has a right to value its own existence and growth, and to value the external conditions that make that existence and growth possible. Thus, values that have to do with public image, with ability to attract and maintain funding, with organizational security and stability, are all relevant to evaluation of programs in being.

This requires an unusual degree of honesty of those who prepare lists of values. Such honesty can be more likely if the evaluator is absolutely explicit about the relevance and appropriateness of selfish values in a value structure. Edwards et al. (1975) found it helpful to obtain two lists of values, one concerned with program impacts and the other concerned with organizational growth and survival, in their evaluation of Office of Child Development research project selection methods. Most of the values in the Community Anti-Crime Program evaluation described below are concerned with the program itself, rather than with its impact on crimes.

Idealists may well complain that selfish or bureaucratic values are not relevant to an outsider's evaluation of a program. Perhaps not, in some Olympian overview. But a relevant evaluation should speak to what, in fact, is happening. And almost every program in being that I have ever seen is eager to survive, regardless of its external effects, and makes every effort to do so. Fortunately, many of those efforts do require the program to address itself to its external goals and clients.

I think that recognition of the importance of such nonidealistic goals may have led Mr. Joseph F. Coates, former Associate Director of the Office of Technology Assessment and a very sophisticated observer of the federal bureaucracy, to deride "the false conclusion that making those values explicit is a worthwhile activity in all public policy processes. . . . Many private motives are in conflict, are latent, are dark, uncongenial, and even unspeakable. Consequently, the universal call for making them explicit in public is really an invitation to hypocrisy" (Coates, 1978). Mr. Coates overstated the problem, but he is quite correct that hypocrisy is the inevitable result of neglecting personal values. In just this sense, many impact evaluations are hypocritical—one of the many reasons evaluations are so often ignored. The alternative, which I advocate, is to recognize and accept as legitimate the internal, as well as external, personal and organizational goals that in fact drive programs and the organizations that implement them. (For a fuller discussion of Mr. Coates's views and my responses to them, see Edwards, 1978).

The process of developing a value tree is both more important and far more difficult if that tree must include values relevant not only to the stakeholders at various comparable levels of power, but also to the various elements of a power hierarchy. This chapter will later summarize an evaluation now in progress of the Community Anti-Crime Program of the Law Enforcement Assistance Administration. The value tree used for that evaluation, after numerous iterations, came to be addressed to the values of stakeholders, including the staff of the House Judiciary Subcommittee on Crime; the staff of Congressman Conyers (chairman of that subcommittee); the administrator of the LEAA; the director of the Community Anti-Crime Program and members of that staff; other LEAA staff members, including especially those funding the evaluation; the evaluation project monitor; and the program people in the various Community Anti-Crime Programs themselves.

In spite of its difficulty and complexity, the idea of structuring a value tree so that its hierarchical organization corresponds to the power structure of the program to which it is relevant makes a great deal of sense. It ensures that the resulting evaluation will speak to the concerns of decision makers at a number of different levels in the power structure, and this greatly improves the chances that the evaluation will, in fact, be used.

Step 5

Rank the dimensions of value in order of importance. If attributes are simply listed, the ranking must include them all. If attributes are arranged in a value tree, it is sufficient to obtain ranks for the values beneath each node of the tree separately, as in the bicycle example. Use of such partial sets of ranks is described at step 6. This ranking job, like step 4, can be performed by program leaders or other stakeholder representatives, acting alone or by some form of group process. Individual judgments may be expected to differ; such differences are the essence of disagreements about values. For that reason, it is important to preserve them—at least until the point at which a decision must be made.

The preceding paragraph conceals a subtle problem: What does "importance" mean? We all have an intuitive idea of its meaning, and in earlier versions of the SMART procedure I relied primarily on that intuition for this step and for step 6. But that intuition can be misleading. For example, the importance of reducing recidivism, relative to the importance of other values relevant to a criminal justice program, should depend heavily on whether the amount of reduction the program might reasonably be expected to produce is, say, 2 percent or 20 percent. A 2 percent reduction may (or may not) be too little to pay much attention to, while a 20 percent reduction would be guaranteed to astonish and delight program people and sponsors. In short, the notion of importance can be given clear technical meaning only in connection with an explicit tradeoff in utility between one change and another. Consider an example. Suppose that, in a particular police jurisdiction, a decision is made to try keeping teenaged drunk drivers out of the court system—perhaps by using courses, counseling, parental discipline, or some combination of these, instead. A suitable baseline for both involvement in the court system and recidivism is available from preprogram records. For convenience, suppose that the preprogram court caseload is 500 cases per year, and that over a five-year follow-up period, 50 of these 500 are picked up for drunk, driving again. The program, if successful, might reduce the caseload in the courts to zero. Thus, the range on the dimension "incidence of court cases" is from 500 to 0. The experts, using caseload information, estimate that the program might as much as double the number of those who are picked up for drunk driving again within five years. So the range on that dimension is from 50 to 100. A statement that, say, keeping the repeat cases down is five times as important as keeping teenaged drunk drivers out of the courts, would imply that an actual reduction of such court cases from 500 to 300 would be barely wiped out in attractiveness by an increase in the current repeat cases from 50 to 54.

For those not familiar with linear functions, I had better explain how I arrived at those figures.

The first step is to assume that utility is linear in the chosen dimensions between their limits, as Figure 7.2 did. This is probably a great oversimplification, but it makes the arithmetic easy enough to be understandable, and a straight line is always an excellent approximation to any smooth monotonic function. For convenience, I normalize all utility functions so that 0 is the worst, and 100 the best, outcome within the set of outcomes given serious consideration.

Now, suppose we consider some location measure L on a dimension of value, and we need its utility. The dimension may be attractive, meaning that more is better than less, or unattractive, meaning the opposite. For attractive dimensions,

$$u_L = 100(L - min_D) / (max_D - min_D). \qquad [1]$$

For unattractive dimensions,

$$u_L = 100(max_D - L) / (max_D - min_D). \qquad [2]$$

Of course, max_D and min_D are the maximum and minimum values on the dimension D, on which L is measured.

In the example at hand, both dimensions are unattractive, so equation 2 applies. Call the number of court cases C, corresponding to L above. Then, from equation 2,

$$u_C = 100 (500 - C) / (500 - 0) = (500 - C) / 5. \qquad [3]$$

Call the number of repeat arrests R, again corresponding to L. Then,

$$u_R = 100\,(100 - R)\,/\,(100 - 50) = 2\,(100 - R). \qquad [4]$$

To say that keeping repeat arrests down is five times as important as keeping cases out of the courts simply means that one unit of u_C has only 1/5 the weight of the one unit of u_R. By substituting into equation 3 and solving for u_C, it is easy to calculate that the reduction of 200 court cases gains us 40 units (called "utiles" in the technical jargon) of u_C. This can just be compensated for by a loss of 8 utiles in u_R. Substituting $u_R = 8$ into equation 4 and solving for R shows that R = 96. This tells us that a tradeoff relation between R and C exists such that a gain of 200 cases reduced in C is compensated by a loss of 4 rearrests in R, and vice versa. The linearity assumption means that this will be true regardless of the starting and ending points of either gain or loss. In the absence of that assumption, we would have to elicit actual utility functions and consider actual starting and finishing points, rather than talk about simple tradeoff ratios.

The tradeoff between R and C could have been calculated much more simply, but in a way that would have contributed less insight. R, in its natural units of rearrests, has a range of 50. C, in its natural units of court cases, has a range of 500. The ratio of ranges in natural units, then, is 10:1. A 10:1 ratio in ranges of natural units multiplied by a 5:1 ratio in importance produces a 50:1, or 200:4, ratio that combines the two, and thus expresses the value tradeoff in natural units rather than in abstract utility units. Lest this apparent simplicity tease the reader into thinking that one can ignore utility and work in natural units, remember that you will be dealing with many different dimensions, and that many of them, being purely subjective, have no natural units. All, however, must trade off against one another; that is the ‑key idea that multiattribute utility measurement in any of its versions is about. Abstract utilities all measured on the same scale are therefore essential.

"Importance," then, means importance of tradeoffs in utiles, not tradeoffs in natural units. That is why ranges are important.

Examples like the preceding one, carefully explained, though without the mathematics, usually make it clear to experts who must estimate the end points of those ranges. All those who estimate weights really need to know is the end points of the ranges and the fact that all measurable quantities will be transformed onto a 0-100 scale.

The need for ranges as elements of the definition of importance presents problems for hierarchically structured value trees. At all levels of the tree except the twigs themselves, the dimensions are abstract and so have no specifiable ranges. Nevertheless, tradeoffs must be made among them—and, if SMART is to be used, rankings and importance weight judgments are necessary.

Fortunately, the twigs, in effect, define the meaning of the abstract dimensions from which they depend, as the bicycle example illustrated. While I know of no convincing algorithm that would permit aggregation of such twig ranges into numbers comparable to ranges for higher levels of the tree, neither have I ever encountered any resistance from those making such judgments. Apparently, the tree structure itself, combined with the evocative labels given to higher-order abstract dimensions, is sufficient to permit importance weight judgments to be made. This fact, of course, implies that the respondents must have strong intuitions about what "importance" means—intuitions sufficiently strong to prevent their being bothered by the inherent vagueness of the concept.

Step 6

Assess importance weights at each twig of the value tree.

How can a respondent compare all the twigs with one another in importance? If there are only a few, a number of direct judgment techniques will work. But the more familiar and difficult case involves a value tree with far too many twigs at the bottom to make direct assessment of tradeoffs among them meaningful or feasible. Just as, at step 5, it was sufficient to rank order only the attributes beneath each node of the value tree, so here it is sufficient to ask for direct comparative assessment of weights only for those nodes that were compared with one another in the ranking at step 5—that is, nodes beneath a single node at the next higher level. By any of a number of elicitation techniques, it is possible to obtain a set of weights for each attribute relative to the weights of the others with which it is compared. These weights are normalized (i.e., summed to 1) over that set of attributes. Thus, a weight is associated with each node (or, equivalently, with each branch or twig) of the value tree. Since, as I explained in presenting the bicycle example, there is a unique path from the top of the value tree to each twig, final twig weights can be obtained by multiplying together the normalized weights at each node of this path. In the discussion of the bicycle example, I called this process "multiplying downward through the tree." These final twig weights will sum to 1 over all the twigs in the tree.

Step 6 is not concerned with the arithmetic described above; the evaluator's task at step 6 is simply to elicit from appropriate respondents the numbers that are raw material for that arithmetic.

Who should assess weights? The problem was discussed above. The weights are the essence of value judgments, and so they should be assessed by the relevant stakeholder representatives. The same people who contribute value dimensions should, if at all possible, assess weights. This implies a two-step process; the value dimension elicitation and the weight elicitation cannot be executed in the same session, since value dimensions from all participants must be consolidated into a single value tree.

In previous publications (e.g., Edwards, 1977), I have proposed a thorough-going ratio judgment procedure as a source of weights. Such a procedure has two advantages. It is thorough and demanding enough to ensure that any respondent who in fact carries it through will think carefully about every dimension and every judgment. Also, ratio judgments are steep—a useful property. That is why, in those previous publications, I preferred ratio judgments to the otherwise more familiar procedure of dividing 100 points among the values to be weighted—a procedure known to produce flat weights. Since these procedures are difficult to validate, no objective case can be made for preferring steep weights to flat ones. But commonsense observation suggests that value dimensions differ enormously in importance; a response mode that preserves that difference seems preferable to one that does not.

Both ratio judgment procedures and divide-100-points procedures are fairly arduous, and therefore discourage busy weighters. For that reason, Stillwell et al. (forthcoming) have proposed an approximation procedure, called rank-exponent weights, that greatly reduces judgmental labor while yielding very good approximations. In addition to the rank ordering collected at step 5, the respondent need make only one more judgment per group of values being compared. In Stillwell, et al., (forthcoming), that additional judgment was the weight of the most important dimension, on a 0-1 scale. However, since that paper was written, I have come to prefer the same model combined with a different elicitation, which I will present here.

First, the model. Suppose that N dimensions of value or attributes are being compared. Let r_i be the inverse rank of the i_{th} dimension; by inverse rank I mean that the least important dimension gets a rank of 1, the next least, a rank of 2, and so on, until the most important dimension gets a rank of N. (Ties are handled as usual.) The approximate model expresses the weight of the i_{th} dimension, W_i, as follows:

$$W_i = \frac{r_i^Z}{\sum_{j=1}^{N} r_j^Z} \qquad [5]$$

Next, the elicitation procedure. Select any two dimensions from the list being compared; symbolize them s and t. These dimensions should be chosen to be far apart in importance (e.g., the highest and lowest in the rank ordering), but also easy to compare with each other from the respondent's point of view. Define dimension s as more important than dimension t. Now, ask the respondent to judge the ratio of their importances. The respondent can do so directly, or, to facilitate judgments of less than 2:1, can be asked to assign an arbitrary weight of 10 to dimension t and then judge what weight should be assigned to s in order to preserve the ratio of the importances.

A bit of algebra on equation 5 shows that, if $R_{s/t}$ is the ratio of the weight of dimension s to that of dimension t, then

$$R_{s/t} = r_s{}^Z / r_t{}^Z;$$

or, taking logarithms and rearranging terms,

$$Z = \log R_{s/t} \ / \ (\log r_s - \log r_t) = \log R_{s/t} / \log (r_s/r_t). \tag{6}$$

Equation 6 is simple to calculate on a hand calculator with a log key. Once the value of Z is recovered from equation 6, the normalized weights for all dimensions compared with each other can be calculated directly from equation 5, changing the numerator appropriately from N down to 1 for the successively lower weights.

The difficulty with the preceding elicitation method is, of course, that various choices of s and t will probably lead to differing values of Z. If the value tree is not too large and bushy, this can be checked by asking the respondent to choose more than one value of s, t, or both. If the values of Z do not differ too much, you may simply want to average them. If they do, a complete set of ratio weights can be obtained by using the technique explained in Edwards (1977). For large, bushy value trees, one cares very little about any single value of Z, and so need not bother with such additional attributes.

In any case, the output of step 6 is a set of weights for sets of lower nodes in the tree that are connected to each higher node. These sets of weights may or may not already sum to 1, depending on how the elicitation was done.

Step 7

Normalize the weights and calculate final weights. If the weights obtained at step 6 did not sum to 1, the first step is to make them do so by adding each set and dividing by the sum.

The second step is to multiply all normalized weights downward through the tree to obtain twig weights. That is, the normalized weights at each twig should be multiplied by the normalized weights at each node above that twig to obtain final twig weights. These will sum to 1 over all twigs in the value tree. If the reader finds this description of the arithmetic too brief, go back to Table 7.2 of the bicycle example for an illustrative set of calculations.

Step 8

Obtain location measures. The location measures, also called single-dimension utilities, are measures of how well each of the objects of evaluation does on each dimension on which it is to be evaluated.

Such numbers can be obtained from a wide variety of sources. The most common source will be expert judgment, since many dimensions of evaluation are obviously subjective. Sometimes an evaluator will find it necessary to use expert judgment, even if a more objective alternative exists, either because the dimension is not important enough to justify the cost of a more expensive measure, or because no time is available for a careful study, or for some other reason.

The numbers that come out of typical experimental evaluations are of this kind. That is, they are measures of how well a program (or other entity being evaluated) performs on some dimension of evaluation. Such numbers are obviously the best inputs into step 8, when and if available.

Figure 7.2 of the bicycle example and the discussion of step 5 pointed out that there are four kinds of location measures, three being functions relating objective measures to utility, and the fourth being a simple subjective assessment of utility. In the first three cases, I know of no good reason not to approximate the location measures by linear or (in the unimodal case) bilinear functions. This means that the location measures for these cases can be calculated, using the linear mathematics explained above, once either two or three numbers are known. (The bilinear calculation is like the linear one, except that the peak of the function is used instead of the minimum or the maximum, depending upon on which side of the peak the location measure falls.)

Step 9

Aggregate. Step 7 produced a set of twig weights that sum to 1. Step 8 produced a location measure for each twig, for each program or other entity being evaluated. Step 9 combines them.

The formal idea is extremely simple. Define U_k as the aggregate utility of the kth entity being evaluated, and suppose that the index j refers to the twigs, of which there are a total of T. Then

$$U_k = \sum_{j=1}^{T} W_j u_{jk} \qquad [7]$$

Note that in equation 7, W_j is the final weight on the jth twig, the output of the calculations in step 7; u_{jk} is the location measure, on a 0-100 scale, of the kth object of evaluation on the jth twig. Equation 7 is nothing more than the equation for a weighted average.

Quite often, equation 7 is too condensed an aggregation. It may be preferable to be able to say how well the kth object of evaluation is doing on each of several higher-order dimensions of evaluation in the value tree (e.g., how well each bike fares with respect to comfort and performance), and thus produce a sort of profile of each object of evaluation with respect to these higher-order values. Moreover, any such higher-order profile will be most informative if its numbers are all on the same 0-100 scale as are the values of u_{jk}. The appropriate calculation is:

$$U_{kB} = \sum_{j=1}^{T(B)} w_j \ u_{jk}/W_B. \qquad [8]$$

In equation 8, U_{kB} is the utility of the kth object on branch B of the value tree. The notation T (B) means that the summation extends only over twigs dependent from that branch, so not all values of j are used. W_B is the normalized weight of branch B. If all values of u_{jk} within branch B are 100, then this calculation ensures that U_{kB} is also 100—as it should be. This technique can produce summaries at any desired level of the value tree, but is most often used at the second level—that is, the most abstract and aggregated values that are still identified by explicit names.

Step 10

Decide. What this step means in an evaluation context depends on the reason for the evaluation. At the beginning of this chapter I claimed that multiattribute utility evaluations are relevant to all four of the purposes for evaluation that I proposed. It is now appropriate to defend the claim.

If an evaluation is for curiosity, multiattribute utility methods serve two main purposes: They help specify what is important and therefore what one should be curious about, and they help provide an orderly way of presenting and summarizing data and judgments bearing on the topics of curiosity. Weighting mechanisms are of relatively minor importance, as is aggregation; the main function of weighting is to guide data collection or judgmental effort.

If an evaluation is to guide fine-tuning, multiattribute utility methods serve to highlight the areas in which fine-tuning is important, and to predict at least to some extent what the result will be. For this purpose, profiles obtained from equation 8 are more likely to be useful than aggregate utilities obtained from equation 7. Weights will be very useful, since they offer candidate topics for intensive study to find out whether or not fine-tuning is needed and feasible. If possible, not only the present program but its retuned version should be evaluated.

If an evaluation is to guide life-or-death decisions about a program, they will usually require one kind of judgment not so far discussed—one that brings the noneconomic benefits of the program (often, the measures obtained as outputs of equation 7) into relation with both economic and noneconomic costs.

The best way to make such assessments is to obtain direct judgments equating amounts of dollar cost to amounts of intangible benefits. Managers are often quite willing to make such judgments. If so, then all costs and benefits can be expressed in equivalent dollars, and the analysis reduces to comparing this program with alternatives to it, all expressed in equivalent dollar terms via equation 7.

If managers are reluctant to equate nondollar benefits with dollar costs, then one can use equation 7 to assess aggregate benefits (noneconomic costs can and probably should be treated as negative benefits and included in that assessment) and also obtain dollar cost figures. These are the raw ingredients of a benefit-to-cost ratio. Note, however, that both benefits and costs must be measured on scales with a true zero point in order for such ratios to be meaningful. Depending on circumstances, zero benefit and zero cost might mean what you would have if no program existed, or the status quo, or perhaps something else. In any case, whatever is taken as defining zero benefit and zero cost must be assessed and subtracted from the benefits and costs of the program being evaluated. A case can be made that, of available options, the one with the highest benefit-to-cost ratio is preferable. The case is relatively weak, though defensible. For that reason, a judgment that equates benefits to dollar costs is a much better resolution of this kind of problem, if it can be had.

Decision analysts commonly, and correctly, emphasize that their procedures, including multiattribute utility measurement, are more often useful for helping the decision maker(s) to clarify and refine thought than for providing a numerical alternative to thought. Any analysis should be iterative; various structures and formulations are tried, and in this process what to do becomes clear. The evolving, interactive character of multiattribute utility analysis contrasts sharply with the "impartial" and uninvolved stance sometimes elaborated in the name of objectivity. In my view, the suspicion with which program people regard that stance is thoroughly appropriate. Lack of thought about, or interest in, the problem at hand prior to collection of data is hardly a recommendation for the would-be evaluator. Openness to new ideas and the new data is a better and more honestly attainable substitute.

For problems that involve multiple, conflicting stakeholders, the main function of multiattribute utility analysis is to specify an agenda for discussion, negotiation, and horsetrading. (It also permits the use of formal tools to specify good trades; that is a technical subject all by itself.) It makes communication about values far easier than any other mode of their study that I know of. For that reason, it has come to be a useful tool in some U.S. negotiations with other countries.

EXAMPLE 1:
THE COMMUNITY ANTI-CRIME PROGRAM EVALUATION

Snapper and Seaver (forthcoming) have reported on an ongoing LEAA-funded evaluation of the LEAA's Community Anti-Crime (CAC) Program. This is the epitome of an umbrella program and is therefore especially interesting to consider. As implemented, its basic idea is that local community organizations interested in adopting some mix of strategies for reducing the incidence of crime can apply for money to the LEAA's Office of Community Anti-Crime Programs (OCAP). One goal of the program is to reduce red tape; consequently, grants go directly from the LEAA to the applying organization—which may not even be sufficiently highly structured to meet normal federal standards of stability and of capability for financial accounting. Another goal of the program is to encourage the invention of innovative anticrime strategies; this gives OCAP every reason to seek a wide variety of different activities among its grantees. Moreover, since yet another program objective is community involvement, any simplistic measure such as crime statistics for the relevant communities would miss a major point of the program. In short, the CAC Program is an evaluator's nightmare—a fact that makes it especially important to evaluate it.

Moreover, Snapper and Seaver introduced several innovations in the basic SMART idea. One arose from the phrase MAUT-Bayes. When it first was used in the social service-delivery program community in the early 1970s, MAUT-Bayes was a slogan rather than a well-thought-through evaluation strategy. The MAUT part meant multiattribute utility—a familiar idea from other evaluation contexts by then. The addition of Bayes was presumably a recognition that Bayesian thinking (see, for example, Edwards et al., 1963) should have something to contribute to evaluation research—but users of the slogan did not know exactly what. (Please note that that slogan did *not* appear in Edwards et al., 1975, or in Edwards and Guttentag, 1975.)

Bayes's Theorem of probability theory is simply a rule whereby prior opinions (probabilities) are revised into posterior opinions on the basis of new evidence. Since evidence enters into SMART at step 8, that is obviously where Bayes should be relevant, if at all. Snapper and Seaver (forthcoming) have proposed that "location measures are given in probabilistic form. For example, a measure could be the probability that a randomly chosen client of the program has benefitted in a certain way.... Probabilistic location measures have the desirable property that subjective probability and Bayesian statistical methods can be employed to express opinions about expected attainment of objectives and that these opinions can be linked to evaluative data subsequently collected." They also point out that the use of probabilities as location measures automatically solves the comparability-of-ranges problem.

To implement this idea, Snapper and Seaver define their operational variables as probabilistic measures, typically in relative frequency form, that can in fact be counted. They collect prior judgments from relevant stakeholders, and express those judgments as prior beta distributions. Then, as evidence becomes available, they propose to revise these betas, using the normal Bayesian algorithm (see, for example, Phillips, 1974). In principle, multiple observations could be brought to bear on a location measure for any single twig, and, indeed, Snapper and Seaver plan just that. This too is a variation on SMART. I admire this imaginative conversion of a slogan into an implementable method.

Whether these variations contribute enough to make them worthwhile, remains to be seen. The limitation of location measures to probabilities is severely constraining—and not necessary to the implementation of the MAUT-Bayes strategy. The full apparatus of Bayesian inference could be brought to bear on location measures. But I am less clear about the usefulness of employing the Bayesian apparatus to relate earlier to later observations in this context. I do not immediately see why prior and posterior observations could not, so to speak, stand on their own feet, leading to earlier and later utility measures, without need for any formal linkage between them. Snapper and Seaver, on the whole, agree.

The value tree that Snapper and Seaver report is extremely interesting. Figure 7.3 shows it. It is obviously responsive to stakeholders at at least three different levels of the CAC hierarchy. The program/policy objectives clearly represent congressional intentions for the program. Many of them can be explicitly extracted from the language of the act that created the program. The OCAP "results sought" objectives, though they grow from the program concept also, are more directly responsive to OCAP concerns. Finally, the project-specific objectives will vary widely from one project to another.

Inspection of weights assigned to the OCAP "results sought" objectives by one weighter illustrates nicely some of the differences between this kind of evaluation and a simplistic "Did CAC reduce crime?" kind of evaluation. The two most important objectives, together accounting for almost 50 percent of the weight, were mobilization of residents and sense of community. These are process objectives, not outcome objectives. The history of the CAC Program strongly implies that, even after the program is over, implementation of its process objectives will probably be considered at least as important as whatever crime-reducing impacts it may have.

The data collection is now in progress, so results of the evaluation cannot be summarized. But in their incomplete form they have already been used to guide one program decision.

EXAMPLE 2:
EVALUATION OF PUMPED STORAGE SITES

Keeney (1977), working with other experts from Woodward-Clyde Consultants, Inc., the geological consulting firm for which he works, and with biologists and other experts from a large utility company in the Southwest (UCS), evaluated a number of potential sites for pumped storage facilities. A pumped storage facility is a plant that makes use of electricity generated during off-peak hours to pump water to a high location. During peak hours, the water

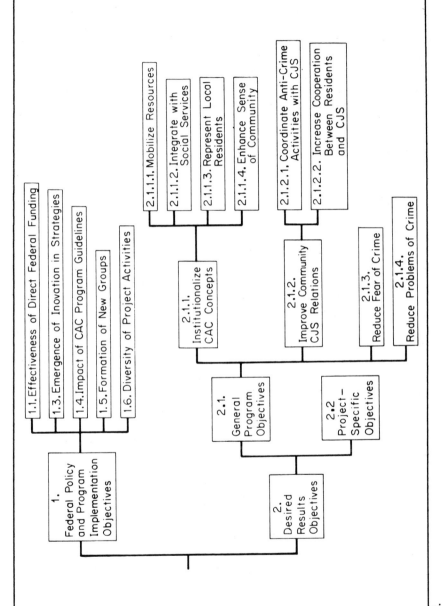

Figure 7.3.

flows back through a hydroelectric plant to its origin, generating electricity. The net effect of such a plant is to even out the electrical load over the day, permitting the utility to avoid building enough power production capacity to cover demand at peak periods. Obviously, an appropriate site for such a facility must include a lower water source and a higher basin-shaped site in which the water can be stored, the two fairly close to each other. Moreover, the facility must be connected to the power grid it serves.

Initial screening identified ten sites worth considering. Out of an initial list of more than sixteen potential value dimensions, four were selected for the analysis. They were: first-year cost in millions of 1976 dollars, transmission line distance in mile equivalents, pinyon-juniper forest in acres, and riparian community in yards. First-year cost includes 18 percent of direct and indirect construction costs plus annual operating costs. Transmission line distance is an aesthetic and ecological factor, since the cost of building lines is included in capital cost, and line losses are included in operating cost. Actual distance to each site from a major UCS load center was the basis for the calculation. However, a mile of actual distance could count as anywhere from 1 to 10 miles, depending on how undesirable the experts considered it to be to have a transmission line there. A rural route traversing unpopulated range land is worth a mile per mile; a route over extraordinarily scenic land is worth 5 miles per mile; a route traversing a park or the habitat of an endangered species is worth 10 miles per mile. Destroying pinyon-juniper forest is also aesthetically and ecologically undesirable. Actual areas that would be destroyed were modified upward to take into account the presence on one site of arroyo seeps and the fact that another was an especially good raptor (bird of prey) habitat. Riparian communities—that is, plants and animals living at the edges of streams that would be destroyed—were also to be preserved if possible.

This study did not use the SMART methodology. For a full description of the multiattribute utility methods used, see Keeney and Raiffa (1976). Since additive independence was violated, Keeney used a multiplicative utility function. He used hypothetical bets to obtain tradeoffs among the dimensions and to obtain nonlinear single-dimension utility functions. While the interpretation of weights is not as easy for multiplicative as for additive utility functions, the weights obtained by averaging judgments of a number of UCS executives, if they had been in additive form, would have been .60, .32, .01, and .07 for the four dimensions. Little would have been lost from the analysis by ignoring the pinyon-juniper forest acreage, and not much more by ignoring the riparian communities. But the ecological and environmental damage caused by building power transmission lines is more than half as important as the cost of the entire facility.

Since one of the value dimensions is money, it is easy to use it as a numeraire for the other dimensions, and Keeney did so. Specifically, he calculated the cost of an imaginary site equivalent in utility to each real site except that no losses for transmission lines, forest destruction, or riparian community destruction would be required. In effect, the difference between this and the real cost is a dollar equivalent of the environmental damage such a plant would cause. He also did extensive sensitivity analyses, showing how variations in plant design and site characteristics would affect the evaluation of each site.

One can summarize Keeney (1977) as follows: The ranking . . . is one of the major inputs to the decision process. Some other factors important to the overall ranking of sites were explicitly not considered here. Such factors include legal considerations in acquiring land and water rights, political factors, and interests of local groups living within the vicinity of proposed sites. This overall decision process is currently underway.

Of course, if I had been doing the study, I would have tried as best as I could to persuade UCS to include those variables as well as the cost and environmental variables in it. If so, use of the multiplicative model and of imaginary bets might have been far more difficult than it was in this relatively simple analysis. For these data, Keeney presents an analysis showing that the use of a multiplicative rather than an additive model made essentially no difference to the ranking of sites.

EXAMPLE 3:
EVALUATING DESEGREGATION PLANS

In 1977, the Los Angeles Unified School District (LAUSD) asked me to prepare and apply an evaluation scheme for school desegregation plans. (For a full report, see the document submitted to the court; for a fairly full one, see Edwards, 1979; for a quite brief one, see Edwards, 1980.) The reason for the request was that the California Supreme Court had ordered the Los Angeles School Board to desegregate, and Superior Court Judge Paul Egly had been appointed to monitor, supervise, and if necessary intervene in the process. The board had submitted a plan to Judge Egly. He rejected it as insufficient, ordered the board to submit another within ninety days, and included in that order a requirement that the board review alternative plans that might be submitted and that it accompany its own plan or plans and the alternatives with, among other things, "all cost and benefit studies." I was asked to prepare an acceptable method of evaluating the benefits of school desegregation plans.

Decision-making responsibility was extraordinarily diffuse; I identified eleven different decision makers (Edwards, 1980), of which, for my purposes, the board was by far most important. The board consisted of seven elected members, strongly supported by a highly sophisticated group of professional LAUSD administrators. With the help of a team that ultimately grew to about eighty LAUSD personnel, I completed a SMART analysis, using the techniques presented in this chapter, in less than two months.

Two LAUSD administrators and I formulated Model 1 of the value tree. In the course of review by board members and other stakeholders, it grew, until Model 8 had 144 twigs.

Since board members, mindful of later elections, could not be expected to include weights expressing explicit tradeoffs between, say, educational quality and racial-ethnic balance in a public document, I obtained the cooperation of five of the seven by keeping their weights secret, reporting only averages. Agreement among board members was surprisingly good, considering their political disagreements.

Overlapping teams of LAUSD experts provided the location measures for all twigs, accompanying each by a written rationale. I judged these numbers to have been carefully assessed and to make sense. Most dimensions of evaluation were primarily or entirely judgmental.

We evaluated seven plans, including the one Judge Egly had rejected. On both benefit and benefit-cost ratio measures, that one scored best. (To be able to calculate benefit-cost ratios, we also evaluated the current state of the district. By subtracting current benefits and costs from each plan, we were able to obtain ratio-scale measures in both numerator and denominator.) The profiles of the various plans for the seven highest-level values were extremely informative about the nature of each plan.

We did not, unfortunately, evaluate the plan the board finally adopted, since it was prepared and agreed to by the board too late for our evaluation mechanism to be used before Judge Egly's deadline.

Probably the major practical consequence of the effort was that the board and those writing the plan it ultimately adopted had available explicit measures of its own values, and used them in preparing a plan that would conform to them. The plan adopted fits in considerable detail the value structure the board's judgments had revealed.

The evaluation mechanism, having met the judge's requirement, has had no further use since 1977. Four of the five respondents no longer sit on the board, so board values collected now would probably be significantly different— especially since Los Angeles has had two years of experience with the plan the board adopted.

EXAMPLE 4:
EVALUATING THE OFFICE OF THE RENTALSMAN

The Province of British Columbia is experimenting with an interesting alternative to the courts for settling disputes between landlords and tenants: the Office of the Rentalsman. All disputes between landlords and tenants concerning noncommercial property go to that office. The office takes complaints easily (i.e., by phone or mail), follows up informally (i.e., by phone, mail, or direct investigation), and mediates whenever possible. It can, if necessary, hear cases; only about 6 percent of cases lead to hearings, and these are informal. Disputed hearing outcomes can be appealed to the courts.

As part of a research program on alternatives to the courts, Newman and Drew (1979) conducted a multiattribute utility evaluation of this program. In fact, they evaluated three things: the office as it was operating when the evaluation was conducted, the office as it should operate, and British Columbia's normal process of settling landlord-tenant disputes, through the courts, before the legislation creating the Office of the Rentalsman passed.

Their respondents for value dimensions, weights, and location measures were twelve local experts, including supporters, critics, and neutrals. They identified sixteen attributes; these were not arranged in a tree structure, but were merely listed. (I sympathize with the experts who had to make ratio weight judgments for sixteen attributes in a single list.) Some question can be raised about overlapping dimensions: For example, two of them were "fairness" and "impartiality"; the definitions do nothing to reduce the concern that these are two verbal statements of the same idea. Unfortunately, data were not collected in a face-to-face meeting at which such problems could have been sorted out. Ratio weights were collected by the SMART technique presented in Edwards (1977). Location measures were judged on seven-point scales: Interjudge reliabilities were relatively high. The evaluation showed that the Office of the Rentalsman was, as of the date of the evaluation, doing better than the courts had done, but that it should do quite a lot better. The pattern of location measures on the specific dimensions fit well with intuition about what might emerge from comparison between administrative and court resolution of such disputes. It also offers strong implications about how to improve the operation of the Office of the Rentalsman. Though the purpose of the study was not to fine-tune that office, the results should be very useful for that purpose.

OTHER MULTIATTRIBUTE UTILITY EVALUATIONS

Two points should be apparent by now. One is that the tools of multiattribute utility analysis are useful in a wide variety of contexts and purposes, of which social service-delivery program evaluation is only one. A second is that most of its other uses have received far more scientific, technological, and decision maker attention than has person-oriented service-delivery program evaluation. To document this further, I list the other applications or would-be applications that I know about. I apologize to those whose work is left out, as I am sure is the case for many important studies. The literature is large, and no one has yet done a serious job of trying to collect it from the widely dispersed journals, and very hard-to-locate technical reports, in which it resides. The following summaries use MAU to mean multiattribute utility measurement.

- Allen et al. (1977) report a very large MAU for evaluating combat readiness of marine battalions.

- Bajgier and Moskowitz (1977) report a MAU of drinking water quality.

- Bauer and Wegener (1975) use MAU to evaluate alternative urban development plans.

- Barclay and Peterson (1976) base a negotiation model for international and other negotiations on MAUs for both sides.

- Bell (1975) develops a MAU for methods of trying to control the budworm pest in East Canadian forests.

- Brown et al. (1975) use a MAU to provide a basis for deciding when NATO should take what actions in response to an attack from the Warsaw Pact powers.

- Brown et al. (1975) use a MAU to choose among hypothetical alternative agreements about oil with Mideastern countries.

- Buehring et al. (1975) use MAU to formulate an approach to making tradeoffs among energy sources, taking environmental considerations into account.

- Chen et al. (1975 develop a MAU indicator for health.

- Chinnis et al. (1975) use MAU to evaluate alternative versions of a kind of army radio.

- Dyer and Miles (1976) use MAU to choose among trajectories for the Mariner fly-by of Jupiter and Saturn.

- Kaplan et al. (1976) report a MAU index of health status.

- Keefer (1976) uses a MAU for research and for product engineering decisions in industrial planning.

- Keeney (1975) proposes MAU for energy policy, and proposes a specific MAU structure for that context.

- Keeney (1976) uses MAU to choose among policies for management of salmon in the Skeena River.

- Keeney and Nair (1976) develop a MAU screening model for potential nuclear power plant sites in the Pacific Northwest.

- Keeney and Raiffa (1976) report a large number of applications or near-applications of MAU in their book. Rather than cite each separately, I will mention their topics and refer the interested reader to the book for more details and references to the original sources. They include: siting of a new Mexico City airport, air pollution control in New York, budget allocations in a small school district, operation of the New York Fire Department, structuring the corporate objectives for Woodward-Clyde Consultants, usefulness of time-sharing computer systems, siting and licensing of nuclear power facilities, policies concerning frozen blood, treatment of cleft lip and cleft palate, water quality, and various other topics cited separately here.

- O'Connor Rhees, and Allen (1976) developed a large and complex computerized MAU model for the U.S. Navy to use in evaluating future mixes of naval aircraft.

The preceding applications are all "for real" in the sense that they are either reports of applications that have already been made or reports based on the development of tools for applications that, I believe, have been made since the time of their reports. Various other lines of thought that should lead to application, and may already have done so, have also been published.

- Aschenbrenner and Kasubek (forthcoming) developed a MAU for evaluating variants of the drug cortisone on the basis of their side effects.
- Beach et al. (1976) report a MAU intended to help with birth-planning decisions.
- Ford et al. (1972) propose a MAU model for job choices.
- Gardiner and Edwards (1975) develop a MAU for land-use decisions in the California Coastal Zone.
- Gustafson and Holloway (1975) develop a MAU for severity of illness. I do not have a good reference, but Gustafson and his collaborators also developed a MAU-based index of medical underservedness that is now the basis for decisions about which locations wishing to receive federal assistance for building new hospitals can do so, and which ones cannot.
- Hoepfl and Huber (1970) develop a MAU for evaluating the performance of faculty members.
- Jauch and Glueck (1975) propose a MAU to evaluate the research productivity of professors.
- Moskowitz et al. (1978) offer a MAU for long-range expansion-planning of generation facilities for electric utilities.
- O'Connor (1973) develops a MAU for measuring water quality for two different uses.
- Otway and Edwards (1977) develop a MAU for nuclear waste disposal sites.

ETIOLOGY OF MULTIATTRIBUTE UTILITY IDEAS

The frequent recurrence of names in the preceding list of applications should invite attention to the scarcity of people in the field relative to the demand for them, and speculation about where such people are trained and located.

The original formal structure was developed by Howard Raiffa (1968), although others were thinking along similar lines. Keeney was Raiffa's most important student. When Raiffa became Director of the International Institute for Applied Systems Analysis, Keeney accompanied him; they wrote their joint book there. Raiffa is now back at Harvard, and Keeney is with Woodward-Clyde Consultants.

Edwards, while at Michigan, trained a number of appliers, including Beach, Chinnis, Fryback, Gustafson, Kelly, O'Connor, Peterson, Seaver, and Snapper. Gustafson and Huber have built a large and enthusiastic group of appliers to medical problems at the University of Wisconsin. Kelly and Peterson, with Robert Eidson, founded Decisions & Designs, Inc., which is now the most successful consulting group in the field. Snapper more recently founded the Decision Science Consortium, Inc., another successful consulting firm, where Seaver, Brown, and Chinnis now work.

Howard, not represented above, teaches decision analysis at Stanford, and has been, with Matheson, the leader of an important and successful group at Stanford Research Institute. That group recently reproduced by fission; a number of companies grew out of it and are now doing well in the Bay region. It is underrepresented above partly because so much of its work is done for corporations and is proprietary, and partly because their usual approach to multiple-value dimensions is to reduce them all to a common scale, dollars first.

Guttentag first was exposed to decision theory and multiattribute utility in Edwards's Michigan laboratory. She did not herself teach any other practitioners, but was an ardently enthusiastic advocate for the ideas in social service-delivery contexts.

Other interest in multiattribute utility can be found in nearly every business school of major importance in the country, but I cannot cite them all. Unfortunately, the rate of application is less dependent on schools than on consulting organizations—and the consulting organizations are limited, not by shortage of funds, but by shortage of those well trained in the relevant skills. Few of those highly skilled at applications have chosen the financial sacrifices of academia. And few undergraduates, or even graduate students, have paid any serious attention to this highly demanded interdisciplinary field.

CONCLUSIONS

The message should now be clear. I began this chapter by expressing surprise at the idea that the multiattribute utility approach to evaluation had died. Obviously, it has not; it is thriving and growing rapidly. Its application to social service-delivery contexts other than medical has lagged far behind its application to other evaluation contexts; even the medical applications have lagged, relative to others.

Why? I think that the skills required to do a good job of multiattribute utility assessment are sufficiently inconsistent that they do not often reside inside the same head. One is some mathematical competence—beyond and quite different from ordinary statistics. The other is an appreciation of, and an ability to elicit, subjective numbers. Both of these ingredients are often lacking from the equipment of those who do person-oriented social service-delivery evaluations. While many evaluators are willing to admit that decision-making is inherently subjective, fewer want to admit that subjectivity can usefully and effectively be translated into numerical form. And social scientists notoriously receive less, and less effective, training in any kind of mathemenatics than do most other kinds of scientists, especially in any kind other than conventional cookbook statistics.

But the blend of subjectivity and numbers offers to those skilled in its use capabilities that would otherwise not be available. This chapter has attempted to sketch one such capability, to make the part of it that deals with numbers less mysterious than it has hitherto been, and to hint at the far-reaching implications that such a capability can have for actually influencing the course of human events outside the academy.

REFERENCES

Allen, J., D. Buede, and M. O'Connor (1977) "Program Completion Research: Advanced Decision Technology Program (1972-1979)." Technical Report 79-3-93, Decisions and Designs, Inc., Cybernetics Technology Office, Defense Advanced Projects Agency.

Aschenbrenner, M. K. and W. Kasubek, *Challenging the Cushing Syndrome: Multiattribute Evaluation of Cortisone Drugs.* University of Mannheim.

Bajgier, S. M. and H. Moskowitz (1977) "Public Risk Assessment and Evaluation of Drinking Water Quality." Report 596, Krannert Graduate School of Management, Purdue University, West Lafayette, Indiana.

Barclay, S. and C. R. Peterson (1976) "Multiattribute Utility Models for Negotiations." Technical Report 76-1, Defense Advanced Research Projects Agency, Arlington, Virginia.

Bauer, V. and M. Wegener (1975) "Simulation, Evaluation and Conflict Analysis in Urban Planning." *Proceedings of the Institute of Electrical and Electronics Engineers* 63: 405-413.

Beach, L. R., B. P. Townes, F. L. Campbell, and G. W. Keating (1976) "Developing and Testing a Decision Aid for Birth Planning Decisions." *Organizational Behavior and Human Performance* 15: 99-116.

Bell, D. E. (1975) "A Decision Analysis of Objectives for a Forest Pest Problem." Research Report 75-43, International Institute for Applied Systems Analysis, Laxenburg, Austria.

Brown, R. V., C. W. Kelly, R. R. Stewart, and J. W. Ulvila (1975) "The Timeliness of a NATO Response to an Impending Warsaw Pact Attack." Technical Report DT/TR 75-7, Advanced Research Projects Agency, Arlington, Virginia.

Brown, R. V., C. R. Peterson, and J. W. Ulvila (1975) "An Analysis of Alternative Mideastern Oil Agreements." Technical Report DT/TR 75-6, Rome Air Development Center, Office of Naval Research and Defense Advanced Research Projects Agency, Arlington, Virginia.

Buehring, W. A., W. K. Foell, and R. L. Keeney (1975) "Energy/Environment Management: Application of Decision Analysis." Research Report 76-14, International Institute for Applied Systems Analysis, Laxenburg, Austria.

Campbell, D. T. and R. F. Boruch (1975) "Making the Case for Randomized Assignment to Treatments by Considering the Alternatives: Six Ways in Which Quasi-Experimental Evaluations Tend To Underestimate Effects," in C. A. Bennett and A. A. Lumsdaine (eds.) *Evaluation and Experience: Some Critical Issues in Assessing Social Programs*. New York: Academic Press.

Chen, M. M., J. W. Bush, and D. L. Patrick (1975) "Social Indicators for Health Planning and Policy Analysis." *Policy Sciences* 6: 71-89.

Chinnis, J. O., C. W. Kelly, R. D. Minckler, and M. F. O'Connor (1975) "Single Channel Ground and Airborn Radio System (SINCGARS) Evaluation Model." Technical Report, Decisions & Designs, Inc.

Coates, J. F. (1978) "What Is a Public Policy Issue?" in K. R. Hammond (ed.) Judgment and Decision in Public Policy Formation. Boulder, CO: Westview Press.

Dyer, J. S. and R. F. Miles, Jr. (1976) "An Actual Application of Collective Choice Theory to the Selection of Trajectories for the Mariner Jupiter/Saturn 1977 Project." *Operations Research* 24, 2: 220-244.

Edwards, W. (1980) "Reflections on and Criticisms of a Highly Political Multiattribute Utility Analysis," in L. Cobb and R. M. Thrall (eds.), *Mathematical Frontiers of Behavioral and Policy Sciences*. Boulder, CO: Westview Press.

——— (1979) "Multiattribute Utility Measurement: Evaluating Desegregation Plans in a Highly Political Context," in R. Perloff (ed.) *Evaluator Interventions: Pros and Cons*. Beverly Hills, CA: Sage Publications.

——— (1978) "Technology for Director Dubious," in K. R. Hammond (ed.) *Judgment and Decision in Public Policy Formation*. Boulder, CO: Westview Press.

——— (1977) "How To Use Multiattribute Utility Measurement for Social Decision Making." *IEEE Transactions on Systems, Man and Cybernetics* 7: 326-340.

——— (1971) "Social Utilities." *Engineering Economist* 6: 119-129.

——— (1965) "A Tactical Note on the Relation Between Scientific and Statistical Hypotheses." *Psychological Bulletin* 63: 400-402.

Edwards, W. and M. Guttentag (1975) "Experiments and Evaluations: A Re-Examination," in C. A. Bennett and A. Lumsdaine (eds.) *Evaluation and Experiment: Some Critical Issues in Assessing Social Programs*. New York: Academic Press.

Edwards, W., and M. F. O'Connor (1975) "On Using Scenarios in the Evaluation of Complex Alternatives." Technical Report 76-17, Decisions & Designs, Inc.

Edwards, W., H. Lindman, and L. J. Savage (1963) "Bayesian Statistical Inference for Psychological Research." *Psychological Review* 70: 193-242.

Ford, D. L., G. P. Huber, and D. H. Gustafson (1972) "Predicting Job Choices with Models That Contain Subjective Probability Judgments: An Empirical Comparison of Five Models." *Organizational Behavior and Human Performance* 7, 3: 397-416.

Gardiner, P. and W. Edwards (1975) "Public Values: Multiattribute Utility Measurement in Social Decision Making," in Schwartz and Kaplan (eds.) *Human Judgment and Decision Processes: Formal and Mathematical Approaches*. New York: Academic Press.

Gustafson, D. H. and D. C. Holloway (1975) "A Decision Theory Approach to Measuring Severity in Illness." *Health Services Research* (Spring): 97-106.

Guttentag, M. and E. L. Struening (1975) *Handbook of Evaluation Research, Volume 2*. Beverly Hills, CA: Sage Publications.

Hoepfl, R. T. and G. P. Huber (1970) "A Study of Self-Explicated Utility Models." *Behavioral Science* 15: 408-414.

Jauch, L. R. and W. F. Glueck (1975) "Evaluation of University Professors' Research Performance." Management Science 22, 1: 66-75.

Kaplan, R. M., J. W. Bush, and C. C. Berry (1976) "Health Status: Types of Validity and the Index of Well-Being." *Health Services Research* 11, 4: 478-507.

Keefer, D. L. (1976) "A Decision Analysis Approach to Resource Allocation Planning Problems with Multiple Objectives." Ph.D. dissertation, University of Michigan.

Keeney, R. L. (1977) *Evaluation of Proposed Pumped Storage Sites.* San Francisco: Woodward-Clyde Consultants, Inc.

——— (1976) "A Utility Function for Examining Policy Affecting Salmon in the Skeena River." Research Report 76-5, International Institute for Applied Systems Analysis, Laxenburg, Austria.

——— (1975) "Energy Policy and Value Tradeoffs." Research Memorandum 75-76, International Institute for Applied Systems Analysis, Laxenburg, Austria.

——— and K. Nair (1976) "Evaluating Potential Nuclear Power Plant Sites in the Pacific Northwest Using Decision Analysis." Professional Paper 76-1, International Institute for Applied Systems Analysis, Laxenburg, Austria.

Keeney, R. L. and H. Raiffa (1976) Decisions with Multiple Objectives: Preferences and Value Tradeoffs." New York: John Wiley.

Moskowitz, H., J. Evans, and I. Jimenez-Lerma (1978) "Development of a Multiattribute Value Function for Long Range Electrical Generation Expansion." Report 670, Krannert Graduate School of Management, Purdue University, West Lafayette, Indiana.

Newman, J. R. and A. B. Drew (1979) Paper presented to the Third Annual Meeting of the Evaluation Research Society, Minneapolis, Minnesota, October 17-20.

O'Connor, M. F. (1973) "The Application of Multiattribute Scaling Procedures to the Development of Indices of Water Quality." Report 7339, Center for Mathematical Studies in Business and Economics, University of Chicago.

O'Connor, M. F., T. R. Rhees, and J. J. Allen, (1976) "A Multiattribute Utility Approach for Evaluating Alternative Naval Aviation Plans." Technical Report 76-16, Defense Advanced Research Projects Agency, Arlington, Virginia.

Otway, H. J. and W. Edwards (1977) "Application of a simple Multiattribute Rating Technique to Evaluation of Nuclear Waste Disposal Sites: A Demonstration." Research Memorandum 77-31, International Institute for Applied Systems Analysis, Laxenburg, Austria.

Phillips, L. D. (1974) *Bayesian Statistics for Social Scientists.* New York: Harper & Row.

Raiffa, H. (1968) *Decision Analysis: Introductory Lectures on Choices Under Uncertainty.* Reading, MA: Addison-Wesley.

Snapper, K. and D. Seaver (forthcoming) "National Evaluation of the Community Anti-Crime Program." Prepared for Social Change, Inc., Grant 77-NI-99-0084, National Institute of Law Enforcement and Criminal Justice/Law Enforcement Assistance Administration, Washington, D.C.

Stillwell, W., D. Seaver, and W. Edwards (forthcoming) "Rank Weighting in Multiattribute Utility Decision Making: Avoiding the Pitfalls of Equal Weights." *Organizational Behavior and Human Performance.*

8

Utility of Process Evaluation: Crime and Delinquency Programs

Barry Krisberg

I. WHAT IS PROCESS EVALUATION?

Process evaluation consists of a comprehensive description and analysis of how crime and delinquency programs are conceptualized, planned, implemented, modified, and terminated. Process evaluations attempt to assess the quality and purpose of program activities relative to the desired outcomes or results of these programs. Since relationships and interactions of the program with its surrounding social environment are crucial to comprehending the quality and meaning of program efforts, process studies also examine issues of context as well as interorganizational linkages. Process studies often render policy-relevant data when implementation of rigorous impact designs proves impractical. Further, process evaluations may be employed during early stages of program development to assist the refinement of program strategies and activities. In this program development role, process studies have been called "formative evaluations."[1] Finally, process evaluation should be routinely integrated with impact studies to enhance the explanatory power of research designed to measure the effects of crime and delinquency programs.

AUTHOR'S NOTE: Preparation of this chapter was partially supported through grants (77-NI–99–007 and 77-JN-99-008) from the Office of Juvenile Justice and Delinquency Prevention. The author wishes to thank James Austin for his detailed critique of an earlier draft of this chapter. Points of view or opinions expressed herein are those of the author and do not necessarily represent the official position or policies of the U.S. Department of Justice.

Process evaluations help realize two important public policy goals:

(1) to produce information about how crime control efforts *actually* operate and the forces impeding or facilitating reform efforts; and

(2) to permit the proper interpretation of impact studies of alternative criminal justice reform programs.

The first goal seems particularly warranted because of the relatively meagre amount of basic research concerning criminal justice agencies, as well as the virtually unexplored character of the more innovative community crime prevention programs. The second goal—to facilitate the policy analysis of impact studies—deserves high priority because of the well-known problems associated with measuring the impacts of crime control programs (Hudson, 1977). Moreover, impact research has reported an apparently consistent pattern of failure in a broad range of crime and delinquency program areas[2] (Martinson, 1974; Wright and Dixon, 1977; Newton, 1978). But even the most rigorous impact studies are unable to explain why many well-intentioned efforts fail. Perhaps the most significant utility of process evaluation would be to provide data and careful analyses of the seeming intransigence of criminal justice agencies to constructive reform efforts. (Nimmer, 1978; Lemert, 1970).

Optimism about process evaluation must be tempered by the observation that the "state of the art" in process evaluation is severely underdeveloped. Rossi and Wright (1977) go so far as to doubt the value of process-evaluative models because "they cannot be articulated as a method." Freeman (1977) asserts that evaluative studies should include both process and impact components, but he notes that few analytic rules apply to process studies. He advises that the researcher should develop a well-conceptualized and carefully designed approach to collecting process data, but admits there exists little structure to guide such inquiries.

> The state of the art with respect to process evaluation in many areas of program interest . . . is exceedingly undeveloped. I do not think it is too bold a position to argue that if one has to choose between directing efforts now at the improvement of process or impact evaluative procedures, the former has a higher priority. [Freeman, 1977: 39].

Central issues for conceptual and practical development of process research include:

(1) providing a framework for data collection and elaborating rules of inference applicable to process data;

(2) articulating modes of analysis linking process and impact data; and

(3) improving the methodological adequacy of qualitative research techniques that often produce the most fruitful process data.

These concerns are critical for the successful application of process evaluation to crime and delinquency programs. Later in the chapter, some preliminary suggestions pertinent to improving process evaluation methods will be offered. But real advances in process evaluation await a broader application of this approach and more serious attention from social scientists to the methodological issues inherent in process studies.[3] Process evaluation must grow beyond an intuitive "logic in use"[4] and become translatable into a "reconstructed logic" comprehensible to researchers, program staff, and policy makers.

II. UNIQUE DATA NEEDS OF PROCESS EVALUATIONS

A. Program Development and Planning

Process evaluations require unique program data along several dimensions. For instance, process studies contain detailed descriptions of program development. Such data include a chronology of how the program evolved and who were the key initiators of program concepts. Analysis of these data help explain features of program design in terms of underlying theories or assumptions of planners, as well as political and practical compromises required to launch and maintain the program. For example, a process study might discover that program planners were required to amend their original goals to fit the expediency of available funding. Good grantsmanship decisions have often produced significant unanticipated consequences when plans are put into action. Analyzing program development might extend to assessments of the quality of the preproject planning—the degree of accurate planning information and the extent of involvement in program development of potential clients, agency staff, other criminal justice agencies, or representatives of the community-at-large.

Contextual factors exert a profound effect on program operations. Thus, it is imperative that process evaluations explore ideological currents underlying the program, historical events, and organizational structures within which the program must function. A related contextual concern includes the special attributes of targeted populations that may be decisive in understanding the program's logic and its apparent results.

Program development data also require descriptions of the methods for translating abstract plans into action. Process evaluations focus on implementation issues revealing programmatic constraints and supports for program objectives. Such data might illuminate the value of certain planning models, thereby facilitating smooth program commencement. Further, data on early stages of implementation are invaluable for programs designated as exemplary and worthy of replication. Information about how facilities were obtained, or techniques for recruitment, selection, and training of staff (or clients), provide heuristic insights into later stages of program development. For example, many "community-based" crime control programs must begin their efforts by gaining the goodwill and support of local residents. Enlisting community support might entail public information campaigns, creating local advisory groups or intensive grass-roots community organizing. The character of these efforts often determines the program's "image" which, in turn, effects staff ability to recruit clients or enlist local resources and support. In some instances, community resistance has pre-cipitously ended community-based programs.

B. Program Operations

Another unique set of process data encompasses the operations, structure and flow of the program under study. Too often, program evaluations provide minimal data about the nature of the social program being measured (Geis, 1975). A review of evaluative research reports on many diverse crime control programs reveals a pattern of insufficient detail about the program operations. Such omissions seriously impede policy-relevant application of research findings.

> If a program is unsuccessful, it may be because the program failed to "operationalize" the theory, or because the theory itself was deficient. One might be highly successful in putting a program into action, but if the theory is incorrect . . . the desired changes may not be forthcoming; i.e., "the operation was a success, but the patient died." Furthermore, in very few cases do action or service programs directly attack the ultimate objective. Rather they attempt to change the intermediate process which is "causally" related to the ultimate objective [Suchman, 1969: 16].

Without detailed descriptions of program operations, the analyst cannot reasonably decide among these potential sources of program failure.

Freeman and Bernstein (1975) argue that the description of program content must respond to the following two questions:

(1) Has the program been directed at the appropriate and specified target population or target area?
(2) Were the various practices and intervention efforts undertaken as speci-fied in the program design or derived from the principles explained in the design?

A survey of delinquency prevention programs explored these concerns and concluded that delinquency prevention programs rarely derived their intervention efforts from a consistent set of design principles. Further, it observed unsystematic client identification procedures which suggested "skimming"–i.e., agencies served the best of the bad kids, leaving the more hostile youth to the criminal justice system or to fend for themselves (Cardarelli, 1977). Data from this national assessment of delinquency prevention enhance our ability to comprehend the image of failure characterizing most delinquency prevention efforts. Moreover, this mode of analysis possesses implications for methods of improved program design in future efforts.

Process evaluation should describe program procedures for identifying and selecting target populations. Descriptions of these procedures are then compared with overall project goals and the intended intervention techniques. Often one finds target selection criteria ambiguously defined in program proposals. Thus, program staff must quickly devise plans to recruit clients and/or focus their service strategies. Methods of recruiting clients for crime and delinquency programs usually depend upon cooperative linkages with other components of the criminal justice system. For example, adult diversion programs require the coordinated efforts of police, prosecutors, public defenders, and probation officers to identify and select clients for these programs. Often crime control programs operate under specific legal or administrative rules which mandate whom they must serve and which intervention alternatives are permissible. Such constraints on client/target selection can produce serious consequences for program operations. Similarly, programs must depend upon other agencies for information about potential clients, referral sources, or the availability of other intervention options.

Full description of project services constitutes an important component of process evaluations. Ideally, the documentation of program operations should reveal if the program is functioning according to its underlying theory or plan. At a minimum, program descriptions should cover the nature and extent of program services as well as provide indicators of intensity and duration of services. One useful approach involves instituting a straightforward data system recording rates of client participation. This data system should be capable of tracking the individual client from intake through release/termination from the program. A more elaborate client-tracking system could include periodic updates of services rendered, as well as measures of client status. Although implementing a relatively simple client-flow data system can provide invaluable information to program planners, attempts to initiate new record-keeping routines often encounter staff and client resistance. The success of these data-gathering efforts requires that all participants understand the *potential value to them* of information systems. Whenever feasible, program clients and staff should be involved in the development of data systems focused on program services.

Documenting program services can be further accomplished through interviews with staff and clients. It is important to be aware of the diverse perceptions held by participants in a common social event such as a crime control program, and the need to triangulate measurements of project services. Whenever possible, the process research should sample all groups that participate in programs. For example, an agency administrator might tell the researcher about the broad goals of a program and the intended staff structure. Program staff, particularly those who actively deliver the service, may provide a better source of information about how the program really works, and what "informal" procedures employed because official plans fail to meet the exigencies of daily operations. Similarly, clients can offer valuable data about what they *perceive* are the services and program rules. Comparisons of contrasting perceptions help provide a more holistic view of program content. Often the researcher discovers large discrepancies between the written descriptions of a program and the verbal descriptions of different program actors. In these instances, the analysis can be substantially enriched by multiple observations of program services. Carefully structured observations might be made by accompanying specific staff members (and observing a typical day), attending program services, and observing staff meetings and planning sessions. Less structured observations could be gathered by "hanging out" at program facilities or in the surrounding community.

In formative stages of program development, the focus on services may assist program planners to monitor the implementation of their concepts. Process research provides useful data about policies, procedures, and agency routines that inhibit or support successful development of program services. One practical result of early process data collection would consist of a well-articulated description of critical decision points within the program. Critical decision points encompass situations within the operation of the program when choices are made about the appropriateness of targets and services. Critical decision points might include the intake interview and subsequent assignment to program status, procedures to review or reclassify, and decisions to terminate services. These decision points often involve several program actors and occur throughout the duration of the program. In microcosm, these decision points produce the distribution of program choices that contribute to ultimate program outcomes. Process research can identify both formal and informal decision points— including descriptions of the decision-making processes, adequacy of information, and results of differing decision alternatives.

III. UNIQUE CONTRIBUTIONS OF
PROCESS EVALUATION

A. Interpreting Impact Findings

Data on program content looms large in efforts to explain positive or negative impact results. For example, Hudson (1977) describes a Minnesota restitution program in which subsequent program developments added parole supervision and various traditional rehabilitation services to the basic restitution model.

The effect on the evaluation research was one of further complicating the independent variables. The problems caused for the research of mixed program interventions were complicated by the serial introduction of these different interventions into the program package with the inception of the Center; residents admitted to the program experienced different "pieces" of the program according to their time of admission [Hudson, 1977: 95].

In many social programs, particularly those aimed at broad objectives (e.g., preventing delinquency) staff may be expected to alter program content constantly in response to their perceptions about client needs or potentially successful intervention strategies. Similarly, law changes or new administrative regulations might profoundly affect program activities. Reform programs rarely stand still long enough to be subject to accurate "snapshots" of their progress. The number and type of independent variables increase as programs evolve, sometimes leaving the impact research design curiously out of synchronization with actual program operations.

Process research cannot solve the methodological problems posed by mixed and chaotic program interventions, unanticipated program changes, or the programmatic consequences of external forces. There are real limits to the flexibility of most impact designs. But process research can record these program changes and provide timely feedback to researchers and administrators hoping for conclusive measures of outcome. In this role, process research can help the impact design achieve a closer fit with program reality, as well as suggest the most strategic points of additional data collection.

B. Interpreting Impact Measures

Process evaluations help form impact research designs (Rutman, 1977) and alert researchers when impact measurements are becoming less valid. Process researchers often investigate the social process generating or producing the conventional outcome measures used in assessing crime and delinquency programs. Paul Lerman's (1970) research on the California Community Treatment Program (CTP) provides an excellent illustration of this situation. Premilinary findings of the CTP apparently showed that the treatment group was possessed with a lower rate of parole revocation than the control group—despite the finding that the experimentals seemed to commit more serious offenses. What Lerman discovered was that the parole officers having a CTP caseload were reluctant to revoke the parole status of their clients, thus producing an artificially lower revocation rate. In fact, the offense rates of the two groups were quite similar. Lerman and other researchers have provided ample evidence that standard measures of recidivism are often heavily dependent upon the law enforcement policies of the jurisdiction under study.

Research on police by Skolnick (1966) illustrated how detectives could manufacture higher rates of burglary or artificially improve their clearance rates by encouraging alleged offenders to take credit for many unsolved crimes in exchange for police requests for judicial leniency. Cicourel (1968) and Emerson (1969) examined the definitional processes employed by juvenile court staff to produce rates of delinquency. In *Society of Captives,* Gresham Sykes (1958) analyzed the subtle co-optative process leading to guards' systematic under-reporting of prison rule violations. Moreover, there exists a rich tradition of research on criminal justice agencies concerning patterns of discretionary deci-sion-making that bears directly on the validity of outcome measures for criminal and delinquency programs. Despite this body of research knowledge, few evalua-tions adequately examine the organizational factors that transform criminal justice events into official statistics. It is not suggested that each evaluation must contain a comprehensive analysis of discretionary behavior within criminal agencies. However, it seems reasonable to expect evaluation researchers to examine policies, procedures, and practices that govern the "production" of the key impact measures of their programs.

Time-series impact designs provide another example of how process data clarify the measuring of impact data. For example, suppose juvenile arrest rates in one jurisdiction change dramatically prior to the beginning of a delinquency prevention program. These statistics later might be employed to measure pro-gram impact. The process evaluation must examine the factors leading to this apparent decline in the juvenile arrest rate. Dramatic changes in official statistics can signal changing laws and/or enforcement policies rather than program impact.

Concern over the validity of outcome measures is not limited to official statistics. Evaluation researchers are well aware of "experimenter effects" that may contaminate measures of impact. Process studies can assist the prudent researcher to understand the limitations of standardized instruments. Qualitative data describing the social situations of surveys, questionnaires, and other mea-surement techniques can facilitate interpretation of these data. Of central interest are data revealing the *meaning* of the instrument to the subject as well as conditions of the administration. Likewise, process data should be collected about the implementation of the design of impact studies. Austin (1977) discovered project staff trying to "fix" the random assignment of clients into an adult diversion program. Lerman (1970) describes how program dropouts are removed from impact measures of some private correctional programs. These examples suggest that researchers must exercise close scrutiny on all aspects of their designs, especially those designs involving client assignment to different experimental groups. While there exist several statistical approaches to assess the validity and reliability of measurement techniques, statistical approaches do not permit substantive interpretations of the many factors supporting or diminishing the strength of measurements of program outcomes.

IV. TOWARD AN ANALYTIC MODEL OF PROCESS EVALUATION

Most researchers would agree that the sorts of data discussed above can enhance program evaluations in the crime and delinquency field. Yet the problem remains—how to sort out from among the virtually infinite data on a program, the most heuristic and policy-relevant information. Moreover, facts do not speak for themselves. Process evaluation requires a conceptual framework to be applied to data.

A. Program Models

One approach to organizing process data is borrowed from the field of operations research. Programs are described in terms of models that specify all relevant variables. The model specifies how the program is supposed to operate in terms of inputs, intervening processes, and expected outcomes. Ideally, the model indicates the most efficient points of data collected for testing the model. Once the program model is fully elaborated, the process researcher proceeds to test the several predicted relationships against available data.

In some cases, fairly detailed program models can be used to estimate the probable impact of altering various aspects of the program. For example, a model depicting the factors contributing to the size of prison populations might include variables such as arrest rates, proportion of convictions, and the distribution of sentencing alternatives. Other factors, such as parole board policies and transfers between penal and mental health facilities, might be incorporated. The actual structure of the model is derived from previous empirical data as well as an underlying theory of how the process actually works. If sufficient data can be gathered to validate the model, the analysis can examine the potential impact of various policy alternatives, such as abolishing parole, expanding community-based diversion programs, or shortening the average length of incarceration for convicted felons.

Program models are attractive to administrators and researchers because they spell out most of the crucial operational factors. Such models focus the process research on the testing of a limited set of hypothesized relationships. Potentially, the program model can assist in forecasting program outcome. Unfortunately, the modeling approach requires a great deal of prior information about how the program functions. Few crime and delinquency programs can be fully described as models. The theoretical and practical "state of the art" frequently precludes employing the modeling approach. All relevant variables are not known, nor is it often possible to specify (in advance) the direction of relationships between inputs, intervening variables, and outputs. Programs most amenable to the modeling approach are generally well systematized, articulated both theoretically and procedurally, *and these programs have been the subject of extensive prior research that helped adumbrate the program model.*

Even where accurate models can be conceptualized, testing the model may depend upon data sources that are difficult to tap. For instance, criminal justice researchers are well aware of the practical dilemmas of trying to follow a single case through the justice process. These kinds of client-flow data are crucial for many program models. Other models may depend upon measuring changes in intrapsychic processes (e.g., developing more positive self-esteem among adjudicated delinquents) that may prove difficult to measure with available techniques. Further, research employing program models must be wary not to overlook informal and implicit processes that exist alongside formal program structures. Latent, as opposed to manifest, program goals and structures must be included in the model, where these are known and capable of schematic description. Despite these cautions, the application of modeling techniques to crime and delinquency programs represents a desirable goal for evaluative researchers. It is suggested that formative evaluations be employed both in the development and in the preliminary testing of modeling techniques.

B. Defining Program Elements

For the vast majority of crime and delinquency programs, process evaluations require a more generic analytic approach to structure research plans and to organize data collection. The national assessment of delinquency prevention programs (Walker et al., 1976), mentioned earlier, provides a useful starting point for interpreting process data. Data collection is designed around the paradigm of elements of program development. The following represent the five components of this analytic approach:

- Context: the set of conditions and assumptions which operationally and conceptually define the distinctive features of the program. Included are the theoretical assumptions guiding service programs as well as physical, financial, historical, and organizational characteristics of the program.

- Identification: the combination of techniques, procedures, and criteria employed to define, select, and admit clients to various decision alternatives within the program.

- Intervention: the full range of activities and services provided by the program toward meeting its objectives.

- Goals: the criteria for determining how effective the program was in meeting its objectives. This element includes data on the measurable outcomes of program activities, as well as decision-making processes employed by staff to improve the program's effectiveness and efficiency.

- Linkages: those formal and informal conditions and relationships that may hinder or support program operations. Linkages may include relations with external agencies or organizations, or may involve issues of coordination within programs. Another aspect of this program element consists of environmental factors (e.g., the sociopolitical environment) influencing program outcomes.

C. A Hypothetical Analysis

Consider how this analytic framework might be employed to evaluate a new method of inmate classification within a jail. For purposes of explication, the new program will be presented in radically simplified terms. Suppose the county jail wishes to institute a new classification system based upon a "just deserts" model—i.e., focusing solely on the characteristics of the offense rather than on the attributes of the offender. Staff at the jail believe that the new system will reduce violence within the jail by assigning inmates to different types of custody by a "fair and open" criterion, thus reducing inmate anxieties and frustrations with seemingly arbitrary classification decisions.

Context. The research would explore with staff the full underlying assumptions of the new program. Where feasible, key policy statements would be collected and analyzed. Process research would also examine the stimuli for bringing the program into existence and document the chronology of program development. Also important would be information about the size of the inmate-staff ratio and past history of violence within the jail. Previous studies or investigations might provide insights into program context. The process research would collect (or construct) an organizational chart of the jail, detailing levels of personnel and chains of command necessary to implement the new classification program.

Identification. The process research would fully describe the formal procedures, data collection methods and classification decision rules. But the research would also examine (by tapping the divergent perspectives of inmates, staff, administrators, and outside agencies, and by direct observation of classification decision ceremonies) whether the system is operating as intended. For example, while the written plan might call for regular reviews of classification decisions, reclassification may, in fact, never take place. Similarly, the plan might envision using only data about prior offenses, but classification officers might continue to make estimates of "probable adjustment" within the jail. Research would pinpoint formal and informal critical decision makers, decision points, and the nature and extent of classification data that are collected and those which are actually employed to make decisions.

Intervention. The range and quality of custody and program assignments would be examined to determine if differential classification decisions actually produce the desired differential care of inmates. Perhaps jail overcrowding or special security problems render classification decisions irrelevant, since these decisions do not reflect housing and program assignments actually available within the jail. Similarly, observations of the various living conditions in custody might suggest insufficient differences in the quality of care afforded inmates. Since the program design assumes that fairer classification decisions will be perceived by inmates, the manner in which different classification levels are perceived by inmates constitutes a key aspect of the process research.

Linkages. Process research would identify the key relationships between agencies or units within the same organization. One question might involve the degree of support for or resistance to the new classification system by other jail personnel or departments. Similarly, one would want to gauge the reactions of external criminal justice agencies playing some role in the classification process. For example, classification often depends upon accurate and timely crime data from police agencies. The cooperation of prosecutors and public defenders would seem important to the successful implementation of the classification system. Judicial endorsement of the new classification procedures is critical, because courts have increasingly exercised their authority, reviewing the merits of jail classification methods. Another important linkage might include public officials or local media representatives. These groups can build public support for a new program as well as promote greater awareness of the aims of the new effort.

The exploration of linkages might begin with a series of interviews with all key actors who helped develop the new program. Subsequent interviews would be conducted with persons whose jobs place them in direct contact with the jail classification process. The interview might compare staff perceptions of the goals and methods of the new classification system with the plans set forth by program planners.

The technique of observing the classification process can pinpoint important linkage issues that might not be immediately obvious to the classification staff. For example, the new classification procedures might produce inadequate data for jail, medical, and social service staff. This might negatively affect these services, causing tension within the jail. Similarly, classification decisions made during certain times might place difficult information demands on law enforcement and court agencies. Observational research can often trigger tentative insights leading the researcher to conduct further interviews or obtain additional statistical data. In general, the process evaluator examines both supportive and constraining linkages as they affect the new classification system.

Goals. The new system is designed to reduce violence within the jail and reduce inmate and staff hostilities. Are these goals fully understood by all relevant parties? Does the jail possess sufficient data collection to determine if these goals are being accomplished? Do classification decision makers receive feedback about the results of their decisions?

These are some of the areas that the process evaluation would explore. Of central importance is whether the goals of the new classification system are clearly formulated and capable of objective assessment. Related to this concern is the question of whether there exists a consensus about the goals. Various participants in a program may hold radically different objectives that are often in conflict. The process researcher should attempt to determine if *goals are displaced*—i.e., if the stated goals are replaced by implicit objectives. For example, staff may support the new classification procedure because it reduces the amount of time to complete classification decisions. Jail officials might place high value on the new program if it produces large grant funds to subsidize their limited operational budgets. In short, a host of "unofficial goals" may take on increased significance as the new system is implemented. Process research must pay close attention to informal goals and informal organizational structures that often exert substantial influence. Special attention should be focused upon how human social processes generate the "data" used to assess program success or failure. As mentioned earlier, there may exist informal norms and values that restrict the reporting of violent incidents within the jail, thereby biasing the assessment of program impact. Likewise, other factors, such as increased levels of custody or gang conflict, may affect the reported rates of jail violence quite independent of the new classification program.

D. Internal Consistency of Program Elements

The paradigm of program elements enables the researcher to examine empirical regularities systematically as the basis for theory-building. For example, one can examine the program elements to determine whether the program possesses internal consistency. Ideally, the program elements ought to be logically related. For instance, client identification methods should relate to the types of services (intervention) offered. Issues of linkages should closely relate to contextual issues as well as program operations. Not infrequently, evaluators find programs in which the program elements are, at best, tenuously connected.

A program may be premised upon one set of policy assumptions but contain intervention methods which imply a different set of policy assumptions. For example, program staff may believe that delinquency is caused by the harm generated by social institutions. Their theory of prevention requires that these negative *institutional practices* be altered. But the actual intervention might only consist of counseling and educational programs aimed at helping *individuals* to cope with *psychological problems*. Incongruencies among program elements should alert the researchers to examine the reasons these apparent contradictions exist. Very often one finds sociopolitical or organizational constraints explaining the disconnections between program elements. Staff may have attempted to implement institutional change strategies, but abandoned them due to lack of experience or resources. The individually oriented services may have emerged because they were easier to implement or because they were requested by the sponsoring agency. More important, the collapse of the theory in practice signals that impact measures are not assessing the intended program.

Process evaluations can point out to program planners apparent lapses of internal consistency and thus permit program modifications at early stages of program development. Moreover, the research can monitor the degree of internal program consistency at various points in program operation. It is important to note that internally consistent programs provide better opportunities for evaluative research to test programmatic strategies, but the most "logical" program can fail because fundamental program assumptions are incorrect. Programs whose program elements appear totally incongruent may yet be responding to environmental conditions or client needs. In this later case the program's theory has not caught up with its praxis.

E. Changes Over Time in Program Elements

Another mode of analysis consists of tracking changes within and between program elements over time. For example, the researcher would make periodic assessments of intervention of identification strategies throughout the life of the program. Observed changes over time become the basis of further theory development. The analyst would attempt to explain why a significant change in a program element occurred at a particular time. Further, one may wish to examine how two or more program elements covary at several points during the program. Table 8.1 (see p. 232) portrays how a process analysis might sort observations of changing program elements over time. The symbols within the table (e.g., L_3) refer to periodic descriptions of the program with respect to that program element. While these descriptions might consist of nominal level data, under some circumstances these aspects of programs might be amenable to scaling. Table 8.1 suggests an analogy to analysis of variance. Using this analogy, program variation (change in program elements) is partitioned into two components:

(1) Within variation: variation among different program elements at the same point in time—i.e., internal consistency.

(2) Between variation: variation among the same program elements across time—i.e., changing program content.

Indeed, one might want to examine interaction effects of particular moments in a program's existence and specific changes in aspects of that program.

Process researchers might further enhance (or complicate) the analysis by replacing the concept of program chronology (in terms of months or weeks since commencement) with a notion of stages of program development. For example, a program might go through the stages of planning, implementation, operations and closure (or transition). Program stages are determined by ascertaining the dominant *kind of problem* that program staff are attempting to solve (see Table 8.2, p. 233).

Analysis of stages of program development permits one to study programs that evolve at different paces as well as programs that skip stages or even go back to prior stages. Taken together with the earlier model of program elements, the concept of program stages provides a more systematic approach to process evaluation. Actual refinement of the process-analytic model requires sufficient field testing to examine potential contributions to the theory of program development. Ideally, this framework for process evaluation permits a bridge to the rich social science literature on organizational analysis and systems theory.

V. METHODS OF PROCESS DATA COLLECTION

Process evaluations employ *both* quantitative and qualitative methods of data collection. Process evaluations generally depend upon extensive review of program documents, numerous in-depth interviews with program participants, and sustained observation of program operations. Qualitative methods often predominate, because the essential task of the research is exploratory. Moreover, the aim of process evaluation is to approximate a naturalistic appreciation of the program and suggest, in turn, methods for getting as close to the social action as possible.

To move from the program elements to data collection procedures, each of the five program elements is transformed into a limited set of research questions. These research questions provide the basis for deriving practical measurement techniques. For instance, for a delinquency prevention program, identification could be focused into two research questions:

(1) What are the recruitment methods used to attract youth into prevention projects?

(2) What screening methods are employed in processing youth for services?

TABLE 8.1

Program Elements	Periodic Description of the Program		
	t_1	t_2	$t_3 \ldots t_n$
Context (C)	C_1	C_2	$C_3 \ldots C_n$
Identification (I)	I_1	I_2	$I_3 \ldots I_n$
Intervention (S)	S_1	S_2	$S_3 \ldots S_n$
Linkages (L)	L_1	L_2	$L_3 \ldots L_n$
Goals (G)	G_1	G_2	$G_3 \ldots G_n$

Specific data collection instruments, including interviews, observation, and review of program records, are designed to answer the research questions. Similarly, the results of identification procedures are captured by the question, "What are the numbers and types of youth utilizing project services?" The process evaluation might collect client participation records yielding quantitative data, and secure qualitative data through observations and interviews with youth and community residents. Multiple measures are warranted because of the serious limitations of readily available criminal justice data sources discussed earlier in this chapter.

Once the preliminary research questions are formulated, the process evaluator identifies data needs, as well as the sources, methods, and timing of data collection. Some researchers argue that early process evaluations should remain relatively open-ended to avoid an artificial theoretical structure that might bias subsequent data collection. However, given the admittedly ubiquitous nature of process evaluation, the researcher should strive to limit the inquiry to avoid the dilemma of amassing mountains of "fascinating data" that defy coherent analysis. The research questions force the analyst to converge data collection on the essential components of the program—the program elements.

It is beyond the limits of this chapter to detail the particular methodological issues concerning the application of qualitative methods to program evaluations. While there exist several excellent texts on qualitative methods (e.g., Schatzman and Strauss, 1973), the systematic application of these methods to crime and delinquency program evaluations is relatively novel (Ball, 1975).

Qualitative methods are difficult to employ with sustained levels of research quality. Interviewing and observational techniques are neither intuitive to most researchers, nor capable of easy transmission. The problem is further exacerbated by the lack of emphasis on qualitative methods in the professional training curricula of evaluation researchers.

Expanded attention to qualitative methods applied to program evaluation probably depends upon the increased utilization of process models in program

TABLE 8.2

Stage of Program Development	Dominant Problem To Be Solved
Planning-conceptualization	Determining what the program is to accomplish, methods for accomplishment, and those whose cooperation will be required.
Implementation-resistance, accomodation	Fitting the program's plans into the real world of people, resources, and organizations.
Operations-transformation	Determining if the programs are working as planned, what modifications are needed, and what results can be expected.
Closure (transition)-termination	Assessing the impact or results of the program and making provisions for program continuation, termination, or transition into another form.

evaluations. Much more knowledge is required about conducting research within crime and delinquency programs, particularly when the methods employed demand intensive scrutiny of all aspects of these programs. Criminal justice personnel, like other professionals, may find research incursions into their "private" worlds disquieting and threatening. Overcoming agency fears and resistance may prove the most serious challenge to process research on crime and delinquency programs.

VI. IMPROVING PROGRAMS THROUGH PROCESS EVALUATIONS

Successful collaborations of research and action staff can produce advances in both *knowledge* and *practice*. Within this framework, the utility of process evaluation can be fully actualized. But both researchers and program staff need to understand clearly the purposes, as well as the limits, of process studies. For example, process evaluations possess only limited utility for securing additional funding. Often the data of process studies reveal that programs are straying from initial designs or that program elements lack consistency. The dialectical process of program and research staff, commonly referred to in the evaluative literature as *feedback,* demands an intellectual confrontation with contradictions or anomalies within the program under study. Commitment to improving the program dictates a serious focus on program failures and areas of needed change. Positive accomplishments should not be minimized or discounted—on the contrary, program strengths may prove clues to solving programmatic deficiencies.

Program and research staff should establish well-defined mechanisms for applying process data to the ongoing planning and development of the program. Without concrete procedures for employing feedback, process studies become merely program autopsies. While the research efforts may contribute positively to theory and practice, the actual testing of process analysis requires the application of these data toward modifying ongoing programs.

The dialectic of program and research is fraught with difficulties. Neither evaluators nor action staff are especially knowledgeable about each other's craft. Initial encounters between the two groups are often filled with suspicion, misunderstanding, and a large dose of paranoia. Sometimes this situation of conflict is structurally defined when the evaluator is under contract to the funders rather than to the program staff; or when the evaluation is employed as an afterthought and not integrated into early program-planning. Another peril of process evaluations involves pressures to provide project-monitoring data under which researchers unintentionally become sources of organizational intelligence for program administrators. Process research often collects data that is subject to abuse. The ethical line separating useful feedback from program-spying is tenuous and ambiguous. Staff may express legitimate concerns about the need to use the confidential data to improve program performance. Process researchers may learn of interpersonal jealousies, sexual peccadilloes, and attempts to subvert program efforts. Some of these data may be relevant to process analysis, but, in general, the researcher must exercise considerable tact and not pass along gossip.

Besides protecting the confidentiality of sources and not engaging in gossip-mongering, researchers must also confront program situations comprised of competing interest groups. Various factions within an agency (or a community) will try to use evaluation data to advance their objectives. It is easy for researchers to be drawn unwittingly into already existing conflicts that may compromise the objectivity of the study. Within a highly politicized research situation, the researcher must understand that there are "sides" and that absolute value-neutrality is illusory. Sociologist Howard Becker (1967) challenged researchers to answer the question, "Who's side are we on?" His provocative paper has stimulated varied responses. The important point for process researchers is to know that there *are* sides and to clarify their own biases rather than deny the essentially political character of the research.

The promise of process evaluation is to provide policy-relevant data and to assist the implementation of constructive reforms in the crime and delinquency field. It remains unclear whether this promise can be fulfilled. Process evaluation awaits broader application as well as extensive conceptual and technical development. Further, the ethical and pragmatic problems of utilizing process data must be reexamined. In the balance, the investment in developing the theory and practice of process evaluation seems justified, given the limited knowledge we have gained through alternative evaluation approaches.

NOTES

1. See Scriven (1972) or Rutman (1977).

2. This constant pattern of program failure also characterizes wide ranges of social service areas, including job training, mental health services, and compensatory education (Weiss, 1972a; Freeman, 1977).

3. Major texts on evaluation research (e.g., Weiss, 1972b; Caro, 1971; Rutman, 1977; Suchman, 1967) provide only passing reference to process methods of evaluation, although these sources provide excellent pleas for the need to conduct process studies.

4. These terms come from Abraham Kaplan (1964).

REFERENCES

Austin, J. (1977) "From Theory to Social Policy: Implementing Diversion within the Criminal Justice System." (unpublished)

Ball, R. A. (1975) "Qualitative Evaluation of Criminal Justice Programs," pp. 97-112 in E. Viano, Criminal Justice Research. Lexington, MA: D. C. Heath.

Becker, H. S. (1967) "Whose Side Are We On?" Social Problems 14: 239-247.

Cardarelli, A. P. (1977) "Delinquency Prevention in the U.S.: A Summary of Findings and Implications for Social Policy." (unpublished)

Caro, F. G. [ed.] (1971) Readings in Evaluation Research. New York: Russell Sage.

Cicourel, A. (1968) The Social Organization of Juvenile Justice. New York: John Wiley.

Emerson, R. M. (1969) Judging Delinquents. Chicago: AVC.

Freeman, H. E. (1977) "The Present State of Evaluation Research," pp. 71-100 in M. Guttentag [ed.] Evaluation Studies Review Annual, Volume 2. Beverly Hills, CA: Sage Publications.

Freeman, H. E. and I. N. Bernstein (1975) "Evaluation Research and Publication Policies." pp. 9-25 in S. S. Nagel (ed.) Policy Studies and the Social Sciences. Lexington, MA: D. C. Heath.

Geis, G. (1975) "Program Descriptions in Criminal Justice Evaluations," pp. 87-96 in E. Viano (ed.) Criminal Justice Research. Lexington, MA: D. C. Heath.

Glaser, B. and A. Strauss (1976) The Discovery of Grounded Theory. Chicago: AVC.

Hudson, J. (1977) "Problem of Measurement in Criminal Justice," pp. 73-100 in L. Rutman (ed.) Evaluation Research Methods. Beverly Hills, CA: Sage Publications.

Kaplan, A. (1964) The Conduct of Inquiry. New York: ITT.

Lemert, E. (1970) Social Action and Legal Change. Chicago: AVC.

Lerman, P. [ed.] (1970) Delinquency and Social Policy. New York: Praeger.

Martinson, R. (1974) "What Works? Questions and Answers About Prison Reform." *Public Interest* (June): 22-25.

Newton, A. (1978) "Prevention of Crime and Delinquency." *Criminal Justice Abstracts* (June): 245-266.

Nimmer, R. T. (1978) *The Nature of System Change.* Chicago: American Bar Foundation.

Rossi, P. H. and S. R. Wright (1977) "Evaluation Research: An Assessment of Theory, Practice and Politics." *Evaluation Quarterly* 1: 5-52.

Rutman, L. (1977) *Evaluation and Research Methods.* Beverly Hills, CA: Sage Publications.

Schatzman, L. and A. Strauss (1973) *Field Research.* Englewood Cliffs, NJ: Prentice-Hall.

Scriven, M. (1972) "The Methodology of Evaluation," pp. 123-136 in C. H. Weiss (ed.) *Evaluating Action Programs.* Boston: Allyn & Bacon.

Skolnick, J. (1966) *Justice Without Trial.* New York: John Wiley.

Suchman, E. A. (1969) "Evaluating Educational Programs." *The Urban Review* 3: 16.

Suchman, E. A. (1967) *Evaluation Research.* New York: Russell Sage.

Sykes, G. (1958) *Society of Captives.* Princeton, NJ: Princeton University Press.

Walker, J. P., A. P. Cardarelli, and D. L. Billingsley (1976) *Delinquency Prevention in the USA: Synthesis and Assessment of Strategies.* Washington, DC: Office of Juvenile Justice and Delinquency Prevention.

Weiss, C. [ed.] (1972a) *Evaluating Action Programs.* Boston: Allyn & Bacon.

——— (1972b) *Evaluation Research.* Englewood Cliffs, NJ: Prentice-Hall.

Wright, W. E. and M. C. Dixon (1977) "Community Prevention and Treatment of Juvenile Delinquency: A Review of Evaluation Studies." *Journal of Research in Crime and Delinquency* 14, 11: 35-62.

9

Planning Models for Analytical Evaluation

Alfred Blumstein

I. THE TWO FACES OF EVALUATION

Most conceptions of evaluation invoke the experimental paradigm whereby the effects of some kind of treatment are compared to another treatment or control in an experimental—or, more often, a quasi-experimental—design. The prospect for widespread experimental evaluations has generated a great amount of wishful thinking, hope, and faith in the potential of evaluations to generate "optimal" programs through what one advocate has called an "experimental society." Indeed, pursuit of that ideal over the past decade has motivated a considerable amount of the effort in the criminal justice system, and in social programs more generally.

The consequence of these efforts has been a much better realization of the great difficulty—if not the futility—in undertaking rigorous experimentation in all but the most exceptional circumstances. It is extremely difficult to maintain stability in the treatment or the control in an operational setting, and this difficulty increases when the technology used as the "treatment" is narrowly defined, which it must be for the results of the evaluation to be generalizable and transferable. It is difficult to create and maintain equivalent control groups, and this difficulty increases as the treatment shows its effectiveness. These and other problems with the experimental paradigm have led to a much more realistic perspective on what can be attained through such evaluations.

Evaluation can also be pursued through an analytical rather than through an experimental paradigm. That approach involves the use of an abstract model of the system being evaluated. The model typically is represented as a system of equations with parameters reflecting the relevant exogeneous uncontrollable variables. Other parameters reflect key aspects of alternative treatments or programs to be evaluated. Such an approach has the obvious advantage of generating the evaluation results quickly and cheaply; a parametric change is accomplished simply by rerunning a set of calculations through some minor manipulations at a computer terminal. Thus, a large number of such combinations can be pursued even before the actual program is implemented. The limitation of this approach derives from the inevitably limited validity of the analytical model as an approximation to the real system being studied. Any such model incorporates only those parameters the analyst chooses explicitly to include, and in the specific functional form he or she creates. These burdens do not fall on the experimenter, since the real system examined through the experimental paradigm provides all the relevant parameters, whether the evaluator thinks of them or not. This represents both a benefit (since it makes the results a much better approximation to reality), and a problem (since it requires complex statistical analysis to sort out the effects of individual parameters and their changes).

Thus, this analytical perspective on evaluation is most useful in evaluating those programs where the basic underlying theory is best developed, and it is weakest where the many complicating features associated with the real world and its operation are most salient. Ultimately, it is best used in concert with the experimental paradigm in a mutually supportive way. Experimentation should be used for initial exploration and for model development as well as for final validity checking. Analytical models should be used for exploration of many combinations of alternatives, partly to focus on and to design the critical experiments of greatest interest, so that the resources committed to experimental evaluation are best applied.

The discussion in this chapter focuses first on an overall description of the planning process which reflects the joint involvement of the experimental and the analytical evaluations, and then focuses on a particular model for analytical evaluation in the criminal justice system, JUSSIM I for downstream flow and JUSSIM II for augmentation with recidivist feedback. The chapter goes on to discuss some issues in implementing that model, and then some of its possible future extensions.

II. THE PLANNING PROCESS

Planning is, first of all, an analytical process in which an organization attempts systematically to make rational choices for the future. The emphasis is on the process by which those choices are made, rather than on the choices themselves. In this case the choices are "rational" in the sense that they address the objectives of the criminal justice system, as opposed to other objectives that may well influence behavior in the criminal justice system (for example, the desire of political figures to be reelected or the desire of civil servants to preserve their jobs). Even though these objectives are real (and are certainly rational from the perspective of the people who are concerned with them), rational planning in the criminal justice system involves concern for questions like crime reduction, enhancement of liberty, and reduction of the total social cost of crime control.

The second principal characteristic of the planning process is the orientation toward the future—toward making choices now for implementation in a future, and therefore uncertain, world. The planning process must face up to that uncertainty. In the criminal justice field, such uncertainty derives partly from the inability to predict the variety of social and political changes that will influence behavior within the criminal justice system, and partly from the effect of the criminal justice system's own influence on criminal behavior. Furthermore, that crime and the actions of the criminal justice system are mutually adaptive results in each influencing the other in ways that are only minimally predictable, while general changes in the political and socioeconomic climate will affect both crime and the criminal justice system.

The uncertainty does not preclude the use of analytical techniques and techniques of statistical estimation any more than the uncertainty about the roll of a pair of dice precludes the experienced gambler as well as the statistician from being able to project that the roll of a "7" is six times more likely to occur than the roll of a "12," even though the next roll might well be a "12." Because the processes in the criminal justice system, however, are far more complex, no analyst can make anything like comparable projections, and therefore considerable judgment must be required in obtaining and using any such projections.

The third principal emphasis in the planning process is on the need to make *choices,* an operation which involves a combination of forecasting, prediction of impact, and attribution of the cost benefits of a given action. Thus, the planning process inherently involves the value considerations of the community. It would be even more useful, however, if that valuation process were applied to factual information about the consequences of alternative courses of action once those consequences are illuminated.

Such a planning process of "making rational choices for the future" involves the following steps:

(1) describing the current system;
(2) projecting the future environment;
(3) developing alternatives among which to choose;
(4) analyzing the impact of the alternatives ("preevaluation");
(5) allocating resources to the choices and implementing them;
(6) evaluating the impact ("postevaluation"); and
(7) repeating the process on a regular and continuing basis.

The need for these seven steps is reasonably logical. First, in order to consider sensibly any revisions or changes in the current system, it is necessary to have some characterization of it. It is necessary to know what the present crime situation is, how the current criminal justice system works, what resources are applied, where and how they are applied, and how the budgets are distributed over the parts of the criminal justice system and over the various crime types.

Because the planning process is concerned about the future, the next logical step would be to project the description of the current system to the future. This involves forecasting anticipated crime rates as well as projecting the future behavior of the criminal justice system. The projection of crime rates might be undertaken by a variety of means, including simply assuming that current crime rates would persist into the future, extrapolating the last few years of data, using more sophisticated time-series analysis techniques, or using more sophisticated models involving the crime rates per demographic group (e.g., age, race, sex combinations) and projecting the demographic mix. Each of these methods has its virtues, the simpler ones being the easier to understand and to implement, the more elaborate ones imposing a considerably greater demand for data and for computational power, although sometimes providing considerably greater predictive power in return.

For the features of the criminal justice system other than crime rates and future behavior of the system itself, it would be desirable to find parameters that are reasonably stable over time. Thus, for example, the number of cases processed will vary from year to year, and hence the number of guilty or innocent dispositions will vary accordingly. In many settings, however, the proportion found guilty or innocent may well be far more stable than the total costs and workloads (which may depend much more on total number of units processed). Here again, the easiest projection would be to assume that next year's branching ratios, costs, workloads, and the like are the same as this year's. If a longer time series on these parameters were available, then one might project that time series in ways similar to the projection of crimes. In other cases, however, the introduction of new programs or new court decisions or new legislation will force a qualitative change in some of those parameters, and that qualitative change must be taken into account in the planning process. In some cases there may be empirical evidence to indicate how a new program affects the value of a system parameter (e.g., experience in other jurisdictions or evaluative reports). In other cases, the best estimate is simply some judgmental guess.

Since the planning process involves choices, one must first define alternatives among which to choose. The development of such alternatives is inherently a creative process whereby new ways of doing things are proposed by staff members of the existing agencies (although they often seem to have a compulsion to continue doing things as they have been); or by staff from the planning agencies, through scanning innovations that have been used successfully in other jurisdictions; or by other means as diverse as citizens' suggestions, brainstorming sessions, and so on.

The choice among these alternatives must be made before they are implemented in the local jurisdictions, and therefore a "preevaluation" process must be undertaken. In that preevaluation, a judgmental process is again called for, but that judgmental process can be enhanced significantly by the use of appropriate analytical tools. The next section contains the discussion of one such tool, the JUSSIM model, which can aid significantly in assessing the impact of a particular change (e.g., a pretrial diversion program) on different parts of the system. Because this preevaluation stage occurs prior to implementation, it is inherently an analytical or abstract process, and so can better employ some form of mathematical "model" that represents abstractly the behavior of the criminal justice system, rather than an experiment imposed on the operating criminal justice system. The preevaluation process provides an initial assessment of the impact of a change, both in the part of the criminal justice system to which it is applied and in other parts of the system. Such an assessment should include not only the "downstream" parts (e.g., the effect of a change in police arrest practice on court workloads), but also the feedback or recidivist effects. Normally, once a planning agency has made such an impact assessment, it then allocates resources to new programs—taking into account the estimate of these impacts and weighing impacts along with the more direct costs and benefits associated with alternative choices.

Having made the choice and implemented it on at least a pilot basis, or possibly throughout a jurisdiction, the planning process can then undertake an experimental "postevaluation" of its impact. This evaluation is modeled on the classic random, controlled experiment. But such experiments in the criminal justice system are limited by the difficulty of their being truly controlled, by the inevitable selection effects that creep into the experiment, and by the multiplicity of influences that prevail in a social setting—all of which influence crime rates or other measures of effectiveness. Despite these problems, the evaluative information represents an important part of the planning process and should be fed back into improvement of all the previous stages for the next planning cycle.

III. A MODEL FOR THE EVALUATION OF
DOWNSTREAM IMPACTS (JUSSIM I)

As described above, a central part of the planning process is the analysis of the impact of alternative choices, and, as suggested, this can best be accomplished with some form of model prior to implementation. The general method whereby this process occurs is reflected in Figure 9.1. A proposed system change

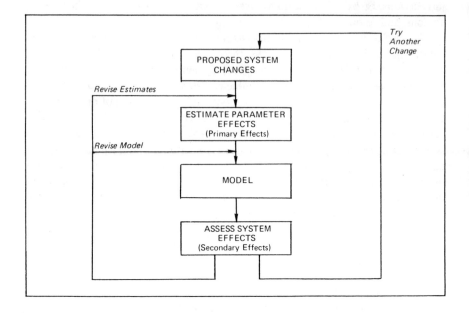

Figure 9.1: General Process of Impact Analysis

is considered; it is translated into estimates of parameter effects which are then put through some kind of model (which may be a mathematical model or some judgmental process) to generate estimates of the system effects or "secondary effects" resulting from that change. After such a calculation and after reviewing those system effects, a user might conclude that the initial parameter estimates were inappropriate, and this reconsideration might result in estimation of different parameter values; or the user might conclude that the model does not adequately reflect some of the complexities he or she is certain do occur, and so may well change the model. After several cycles through this process, the user may be satisfied with the estimate of those system effects and go through the same process for another system change.

This is a totally general characterization of any analysis of a proposed system change. The critical aspect, however, is the use of a model that provides the basis for translating a programmatic change in the criminal justice system to an estimate of the impact of that change on performance measures of the system. In a sense, the model may be viewed as a "black box" in which the parameter estimates are the knobs (reflecting measures like arrest policy, punishment policy, resource allocation, and so on) and the system effects are the dials (representing measures of output effectiveness such as crime rate and costs). This conceptual "black-box" simulation of the criminal justice system enables the planner to twist the knobs, note the dial readings that result, and then to use that experience to choose the next knob settings to explore.

The crucial stage of this process is the formulation and use of the model. One model that has been used in a number of jurisdictions is the Justice System Interactive Model (JUSSIM). The model uses a computer in an "interactive" mode, with a user sitting at a terminal, calling a stored data base characterizing the user's criminal justice system, and interacting in a conversational way with the computer program, without needing special technical training or computer programming skills, since the entire process goes on in plain English.

A. Single-Stage Analysis

The operation of the JUSSIM model can best be explained by examination of a single stage in the flow diagram of cases moving through a criminal justice system. Consider, for example, the jury trial stage for a single crime type (say, robbery). Let us assume for the moment that 100 robbery cases come to the jury trial stage, a number calculated based on flows from the earlier stages.

As shown in Figure 9.2, there are two output flow paths from the jury trial: "acquittal" and "guilty." If the branching ratios from jury trial to these two paths are .4 (probability of acquittal) and .6 (probability of conviction), then the jury trial stage feeds 60 offenders to the sentencing stage (which also receives offenders coming from guilty plea and bench trial). This same branching and collection process at the earlier stages provided the basis for calculating the 100 cases coming to jury trial. In this simple computation, the branching ratios (the probabilities of conviction and acquittal) are required input data. All input data are shown circled in Figure 9.2.

We are now interested in calculating the workloads, costs, and resource requirements associated with the two principal resources used to process cases at jury trial: judges and prosecutors. Let us assume that the average *unit workload* for judges in robbery jury trials is 6 hours, and that the prosecutor (with more preparation time) must spend an average of 20 hours per case. These numbers also are necessary input data, and so are also circled.

Focusing on the *judges* now, their *workload* in handling robbery jury trials, at 6 hours per case, for 100 cases, is then 600 judge-hours. If a judgeship-hour (including support staff and facilities) costs $100 (also an input datum), then the cost of the 600 judge-hours is $60,000. If a judge is available 1,000 hours per year for processing cases, then the *resource requirement* is the workload (600 judge-hours) divided by this *annual availability,* or 0.6 of a full-time judge is required to process robbery jury trials. Similar computations are made for *prosecutors,* and these are also shown in Figure 9.2.

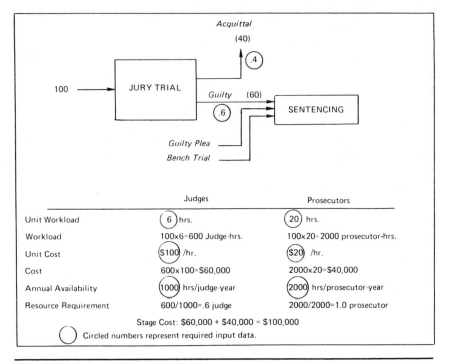

Figure 9.2: An Illustrative JUSSIM Stage: Robbery Jury Trials

The robbery jury trial cost, then, is the sum of the resource costs associated with that stage, $60,000 for judges and $40,000 for prosecutors, for a total of $100,000. Similarly, the *court costs* associated with *robbery* can be computed as the sum of the resource costs for all stages in the court system. Then, the *total court costs* would simply be the sum of those costs for all the various types of crime.

B. Basic Operation of the Model

The operation of the JUSSIM model begins with a "base case" reflecting the current operation of the system. All the data on the base case parameters must be collected and stored. The user of JUSSIM—the criminal justice system planner—then creates a "test case" by making changes in any of the base-case parameters at the computer terminal. The program then reports the changes in flows, costs, workloads, and resource requirements resulting from the changes introduced. The designer thus uses the model as a very flexible design tool by making contemplated changes, rapidly obtaining an assessment of the effects of those changes, and then trying another change suggested by reconsideration of the previous try. If the designer does not like the implications of a proposed change, he or she can reject it immediately and try another.

Operating the model to assess the consequences of a system change, a user necessarily has to make assumptions about the detailed primary consequences of the change as they are reflected in changes in the system's parameters. For those changes that initially appear desirable to make, the user may want to explore the assumed consequences more carefully. Several system planners can explore the same system changes, each using his or her own assumptions. If a threshold of acceptance or rejection lies outside the range of consequences calculated by this group, then acceptance or rejection is clear and further exploration is not necessary. If it lies within the range, then closer examination is required to assess the validity of the various assumptions made.

One of the virtues of this process is that it forces the planners into a debate over their assumptions and estimates, rather than on the generalized goodness of a possible change. Thus, the model serves the same function as any other model—it lowers the level of argument to issues that are more fundamental and empirically testable than those that arise without the model.

C. Model Structure

To generalize the previous example, we describe here the operation of the model in terms of its inputs, its outputs, and the relationships between them.

Inputs. The basic inputs for JUSSIM are enumerated below:

(1) a listing of the *crime types* considered;
(2) an enumeration of system *stages;*
(3) for each stage, a listing of the stages it feeds and specifications of the *branching ratios* characterizing the proportion of flow along each of those flow paths for each crime type;
(4) a listing of *resources,* and their associated
    (a) *annual unit availability* (say, hours per year per resource),
    (b) *cost per unit time* (say, dollars per hour), and
    (c) *"capacity"* (the maximum amount of the resource that might be made available);
(5) a tabulation of the *unit workloads,* or times for processing a unit of flow, at any stage or flow path, by each resource applied for each crime type; and
(6) a *reference flow*—typically, the number of reported crimes by crime type (or the number of arrests) that sets an absolute level of flow throughout the rest of the system when the branching ratios are specified.

The branching ratios, the unit processing times, and the reference flow are all specified for each crime type.

Outputs. The outputs of the JUSSIM model are presented to the user in whatever order and organization the user specifies. The potential outputs include the following variables:

(1) *flow* through each processing stage;
(2) *costs* associated with each stage for any aggregation of stages grouped into specified "subsystems," including the complete aggregation into a single, "total system";
(3) *resource costs,* indicating the costs associated with each of the resources;
(4) *resource workloads* – the number of labor hours per year imposed on each of the resources; and
(5) *resources required* – the numbers of each of the specified resources that would be required to handle the workload.

All of these output measures are functions of crime type, and therefore each can be presented either for each individual crime type or as a single value summed over all the crime types.

Basic Relationships. Assuming one has knowledge of all the input parameters, one can then calculate the output measures by means of the following relationships:

- One knows the basic input flow (say, reported crimes) and the branching ratios. The *flow* at each stage is calculated as the sum from each of the stages feeding it. These are the flows in the preceding stage, multiplied by the corresponding branching ratio.

- The resource workload is the flow at each stage or flow path where the resource is applied, multiplied by its unit workload there. The total resource workload is then calculated as the sum of these resource workloads over all the stages and flow paths.

- The number of *resources required* per year is the resource workload divided by the annual availability of an individual unit of resource.

- The processing *cost* at a stage is the flow through the stage, multiplied by the workloads and the unit costs for each resource applied at that stage. The subsystem costs associated with a "subsystem" (or any aggregation of stages) is simply the sum of all the costs associated with its constituent stages.

D. Operation of a Run

In the operation of a JUSSIM run, the user's basic role is to create a "test case" to compare with a "base case" already stored. The base case is a complete set of data describing a criminal justice system and is developed individually for each jurisdiction. Once the user has drawn a base case from a data file, he or she then generates a test case, modifying the base case. Sitting at a terminal, the user is asked a sequence of questions about what changes he or she wants to make.

Each of these questions is an entry to a "phase," which leads the user by a sequence of hierarchical steps directly to the parameters to be changed. A separate phase is provided for changing each of the following parameters:

(1) branching ratios,
(2) unit workloads,
(3) annual unit resource availability,
(4) resource unit costs,
(5) resource capacity constraints, and
(6) reference flow.

Once a phase is entered, further detailed questions permit the user to specify precisely which parameters he or she wants to change, and the crime type(s) for which the change is to be made. All the questions are in clear language, and the answers regarding stage numbers, resource numbers, crime groups, workload numbers, and other code numbers are based on the code numbers in the base-case data file. The program then displays the base-case value for the parameters the user identifies and asks the user to type in the new or test-case values.

In dealing with the multiple parallel channels of flow for all the crime types,[1] most users, at least initially, do not want to sit through the complete, detailed output for each crime type. In a separate phase, JUSSIM permits them to choose one of a number of standard complete partitions of the crime types (e.g., into felonies and misdemeanors or Part I and Part II crimes) or to specify their own crime groupings. Thus, a user may choose to have the complete details on one or a few individual crime types, but to combine the remainder into a single group. The standard groupings are specified in the data file.

In another phase, the user specifies the output tables to be displayed. The output tables present calculated results on flows, costs, workloads, and resource requirements. The data are listed for the base case, the test case, and the absolute and percentage changes in going to the test case. These results can be presented by crime group or summed over all crime groups. In the early stages of an exploration, a user will presumably want to conserve time and will examine results only for the total system or for a few critical subsystems. At the end of an exploration, the user is more likely to want more detail.

At the end of a run, the user is asked if he or she wishes to rerun the model. In addition to using this to explore a new issue, users will do this iteratively if they are dissatisfied with the implications of some of their assumptions and would like to reconsider some of them. In a rerun, users are given considerable flexibility in respecifying a new base case (e.g., calling a data file, using the latest test case), and then begin again to create a new test case.

IV. A FEEDBACK MODEL (JUSSIM II)

The JUSSIM linear model discussed so far looks only at the downstream consequences of a change in the criminal justice system. It cannot explicitly calculate the effects on the future load on the criminal justice system of new programs that might change either the probability of rearrest of released individuals, or the time between release and rearrest. For example, on the one hand, a pretrial probation program might reduce the probability of arrest for some of the treated individuals. (This could occur if the threat of prosecution for the deferred charges acted as a deterrent, or if the treatment provided during the probation were more successful in rehabilitation than any of the alternative treatments that the defendant might have received.) On the other hand, these released individuals would return to the street more quickly than they might otherwise, and so the opportunity for earlier rearrest is increased.

Because so many programmatic and procedural changes under consideration by criminal justice planners involve these kinds of considerations, an extension of the JUSSIM model (designated "JUSSIM II") incorporates these feedback flow paths into the model.

A simple flow chart of the feedback version of JUSSIM is shown in Figure 9.3. The new feedback flow paths can now be characterized simply as a branching ratio, i.e., the average proportion of individuals, released from some point of the criminal justice system, who will ever be rearrested. We must also associate an average time until rearrest for each of the feedback flow paths. Such a concern for elapsed time was not necessary in the linear model.

Also, since a vital aspect of the JUSSIM structure is its crime-specific characterization of systems operation, the feedback JUSSIM model must specify the new offense for which recidivists are rearrested. This requires the inclusion in the model of a "crime-switch matrix," a matrix which distributes the flow of individuals released from the criminal justice system after arrest for one crime type, into a flow of individuals rearrested for another (or possibly the same) crime type.

In addition to the flow of recidivists, the feedback model also requires specification of the input flow of virgin arrests—the individuals arrested for the first time who may subsequently reappear as recidivists. This is a distinction rarely made in the conceptualizations of the criminal justice system, and less often in available data.

Thus, the principal new elements required to extend the linear JUSSIM model to incorporate the feedback flow of recidivists are:

(1) the probability of rearrest by crime type of first arrest;
(2) the average time until rearrest by crime type of first arrest;

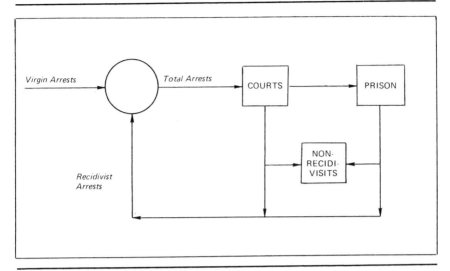

Figure 9.3: Basic Feedback Model

(3) a crime-switch matrix linking the prior and subsequent crime types for recidivists; and

(4) the number of virgin arrests by crime type.

In addition to these extensions to the basic model, the feedback JUSSIM II model requires significant changes in the use of the model. The linear JUSSIM model is a one-period model, typically a one-year model. Because of the significant time delays in the recidivism process, the feedback version must be a multiyear model. Thus, a new user option has been added to the feedback version. The user can request a printout of selected results at the end of each intermediate year in the multiyear run, and can examine these results before their impact (in the form of a new queue of recidivists) has been registered on subsequent years. This is in keeping with the interactive character of the JUSSIM planning tool that encourages users to reexamine their assumptions if results do not seem either plausible or satisfactory.

The most significant change in the operation of the model, however, is that new data demands are placed on the user. Obviously the user must now come to grips with the problem of identifying virgin arrests, recidivism probabilities, recidivism time constants, and elements in the crime-switch matrix.[2]

This feedback version, JUSSIM II, is currently operating, but it has not been implemented as widely as JUSSIM I. This is partly because of its greater data demands and partly because its use requires somewhat more sophistication on the part of the user as a result of its more complex structure.

V. ISSUES IN IMPLEMENTATION

As expected, the response to the interactive JUSSIM model was far more positive than the response to a previous batch-processed model from which it was derived. A number of states (e.g., California and Alaska), cities (e.g., Pittsburgh, Philadelphia, and Denver), and countries (e.g., Canada and Sweden) have organized data collection efforts to describe their systems as base cases for the JUSSIM model, and plan to use a version of the model for their own planning. The Alaska model focuses on the corrections system and therefore represents the police and court subsystems as only a small number of stages, and therefore also provides greater detail (e.g., a separate stage for each institution) for the corrections subsystem. In some cases, staff changes in these organizations resulted in discontinued use of these models.

An important use of the model is as a teaching tool for system planners. The Urban Systems Institute of Carnegie-Mellon University has used it in one-week short courses on systems analysis for criminal justice planning. The planners have readily learned to operate the terminal, to respond to the program's interrogations, to translate their project ideas into judgments about model-parameter changes, and to operate the model effectively as a design tool. The model then plays the important role of forcing planners to consider the entire system and the interdependency of its parts in their planning. One retired police officer commented, "This was the first time I've thought much about what happens to the people I arrested."

In Pittsburgh, three masters degree students at Carnegie-Mellon's School of Urban and Public Affairs developed a base-case data file of the Allegheny County criminal justice system over a three-month summer internship with the Allegheny County Regional Planning Council of the Pennsylvania Governor's Justice Commission. A follow-on student team, as part of a second-year project course, used that data base to perform a variety of analyses regarding potential improvements in the system.[3] New projects considered included bail reform, diversion of less serious cases from the higher court to the minor judiciary, and diversion from a juvenile detention home. Upon graduation, one of the students became a member of the planning staff of the council. There, he continued to work at integrating the model into the council's planning process. Upon his departure after one year, the model was continuously maintained, used, updated, and extended by a staff member with no special technical training.

VI. SOME TYPICAL USES OF JUSSIM

Once one has a JUSSIM model, there are a variety of kinds of uses to which it might be put. For example, it could be used to estimate the downstream implications of an incremental decision at any stage, by calculating the average or expected cost per additional arrest (or reported crime, charge, conviction, and so on)—taking into account the fact that some of the arrestees will be dismissed without charge, some will be acquitted in the courts, and some will penetrate through to a correctional institution. An average cost would reflect these various probabilities of penetration and the costs associated with each degree of penetration.

Users are often interested in the distribution of costs (or workload) associated with the various portions of the criminal justice system, since knowing those distributions in a jurisdiction might suggest a reallocation. Such a reallocation consideration might be influenced by comparing local or state distributions to national distributions.[4]

An important value of the JUSSIM model is that it provides the "entry price" in the development of a statistical data base for a wide variety of research projects. Any single project may not be able to justify the costs of collecting the total base of information it needs, but the aggregate needs represented by a range of users who might then make use of that collected base could usually more than justify that expense. Even more important than the expense is the time and effort that various potential users would require to collect their information individually, which would effectively deter any serious quantitative inquiry into the operation of the system. With the ready availability of a planning data base in a well-structured format such as JUSSIM, any potential user can inquire directly to obtain an estimate of a particular parameter or of any calculated value, or to obtain a quick estimate of the impact of one or another potential system change.

The JUSSIM model is particularly helpful in evaluating a wide variety of potential system changes. The user introduces these changes one at a time or in combination, and receives a quick estimate of the downstream implications of such changes. Different users, particularly those on different sides of a particular policy question, can come together to develop estimates of the favorable and unfavorable values of parameter changes associated with a system revision. The cost, resource, and flow implications of those alternative estimates can then be calculated with the JUSSIM program. In many cases, the original basis of disagreement may disappear. Each of the advocates may develop new insights into some of the implications of the change he or she was endorsing or opposing; or the basis of disagreement may boil down to a particular parameter value, and that value might then be developed more carefully empirically, either by a test project in that jurisdiction or by obtaining estimates that may have been derived in another jurisdiction.

The JUSSIM program also has significant potential value for conducting cross-jurisdictional comparisons. Since the data are in a consistent, comparable format across jurisdictions—particularly within a state which has the same criminal justice structure—the State Planning Agencies (SPA) can generate data files for the different jurisdictions or regions within their purviews and can conduct cross-jurisdictional comparisons by searching for jurisdictions which have deviant parameters.

As it develops new standards and goals procedures, each SPA will be seeking to find a means of assessing the cost and workload implications of the various standards and goals being considered by state or national commissions, or promulgated by them. One of the shortcomings identified in the reports of the National Advisory Commission on Criminal Justice Standards and Goals has been the absence of some of the cost implications associated with the standards promulgated. With a JUSSIM model for the state and its component jurisdictions, the SPAs as well as the Standards and Goals Commission can begin to address some of those implications, particularly for those standards or goals that can be translated into branching ratio, workload, or unit cost parameters. A study conducted by the American Bar Association Commission on Correctional Standards used the JUSSIM model for precisely that purpose: to assess the cost implications of the correctional standards in the National Advisory Commission's report.

VII. JUSSIM LIMITATIONS

It should be recognized that all models are finite and limited. The limits come from the inherent necessity to abstract reality rather than to represent it literally in any computational model. Given this, one could try to build an extremely elaborate and complex model which pushes toward an extensive representation of reality. Experience in such modeling efforts has shown that almost always such models fail to be very useful because of their elaborateness and complexity. Such elaborateness requires more data than can be reasonably obtained; and enormous complexity clouds the bases for an observed calculated result. Experience with modeling of other systems has made it clear that it is important to limit the size of any model.

This philosophy has been reflected in the JUSSIM model by limiting its size to 32,000 words of computer storage. Doing so makes the computer program accessible to most commercial time-sharing computing services. More fundamentally, however, it restricts the complexity by restricting the number of crime types, stages, flow paths, resources, workloads, and the like, that can be incorporated. If a user wants to increase the complexity of one kind of structure (to create more stages, for instance), then another must be given up (for example, the number of resources or the number of crime types must be decreased). Of course, a user with greater computer capacity who is prepared to deal with the greater complexity can readily go in and revise the dimensions of those parameters if he or she is prepared to deal with the more complex model.

In its operation, JUSSIM I (as well as the downstream portion of JUSSIM II) ignores the passage of time. In particular, this calculates the downstream impact of a crime in the year in which it was committed. Thus, a three-year sentence for a robbery committed in 1979 is counted in 1979, even though part of the time is served in 1980 and later. This would still give a good estimate of corrections cost if the system is not changing radically over time, since people sentenced in 1978 and earlier serve time in 1979, thereby roughly compensating for the 1979 crimes whose impact occurs in later years.

This structure makes the model simpler and much of the computation considerably easier and less expensive. But the structure does not allow the JUSSIM model to deal with queueing or delay problems, which explicitly focus on the passage of time and which are often of considerable concern to courts. There are a variety of "job shop simulation" programs which can be used much more effectively for this purpose. These include the General Purpose Simulation Systems (GPSS) models and various other simulation programs that specifically address these delay issues. When focusing on queueing issues, it would be far more efficient for a planner to use a separate model addressed to that purpose rather than to try to complicate a single model with all the complexity necessary to provide this wide range of flexibility.

VIII. POSSIBLE FUTURE EXTENSIONS

The JUSSIM models discussed here clearly represent only a basic framework on which a more extended analytical evaluation process can develop. These models, as currently formulated, include far less of the features of criminal behavior, or even of the behavior of the criminal justice system, then one would like for realistic evaluation.

A. Determinants of Crimes

In both JUSSIM I and JUSSIM II, the initiating exogeneous factors are those associated with the numbers of crimes (or the associated arrests in JUSSIM II), but there is no explicit incorporation of determinants of crimes or of arrests. Thus, the creation of a richer "front end" of the model represents the extension that would appear to be most appropriate for consideration. The opportunities on this agenda include the following, in the order of the difficulty of estimating them and of developing the requisite relationships:

(1) incorporation of demographic factors associated with the occurrence of crime;

(2) incorporation of the crime-reduction consequences of increased sanctions through their incapacitating effects, in order to bring about a link

between crime control effectiveness of the criminal justice system and, especially, of its sanction policies, and the crime-generation process;

(3) incorporation of the deterrent effects resulting from changes in the sanction policy of the criminal justice system; and

(4) incorporation of exogeneous socioeconomic "causes" of crime.

JUSSIM I begins with the crime process and JUSSIM II begins with the associated arrest process. These models simply depend on whatever projection might be provided of crimes (for JUSSIM I) and of virgin arrests (for JUSSIM II). Future estimates of those variables could be provided by simple time extrapolation of recent values. As the theory on crime causation develops and the fundamental determinants of crime are identified, these can provide a more solidly based basis for extrapolation. The effects of demographic shifts on those rates can be provided by using demography-specific arrest rates and by projecting the numbers of arrests based on changes in the demographic composition.[5] This form of projection is especially important to the current evaluation of programs, particularly those that are oriented toward particular demographic groups, in view of the significantly shifting demographic structure of the population associated with the postwar baby boom, and their aging out of the high-crime ages (but into the high-imprisonment ages) anticipated for the 1980s.

The critical problem in estimating the incapacitative effects of imprisonment involves the determination of several key parameters characterizing individual criminal careers. The most important of these is the mean individual crime rate of the people sent to prison, since each person-year of imprisonment implies that many crimes averted per year. If we had estimates of that parameter, an initial crime-generating function could then be elaborated to reflect a reduction of that many crimes per person-year in prison. Thus, a shift in the imprisonment rate would be reflected in that crime function.

A second important parameter associated with incapacitation is the mean duration of individual criminal careers. Since individuals do drop out from criminal activity as they age, an evaluation model, especially one focused on sanction policy, should reflect those dropouts. This would reflect the fact that the use of imprisonment to lock up individuals who are past their period of criminal activity would have no crime-reduction effects. Estimates of the duration of criminal careers are even less available than estimates of individual crime rates. As estimates of these parameters become available, they can be incorporated into the projection of crime rates and the evaluation of programs that affect imprisonment.

The effect of deterrence, i.e., of crime-reduction consequences associated with a particular sanction policy, is reflected in an empirically measured "elasticity" representing the percentage of reduction in crime commission associated with a percentage of increase in sanction level. As the sanction level is increased, one should notice a corresponding reduction in crime rate. A number of econometric studies have attempted to estimate this elasticity, but none of them are yet sufficiently valid[6] to warrant incorporation into an evaluation model. As valid estimates of the elasticity are developed, those could be similarly incorporated into the crime-generating function.

When one tries to incorporate the variety of socioeconomic factors that could be viewed as "causes of crime," one moves into an extremely complicated morass of rich correlations and associated theoretical confusion. Many socioeconomic variables are strongly correlated with crime, as are virtually all measures of social or economic disruption or deprivation (unemployment, broken homes, low education, low income, and so on). The fundamental problem is one of isolating these factors which are highly intercorrelated with each other to provide estimates of the reduction in crime that would result from a change in any of those variables. The state of knowledge in these areas is extremely primitive, and it will probably be a long time before one can generate causal models that permit evaluators to assess the elasticity that reflects the quantitative reduction in crime associated with an improvement in any of these factors.

SUMMARY

This chapter has presented an approach to evaluation that invokes the use of analytical models as an evaluative tool. The models used reflect the currently available theoretical knowledge associated with the influences on crime and the criminal justice system of various policy or programmatic changes. Such models are inherently limited by the state of theoretical knowledge associated with the causal consequences of any such policy change. In the experimental paradigm, such causal knowledge or theory is not necessary, because it is provided by the real system, which keeps that knowledge well hidden and reveals it implicitly. When analytical models are used to provide a valid evaluation, they are far more efficient and speedy. Ultimately, such approaches must be pursued, partly because they do provide reasonable approximations to knowledge in many areas. Results of such evaluations must be treated with the limited degree of certainty associated with the limits in the theoretical understanding. They do, however, provide a valuable contribution in the policy evaluation process.

NOTES

1. The FBI's Uniform Crime Reports (UCR) system organizes its data into 29 separate crime types. JUSSIM permits 30 crime types.

2. Some preliminary estimations of values of these parameters are explored in Belkin et al. (1973).

3. See (1) Fields et al. (1972), (2) Cohen et al. (1972), and (3) Cohen et al. (1973).

4. As reflected, for example, in National Criminal Justice Information and Statistics Service (1975).

5. See, for example, Blumstein et al. (1980).

6. See Blumstein et al. (1978).

APPENDIX: REFERENCES ON JUSSIM

For those interested in more detail on the JUSSIM model than can be presented here, a number of references are available. The original flow model from which the JUSSIM model was derived was developed by Blumstein and Larson (1969) as an outgrowth of the work of the Science and Technology Task Force of the President's Commission on Law Enforcement and Administration of Justice (1967: especially ch. 5). That original model existed in batch-processing mode, which made it relatively inaccessible to most nontechnical users. The JUSSIM model was reprogrammed in an interactive mode by William Glass and is described in Belkin et al. (1973a) and Blumstein (1973). Its particular implementation in Allegheny County was described by Cohen et al. (1973) and in the juvenile justice system there by Blumstein and Stafford (1973). Other implementations have been described by Cassidy et al. (1973) for Canada, and by others. Sections of some of these references have been used in this chapter.

User's manuals for JUSSIM I (the downstream model; see Belkin et al., 1971) and for JUSSIM II (the feedback model; see Belkin et al., 1973a) are available from the Urban Systems Institute at Carnegie-Mellon University. Copies of the JUSSIM programs, written in dialect-free FORTRAN IV and dimensioned to a computer with 32k words of core storage, are also available. The programs are well documented internally and contain a basic data file so that they can be operated immediately. Interested agencies can write for order forms to the Urban Systems Institute, Carnegie-Mellon University, Pittsburgh, PA 15213.

Parts of the materials in this chapter are derived from various segments of the earlier documents referred to in this appendix.

REFERENCES

Belkin, J., A. Blumstein, and W. Glass (1973a) "JUSSIM II: An Interactive Feedback Model for Criminal Justice Planning." Urban Systems Institute, Carnegie-Mellon University, Pittsburgh, Pennsylvania.

——— (1973b) "Recidivism as a Feedback Process: An Analytical Model and Empirical Validation." *Journal of Criminal Justice* 1, 1: 7-27.

——— (1971) "JUSSIM: An Interactive Computer Program for Analysis of Criminal Justice Systems." Urban Systems Institute, Carnegie-Mellon University, Pittsburgh, Pennsylvania.

——— and Michel Lettre (1972) "JUSSIM: An Interactive Computer Program and Its Uses in Criminal Justice Planning," pp. 467-477 in G. Cooper (ed.) *Proceedings, International Symposium on Criminal Justice Information & Statistics Systems*. Sacramento, CA: SEARCH Group, Inc.

Blumstein, A., H. Miller, and J. Cohen (1980) "Demographically Disaggregated Projections of Prison Populations." *Journal of Criminal Justice* 8, 1: 1-26.

――― and R. Larson (1969) "Models of a Total Criminal Justice System." *Operations Research* 17, 2: 199-232.

Blumstein, A. and R. Stafford (1973) "Application of the JUSSIM Model to a Juvenile Justice System," pp. 60-84 in *Proceedings of the National Symposium on Computer Applications in the Juvenile Justice System.*

Blumstein, A., J. Cohen, and D. Nagin [eds.] (1978) *Deterrence and Incapacitation: Estimating the Effects of Criminal Sanctions on Crime Rates.* Washington, DC: National Academy of Sciences.

Blumstein, A., H. Miller, and J. Cohen (1980) "Demographically Disaggregated Projections of Prison Populations." *Journal of Criminal Justice* 8, 1: 1-26.

Cassidy, R. G., R. G. Hopkinson, and W. Laycock (1973) "A Preliminary Description of the Canadian Criminal Justice System." Report of the Ministry of State for Urban Affairs and Ministry of the Solicitor General, Ottawa.

Cohen, J., M. Lettre, and R. Stafford (1972) "Analysis of the Allegheny County Criminal Justice System: Present Operations and Alternative Programs." Urban Systems Institute, Carnegie-Mellon University, Pittsburgh, Pennsylvania.

Cohen, J., K. Fields, M. Lettre, R. Stafford, and C. Walker (1973) "Implementation of the JUSSIM Model in a Criminal Justice Planning Agency." *Journal of Research in Crime and Delinquency:* 117-131.

Federal Bureau of Investigation (annual) *Uniform Crime Reports.* Washington, DC: Government Printing Office.

Fields, K., M. Lettre, and R. Stafford (1972) "A Description of the Allegheny County Criminal Justice System." Urban Systems Institute, Carnegie-Mellon University, Pittsburgh, Pennsylvania.

National Criminal Justice Information and Statistics Service (1975) *"Expenditure and Employment Data for the Criminal Justice System: 1972-73.* Washington, DC: Government Printing Office.

President's Commission on Law Enforcement and Administration of Justice (1967) *Report of the Task Force on Science and Technology.*

10

Criminal Justice Evaluation Techniques: Methods Other Than Random Assignment

Gloria A. Grizzle and Ann D. Witte

The strongest single evaluation technique is the true experimental design. However, to date, the true experimental design has been used only occasionally in criminal justice evaluation. (See Rezmovic, 1979, for a review of criminal justice evaluations which have used this technique, and either Campbell and Stanley, 1966, or Rezmovic, 1979, for further description of the technique.) The infrequent use of this technique has been due mainly to moral, legal, and administrative restrictions which make random assignment difficult if not impossible in many criminal justice settings. For example, it is difficult to imagine a judge assigning convicted offenders randomly to alternative sentences. Even when random assignment has been used in criminal justice, it has at times broken down in the course of program implementation (see Empey and Erickson, 1972, for an example). In addition, random assignment may at times (particularly when sample sizes are small) produce a nonequivalent control group.

For the reasons cited above, criminal justice and other evaluations have sought alternatives to the true experimental design. These alternative techniques have often been called quasi-experimental designs. The alternative design which has been most used in criminal justice evaluation is the nonequivalent control group. This evaluation design uses a group of individuals (the comparison group) that is as much like the group of program participants studied as possible. It compares the activities of both groups after the program participants have completed the program. *If the comparison group is not different from the program group in any characteristic that is related to the follow-up activities studied,* then one may attribute significant differences in activities of the two groups during the follow-up period to program participation. The first phrase of the last sentence is important. Many if not all criminal justice evaluations which have used the nonequivalent control group design are subject to the criticism that the program participant and comparison groups are not truly comparable. If the groups do differ in characteristics related to program effects, then the comparison of activities of the two groups during the follow-up period does not provide an accurate measure of program effects. (See Brody, 1976 for a recent listing of criminal justice evaluations which use this technique and Rezmovic, 1979, for a further discussion of the technique.)

While the experimental and nonequivalent control group designs are now quite familiar to criminal justice researchers, other evaluative techniques which seek to extend and strengthen these designs are less well known. It is six of these techniques which the authors survey in this chapter.[1]

In the first section of the chapter, we discuss process evaluation. In contrast to most criminal justice evaluative techniques, which seek to determine the ultimate impact of criminal justice programs, this technique seeks to describe the way in which a program is carried out. This technique may be used to extend experimental and nonequivalent control group designs by providing more complete descriptions of the program evaluated. Sections 2 and 3 describe two techniques, multivariate statistical techniques and time-series analysis, which have been used to improve the accuracy with which experimental and nonequivalent control group designs measure program effects. In addition, the techniques discussed in these two sections have been used to evaluate programs when no comparison group is available.

Section 4 contains a description of cost-effectiveness analysis. This technique extends traditional impact analysis by considering the cost at which various program outcomes are obtained. Finally, the last two sections of this chapter describe two techniques, benefit-cost analysis and multiattribute utility analysis, which allow one to obtain a single measure of program effects even when program outputs are originally measured in diverse ways. Benefit-cost analysis does this by converting all program costs and benefits to dollar values, while multiattribute utility analysis uses subjective evaluations of the worth of various program outputs.

I. THE USE OF PROCESS EVALUATION
IN CRIMINAL JUSTICE EVALUATION

In contrast to experimental design, multivariate statistical analysis, and time-series analysis, where the phenomenon of interest is usually the effect or impact of a program intervention, process evaluation focuses upon how a program was implemented. A process evaluation describes the content of the program, assesses the quality of the program, and defines the character and quantity of the program's immediate products.

1. Uses of Process Evaluation

Process evaluation has been used as a monitoring device to determine whether a program is being carried out in conformance with program plans. For this purpose, the evaluation might look at whether personnel and equipment were acquired as scheduled, whether the activities proposed are being conducted in the quantity and mix proposed, and whether the target group is being reached to the extent proposed.

Process evaluation can also be used to learn about why programs succeed or fail. Experimental, multivariate statistical, time-series, and other quasi-experimental designs can be used to evaluate program intervention itself. Such designs can produce information about whether a given program was successful or unsuccessful in producing certain impacts, but they cannot produce information about *why* a program was successful or unsuccessful. By knowing how and why change does or does not occur, one has a better chance both of modifying unsuccessful programs so that they can in the future obtain the objectives set for them, and of replicating successful programs in other geographic areas.

2. The Technique

A synthesis of writings about how to do process evaluation[2] suggests that a thorough process evaluation would answer these questions:

(A) What was the political, economic, and social milieu into which the program was introduced?
(B) What people and institutions became involved, what roles did they play, and how did the program affect their relationships with each other?
(C) What did the program actually do, and were the program's various activities undertaken as specified in the program design?
(D) Was the program directed at the specified population or target area?
(E) Why did the program reach some people in the target group and not others? What were the characteristics of nonparticipants and dropouts?

.Specific data collection techniques suggested for process evaluation include interviews, observation of events, tests and questionnaires, and analysis of existing documents.[3] Weiss and Rein (1970) suggest that three mutually complimentary conceptual frameworks—systems theory, the dramalike unfolding of events, and the interaction of political forces—be used to guide one's data collection and reporting of what happens during program implementation.

3. Use of the Technique in Criminal Justice Evaluation

One problem in reviewing process evaluations in the criminal justice literature is that space restrictions in journals often prohibit presenting the detailed information needed to answer the questions listed above. This space restriction, coupled with the belief that experimental design methods produce more objective and conclusive and therefore valid findings, has resulted in an underrepresentation of process evaluations in criminal justice and evaluation-oriented periodicals. Given a choice between reporting a process evaluation or an impact evaluation, the researcher who has evaluated both a program's impacts and its processes will usually choose to describe the program briefly and reserve most of the space to present the methods and findings related to impact rather than process. Process evaluations are more likely to appear in technical reports than in periodicals.

Many process evaluations of criminal justice programs have been produced, though their comprehensiveness and quality vary greatly. Among those worth mentioning are reports on the Minnesota ombudsman for corrections (as an example that combines records and structured interviews to reconstruct the process by which requests for assistance are handled); the Middlesex Treatment Release Program for inmates with drug and alcohol problems (as an example of interviews and questionnaires used in conjunction with records to present an account of the previous conflicts and organizational structures that affected the functioning of the program); the Dreyfous halfway-in house for juveniles (as an example of a narrative history based upon records, interviews, and observation that explains why a program was not implemented in conformance with the plan); the Marin Treatment Alternatives to Street Crime Project (as an example of systems theory used to evaluate the project in terms of its basic components, staff behavior, and decision-making, with decision-making being the central process tying the system together); and the Wilmington Split-Force Police Patrol Experiment (as an example of careful measurement of the quantity and quality of the tasks that make up the program, included in an evaluation that also looks at the program's impact on crime).[4]

When successful programs are to be replicated elsewhere, it is important that potential replicators understand in some detail what the program did and the environment in which it was successful. The reporting of the Seattle Community Crime Prevention Program as a LEAA exemplary project (Cirel, 1977) is an excellent example of the integration of process and impact evaluation. Not only does the report cover the needs which the Seattle program addressed, the development of the program and how it operated, what the program cost and its results in terms of burglary rate reductions; it also emphasizes the environmental, program, and legal factors that others should take into account when considering developing such a program for their community.

Although process evaluations can provide necessary information for developing, monitoring, and replicating criminal justice programs, this method must be used with caution. Whether the data supporting the evaluator's conclusions are primarily qualitative or quantitative, both the conclusions as to a program's success or failure and the reasons alleged for the success or failure may depend upon what the evaluator "sees." Although the interpretation of findings from experimental and multivariate statistical designs can also become controversial, there seems to be more latitude with process evaluation techniques in perceiving what events and outcomes are important.

Consider the example of the Pilot Cities Program, which was evaluated both by the General Accounting Office and the American Institutes of Research. Both evaluators relied primarily upon existing records and personal interviews to obtain information about the program. Yet, their conclusions about the program's success or failure were quite different. The General Accounting Office recommended that the program be terminated ahead of schedule, saying, "we do not believe the cumulative experience of the eight teams, either in terms of the innovativeness of the research undertaken or the demonstration projects implemented, has been very successful in accomplishing the program's goal of developing efforts with national applicability" (Comptroller General of the United States, 1975: 53). The American Institutes for Research, in contrast, concluded: "The central concept of the Pilot Cities Program is sound; it is an effective approach to improving local law enforcement and criminal justice systems, and one which should be applied further" (Murray and Krug, 1975). Tharp and Gallimore's (1979: 48) comment on qualitative methods of knowing may be appropriate here: "In its highest form it is wisdom, in its lowest, delusion."

4. Future Use of the Technique

Process evaluations will continue to be used for monitoring program development and in conjunction with impact evaluation. As a control tool, process evaluation may be the only type of evaluation needed when the funding agency simply wants to know whether the program was implemented in conformance with the plan that served as the funding basis. When programs are in a developmental stage or are unstable and subject to change in midstream, it may be more important to do process evaluation to find out what happened and why, than to do impact evaluation. Finally, process evaluation will be a useful complement to impact evaluation for those programs where it is not certain that the program will be carried out as described.

II. THE USE OF MULTIVARIATE STATISTICAL TECHNIQUES IN CRIMINAL JUSTICE EVALUATION

Multivariate statistical techniques have been relatively little used in criminal justice evaluation to date, but can be of great value, particularly when experimental designs are not possible. The techniques have been most frequently used in evaluation to obtain predicted values of an outcome variable of interest and to "control" for the effect of factors other than treatment on an outcome of interest.[5] These two uses of multivariate technique are quite similar and subject to similar difficulties. However, because they have developed separately, we treat them separately below. We discuss predictive modeling first and deal with basic issues here. We treat more advanced issues when discussing statistical control. Most of the issues raised in each section are relevant to both techniques. The essential difference between the two techniques is that predictive modeling generally relies on relationships established before treatment (a "before the fact" or ex ante design), while statistical control relies on relationships which exist after treatment has occurred (an "after the fact" or ex post design). The nontechnically oriented reader may wish to skip subsections 2.A and 2.B below.

1. Predictive Modeling

Probably the earliest use of multivariate statistical techniques (often informal rather than formal) in criminal justice was to develop models to predict future criminal activity. Early predictive models were generally designed to isolate potential delinquents amongst school children (Glueck and Glueck, 1960), or as aid to selection for parole (Gottfredson and Beverly, 1962; Ohlin, 1951).[6] Mannheim and Wilkins (1955) seem to be the first individuals to use predictive models to evaluate a criminal justice program. This technique has been used sporadically since Mannheim and Wilkins's early work,[7] but has failed to gain widespread popularity for a number of reasons.

A. The Technique. Predictive models can be used to evaluate criminal justice programs in basically one of two ways. First, they can be used to find a "matched" comparison group when one is evaluating a program using a nonequivalent control group design. One would use a predictive model and obtain predictions of future activity for both program participants and nonparticipants. Nonparticipants with future predictions most like the program participant group would be selected for the comparison or nonequivalent control group. If prediction models contain all variables other than treatment impinging differentially on the treatment and comparison group, and the factors related to treatment affecting the activity of interest remain unchanged (both in terms of variables and relative effects), any difference between the participant and "matched" nonparticipant group can be attributed to program participation.

A second possible use of predictive models is for predicting future activity and for comparing directly this activity to actual future activity after program participation or treatment. If prediction models contain all variables related to the outcome of interest, and the factors affecting the activity of interest remain unchanged (both in terms of variables and relative effects), a significant difference between predicted and actual levels of the activity of interest may be interpreted as due to treatment. In what follows, we will first discuss this latter use of prediction and then deal more briefly with the former use of the technique.

B. *Obtaining Predictions.* There are three basic approaches for initially specifying prediction equations. The first and most generally used is to specify an equation based on the findings of previous empirical research and present data availability. The second relies on theory to indicate what factors determine (and thus predict) a particular outcome of interest. This latter approach has been relatively seldom used in criminal justice evaluation, in part due to the paucity of quantifiable theory. Most individual prediction models[8] rely on the first approach, while some crime-rate models use the second approach.[9] A third approach is even less theoretical than the first. It finds a correlation between the activity of interest in two areas and makes future predictions for one of the areas, the treatment area, based on the future activity level in the other.[10]

After determining an original specification, it is next necessary to utilize a multivariate statistical technique to determine how each predictor variable affects the activity of interest. Techniques used in the criminal justice area have ranged from simple ad hoc weighting formulas to discriminant analysis, ordinary least squares regression, predictive attribute analysis, and maximum likelihood techniques. The latter techniques are generally preferable, as they allow one either to obtain more accurate estimates of program effects or to judge accurately the significance of any effects found. Selection among techniques should be based on the nature of the activity one is analyzing and available computational and statistical skills.[11]

Finally, the list of predictor variables is usually reduced to a small set which is "significantly"[12] related to the activity of interest.

C. *Activities Predicted.* Prediction research in criminal justice has dealt almost solely with prediction of various measures of the level of individual criminal activity or with area crime rates.

To date, most individual prediction models have sought to predict whether or not an individual would return to crime (e.g., whether an individual would be arrested during a follow-up period) or the probability of return to crime (e.g., the probability that an individual would be arrested during a follow-up period).

Prediction for such relatively simple measures of criminal activity may be most fruitfully obtained by using discriminant analysis, or the probit or logit models.[13] However, to date, many criminal justice researchers have used ordinary least squares (OLS) regression for such analyses.[14] While this may be acceptable as preliminary analysis and may be unavoidable where more sophisticated techniques are not available, the use of OLS with such variables is fraught with both logical and statistical problems.[15] Perhaps most important is the fact that the use of such techniques to predict dichotomous measures of criminal activity (e.g., rearrest/no rearrest) allows no accurate tests of significance to be made.

Evaluations of criminal justice programs should deal with more complex measures of recidivism than the simple dichotomous measures described above.[16] At least the timing, frequency, and seriousness of criminal activity should be considered. The development of prediction models for these more complex measures of criminal activity is in its infancy. This lack of development is due to both the concentration on dichotomous models, noted above, and the difficulty of modeling more complex measures of criminal activity because they tend to be either qualitative or limited (truncated or censored) in nature. For example, the Sellin-Wolfgang measure of the seriousness of criminal activity does not allow negative values (it is truncated) and tends to have a "pile-up" of observations at zero (no criminal activity). Qualitative and limited dependent variables require specialized statistical techniques, many of which have been developed only in recent years. Specialized techniques are necessary because the variable to be predicted (the dependent variable) is not normally distributed. Normal distribution is required when using such standard techniques as OLS regression, so that accurate tests of significance can be made. In our example above, Tobit analysis might be a suitable modeling technique.[17] This technique would also be useful in modeling such measures of the frequency of criminal activity as conviction and arrest rates (the number of convictions [arrests] per unit time free).

Measures of the timing of criminal activity present different statistical difficulties. These measures, such as the length of time until arrest (conviction), are nonnegative by definition and positively skewed. The positive skewness results from the fact that most individuals who return to the criminal justice system do so quite quickly, although some do not return for long periods, if ever. A further complication is that we cannot observe a value longer than the length of the individual's follow-up period. Indeed, for individuals who do not return to criminal activity during their follow-up periods, we observe no value for the dependent variable. Witte and Schmidt (1977) have explored a number of possible distributions for modeling such a dependent variable and have found the truncated log normal distribution to be most appropriate. In the context of criminal justice evaluation, the modeling of the dependent variable is attractive because it can provide sequential predictions of recidivism rates, thus allowing simultaneous evaluation of the timing and extent of posttreatment criminal activity.[18]

Aggregate prediction models which seek to predict such things as area crime rates run into statistical difficulties of a different sort. To predict accurately an area's crime rate, it is necessary to understand the factors which affect crime rates. Unfortunately, the factors affecting area crime rates are poorly understood and often relatively difficult to measure. In addition, the relationship between crime rates and measures of the level of criminal justice system activity (e.g., clearance rates and conviction rates) are quite complex. Although the level of criminal justice system activity affects the crime rate, it may also be affected by the crime rate due to "workload" effects. This interaction is the simultaneity problem extensively discussed in the deterrence literature.[19]

In addition to the statistical problem discussed above, crime-rate prediction suffers from quite serious data problems.[20] Reported crime rates are not measures of the true level of criminal activity, and the degree to which they approximate the "true crime rate" may vary in nonrandom ways both across jurisdictions and through time, due to such things as reporting conventions. In addition, errors in the measurement of crime are quite likely to result in a negative relationship between reported crime rates and traditional measures of the level of police activity (the clearance rate), even in the absence of a causal relationship. See either Blumstein et al. (1978) or Cook (1977) for more detailed treatment of this data problem.

To date, crime-rate models have been used most frequently to evaluate changes in police activity. However, even assuming that all of the problems discussed above have been adequately dealt with, one may not unequivocally interpret a predicted crime rate which is greater than the actual crime rate as due to increased deterrence caused by higher clearance rates or police presence. The observed decrease in the crime rate may be due to the fact that more criminals are staying in prison (i.e., are incapacitated), rather than to the increased deterrence associated with police activities. See Chaiken (1977) for a survey of research investigating the deterrent effects of police activities.

Given the difficulties discussed above, some researchers have abandoned the effort to predict crime rates by using theoretically suggested predictive models, and have instead resorted to purely empirical prediction techniques. Many of these efforts use time-series techniques such as the Box-Jenkins technique, and are discussed in the next section of this chapter; however, others make more traditional use of multivariate statistical techniques and are discussed here. Budnick's (1973) crime-correlated area analysis, which has been used to evaluate the High Impact Anti-Crime Program (Chelimsky, 1976), is a good example of this latter approach. This approach is atheoretical and seeks to predict an area's crime rate based upon the fact that the area's crime rate has behaved similarly to the crime rate in other areas in the past. To use this technique, one estimates an ordinary least squares regression relating the area's crime rate to the crime of other areas in the past. One then uses the coefficients obtained in this estimation and observed crime rates in other areas during the experimental period to predict a crime rate for the experimental area. If this predicted crime rate exceeds the actual, the model will attribute the difference to the experimental condition.

   D. The Strengths and Weaknesses of the Technique. The weaknesses of the prediction techniques outlined above for evaluation are many. First, the inadequacy of current theoretical understanding of the causes of crime means that it is *very* difficult on a priori grounds to know for what variables it is necessary to control. If one doesn't control adequately for variables affecting the level of crime other than the experimental condition one is evaluating, then differences between predicted and actual crime levels may be due to these omitted causal factors and not to the experimental condition. Second, even if one adequately controls for all causal factors, the relationship between the crime level and the causal factors may not be constant either across time or across groups. In the terminology of Campbell and Stanley, external validity may be a serious problem. External validity of predictive models should be carefully assessed and continually checked. The most effective test of external validity is to use a model to predict the level of criminal activity for a randomly selected group or area not used to estimate the model. The level of activity predicted for this external group should be insignificantly different from the actual level if the models are adequate. Such predictions for random groups of interest should be continually made and checked against actual activity. When prediction for such random groups becomes significantly different from actual performance, it is necessary to reestimate the predictive model. Third, modeling requires that both the level of criminal activity and the factors affecting it can be accurately and quantitatively measured.

   The strengths of the prediction technique are the relationship that it reveals and the relative cheapness and rapidity with which evaluations can be made. The relationship revealed by predictive models can be extremely valuable for future theoretical development. Predictive models are relatively cheap and quick to implement, because it is not necessary to follow the activity of a control or comparison group.

   E. Future Use of the Technique. The above prediction technique is a relatively weak evaluation design and is only appropriate when stronger alternatives are not available. However, when it is not possible to identify and follow the activities of a comparison group, the above technique is useful and appropriate. In addition, predictive modeling can be used to aid decision makers and to help develop theoretical models of the causes of crime, and its use should be encouraged in these areas.

   Future predictive models can be substantially stronger than most current models if researchers: (1) take great care to develop models of the outcome of interest that are as complete as possible; (2) carefully select a statistical technique appropriate to model the variable of interest; and (3) carefully check the external validity of the models to ensure that they predict accurately. A number of researchers (e.g., Monahan, 1978; Simon, 1971) have suggested that predictions can be improved by including environmental variables.

   F. *The Use of Predictive Models to Obtain Comparison Groups.* A stronger evaluative design using predictive models is possible if one uses such models to obtain a "matched" comparison group. The postparticipation activities of this matched comparison group may be compared with those of a treatment group, in order to evaluate a treatment. This design is stronger than the previously discussed simple predictive design, because factors omitted from the prediction equation which impinge equally on both groups are controlled. However, as in the previous design, this design is only as strong as the models upon which it is based. Sherwood et al. (1975) have suggested a sophisticated version of this design which could provide a relatively strong evaluation.

2. Statistical Control

   When one is using either no comparison group or a nonequivalent comparison group, using multivariate statistical techniques to control for known and quantifiable differences between the experimental and comparison group is extremely valuable. In addition, such techniques can be used, even when true experiments are possible, to decrease the variance (increase the efficiency, in statistical terminology) of our estimate of the treatment effect.

   Adequate statistical control in the absence of any comparison group requires three things: First, it requires a model which indicates the factors likely to affect the outcome of interest other than the treatment being evaluated. Second, it requires an accurate quantitative measure of the factors for which it is necessary to control. Finally, it requires an appropriate statistical technique to control for the factors identified.

   Evaluations which use purely statistical control are relatively rare in criminal justice but quite prevalent in economics, where researchers are generally forced to be relatively passive observers of the passing scene. Economists have used multivariate statistical techniques (primarily ordinary least squares regression and its derivatives) to judge the effect of such things as taxes and government spending on output and employment in the economy (Klein, 1969), and to evaluate the effect of training programs on earnings (Goldstein, 1972; Hall, 1976) and union membership on wages (Lewis, 1963). Economists are, perhaps, in a better, or at least more comfortable, position to use statistical control, because of the large body of theory (albeit of varying quality) upon which they have to draw. Economists have large-scale models of the determinants of output and employment in the economy,[21] and neoclassical economic theory offers a well-developed theory of wage determination. Due to the existence of this theoretic base, economists are better able to know for what variables to control. The weakness of theory in the criminal justice area makes such knowledge much more difficult to ascertain.[22] Economists are further blessed with relatively more quantifiable concepts than are researchers in criminal justice.[23] Such things as wage rates and number of years of schooling can be relatively well measured quantitatively, while concepts central to criminal justice, such as criminality and social adjustment, are much more nebulous and qualitative variables. A final advantage economics has over criminal justice in using statistical control is that the variables of interest in economics (e.g., wages, GNP) are generally normally or near-normally distributed and hence more amenable to use of standard multivariate statistical techniques (e.g., ordinary least squares regression) than are the variables of interest in criminal justice (indicators of crime and criminality which are often dichotomous, skewed, and/or truncated).

In summary, it is probably too early for purely statistical control (control in the absence of a comparison group) to be extensively used in criminal justice evaluation. Given the current state of theory and measurement in criminal justice, purely statistical control is a weak evaluative design. However, it is better than no control at all, and is a stronger, although more expensive (because a model must be estimated rather than a simple prediction made), evaluative design than are simple predictive designs (discussed in subsection 1), which assume the continuance of historical relationships and that the factors other than treatment affecting the outcome of interest do not change. Cook (1975) and Clarke et al. (1976) provide examples of the use of this technique in criminal justice evaluation.

Rossi (1978) has advocated "a progressive series of tests . . . starting with a tight experimental design for the evaluation of the effectiveness of a treatment under the best possible mode of delivery, through a final evaluation through correlational designs of the effectiveness of a human services program that has been enacted into social policy." Rossi's correlational design is our pure statistical control model, and, indeed, such a model is, as Rossi suggests, most useful as a fall back design when evaluating long-standing programs.

A stronger design is possible when multivariate statistical control is used in conjunction with a nonequivalent control group.[24] If one is able to control completely for all selection factors which are correlated with the treatment, then this design is conceptually similar to a true experimental design, although it is less efficient in a statistical sense. In point of fact, one is unlikely both to know and to be able to model the selection process completely.[25] If one does not fully model the selection process, one will obtain biased estimates of the effect of treatment. Campbell and Boruch (1975) and Cook and Campbell (1976) have pointed out the most likely difficulties: omitted variables and errors in the measurement of included variables. We will discuss each in turn.

A. *Omitted Variables.* It is well known that when a relevant variable is omitted from a model, the coefficients obtained for all other variables that are correlated with this variable are inaccurate. In formal statistical terminology these coefficient estimates are biased. Thus, if one fails to control for a selection factor which is correlated with treatment, one will be unable to estimate the true effect of the treatment on the outcome of interest. However, one may be able to estimate the direction of bias (whether the coefficient estimate overestimates or underestimates the true treatment effect) in the estimation of the treatment effect and, thus, be able to make valuable statements about the nature, if not the size, of the treatment effect. Suppose that selection for a rehabilitative program was based solely on previous behavior and that the program was designed to lower the level of future criminal activity. In order to obtain an unbiased estimate of the program's effect using statistical control, one should estimate the following model, using data for all members of the experimental and nonequivalent control groups:

$$Y = \beta_0 + \beta_1 T + \beta_2 PB + \epsilon, \qquad [1]$$

where Y is a measure of posttreatment criminal activity, T is a measure of treatment, PB is a measure of the previous behavior upon which selection is based, ϵ is a stochastic error term, and β_0, β_1, and β_2 are parameters to be estimated. β_1 will be an unbiased estimate of the effect of participation in the rehabilitative program upon future criminal activity, if we have measured PB without error and if it is the sole selection criterion. However, if PB is unmeasurable, or, because we are ignorant of the selection procedure, we estimate instead

$$Y = \gamma_0 + \gamma_1 T + \epsilon^*, \qquad [2]$$

then $\epsilon^* = \beta_2 PB + \epsilon$ and will be correlated with T, if PB is correlated with T (which it would be under our assumptions). If such correlation exists, γ_1 is a biased estimate of β_1, the true effect of treatment. The direction of this bias will depend on the direction of the effect of previous behavior on future criminal activity (the sign of β_2) and the direction of the correlation between the omitted variable (PB) and the treatment variable (T). Assuming that a higher value of PB indicates better previous behavior and that better previous behavior is associated with lower levels of future criminal activity, one would expect β_2 to be negative. Assuming, further, that selection for the program is based on poor previous behavior (low value of PB), then one knows that γ_1 is an underestimate of the true treatment effect, β_1. If γ_1 is negative and significant, one can conclude that the program works, although one does not know how well.

In general, the relationship between the true treatment effect (β_1) and the measure (γ_1) obtained from equation 2 is

$$\gamma_1 = \beta_1 + \beta_2 d, \tag{3}$$

where d is equivalent to the coefficient one would obtain if the following regression[26] were run:

$$PB = a + dT. \tag{4}$$

Here, a is the intercept, T is a measure of treatment, and d is the estimated coefficient for treatment. Using equation 3, one may estimate the direction of bias in an estimate of treatment effects when one knows that relevant variables have been omitted. Knowing the direction of bias, one may make qualitative statements about likely treatment effects.

B. *Errors in Measurement.* Errors in the measurement of selection variables are somewhat more difficult to handle. It can be shown that, in general, estimates of the treatment effect obtained from a regression like equation 1 when the selection variable (PB) is measured with error, will lead to biased estimates of the treatment effect (Kmenta, 1971: 307-309). However, in some cases it is possible to obtain unbiased estimates of the treatment effect by using more sophisticated techniques such as multiple-indicator models developed by Joreskog (1973); and the instrumental variable technique of econometrics (Klein, 1969) and its extension, multiple-cause models (Goldberger, 1974). These approaches, however, require relatively strong theoretical knowledge which is not currently available in most areas of criminal justice evaluation. As far as the authors are aware, multiple-indicator models have not been used in criminal justice research to date. Magidson (1977) provides an example of the use of the multiple-indicator model in educational evaluation. A variant of the multiple-cause model has been used in the deterrence literature by Carr-Hill and Stern (1973) and in the economics literature by Griliches and Mason (1972).

C. *Future Use of the Technique.* The above discussion should not lead one to abandon statistical control when using a nonequivalent control group; rather, it should indicate that great care should be taken to learn what process operated in selection for treatment. Statistical control with nonequivalent control groups is not as strong a design as a true experiment, but if one knows something about the selection process, such control greatly strengthens a nonequivalent control group design.

Statistical control with a nonequivalent control group is, in general, the strongest design discussed in this section. Its superiority to simple predictive models and to statistical control alone is relatively obvious. Its superiority to the prediction-matched nonequivalent comparison group is less obvious and hinges on two factors. First, treatment selection processes are generally simpler to model than criminal outcomes. This fact means that we are likely to have more complete models, and hence a stronger design, using statistical control and a nonequivalent control group than we are using a prediction-matched nonequivalent control group. Second, after treatment, statistical control does not require one to assume that statistical relationships have remained constant through time. This assumption is generally required if the prediction-matched nonequivalent comparison group is to adjust adequately for the effect of factors other than treatment on the outcome of interest.

III. TIME-SERIES ANALYSIS

Time-series analysis deals with a set of observations that have been recorded at regular intervals over time. Unlike multivariate analysis, where the objective is to estimate a dependent variable as a function of two or more independent variables, the objective in time-series analysis is to estimate future observations based upon prior observations of the same variable. Time-series analysis has been used in the business sector for forecasting and control purposes, and has been more recently advocated in the public sector as an evaluation method for detecting program effects. When used for program evaluation purposes, this technique looks for an intervention effect in a time series by establishing the trend in the data and determining whether a deviation from this trend occurred when the program intervention took place.

1. Uses of Time-Series Analysis

Time-series analysis has been used to detect the effects of program interventions in some situations where experimental designs are impossible. At least fifty, and preferably one hundred or more, observations are needed (Box and Jenkins, 1976: 18). This technique can be most successfully used when the intervention effect is large and long-term and when program implementation is not gradual. The statistical technique for detecting deviations from the trend is conservative, in that it cannot readily detect small or gradual changes. While time-series analysis can detect a deviation from the trend, it cannot ascribe any portion of this deviation to any particular event. Such interpretation is left to the researcher, who must, aided by whatever other evidence is available, conclude to what extent the program intervention caused the deviation.

Perhaps the best known of the earlier evaluations using time-series analysis is the work by Glass (1968) and Campbell and Ross (1968) that looks at the effect of a crackdown on speeding motorists in the State of Connecticut. Since the publication of those articles, Ross (1973, 1976) has continued using time-series analysis to examine the effect of changes in penalties for drinking and driving in Britain and the Scandinavian countries. Zimring (1976) and Deutsch (1977) have used the technique to evaluate the effect of gun control legislation upon the incidence of assaults, homicides, and armed robberies. Other evaluations of the effects of legislation include the 1973 New York State laws on heroin use (Sajovic and Goldsmith, 1978) and the 1900 German divorce law (Glass, 1971). In the police area, time-series analysis has been used to identify the effects upon burglary rates of a specialized home-burglary patrol and the effects of a police walking patrol upon reported crime (Schnelle, 1975), to determine the effects upon subway crime of a fourfold increase in patrol officers (Chaiken, 1974), and to examine the effects upon street crime of a 40 percent increase in the police labor force (Press, 1971). In the judicial area, the technique has been used to evaluate the effect upon motor vehicle fatalities of seven-day jail terms and license suspensions for driving while intoxicated (Robertson, 1973).

2. The Technique

Time-series analysis includes four major steps.

A. Identifying the Statistical Model. The first step requires identifying a statistical model that adequately represents the process that generated the time series being examined. The desired model, following Occam's Razor, is the one that uses the smallest number of parameters for adequate representation. If a process were completely understood, it might be possible to write a theoretical model that would adequately represent it. If, as is typically the case in criminal justice evaluation, our theoretical knowledge is inadequate to identify the one best model, it may still be possible to use what knowledge is available to suggest a suitable class of models.

The various classes of models differ principally in terms of four factors:

(1) the number of previous observations that influence the observation to be predicted;
(2) whether the time series is nonstationary (i.e., has an upward or downward trend) or stationary;
(3) the number of observations over which a moving average is calculated;
(4) whether seasonal influences on the time series are included.

Deutsch's models describing crime patterns in ten cities illustrate two useful classes of models. Figure 10.1 graphs total crimes for Los Angeles by month, over a nine-year period. It is apparent from looking at this graph that the series of observations is not stationary, because it has an upward trend. It is also apparent that a seasonal pattern exists, with certain months in each year tending to be higher than average across the nine-year period, and others tending to be lower. The model that Deutsch developed to fit this time series predicts the number of crimes on the basis of a moving average of one parameter, and takes into account the upward trend and seasonal variation. This model was appropriate for describing robbery, burglary, assault, larceny, and vehicle theft patterns in the ten cities studied (Deutsch, 1977: 48-51). Homicide and forcible rape patterns were best described by a simpler model, one that excluded seasonal variations (Deutsch, 1977: 47).

The simplest model of a time series would be one that predicted on the basis of a single previous observation and assumed no upward or downward trend, no moving average, and no seasonal influence. Sajovic and Goldsmith (1978) used such a model to describe the pattern of narcotic deaths and admissions to treatment in New York State from 1970 through 1976. They used a second class of model in describing the pattern of serum hepatitis cases in New York State. This model predicts on the basis of a single previous observation, and also takes trend into account. For describing the pattern of admissions to detoxification and methadone maintenance programs in Maryland, they added to this second model another factor, a moving average (Sajovic and Goldsmith, 1978: 92-96).

B. Estimating the Parameters. Once a model form has been tentatively formulated, based upon data and knowledge of the process, the model is then fitted to data in order to estimate the parameters. A least squares estimation procedure is generally used to estimate the parameters. From a number of models, the best fit would be the model that minimizes the mean square error. Evidence of model adequacy can also be provided by the confidence intervals set around the parameters and the chi-square statistic based upon the residual autocorrelations.

C. Checking the Model. In the third step, the fitted model is checked to determine whether it adequately represents the process underlying the time series. Two techniques for diagnostic checking are overfitting (fitting a more elaborate model and comparing its mean square error with that of the fitted model) and analyzing the residuals of the fitted model. If the residuals are not distributed normally and there is some pattern to the variation, the model may have been incorrectly identified. In such a case, the researcher would need to go back to the first step—model identification.

3. The Use of the Technique in Criminal Justice Evaluation

Zimring's careful interpretation of the effect of the Federal Gun Control Act of 1968 illustrates an approach that may be followed when using time-series analysis to evaluate program interventions.[27] After reviewing the history of gun control legislation, he described the purposes and provisions of the act and documented its enforcement by the Alcohol, Tobacco, and Firearms Division in the Treasury Department. Rather than simply examining trends of firearm assaults and handgun homicides, he sought to link a chain of series, beginning with measures of enforcement activity, to the assault and homicide series. Cases recommended for prosecution, indictments, and convictions did increase sub-

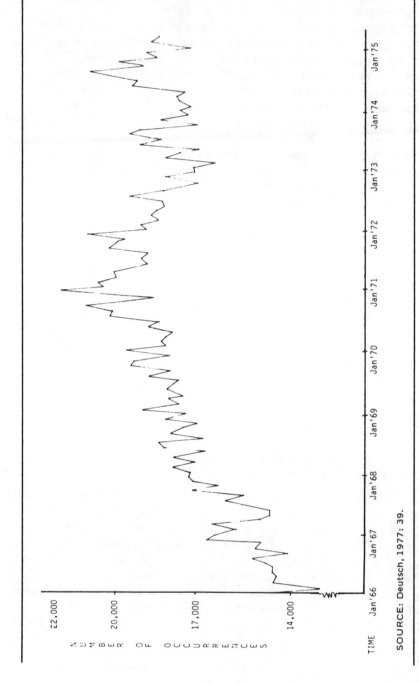

SOURCE: Deutsch, 1977: 39.

Figure 10.1: Monthly Occurrences for Total Los Angeles Crimes

stantially after the 1968 legislation; handgun importation did show a dramatic reduction; handgun homicides and gun assaults continued to increase but at a lower rate after 1969.

Turning to the question of the act's effect on interstate gun traffic, Zimring then compared trends in handgun homicides and firearm assaults for the two cities with the most restrictive handgun-licensing statutes, with trends for a 57-city average. While these two cities showed higher rates than the 57-city average, the difference in baselines made the comparisons misleading. Zimring then attempted to find better comparison cities and discovered that the postact rate for the one city found to be comparable was similar to that for the city in the restrictive handgun licensing state, thus failing to support a conclusion that enforcement of the Gun Control Act led to a reduction of interstate firearms traffic. In looking at why the rate of handgun crime continued to increase in tight-control cities, he showed that 95 percent of the handguns confiscated in the restrictive handgun licensing state were originally bought outside of the state, and that over half were bought at retail after the Gun Control Act.

Approaching the question from still another angle, Zimring focused upon time series for homicides and assaults in a city where the Alcohol, Tobacco, and Firearms Division's enforcement effort was about ten times greater than it was for other cities. A comparison of gun homicide with nongun homicide monthly time series showed that gun killings did decrease substantially during the enforcement effort, while nongun killings did not. Not enough observations were available to do a similar time-series analysis for assaults, but visual inspection did not show a similar dip in the level of assaults while the enforcement effort was in place.

As this research indicates, time-series analysis can be a valuable tool in criminal justice evaluations, but it may leave unanswered many questions which must be addressed by other means. Among the problems that the evaluator must face when deciding whether to use time-series analysis, the quality of the data series is frequently paramount. Changes during the time series in the way events are recorded make interpretation particularly difficult when the program intervention is limited to a single jurisdiction which has changed the way data are recorded during the time series. Researchers who have attempted to use reported offense data to examine the impact of local programs are well aware of the possible instrumentation changes that the data series may reflect. Not only may the rate of total offenses which are reported to the police change, but the police themselves have been known to change the way offenses are classified. For example, if the objective of a program is to reduce burglaries, there is the temptation to record some burglaries as acts of vandalism instead of burglary, thereby causing the burglary rate to appear to decrease.[28] Because the data used in time-series analysis are usually collected by an administrative agency rather than by the researcher, it is important that the researcher look into the way the data were actually collected and recorded, and decided whether data inconsistencies would mislead someone interpreting the results of time-series analysis.

Given an adequate data base, the researcher can proceed to identify, estimate, and check the statistical model that represents the process underlying the pertinent time series. When identifying the model, it is important that the researcher postulate the way in which the program intervention would occur. While sudden and dramatic changes can be readily detected, it may also be possible to detect a more gradual but cumulative effect of the intervention, provided the model fitted is specified to account for such a cumulative effect.[29] When the outcome of interest is being measured indirectly, the finding that there was a change can be strengthened if multiple measures are analyzed and they all show similar changes.

Given a finding from the time-series analysis that there indeed was a shift in the data series after program intervention, the researcher must conclude whether the change was in fact caused by the program intervention. It is in arriving at this conclusion that some of the approaches Zimring used are particularly helpful. If the immediate products or outputs of the program actually occurred in the magnitude expected, and if these products can be logically linked to the outcomes (e.g., number of handgun homicides) either directly or through one or more intervening events, additional support is obtained for the assumption that the program caused the change.

Fashioning after-the-fact comparison groups can also help to strengthen the conclusion. Some of these comparisons have been ingenious, as was Ross's work (1973) on the effect of the British Road Safety Act. While random assignment between experimental and control groups was clearly impossible, Ross was able to break down fatalities and serious injuries by day and time of day. He compared casualties during weekday commuting hours (when pubs were closed and drinking while driving was therefore more likely to be minimal) with casualties during Friday and Saturday nights (when alcohol is most likely to be consumed). By demonstrating that there was a sharp drop in weekend casualties but not in commuting-hour casualties, he strengthened his conclusion that the reduction in total casualties reflected a reduction in alcohol-related casualties, an outcome that would be expected if the act had had the desired intervention effect (Ross, 1973: 33-34).

4. *Future Use of the Technique.* All the time-series analyses mentioned were conducted in situations where the experimental approach was clearly impossible. It will continue to be the case that the experimental approach will frequently not be possible and that evaluations must nevertheless be conducted. In such situations, time-series analysis can be a valuable tool for the evaluator when the following conditions hold:

(a) At least fifty observations of the outcome of interest are available at regular time intervals and the data collection and record-keeping procedures are consistent over that time-span.

(b) A model can be adequately fitted that describes the process that generated the data series.

(c) The program implementation is carefully documented and its immediate products measured.

(d) The time-series analysis is supplemented by additional evidence linking program products to outcomes and discounting other factors that might have caused the change in the time series.

Although all the time-series analyses discussed here used police data (homicides, assaults, traffic accidents, and so on), the technique is applicable to data from other sources. While police data on crime rates may be the only readily available time series that reflect the performance of the total criminal justice system, time series reflecting more specific phenomena, such as the pattern of serum hepatitis in the Sajovic and Goldsmith study, can be a valuable component in evaluating a program's effect. We expect to see time-series analysis used in evaluating an increasing number and a more diverse set of criminal justice programs in the future.

IV. COST-EFFECTIVENESS ANALYSIS

Cost-effectiveness analysis became a popular tool for analyzing public-sector programs in the 1960s when first the U.S. Department of Defense, and later the rest of the federal government and many state and local governments, sought to link planning and budgeting through a Planning Programming Budgeting System. A central concept underlying PPBS was the belief that alternative ways of accomplishing program objectives should be compared in terms of what they cost relative to what they accomplished.

1. Uses of Cost-Effectiveness Analysis in Criminal Justice Evaluation

Although the focus of cost-effectiveness analysis, as used with PPBS, was primarily prospective—anticipating what the costs and accomplishments of a program would be if it were funded and implemented—it can be equally useful when the focus is retrospective—determining what the costs and accomplishments of a program were after the program was implemented. This method is essentially the same as benefit-cost analysis, with one major exception. In benefit-cost analysis, the benefits are all quantified in terms of dollars, permitting a summation of benefits into a single quantity that can be compared with cost, also measured in terms of dollars. In cost-effectiveness analysis, it is recognized that some important program impacts may not reasonably be translated into dollar benefits. The benefits are quantified and aggregated to the greatest extent possible; but, when aggregation is not possible, an array of impacts is presented rather than the single benefit measure used in benefit-cost analysis.[30]

A few examples will suffice to demonstrate the range of programs whose evaluations have included cost-effectiveness data. These programs include a bail reform (release on recognizance); drug-abuse prevention, treatment, and enforcement programs; community crime prevention; pre- and posttrial alternatives to jail; and outreach offices for reintegrating offenders into the community. The Seattle Community Crime Prevention Program report (Cirel, 1977) provides the simplest example, i.e., cost compared to a single effect for a single program. Annual cost to operate the program ($250,000) is related to one effect (an estimated 350 burglaries prevented). The bail reform study (Friedman, 1976b) suggests that a release-on-recognizance program includes two main cost components (the cost of operating the program and the cost incurred when defendants fail to appear in court) and two main effects (the value of freedom and the cost to the state of keeping defendants in jail until they appear in court).

The Philadelphia outreach program evaluation (Pennsylvania Governor's Justice Commission, 1976) compares the performance of suboffices, which make possible more localized delivery of services, to that of the district office. The two modes of service delivery are compared in terms of average societal cost per client per year. Included in these costs are supervision costs borne by the Pennsylvania Board of Probation and Parole, welfare payments to clients less income taxes paid by clients, plus detention costs incurred by the state for clients jailed for new violations or offenses. As is the case for the two benefit-cost studies summarized in the next section, this study uses average cost rather than the more appropriate marginal cost. This type of evaluation is more useful than one that simply cites the number of clients supervised, but it merges the beneficial effects of the program—reduced welfare payments, reduced detention costs, increased productivity of the probationer or parolee—with the outreach program costs of the Board of Probation and Parole. As in benefit-cost analysis, it is important in cost-effectiveness analysis to ask from whose viewpoint costs and effects are being calculated. From a societal viewpoint, welfare payments are transfers of wealth and not really costs. From the Board of Probation and Parole's viewpoint, detention costs incurred by another state agency may not be considered costs. Laying out separately the various costs and effects would make the findings more useful to readers having different viewpoints.

In evaluating alternatives to jail, Galvin et al. (1977) relate costs for various diversion programs to the number of successful terminations. This approach permits the comparison of different programs of the same type as well as programs of different types in terms of cost per successful termination. "Successful termination," though more informative than a simple unit-of-service measure, still leaves to the reader's imagination the good effects presumed to flow from a successful termination. If the same impacts, on the average, occur as a result of successful terminations in one program as opposed to another, then cost per successful termination is an adequate way of taking these impacts into account when comparing programs.

The drug-abuse program analysis (Grizzle, 1975) looks at effects of different education, treatment, and law enforcement programs per $100,000 spent. These programs are compared in terms of total years of addiction prevented, number of people emotionally rehabilitated, number of people for whom frequent drug usage is prevented, dollar value of theft prevented, dollar value of increased economic productivity, and number of heroin addicts motivated to accept treatment per $100,000 spent in each program. The relationship of cost to impact is also expressed in terms of the cost per year of addiction prevented by each program.

This study raises an interesting dilemma. On the one hand, we would like to broaden the range of programs having commensurable measures. This study applies a common measure, cost per year of addiction prevented, to both prevention and treatment programs. The impacts of prevention programs, however, often occur much farther in the future than do the impacts of treatment programs. If we truncate consideration of impacts five or even ten years downstream, we may be stacking the deck in favor of treatment programs. On the other hand, we do need to take into account the fact that events that occur far into the future are usually surrounded by more uncertainty than events that occur in the near future. Not to do so may reduce the credibility of the evaluation in the eyes of potential users. Perhaps the solution is to identify both short-term and long-term effects and to devise some appropriate way of discounting long-term nondollar effects back to present value.

2. Future Use of the Technique

Cost-effectiveness information in criminal justice program evaluations is still the exception rather than the rule. This technique may be the most important one discussed in this chapter for making impact evaluations more useful to policy makers as an aid in resource allocation. To be most useful in allocating resources, evaluations need to show impact relative to cost. Cost data ought to be regularly reported in impact evaluations. As cost-effectiveness information becomes more regularly available, two points need to be kept in mind:

(a) Data on effects will be no better than the impact evaluation that produced them.
(b) Data on costs will be no better than the cost-accounting or cost determination systems that produced them.

When a program has multiple effects, weights can be assigned to each effect in order to aggregate them into a single measure. Some people object to arbitrary or evaluator-imposed weights and recommend either that there be no aggregation or that several different weighting schemes be used, so that the person using the evaluation findings can choose the weighting scheme that matches his or her own values. While leaving effects unaggregated makes it possible for users to assign weights that conform to their own values, an array displaying many different effects can become confusing. Multiattribute utility analysis, discussed in section VI, provides a method for weighting (and therefore permitting the aggregation of) program effects that can incorporate the user's values and also preserve value differences among different users.

V. BENEFIT-COST ANALYSIS

It has been noted that process evaluation can serve to make the findings of impact evaluation more useful to people who decide whether to implement, expand, or curtail criminal justice programs. Benefit-cost analysis, as well as cost-effectiveness analysis, can also increase the utility of impact information for these decision makers. These two methods relate impact to cost in order to answer the question, "What did the program cost per unit of impact?"

Benefit-cost analysis evolved from welfare economics and is, as its parent, mainly concerned with questions of efficiency rather than equity. Benefit-cost analysis deems a project beneficial if the sum of the value of the appropriately discounted benefits exceeds the value of the sum of the appropriately discounted costs. Benefits include both direct increases in real output which occur as a result of the project, and indirect beneficial effects. The indirect effects are termed externalities.[31] Costs include the opportunity cost (cost in the best alternative use) of all resources utilized, plus detrimental indirect or externality effects. Benefit-cost analyses will often be supplemented by a section which analyzes and catalogues any income redistribution which occurs as a result of the program evaluated.[32]

1. Uses of Benefit-Cost Analysis

Modern techniques of benefit-cost analysis evolved mainly in the water resource projects area as a result of the Flood Control Act of 1936 which required that water projects be undertaken only if "the benefits to whomsoever they may accrue are in excess of estimated costs." As a result of the requirements of this act, most of the original techniques of benefit-cost analysis were developed to evaluate large-scale capital investment projects. Benefit-cost analysis has been used extensively to evaluate human resources programs and noninvestment government activities only since the 1960s. The use of benefit-cost analysis for criminal justice evaluation is even more recent. As far as the authors are aware, the first application of the benefit-cost technique for criminal justice evaluation was Cooper's (1968) analysis of North Carolina's prisoner work release program. Cooper details the historic costs and benefits of the work release program and compares them to an alternative program, prison industries. He finds that the work release program increases efficiency, that benefits exceed costs. Specifically, he estimates that, considering only benefits and costs accru-

ing while an individual is imprisoned, transferring one man from prison industries to work release results in a $2056 yearly net gain to society.

Benefit-cost analysis has not been used extensively to evaluate criminal justice
programs since Cooper's work, although the number of such analyses has
increased moderately since 1972.[33] The relatively infrequent use of benefit-cost
analysis for criminal justice evaluation stems from a number of factors. First, the
application of the technique requires reliable knowledge of program costs which
is often not available in the criminal justice area.[34] Second, the technique is
relevant only where positive, quantifiable benefits result from a criminal justice
program. To date, many evaluations of criminal justice programs have used such
weak designs that they have yielded no reliable quantitative estimate of program
effects. Often when strong designs have been used, no significant program effects
have been found.[35] Finally, benefit-cost requires that a dollar figure be placed
on most program benefits and costs.[36] We will consider these factors in more
detail below.

2. The Technique

Benefit-cost analysis may be divided into four distinct steps.

A. Listing All Benefits and Costs. The first step of a benefit-cost analysis
requires that the analyst make a complete list of all costs and benefits, regardless
of who or where their recipient is. This social perspective is central to classical
benefit-cost analysis, but, as we will see below, it is possible to conduct a
benefit-cost analysis using a narrower perspective (e.g., the funding agency). All
items which increase real output (e.g., increased output due to the training
received in a vocational training program for prison inmates) or which lead to a
beneficial effect on individuals not directly involved in the program (i.e., a
beneficial change in externalities) should be counted as benefits. An example of
this later type of benefit would be a reduction in future crime of participants as
a result of the vocational training program. All uses of resources and detrimental
effects on people not involved in the program should be counted as costs. An
example of the former would be the services of teachers and buildings used in a
vocational training program. An example of the latter, in a similar setting, would
be the decreased incapacitation which would result from placing offenders in an
external training program rather than in a prison.

B. Measuring the Dollar Value of Benefits and Costs. The second step
involves placing dollar values on as many of the benefits and costs identified in
step A as possible. The values of new or improved productive resources are
relatively easy to measure. For example, the productive value of increased
training is generally measured by the increased income earned as a result of the
training.[37] The value of increased consumption is more difficult to measure if
the good under consideration does not change hands in the market. For
example, the pleasure one obtains from learning a new skill could only be
indirectly evaluated. The general rule for evaluating such nonmarketed consump-

tion benefits is to value them at the amount the individual would be willing to pay rather than do without the benefits—here, the pleasure of the learning experience. This amount is known in the literature as the "compensating variation."[38]

External benefits or spillovers are generally difficult to value because they are by definition not directly related to the activity being evaluated. In general, these effects, like nonmarketed consumption effects, should be valued at the amount the individual would be willing to pay rather than do without the effect, the compensating variation. In point of fact, these effects are often not valued, and when valued are often valued indirectly rather than directly through determination of the compensating variation. For example, a vocational training program might yield benefits by reducing the future criminal activity of participants. The correct way of valuing this benefit is to find out what people would be willing to pay rather than forego the reduction in crime caused by the program. This measure has not been used in the criminal justice literature to date.

In general, program costs are more easily valued than program benefits, because many program inputs are purchased in the market. However, difficulties can arise in allocating the cost of resources used for more than one activity (e.g., buildings). As noted above, knowledge of program costs requires good cost-accounting or cost determination systems.

Benefit-cost analysis requires that all program inputs be given a value equal to the value of their use in their next best use, i.e., at their opportunity cost. If markets are competitive and if the purchase price of an input has not been affected by subsidies or by taxes, then the market price of an input will reflect its opportunity cost and can be used to value the cost.

External costs of a program are generally difficult to value, as are external benefits, but cause fewer problems, since they are generally fewer in number. As indicated above, an external cost of an external vocational training program for prison inmates would be the crimes committed by those inmates that would not have occurred if they had been "behind bars."

C. Discounting Benefits and Costs. The third step in a benefit-cost analysis requires the analyst to discount benefits and costs which occur in the future so as to make them comparable in value to costs and benefits which occur today. Future costs are less onerous than those that occur today, and future benefits are less valuable than those that occur today. Appropriate discounting allows one to determine the value today (present value) of future benefits and costs.

The appropriate discount rate to use has been the source of much debate in economics.[39] Theoretically, the rate of discount should be the return obtainable if the funds were devoted to their best alternative use. Practically, it is difficult to determine what the best alternative use is (e.g., current consumption, private investment) for funds used for public programs. Even if it is possible to determine what the next best use is, it is often difficult to know what return this alternative would yield. Market interest rates are of little help, as these are greatly influenced by taxes (tax exemption for interest paid) and subsidies (tax-free status of municipal bonds) and, thus, do not generally reflect opportunity cost. The currently accepted practice is to report results which use different discount rates.[40]

Given a discount rate, the net present value of a program may be calculated as follows:

$$NPV = B_0 - C_0 + \frac{B_1 - C_1}{(1+r)} + \frac{B_2 - C_2}{(1+r)^2} + \ldots + \frac{B_n - C_n}{(1+r)^n},$$

where NPV is the net present value, B and C are measures of benefits and costs, respectively, r is the discount rate, and subscripts 0, 1, 2 . . . n indicate time periods. If one does not wish to favor large projects, the net present value calculated above should be divided by project costs.[41]

D. Comparing Alternative Programs. The next step in a benefit-cost analysis is to compare the net present value per dollar of cost obtained in step C with similar values for alternative uses of public funds.[42] Those projects should be selected which will yield the highest net present value per dollar spent, given the budget constraint.[43]

3. The Use of the Technique in Criminal Justice Evaluation

Two benefit-cost analyses (Friedman, 1977; Mallar and Thornton, 1978) of criminal justice programs well illustrate the difficulties of using this technique in the criminal justice area, as well as the strengths and weaknesses of the technique. The earlier of these two studies conducted a cost-benefit analysis of the Support Work Experiment carried out by the Vera Institute of Justice in New York City between June 1972 and June 1974. The latter conducted a benefit-cost analysis of the Living Insurance for Ex-Offenders (LIFE) experiment carried out by the Bureau of Social Science Research in Baltimore between 1971 and 1974. There are a number of similarities between these two projects which provide valuable insights into potential uses of benefit-cost analysis for criminal justice evaluation. First, both programs were designed to improve the labor market performance of participants as well as to reduce their future criminal activity. In general, it will be true that benefit-cost analysis will be most usefully and easily applied to programs which are designed to increase real output (as these programs were improving labor market skills), as well as to lower the level of negative externalities, e.g., crime. Thus, we would expect more and more successful benefit-cost analyses of work-related programs than of psychological or psychiatric programs designed to improve the adjustment of potential criminals.[44] The reason for this phenomenon is simple: Benefit-cost evaluations are most easily carried out where benefits are evaluated by the market as they are when we observe an individual's wage rate. Second, results of an evaluation using an experimental design were available for both programs. Benefit-cost analysis is designed to value the changes due to a program. Such valuation is obviously not possible if an evaluation using an experimental, or strong quasi-experimental or statistical, design has not been conducted. Thus, the cost of benefit-cost analysis is not justified if we do not have firm evidence of positive program effects.

Both the Friedman and the Mallar and Thornton studies conduct benefit-cost analyses from a number of perspectives, including the classical social perspective advocated by most economists. Friedman conducts additional analyses from the perspective of the taxpayer, the main supporting agency (Welfare Department) and the program participant, while Mallar and Thornton conduct additional analyses from the perspective of the budget of all levels of government, the taxpayer, and the program participant. From what perspectives in addition to the societal it is necessary or indeed desirable to conduct benefit-cost analyses will depend on the particular problem at hand. However, an additional analysis conducted from the point of view of the administering agency or funding government body would seem generally valuable. In what follows, we will be considering only the analyses conducted from a societal point of view, as this is the main analysis and basic to all others.

Both of the studies under consideration relied upon relatively short follow-ups—four months[45] to a year, for most data—to obtain their estimates of behavioral change. A number of important questions arise when obtaining follow-up data for use in a benefit-cost analysis. First and most important, how far in the future can one attribute changes in behavior to program effects? Second, how far in the future can one realistically expect follow-up information to be available? Third, if extended follow-up information is not available, can we project early findings into future periods?

Both studies list and attempt to value a large number of positive external effects, as well as the directly productive effects of improved labor market performance for the programs considered. Consider first the labor market effects and their valuation. Labor market effects are of two types: a lowered unemployment rate and a raised wage. Both analyses under consideration obtained a single estimate for these combined effects. These analyses would be improved if they separated employment from wage effects.[46] A discussion of conditions in the local labor market should preface the employment analysis so that the reader will have some idea of the conditions under which employment effects of the estimated magnitude are likely.

Both studies list and try to value a number of positive externality changes caused by the program.[47] The major such change expected, and the only one we will consider here, is reduced crime. Due to the short follow-up periods mentioned above, both studies were forced to use arrest differences between the experimental and control group as an indicator of the reduction in criminal activity due to the program. Most efforts of which the authors are aware provide far from satisfactory estimates of the social value of avoided crime. Consider three broad types of offenses: offenses involving the destruction or damage of people (e.g., assault) or things (e.g., arson), offenses involving the transfer of property (e.g., larceny); and offenses which mainly involve a violation of social mores (e.g., prostitution). In order to value any of these, it is first necessary to estimate the reduction in offenses as a result of the program.

Second, the offenses avoided must be valued. The social cost of any offense may be divided into three conceptually distinct parts: First is the direct productive loss suffered by society as a result of the offense, e.g., the lowered production due to elimination of or damage to a human or nonhuman resource. Second is the use of resources occasioned by society's efforts to prevent, deter, or punish offenders. These resources include those devoted to the criminal justice system and those used in private efforts (e.g., locks, guards). Finally, there are other externality effects of crime.[48] These other externalities include the fear and anxiety caused by crime, as well as its work disincentive and resource allocation effects.

Given the difficulties of obtaining direct measures of all three parts of the social cost of crime, it might be useful to consider two alternative methods of estimating the value of a crime prevented. The first method would require that one obtain a direct estimate of the amount people would be willing to pay to prevent an offense.[49] The second measure would require that we obtain estimates of the extra cost we see society incurring in order to prevent one offense. If criminal justice expenditures are at an optimal level and optimally allocated, this amount should be equal to the social cost of crime.[50] Neither of the above measures of the social cost of crime has, as far as the authors are aware, been utilized to date.

4. Future Use of the Technique

Benefit-cost analysis is a potentially valuable and, to date, relatively little used tool for evaluating criminal justice programs. While the utilization of the full technique is only appropriate for certain types of evaluation (e.g., those with large productive effects) when the results of experimental or strong quasi-experimental or statistical evaluations are available, many of the insights of benefit-cost analysis should be incorporated into more traditional evaluation designs. First, benefit-cost analysis points up the importance of program costs. All criminal justice evaluations should provide information on the cost of program operations. Second, benefit-cost analysis indicates that these cost figures should reflect the opportunity cost of all resources utilized and should not be merely expenditure figures. Third, benefit-cost analysis indicates that benefits that occur in the future are less valuable than those that occur today, and must be discounted if they are to be correctly valued. Finally, and perhaps most important, the benefit-cost technique forces an evaluator to consider carefully both the nature of the benefits and costs emanating from his program and the value society is likely to place on them.

VI. MULTIATTRIBUTE UTILITY ANALYSIS

Of all the evaluation methods discussed in this chapter, multiattribute utility analysis is the newest to come on the criminal justice evaluation scene. This method enables the researcher to incorporate explicitly into an impact evaluation the values held by different potential users. The user is thereby able to identify from among alternative programs those that maximize the values he or she finds most important.

1. Uses of Multiattribute Utility Analysis in Criminal Justice Evaluation

The technique is presented by Ward Edwards in another chapter of this book and will not be repeated here. To our knowledge, there are no completed impact evaluations of criminal justice programs that apply this technique. There are, however, two promising criminal justice research efforts in progress that do make use of the method. In the first effort, the National Community Anti-Crime Program Evaluation Project, Snapper proposes to use multiattribute utility analysis in conjunction with Bayesian statistics (Research for Social Change, Inc., 1978). At the beginning of the evaluation, the extent to which project goals are attained is unknown. Subjective estimates of goal attainment are therefore used in order to calculate utilities that can guide decisions until more objective data can be obtained. Three data collection cycles are planned during the evaluation. At each cycle, 20 persons will be added to the sample pool for each project selected to participate in the evaluation. Data will be collected from these people, using a variety of techniques (e.g., in-person, telephone, mail surveys). When the data have been collected at each cycle, the utilities are to be recalculated, using Bayesian statistics to integrate the original subjective estimates of goal attainment with the interview data.

In some instances, introducing Bayesian statistics may not be worth what it costs in terms of making the evaluation process more complicated and therefore more difficult to explain to potential users of the evaluation. When the initial subjective estimate is weakly held and assumed equal to a single trial, the objective data will swamp out the subjective estimate when the number of people on which data are collected is large. Assume, for example, that an escort service for the elderly is provided in order to reduce restricted mobility caused by fear of crime. Assume further that the initial subjective estimate is that the probability of success is .5, and that the first-cycle data collection effort shows that 19 program participants out of 20 were successes (i.e., they said they were no longer afraid to go out). The posterior probability, using Bayesian statistics to estimate the revised success rate and assuming $x = \beta = 1$ for the prior, would be:

$$\frac{(1 + 19)}{(1 + 1 + 19 + 1)} = .91$$

Ignoring the earlier subjective estimate of .5 and looking only at the interview data, one would have estimated the probability of success to be .95 instead of .91.

Assume further that at the end of the third cycle, 60 people have been interviewed and that 50 out of the 60 are determined to be successes. The posterior probability would then be

$$\frac{(1 + 50)}{(1 + 1 + 50 + 10)} = .82$$

Ignoring the .5 subjective estimate, one would have estimated the probability of success based upon the interview data to be 50/60 or .83.[51] This small difference between the two methods of estimating the success probability hardly makes it worth the effort to incorporate Bayesian statistics into the multi-attribute utility analysis. This conclusion would not hold, of course, in those instances where prior views are strongly held.

A second effort making use of multiattribute utility analysis evaluates different dispute resolution strategies (Johnson, 1978: 12-14, 21-23). For example, in deciding how successful mediation is compared with court adjudication in the Wayne County (Michigan) Circuit Court, one goal in terms of which the two strategies will be evaluated is speed of settlement. Another goal might be impartiality. Utilities for each strategy will be calculated for each expert, using that expert's judgment of the importance of each goal and the extent to which the strategy achieves that goal. From this information, the method receiving the highest utility can be compared for various subgroups, such as defense attorneys, plaintiff attorneys, and judges.

The potential for using this technique to make explicit differences in values held by different groups is particularly intriguing. On the one hand, groups holding different values could use the same impact information to arrive at different conclusions about which program alternative provides the greatest utility (Guttentag and Snapper, 1974: 73). This feature of multiattribute utility analysis has the advantage of making the evaluator's findings about program impact useful to a wider range of people than would aggregate utilities based upon arbitrary or evaluator-imposed weights. Another possible outcome when groups do not agree on their conclusions about program success or failure, however, is to make explicit their differences in values and thereby increase the level of conflict in the decision-making process.

On the other hand, we may find that "the magnitude of interpersonal disagreement produced by this procedure would be less than that produced by simply arguing about what to do" (Edwards, et al., 1975: 158).[52] The reasoning supporting this possibility is that people with strong viewpoints will, without multiattribute utility analysis, judge a program's success solely upon the extent to which that program is believed to achieve the particular goal they are most interested in. When those holding strong and conflicting viewpoints on a single goal assign utilities, through the multiattribute utility procedure, to all the goals pertinent to a given program, they will probably agree in their evaluation of some of the other goals that they do not feel as strongly about. This agreement on other goals would lead to total program utilities for the groups holding conflicting viewpoints that were more similar than utilities for these groups based upon the single controversial goal.

3. Future Use of the Technique

Theoretically, there is no reason criminal justice programs cannot successfully combine the elements of impact evaluation, process evaluation, benefit-cost analysis, and multiattribute utility analysis. The usual methods of determining impact (i.e., experimental, quasi-experimental, and multivariate statistical designs) can be used to generate the data used in multiattribute analysis for measuring the extent to which program goals are achieved. Once utilities are calculated, the need to make funding decisions subject to budget constraints can be acknowledged by ranking program alternatives in terms of each program's utility divided by cost. Finally, process evaluations can provide information helpful in expanding or replicating programs in other geographic areas. Whether multiattribute utility analysis can become widely used will ultimately depend upon whether decision makers will accept it.

VII. SUMMARY AND CONCLUSIONS

In this chapter, we have reviewed six methods which have been used to extend and strengthen traditional criminal justice evaluations which use experimental or nonequivalent control group designs.

Process evaluation extends traditional evaluation by providing detailed information on the nature of the program evaluated. This technique is of great value in the development of effective programs and in monitoring ongoing projects. In addition, complete process analyses are essential if one is to replicate effective programs successfully. The authors recommended that criminal justice program administrators carefully document the nature and evolution of the programs they administer. If such process evaluations are not carried out, it is impossible to know what caused any positive effects which may be obtained.

Multivariate statistical techniques and time-series analysis may be used either to strengthen traditional evaluative designs or to evaluate programs when no control or comparison group is available. When used in conjunction with a control or comparison group, these techniques increase the accuracy with which program effects can be measured. When used in the absence of a control or comparison group these techniques provide relatively weak evaluative designs unless there are special circumstances. For multivariate statistical techniques, favorable circumstances are extensive, quantifiable theoretical knowledge or quantifiable knowledge of decision-making processes. Time-series analysis produces strongest evaluations when good, consistent time-series data are available, program implementation is relatively abrupt, and the nature of program effects are relatively well understood. The authors recommend that these two techniques be used in conjunction with comparison or control groups whenever possible. The practicing evaluator should be warned, however, that both techniques require relatively advanced statistical skills to be used properly and effectively. The evaluator planning to use these techniques for the first time should either put aside adequate time to master them or hire someone who has mastered them. If it is not possible to establish either a control or comparison group, the authors recommend that multivariate statistical techniques or time-series analysis be used to evaluate correctional programs. Such evaluations should be careful to point out the relative weakness of the design and discuss inaccuracies which are possible in the measures of program effects obtained.

Cost-effectiveness analysis extends traditional evaluative designs by considering the cost at which any beneficial program effects have been purchased. This technique provides a cost per unit of impact by dividing various program output measures into the costs incurred to obtain them (e.g., cost-crime prevented). This technique is relatively simple to use and understand, and in this period of financial stringency should be increasingly utilized. The relatively poor quality of cost-accounting systems in many criminal justice areas means that this technique will be less accurately and widely utilized than it should be. The authors recommend increased use of this technique and improved criminal justice cost-accounting systems.

Benefit-cost analysis and multiattribute utility analysis extend traditional evaluative designs by converting various program outputs to a common unit of measure and summing to obtain an overall measure of program effectiveness. Benefit-cost analysis uses the dollar as the common unit of measure, while multiattribute utility analysis uses subjective evaluations of the worth of various program outputs.

Benefit-cost analysis is relatively difficult to use in many criminal justice settings and requires relatively advanced technical skills. As a result, the use of the complete techniques should be limited to evaluation of successful programs designed to increase marketed output (e.g., work-related programs). However, various portions of the techniques can be used more extensively. First, a complete listing of expected program benefits and costs is a useful organizational device. Second, the lesser value of future benefits and costs should be considered. Finally, opportunity costs rather than budgetary outlays provide a true measure of program costs. We recommend that the above insights of benefit-cost analysis be more extensively used in criminal justice evaluations.

Multiattribute utility analysis is a relatively new evaluative technique which is only now being used in criminal justice evaluations. The technique is relatively easy to use and understand. It uses either subjective or objective evidence of program effects and values these effects subjectively. Thus, this technique may be used to extend traditional evaluative designs or it may be used as a substitute for them. The accuracy of the results obtained by this technique depends on the accuracy of measurement of program effects and subjective values of these effects. The technique is weak if only subjective measures of program effects are used and group values are poorly articulated. The technique is strong if program effects have been measured by an experimental design and group values are agreed upon and well articulated. The technique offers intriguing possibilities for aiding in establishing generally accepted group values and for combining subjective and objective knowledge of program effects. We recommend the continued development of this technique.

The six techniques discussed in this chapter should not be considered mutually exclusive, but rather in large part complementary. A useful combination of the techniques described which would provide a complete evaluation of a criminal justice program might be the following: First, while a program is in its formative stages, process analysis might be used to determine the degree to which the program design is being implemented, to improve coordination of various program components, and to discover methods of improving program performance. Tharp and Gallimore (1979) provide an excellent example of the use of process evaluation in this manner. After a program has been completely developed, its impact should be evaluated. The true experiment is the strongest single method for determining the impact of a program, and this method should be used whenever possible. If the random assignment required for a true experiment is not possible, a nonequivalent control group design combined with statistical techniques can provide a strong alternative.

Program costs should be thoroughly documented, and if beneficial program impacts are found, cost-effectiveness ratios should be calculated to determine relative program effectiveness.

Finally, the question of the relative value of various program effects may be addressed by using benefit-cost analysis if program effects can be valued in monetary terms, or multiattribute utility analysis if they cannot.

The complete program evaluation outlined above will rarely be possible. However, at a minimum, criminal justice evaluations should contain an accurate description of the program evaluated, as strong an impact evaluation as possible, and information on program costs.

NOTES

1. Simulation models, which make use of a number of the techniques discussed in this chapter, are not considered separately in this chapter because J. Chaiken et al. (1976) have made a recent survey of simulation models in the criminal justice area. See Richard C. Larson et al. (1976) for a use of simulation to evaluate a police vehicle-monitoring system.

2. For more detailed discussion of the technique, see Brooks (1971); Weiss and Rein (1970); Chommie and Hudson (1974); Bernstein and Freeman (1975: 18-19, 65-81); Morris and Fitz-Gibbon (1978); Stufflebeam (1967); and Krisberg's chapter in this volume.

3. McCall (1975) has developed a good manual that explains how to use these techniques when studying criminal justice programs. See Tharp and Gallimore (1979) for an explanation of how the techniques of process evaluation can be integrated into a research and development effort that includes a lengthy succession of methods for obtaining information about programs.

4. These five evaluations are reported in the Governor's Commission on Crime Prevention and Control (1974), Thomas (n.d.), Slotnick (n.d.), Pick and Billings (1975), and Tien et al. (1978), respectively.

5. There has been considerable work designed to model the timing of recidivism for a treatment and comparison group. For examples, see Stolmack and Harris (1974), Maltz and McCleary (1977), and Bloom (1978). Significant differences in model parameters for the two groups are interpreted as treatment effects. Models of this type of which the authors are aware assume that individual characteristics do not affect the time path of recidivism. As the individual models surveyed here do not make this assumption, and allow group predictions to be built on the basis of individual results, these models seem more satisfying. Because of their assumptions, these recent recidivism timing models seem to be most applicable to situations where an experimental design is used.

6. See Wilkins (1967) for a review of early prediction models.

7. See Brody (1976: 42-48) for a list of criminal justice evaluations which use this technique. Budnick (1973) surveys some models which seek to predict crime rates. Gottfredson (1967) surveys predictive models in the juvenile area, while Simon (1971) provides a survey of models for adult offenders.

8. See Mannheim and Wilkins (1955) and Gottfredson and Beverly (1962) for early uses of this approach. Schmidt and Witte (1979) provide a more recent example. Monahan (1978) provides a survey of work on prediction of violent criminal behavior.

9. See Budnick (1973) for a survey.

10. See Budnick (1973) for the development of this technique and an example of its use to evaluate intensive police patrol activities in Washington, D.C., in 1970. Chelimsky's

(1976) evaluation of the High Impact Anti-Crime Program provides a more recent illustration of this technique.

11. Simon (1971) compares a number of techniques as well as surveying previous comparisons. Her work seems to indicate that ordinary least squares analysis and predictive attribute analysis perform most satisfactorily. However, she does not compare the above techniques with the more advanced techniques (e.g., maximum likelihood estimation, descriminant analysis). The authors' own work indicates that these latter techniques provide more accurate predictions. See Witte and Schmidt (1979).

12. This term has been variously defined—e.g., significant at the 10 percent level, two-tailed test. Theil (1971: 543-545) suggests maximizing adjusted R^2. The criterion is equivalent to minimizing the standard error of the residuals and will "on the average" choose the correct model. A more desirable criterion is to select the model which gives the most accurate prediction for a sample not used to estimate the model (external predictions). Simon (1971) presents a number of model comparison techniques.

13. See van de Geer (1971) for a description of discriminant analysis. Pindyck and Rubenfeld (1976) give a simple description of the probit and logit models, while Theil (1971) gives additional details. See Palmer and Carlson (1976) or Witte and Schmidt (1978) for examples of the use of logit analysis in a criminal justice setting, Cook (1975) for an example of probit analysis, and Fair Isaacs, Inc. (1971) for an example of discriminant analysis.

14. See Gottfredson and Beverly (1962), Wolfgang et al. (1972), and Blumstein and Cohen (1974) for examples.

15. The logical problem is that the probability of an event (e.g., return to crime) cannot exceed 1 nor be less than 0, while an OLS model can clearly yield a prediction outside this range. The statistical problem involves the violation of two assumptions underlying the OLS model, normality of the residuals and their constant variance across observations (homoskedasticity). See Theil (1971) or Pindyck and Rubenfeld (1976) for details. The violation of these assumptions means that coefficient estimates remain unbiased and consistent, but that such estimates are not either efficient or asymptotically efficient. Furthermore, all estimates of variances are biased, and no tests of significance or confidence intervals may validly be constructed.

16. This is a recommendation of the National Academy of Sciences' Panel on Research on Rehabilitative Techniques.

17. This techniques was developed by Tobin (1958) and has been refined by Amemiya (1973). For an example of the use of this technique in criminal justice, see Witte et al. (1978).

18. See Schmidt and Witte (1979) for an illustration of the use of these models in this way.

19. See Cook (1977) or Blumstein et al. (1978) for extensive discussions of this problem.

20. Individual prediction also suffers from similar data problems, but such problems may be less serious (due to the randomness of measurement error) and have been less discussed. Self-reports have not, as far as the authors are aware, been modeled.

21. Unfortunately, these models do not predict as well as one would like. See Cooper (1972) for a review.

22. There have been a number of recent calls for more and better theory in the criminal justice area. See Sechrest et al. (1979) and Glaser (1977).

23. This distinction should not be overdrawn. Many concepts in economics are very difficult to measure, e.g., tastes, capital inputs. Economists have simply been less concerned about measurement error and errors in variables than have psychologists and sociologists who have traditionally dominated criminal justice research. See Goldberger (1974) for a discussion of why this may be so.

24. See Cain (1975) or Alwin and Sullivan (1976: 83-106) for recent discussion of this evaluative technique.

25. Gottfredson et al. (1975) have made some interesting advances in modeling the parole selection process.

26. See Kmenta (1971: 391-394) for additional details and an extension to cases involving larger numbers of explanatory variables. The treatment here is similar to Cain's (1975).

27. For a complete account of this evaluation, see Zimring (1976).

28. For an example in which record-keeping improvements led to a higher reported crime rate, see Campbell (1971: 146-147). For an example in which the police changed reporting practices to make programs appear more effective, see Morrissey (1972).

29. For an illustration of a model developed by Gene V Glass that recognizes a cumulative impact, see Zimring (1976: 567-569).

30. For a recent overview of cost-effectiveness analysis, see Levin (1975).

31. An externality is an effect on an individual or institution not directly involved in a transaction. Such an effect is sometimes termed a "neighborhood effect" or "spillover."

32. Mishan (1976) provides a good description of present practices in benefit-cost analysis, and Aldine has published a compilation of current benefit-cost studies under the title, *Benefit-Cost and Policy Analysis*. The Correctional Economics Center of the American Bar Association has been most active in promoting the use of benefit-cost analysis in the criminal justice area. Part I of their *Handbook of Cost-Benefit Techniques and Applications* (1975) discusses the adoption of this technique in the criminal justice area.

33. See Weimar and Friedman (1979) for a survey of this literature. Perhaps the most thorough and thoughtful benefit-cost analysis completed to date in the criminal justice area is John Holahan's (1971) analysis of Project Crossroads.

34. A recent survey by Witte et al. (1977) of ten states and the federal prison system found that only the federal system included depreciation of buildings and equipment in their cost data. Further, many state systems had no data available at the prison unit or program level. Much data that were found to be available were very difficult to access, e.g., hard copy, archived data.

35. See Lee Sechrest et al. (1979) for a survey.

36. Minor benefits may be catalogued with an indication of a direction of effect, but without direct quantification. For example, see Rothenberg's (1967) evaluation of urban renewal.

37. The use of this measure requires that workers are paid their marginal product. This may not occur if competition does not prevail in product and factor markets or if taxes and subsidies affect wage payment.

38. It is defined by Mishan (1976: 134) as "a measure of the money transfer necessary, following some economic change, to maintain the individual's welfare at its original level."

39. See Mishan (1976) for an extended discussion of this problem, and Rothenberg (1975) for a briefer treatment.

40. Many current analyses use 5 percent, 10 percent, and 15 percent as alternative discount rates. An alternative to selecting a discount rate is to determine the internal rate of return for a program. The internal rate of return is defined as that discount rate which makes the present value of the net benefits (present value of benefits minus costs) equal to zero. See Mishan (1976: ch. 28) for additional details.

41. Use of the net present value per dollar cost rather than the internal rate of return criterion may yield different project ranking. Mishan (1976) has developed a normalization procedure that will make both techniques yield the same ranking. If possible, this normalization procedure should be used.

42. This step is only necessary if public funds are not adequate to cover all projects with NPVs > 1, which is likely to be the case always.

43. Because the estimates of future benefits and costs, their valuation, and the discount rate are all generally point estimates of a distribution of possible values, it has been suggested that a probability distribution of possible values of the net present value per dollar cost be presented (Mishan, 1976: ch. 56). This is highly desirable, particularly where uncertainty is great, as it is likely to be in criminal justice evaluations.

44. This observation is supported by the existing literature. See Weimar and Friedman (1979) for review.

45. Friedman plans a three- to five-year follow-up period, and the current paper is an interim report.

46. This approach is generally advocated for regional development projects and accords with the separation of efficiency from equity and stability considerations, advocated my Musgrave and Musgrave (1973).

47. In addition to reduced crime, Friedman tries to value health and educational benefits (these are not externalities in the economic sense), while Mallar and Thornton value some decreased administrative expenses.

48. See Friedman (1976a) or Holahan (1971) for excellent discussions of these latter effects. This category should also include the administrative cost of insurance schemes. See Mallar and Thornton (1978) for a discussion.

49. Acton (1976) has advocated this approach for valuing life in medical evaluations. He also presents some results of a survey which attempts to obtain such estimates.

50. For the original development of this position, see Becker (1968). Stigler (1974) further develops Becker's ideas and suggests that in many areas of criminal justice enforcement allocation may be optimal.

51. Another example of the prior estimates being swamped by the empirical data is contained in Research for Social Change, Inc. (1978: 65-66).

52. An instance in which the method was applied and resulted in less disagreement is described in Edwards et al. (1975: 158-159).

REFERENCES

Acton, J. (1976) "Measuring the Monetary Value of Lifesaving Programs." *Law and Contemporary Problems* 40: 46-72.

Alwin, D. F. and M. J. Sullivan (1976) "Issues of Design and Analysis in Evaluation Research," pp. 83-106 in I. N. Bernstein (ed.) *Validity Issues in Evaluative Research.* Beverly Hills, CA: Sage Publications.

Amemiya, T. (1973) "Regression Analysis When the Dependent Variable is Truncated Normal." *Econometrica* 41: 997-1016.

American Bar Association, Correctional Economics Center (1975) *A Handbook of Cost-Benefit Techniques and Applications.* Washington, D.C.: American Bar Association.

Becker, G. S. (1968) "Crime and Punishment: An Economic Approach." *Journal of Political Economy* 76: 169-217.

Bernstein, I. N. and H. E. Freeman (1975) *Academic and Entrepreneurial Research.* New York: Russell Sage.

Bloom, H. S. (1978) "Evaluating Human Service and Criminal Justice Programs by Modeling the Probability and Timing of Recidivism." Discussion Paper D78-9, Department of City and Regional Planning, Harvard University.

Blumstein, A. and J. Cohen (1974) "An Evaluation of a College-Level Program in a Maximum Security Prison." Working Paper, Urban Systems Institute, School of Urban and Public Affairs, Carnegie-Mellon University.

——— and D. Nagin [eds.] (1978) *Deterrence and Incapacitation: Estimating the Effects of Criminal Sanctions on Crime Rates.* Washington, DC: National Academy of Sciences.

Box, G.E.P. and G. M. Jenkins (1976) *Time Series Analysis: Forecasting and Control.* San Francisco: Holden-Day.

Brody, S. R. (1976) *The Effectiveness of Sentencing: A Review of the Literature.* London: Her Majesty's Stationary Office.

Brooks, M. P. (1971) "The Community Action Program as a Setting for Applied Research," pp. 53-62 in F. G. Caro (ed.) *Readings in Evaluation Research.* New York: Russell Sage.

Budnick, F. S. (1973) "Crime Correlated Areas: An Evaluation of the Impact of High Intensity Police Patrol Operations." D.B.A. dissertation, University of Maryland.

Cain, G. G. (1975) "Regression and Selection Models to Improve Nonexperimental Comparisons," in C. A. Bennett and A. A. Lumsdaine (eds.) *Evaluation and Experiment.* New York: Academic Press.

Campbell, D. T. (1971) "Reforms as Experiments." *Urban Affairs Quarterly* 7, 2: 133-171.

——— and R. F. Boruch (1975) "Making the Case for Randomized Assignment to Treatments by Considering the Alternatives: Six Ways in Which Quasi-Experimental Evaluations in Compensatory Education Tend to Underestimate Effects," pp. 195-296 in C. A. Bennett and A. A. Lumsdaine (eds.) *Evaluation and Experiment.* New York: Academic Press.

Campbell, D. T. and H. L. Ross (1968) "The Connecticut Crackdown on Speeding: Time-Series Data in Quasi-Experimental Analysis." *Law and Society Review* 3, 1: 33-53.

Campbell, D. T. and J. C. Stanley (1966) *Experimental and Quasi-Experimental Designs for Research.* Skokie, IL: Rand McNally.

Carr-Hill, R. A. and N. H. Stern (1973) "An Econometric Model of the Supply and Control of Recorded Offenses in England and Wales." *Journal of Public Economics* 2: 289-318.

Chaiken, J. (1977) *What's Known about Deterrent Effects of Police Activities.* Santa Monica, CA: Rand Corporation. (P-5735-1)

Chaiken, J. et al. (1976) *Criminal Justice Models: An Overview.* Washington, DC: Government Printing Office.

——— (1974) *The Impact of Police Activity on Subway Crime: Robberies on the New York City Subway System.* New York: Rand Institute. (R-1424-NYC)

Chelimsky, E. (1976) *High Impact Anti-Crime Program.* Washington, DC: Government Printing Office:

Chommie, P. W. and J. Hudson (1974) "Evaluation of Outcome and Process." *Social Work* 19, 6: 682-687.

Clarke, S. H., J. L. Freeman, and G. G. Koch (1976) "Bail Risk: A Multivariate Analysis." *Journal of Legal Studies* 5: 341-385.

Cirel, P. et al. (1977) *Community Crime Prevention: An Exemplary Project.* Washington, DC: Government Printing Office.

Comptroller General of the United States (1975) The Pilot Cities Program: Phaseout Needed Due to Limited National Benefits. Washington, DC: General Accounting Office. (B-171019)

Cook, P. J. (1977) "Punishment and Crime: A Critique of Current Findings Concerning the Preventive Effects of Punishment." *Law and Contemporary Problems* 41: 164-204.

Cook, T. D. and D. T. Campbell (1976) "The Design and Conduct of Quasi-Experiments and True Experiments in Field Settings," pp. 223-326 in M. D. Dunnette (ed.) *Handbook of Industrial and Organizational Psychology.* Skokie, IL: Rand McNally.

Cooper, R. L. (1972) "The Predictive Performance of Quarterly Econometric Models of the United States," pp. 813-926 in B. G. Hickman (ed.) *Econometric Models of Cyclical Behavior.* New York: National Bureau of Economic Research.

Cooper, W. D. (1968) "An Economic Analysis of the Work-Release Program in North Carolina." Ph.D. dissertation, North Carolina State University, Raleigh, North Carolina.

Deutsch, S. J. (1977) "Stochastic Models of Crime Rates," pp. 32-63 in *A Proposal for Stochastic Modeling and Analysis of Crime—Phase II.* Atlanta: Georgia Institute of Technology.

Edwards, W. and M. Guttentag (1975) "Experiments and Evaluations: A reexamination," pp. 409-463 in C. A. Bennett and A. A. Lumsdaine (eds.) *Evaluation and Experiment.* New York: Academic Press.

Edwards, W. (1979) "Multiattribute Utility Measurement: Evaluating Desegregation Plans in a Highly Political Context," in R. Perloff (ed.) *Evaluator Interventions: Pros and Cons.* Beverly Hills, CA: Sage Publications

——— M. Guttentag, and K. Snapper (1975) "A Decision-Theoretical Approach to Evaluation Research," pp. 139-181 in E. L. Struening and M. Guttentag (eds.) *Handbook of Evaluation Research Volume 1.* Beverly Hills, CA: Sage Publications.

——— Edwards, W. et al. (1963) "Bayesian Statistical Inference for Psychological Research.' *Psychological Review* 70, 3: 193-242.

Empey, L. T. and M. L. Erickson (1972) *The Provo Experiment: Life and Death of an Innovation.* Lexington, MA: D. C. Heath.

Fair Isaacs, Inc. (1971) "Development of a Scoring System to Predict Success on Work Release." Prepared for the District of Columbia Department of Correction.

Fay, M. et al. (1978) *Second Annual Report of the National Supported Work Demonstration.* New York: Manpower Demonstration Research Corporation.

Freeman, H. E. (1977) "The Present Status of Evaluation Research," pp. 19-51 in M. Guttentag (ed.) *Evaluation Studies Review Annual, Volume 2.* Beverly Hills, CA: Sage Publications.

Friedman, L. S. (1977) "An Interim Evaluation of the Supported Work Experiment." *Policy Analysis* 3: 147-170.

——— (1976a) *The Economics of Crime and Justice.* Morristown, NJ: General Learning Press.

——— (1976b) "The Evolution of a Bail Reform." *Policy Sciences* 7: 281-313.

Galvin, J. L. et al. (1977) *Instead of Jail: Pre- and Post-Trial Alternatives to Jail Incarceration, Planning, Staffing, Evaluating Alternative Programs, Volume 5.* Washington, DC: Government Printing Office.

Glaser, D. (1977) "Concern with Theory in Correctional Evaluation Research." *Crime and Delinquency* 23: 173-179.

Glass, G. V (1968) "Analysis of Data on the Connecticut Speeding Crackdown as a Time-Series Quasi-Experiment." *Law and Society Review* 3, 1: 55-76.

——— et al. (1971) "The 1900 Revision of the German Divorce Laws: Analysis of Data as a Time-Series Quasi-Experiment." *Law and Society Review* 5: 539-562.

Glueck, S. and E. Glueck (1960) *Predicting Delinquency and Crime.* Cambridge, MA: Harvard University Press.

Goldberger, A. S. (1974) "Unobservable Variables in Econometrics," pp. 193-213 in P. Zarembka (ed.) *Frontier in Econometrics.* New York: Academic Press.

Goldstein, J. H. (1972) "The Effectiveness of Manpower Training Programs: A Review of Research on the Impact on the Poor," pp. 338-393 in W. A. Niskanen et al. (eds.) *Benefit-Cost and Policy Analysis.* Chicago: AVC.

Gottfredson, D. M. (1967) "Assessment and Prediction Methods in Crime and Delinquency," Appendix to President's Commission on Law Enforcement and the Administration of Justice, *Juvenile Delinquency and Youth Crime*. Washington, DC: Government Printing Office.

––– and R. F. Beverly (1962) "Development and Operational Use of Prediction Methods in Correctional Work." *Proceedings of the American Statistical Association*.

Gottfredson, D. M. et. al. (1975) "Making Paroling Policy Explicit." *Crime and Delinquency* 21: 34-44.

Governor's Commission on Crime Prevention and Control (1974) "Minnesota Ombudsman for Corrections."

Griliches, Z. and W. Mason (1972) "Education, Income and Ability." *Journal of Political Economy* 80: S74-S103.

Grizzle, G. A. (1975) "Preventing Drug Abuse: A Comparison of Education, Treatment, and Law Enforcement Approaches." *Criminal Justice and Behavior* 2, 4: 372-382.

–––– (1974) *Using Time Series Analysis to Evaluate the Impact of Team Policing*. Chapel Hill: Institute of Government, University of North Carolina.

Guttentag, M. (1973) "Subjectivity and Its Use in Evaluation Research." *Evaluation* 1, 2: 60-65.

––– and K. Snapper (1974) "Plans, Evaluations, and Decisions." *Evaluation* 2: 58-64, 73-74.

Hall, R. E. (1976) "The Effectiveness of Training Programs in Raising Earnings." Prepared for the Secretary of Labor's Invitational Conference, Washington, D.C.

Harberger, A. C. (1971) "Three Basic Postulates for Applied Welfare Economics: An Interpretive Essay." *Journal of Economic Literature* 9: 785-797.

Holahan, J. (1974) "Measuring the Benefits of Prison Reform," in R. H. Haveman et. al. (eds.) *Benefit-Cost and Policy Analysis*. Chicago: AVC.

––– (1971) *A Benefit-Cost Analysis of Project Crossroads*. Washington, DC: National Committee for Children and Youth.

Johnson, E. C. (1978) "Alternatives to Adjudication: An International Study." Grant application submitted to the Law Enforcement Assistance Administration by the Social Science Research Institute, University of Southern California.

Joreskog, K. G. (1973) "A General Method for Estimating a Linear Structural Equation System," pp. 85-112 in A. S. Goldberger and O. D. Duncan (eds.) *Structural Equation Models in the Social Sciences*. New York: Seminar.

Klein, L. R. (1969) "Econometric Analysis of the Tax Cut," in J. S. Duesenberry et. al. (eds.) *The Brookings Model: Some Further Results*. Chicago: AVC.

Kmenta, J. (1971) *Elements of Econometrics*. New York: MacMillan.

Larson, R. C. et. al. (1976) "Evaluation of an Implemented AVM System: Phase I." Prepared by Public Systems Evaluation, Inc., Cambridge, Massachusetts, for the National Institute of Law Enforcement and Criminal Justice.

Levin, H. M. (1975) "Cost-Effectiveness Analysis in Evaluating Research," pp. 89-122 in M. Guttentag and E. L. Struening (eds.) *Handbook of Evaluation Research, Volume 2*. Beverly Hills, CA: Sage Publications.

Lewis, H. G. (1963) *Unionism and Relative Wages in the United States*. Chicago: University of Chicago Press. (This work is currently under revision.)

Magidson, J. (1977) "Toward a Causal Model Approach for Adjusting for Pre-Existing Differences in the Nonequivalent Control Group Situation: A General Alternative to ANCOVA." *Evaluation Quarterly* 1: 399-420.

Mallar, C. D. and C.V.D. Thornton (1978) "An Estimate of an Average Cost Curve for from the Life Experiment." *Journal of Human Resources* 13: 208-236.

Maltz, M. D. and R. McCleary (1977) "The Mathematics of Behaviorial Change." *Evaluation Quarterly* 1: 421-438.

Mannheim, H. and L. T. Wilkins (1955) *Prediction Methods in Relation to Borstal Training.* London: Her Majesty's Stationary Office.

McCall, G. J. (1975) Observing the Law: Applications of Field Methods to the Study of the Criminal Justice System. Washington, DC: Government Printing Office.

McGuire, W. J. and A. D. Witte (1978) "An Estimate of an Average Cost Curve for Large-Scale Correctional Institutions." Working Paper, Department of Economics, University of North Carolina at Chapel Hill.

Mishan, E. J. (1976) *Cost-Benefit Analysis: New and Expanded Edition.* New York: Praeger.

Monahan, J. (1978) "The Prediction of Violent Criminal Behavior: A Methodological Critique and Prospectus," pp. 244-269 in A. Blumstein et al. (eds.) *Deterrence and Incapacitation: Estimating the Effects of Criminal Sanctions on Crime Rates.* Washington, DC: National Academy of Sciences.

Morris, L. L. and C. T. Fitz-Gibbon (1978) *How to Measure Program Implementation.* Beverly Hills, CA: Sage Publications.

Morrissey, W. R. (1972) "Nixon Anti-Crime Plan Undermines States." *Justice Magazine* 1, 5/6: 8-11.

Murray C. A. and R. E. Krug (1975a) *The National Evaluation of the Pilot Cities Program: A Team Approach to Improving Local Criminal Justice Systems.* Washington, DC: American Institutes for Research.

Murray, C. A. and R. E. Krug (1975a) *The National Evaluation of the Pilot Cities Program: Executive Summary.* Washington, DC: National Institute of Law Enforcement and Criminal Justice.

Musgrave, R. A. and P. B. Musgrave (1973) *Public Finance in Theory and Practice.* New York: McGraw-Hill.

Myers, S. L., Jr. (1976) "Victimization Reporting Behavior: The Case of Illegal Transfers." Working Paper, Department of Economics, University of Texas at Austin.

Ohlin, L. E. (1951) *Selection for Parole.* New York: Russell Sage.

Ostrom, C. W. (1978) *Time Series Analysis: Regression Techniques.* Beverly Hills, CA: Sage Publications.

Pennsylvania Governor's Justice Commission (1976) *Establishment of a District Office and Outreach Centers in the Philadelphia Area for the Pennsylvania Board of Probation and Parole: Final Report*

Palmer, J. and P. Carlson (1976) "Problems with the Use of Regression Analysis in Prediction Studies." *Journal of Research in Crime and Delinquency* 13: 64-81.

Pick, D. J. and C. Billings (1975) *A Systems Approach to the Evaluation of the Marin County TASC Program.* San Rafael, CA: Equinox Systems, Inc.

Pindyck, R. S. and D. L. Rubinfield (1976) *Econometric Models and Economic Forecasts.* New York: McGraw-Hill.

Press, S. J. (1971) *Some Effects of an Increase in Police Manpower in the 20th Precinct of New York City.* New York: Rand Institute. (R-704-NYC)

Research for Social Change, Inc. (1978) National Community Anti-Crime Program Evaluation Project Work Plan. Washington, DC: Author.

Rezmovic, E. L. (1979) "Methodological Problems and Prospects in Correctional Rehabilitation Research," in L. Sechrest et al., *Rehabilitation of Criminal Offenders: Problems and Prospects.* Washington, DC: National Academy of Sciences.

Robertson, L. S. et al. (1973) "Jail Sentences for Driving While Intoxicated in Chicago: A Judicial Policy That Failed." *Law and Society Review* 8, 1: 55-67.

Ross, H. L. (1977) "The Neutralization of Severe Penalties: Some Traffic Law Studies," pp. 569-580 in M. Guttentag (ed.) *Evaluation Studies Review Annual, Volume 2.* Beverly Hills, CA: Sage Publications.

––– (1976) "The Scandinavian Myth: The Effectiveness of Drinking-and-Driving Legislation in Sweden and Norway," pp. 578-604 in Gene V Glass (ed.) *Evaluation Studies Review Annual, Volume 1.* Beverly Hills, CA: Sage Publications.

––– (1973) "Law, Science, and Accidents: The British Road Safety Act of 1967." *Journal of Legal Studies* 2, 1: 1-78.

Rossi, P. H. (1978) "Evaluating Human Services Delivery Systems." Working Paper, Social and Demographic Research Institute, University of Massachusetts, Amherst. (un published)

Rothenberg, J. (1975) "Cost-Benefit Analysis: A Methodological Exposition," pp. 55-88 in M. Guttentag and E. L. Struening (eds.) *Handbook of Evaluation Research, Volume 2.* Beverly Hills, CA: Sage Publications.

––– (1967) *Economic Evaluation of Urban Renewal.* Washington, DC: Brookings.

Sajovic, M. I. and R. M. Goldsmith (1978) "The Effects of the 1973 Drug Laws on Heroin Use in New York City," pp. 1-96 in *Staff Working Papers of the Drug Law Evaluation Project: A Companion Volume to the Final Report of the Joint Committee on New York Drug Law Evaluation.* Washington, DC: National Institute of Law Enforcement and Criminal Justice.

Schmidt, P. and A. D. Witte (1979) "Models of Criminal Recidivism and an Illustration of Their Use in Evaluating Correctional Programs," in L. Sechrest et al., *Rehabilitation of Criminal Offenders: Problems and Prospects.* Washington, DC: National Academy of Sciences.

Schnelle, J. F. et al. (1975) "Social Evaluation Research: The Evaluation of Two Police Patrolling Strategies." *Journal of Applied Behavior Analysis.* 8, 4: 353-365.

Sechrest, L. et al. (1979) *Rehabilitation of Criminal Offenders: Problems and Prospects.* Washington, DC: National Academy of Sciences.

Sherwood, C. C., J. N. Morris, and S. Sherwood (1975) "A Multivariate, Nonrandomized Matching Technique for Studying the Impact of Social Interventions," pp. 183-224 in E. L. Struening and M. Guttentag (eds.) *Handbook of Evaluation Research, Volume 1.* Beverly Hills, CA: Sage Publications.

Simon, F. H. (1971) *Prediction Methods in Criminology.* London: Her Majesty's Stationary Office.

Slotnick, M. (n.d.) "Community-Based Residential Treatment Facilities: The Case of Dreyfous House," pp. 45-96 in Mayor's Criminal Justice Coordinating Council, *Evaluating Demonstration Programs: Two Case Studies.*

Stigler, G. J. (1974) "The Optimum Enforcement of Laws," pp. 55-67 in G. S. Becker and W. M. Landes (eds.) *Essays in the Economics of Crime and Punishment.* New York: National Bureau of Economic Research.

Stolmack, S. and C. M. Harris (1974) "Failure Rate Analysis Applied to Recidivism Data." *Operations Research* 22: 1192-1205.

Stufflebeam, D. S. (1967) "The Use and Abuse of Evaluation in Title III." *Theory in Practice* 6, 3: 126-133.

Tharp, R. G. and R. Gallimore (1979) "The Ecology of Program Research and Development: A Model of Evaluation Succession," in L. Sechrest et al. (eds.) *Evaluation Studies Review Annual, Volume 4.* Beverly Hills, CA: Sage Publications.

Theil, H. (1971) *Principles of Econometrics.* New York: John Wiley.

Thomas, E.M.P. (n.d.) 'Evaluation of the Treatment Release Program, Middlesex County House of Correction." Report to the Eastern Middlesex, Massachusetts, Criminal Justice Development Agency.

Tien, J. M., J. W. Simon, and R. C. Larson (1978) *An Alternative Approach in Police Patrol: The Wilmington Split-Force Experiment.* Washington, DC: Government Printing Office.

Tobin, J. (1958) "Estimation of Relationships for Limited Dependent Variables." *Econometrica* 26: 24-36.

van de Geer, J. P. (1971) *Introduction to Multivariate Analysis for the Social Sciences*. San Francisco: Freeman.

Walzer, N. (1976) "Economies of Scale and Municipal Police Services: The Illinois Experience," in L. R. McPheters and W. B. Stronge, *The Economics of Crime and Law Enforcement*. Springfield, IL: Charles C Thomas.

Weimar, D. L. and L. S. Friedman (1979) "Efficiency Considerations in Criminal Rehabilitation Research: Cost and Consequences," in L. Sechrest et al. *Report of the Panel on Research on Rehabilitative Techniques*. Washington, DC: National Academy of Sciences.

Weiss, R. S. and M. Rein (1970) "The Evaluation of Broad-Aim Programs: Experimental Design, Its Difficulties, and an Alternative." *Administrative Science Quarterly* 15: 97-104.

Wilkins, L. T. (1967) "Survey of the Field from the Standpoint of Facts and Figures," in *The Effectiveness of Punishment and Other Measures of Treatment*. Strasbourg: Council of Europe.

Witte, A. D. (1977) "Work Release in North Carolina—a Program That Works!" Law and Contemporary Problems. 41: 230-251.

——— (1976) "Earnings and Jobs of Ex-Offenders: A Case Study." *Monthly Labor Review* 99: 31-39.

Witte, A. D. and P. Schmidt (forthcoming) "Determinants of the Seriousness of Criminal Activities: The Misdemeanor Felony Distinction," in *Proceedings of the National Conference on Criminal Justice Evaluation*. Washington, DC: Government Printing Office.

——— (1979) "An Analysis of the Type of Criminal Activity Using the Logit Model." *Journal of Research in Crime and Delinquency* 16: 164-179.

——— (1977) "An Analysis of Recidivism, Using the Truncated Lognormal Distribution." *Journal of the Royal Statistical Society, Series C (Applied Statistics)* 26: 302-311.

Witte, A. D., W. J. McGuire, and R. A. Hofler (1977) "An Empirical Investigation of the Short and Long Run Cost Functions Characterizing Criminal Correctional Institutions: Conventional and Frontier Analysis." Grant Proposal to the National Institute of Law Enforcement and Criminal Justice.

Witte, A. D., P. Schmidt, and R. Sickles (1978) "An Analysis of Time Sentenced After Release from Prison," in *Proceedings of the Criminal Justice Statistics Association*.

Wolfgang, M. E., R. M. Figlio, and T. Sellin (1972) *Delinquency in a Birth Cohort*. Chicago: University of Chicago Press.

Zimring, F. E. (1976) "Firearms and Federal Law: The Gun Control Act of 1968," pp. 511-577 in Gene V Glass (ed.) *Evaluation Studies Review Annual, Volume 1*. Beverly Hills, CA: Sage Publications.

11

Evaluation as Knowledge-Building—
and Vice Versa

James F. Short, Jr.

It is also a good rule not to put overmuch confidence in the observational results that are put forward until they are confirmed by theory [Sir Arthur Eddington].[1]

Nothing is so practical as a good theory [Kurt Lewin].

INTRODUCTION

Theory-testing and what has come to be known as evaluation research are in essential ways the same. The two enterprises typically are carried out by different researchers, with little cross-fertilization. Yet, each time a program is evaluated, some theory—often implied—is in some manner "tested." Failure to recognize this fundamental identity has weakened the contributions of the social and behavioral sciences and social policy to one another.

Gene V Glass, editor of the first volume of *Evaluation Studies Review Annual,* reflects on the confused state of the field in this respect when he identifies as unsolved problems of evaluation research two broad issues (the second and third of seven listed; 1976: 12):

2. What are the differences between evaluation and research? Is evaluation the same as building theories? Or is it dependent on theories? Or is it unaffected by theories?

3. How does evaluation differ from the explanation of why an endeavor produced its results? How does it differ from the narrative portrayal of the endeavor? In what sense is a narrative portrayal evaluative?

AUTHOR'S NOTE: I am grateful for critical readings of drafts of this chapter to Washington State University colleagues Lee Freese, Robert Meier, and Peggy Thoits, and to editor Malcolm Klein. Because I have no special expertise in either evaluation research or in formal theory, their suggestions have been most helpful. They are not, of course, to blame for such inadequacies as remain in the chapter.

Answers to these queries are, of course, complex. Surely all evaluation involves research, though much of it may be of poor quality. The identity or dependency between theory-building/-testing and evaluation research constitutes a broad agenda for this essay, as does the relationship between evaluation and explanation.

If additional evidence of the importance of such issues is required, the Evaluation Research Planning Committee of the Social Science Research Council notes the importance of assessing "the interrelationships between social science theory and social experiments." Specifically, "the degree to which social experiments are explicitly or implicitly based upon social science theory and knowledge needs to be clarified, and the degree to which social experiments contribute to the development of social science theory needs to be examined" (Social Science Research Council, 1979: 16). Numerous other examples of evaluation researchers' concern over the relationship of their discipline and their practice to the theories, perspectives, and bodies of knowledge of the several social sciences, including those in this volume, might be cited. Let it suffice to say that the problem is widely recognized. Regrettably, it is even more widely ignored in practice. Nor, to observe the obvious, is the problem restricted to the field of criminal justice. Indeed, some evaluation research in criminal justice has been noted as exemplary. Glass (1976: 11) writes:

> Evaluation in law enforcement and criminal correction has the best record of findings with clear payoff. Studies of police work and criminal rehabilitation have uncovered potentially huge savings. One feature after another has been altered experimentally, and crime and recidivism rates have remained unchanged. These "no difference" findings, the bane of the experimental scientist, are grist for the evaluator's mill. If cutting reformatory sentences in half does not produce increased recidivism, then shorter sentences are 100% more cost-effective, ceteris paribus. *Doing as well as in the past but doing it more cheaply is a gain in value as surely as is doing better at a greater cost.* A growing body of evaluation research in legal studies exemplifies meticulous scholarship and imaginative data analysis. Sociologists and jurists are verifying the social consequences of enacting laws: no-fault divorce, gun control, decriminalization of alcoholism. This evaluation work is perforce nonexperimental. These evaluators have advanced the art of drawing causal inferences from nonexperimental evidence. Data analysis is like detective work, and greater imagination and care are needed where conventional experimental designs cannot be used. Although only recently seriously undertaken, these studies are already profoundly affecting conceptions of how laws change society [emphasis added].

One can accept this conclusion—and be grateful for it—without resting content. A primary result of years of innovative correctional and preventative concepts and programs is the widely accepted conclusion, expressed in the desultory phrase, "nothing works." Glass's assessment, therefore, might be rephrased in this way: "Doing as poorly as in the past but doing it more cheaply is a gain in value." Acceptance of the implied judgment that value thus gained is the equal of "doing better at a greater cost" clearly is more problematic. An alternative formulation which some find more attractive has it that "everything works with some people and under some conditions." Without theoretically grounded specification of what people and what conditions, the state of the art—let alone the science—is advanced very little. Further, while the economic standard of value is extremely important, it is not the only standard, and we do our disciplines a disservice if we accept it as such.

LIMITATIONS OF ECONOMIC APPROACHES TO EVALUATION

The limitations of economic approaches to evaluation, despite their popularity and their undeniable strength in terms both of theory and method, in fact provide a good example of more general problems of relating evaluation research to the cumulative development of knowledge. Toward this end, a brief examination of two prominent economic approaches follows: (1) cost-effectiveness and (2) the theoretical approach of economics identified most prominently with Becker (1976) and Ehrlich (1979).

The importance to social policy of cost-benefit or -effectiveness analysis is undeniably considerable. It should be recognized, however, that this type of analysis, as such, contributes little to knowledge. In the latter respect, the chief value of cost-benefit analysis is as data—facts our theories must fit, with qualifications concerning the extent to which the data are reliable and valid and the analyses properly done. The qualifications are not trivial—witness the often disputed reliability and validity of data concerning the distribution of crime and delinquency, e.g., by age, race, sex, and social class.

An example from the delinquency prevention literature is apposite. Adams's (1967: 166) cost-effectiveness analysis of a detached worker program in Los Angeles compared correctional costs for one hundred core members of three "comparable gangs" which had received varying degrees of service from the program, ranging from "full service" to "partial service" to "no service." Auditors' estimates of the costs of actions and services were used to determine a "career correctional cost for each boy over the six-year follow up" covering roughly the fourteenth through the twentieth year in the boys' lives. The analysis concluded that after the experiment, correctional costs had decreased for the fully treated group, while for the untreated gang "correctional costs rose from before to after." The partially treated gang members were between these two extremes. Overall correctional costs also varied, the lowest being for the fully treated group and the highest for the untreated group. Of equal interest, data on the younger brothers of the fully and partially treated gangs suggested that the project had an impact of considerable magnitude on these boys, with the greatest impact on the younger siblings of the fully treated gang. This finding suggested that the project might have had an impact on the subculture as well as the gang.

These positive findings—virtually unique in this respect—are challenged by more systematic research on the same detached worker program which found that the overall effect of the project—beyond the three gangs studied by Adams and his colleagues—was to increase delinquency and strengthen the delinquent subculture (Klein, 1971). While the efficacy of these two studies—the reliability and validity of their data, the adequacy of their samples and analyses (particularly the selectivity involved in Adams's choice of gangs to be studied)—require justification in view of apparently contradictory findings, it is quite conceivable that the findings are, in fact, equally valid. The studies are of different "samples" and they employ different criteria and methods of evaluation. The Klein study is the much the broader of the two in questions addressed and data gathered and analyzed. Both, however, are essentially descriptive, leaving much room for "theoretical" and social policy interpretation. Indeed, they lead to very different speculations in both respects. The major point I wish to make is that both yield important facts our theories must fit (subject to the usual caveats) rather than theoretically established principles empirically verified. At the very least, they suggest the extreme caution that should be taken in social policy implementation and the need for far more carefully designed experimentation—conclusions shared by Adams and Klein.

THE ECONOMIC THEORY OF BEHAVIOR, AS APPLIED TO CRIME.

Cost analysis need not be limited to monetary costs of program activity, as Phillips's chapter in this volume amply demonstrates. Going beyond these costs, however, often necessitates converting quite subjective phenomena into "objective" indexes for purposes of analysis, and ignoring others. Unfortunately, the variables ignored or "objectified" in this process may prove to be intransigent with respect to questions of reliability and validity, and most difficult to understand or change in the "real world." These problems lie at the heart of the second economic approach to crime, an application of a general economic theory of behavior. The "fundamental hypothesis" of this approach, in the words of one of its most distinguished contributors, "is that offenders and those who attempt to control crime on the whole respond to measurable opportunities, or incentives" (Ehrlich, 1979: 25). Ehrlich's elaboration of the assumptions and basic components of the model, his research on crime, and that of others within this framework, have contributed significantly to scholarly and public debate on several important issues while raising serious questions among scholars from other disciplines. Messinger and Bittner point out,(1979: 22) for example, that while the fundamental hypothesis is entirely plausible ("indeed, it strikes us as a truism"), the point is that "[people] respond specifically to specific incentives." Determination of the nature of these incentives under varying structural- and individual-level conditions is a formidable task, as many critics have pointed out. Further, many would regard the assumptions of the model as basic questions, the answers to which constitute important facts theory must fit and/or basic theoretical components. Thus, the assumption (Ehrlich's first) that "offenders ... behave as if they seek to maximize their expected utility" (Ehrlich, 1979: 34) is a beginning point for inquiry into the nature of utility for different individuals under different conditions. To what extent is such utility a function of structurally determined conditions (Harris, 1977) or of emerging situations (Short and Strodtbeck, 1965; Berk, 1974)?

Similar questions, and others concerning measurement, can be raised concerning other assumptions of the economic model. The following brief comments are meant to be illustrative. Their theoretical cogency certainly is debatable; indeed, that is the point. What the economist assumes, other social scientists may regard as problematic. Answers to such questions are required before the response of individuals and groups to incentives can be understood, explained, predicted, or controlled—whatever the aim of theory, policy, or practice.

The assumption of stable preferences:

"The assumption that lends the economic approach its explanatory or predictive power, therefore, is that this distribution of individual preferences for crime—penchant for violence, preference for risk, benevolence, malevolence, or envy, to mention a few—is, to a significant degree, stable across different communities at a point in time or in a given community over reasonable periods of time" (Ehrlich, 1979: 34). Does this assumption envision a polarized and unchanging populace where "criminal choice" is unvarying (and unchanging) between individuals or groups of individuals? If so, the evidence suggests otherwise (see, for example, Harris, 1975). And how are we to interpret the further specification that "at the very minimum, the assumption is that changes in preferences for crime are uncorrelated with the observed changes in measurable opportunities for criminal endeavors"? Such an assumption invests preference for crime with an absolute quality which surely is problematic. In any case, preferences—their nature, distribution, and relative stability or change—surely are subject to systematic study (see MacRae, 1978).

Stability is also an issue with respect to Ehrlich's fourth assumption, "market equilibrium," much of the first part of which, I suspect, is acceptable to most behavior scientists—that "An implicit 'market' for criminal activity exists, that coordinates the behavior of offenders, potential victims, and law enforcement authorities, and makes it mutually consistent through the effect of explicit prices (as in most law enforcement and private protection activities), and that the ensuing market equilibrium is stable" (Ehrlich, 1979: 35). The most suspect aspect of this assumption is, of course, the stability of the equilibrium, since the behavior of criminals and of law makers, enforcers, and "victims" is subject to change in response to changes in the larger society, e.g., changing fads and fashions, changing legal definitions, policies, and practices (see DeFleur, 1975, for data concerning changing law enforcement practices with respect to drug traffic), and a variety of other macro-level phenomena.

While less suspect, the earlier part of this assumption poses many problems of interest to policy makers as well as to social scientists. The *nature* of the "market" appears crucial, for surely it varies greatly for different types of criminal behaviors. Compare, for example, professional, organized, and white-collar crime, or violent gang delinquency with drug-using groups. For many of us the nature of the market is precisely what is most interesting and important in explaining the differences in such behavior and changes in their incidence and social distribution (see Cressey, 1969; Ianni, 1972; Klockars, 1974; Finestone, 1957).

Another of the assumptions of the economic model is that "because criminal decisions are made under uncertainty, maximizing behavior involves assessment of probability of 'success' " (Ehrlich, 1979: 34-35). Few behavioral scientists would quarrel with this assumption. Its elaboration, however, poses problems with which students of criminal justice are all too familiar. Ehrlich continues, "Such assessment is subjective to the offender, however, whereas the risk measures utilized in empirical research are based on objective observations" (1979: 35). But note that the latter are subject to a great deal of measurement error. A further assumption necessary to the model is that subjective and objective assessments "tend to be identical or, at least, systematically related" (1979: 35). This is precisely the sort of question which has occupied so much attention as scholars have sought to understand the relationship of various measures of crime and delinquency to the behaviors to which they refer (see Riess, 1976; Elliott and Ageton, 1978; Hindelang, Hirschi and Weis, forthcoming). Decades of research have failed to resolve the issue, though it appears substantial progress is being made. At the very least we must question the nature of the relationship between subjective and objective assessments of risk which is assumed by economists (see MacRae, 1978).

The final assumption of the economic model listed by Ehrlich concerns "the concept of crime":

Whereas the concept of crime relevant for the theoretical analysis of offenders' behavior can be defined as any unlawful activity punishable by a legal sanction, in the theoretical analysis of the demand for public enforcement crime is defined as an activity that imposes external diseconomies in either wealth or utility. External diseconomies (or negative externalities) are said to arise in all those circumstances where an activity by one person imposes costs on other persons, for which it is not feasible to make him compensate them—an activity which cannot be controlled through voluntary exchanges between the parties involved. An illegal activity is thus conceived of in the analysis as one which imposes costs on society in excess of the direct costs borne by the perpetrator [1979: 35-36].

We have not the space to discuss fully the meaning or the implications of this concept of crime for more traditional concepts or, for that matter, for other aspects of economic life in modern societies which are not included under the rubric of crime. Students of crime are particularly concerned to know which types of crime, law-making, and law enforcement are included and which excluded by this assumption. Apparently no crimes are excluded, for Ehrlich next states, "Central to the economic approach is the assumption that despite the diversity of activities defined as illegal, all such activities share some common characteristics, which form the basis for a general analysis of individual participation in crime" (1979: 36).

The point of this discussion is not that assumptions should not be made in either evaluation research or theoretical inquiry. One of the most admirable characteristics of the economic approach to crime is the fact that assumptions are made explicit. They are therefore subject to challenge and, through challenge, modification.[2] Several theoretical and empirical studies of the economics of crime have contributed much to scholarly and public discussion of important issues (see Becker, 1976; Friedman, 1979). The model and its methods have stimulated inquiry into noneconomic factors and, in so doing, have injected rigor into sociological research and theorizing concerning crime (see Cohen et al., forthcoming; Cohen and Felson, 1979).

This brief discussion is intended only to suggest: (1) that while cost effectiveness can be an important tool in evaluation, as it is currently most often practiced it does not explain phenomena which are the focus of social policy; and (2) that the economic approach to crime outlined by Ehrlich also is deceptively simple as a guide to evaluation. Theoretically, the approach offers promise in conjunction with traditional psychological and sociological approaches. I must stress that my queries concerning the assumptions of the economic approach to crime, as sketched by Ehrlich, are not directed at theoretical assumptions per se, or at making them explicit, in the theoretical enterprise. Both are, of course, necessary. Noam Chomsky's discussion of "ideal-ization" in science, while directed toward sociolinguists, is appropriate to other social and behavioral sciences. The questioner asks Chomsky to comment on the fact that some sociologists reject "idealization" (the essence of which lies in the kinds of assumptions made) because it removes language from social reality. Chomsky's reply follows:

> Opposition to idealization is simply objection to rationality, it amounts to nothing more than an insistence that we shall not have meaningful intel-lectual work. Phenomena that are complicated enough to be worth study-ing generally involve the interaction of several systems. Therefore you must abstract some object of study, you must eliminate those factors which are not pertinent. At least if you want to conduct an investigation which is not trivial. In the natural sciences this isn't even discussed, it is self-evident. In the human sciences, people continue to question it. That is unfortunate. When you work within some idealization, perhaps you over-look something which is terribly important. That is a contingency of rational inquiry that has always been understood. One must not be too worried about it. One has to face this problem and try to deal with it, to accommodate oneself to it. It is inevitable [Chomsky and Ronat, 1979: 57].

The problem thus is one of refinement of theory by questioning the efficacy of assumptions and developing the implications for theory and the modifications of it that are required by the addition of knowledge. It is perhaps inevitable that the unproblematic assumptions of one discipline may be at the heart of another's research and theory.

A more basic problem lies in the failure of social and behavioral sciences—and the criticism applies with special force to criminology and its applications and evaluations in criminal justice—to develop cumulative knowledge. We do not have to be reminded by a structural linguist—eminent though the person may be—that the object of a science is to arrive at explanatory principles, as distinct from observations, intuitions, impressions, or even valid generalizations, though each of the former surely contributes to the latter, and all may contribute to explanatory principles at some stage of the theory-building process. Chomsky's further observations again are apposite. Responding to the somewhat presump-tuous question, "Aren't sociologists seeking to preserve the methods they use at present, their interviews, surveys, statistics, and so on, which take the place of scientific practice?" Chomsky (Chomsky and Ronat, 1979: 59) replies:

> Again in itself this type of approach is neither good nor bad. The question is whether it leads to the discovery of principles that are significant. We are back to the difference between natural history and natural science. In

natural history, whatever you do is fine. If you like to collect stones, you can classify them according to their color, their shape, and so forth. Everything is of equal value, because you are not looking for principles. You are amusing yourself, and nobody can object to that. But in the natural sciences, it is altogether different. There the search is for the discovery of intelligible structure and for explanatory principles or of hidden structures that have some intellectual interest. I think this whole discussion comes down to a confusion between two senses of the word interesting. Certain things are interesting in themselves—for example: human action. When a novelist deals with human actions, that's interesting; the flight of a bird, a flower, that's interesting. In this sense, natural history and descriptive sociology are interesting, just like a novel. Both deal with interesting phenomena, and display these to our view, perhaps even yield insight into them somehow.

But there is another meaning of the word interesting, in physics, for example. A phenomenon in itself does not have interest for a physicist. In fact, physicists are generally interested, at least in the modern period, in "exotic" phenomena, of virtually no interest in themselves, in the first sense of the word interesting. What happens under the conditions of a scientific experiment is of no importance in itself. Its interest lies in its relation to whatever theoretical principles are at stake. Natural science, as distinct from natural history, is not concerned with the phenomena in themselves, but with the principles and the explanations that they have some bearing on. There is no right or wrong in the choice of one of these definitions of the word interesting (or some other sense, relating to utility, for example). It is not wrong to be interested in human actions or right to be interested in human actions or right to be interested in particle accelerators. There are simply two entirely different things. The attraction of sociology should not be based on a confusion between the two senses of the word.

The ultimate "attraction" of sociology—its promise (and to some its threat)—lies not in the accumulation of data about "ordinary cases," but in the development of explanatory principles that make possible cumulative knowledge (Freese, 1980). Without theory, in this sense, the welter of observations and facts becomes more confusing than enlightening, particularly to the policy maker, politician, community leader, or concerned citizen who must "make sense" of them as a basis for decisions. This is not an argument against descriptive research and data concerning ordinary cases. The argument is for research strategies which go beyond the collection of data about ordinary cases, for purposes either of theory illustration or of a theoretically informed "real world"—which go beyond by formalizing theory so it is potentially falsifiable, and by designing test cases in the terms of the theory so that measurement error can be specified (Freese and Sell, 1980).

As matters now stand, with few exceptions (and even fewer of these have as yet been directly applied in criminal justice), the state of most sociological theories is such that the design of test cases is problematic. The appalling theoretical weakness of sociological research is apparent to all who are willing to question their assumptions, no more so than among those who "wrestle with the beast," as Joe Lohman used to refer to the "real world" of social action. It was painfully so to those of us who served with the National Commission on the Causes and Prevention of Violence, in 1968-1969 (see Short, 1975). Despite decades of fact-gathering and winnowing the known "facts our theories must fit," we were unable to present convincing theoretical or empirical evidence as to either causes or the "prevention" of many types of violence. Our data were relevant, to be sure, as were our theories, and our reports have continued to be cited by scholars and policy makers alike. But in the absence of formal theory, having empirical support, and confronted with a bewildering array of not-al-together-consistent findings, the commissioners could not reach consensus on important matters. Ideological differences among them, and between them and the staff, very likely would have prevented consensus on some matters in any case. My point, however, is that we often abandon sociology to ideology when we fail to design our research in a context of convincing theory—convincing logically and empirically.[3]

In the remainder of the chapter I will attempt to develop some of the ideas which to this point have been implicit. I will begin with an example from personal experience which, though not entirely successful (for reasons I will discuss), provides a possible model for collaboration between policy makers, practitioners, and social scientists. This will be followed by a (theoretically) more successful model, and a concluding discussion of an idealized model which extends ideas I have previously expressed on the topic.

THE STUDY OF DELINQUENT GANGS AND
DETACHED WORKER PROJECTS

Klein has discussed, with considerable feeling and insight, the temptations and pitfalls of various strategies of "action research" (Klein, 1971: ch. 8). He orients his discussion around the poles of "research purity" versus "action seduction." He characterizes my position as "the extreme academic view point . . . that the most important contribution of the researcher in these programs is the contribution to knowledge." The characterization is, I suppose, accurate for the time it was written. I hope by now that this position is less extreme and less academic than was the case a decade ago. My hope is based both upon my experience in "evaluating" the Program for Detached Workers of the Metropolitan Chicago YMCA and my conviction that contributions to knowledge are the most important products of research for policy makers and practitioners as well as scientists. Good theory thus not only is practical; it is necessary if knowledge (of social problems, policies, and practices) is to be cumulative (which, in turn, greatly enhances its practicality).

I defended this point of view, in contradistinction to the value of lack of "impact" conclusions of four evaluation studies concerned with delinquency prevention: Miller's (1958, 1962) study of the Roxbury Project in Boston, the Cambridge-Somerville project evaluated first by Powers and Witmer (1951) and later by the McCords (1959), Mattick and Caplan's (1967) work on the Chicago Boys' Club project, and Klein's (1971) study of gang projects in Los Angeles. Here I wish to discuss the strategies developed in our action research with the Chicago YMCA, and the sorts of results which I believe justify those strategies.

From its inception, the collaboration on this project between the YMCA and the research team from the University of Chicago was characterized by intellectual purpose and excitement and a spirit of experimentation (see the preface to Short and Strodtbeck, 1965). Competing theories of delinquency and perspectives on urban sociology played an important role in the very first discussions of the project, and they continued to do so throughout its existence. While there was some early discussion of evaluating the effectiveness of the program, in terms of feasibility, implementation, and outcome measures, this idea was never encouraged by the research team for a variety of reasons. Chief among those reasons were the following: (1) While the detached worker program was based loosely on the "opportunity theory" framework developed by Cloward and Ohlin (published in 1960, two years after our project began in the fall of 1958), the connection was tenuous and the theory was not then formally developed (nor has it been since). (2) Competing theoretical positions such as those proposed by Cohen (1955) and Miller (1958) seemed worthy of exploration, both to researchers and YMCA policy makers and implementers. (3) The very fact that the YMCA regarded the detached worker programs as experimental *within the framework of the YMCA* led them to see the research program as "a basis for evaluation and the accumulation of knowledge for further implementation" (Short and Strodtbeck, 1965: vi) rather than as an end in itself.[4] (4) The program was evolving, even as we discussed the research and it continued to change throughout our association with it; researchers agreed that this made sense in view of the lack of clear and precise theoretical directives for action and in view of changing conditions, some of which might be revealed by the research. (5) It was clear from the beginning that evaluation by means of the traditional feasibility, implementation, and outcome measures would be meaningless in view of other objectives of the program, in the absence of a formal and explicit design for the action program and its implementation to conform with theory to be tested. This would be true even if the program were to be judged successful by the traditional criteria, for we would not know what it was that had been "tested." (6) Finally, with the exception of Miller's work—only then beginning to be published—little recent empirical work on gangs had been done since Thrasher (1927), and we felt new theoretical perspectives might emerge from adopting a strategy of discovery in this respect.

In the final analysis, then, we agreed that the research team would have access to all phases of the program, from the highest policy levels to field operations. To the best of my knowledge, that access was never compromised, though our success at observation with different workers, was uneven. "At the close of the first meeting (of academicians and YMCA personnel, convened to consider the research opportunity and what might be done with it) the essential design was clear. We were to open a window on the gangs being worked with by the detached workers and, among other things, collect observations in Chicago to test propositions of the type we had reviewed at the two-day meeting" (Short and Strodtbeck, 1965: vii). Details of research designs, methods of observation and analysis, and findings are available elsewhere (see Short and Strodtbeck, 1965, 1974; Short et al., 1965; Rivera and Short, 1967a, 1967b; Short and Moland, 1976). Following the initial project, which extended from 1959 through 1964, researchers, program administrators, and field personnel parted good friends. I was, in fact, welcomed back when in 1971 I returned to the YMCA to pursue a modest follow-up study of some of the gang members we had observed a decade earlier (see Short and Moland, 1976). And I have subsequently been invited back as a consultant on "current [1979] gang related problems" in Chicago. This is important, I think, because it reflects a quite different posture and result from that which often occurs, where the researcher is pictured as "a snarling watchdog ready to oppose alterations in program and procedures that could render his evaluation efforts useless" (Freeman and Sherwood, 1965: 16).

It would be too easy, I think, to dismiss these observations as either fortuitous because of the personalities involved, or banal because our research was nonthreatening. We were not completely nonthreatening, as evidenced by the fact that, nearly two years after coming to Chicago, I discovered that a research committee of lay and professional YMCA people I worked with beginning in the summer of 1959 was in fact a "watchdog" committee that was prepared to halt access to the program by the researchers if "necessary." The criteria of necessity were not altogether clear, but no effort ever was made to prevent or curtail research operations. From the beginning we viewed program personnel as partners in the research enterprise, and we encouraged them to view us as a resource for their own enlightenment.

Early in the project we were occasionally asked to advise program personnel on what should be done about a variety of problems. We steadfastly refused to do so—with one important exception, to be discussed below—but we continued to share observations and analysis as they became available. The fact that data-gathering was slow and tedious made our findings of less relevance to immediate policy or field practice problems, and therefore easily presented as relevant information rather than evaluation. The fact that we were dependent on the program for access to gangs—and at times to nongang boys as well—often involving considerable effort, made program personnel perceive their partnership as real rather than merely symbolic. We often spoke to YMCA groups about our research—what we were doing and finding—which contributed to an atmosphere of openness rather than secretiveness concerning the research. Finally, there is reason to believe that the YMCA's willingness to support the research effort was important to the organization, symbolically and probably in monetary terms as well. Our relationship was, after all, prima facie evidence of the willingness of the YMCA to subject itself to inquiry from outside the organization (the entire research effort was located at the University of Chicago and was funded almost entirely from external sources—the National Institute of Mental Health, the Ford Foundation, and the President's Committee on Juvenile Delinquency and Youth Crime).

I referred above to a single exception to our general rule of not advising detached worker program personnel "what to do." This rule was violated upon one occasion as a quasi-experiment in the interest of "testing" an emerging theory. The theory concerned the response of gang leaders—later extended to include entire groups—to status threat (see Short and Strodtbeck, 1965: chs. 8, 9). We had observed a series of incidents in which gang leaders had instigated aggressive actions. We first became interested in the phenomenon because a previously "cool" leader of one gang reacted to a situation violently and quite out of character. In other instances the action was not so much out of character as without clear provocation. The notion that these boys were reacting to threats to their status in the group occurred to us after one boy turned from aggressive behavior directed at gang participation in a party, to dramatic action in assisting the detached worker in bringing about order at the party after a fight broke out between a member of his gang and a rival gang member. The initial aggression, we believed, derived from the fact that the boy had no money for the "quarter party," and his position in the group made asking for money from another group member untenable. The worker mollified the boy initially by unobtrusively loaning him money; he further removed the status threat implied in poverty-enforced nonparticipation in the party by turning to the boy for assistance in averting serious violence.

Our "experiment" occurred when a worker reported that his strategy of "putting down" one of his boys, who had been behaving aggressively, had not paid off. Based on the status threat "theory," we suggested he adopt a different strategy by shifting to a nurturant relationship with the boy and impressing upon him his responsibility as a leader in the gang, thus enhancing his status. Much to our relief, the strategy worked. When communicated to the other workers, the "theory" made sense. Our intervention thus served both theoretical purposes for us and program purposes for the detached workers. Beyond this, regrettably, we did not formalize the theory.

WHEN EMPIRICAL FINDINGS DIFFER

Empirical findings regarding apparently similar phenomena often differ, thereby enhancing the image of social sciences as confused and scientifically immature. The problem stems from several sources, but primarily, I believe, from the lack of rigor in theoretical conceptualization, research design, and execution. Measurement error of unknown dimension is present in nearly all criminological research, and scope conditions of theories are rarely specified so as to permit conclusive evaluation of the theoretical significance of empirical findings. The problem is exacerbated when, as usually is the case, empirical observations are of ordinary cases rather than theoretically designed test cases.

Again, an example from the gang literature is instructive. Jansyn (1966) reported significant increases in gang activity (of both delinquent and nondelinquent behavior) following periods of exceptionally low gang cohesiveness (as measured by the number of gang members on the street and the time they spent "hanging out" together). Increased activity, in turn, was followed by an increase in cohesiveness and lowered activity. Jansyn interpreted these findings as a type of reaffirmation of the gang's value to its members. Klein (1971: ch. 10), however, found that gang activity, including delinquency involvement, did not increase in response to efforts to dissolve the gang (reduce cohesiveness) by a variety of programmed activities.

Both social scientists and policy makers must be concerned with such apparently discrepant findings. The policy makers would be well advised not to make too great an investment in programs on the basis of either set of findings until the differences are better understood theoretically. For the scientist, empirical differences of this sort provide an opportunity for theoretical advance, but only if the effort is made to specify such differences theoretically. What, exactly, are the alternative assumptions and scope conditions of competing theories that would enable one to explain these differences, and how do empirical observations fit with those assumptions and conditions? What, for example, is the significance of the different community settings of the two studies: one in Chicago, the other in Los Angeles? What of the ethnic composition of the gangs, their differing histories and traditions? To what extent is worker-style related to the empirical results? (I have the impression that Jansyn was a very passive worker, more an observer—a very perceptive one—than a "programmer," in contrast with Klein's worker; see Klein, 1971: ch. 9.) What of the history of the gangs observed? (Jansyn's gang existed long before he became associated with it, and the tradition of such gangs was well established in the community; Klein's gang appears to have been of more recent origin, and the tradition of ganging was probably less well established in this community.) Attention to questions such as these, if they are abstractly formulated, and incorporation of relevant concepts and conditions into the "theories" in question, might reconcile the observed differences (compare Cohen, 1980). More important, theories which now appear to be contradictory—and therefore of little "practical" value—might turn out, upon formalization, to be not only compatible, but more powerful as well.

Earlier I described the model implied by the Chicago project as less than entirely successful. I believe it was successful as a "strategy for discovery," as opposed to a "strategy of proof" or a "strategy of action" (in which the fact that *something* is being done is regarded as more important than *what* is being done). The argument which I have made, however, calls ultimately for strategies of proof—related, it must be added, to the accumulation of knowledge rather than to outcome variables per se. I believe it will be necessary in most evaluation research to pursue strategies of discovery for the forseeable future; indeed, such strategies will always be important in view of social change. In the meantime, formally designed experimental social programs are possible and have in a few instances taught us a great deal: there are examples in criminal and juvenile justice (see Rossi et al., forthcoming; Empey and Erickson, 1972; Empey and Lubeck, 1971; Klein, 1971). None of these fully meets requirements for the generation of cumulative knowledge, either because the treatment programs were not based on formal theory or the primary theoretical contribution was post hoc. Perhaps the best example—because of its programmatic nature and its more formal and cumulatively developed theory—comes from a series of experiments in educational settings based on status characteristics (or expectation states) theory, as reported by Elizabeth Cohen and her associates.

EXPECTATION STATES AND RACIAL INTERACTION

Briefly, expectation states theory holds that, in mixed status situations, diffuse status characteristics organize and dominate activity and influence within groups (Berger et al., 1972, 1977). Age, sex, and race, for example, are characteristics on the basis of which expectations of competence may be generalized over a wide variety of situations. Thus, task groups composed of blacks and whites tend to be dominated by whites, not because of task-specific differences in individual abilities, but because expectations about task performance are generalized from the diffuse status characteristic of race.

Cohen and her associates set out to modify expectations based on race and to produce equal status interaction in small mixed-race (black and white) groups of junior high school boys (see Cohen and Roper, 1972). Success in this venture was followed by experiments with other racial mixtures and by field experiments in ongoing "natural" school situations. Study of these situations led to further theoretical development and further experimentation, concerning, for example, the relevance to expectation states and equal status behavior of single versus multiple abilities related to group tasks, and of authority patterns and numerical and social dominance within the school (see Cohen, 1979). Results of this carefully conceptualized and executed research program have been encouraging. Much work remains to be done, but as Cohen notes, we now know it is possible to structure situations so as to produce equal status behavior. Further,

> many classrooms and schools have demonstrated that they are successful in teaching conventional academic skills to poor, minority students (Brookover et al., 1978). Although it is unlikely that school can solve the problems of society, they need not be faithful mirrors of the inequities of society. With the sharpened diagnostic and analytical tools in our possession, there is much that can be done in the deliberate design of desegregated situations moving toward an equal status model [Cohen, 1979: 43].

I doubt that it is possible to defend a similarly optimistic assessment of any phase of criminal justice. The reason is not that there are neither good ideas nor promising theories in criminology. Rather, I believe, it is because we have no comparably systematic and incrementally developed theoretically based research programs, such as the Status Equalization Project at Stanford.[5]

WHERE DO WE GO FROM HERE?

More than a decade ago I offered the somewhat brash (and perhaps presumptuous) suggestion that evaluation research ought to be more "sociological":

> Sociological evaluation . . . should "make sense" in sociological terms. In order for this to be the case, research must be guided and designed for the purpose of *theory* testing rather than *action program* testing alone. Sociologists . . . complain of the *gap* between the vast amount of research in particular areas of study and its application to effective action. I take strong issue with the statement: "Knowing the forces that *contribute* to a social evil tells us nothing about how to eradicate the evil" (Rosenfeld, 1965). Nevertheless, it is of course true that there is no simple or direct translation of research findings into action. This is particularly true, however, if the research has not been guided by general theoretical notions. In much the same sense, for research to contribute to action, the theory underlying action must be made explicit, and the "fit" of theory and action carefully examined. Theoretical relevance, and compatibility between action and research interests, are likely to make research findings a good deal more relevant to both. . . . By sociological evaluation I [mean,] first of all, *the extent to which research findings concerning the phenomena under study* (and with which the action program is concerned)

are consistent with the assumptions of the action program. For example, does the problem possess the dimensions and characteristics attributed to it by the action program? Do findings concerning etiology confirm the assumptions upon which the action program is proceeding? Does the program have an impact on research-identified etiological processes, and what is the nature of that impact?

Secondly, and related to the first type of sociological evaluation, *how does the action program adjust to research findings?* An important criterion of sociological evaluation, I should like to suggest, is demonstration of flexibility, of adjustment to the findings of social science, as opposed to doctrinaire practice in the face of such findings. Adoption of such a posture by action agencies would [help to] overcome one of the primary weaknesses of a great deal of agency effort, *viz.,* rigidity of structure and program in the face of changed conditions—the cultural lag between practice and changing problem conditions. Change is a dominant characteristic of present-day cultures and civilizations, and of their problems. The adjustment of social action programs to these conditions is an important aspect of sociological evaluation [Short, 1967: 52-3, emphasis in the original].

I might have added that, ideally, action programs should adjust to changing theories, presuming there is enough good theory to adjust to. Those words were part of an address to an audience of sociologists. I still believe what I said upon that occasion, but I would broaden the notion of sociological evaluation to include other social and behavior sciences that may be appropriate to the phenomena under study. The qualification, "that may be appropriate," is not as limiting as it may at first appear, for any behavior may be "explained" at more than one level. Sociologists, for example, have approached the study of crime and juvenile delinquency from macro- and microsociological levels, and from the levels of individual socialization, adjustment, "definitions of the situation," and so on. So, too, have psychologists on occasion, though their primary focus typically is at the individual level. Economics has both micro- and macro-foci, as well. Even biologists, though their chief focus is on biological characteristics of individuals, must perforce examine generational relationships and other associational characteristics of individuals as revealed, for example, in epidemiological studies. Many programs to ameliorate some human condition typically are aimed at individuals, or are efforts to evaluate their effects. Yet, rarely is one level of explanation sufficient fully to elucidate the nature of either a problem or a program or that program's effects.

Exclusion of other sciences in my 1967 prescriptions was a minor error, given the audience I was addressing. Perhaps my most egregious error was the presumption that sociology might soon be ready, or even interested, in such an approach. I did hedge my advice with the observation that I was aware "that the social sciences have not reached that state of maturity or certainty which would justify immediate and full-scale acceptance" of my proposals (1967: 53). I still believe that their "achievement would enable us to answer the query, 'Knowledge for what?' with a clear conscience and with immense profit to our discipline" (1967: 53).

The evaluation researcher, however, does not often have the choice of eschewing evaluation in conventional terms. And since, at the moment—and for the forseeable future—we do not have theories powerful enough to guide social policy or practice, alternative strategies must be found if we are to advance the goals of accumulating knowledge and of better informing policy and practice.

With respect to these goals, evaluation research in criminal justice would appear to be in somewhat the same shape as is the field of education and race. Cohen and Weiss's (1978) analysis of two decades of research in this area finds that a large volume of research and increasingly sophisticated methods failed to generate pertinent knowledge that was cumulative. Instead of providing guidance for social policy and practice, the research revealed the complexity of race and education issues. Revealing the complexity of any issue, an important part of "demystification" (Berk and Rossi, 1976), constitutes a substantial gain, especially concerning emotionally charged issues for which simplistic solutions are so often urged in the political arena. If the *nature* of the complexity can be systematically documented, so much the better. At least then we have an idea of what it is we are arguing about. Here again, however, such findings are in the nature of "facts our theories must fit." They do not constitute explanatory principles, and they contribute to cumulative knowledge only peripherally.

Cohen and Weiss (1978: 55) conclude that the failure of methodologically more sophisticated research to lead to effective action results from "misconception of the research process." Perhaps, however, other conceptions also are responsible, e.g., perceived political and ideological threats and, more fundamentally from a social science perspective, the failure of research to be conceived in theoretical terms. From the latter perspective, the major failure lies in the theory-building process, which is to say in this instance and in the field of criminal justice evaluation, the failure to imbed research in theory aimed at explanatory principles.

Perhaps because methodological sophistication in the social sciences has so far outstripped theoretical advances, concern with theoretical weaknesses in evaluation research has been a common theme of several recent assessments (Glass, 1976; Gordon and Morse, 1975), including many of those published in this volume. Evaluation of past research is at least consistent in recognizing that a severe problem exists.

Gordon and Morse note, for example, that even the selection of variables to be studied is extremely difficult, "given the inadequacies of the theoretical base," and that "the rather limited knowledge in regard to the identification of relevant variables is a cause for concern—a concern which will continue until viable analytic and theoretical frameworks in regard to evaluation and behavior change are developed" (1975: 344). They sampled evaluation studies listed in *Sociological Abstracts* during 1969, 1971, and 1973, concluding that "in terms of frequency of publication in major journals, evaluation research is not receiving widespread attention in sociology" (1975: 351). Of 93 studies in the survey, 13 concerned "social control (delinquency, prisons, etc.)" and, while the studies were not analyzed by content areas, there is little reason to believe that those concerned with social control and the like were any more rigorous than the others. Findings of the survey in this respect were not encouraging: "75% of the studies do not have formally derived hypotheses (excluded testing of null hypotheses), 63% do not examine the assumptions underlying the intervention, and 84% do not test theory" (1975: 346).

Diagnoses of the nature of the problem vary, as do prescriptions for its remedy. In this volume Glaser, for example, argues persuasively for the value of "universalistic" versus "particularistic" evaluations, on the ground that the former "have more potential utility for guiding policy and practice." More important, if my argument is correct, universalistic evaluations are, I take it by definition, grounded in explanatory principles rather than in specific program outcome variables. Kobrin's thoughtful analysis of outcome variables is grounded in fundamental concerns over social control, currently the most popular theory in criminology and criminal justice (see Kornhouser, 1978).

Krisberg is concerned with formative evaluation, in contrast with traditional impact, or "black-box," models. In retrospect, though we did not call it that, the strategy we adopted in the Chicago gang project was a type of formative evaluation. We wanted to be able to describe for the YMCA program what it was that was happening in their program. In addition, our role, as we conceived it, was to inform the program theoretically, in terms of existing theoretical formulations and even of theoretical insights generated by our research. We enjoyed some success toward this goal, as I have suggested. We did, however, "tinker with the program," contrary to Krisberg's admonition. We did so in the joint interests of knowledge-building and program goals. Our tinkering was modest, and quite inadequate to the accomplishment of the lofty theoretical goals advocated in this chapter. The latter require much more than tinkering with the program variables. They require, first of all, formalization of theory and design of test cases which ensure potential falsification and specification of measurement error. Both the state of theory and the nature of our relationship with the YMCA program prevented this. Perhaps we could have done more toward this end had we been more alert to the problems posed in this chapter. Stepping into a research role with an ongoing program necessitated certain compromises, and once into the program we were limited as to the amount of program manipulation which was possible in response to theoretical concerns, though the program did its best to accommodate our theoretically based research designs (see Short and Strodtbeck, 1965: 1) Our "test cases" of the responses of gang leaders, and of gangs, to status threats were more illustrative than normal test cases, though they took advantage of quasi-experimental natural situations.

More is called for, however. Klein has suggested to me, in correspondence, that a step in the right direction would be to require that all evaluations place programs being evaluated, or specific aspects of programs which are the basis for theoretical inquiry, within a universe of cases, situations, or variables which are the subject of such inquiry (see also Weiss, 1977). Doing so might also aid the process of theoretically designed test cases.

Rossi et al. (1978: 172) suggest that "in applied research, the standard is whether the variables contributing to R^2 are manipulable by policy makers." My strictures imply more, i.e., that the standard ought also to include whether the variables contributing to R^2 (or any other statistical criterion) are theoretically significant—not merely "interesting" or "suggestive," or even manipulable by policy makers. Theoretical significance, in turn, may be judged by a variety of criteria, including relevance to a body of knowledge and, ideally, to formal theory with specified scope conditions and measurement error. For although strategies to enhance theoretical relevance, such as those suggested in this volume, may enhance the goal of cumulative knowledge, in the final analysis this goal can be reached only by rigorous formalization of theory and the closest collaboration of researchers, policy makers, and practitioners. Formalization of theory is the primary responsibility of the basic disciplines, but there is reason to argue that its achievement will be enhanced by the opportunities provided by problem-oriented research, such as often is possible in evaluation research settings. Gordon and Morse (1975: 351) note, for example, Ben-David's (1964: 475) finding that "not only were growth and innovation in medicine stimulated by science systems that were open and free of 'defenses against an external influence,' but . . . the major breakthroughs occurred through problem-oriented research." Certainly, social policies and practices, and their evaluation, are problem-oriented, though the nature of the problem(s) is often not clearly understood.

Evaluation research is rarely, if ever, free of external influences. My argument is that theoretical weakness in the social sciences is especially critical in view of increasing (?) political influences on evaluation (Weis, 1977). The social scientist is not without options or resources in dealing with these influences, as Berk and Rossi (1976) demonstrate. Ultimately, however, if evaluation research is to have cumulative effects, the design of test cases must become a joint enterprise of researchers, policy makers, and practitioners. All have much to gain if we are serious about a social science and about effective social programs.

CONCLUSION

This chapter has examined a variety of issues related to the contribution to knowledge of evaluation studies, and the contribution of knowledge to evaluation strategies and criteria. I have argued that evaluation which lacks theoretical guidance contributes little either to the base of knowledge in the social and behavioral sciences or to scientifically based social policy. I do not argue that scientifically based social policy is always to be desired. If we are to engage in evaluation research, however, we have an obligation not only to demystify the phenomena which are the objects of social programs, and the nature and effects of those programs, but to advance basic knowledge cumulatively as well. In the absence of such knowledge we learn more about the collective behavior of program participants, especially their political behavior, than about the behaviors at issue in social policies and programs. The sociology of political behavior is thereby enriched, as are social constructionist views of social problems (Mauss, 1975; Spector and Kitsuse, 1977). But questions of the etiology of behaviors which are the focus of social programs, and knowledge as to the nature and effects of such programs, remain unanswered. For too long we have "put overmuch confidence in . . . observational results" without theoretical confirmation. As a result, neither the cumulation nor the practicality of knowledge have been well served.

NOTES

1. Quoted from Judson (1979).
2. This is all well and good for scholars engaged in intellectual debate. Practitioners, however, may feel themselves in sympathy with the shipwreck victim who upon inquiring of his fellow victim, the economist, "What shall we do?" received the reply, "First, let's assume a ship." The answer to this somewhat facetious example, of course, is that all theories make assumptions, as do all policies and practitioners. All are ill-served by failing to make explicit their theoretical assumptions and premises.
3. Ideological biases in social program evaluation have been the subject of extensive commentary and thoughtful analysis. Berk and Rossi (1976: 89) argue that since "political and methodological considerations are inextricably linked" it is important to adapt methodology so as to enhance the liberating potential of evaluation research. They argue that research which ignores ideological convictions thereby necessarily enhances them.
4. The detached worker program, its planners and implementers, were in fact responsible for extensive policy changes in the YMCA, a process documented by Zald (1968).
5. Directed by Elizabeth G. Cohen and James Deslonde.

REFERENCES

Adams, S. (1967) "A Cost approach to the Assessment of Gang Rehabilitation Techniques." *Journal of Research in Crime and Delinquency* 4 (January): 166-182.

Becker, G. S. (1976) *The Economic Approach to Human Behavior*. Chicago: University of Chicago Press.

Ben-David, J. (1964) "Scientific Growth." *Minerva* 2: 475.

Berger, J., B. Cohen, and M. Zelditch, Jr. (1972) "Status Conceptions and Social Interactions." *American Sociological Review* 37, 3: 241-255.

Berger, J., and M. Fisek (1974) "A Generalization of the Theory of Status Characteristics and Expectation States," pp. 163-205 in *Expectations States Theory: A Theoretical Research Program*. Englewood Cliffs, NJ: Prentice-Hall.

Berger, J., M. Fisek, R. Z. Norman, and M. Zelditch, Jr. (1977) *Status Characteristics and Social Interaction*. New York: Elsevier.

Berk, R. A. (1974) "A Gaming Approach to Crowd Behavior." *American Sociological Review* (June): 355-373.

––– and P. H. Rossi (1976) "Doing Good or Worse: Evaluation Research Politically Examined." *Social Problems* 23 (February): 337-349.

Brookover, W., J. Schweitzer, J. Schneider, D. Beady, P. Flood, L. Wisenbaker (1978) "Elementary School Social Climate and School Achievement." *American Educational Research Journal* 15, 2: 301-318.

Chomsky, N. and M. Ronat (1979) *Language and Responsibility*. New York: Random House.

Cloward, R. and L. E. Ohlin (1960) *Delinquency and Opportunity: A Theory of Delinquent Gangs*. New York: Free Press.

Cohen, A. K. (1955) *Delinquent Boys: The Culture of the Gang*. New York: Free Press.

Cohen, B. P. (1980) "The Conditional Nature of Scientific Knowledge," pp. 71-110 in L. Freeze (ed.) *Theoretical Methods in Sociology*. Pittsburgh, PA: University of Pittsburgh Press.

Cohen, D. K. and A. Weiss (1978) "Social Science and Social Policy: Schools and Race," pp. 42-58 in T. D. Cook et al. (eds.) *Evaluation Studies Review Annual, Volume 3*. Beverly Hills, CA: Sage Publications.

Cohen, E. G. (1979) "Design and Redesign of the Desegregated School: Problems of Status, Power, and Conflict," in E. Aronson (ed.) *Desegregation, Past, Present and Future*. New York: Plenum.

Cohen, E. and S. Roper (1972) "Modification of Interracial Interaction Disability: An Application of Status Characteristics Theory." *American Sociological Review* 37, 6.

Cohen, L. E. and M. Felson (1979) "Social Change and Crime Rate Trends: A Routine Activity Approach." *American Sociological Review* 44 (August): 588-608.

––– and K. Land (forthcoming) "Property Crime in the United States: A Macrodynamic Analysis, 1947-1977, with Ex Ante Forecasts for the Mid-1980's. *American Journal of Sociology*.

Cressey, D. R. (1969) *Theft of a Nation*. New York: Harper & Row.

DeFleur, L. B. (1975) "Biasing Influences on Drug Arrest Records: Implications for Deviance Research." *American Sociological Review* 40, 1: 88-103.

Ehrlich, I. (1979) "The Economic Aproach to Crime: A Preliminary Assessment," pp. 25-60 in S. Messinger and E. Bittner (eds.) *Criminology Review Yearbook, Volume 1*. Beverly Hills, CA: Sage Publications.

Elliott, D. S. and S. S. Ageton (1978) "The Social Correlates of Delinquent Behavior in a National Youth Panel." Project Report 4, Behavior Research Institute, Boulder, CO.

Empey, L. T. and M. L. Erickson (1972) *The Provo Experiment: Evaluating Community Control of Delinquency*. Lexington, MA: D. C. Heath.

Empey, L. T. and S. Lubeck (1971) *The Silverlake Experiment: Testing Delinquency Theory and Community Intervention*. Chicago: AVC.

Finestone, H. (1957) "Cats, Kicks and Color." *Social Problems* (July): 3-13.

Freeman, H. E. and C. C. Sherwood (1965) *Social Research and Social Policy*. Englewood Cliffs, NJ: Prentice-Hall.

Freese, L. (1980) "Formal Theorizing." *Annual Review of Sociology* 6.

——— (1972) "Cumulative Sociological Knowledge." *American Sociological Review* (August): 472-82.

——— and Jane Sell (1980) in *Theoretical Methods in Sociology: Seven Essays*. Pittsburgh, PA: University of Pittsburgh Press.

Friedman, L. (1979) "The Use of Multiple Regression Analysis To Test for a Deterrent Effect of Capital Punishment: Prospects and Problems," pp. 61-87 in S. Messinger and E. Bittner (eds.) *Criminology Review Yearbook, Volume 1*. Beverly Hills, CA: Sage Publications.

Glass, G. V (1976) "Introduction," pp. 9-12 in *Evaluation Studies Review Annual, Volume 1*. Beverly Hills, CA: Sage Publications.

Gordon, G. and E. V. Morse (1975) "Evaluation Research," pp. 339-61 in A. Inkles et al. (eds.) *Annual Review of Sociology, Volume 1*. Palo Alto, CA: Annual Reviews, Inc.

Harris, A. R. (1977) "Sex and Theories of Deviance: Toward a Functional Theory of Deviant Type Scripts." *American Sociological Review* (February): 3-15.

Hindelang, M., T. Hirschi, and J. Weis (forthcoming) The Measurement of Delinquency by the Self-Report Method.

Ianni, F.A.J. (1974) *Black Mafia*. New York: Simon & Schuster.

——— (1972) *A Family Business*. New York: Russell Sage.

Jansyn, L. (1966) "Solidarity and Delinquency in a Street Corner Group." *American Sociological Review* 31 (October): 600-614.

Judson, H. F. (1979) *The Eighth Day of Creation: Makers of the Revolution in Biology*. New York: Simon & Schuster.

Klein, M. W. (1971) *Street Gangs and Street Workers*. Englewood Cliffs, NJ: Prentice-Hall.

Klockars, C. B. (1974) *The Professional Fence*. New York: Free Press.

Kornhauser, R. R. (1978) *Social Sources of Delinquency: An Appraisal of Analytic Methods*. Chicago: University of Chicago Press.

MacRae, D., Jr. (1978) "The Sociological Economics of Gary S. Becker." *American Journal of Sociology* 83, 5: 1244-1253.

Mattick, H. W. and N. S. Caplan (1967) "Stake Animals, Loud Talking, and Leadership in Do-Nothing and Do-Something Situations," in M. Klein and B. Myerhoff (eds.) *Juvenile Gangs in Context: Theory, Research and Action*. Englewood Cliffs, NJ: Prentice-Hall.

Mauss, A. L. (1975) *Social Problems as Social Movements*. Philadelphia: J. B. Lippincott.

McCord, W. and J. McCord (1959) *Origins of Crime: A New Evaluation of the Cambridge-Somerville Youth Study*. New York: Columbia University Press.

Messinger, S. and E. Bittner [eds.] (1979) *Criminology Review Yearbook*. Beverly Hills, CA: Sage Publications.

Miller, W. B. (1962) "The Impact of a 'Total-Community' Delinquency Control Project." *Social Problems* 10 (Fall): 168-191.

——— (1958) "Lower Class Culture as a Generating Milieu of Gang Delinquency." *Journal of Social Issues* 14: 5-19.

Powers, E. and H. Witmer (1951) *An Experiment in the Prevention of Delinquency: The*

Cambridge-Somerville Youth Study. New York: Columbia University Press.

Riess, A. J., Jr. (1976) "Settling the Frontiers of a Pioneer in American Criminology: Henry McKay, pp. 64-88 in J. F. Short (ed.) *Delinquency, Crime, and Society*. Chicago: University of Chicago Press.

Rieker, P. P. (1979) "Review of 'Using Social Research in Public Policy Making,' by Carol H. Weis (ed.)." *Contemporary Sociology* 8, 4: 634-635.

Rivera, R. J. and J. F. Short, Jr. (1967a) "Significant Adults, Caretakers, and Structures of Opportunity: An Exploratory Study." *Journal of Research in Crime and Delinquency* 4 (January): 76-97.

——— (1967b) "Occupational Goals: A Comparative Analysis," pp. 70-90 in M. W. Klein (ed.) *Juvenile Gangs in Context: Theory, Research, and Action*. Englewood Cliffs, NJ: Prentice-Hall.

Rosenfeld, E. (1966) "Social Research and Social Action in Prevention of Juvenile Delinquency," pp. 367-380 in A. W. Gouldner and S. M. Miller (eds.) *Applied Sociology: Opportunities and Problems*. New York: Free Press.

Rossi, P. H., R. A. Berk, and K. J. Lenihan (forthcoming) *Money, Work and Crime: A Field Experiment in Reducing Recidivism through Post-Release Financial Aid to Prisoners*. New York: Academic Press.

Rossi, P. H., J. D. Wright, and S. R. Wright (1978) "The Theory and Practice of Applied Social Research." *Evaluation Quarterly* (May): 171-191.

Short, J. F., Jr. (1975) "The National Commission on the Causes and Prevention of Violence: Reflections on the Contributions of Sociology and Sociologists," in M. Komarovsky (ed.) *Sociology and Public Policy: The Case of Presidential Commissions*. New York: Elsevier.

——— (1967) "Action-Research Collaboration and Sociological Evaluation." *Pacific Sociological Review* 10 (Fall): 47-53.

——— and J. Moland, Jr. (1976) "Politics and Youth Gangs." *Sociological Quarterly* 17, 2: 162-179.

Short, J. F., Jr., and F. L. Strodtbeck (1965) *Group Process and Gang Delinquency*. Chicago: University of Chicago Press.

Short, J. F., Jr., R. Rivera and R. A. Tennyson (1965) "Perceived Opportunities, Gang Membership, and Delinquency." *American Sociological Review* 30, 1: 56-67.

Social Science Research Council (1979) *Annual Report, 1977-78*. New York: Author.

Spector, M. and J. I. Kitsuse (1977) *Constructing Social Problems*. Menlo Park, CA: Cummings.

Thrasher, F. (1927) *The Gang: A Study of 1,313 Gangs in Chicago*. Chicago: University of Chicago Press.

Weiss, C. H. [ed.] (1977) *Using Social Research in Public Policy Making*. Lexington, MA: D. C. Heath.

Zald, M. N. (1968) *Organizational Change: The Political Economy of the YMCA*. Chicago: University of Chicago Press.

PART III

ON UNIQUENESS IN
CRIMINAL JUSTICE EVALUATION

Malcolm W. Klein and Katherine S. Teilmann

While it has been fashionable in recent years to speak of the "nonsystem" of criminal justice, the term is really incorrect. There is a criminal justice system with denotable components, interdependencies, and semipermeable boundaries helping to distinquish system from nonsystem elements. The permeability of the boundaries and the often reactive rather than proactive nature of the interdependencies should not blind us to the overall appropriateness of system terminology and analysis.

However, there has been a propensity among many to assume that one system is much like another. In particular, researchers whose experiences have been in other realms come to the evaluation of criminal justice programs with assumptions—generally acceptable elsewhere—that simply overlook the very special nature of the criminal justice system. Backgrounds in operations research, engineering, and economics in particular, seem associated with these incorrect assumptions.

Systems analysts are used to thinking in terms of system coordination, efficiency, and relative homogeneity of clientele and/or product. The world of crime does not lend itself readily to such thinking, and the five chapters in Part III are designed to alert our varied audiences to some of the relatively unique aspects of our system.

Morse reminds us that the adversarial system *deliberately* instills inefficiency and lack of coordination in order to protect the individual rights of citizens against the more powerful criminal justice establishment. The implications for evaluation can be very substantial.

Reiss describes the variability of subsystems that mark our approach to criminal processing, and carefully delineates the difficulties and the advantages this poses for evaluation research. While other systems—health, education, military, welfare—also exhibit subsystem variability, probably none does so quite as deliberately as ours.

Tittle's chapter on evaluating the efficacy of deterrence programs speaks not only to the special character of this concept, but also to the paucity of well-grounded theory which could guide useful evaluations. The criminal justice system is the only major social system which attempts to achieve its goals principally through the application of negative sanctions. This unique approach seems to call for unique forms of evaluation, and Tittle helps lay the conceptual groundwork for these.

Geis's chapter on victimless crimes and Gibbons's description of bias and discretion in the processing of clients provide further evidences that proper evaluation requires substantial knowledge of the *substance* of criminal justice matters. It is clearly not sufficient to move into criminal justice evaluation with methodological or conceptual "overlays" developed elsewhere. Substance and method are interrelated, each informing the other in the evaluation process.

While these five chapters should provide the antidote we seek for inappropriate evaluation treatments, their topics are certainly not exhaustive. Two additional examples deserve mention. The first is the question of special sampling issues. By their nature, many crimes tend to be unreported and only differentially detected. Thus, to sample from a known universe of crimes is problematic at best. Similarly, some processes are secret and seldom available, except selectively, to evaluators. Examples include plea-bargaining conversations, jury deliberations, and field interrogations. These forms of nonaccessibility of basic data place very special burdens on evaluators who are concerned, as all should be, with the generalizability of their findings.

The second example of the special nature of the justice system is the differentiation between its juvenile and its adult structures. While it is true that recent years have seen movement toward decreased separation between the two, it remains true that application of findings from the one to the other should be undertaken with great caution. Assumptions underlying processing of juvenile and adult suspects differ considerably (e.g., competence, responsibility, culpability, potential for rehabilitation). Patterns of criminal activity differ in type, form, timing, peer association, sophistication, and so on. Legal requirements and safeguards differ between the two systems, as does the attitude of the public toward juvenile versus adult perpetrators. Failure to understand differences of these types is a good predictor of invalid evaluations or inappropriate conclusions.

Finally, it seems to us that most of the comments above are no less applicable to any one of our reader audiences than to another. The requirement for a working knowledge of the relatively unique aspects of the criminal justice system applies equally to student and teacher, to funder and program director, to policy maker and to evaluator. While evaluators may differ with respect to what to make of this uniqueness, they should not differ with respect to familiarity with it.

12

Understanding Adversary Process and Conflict in Criminal Justice

Stephen J. Morse

Because few criminal justice evaluators are trained in law, they often are not aware of the theory of the adversary system, imbued with its spirit, or fully cognizant of its adversary and *nonadversary* operation. This chapter will explore the theory and practice of our adversary system of criminal justice, including both its adversary and nonadversary aspects. The major point to be made is that our criminal justice system is predicated upon tensions and conflicts between the goals of the system and the values underlying it. Evaluation depends on the clear, empirical specification of the process or outcome goals of the program under investigation. The clear, empirical specification of goals necessary for good evaluation is particularly difficult in a system that is committed to conflicting goals and values, some of which, such as fairness or justice, are probably impossible to quantify in a sensible fashion. Indeed, to paraphrase Mr. Justice Stewart's observation on the difficulty of defining obscenity and pornography, perhaps we do not even know justice when we see it (Jacobellis v. Ohio, 1964). Evaluators must be clearly cognizant of such difficulties or their work will run the risk of appearing limited or beside the point. It is hoped that a better appreciation of the nature of our criminal justice system will help evaluators

AUTHOR'S NOTE: I should like to thank my colleague, Professor Charles Whitebread, for his excellent suggestions, and my research assistant, Ms. Joan Mussoff, for her invaluable assistance.

become more sophisticated and sympathetic observers when they attempt empirically to determine how the system is operating and what impact it is having.

Before continuing, a *caveat* is necessary. When lawyers refer to the "adversary system," they are using a term of the art, which refers to the common-law trial method of truth-finding and dispute resolution and which, in turn, relies on the confrontation and cross-examination of witnesses and the like. In this chapter, however, the term *adversary* will be used more broadly, to refer to the conflict between the state and the citizen that is inherent at every stage of the criminal justice system. Nevertheless, it should be remembered that the notion of an adversary system is a technical one that refers specifically to trial-related procedures.

I. INTRODUCTION

It is a commonplace that our legal system, and especially its criminal justice component, is an adversary system. An underlying assumption pervades the system: The state and its citizens are in conflict. In its broadest, nontechnical sense, an adversary system of criminal justice means that when the state has the power to deprive citizens of privacy, liberty, and their good names, the state and the accused are opponents of one another (In re Winship, 1970). There is no pretense that lawbreakers should willingly expose themselves to investigation, or aid the state in regulating the social order by helping its agents to convict them (Uviller, 1975; Fortas, 1954).

In a society that values the dignity, privacy, and liberty of its citizens at least as highly as it values the power of the state to preserve the social order and safety, the criminal justice system will develop a complex set of rules to ensure that, within reasonable limits, the system protects its citizens against unwarranted intrusions by the state and proceeds against the individual fairly when such intrusions have begun (Bill of Rights; Federal Rules of Criminal Procedure). The fundamental tension in all societies between individual rights and social order is balanced differently from place to place and from time to time. From the beginning of our history, our system of criminal justice, which pits the state against the citizen and grants the latter substantial rights at all stages of the system, has been a primary means of preserving the American preference for protecting the rights of individuals (Pound, 1930).

As noted, the adversary system also means specifically that the criminal justice system employs a particular means of adjudicating disputes between the citizen and the state about the guilt of the accused. Briefly, it envisions a process whereby opposing sides of relatively equal power, the state and the accused, confront each other and try to convince a neutral factfinder (i.e., judge or jury) of the truth of their respective positions (Gideon v. Wainwright, 1963). Neither side is expected to aid the other or to expose weaknesses in its own case; rather, each is to present its own side as strongly as possible, leaving to the other side the tasks of presenting the opposite view and exposing weaknesses in the opponent's case through cross-examination and other techniques (Brennan, 1963; Freedman, 1975). It is believed that this method of proceeding is more likely to elicit truth than a system wherein the state, the accused, and the judge are all engaged in a more or less cooperative effort (Freedman, 1975).

Before entering the labyrinth of the system, however, it will be useful to take a brief detour to explore just which system it is that we are talking about. As is well known, the American criminal justice system is a direct descendant of the criminal justice system that developed in England (Kimball, 1966). However, whereas there is still largely one system in England, the American offshoots of the English experience have branched out in many different ways. It is, of course, true that the Constitution and especially the Bill of Rights are the final arbiters of how the criminal justice system may and will proceed. Nevertheless, within the enormous range of questions that might be presented by our system for adjudication, only a relatively small number have been finally adjudicated by the U.S. Supreme Court in opinions that are binding on the system throughout the United States.[1]

One of the alleged glories of our system, as many judges have fondly noted (Malloy v. Hogan, 1964: Harlan dissent), is that it is a federal system. The states, each governed by its own independent state constitution (Brennan, 1977), provide fifty "laboratories" in which society can experiment with criminal law and procedure. Furthermore, federal jurisdiction is divided among eleven judicial circuits, providing eleven more opportunities for courts to express different views about how federal law ought to be interpreted.

Although our whole system is descended from a common ancestor, the criminal law and procedures of the states vary enormously, and there is often much conflict among the federal judicial circuits over questions not yet decided by the Supreme Court. Consider the following, brief examples. First, discovery practice, the right of each side to gain pretrial access to information held by the opponent, is widely divergent from state to state. Some states provide easy access to much of the information held by the opposing party (Discovery in Criminal Cases, 1967), while others allow almost no discovery (State v. Johnson, 1966; People v. Johnson, 1976). Second, in the federal circuits there is a wide split of authority over the appropriate standard by which to judge the competence of counsel (Maryland v. Marzullo, 1978). Some circuits apply the traditional test, whereby counsel will be found competent unless the representation made a "mockery, sham or farce" of the trial (United States v. Ramirez, 1976; Rickenbacker v. Warden, 1976; Gillihan v. Rodriquez, 1977). Others have applied the much higher standard of "reasonably competent" assistance (United States v. De Coster, 1973; United States v. Fesell, 1976; United States v. Easter, 1976).

The examples could be easily multiplied, but the point is simple: There are many jurisdictions, all differing to some degree in their rules of law and practice and thus in their degrees of adversariness. For example, the ease of discovery will have a distinct effect on the degree to which a criminal trial is a contest between true adversaries who have independently investigated and prepared their own cases. Moreover, much of the practice within a state or federal circuit will not be uniform, because many aspects of practice will not be authoritatively settled by constitutional law, statutes, or administrative regulations. For instance, although there are clear constitutional limitations on various aspects of plea-bargaining (Brady v. United States, 1970; Santobello v. New York, 1971; Bordenkircher v. Hayes, 1978), the law still allows a wide range of practices among the many prosecutorial offices (e.g., deciding which cases are appropriate for plea agreements; Alschuler, 1968).

In sum, the diversity of systems means that, by necessity, one must generalize quite broadly when analyzing the implications of the functioning of any aspect of the adversary system. By contrast, however, criminal justice evaluators should be alert to the need for caution when generalizing from a study in one locale or when assessing the implications of *the* adversary system in the locale they are studying.

II. ADVERSARY AND CONFLICT ASPECTS OF THE AMERICAN CRIMINAL JUSTICE SYSTEM

The overriding goal of the criminal justice system appears easy to state: Criminals should be apprehended, convicted, and sanctioned according to the rule of law. Value tensions are imbedded in this goal at every stage of the process, however, especially the tension between the need efficiently to deal with lawbreakers and the need fairly to protect the rights of the citizens against the substantial power of the state. This section will examine the "adversary" aspects of the various stages of our system, with special reference to the conflicts within it. After examining police procedures, it will turn to an examination of the adversary system in its technical sense, our trial system.

In the investigative stage, there is extraordinary conflict between the legitimate needs of law enforcement and the equally legitimate right of citizens to be free from state intrusion. For example, the police may only engage in full-scale search and seizure if there is "probable cause," which has been defined as existing where "the facts and circumstances within their [the officers'] knowledge and of which they had reasonably trustworthy information [are] sufficient in themselves to warrant a man of reasonable caution in the belief" (Carroll v. United States, 1924: 162) that an offense had been or is being committed, or that fruits, instrumentalities, contraband, or evidence of crime is to be found in the place to be searched. Furthermore, there is a requirement that probable cause should be determined by a neutral and detached magistrate (Johnson v. United States, 1948; Coolidge v. New Hampshire, 1971; United States v. United States District Court, 1972; Shadwick v. City of Tampa, 1972), except in the cases of certain narrow and carefully drawn exceptions (plain view: Coolidge v. New Hampshire, 1971; consent: Schneckloth v. Bustamonte, 1973; automobile: Cady v. Dombrowski, 1973; hot pursuit: Warden v. Hayden, 1967; stop and frisk: Terry v. Ohio, 1968; search incident to a lawful arrest: United States v. Robinson, 1973).[2] Even the limited intrusion of a "stop and frisk" must be founded on reasonable suspicion based on "specific and articulable facts which, taken together with rational inferences from those facts, reasonably warrant that intrusion" (Terry v. Ohio, 1968; Dunaway v. New York, 1979).

This requirement has been reaffirmed by two recent Supreme Court holdings—that the police may not randomly demand that a pedestrian, even one in a high-crime area, identify him- or herself, without reasonable suspicion that the person is engaged in criminal activity (Brown v. Texas, 1979), or randomly detain a motorist to check license and registration without reasonable suspicion that either the license or the registration is faulty, or that other criminal activity is in progress (Delaware v. Prouse, 1979). Finally, the scope of all searches must be reasonably limited to what is necessary to achieve the purposes of the search; general searches are prohibited (Lo-Ji Sales, Inc. v. New York, 1979).

These constitutional limitations on the power to search and seize, founded in the Fourth Amendment (Amsterdam, 1974), substantially hinder the efforts of the police to detect crime and to catch alleged wrongdoers, but they also protect the citizen's right to be free from unwarranted state intrusion, a right highly valued in our society because of our fear, rooted in the colonial experience, of tyranny exercised by the state and police over the individual. Indeed, the right is so highly valued that the remedy is the exclusionary rule: If the police offend the dictates of the Fourth Amendment, even in good faith, any evidence seized or later-discovered fruits of that evidence will be excluded from the trial (Mapp v. Ohio, 1961; Wilkey, 1978, 1979; Kamisar, 1978, 1979; Canon, 1979; Schlesinger, 1979; Canon and Schlesinger, 1979). Thus, highly probative evidence of guilt, which is often the only evidence, will be deemed inadmissible; the criminal will be freed because the constable has blundered (People v. DeFore, 1926).

The wrongdoer harboring illegal instrumentalities, contraband, or evidence in his or her house or on his or her person, may bar the state from searching for that evidence or seizing it unless the state's agent has probable cause. What, therefore, is the social goal to be implemented at the investigative stage of the criminal justice system? Clearly, there is not one goal but many, and the major goals— detection of crime and protection of privacy—are terribly in conflict. The police could clearly be more effective as crime control agents if they were empowered to stop and search citizens at will or to rummage through their homes and effects upon slight suspicion, but the costs in terms of privacy or liberty would be immense. To study the police and to evaluate their performance, then, is to study a social organization that is placed uncomfortably on the horns of a dilemma, between crime control and individual rights goals, that is nearly impossible to resolve to the satisfaction of all parties concerned (Davis, 1969; Allen, 1976; Hyman, 1979).

It is easy to say that the proper goal of the police is to investigate crime and apprehend criminals within the confines of constitutional limits on police behavior, but such a statement ignores the realities of the nature of policing. Moreover, it ignores political realities. Suppose the police decide to institute aggressive patrol practices of dubious constitutionality in a high-crime area. Although the practice may be barely within the limits of the law, and even effective in reducing street crime, it may be widely resented by citizens of the community, leading to political pressure to terminate it. Or, although the practice may be unlawful, the police may be employing it primarily to control the "turf" rather than to detect crime and apprehend criminals (Terry v. Ohio, 1968). Thus, arrests and convictions may not result, but the area may become safer, much to the relief of the residents. Again, which of the above outcomes is successful, and according to whom? Note, too, that conflict about goals will lead to tension in the operation of the system. Citizens will be at odds with the police or the police will be at odds with the law. In either case, it will be difficult to determine precisely what the goals of the system are or how it is attempting to achieve them in fact.

The full tensions of the adversary system become most apparent if we consider both the implications of the Fifth Amendment's right against self-incrimination and the nature of our criminal trial process. What will become readily manifest is that the system's goals of accurately identifying criminal offenders and of determining the truth are in marked conflict with our societal desire to protect the dignity of accused persons and to ensure that convictions are factually and legally correct.

The Fifth Amendment provides, in pertinent part, that "no person shall be . . . compelled in any criminal case to be a witness against himself." As interpreted by our courts over the centuries, this language means much more than a prohibition against using physical force to extract a confession from the lips of the accused; it refers to the protection of a wide range of values that may be loosely collected under the headings of dignity values and adversary values (Murphy v. Waterfront Commission, 1964; Gerstein, 1970, 1971, 1979; Levy, 1968; New York Times, 1968). Thus, in order fully to protect the dignity of the accused and the adversariness of the system, unless immunity is granted the state may not use any compulsion to elicit incriminating information from the accused (Brown v. Mississippi, 1936; New Jersey v. Portash, 1979). As is well known, suspects in custody are entitled to explicit Miranda warnings that they have the right to remain silent, that anything they say may be used against them in evidence, that they have the right to have an attorney present during questioning, and that an attorney will be provided for those who are unable to afford one (Miranda v. Arizona, 1966). Furthermore, the accused may not be called as a witness without his or her consent, and if the accused chooses not to consent, neither the judge nor the prosecution may comment on this fact to the jury, for any comment would jeopardize the right of the accused to remain silent (Griffin v. California, 1965; Lakeside v. Oregon, 1978).

Although statements obtained in violation of the Fifth Amendment were once excluded because it was believed that they were unreliable, this rationale has largely evaporated with the abolition of third-degree methods of interrogation (McKay, 1967; Miranda v. Arizona, 1966). Although a confession beaten out of a person may not be reliable because the person would perhaps falsely admit to having committed a crime in order to terminate his or her mistreatment, statements given without Miranda warnings or after subtle psychological pressures are not necessarily unreliable. Again, the rationale for the Fifth Amendment is now the protection of dignity, our hostility to coercive techniques whether or not they produce reliable statements, and the adversary nature of our system. More specifically, the autonomy of the accused is allegedly violated if he or she is in any way compelled to incriminate himself or herself, and the fundamental nature of our adversary system is upset unless the prosecution independently shoulders the whole load of proving the defendant's guilt (Wigmore, 1961; Miranda v. Arizona, 1966).

The protection of the Fifth Amendment is in many ways extraordinary. The accused is clearly in the best position to help determine whether or not he or she is guilty, yet the amendment utterly prohibits the criminal justice system from using the accused's compelled testimonial communications to determine the truth of the charge. This is so even if the state has not physically abused the defendant or behaved in other ways that are simply repugnant to a civilized society.[3] Indeed, even highly reliable confessions will be excluded from use at trial if the strict dictates of the Fifth Amendment and its surrounding prophylactic rules have not been complied with in order to ensure that the police meticulously respect the dignity and autonomy of the accused. The search for truth in the criminal justice system is balanced against other values in a fashion that may often promote the acquittal of factually guilty persons.

The tension in values also promotes tension in the very operation of the system. How careful are the police in ensuring that suspects understand their Miranda rights? If a suspect desires to terminate interrogation, how scrupulously will the police honor that desire (see Michigan v. Mosley, 1975)? Will they begin questioning relatively shortly thereafter, or will they wait a longer time to give the suspect a "breather"? Often there will be no clear answer to the legality of a particular practice, and thus the system may be promoting, in polar and simplistic terms, "truth" at the expense of the suspect's rights, or the reverse. There will be pressures in both directions, with no obviously correct balance to be struck.

As a constitutional matter, almost no information must be revealed to the opposite side before trial,[4] nor must any particular information damaging to one's case be presented at trial. Indeed, the prosecution's only burden at trial is affirmatively to prove all the elements of the crime charged, and the defendant need not present any defense at all (In re Winship, 1970; Mullaney v. Wilbur, 1975). Before trial, the prosecution's only duty to the defendant is to reveal significantly exculpatory information about the defendant that is in the possession of the prosecution—say, a statement by an eyewitness to the crime that appears to exonerate the accused (Brady v. Maryland, 1963; United States v. Agurs, 1976). Further discovery is a matter of state and federal law, which varies from jurisdiction to jurisdiction. Some jurisdictions are relatively free in allowing each side access to the information possessed by the adversary, but others are highly restrictive. Nowhere, however, are parties entitled to access before trial to all pertinent information in the adversary's possession.

From the standpoint of those trained in the natural and social sciences, the adversary method of litigation procedures for determining the truth is another curious feature of our system (but see Levine, 1974). Readers of this volume are of course familiar with the generally nonadversary nature of scientific investigation which assumes that there is an empirical reality waiting to be discovered if investigators can develop the necessary conceptual and technological armamentarium. By contrast, as noted above, a criminal trial proceeds largely noncooperatively, with each side trying to prove very different, often inconsistent, cases, to assert very different empirical realities.

At the trial itself, each side tries to convince the judge or jury of its own one-sided view of the facts, by two methods: affirmative presentation of the version most favorable to it, and vigorous cross-examination of the opposing witnesses. Again, this system of trials is what is technically meant by the adversary system. There is no duty in the affirmative presentation of one's case to reveal its weaknesses; that is the duty of the adversary. Moreover, it is an adversary's duty fully to cross-examine opposing witnesses in order to cast doubt on their testimony, even if the cross-examining attorney may believe that the opposing witness is telling the truth (see Pye, 1978; Freedman, 1966; Frank, 1963; contrast American Bar Association, 1974a). Indeed, defense counsel must do everything possible, short of suborning or condoning perjury, to convince the judge or jury of the innocence of the client, even if the defense attorney fully believes the client committed the offense charged (Pye, 1978). Since the adversary method of litigation is counterintuitive to many persons, let us examine its rationale.

As one would expect, there has been heated debate concerning whether the adversary method is a valid means for determining the truth (Frankel, 1975; Freedman, 1975; Uviller, 1975; Weinreb, 1977; Johnson, 1977; Tullock, 1975; McChesney, 1977). Although the system is relatively incomprehensible to scientists and to those who seek mainly to maximize efficiency goals, the adversary method of adjudicating guilt makes much more sense and is harder to condemn if one remembers that its purpose is to serve values other than "truth." To explore this point, it is useful to draw Professor Packer's distinction between factual and legal guilt (Packer, 1964, 1968; Goldstein, 1974). *Factual guilt* refers to whether the defendant actually committed the crime charged. *Legal guilt* refers to a finding by a judge or jury that the accused is guilty after a process whereby the accused is entitled to raise an extraordinary number of substantive and procedural barriers to conviction. Legal guilt is not meant necessarily to reflect only factual guilt. The obstacles to a finding of legal guilt are meant to uphold the autonomy of the citizen and to protect him or her when the state is using its power to deprive him or her of liberty, even if the defendant is clearly factually guilty (Hazard, 1978). Some of the barriers are clearly inconsistent with the goal of determining the truth. The exclusionary rule, for example, allows the accused to object to and prevent the admission of highly probative evidence if it has been obtained in violation of the Constitution.

Let us take another example. After all the evidence and arguments have been presented, the outcome of the trial depends on who bears the burden of persuasion. In our system, due process requires that the prosecution bear the burden of convincing the judge or jury, beyond a reasonable doubt, of all the elements of the offense charged (In re Winship, 1970). The reasonable doubt standard does not have a precise mathematical definition. As a moral, legal, and commonsense matter, it means that the accused may be convicted only if the prosecution has defeated every reasonable doubt the factfinder may have about whether the conduct of the accused satisfied all the elements of the crime charged. It is not unlike the social scientist's burden to reject the null hypothesis at a probability level of .05 or less.

The result in the criminal process is that some defendants who are probably guilty are acquitted, although only a small doubt has been cast on their guilt. The "beyond a reasonable doubt" standard clearly makes it more difficult to convict defendants who are factually guilty, especially in light of all the other protections to which the accused is entitled. It would be far easier for the state to convict if its burden of proof were set at a lower standard, such as "more probable than not," which is the burden on plaintiffs in civil cases, or the intermediate standard of "clear and convincing" evidence, which is mandated in civil commitment cases (Addington v. Texas, 1979; California Evidence Code § 115).

Most of the purposes of the criminal sanction—retribution, deterrence, incapacitation, rehabilitation, education (Hart, 1958)—would be better served if convictions of defendants, nearly all of whom are factually guilty, were easier to secure. But the difficulties in obtaining convictions are justified because our system has such a strong preference for preserving the liberty and good name of the citizen and such a commitment to fair play. The high burden of proof placed on prosecutors increases the probability of factually erroneous acquittals, but it decreases the probability of factually erroneous convictions (Speiser v. Randall, 1958; Mullaney v. Wilbur, 1975). In our society, the latter type of error is considered far more serious. It is better, as the saying goes, to free ten guilty persons than to convict one innocent person (see In re Winship, 1970: Harlan concurrence).

The values that make legal guilt relatively hard to prove are clearly in conflict with the values that would promote efficient determinations of factual guilt. Given sufficient resources, it would arguably be possible to establish the degree to which the system was accurately determining factual guilt, but how does one measure the degree to which the system is fair, to which it strikes an equitable balance between the needs of society and the rights of the citizen? Again, the particular balance struck may differ from time to time as social values change. In the 1960s, under the aegis of Chief Justice Warren, the Supreme Court largely expanded the rights of the accused; in the 1970s, under Chief Justice Burger, the Court has been far more willing, although by no means totally so, to limit the protections granted the accused and to enhance the powers of the state (Chase, 1977; Israel, 1977). For instance, the exclusionary rule was applied to the states by the Warren Court. The Burger Court has not yet abandoned this rule, but it has allowed the state to use illegally obtained evidence for collateral pruposes, such as impeaching a witness (Harris v. New York, 1971).

In sum, the criminal justice system is not predicated on the single goal of finding "truth," but on a complex set of goals which are often in conflict and in a state of flux. It may be quite difficult, therefore, perfectly to identify the goals of even a small part of the system at any one time because they too will be in a constant state of readjustment, depending on the constitutional, social, and political pressures of the moment. The adversary system is a fundamental means to test the balance of the moment and to reach new adjustments, as well as to protect the rights of the accused.

In addition to the constant tension between the search for factual guilt and the stringent requirements for a finding of legal guilt, the very concept of factual guilt itself is extremely problematic in law, because legal decisions must depend on the application of relatively soft, normative rules to facts (Uviller, 1975). For this reason, too, the adversary method may be quite appropriate for adjudicating legal guilt. The crime of homicide will furnish an example to explain this point. Guilt for criminal homicide requires more than proof beyond reasonable doubt that the defendant was part of the causal chain that led to the death of another human being (Damaska, 1973). Assume the following set of facts: Able, a nurse, is walking through a high-crime urban area late at night, from the hospital to a bus stop. As he walks alone along a deserted and dark street, three young, tough-looking kids approach him from the opposite direction. As they pass they ask him for some change. When he refuses, they make what he believes are menacing remarks. Furthermore, he sees light glittering off an unidentified metal object one of the kids has seemingly removed from his pocket. Believing he is about to be knifed or shot, Able pulls out a gun he lawfully carries for his own protection, and shoots the fellow holding the metal object. The metal object is later found to be a large ring, and Able is charged with second-degree murder— the intentional killing of another without premeditation and deliberation (e.g., see California Penal Code § 189; People v. Holt, 1944). He defends on the grounds of self-defense, a defense which is available to excuse his deed only if his belief that his life or safety was seriously in danger was reasonable (e.g., see California Penal Code § 197; People v. Sonier, 1952).

Is Able guilty? Whether his belief was reasonable in some ultimate sense is hardly a purely factual question. The law is concerned with whether it was sufficiently reasonable to excuse him. There are no value-neutral empirical techniques, no canons of scientific method or statistics, to which we can turn to resolve the issue. A factually based but normative question is being asked, one whose answer depends on an appeal to social and moral intuitions as well as an appeal to legal and empirical principles. In such cases there may be a great deal of virtue in having adversaries present "biased" views of how the issue ought to be resolved.

The adversary method may ensure that a broad range of considerations, arguments, and counterarguments are presented to the judge or jury to help them decide normative issues, such as whether Able is legally guilty or innocent. Indeed, a vast proportion of the issues raised by every stage of the criminal justice system, not only by the trial stage, are of the normative variety, capable of resolution not by appeal solely to facts, but by appeals to reason and to social and moral standards. To take another, nonjury question as an example, recall the probable cause standard which must be met before search and seizure is authorized. What inference would an officer of "reasonable caution" draw from certain facts? Again, when is a suspect's right to remain silent "scrupulously honored"? Decisions about whether to continue an investigation or a prosecution, as well as the ultimate outcome of a criminal case, often turn upon the resolution of such issues.

When we consider appellate procedure, this point becomes most obvious. Although there is a great virtue in the finality of legal decisions (Bator, 1963), our system considers a criminal conviction an outcome of such awesome moment to the accused that it provides an extensive assortment of mandatory and discretionary appeal mechanisms (Carrington et al., 1976). An appellate court does not hear the case anew; rather, it renders its decision on the basis of the record from the lower court proceeding and the written and oral arguments of counsel. The questions on appeal are explicitly legal and normative. Unless the lower court verdict was clearly contrary to the great weight of the evidence, a conclusion reached only hesitantly by appellate courts, the appellate court will leave undisturbed the factual finding. Thus, in theory, appellate courts are concerned with whether legal errors were committed by the lower court and, if they were, what the appropriate remedy should be.

Here, too, there is no cooperative effort by counsel on appeal to determine what the law is or should be. Rather, opposing counsel argue strenuously, in light of the facts found and the applicable legal principles, for the legal correctness of the position they are asserting. Because the law itself is rarely clear, appellate judges have great discretion to decide cases as they see fit. Consequently, decision-making will be normative.

In all the examples of normative decision-making, where there is no ultimate appeal to "correct" or "true" facts, the adversary system is an admirable means of ensuring a full consideration of the issues that should bear on the legal decision. Counsel committed to discovering the most persuasive arguments for opposing positions will produce a dialectic of reasoning that cannot help but shed much light on the case at hand. In sum, the adversary process is quite well suited to a system that includes inherent goal conflicts and that must decide normative issues.

III. NONADVERSARY AND COOPERATIVE ASPECTS OF THE AMERICAN CRIMINAL JUSTICE SYSTEM

In the previous section, the nature of the adversary system was explored with special reference to the value and goal conflicts inherent in such a system. In this section, the nonadversary aspects of the system will be examined in order to distinguish the system in theory from the system in fact. Here we shall focus mainly on the adjudicative stage of the system, when a suspect has been charged with crime and the adversary system formally begins (Kirby v. Illinois, 1972).

Although one often thinks of the adversaries as the "state" and the "accused," in fact, the primary adversaries are the prosecuting and defense attorneys. Lawyers are the crux of an adversary system. Where the system assumes that the best result is reached if each side presents its own case and protects its own rights, and where the outcome of the system depends on a contest governed by complex and often arcane rules and procedures, it is inconceivable that the system will operate properly unless it is run primarily by those trained in its assumptions and methods (Gideon v. Wainwright, 1963).

In nearly all cases the state is represented by the prosecuting attorney. To equalize the contest, at least to some reasonable degree, the U.S. Supreme Court has held that the Constitution requires that counsel should be provided to all indigent defendants charged with a felony, or in any other case where imprisonment will result. In the words of the Court:

> The right to be heard would be, in many cases, of little avail if it did not comprehend the right to be heard by counsel. Even the intelligent and

educated layman has small and sometimes no skill in the science of law. If charged with crime, he is incapable, generally, of determining for himself whether the indictment is good or bad. He is unfamiliar with the rules of evidence. Left without the aid of counsel he may be put on trial without a proper charge, and convicted upon incompetent evidence, or evidence irrelevant to the issue or otherwise inadmissible. He lacks both the skill and knowledge adequately to prepare his defense, even though he have a perfect one. He requires the guiding hand of counsel at every step in the proceedings against him. Without it, though he be not guilty, he faces the danger of conviction because he does not know how to establish his innocence. If that be true of men of intelligence, how much more is it true of the ignorant and illiterate or those of feeble intellect [Powell v. Alabama, 1932: 68-69].

In our adversary system of criminal justice, any person haled into court, who is too poor to hire a lawyer, cannot be assured a fair trial unless counsel is provided for him. This seems to us to be an obvious truth. Governments, both state and federal, quite properly spend vast sums of money to establish machinery to try defendants accused of crime. Lawyers to prosecute are everywhere deemed essential to protect the public's interest in an orderly society. Similarly, there are few defendants charged with crime, few indeed, who fail to hire the best lawyers they can get to prepare and present their defenses. That government hires lawyers to prosecute and defendants who have the money hire lawyers to defend are the strongest indications of the widespread belief that lawyers in criminal courts are necessities, not luxuries. The right of one charged with crime to counsel may not be deemed fundamental and essential to fair trials in some countries, but it is in ours. From the very beginning, our state and national constitutions and laws have laid great emphasis on procedural and substantive safeguards designed to assure fair trials before impartial tribunals in which every defendant stands equal before the law. This noble ideal cannot be realized if the poor man charged with crime has to face his accusers without a lawyer to assist him [Gideon v. Wainwright, 1963: 344].

Although criminal defendants have a constitutional right to represent themselves if they so choose (Faretta v. California, 1975), few defendants are foolish enough to do so.

The lawyers are the players, and to understand the workings of the system, one must understand the relationship between the contending lawyers. In most jurisdictions, especially in high-volume urban areas, the bulk of criminal cases will be defended by three groups of lawyers: private attorneys retained by defendants, public defenders appointed to represent indigents, and criminal court regulars who earn their livings by court appointment. All three will appear regularly, and inevitably will begin to develop some type of relationship with the prosecuting attorneys (Alschuler, 1975).

In order to understand the relationship better, we must understand the practical operation of the system and the goals of the attorneys. First, the adjudicative stage of the criminal justice system is in most places vastly over-burdened because of three factors: increased rights for defendants, increased criminalization of behavior, and increased levels of crime. Let us briefly explore these. In the past two decades, constitutional criminal procedure doctrine has expanded enormously (Allen, 1975). For the most part, these decisions have substantially enlarged the rights of defendants, enhancing their ability to fight the state at every stage of the process, thereby creating increased costs and delay for the system. At the same time, the scope of criminal law has also expanded; there is widening use of the criminal sanction to effect social goals (Kadish, 1963). It is now considered useful, for instance, to control corporate conduct through the use of criminal law (Harvard Law Review, 1979). Finally, the crime rate has apparently increased substantially over the last two decades (Los Angeles Times, 1978; Federal Bureau of Investigation, 1977), and, in any event, the absolute volume of crime has risen, although the resources allotted to the adjudicative process have not kept pace (Alschuler, 1968). The overall result of these factors has been an astonishing burden on what was already an over-burdened and generally inefficient system (Burger, 1970).

The goals of the attorneys must also be explored. Prosecutors aim to convict as many defendants and to lose as few cases as possible. Whether they are elected or appointed, achieving a high "win" rate is one of their overriding considera-tions (Alschuler, 1968). On the other side, the goals among defense attorneys vary from group to group. Privately retained attorneys also like to win; winning is what builds their reputation and ensures a steady supply of clients. On the other hand, they do have to work with the prosecutors who have the power to make things easier or harder for them. Thus, to some extent even private attorneys will develop a working relationship with the prosecutors (Alschuler, 1975). Such relationships are usually more developed in the case of the appointed lawyers, both the "regulars" (Alschuler, 1975) and the public defend-ers (Alschuler, 1975; Denver Law Journal, 1973), who are typically vastly overburdened and work opposite the same prosecutors again and again. They are thus more in need of the cooperation of the prosecutor and are therefore more likely to give it in return. In addition, appointed attorneys have as a primary goal the speedy disposition of cases because they are so overburdened. Furthermore, the vast majority of defendants are factually guilty, thereby creating great incentive for overburdened attorneys to convince their clients that a guilty plea is the wisest course. Finally, court-appointed "regulars" have an economic incentive for advising guilty pleas (Alschuler, 1975); the economics of their reimbursement are such that they make more money if they can quickly dispose of a high volume of cases.

As a result of all these factors, the system is less adversary in practice than in theory. The system does not possess sufficient numbers of attorneys, investigators, judges, and courtrooms to provide the type of pretrial investigation and preparation and the full-scale trials that are theoretically envisioned by an adversary system. Even the state, with all its resources, lacks the wherewithal in a majority of cases to mount the investigations and preparations necessary effectively to go to trial (Fetter, 1978); and although the accused may have an attorney, the attorney probably has too many clients to enable him or her to prepare properly in all cases, and all too often there are insufficient funds to pay for an investigation.

The final outcome is that much of the attorney's time is spent on negotiating pleas, thereby avoiding trials (Newman, 1966; Alschuler, 1968, 1975, 1979; Uviller, 1977). Attorneys do represent the opposing interests of their sides, but functionally they are often "working together" to clear the system by encouraging guilty pleas. To encourage pleas, the prosecutor will disclose much of his or her case. To maintain the working relationship and to obtain favorable deals, the defense attorneys will often not press their cases to the extent that would be possible if resources permitted. The result is that many important legal and factual issues, including constitutional claims, are not litigated. Rather, if the defense is strong in one respect or another, this strength will be expressed by a concession offered by the prosecutor in return for a plea of guilty; charges will be dropped or lesser sentences will be recommended (Alschuler, 1968, 1975; Newman, 1966). Indeed, depending upon the jurisdiction, 65 to 95 percent of all cases will be disposed of by pleas of guilty, often through plea-bargaining (American Bar Association, 1974c; Newman, 1966). This is not the appropriate forum for analyzing the legal or social desirability of plea-bargaining, but it is necessary to note that a vast percentage of guilt adjudication takes place by means that are only a shadow of a fully adversary method. The system would probably break down if this were not true.

An extremely interesting nonadversary aspect of the system is the large number of cases wherein the defendant is not represented by an attorney, despite the strong language of Supreme Court cases indicating that attorneys are vitally necessary to the fair operation of the system. The large majority of cases brought into the criminal justice system are misdemeanors or other petty offenses. The Supreme Court has recently held that an attorney need not be appointed to represent an indigent defendant in such cases if no term of imprisonment is imposed (Scott v. Illinois, 1979). Consequently, if the state will be satisfied with a fine or any other sanction not entailing incarceration, the accused may be forced to face the state alone. Moreover, these cases are typically tried in a rather summary fashion by the most inferior court of a jurisdiction. Anyone who has spent time observing the business in the municipal courts of our larger cities recognizes that, even if the accused is represented by an attorney, often very little of a truly adversary nature is occurring (except that the accused is undergoing a process and perhaps a sanction that in nearly all cases he or she would rather avoid at all costs; see Harris, 1973; Jacob, 1973; Gazell, 1975; Fetter, 1978).

The sentencing proceeding is a final example of a less than fully adversary stage of the adjudicative process. It deserves attention here because nonlegal students of the criminal justice system tend to be especially concerned with corrections. Although, as always, practice varies from jurisdiction to jurisdiction, the usual procedure after a guilty verdict is for the court to have prepared a presentence report on the now-convicted defendant. The report is based on an investigation of variable thoroughness and may contain much information based on hearsay and other types of evidence that would be inadmissible at a trial. The judge uses the report to render a supposedly rational sentencing decision based on the defendant's particular characteristics and correctional needs.

The sentencing decision is probably the most important one to the defendant because it will have the greatest impact upon his or her life. One would expect, therefore, that in an adversary system committed to the protection of the rights of the accused, the defendant would have access to the report and an opportunity formally to challenge it, especially since it may be based on evidence deemed improper for admission at trial. However, except in very limited cases, the Constitution does not compel access by the defendant to the report, nor do most states provide for such access as a matter of state law (Williams v. New York, 1949; Gardner v. Florida, 1977; but contrast American Bar Association, 1974b). The defendant is allowed to make arguments on his or her own behalf at the sentencing hearing, but is still denied a full adversary challenge to a vital part of the proceedings against him or her. This is an extraordinary limitation on the adversary nature of the system. In terms of the rights of the accused, it also appears to be an unfair limitation. Nevertheless, this limitation is the predominant practice, and at least it has the virtue of saving the system the sizable cost and delay that would be occasioned if sentencing proceedings become fully adversary.

IV. IMPLICATIONS OF THE ADVERSARY SYSTEM

A. The Implications of Value Conflict

Having discussed the adversary and nonadversary features of our criminal justice system, it is now time to turn more specifically to some of the implications of the analysis for criminal justice evaluators.

The first thing to recognize is that the conceptual approach of most evaluators is markedly different from that of the participants in the system they are studying. Evaluators are trained largely in the social sciences which seek their legitimacy on the basis of relatively value-neutral investigations performed according to evenhanded empirical techniques. They study conflict in reality but do not accept that conflict is the most appropriate way to study reality. As empiricists, they also tend to be instrumentalists, concerned with what works. By contrast, lawyers consider truth to be quite relative and often view the search for truth as a normative quest (Uviller, 1975). Trained in the spirit of the adversary system, they cannot avoid seeing both sides to most questions. Furthermore, on the whole they believe the adversary system is well suited to searching for normative truths. Finally, since the law is a normative enterprise, lawyers are familiar with the tension between justice and utility. Arguments that utility must be subordinated to justice are part of their everyday working equipment, rather than positions that can be asserted only by leaving one's role as a "neutral" social scientist.

Justice claims are ambiguous (cf. Rawls, 1971), not lending themselves to empirical adjudication and resolution. Moreover, they often interfere with efficient outcomes; nearly always the price of justice is some disorder and delay. Criminal justice system evaluators must recognize that many of the theoretically and morally most important aspects of the criminal justice system cannot be easily quantified for empirical evaluation. "Was justice done?" is a very hard issue to evaluate indeed. Clearly, then, evaluators must design their studies and assess their conclusions with the goal conflicts of the system in mind, and should hesitate before condemning out of hand some of the inefficiencies of the system. Conflicts and inefficiencies are the inevitable products of an adversary system dedicated to protecting individual rights.

Because the criminal justice system is a normative enterprise, it will be particularly responsive to social and political pressures. For every proponent of some point of view, there will be an opponent, and often the dispute will not be resolvable on empirical grounds. Take a diversion or work-release program, for example. Such programs attempt to decrease crime by avoiding the "criminogenic" effects of the criminal justice system, particularly imprisonment. While such programs may "work"—that is, may decrease recidivism—for some persons that is not the issue. Rather, critics may believe that offenders should be punished without mitigation because they deserve to be, even if there are some negative consequences that ensue.

For instance, in an excellent evaluation study, Waldo and Chiricos (1977) examined whether work-release programs were effective in decreasing recidivism. Using careful, sophisticated methodology and analysis, the investigators concluded that work-release programs were unsuccessful. In their conclusion, however, it was not recommended that most such programs should be abandoned or even temporarily suspended. Rather, the authors suggest that such programs should not be, and probably will not be, abandoned, because they reduce the costs of corrections and because they also might be justified on humanitarian grounds.

It is worth noting that this study assumes that the correctional system has mainly consequentialist goals—cost-saving or "people changing" (to use a phrase the authors have borrowed from Daniel Glaser). But many people might object to work-release programs on the ground that by providing lenient conditions to prisoners, they undermine the retributive goals of the system (see La Patra, 1978). If work release is both rehabilitative and cheap, then perhaps it will satisfy those who accept retributive goals as partial components of the system. But if the only benefit of work-release programs is economic, those who accept retributivism may reach a different conclusion about the desirability of maintaining them. Thus, the study under consideration makes tentative policy suggestions but entirely ignores retributive goals in its analysis of corrections. At a time when retributive goals for corrections are increasingly popular, this is perhaps an important omission. The authors' ultimate conclusion may be sensible, but one wishes that this otherwise excellent study had paid more attention to other important factors.

Within the criminal justice system, it is inevitable that there will be participants who hold different normative positions on any issue, measure, or program, thus inherently creating in all cases a group of players opposed to the full effectuation of any program (Freeman, 1977). Rather than bemoaning this fact and the difficulties it causes them, evaluators should recognize its inevitability in a normative system. Moreover, they should remember that because political viewpoints cycle, their findings may soon lose value or be ignored by those in ascendance. An evaluator should not lose heart, for example, if a diversion or work-release program evaluated as highly successful is abandoned soon thereafter.

A related point concerns the political impact evaluators wish to have. Changes in the criminal justice system are accomplished mainly by lawyers who are accustomed to deciding issues on the basis of adversary procedures wherein normative questions are explicitly taken into account. Evaluators who wish to influence policy, as well as to provide data on how the world works, need to become comfortable with adversary modes of presentation. Furthermore, unless they identify and disclose their own value positions and how these have affected their work, they face a (possible) loss of credibility. Evaluators will have to learn how to convince decision makers, in nontechnical language, that their work is reliable and valid. Finally, because they will be participants in a system that uses adversary methods, they must be prepared for an explicit contest with opposition experts. In sum, evaluators will have to become increasingly proficient scientists *and* advocates if they wish to have maximum impact on the system.

B. The Need for Data

Criminal justice decisions are often based on empirical assumptions about the world. Judicial decisions and legislative hearings are replete with examples of the decision makers citing common wisdom or empirical studies (Ballew v. Georgia, 1978: Blackmun plurality; but contrast Powell concurrence). Although legal rules are normatively based, the law cannot be divorced from reality. For example, the balance between state authority and individual rights will vary according to the nature of the political and social climate at a given time. In a time of significantly rising crime, for instance, one expects to find more proponents of enhanced state power, even if this may work hardships on individual defendants. The stakes in the criminal justice system are high, rendering it imperative that the system should operate on the basis of good data. Thus, although it is a cliché, there is a powerful need for high-quality data about the system's assumptions and performance.

Unfortunately, the same value and goal conflicts that produce opponents who hinder the successful implementation of various programs are also likely to produce opponents who block the efforts of the evaluators. One interest group or another concerned with the program under investigation will perceive, correctly or incorrectly, that its interests are likely to be harmed by the evaluation and therefore will overtly or covertly oppose it. This, again, appears to be inevitable in any system, and perhaps is especially likely in a highly politicized system such as criminal justice.

V. SOME BRIEF SPECULATIONS ABOUT THE FUTURE

The adversary system has many critics who wish to reform the system in a nonadversary fashion (Weinreb, 1977; Tullock, 1975). They believe that factual truth is valued too little and that justice is ultimately inhibited by the inefficiencies, costs, and delays of our system (Frankel, 1975). There is increasing interest in what the continental, so-called inquisitorial, system might have to teach us (Damaska, 1973; Weinreb, 1977). At the same time, the adversary system has its stout defenders, who are dubious about the ability of a system less committed to adversary principles either to find truth or to protect individual rights long cherished in this nation (Johnson, 1977; Freedman, 1975).

It is difficult to foretell the outcome of the present ferment. On the one hand, one can easily point to movement toward less adversary procedures (Aaronson, 1977a, 1977b; Felstiner and Drew, 1976).[5] Increasingly liberalized discovery procedures (American Bar Association, 1974a) and recent limitations on the scope of the Fifth Amendment privilege against self-incrimination by the U.S. Supreme Court (Andresen v. Maryland, 1976; Fisher v. United States,

1976) are examples of this movement. On the other hand, one can as easily point to examples of changes promoting adversariness, such as expansion of the scope of the right to counsel by the Supreme Court (Argersinger v. Hamlin, 1972; Holloway v. Arkansas, 1978) and suggestions that certain grand jury witnesses be provided with counsel (Opinion of the Justices to the Governor, 1977; American Bar Association Journal, 1979).

Whichever way the system moves, however, I believe social science data will be increasingly relied upon for decision-making at all levels. Lawyers understand that law is imbedded in its social context, and many law schools have become explicitly more interdisciplinary in their approach. Judges, too, are increasingly willing to use social science data in their decision-making (Kirp, 1977; Ballew v. Georgia, 1978: Blackmun plurality). Finally, the complexities, burdens, and costs of the criminal justice system indicate the clear need for rigorous empirical analyses. There is special concern for cost-benefit analysis: Are we getting what we pay for and is it worth it (Nagel, 1973)?

The implication for evaluators and all social scientists, as they increasingly offer their services, is that they must do so with a sophisticated understanding of the system they are evaluating. They should know something about criminal law and procedure and should understand legal reasoning and methods. I am not suggesting, of course, that evaluators should become lawyers. But for their work to be most useful and successful, evaluators should be able to understand what is "really going on" in the system. Consequently, for example, one-sided critiques or studies that are methodologically sound but fail to address important and relevant aspects will thereby be avoided. A fundamental part of that understanding must be an appreciation of adversary process and conflict in the system and the system's operation in fact, including its costs and benefits. One hopes that evaluators will learn to understand the conceptual approach and to speak the language of lawyers, and vice versa.

NOTES

1. Accepting the position that almost all of the constitutional protections afforded the criminal defendant by the Bill of Rights have been "incorporated" into the Fourteenth Amendment, the Supreme Court has held in a series of opinions that those protections apply to the fifty states via the Due Process clause of the Fourteenth Amendment to the same degree and force as they apply to the federal government. Although the historical justification and wisdom of selective incorporation have been hotly debated, the result has been that, for example, the rights to counsel, to jury trial, to be free from compelled self-incrimination, and to be free from unreasonable searches and seizures, have been applied to the states with the full force of a constitutional requirement (see Duncan v. Louisiana, 1967; Henkin, 1963; Friendly, 1965). In fact, only two guarantees in the Bill of Rights, the rights to reasonable bail and grand jury indictment, have not been incorporated, thus leaving

the states more flexibility in these areas. Still, although most of the broad guarantees have been incorporated, the specific meaning of these rights is uncertain until the Supreme Court decides specific cases. When it does so, such decisions are binding on the states. Nevertheless, until specific questions are ultimately decided by the Supreme Court, individual states may decide for themselves how the broad guarantees of the Bill of Rights are to be interpreted to apply in those specific cases.

2. It should be recognized, however, that the majority of searches occur in the "exceptional" cases that do not require a warrant. This is largely because most crime detection takes place under exigent circumstances; returning to a magistrate for a warrant would be impractical. On the other hand, agencies such as the FBI that engage in more deliberate, long-term investigations in order to develop a case before initiating searches or arrests, often are able to secure warrants for their intrusions.

3. Thus, in Miranda v. Arizona itself, no element of extreme brutality or psychological coercion was present. Instead, after being arrested at his home and taken to the police station, Ernesto Miranda was identified by a complaining witness and then interrogated by two police officers for two hours. He was not informed of his right to have an attorney present during the interrogation. When he confessed orally, Miranda was read a statement, which he subsequently signed, that his confession was made voluntarily and with full knowledge of his legal rights. He was convicted after a trial during which the written confession was introduced into evidence over his attorney's objections.

4. Several state and federal statutes require a defendant to notify the prosecution of his or her intention to offer evidence of an alibi and/or to plead not guilty by reason of insanity (e.g., Federal Rules of Criminal Procedure, § 12.1, requiring the defendant to specify particulars of a proposed alibi, including time, place, and supporting witnesses; and § 12.2, requiring the defendant to register his or her intended insanity defense, including any expert witnesses he or she plans to have testify in his or her behalf).

5. Although special problems exist in the use of nonadversary procedures in the criminal justice system (e.g., those posed by constitutional requirements), some examples of the variety of nonadversary procedures are both voluntary and mandatory arbitration (Rosenberg, 1972; Getman, 1979).

CASES

ADDINGTON v. TEXAS (1979) 441 U.S. 418
ANDRESEN v. MARYLAND (1976) 427 U.S. 463
ARGERSINGER v. HAMLIN (1972) 407 U.S. 25
BALLEW v. GEORGIA (1978) 435 U.S. 223
BORDENKIRCHER v. HAYES (1978) 434 U.S. 357
BRADY v. MARYLAND (1963) 373 U.S. 83
BRADY v. UNITED STATES (1970) 397 U.S. 742
BROWN v. MISSISSIPPI (1936) 297 U.S. 278
BROWN v. TEXAS (1979) 443 U.S. 47
CADY v. DOMBROWSKI (1973) 413 U.S. 433
CARROLL v. UNITED STATES (1924) 267 U.S. 132
COOLIDGE v. NEW HAMPSHIRE (1971) 403 U.S. 443
DELAWARE v. PROUSE (1979) 440 U.S. 648
Discovery in Criminal Cases (1967) 44 F.R.D. 481

DUNAWAY v. NEW YORK (1979) 442 U.S. 200
DUNCAN v. LOUISIANA (1967) 391 U.S. 145
FARETTA v. CALIFORNIA (1975) 422 U.S. 806
FISHER v. UNITED STATES (1976) 425 U.S. 391
GARDNER v. FLORIDA (1977) 430 U.S. 349
GIDEON v. WAINWRIGHT (1963) 372 U.S. 335
GILLIHAN v. RODRIGUEZ (1977) 551 F.2d 1182
GRIFFIN v. CALIFORNIA (1965) 380 U.S. 609
HARRIS v. NEW YORK (1971) 401 U.S. 222
HOLLOWAY v. ARKANSAS (1978) 435 U.S. 475
JACOBELLIS v. OHIO (1964) 378 U.S. 184
JOHNSON v. UNITED STATES (1948) 333 U.S. 10
KIRBY v. ILLINOIS (1972) 406 U.S. 682
LAKESIDE v. OREGON (1978) 435 U.S. 433
LO-JI SALES, INC. v. NEW YORK (1979) 442 U.S. 319
MALLOY V. HOGAN (1964) 378 U.S. 1 (Harlan Dissenting)
MAPP v. OHIO (1961) 367 U.S. 643
MARYLAND v. MARZULLO (1978) 435 U.S. 1011
MICHIGAN v. MOSLEY (1975) 423 U.S. 96
MIRANDA v. ARIZONA (1966) 384 U.S. 436
MULLANEY v. WILBUR (1975) 421 U.S. 684
MURPHY v. WATERFRONT COMMISSION (1964) 387 U.S. 52
NEW JERSEY v. PORTASH (1979) 440 U.S. 450
Opinion of the Justices to the Governor (1977) 371 N.E.2d 422
PEOPLE v. DeFORE (1926) 150 N.E. 585
PEOPLE v. HOLT (1944) 153 P.2d 21
PEOPLE v. JOHNSON (1976) 546 P.2d 1259
PEOPLE v. SONIER (1952) 248 P.2d 155
POWELL v. ALABAMA (1932) 287 U.S. 45
RICKENBACKER v. WARDEN (1976) 550 F.2d 62
SCHNECKLOTH v. BUSTAMONTE (1973) 412 U.S. 218
SCOTT v. ILLINOIS (1979) 440 U.S. 367
SHADWICK v. CITY OF TAMPA (1972) 407 U.S. 345
SPEISER v. RANDALL (1958) 357 U.S. 513
STATE v. JOHNSON (1966) 192 So.2d 135 (cert. den. 388 U.S. 923)
TERRY v. OHIO (1968) 392 U.S. 1
UNITED STATES v. AGURS (1976) 427 U.S. 97
UNITED STATES v. DeCOSTER (1973) 487 F.2d 1197
UNITED STATES v. EASTER (1976) 539 F.2d 663
UNITED STATES v. FESELL (1976) 531 F.2d 1275
UNITED STATES v. RAMIREZ (1976) 535 F.2d 125
UNITED STATES v. ROBINSON (1973) 414 U.S. 218
UNITED STATES v. UNITED STATES DISTRICT COURT (1972) 407
    U.S. 297
WARDEN v. HAYDEN (1967) 387 U.S. 294

WILLIAMS v. NEW YORK (1949) 373 U.S. 241
In re WINSHIP (1970) 397 U.S. 358

REFERENCES

Aaronson, D. E. et al. (1977a) *The New Justice: Alternatives to Conventional Criminal Adjudication*. Washington, DC: National Institute of Law Enforcement and Criminal Justice.

——— (1977b) *Alternatives to Conventional Criminal Adjudication: Guidebook for Planners and Practitioners*. Washington, DC: National Institute of Law Enforcement and Criminal Justice.

Allen, F. A. (1975) "The Judicial Quest for Penal Justice: The Warren Court and the Criminal Cases." University of Illinois Law Forum: 518-542.

Allen, R. J. (1976) "The Police and Substantive Rulemaking: Reconciling Principle and Expediency." *University of Pennsylvania Law Review* 125: 62-118.

Alschuler, A. W. (1979) "Plea Bargaining and Its History." *Columbia Law Review* 79: 1-43.

——— (1975) "The Defense Attorney's Role in Plea Bargaining." *Yale Law Journal* 84: 1179-1314.

——— (1968) "The Prosecutor's Role in Plea Bargaining." *University of Chicago Law Review* 36: 50-112.

American Bar Association Journal (1979) "Grand Jury Counsel Spurs Multiple-Defense Rifts." 65: 24.

American Bar Association (1974a) "Discovery and Procedure Before Trial," in *Standards Relating to the Administration of Criminal Justice*. Chicago: Author.

——— (1974b) "Sentencing Alternatives and Procedures," in *Standards Relating to the Administration of Criminal Justice*. Chicago: Author.

——— (1974c) "Pleas of Guilty," in *Standards Relating to the Administration of Criminal Justice*. Chicago: Author.

Amsterdam, A. G. (1974) "Perspectives on the Fourth Amendment." *Minnesota Law Review* 58: 349-477.

Bator, P. M. (1963) "Finality in Criminal Law and Federal Habeas Corpus for State Prisoners." *Harvard Law Review* 76: 441-528.

Brennan, W. J., Jr. (1977) "State Constitutions and the Protection of Individual Rights." *Harvard Law Review* 90: 489-504.

——— (1963) "The Criminal Prosecution: Sporting Event or Quest for Truth?" *Washington University Law Quarterly* 1963: 279-295.

Burger, W. E. (1970) "The State of the Judiciary–1970." *American Bar Association Journal* 56: 929-934.

Canon, B. C. (1979). "The Exclusionary Rule: Have Critics Proven That It Doesn't Deter Police?" *Judicature* 62: 398-403.

——— and Schlesinger, S. R. (1979) "A Postscript on Empirical Studies and the Exclusionary Rule." *Judicature* 62: 455-458.

Carrington, P. D. et al. (1976) *Justice on Appeal*. St. Paul, MN: West.

Chase, E. (1977) "The Burger Court, the Individual, and the Criminal Process: Directions and Misdirections." *New York University Law Review* 52: 518-597.

Damaska, M. (1973) "Evidentiary Barriers to Conviction and Two Models of Criminal Procedure: A Comparative Study." *University of Pennsylvania Law Review* 121: 506-589.

Davis, K. C. (1969) *Discretionary Justice: A Preliminary Inquiry.* Baton Rouge: Louisiana State University Press.

Denver Law Journal (1973) "Comparison of Public Defenders' and Private Attorneys' Relationships with the Prosecution in the City of Denver." 50: 101-136.

Federal Bureau of Investigation (1977) *Uniform Crime Reports.* Washington, DC: Government Printing Office.

Felstiner, W.L.F. and A. B. Drew (1976) *European Alternatives to Criminal Trials and Their Applicability in the United States.* Washington, DC: National Institute of Law Enforcement and Criminal Justice.

Fetter, T. J. [ed.] (1978) *State Courts: A Blueprint for the Future.* Washington, DC: National Center for State Courts.

Fortas, A. (1954) "The Fifth Amendment: Nemo Tenetur Prodere Seipsum [no one is bound to betray himself]." *Cleveland Bar Association Journal* 25: 91, 96-104.

Frank, J. (1963). *Courts on Trial: Myth and Reality in American Justice.* New York: Atheneum.

Frankel, M. E. (1975) "The Search for Truth: An Umpireal View." *University of Pennsylvania Law Review* 123: 1031-1059.

Freedman, M. H. (1975) "Judge Frankel's Search for Truth." *University of Pennsylvania Law Review* 123: 1060-1066.

––– (1966) "Professional Responsibility of the Criminal Defense Lawyer: The Three Hardest Questions." *Michigan Law Review* 64: 1469-1484.

Freeman, H. E. (1977) "The Present Status of Evaluation Research," pp. 17-51 in M. Guttentag and S. Saar (eds.) *Evaluation Studies Review Annual, Volume 2.* Beverly Hills, CA: Sage Publications.

Friendly, H. J. (1965) "The Bill of Rights as a Code of Criminal Procedure." *California Law Review* 53: 929-956.

Gazell, J. A. (1975) *State Trial Courts as Bureaucrats: A Study in Judicial Management.* Port Washington, NY: Dunellen.

Gerstein, R. S. (1979) "The Self-Incrimination Debate in Great Britain." *American Journal of Comparative Law* 27: 81-114.

––– (1971) "Punishment and Self-Incrimination." *American Journal of Jurisprudence* 16: 84-94.

––– (1970) "Privacy and Self-Incrimination." *Ethics* 80: 87-101.

Getman, J. (1979) "Labor Arbitration and Dispute Resolution." *Yale Law Journal* 88: 916-949.

Goldstein, A. S. (1974) "Reflections on Two Models: Inquisitorial Themes in American Criminal Procedure." *Stanford Law Review* 26: 1009-1025.

Harris, R. (1973) "Annals of Law: In Criminal Court, I." *New Yorker* 49: 45-88.

Harvard Law Review (1979) "Developments in the Law–Corporate Crime: Regulating Corporate Behavior Through Criminal Sanctions." 92: 1227-1375.

Hart, H. M. (1958) "The Aims of the Criminal Law." *Law and Contemporary Problems* 23: 401-441.

Hazard, G. C., Jr. (1978) *Ethics in the Practice of Law.* New Haven, CT: Yale University Press.

Henkin, L. (1963) " 'Selective Incorporation' in the Fourteenth Amendment." *Yale Law Journal* 73: 74-88.

Hyman, E. M. (1979) "In Pursuit of a More Workable Exclusionary Rule: A Police Officer's Perspective." *Pacific Law Journal* 10: 33-68.

Israel, J. H. (1977) "Criminal Procedure, the Burger Court, and the Legacy of the Warren Court." *Michigan Law Review* 75: 1319-1425.

Jacob, H. (1973) *Urban Justice: Law and Order in American Cities.* Englewood Cliffs, NJ: Prentice-Hall.

Johnson, P. E. (1977) "Importing Justice." *Yale Law Journal* 87: 406-414.

Kadish, S. H. (1963) "Some Observations on the Use of Criminal Sanctions in Enforcing Economic Regulations." *University of Chicago Law Review* 30: 423-449.

Kamisar, Y. (1979) "The Exclusionary Rule in Historical Perspective: The Struggle To Make the Fourth Amendment More than 'an Empty Blessing.' " *Judicature* 62: 337-350.

——— (1978) "Is the Exclusionary Rule an 'Illogical' or 'Unnatural' Interpretation of the Fourth Amendment?" *Judicature* 62: 66-84.

Kimball, S. L. (1966) *Historical Introduction to the Legal System.* St. Paul, MN: West.

Kirp, D. L. (1977) "School Desegregation and the Limits of Legalism." *Public Interest* 47: 101-128.

LaPatra, J. W. (1978) *Analyzing the Criminal Justice System.* Lexington, MA: D. C. Heath.

Levine, M. (1974) "Scientific Method and the Adversary Model: Some Preliminary Thoughts." *American Psychologist* 29: 661-677.

Levy, L. W. (1968) *Origins of the Fifth Amendment.* New York: Oxford University Press.

Los Angeles Times (1978) "Crime Rate in L.A., Nation Up Dramatically." July 11: 3.

McChesney, F. A. (1977) "On the Procedural Superiority of a Civil Law System: A Comment." *Kyklos* 30: 507-510.

McKay, R. B. (1967) "Self-Incrimination and the New Privacy." *Supreme Court Review:* 193-232.

Nagel, S. S. (1973) *Minimizing Costs and Maximizing Benefits in Providing Legal Services to the Poor.* Beverly Hills, CA: Sage Publications.

New York Times (1968) "Court Scored by Top Judge Here." November 10: 73.

Newman, D. J. (1966) *Conviction: The Determination of Guilt or Innocence Without Trial.* Boston: Little, Brown.

Packer, H. L. (1968) *The Limits of the Criminal Sanction.* Stanford, CA: Stanford University Press.

——— (1964) "Two Models of the Criminal Process." *University of Pennsylvania Law Review* 113: 1-68.

Pound, R. (1930) *Criminal Justice in America.* New York: Holt, Rinehart & Winston.

Pye, A. K. (1978) "The Role of Counsel in the Suppression of Truth." *Duke Law Journal:* 921-959.

Rawls, J. (1971) *A Theory of Justice.* Cambridge, MA: Harvard University Press.

Rosenberg, M. (1972) "Let's Everybody Litigate?" *Texas Law Review* 50: 1349-1368.

Schlesinger, S. R. (1979) "The Exclusionary Rule: Have Proponents Proven That It Is a Deterrent to Police?" *Judicature* 62: 404-409.

Tullock, G. (1975) "On the Efficient Organization of Trials." *Kyklos* 28: 745-762.

Uviller, H. R. (1977) "Pleading Guilty: A Critique of Four Models." *Law and Contemporary Problems* 41: 102-131.

——— (1975) "The Advocate, the Truth, and Judicial Hackles: A Reaction to Judge Frankel's Idea." *University of Pennsylvania Law Review* 123: 1067-1082.

Waldo, G. P. and T. G. Chiricos (1977) "Work Release and Recidivism: An Empirical Evaluation of a Social Policy." *Evaluation Quarterly* 1: 87-108.

Weinreb, L. L. (1977) *Denial of Justice: Criminal Process in the United States.* New York: Free Press.

Wigmore, J. H. (1961) *Evidence in Trials at Common Law.* Boston: Little, Brown.
Wilkey, M. R. (1979) "A Call for Alternatives to the Exclusionary Rule: Let Congress and the Trial Courts Speak." *Judicature* 62: 351-356.
——— (1978) "The Exclusionary Rule: Why Suppress Valid Evidence?" *Judicature* 62: 214-232.

13

Variation in Criminal Justice Research Designs

Albert J. Reiss, Jr.

INTRODUCTION

Criminal justice in the United States is organized as a loosely articulated network of hierarchical relationships among functionally differentiated organizations or participants, each making decisions about whether and how people and information are to be processed in the network. Seven major subsystems are organized in the network, including citizen and police law enforcement, defendant and public prosecution, trial and appellate court, and corrections (Reiss, 1974: 679-680).

In addition to its lack of central organization and coordination, the network and its subsystems are characterized by much organizational variability. There are a number of sources of this variability. The main source is our federated system of government, which allows enormous variability in our legal culture and its organizations. Each state is permitted a latitude through its state constitution that is constrained only by federal constitutional mandates. The states, in turn, generally permit considerable local variation. Moreover, constitutional separation of legislative, executive, and judicial powers allows each branch of government to foster considerable variation.

Somewhat separable from these sources of variation are those that distinguish a much larger class of formal organizations. Variation may arise from the surrounding order affecting the structure of an organization, such as its size, or variation may emerge developmentally and by design, as with the degree of bureaucratization and form of management style.

Whatever its source, it is apparent that the most one can do to describe the organization of criminal justice in the United States is to characterize it in terms of some central tendencies. No one is able to offer a detailed and concise description of the nature of its variability.[1] Yet the advent of federal support for innovations and changes in criminal justice has brought with it requirements for evaluation, and this, in turn, has served as an impetus to map some of the variability in criminal justice organization. Such efforts have not been systematically organized, however. They have perhaps been more extensive in juvenile than in adult justice, and in policing and jails than in courts and prosecution.

Our concern in what follows is to assess how variability in the criminal justice network enters in important ways into evaluation research. Two major ways are examined. We first inquire into how variability is an important element in assessing or evaluating either proposed or actual changes in a criminal justice network. The argument basically is that experiments and trial changes may take advantage of variability in criminal justice organization. Later we inquire into the ways that organizational variability must be taken into account in evaluation, particularly in the development and use of evaluation measures. In the background will lie the argument that without substantial and concise knowledge about the nature and amount of variability in the organization of criminal justice in the United States, evaluation is subject to serious limits.

I. ADVANTAGES AND LIABILITIES OF VARIABILITY IN EVALUATION RESEARCH

Variability generally offers the opportunity to examine the conditions and limits for any conclusion. It is perhaps rather naive of much evaluation research that it assumes that any intervention or change should have the same effect under all conditions, rather than searching for the conditions under which a given effect takes place. Long's (1979) reevaluation of an evaluation of an entensive vocational services treatment program (Bell et al., 1969) demonstrates quite nicely that variability within treatment populations may mask treatment effects when they occur for only some subgroups of a population, and that there are opposite and offsetting treatment effects for other subgroups. These kinds of variability within a population of members of criminal justice organizations can occur, likewise, among organizational units. Yet, they are rarely investigated.

Apart from the limits that variability ordinarily sets for any test condition or proposition, one must be aware, secondly, that natural variability among organizations poses problems for both natural and contrived experiments in field settings. All too often, evaluations of an intended or anticipated effect of some innovation or social change fail to separate out or control for the effects of changes in concomitant variables. To overcome such effects, a randomized controlled field trial design often is recommended (Fienberg et al., 1976: 131).

Many field experiments, in failing to control for various sources of variability, end up by supporting the null hypothesis. The probability of rejecting the null hypothesis often is set at a low value so that the probability of failing to detect the alternative hypothesis when it is true is problematic. Unless that probability is small, an experiment is weighted in favor of the null hypothesis. This was the case, Fienberg et al. (1976) argue, in the experimental design of the Kansas City Preventive Patrol Experiment, where there was no control over important sources of variability (Kelling et al., 1974).

There is no single solution to this problem of variability in designing social experiments or evaluation studies, since organizations often do not lend themselves to randomized experiments. Our proposed redesign of the Kansas City Preventive Patrol Experiment used a randomized controlled field trial design which had two key features (Fienberg et al., 1976: 131). Different treatments were to be applied to the same experimental police beats during different time periods, resulting in a crossover or changeover design where each police beat was its own control. Additional control was achieved by insulating each experimental beat by surrounding it with a set of beats where the experimental treatments did not take place. The effects of the several treatments were then examined in both primary and secondary beats. Designs such as this one have greater control over different sources of variability, but they are more costly, take longer periods of time to complete, and involve greater use of repeated measures than does a simple experimental design.

There is, third, the problem that one cannot capitalize on variability by experimentation, because of limits on experimentation or on some conditions that are integral to an experiment. Within a country, these limits stem from natural conditions of organizations, e.g., exclusion on grounds of organizational size, cultural or social system limits which may be dealt with by cross-national research, and constitutional or legislative prohibitions. Even when no such barriers to capitalizing on variability in evaluation designs exist, there are important practical considerations that restrict the evaluation design.

First, given our relatively limited descriptive knowledge of variability in a criminal justice network or national system, we lack information to design studies that take variability into account. Lacking sampling frameworks that would permit stratification of organizations or networks, we are reduced to inelegant modes of selecting organizations for research, ones that do not permit precise estimates for a known population.

Second, even when the sources of variability are known, the cost of each experimental treatment or evaluation may be high enough to make the cost of doing it under the variable conditions prohibitive. The design in this case compromises external validity.

Third, often one cannot take variability into account systematically because of resistance to, or acceptance of, the innovation. Extraneous criteria such as political sponsorship of innovation, resistance from selected organizations, or simply the size of an organization, may determine which are the treatment organizations and which, if any, the controls. Little control over source of variability is possible under such conditions—least of all over the effect of program designation as "experimental" or "treatment." It is not uncommon to discover that the organizations most needed for a particular design are the least accessible or open. In some areas of evaluation, the same organizations tend to become the ones selected for treatment precisely because they are open or accessible (Klein, 1979: 177). Thus, there are a larger number of police evaluation studies undertaken in Kansas City, San Diego, Washington, D.C., and New York City because these cities have been the most receptive to police research by outside investigators, while almost no studies have been undertaken in Los Angeles, San Francisco, or Philadelphia, where strong resistance is encountered.

There seems to be little need to argue for the importance of taking advantage of variability in criminal justice organization in designing evaluations, since variability is what makes it possible to assess external validity by examining the conditions and limits under which innovations and interventions have effects. Rather than explore those arguments further, we shall turn to cases where, when elaborate designs are infeasible and it becomes necessary to sacrifice external validity as an element in the design, we can take advantage of variability in the criminal justice network to evaluate anticipated or intended effects of social programs or changes in the organization of criminal justice. Most of my examples are drawn from evaluations of "system changing" investigations.

Before continuing, it is worth noting that the most common conclusion of evaluation studies of social programs in the criminal justice network is that "nothing works." We have already suggested that this may arise from designs that are too simply constructed as tests of the null hypothesis. But often it is argued that the conclusion that nothing works is based on a false presumption that the experimental condition actually occurred. Klein, in a cogent analysis of evaluations of deinstitutionalization and diversion programs, focuses on five major impediments to the implementation of these programs (1979: 157-181). What is surprising is how infrequently evaluation studies search for major organizational sources of variability that account for such impediments and then take them into account in assessing the effects of changed conditions. Ohlin et al. (1977) are reasonably successful in doing so in their study of deinstitutionalization in Massachusetts.

It is exceedingly rare to find an evaluation study that provides careful and concise documentation of the experimental or treatment condition. This is partly because most studies focus on "outcome variables" to evaluate experimental treatments rather than upon process variables. Where processes are examined, they ordinarily are for the effects of treatment rather than of the treatment condition itself. As sophistication in evaluation studies and their design grows, it becomes increasingly apparent that one must have concise measures of the treatment conditions over the life of the experiment, i.e., of whether the treatment is occuring and how, of the effect of the treatment variables over time as well as at some terminal point, and of concomitant changes that may affect both treatment and outcome variables, e.g., bureaucratic resistance to change.

II. TAKING ADVANTAGE OF NATURAL VARIABILITY IN EVALUATION RESEARCH

Fortunately, not all research on intervention in ongoing organizations need rely upon post hoc examination of the effects of intervention. The natural variability in a criminal justice network provides a number of opportunities to design and evaluate actual or proposed interventions. Three of these are discussed below, using examples from research on the American legal system, both civil and criminal.

We first show how variation within natural settings permits experimental studies without changing the organizations. Then we examine how anticipated changes can be evaluated by investigating them under conditions provided by variability in the criminal justice network. We shall not attempt to define the limits of the "forms of experimentation" used in our examples. Excellent treatment of the limits of experiments in legal research is found in the writings of Zeisel (1956, 1967) and Zeisel and Diamond (1974).

A. Experimental Studies Capitalizing on Natural Variation Within Organizations

Often it is very difficult to convince an organization that it should change its form or functioning and, with a simple before-after experimental design, assess whether it should adopt the changed conditions or return to former ones. This resistance would be understandable if one were to take seriously the possibility that proposed changes might not make a difference or might actually leave the organization worse off.

It is somewhat surprising that experimenters do not take this resistance more seriously, since in the natural form of an experiment the most likely result is that the experimental condition does not have its intended effect. When effects are observed, it often is reasonable to expect that they may be in a direction opposite from that intended. The only experiments that consistently produce intended effects are those that in the past have been demonstrated to occur invariably under those conditions. They are the classic laboratory exercises and the "priors" in proof. (Yet, students soon learn that the classic experiments may fail in a laboratory test because they have not ensured that all conditions have prevailed.)

Were students of evaluation studies to recognize this likely result in the design of "new" experiments, they would abandon attempts to "evaluate" single trials on the grounds that only with continuing opportunity to manipulate treatment variables or other experimental conditions can one produce an intended effect. Experimentation is cumulative, not disjunctive. And evaluation research investigators might well bear that model in mind, since in the face of failure the critical question is what to look at next. Note that most evaluation studies ignore this injunction on the grounds that the evaluation does not "control" the change conditions. But that is hardly adequate justification for doing so, and only adds to the artificial distinctions between classic experiments and evaluation research.

Moreover, the presumption in evaluation studies that one must await the "conclusion" of an "intervention" to observe intended effects is a false and misleading one. Since World War II, when Wald et al. (1945) developed statistical decision theory, it has been possible to undertake continuing evaluation with sequential analysis models. Where interventions are likely to produce harmful effects or to be discriminatory, the design of the research should provide for sequential analysis and, on the basis of it, decisions made on whether to continue a treatment or experiment of the form under evaluation.

B. Taking Advantage of Natural Innovation
to Assess Prospective Changes

Early on, we noted that it was characteristic of the American system of criminal justice that it has considerable variability in its form of organization, mandates, and practices. This variability often provides opportunity to evaluate prospectively the consequences of introducing change in *other* organizational units or contexts. History provides institutionalized innovations that can be evaluated for their effects, using the "prospective organizations" for comparison or control (Zeisel, 1977: 326). Several examples of evaluating historical innovations are given below to illustrate how they were used to shed light upon proposed system changes.

Perhaps one of the earliest of the studies attempting to view prospectively the effect of a statutory change is the now classic study of Thorsten Sellin (1953) on the deterrent effect of capital punishment. Comparing the homicide rates of abolitionist with retentionist capital punishment states, Sellin cast doubt upon the idea that either abolition or retention of capital punishment would have a substantial deterrent effect on the homicide rate, given the structure of sanctions for "capital" crimes. More recently, Forst (1976) substantially undermined Ehrlich's (1973) use of aggregate data to examine the deterrent effect of capital punishment by showing that the crime rate during the 1960s rose in a similar way for states with and without executions during that period.

Zeisel has ingeniously capitalized on these natural opportunities in organizations to evaluate prospective changes in criminal justice. During the controversy over proposed, and later actual, changes in federal use of six-person juries in criminal trials, he was aware that some states used six-person juries in civil and/or criminal trials. He set about to learn as quickly as possible what differences a six-person jury might make on jury decision-making, and hence its consequences for both the prosecution and defendants. He was able to show, for example, that hung juries in the Miami Circuit Court were only about half as frequent among six-person juries as they were among twelve-person juries (Zeisel, 1971a: 720). But he also went on to show that while such natural experiments can lead to important answers to some of the questions raised (Zeisel, 1971a), the evaluations of them often turn out to be faulty in design and analysis (Zeisel and Diamond, 1974).

One of the perennial issues of sentencing in the criminal courts is whether there are invidious disparities in sentencing, and what the effect of this inequality is. Central to an understanding of inequality in sentencing is knowledge of whether one of the proposed resolutions—the use of sentence review—has a substantial effect on reducing disparity in sentences. The natural world of criminal justice provided Zeisel with two different opportunities to assess the effects of judicial disparity in sentencing.

Zeisel and Diamond first examined whether sentencing councils in the federal courts reduced sentencing disparities. Of four districts that had voluntarily created sentencing councils, Diamond and Zeisel (1975) compared the Chicago and New York councils, since they also offered the opportunity to assess differences in participation by federal judges in the two councils. Zeisel and Diamond concluded that sentencing councils have a relatively small effect on reducing disparities in sentencing (1975: 147). In a second study, these investigators evaluated the effect sentence review boards in two states—Massachusetts and Connecticut—had upon reducing disparities in sentences of convicted offenders who appeal their sentence, and the effect of sentence review on the practices of trial courts. Their conclusions were rather similar with respect to effect on reduction of disparity (Zeisel and Diamond, 1977). Although such studies provide only limited answers to the question of what effect these historical innovations might have if introduced into new contexts, they are extremely important in directing arguments to the facts germane to the issues of innovation. As Zeisel plaintively notes in his study of the six-person jury, however, the evidence is easily ignored or distorted (Zeisel and Diamond, 1974: 293).

What seems surprising is how little evaluation there is of these historic changes in American criminal justice, despite an abundance of examples at every level of the criminal justice network. We have little evidence on shifts from public to other forms of law enforcement, such as private policing, indictment by grand jury compared with proceeding on the arrest or by filing of information, judicial compared with state public defender systems, lay versus professional judges, or private versus public corrections—to cite but a single illustration for each of the major levels in the hierarchy. What this absence of attention suggests is that much evaluation research has been dictated by current government policies on criminal justice innovation and by funding sources, rather than by a consideration of what evaluation studies might enable us to understand and innovate in the several systems of justice.

At least one major caution is in order in considering the evaluation of natural historical experiments as a means of understanding what effect the transfer of these experiments to other organizational contexts may bring. It is well recognized that, over time, innovations lose their original effects, if indeed they had any, or concomitant changes alter substantially what would have been the effects, had they been introduced in a new context. Indeed, this might suggest that the proper control for an evaluation of historical innovations is the historical period of introduction. Clearly, such designs are fraught with problems of proof and inference that are not easily overcome. What these difficulties pinpoint, however, is that evaluation is clearly not a point-in-time event, but a continuing enterprise. The cardinal principle of all audits is their repetition over time. That is the principle underlying the use of interrupted time series to evaluate historical or contemporary innovations or changes by legal intervention in ongoing systems (Campbell, 1976; Campbell and Ross, 1968; Ross, 1973).

III. TAKING ORGANIZATIONAL VARIABILITY INTO ACCOUNT IN EVALUATION RESEARCH

The varible properties of criminal justice organizations in which treatments or changes are to be evaluated are commonly disregarded in the design of research. The most frequent way that they *are* taken into account is in the analysis of effects—by statistical control of these properties as sources of variation or by measuring the relative effect of each property on the effect variables.

One reason properties of organizations are so frequently scanted in the design of evaluation studies is that the investigator had little or no control over where the treatments took place. Unfortunately, this is just one of a number of limits on post hoc evaluation studies that restrict their utility; and despite the ways even careful prior selection of organizations affects the external validity of evaluation studies, there are important ways that organizational properties affect the validity and accuracy of evaluation measures that cannot be ignored.

Where organizational variability may be taken into account by design, some common ways of doing so are by the design of a sample, by the use of complex designs (such as randomized controlled field trials), by contriving comparisons to eliminate organizational sources of variability in the treatment or change condition, and by standardizing observations in natural field settings.

We begin below by showing that when evaluation studies use statistical analysis to take organizational variability into account, they often fail to examine other, equally important, sources of organizational variability—the effects of organizational properties on the accuracy of measures that are used to evaluate treatments or effects of changes. This is followed by an examination of some ways that organizational variability may be taken into account in the design of evaluation studies, although such procedures are in no way unique to evaluation research.

A. Organizational Variability and the Accuracy of Evaluation Measures

The most prevalent means of taking into account variability among organizations is either to control statistically for the properties of organizations or to measure their relative effect on the behavior under investigation. Either one or both of these statistical procedures are ordinarily used when there is a considerable body of comparable information available about the organizations. Taken into account less frequently is that organizations also vary considerably in the properties of their *intelligence or information systems,* and the ways that variability affects the validity and accuracy of information used to test theories. Indeed, in evaluation research it is relatively rare to examine the effect that these information systems have on the information produced by the organization or obtained from it by other means—at least in any precise way.

Yet, the use of statistical procedures of analysis depends very much upon the accuracy or reliability of the data, a matter that is especially problematic when the information used in testing for effects is collected by and reported through the very same organizations. In recognition that when information collected by any organization is to be compared or collated with that of others, or its accuracy is to be affirmed, provision often is made to *standardize* the substance and procedures each organization employs to create information *and* to *audit* the degree to which these standards and procedures are in fact followed. Audits are common in the world of commerce, nonprofit organizations, and government. Their techniques include public accounting by inspection and fiscal audit, testing and controlling for the quality of goods and services, and documenting salient characteristics of transactions by independent means.

Although most of the information that we have about organizations within a criminal justice network is produced solely by the organization that has an interest in producing it, audits are rare and provision for them is resisted. Yet we know that it is not safe to rely on information collected by different organizations without knowing the ways that each organization affects the reliability of the data.

Over the past decades, some research investigators have turned their attention to how reliability of information is affected by organizations in the criminal justice network, particularly by the variability in their intelligence or information systems. One set of investigators has focused on how the perspectives of criminal justice agents affect the quality and quantity of information produced by a given organization or system. The others assess the statistical unreliability of information in a system or of time series based on them. Much effort, for example, has gone into assessments of the FBI Uniform Crime Reports, a statistical reporting system based on aggregated reports from local police departments in the United States. Each group of investigators has developed a substantial literature, but here we shall concern ourselves only with its contribution to estimating the effect that variability in organizational properties has on information developed by operating criminal justice systems.

Investigators in the United States who are identified with "phenomenological" and "labeling" perspectives, and those in the United Kingdom identified with "radical criminology" have focused on how criminal justice organizational perspectives introduce error or bias into information about crime and justice. They pay less attention, however, to ways that organizational variability produces unreliability in information. This is partly the case because these investigators hold that the concept of unreliability itself arises from a perspective that is incompatible with organizational processes for producing information, such as organizational and professional ideologies. Unreliability, they maintain, begins with preconceived notions of validity and reliability that are themselves products of an organizational system. This perspective on organizational information in criminal justice perhaps is best set forth in Cicourel's work (1968) on how the organization of two different cities and their juvenile justice systems transforms communications between juveniles and official agents into bureaucratically organized and reported information.

Cicourel argues that "both the researcher's and the actor's rules of procedure [are] problematic elements in all research" (1968: 1), and that "the problems of objectification and verification cannot be resolved by appeals to technical skills in capturing or 'bottling' the phenomena invoked as observational sources of data" (1968: 15). He assumes that "the critical task of the researcher is to show the reader how the research materials are always understood by reference to unstated and seen (but unnoticed) background expectancies both members *and* observers *always* employ to recognize and to understand their activities" (1968: 15).

Put another way, both phenomenological and labeling perspectives in criminology challenge the notion that one can examine how organizational processes and variability among organizations affect the *accuracy* of information by concluding there is no definition of validity or accuracy, apart from organizational perspectives, that transform information. This view chooses to ignore the fact that any statistical assessment must take into account errors introduced by actors *and* investigators, including organizational actors.

Any source of error in data must be documented for each organization, including those sources emphasized by labeling theorists, whether or not there is a statistical assessment of these sources of error. Excellent examples of documenting organizational sources of error are found in the work of Sellin and Wolfgang. Their 1964 study of errors in information on juveniles referred to the Philadelphia Police Department may serve as an example. By observation, interview, and an examination of the official records, Sellin and Wolfgang call attention to five major sources of error in juvenile referrals to the police department's Juvenile Aid Division: (1) changes in the environment of the police department that affect initial reporting or referral of cases to the police by the public or agencies; (2) errors by citizens in reporting information to the police, and by the police in transforming that information to the police record; (3) errors in classifying information into standard classifications, such as offense classifications; (4) errors due to variations over time in police enforcement policies and practices; and (5) errors in creating and maintaining a central information system (1964: 106-113). Unfortunately, where some statistical measure of the error in organizational information is given, it is ordinarily limited to measures of classification, such as the accuracy of classifying information into standard codes. Although studies of organizational sources of error are extremely useful in sensitizing investigators to these sources of error in data, their usefulness is limited unless they provide an accurate measure of the amount of such error that can be included in an overall statistical model of amount of error or in an error profile.

Quite frequently, organizational differences in decision-making account for considerable variation in information. But the kind and quality of information and the standards of classification also may have a considerable effect. Jacoby and her colleagues (1979a: 13) note that for the early years of the PROMIS system in Washington, D.C., the error rate for data elements from the assistant prosecutors and the police ranged from 15 to 30 percent. Even greater inaccuracy was found for many of the data elements in the Uniform Parole Reports. Wainer (1978) reports that the nature of the unreliability was such as to render quite useless reports of case stocks and case flows in federal parole, a condition that has since been corrected.

This kind of finding on inaccuracy in classification, while almost commonplace, rarely is taken into account when the information is used to test substantive hypotheses about criminal justice organizations. Yet, as Long's (1979) reevaluation of an evaluation study demonstrates, these kinds of errors may lead to incorrect conclusions.

The Long evaluation may serve to introduce the second kind of study, wherein there is a statistical assessment of sources of error due to organizational variability. Long reexamines the conclusions about treatment effects in a criminal rehabilitation program (FOR) in ten project sites across the United States (Bell et al., 1969) by taking into account errors in the criterion measure arising from the organization of the treatment research project and the fact that ten different programs provided the data for evaluation. Like the McCords (1959) and Lerman (1975), Long demonstrates that a project's contact with treatment subjects brings greater knowledge of their activities—including criminal violations—than is true for the controls (Long, 1979: 2, 4). But also by comparing FBI rap sheet and FOR treatment project data on recidivism for the same treatment and control subjects, she is able to demonstrate that while arrests are seriously undercounted in both FOR and rap sheet systems, the undercount in both is greater for control than treatment subjects and for rap than FOR counts. Moreover, as labeling theorists would argue, Long shows that the volume of reporting was related to the mandate and sponsorship of each organization. Thus, the FOR treatment project which was sponsored by federal treatment and correctional agencies had more complete information on federal revocations, while the FBI had higher reporting rates for serious arrests (Long, 1979: 4-5). Even though the FOR counts of recidivism provided higher estimates of recidivism for both treatment and control subjects than did the FBI rap sheets, to avoid the bias of evaluating treatment projects by using project-developed counts for the criterion measure of recidivism, Long quite appropriately uses the recidivism count independently derived from FBI rap sheets for both treatment and control subjects (Long, 1979: 6, 10). As Long observes, "more is not necessarily better" for evaluation, as less complete data are to be preferred over more complete data with a bias on matters under evaluation (Long, 1979: 14). Her results in the reevaluation demonstrate the wisdom of these changes. The bias in the original test based on FOR measures, when coupled with the failure to test for differential treatment effects (Bell, 1969), masked very large and significant treatment effects (Long, 1979: 8-11). Equally to the point, for our purposes, Long shows that differences among the ten FOR Projects generating the data had no effect on the demonstration of the differential treatment effects when the FBI measure of recidivism was employed; i.e., despite the variability among the ten projects, the differential treatment effects remain (Long, 1979: 12).

Given the substantial amount of error in criminal justice data generated by interested agencies, it is vital that there be independent means to test the accuracy of evaluation measures. The technique that Long used in comparing FOR with FBI data is not always possible, since it requires unique identification of cases to assess precisely the degree of overlap in systems of reporting—a minimum degree of nonoverlap can be assessed by aggregate comparisons.

The accuracy of information can also be assessed by comparing aggregate counts derived from independent organizations for the same case domain. Three such comparisons are discussed briefly below to illustrate the relevance of investigating organizational sources of error in criterion measures by comparing the criterion measures derived from two independent organizational sources.

Two studies, one by Cantor and Cohen (1979) and the other by Sherman and Langworthy (1979), use the National Center for Health Statistics (NCHS) as the standard for assessing possible biases or errors in police-generated statistics on homicide. The Cantor and Cohen study compares the reports of criminal homicide (murder and nonnegligent manslaughter) in UCR with those of homicides in NCHS for selected time periods and for the 1933-1975 interval. The Sherman and Langworthy study compares (1) the estimates of homicides by police officers, derived from different local and state police department reports of investigations of shootings by police officers, with (2) those reported as law enforcement-related deaths by coroners, on death certificates filed with local or state vital statistics offices, who in turn file them with the NCHS.

Although each of these comparisons was originally based on the assumption that the reliability of the estimates from police sources could be evaluated by using an independent source of information—the NCHS—the Sherman and Langworthy study shows substantial undercounting for the subclass of homicides—homicide by police officers—in NCHS statistics. An aggregate undercount of at least 50 percent fewer homicides in NCHS estimates is traced, in part, to the coroner's lack of independence from the police system in determining and filing cause of death as "law enforcement-related" on the death certificate. Sherman and Langworthy confirmed that coroner's judgments were influenced by their working relationship with police departments and their officers. Through interviews they learned that coroners are very reluctant to classify a death as police officer-related because they rely substantially upon the police for information in almost all homicide cases, and believe that relationship might be jeopardized by complete counts.

There also are important cautionary notes that result from the foregoing investigations of organizational biases in evaluation measures. The first is that the organization that is presumed to have an obvious investment in producing the information—in the above case, a police department investment in under-reporting homicides by police officers—may produce more accurate information than the organization used as the independent standard for evaluating the accuracy of information. In the above case, the presumption of independence by coroners who were thought to have little or no investment in reporting deaths produced by police officers turned out to be false. The second caution derives from the Long investigation (1979). Since investigator investments often produce a biased set of statistics of the outcome measures, they should always be designed so that at least some of the measures can be assessed (evaluated!) by independent sources of information. Third, it is well for evaluators to bear in mind that the comparison of two or more organizational sources of information on the same matters requires careful investigation of presumptions of those sources' independence. Finally, to the degree possible, the extent of organizational differences in information and measures of error should be obtained for any measure used as a criterion variable in evaluation research.

A national reporting system, moreover, which invites invidious comparisons among information-producing units, as do both NCHS and UCR, may well foster inaccuracy of information. We return to our example from Sherman and Langworthy (1979). Since police departments do not report homicides by police officers to UCR, as strictly local reports they may be more reliable. Whether national reporting systems that provide for local comparison generally enhance self-interest errors in reporting is itself a complex matter for evaluation.

Cantor and Cohen compare homicides reported by UCR and by NCHS and conclude that, while over time the two series provide similar counts of criminal homicide, particularly when law enforcement-related deaths are excluded, there are nonetheless short-term fluctuations which suggest differences in their error structures (1979: 11-17). Since the coverage for UCR statistics on homicide is less complete than that in vital statistics death certificates, the estimating procedures of UCR lead to both over- and undercounts for local areas (Chilton, 1978: 60-72). Given this lack of coverage, UCR estimates probably are less reliable for local area (SMSA), state, and national estimates than are those of NCHS, which has virtually complete coverage. The extent to which unreliability varies among local reporting units also is documented in the Sherman and Langworthy study (1979). It finds that while NCHS ordinarily undercounts law enforcement-related deaths for local units, there are some for which the NCHS count is greater than that provided by the law enforcement agency.

Both studies, nevertheless, demonstrate that it seemingly makes little substantive difference which homicide indicator—the NCHS death certificate-based indicator or the police-based indicator—is used with respect to the statistical significance of the independent variables employed (Cantor and Cohen, 1979: 23; Sherman and Langworthy, 1979: 559). The magnitude of differences is, however, affected by the choice of series, although as Cantor and Cohen nicely show, a difference in magnitude may be spurious—a statistical artifact due to multicolinearity, for example—as well as demonstrative of a genuine difference in relationship (Cantor and Cohen, 1979: 23-24).

Both sampling and forms of estimation, particularly snythetic estimation, are sources of error or bias in producing criminal justice information or statistics. Just how sampling may serve to bias estimates in ways that serve an agency's objectives is nicely demonstrated in Zeisel's (1971b, 1973) evaluations of the FBI's use of the criminal career data file in the UCR annual reports. In the 1971 report to the President's Commission on Federal Statistics, Zeisel took note of the fact that the FBI reported that the Careers in Crime Program made a contribution to evaluation of the criminal justice network. In the language of the 1969 UCR reports,

> since 1963 the Careers in Crime Program has been used in this publication to document the extent to which criminal repeating over a period of time contributes to annual crime counts. . . . Although the criminal history process requires tighter control standardization, and more complete data, the Careers in Crime Program has demonstrated the potential use of criminal history information to measure success or failure of the criminal justice system [Federal Bureau of Investigation, 1970: 35].

Zeisel went on to observe that the FBI's evaluation commonly took the form of using rearrest rates to imply that the courts are "soft" on crime (Zeisel, 1973: 38) and to comment:

> An interesting result if true . . . But since it is a highly self-serving statistic from the FBI's point of view, on a controversial point, its presentation and analysis merit somewhat more care" [1971: 550].

By 1973, Zeisel's suspicions were further aroused by his inquiries into the "curious consistency [that] delayed cases showed a higher rearrest rate than the cases whose reporting had not been delayed" (1973: 39). In correspondence with the FBI he learned that, indeed, a bias in sampling cases for criminal careers was likely. In this exchange of views, the FBI provided Zeisel with the independent confirmation of the sampling bias he sought. A comparison of the FBI data on "dismissed and acquitted" with those in the same class in the reports of the Administrative Office of the U.S. Courts confirmed that the FBI data contained too many persons in the crime groups for which rearrest rates are high, and not enough where they are low (Zeisel, 1973: 40). Difficult as it may have been for Zeisel to secure confirmation of sampling bias, it usually is even more difficult to detect, and harder to demonstrate, in the absence of a time series, as time series are useful for detecting the likelihood of error, if not in pinpointing its source.

That the evaluation of the accuracy of any organization's statistical reporting system is no simple matter is apparent from the history of surveying crime victimization. The crime victim survey was originally intended as a means to assess the accuracy of reporting of crime by local police organizations, and thereby to evaluate also national estimates of U.S. crime from the Uniform Crime Reports. Early use of crime victim surveys by Biderman et al. (1967) and Reiss (1976) tried to assess the accuracy of crime reports of local police organizations by adjusting survey data to a base comparable to that for police estimates of offenses known to the police. To achieve such modest comparability, it was necessary to introduce modifications in the survey data that take into account such matters as the fact that survey figures are based on incidences of person-victimizations rather than events or offenses which can involve more than one person; that police statistics locate crimes by their place of occurrence, while the survey in the first instance does so by place of residence of the victim; and that some reports of victimization are false or baseless (Biderman et al., 1967: 61-65).

Such difficulties in introducing strict comparability between police organiza- tion and survey estimates make it more plausible to regard the NCS as an *independent* means of estimating crime—both crimes reported and unreported to the police—recognizing that different approaches have different error properties. An understanding of how these different organizations (police departments and survey research organizations) acquire different error structures and of how that affects estimates, provides an ever closer approximation of the "true" phe- nomena that can only be approximated and never measured.

One consequence of such a multimethod approach to estimating crime is that each organization moves toward an assessment of sources of error in its measure- ment of crime. The IACP has made efforts to introduce audits of the Uniform Crime Reports into local police jurisdictions in the United States, though thus far this effort has remained of little consequence. The NCS has invested con- siderably more resources in assessing the sources of error in crime victim surveys, seeking to develop an error profile for NCS estimates of crime.

The elaborate efforts to assess the error structure of crime victim surveys and their effects on victimization estimates—whether of rates or risks—might also be viewed as a caution to those who would utilize crime victim surveys as a tool to evaluate intervention programs in organizations where victimization is used as a criterion measure. The technology of victim-surveying is as yet inadequate to the task of serving as a precise instrument of evaluation (compare its use in the Kansas City Preventive Patrol Experiment; Kelling et al., 1974: 232-238).

B. Variability and Contrived Comparison

Although statistical manipulation of the sources of variability can often be used to account for variability among organizations, it is not always recom- mended for making comparisons among different units within the criminal justice system. This is so for a number of reasons. One is that it is often far too costly to attempt to assess all of the sources of error in the data for each particular organization. Thus, in comparing organizations one may make false comparisons by capitalizing on different sources of error. Indeed, where one lacks an error profile for the data of each criminal justice agency on which comparison among them is to be based, it seems wiser to develop or adopt a common means of data collection where errors can be measured for making these comparisons. While no means of data collection is free of error, one should opt for the procedure where the error is known or can be accurately measured.

Some alternative means of data collection that is uniform for all of the agencies to be compared, is particularly recommended where one wishes to compare properties of organizations or of their agents, and where the errors concerning these in existing organizational records are not known or cannot be measured in any precise way. Two alternative procedures for making comparisons are discussed below: simulation and standardized testing.

A major means of obtaining comparable information from diverse organizations of a common form is to develop a simulated procedure using a standardized instrument that elicits behavior from members of comparison groups. A major area wherein such simulation testing has been undertaken is decision-making in criminal justice agencies, such as police departments, prosecution offices, courts, and parole boards. The simulation may be accomplished with the use of computers that present the tasks and record the decision, or by standardized test procedures.

Studies of parole board members and of police executive decision-making provide examples of computer-assisted simulations of decision-making. The work of Gottfredson et al. (1978), in collaboration with members of the U.S. Parole Commission, illustrates how both the general characteristics of information-processing—e.g., the capacity of persons to process differing amounts of information—and the way in which members pay selective attention to particular attributes of the cases they process, can be studied in relation one to another. Computer-assisted simulation is important in such instances, as computers have the capacity to store and process large numbers of individual sequential decisions.

A somewhat similar simulation procedure is currently being followed by Ward and his coworkers (1978) to investigate the types of information that middle-level executives in police departments utilize to make decisions. Alternative designs would make it almost impossible to make comparisons among middle-level decision makers in different police departments, since information on decisions is not systematically recorded by police departments, particularly in a form that would allow one to determine what information is used in making each decision. The alternative of observational studies of executive decision-making is both burdensome and costly if one seeks to observe a range of cases, some of which occur only infrequently. Moreover, one would be faced with the difficult problem of equating different decision tasks across different police organizations in both of these designs. A simulation study of police executive decision-making, using standardized decision tasks and alternatives, provides an opportunity to make precise comparisons to evaluate both individual and organizational differences in processing information.

The recent work of Jacoby and her coworkers in their studies of prosecutorial discretion (1979a, 1979b) provides an example of how a standardized test without simulation can be used to make comparisons across different prosecution offices that vary considerably in structure and caseloads. Jacoby and her coworkers developed both a standardized case set and a case evaluation form to be administered to samples of prosecutors in different prosecution offices. The standard case set is comprised of 160 criminal cases that vary in the type and seriousness of crime. Each case has information sufficient to satisfy a probable cause hearing in an adversary proceeding, but not always enough for proof beyond a reasonable doubt at a trial. The set also includes criminal histories for 100 defendants similar to that provided in police arrest records. The common task is to complete a case evaluation form for each of the cases. The case evaluation form collects information about each case's priority for prosecution, acceptance for prosecution, and expected disposition (Jacoby et al., 1979a: 10-11).

As Jacoby and her coauthors note, the standardized case set either resolved or minimized problems that ordinarily are encountered in using actual case records in prosecutors' offices. Not the least of these was the ability to ensure that the quality, content, format of information, and order of presentation was standardized, thereby making for better controlled comparison among prosecution offices (1979a: 14). At the same time, such studies make clear at least some of the tradeoffs in using case and decision data from a standardized, as contrasted with an actual, set of cases. Clearly, information on actual processing time, actual decisions, and actual ordering of steps in making decisions, might well vary from those in a simulated task or standardized test.

Though none of these studies has made note of the fact, it should be apparent that simulated studies provide an opportunity to ensure that tasks which occur in only some of the task environments of a group of organizations can be evaluated for members of every group. In addition,the Gottfredson et al. (1968) demonstrate that it is possible to organize tasks in such a way as to alter a decision-making system permanently. This was actually accomplished in the development of a policy control method in a cooperative study with the U.S. Parole Commission, where a matrix model was developed to guide parole commission decisions (Gottfredson et al., 1978). Subsequently, using state parole boards, both matrix and sequential models were developed as guidelines for their decisions (Gottfredson et al., 1978). These latter investigations show how it is possible to evaluate a procedure that takes account of both uniformity and diversity among the same kinds of organizations.

C. Variability and Standardized Observations in Natural Settings

Each mode of measurement carries with it some sources of error and some costs for what is measured and how. We have noted that the advantage of statistical control and analysis of variability among organizations carries with it problems of unreliability of data derived from organizational sources and problems in equating contexts and variables, among others. Likewise, we have noted that while standardized or simulated task forms of measurement solve some of these problems of unreliability and equating tasks, they have the distinct limits of distorting natural conditions and of obscuring the effects of different mixes among tasks that arise as a function of natural variation among organizations. Procedures for eliciting information, such as the standardized interview survey, likewise are encumbered by many of these limitations (Reiss, 1976).

One procedure that purports to take advantage of natural variability while standardizing measurement is systematic social observation of natural social phenomena (Reiss, 1968; 1971; 1976). By developing standardized observation instruments and standardizing training of observers, comparable information can be obtained by direct observation in different organizations or natural settings. Because one can examine sources of error in data collection, such as the effect of variability among observers (Reiss, 1968), and yet ensure that comparable information is collected in natural settings, independent of each organization's interest in the information (Reiss, 1976), one overcomes much of the synthetic nature of other forms of standardization. Indeed, it is axiomatic in science that indirect modes of observation should not be substituted for direct observation; yet, typically in social science we have developed indirect modes of observation. Whatever their errors may be, the records of criminal justice agencies and those acquired independently by systematic social observation are direct observations of human behavior or activity.

What is somewhat surprising is that systematic social observation has been most widely used in the study of criminal justice agencies and agents, particularly in studies of policing. One review of systematic social observation studies (Reiss, 1979) found at least ten studies of systematically observed police behavior, such as the behavior of men and women on patrol, police control of juveniles, field interrogation practices, and police response time to citizen mobilizations for service.

A major advantage of systematic social observation in organizational settings is that it provides opportunities for exact replication in different settings. Although the studies have not conformed in all respects to the canons of exact replication, the replication of Lundman et al. (1978) confirms almost all of the findings on police control of juveniles reported by Black and Reiss (1970). Similarly, many of the initial findings by direct observation and survey concerning the behavior of police women on patrol (Block and Anderson, 1974) have been confirmed by more rigorously designed police observation studies (Sichel et al., 1977).

CONCLUDING REMARKS

Throughout, we have stressed a theme about how organizational variability may become a more animating source in the design and analysis of interventions in the criminal justice network. We have illustrated how investigators might become more proactive in their selection of problems for inquiry and in approximating experimental designs by taking advantage of the opportunities that exist, arise, or are created by organizations in the criminal justice network. Likewise, we have emphasized that in the evaluation process it is important to develop independent means for assessing the reliability of indicators in our investigations and to consider designs that take variability into account by other than analytical statistical strategies. Our strategies, to be sure, depend also upon how proactive we may become in the design and execution of evaluation studies.

Above all, we hope it is clear that investigators often create conditions that make it difficult to do appropriate interventions, to monitor them, and to evaluate them, and they are to be warned that evaluation should not be a point-in-time event but a continuing process. For if things persist, then the longer we monitor them, the more we will understand about them—as the rest of the world does not stand still. If they change, even disappointingly so, we must learn more about how moving rather than standing still may be responsible.

To be sure, without variability, there is little of interest to explain. It is hoped that the foregoing observations have provided some sensitization to ways that attention to organizational variability may enter into evaluation studies of the criminal justice network.

NOTE

1. There is considerable variability in criminal justice in the United States stemming from differences among federal, state, and local jurisdictions and from organizational structure and mandates. Examples of variation in major forms of organizational structure and process in criminal justice abound. There are lay and professional magistrates, private and public prosecution, private, court-appointed, and public defender defense counsels, and private and public police. Criminal proceedings may proceed with the police record of arrest constituting information, with the filing of a formal charge by a public prosecutor, or upon indictment by a grand jury. Trial organizations may vary in their jury sizes, their decision rules, whether or not a determination is made on oral testimony or a transcript of a hearing, and whether the decision is reached in a court of record. At every level of the hierarchy officials may hold office by election, by merit, or by appointment. Although there are typical separations of judicial and executive prerogatives and practices, public prosecutors may serve at the pleasure of a judicial as well as an executive appointing authority. Indeed, it is not much of an exaggeration to say that many of what are assumed to be differences between the legal systems of common and civil law countries exist as differences somewhere in the American legal system. Though this is not the place to pursue the matter, the

enormous variability among civil law systems, such as the variation produced by whether criminal justice is organized around a principle of legality or opportunity, facilitates comparison among civil and common law countries.

REFERENCES

Bell, P. B., M. Matthews, and W. S. Fulton (1969) A Future for Correctional Rehabilitation? Federal Offenders Rehabilitation Program Final Report. Olympia, Washington: Division of Vocational Rehabilitation.

Biderman, A. D., L. A. Johnson, J. McIntyre, and A. W. Weir (1967) "Report on a Pilot Study in the District of Columbia on Victimization and Attitudes Toward Law Enforcement," in *Field Surveys I. A Report of a Research Study Submitted to the President's Commission on Law Enforcement and Administration of Justice.* Washington, DC: Government Printing Office.

Black, D. and A. J. Reiss, Jr. (1970) "Police Control of Juveniles." *American Sociological Review* 34: 63-77.

Block, P. and D. Anderson (1974) *Policewomen on Patrol, Final Report.* Washington, DC: Police Foundation.

Campbell, D. T. (1976) "Focal Legal Indicators for Social Program Evaluation." *Social Indicators Research* 3: 237-256.

––– and L. H. Ross (1968) "The Connecticut Crack down on Speeding: Time-Series Data in Quasi-Experimental Analysis." *Law and Society Review* 33: 33-53.

Cantor, D. and L. E. Cohen (1979) "Comparative Measures of Homicide Trends: Methodological and Substantive Differences in the Vital Statistics and Uniform Crime Report Time Series (1933-1975)." Working Papers in Applied Statistics 7821, University of Illinois.

Chilton, R. (1978) "Criminal Statistics: Federal Efforts To Produce Statistical Information about Crime and Persons in the United States. Final Report to the Subcommittee on Criminal Justice Statistics of the Social Science Research Council." University of Massachusetts, Amherst. (unpublished)

Cicourel, A. V. (1968) *The Social Organization of Juvenile Justice.* New York: John Wiley.

Diamond, S. S. and H. Zeisel (1975) "Sentencing Councils: A Study of Sentence Disparity and Its Reduction." *University of Chicago Law Review* 43: 109-149.

Ehrlich, I. (1973) "The Deterrent Effect of Capital punishment: A Question of Life and Death." Working Paper 18, National Bureau of Economic Research.

Empey, L. T. and J. Rabow (1961) "The Provo Experiment in Delinquent Rehabilitation." *American Sociological Review* 26: 679-696.

Federal Bureau of Investigation (1970) *Uniform Crime Reports–1969.* Washington, DC: Government Printing Office.

Fienberg, S. E., K. L., and A. J. Reiss, Jr. (1976) "Redesigning the Kansas City Preventive Patrol Experiment." *Evaluation* 3: 124-131.

Forst, B. (1960) "The Deterrent Effect of Capital Punishment: A Cross-State Analysis of the 1960's." Institute for Law and Social Research, Washington, D.C.

Gottfredson, D. M., L. T. Wilkins, and P. B. Hoffman (1978) *Guidelines for Parole and Sentencing: A Policy Control Method.* Lexington, MA: D. C. Heath.

Gottfredson, D. M. et al. (1978) *Classification for Parole Decision Policy.* Washington, DC: Government Printing Office.

Jacoby, J. E. and L. R. Mellon (1979b) *Policy Analysis for Prosecution.* Washington, DC: Bureau of Social Science Research, Inc.

Jacoby, J. E., E. C. Ratledge, and S. H. Turner (1979a) *Research on Prosecutorial Decision Making, Phase I: Final Report.* Washington, DC: Bureau of Social Science Research, Inc.

Kalven, H. Jr. and H. Zeisel (1966) *The American Jury.* Chicago: University of Chicago Press.

Kelling, G., T. Pate, D. Dieckman, and C. E. Brown (1974) *The Kansas City Preventive Patrol Experiment: A Technical Report.* Washington, DC: Police Foundation.

Klein, M. W. (1979) "Deinstitutionalization and Diversion of Juvenile Offenders: A Litany of Impediments," in N. Morris and M. Tonry (eds.) *Crime and Justice: An Annual Review of Research.* Chicago: University of Chicago Press.

Lerman, P. (1975) *Community Treatment and Social Control: A Critical Analysis of Juvenile Correctional Policy.* Chicago: University of Chicago Press.

Long, S. B. (1979) "Rehabilitating Criminals: Is It Treatment or Our Evaluation Methods Which Have Failed?" University of Washington and Bureau of Social Science Research.

Lundman, R. J., R. E. Sykes, and J. P. Clark (1978) "Police Control of Juveniles: A Replication." *Journal of Research in Crime and Delinquency* 15: 74-91.

McCord, J. and W. McCord (1959) "A Follow-Up Report on the Cambridge-Sommerville Youth Study." *Annals of the American Academy of Political and Social Science* 24: 672-682.

Ohlin, L., A. D. Miller, and R. B. Coates (1977) *Juvenile Correctional Reform in Massachusetts.* Washington, DC: Government Printing Office.

Reiss, A. J., Jr. (1979) "Systematic Social Observation in Police Research," pp. 271-305 in J. Knutsson et al. (eds.) *Police and the Social Order: Contemporary Research Perspectives.* Stockholm, Sweden: National Swedish Council for Crime Prevention.

——— (1976) "Systematic Social Observation Surveys of Natural Social Phenomena," in A. W. Sinaido and L. A. Broedling (eds.) *Police and the Social Order: Contemporary Research Perspectives.* Stockholm, Sweden: National Swedish Council for Crime Prevention.

——— (1974) "Discretionary Justice," pp. 679-704 in D. Glaser (ed.) *Handbook of Criminology.* Skokie, IL: Rand McNally.

——— (1971) "Systematic Social Observation of Natural Social Phenomena" pp. 3-33 in Herbert Costner (ed.) Sociological Methodology, 1971. San Francisco: Jossey-Bass.

——— (1968) "Stuff and Nonsense About Social Surveys and Observation" pp. 351-367 in H. Becker et al. (eds.) *Institution and the Person.* Chicago: AVC.

——— (1967) "Measurement of the Nature and Amount of Crime," in *Field Surveys III. Crime and Law Enforcement in Major Metropolitan Areas. A Report of a Research Study Submitted to the President's Commission on Law Enforcement and Administration of Justice.* Washington, DC: Government Printing Office.

Ross, H. L. (1973) "Law, Science, and Accidents: The British Road Safety Act of 1967." *Journal of Legal Studies* 2: 1-78.

Sellin, T. (1953) "The Deterrent Value of Capital Punishment," Appendix 6, Report of the Royal Commission on Capital Punishment. (Command 8932)

——— and M. E. Wolfgang (1964) *The Measurement of Delinquency.* New York: John Wiley.

Sherman, L. W. and R. H. Langworthy (1979) "Measuring Homicide by Police Officers." *Journal of Criminal Law and Criminology* 70: 546-560.

Sichel, J. L., L. N. Friedman, J. C. Quint and M. E. Smith (1977) *Women on Patrol: A Pilot Study of Police Performance in New York City.* New York: Vera Institute of Justice.

Statistical Research Group (1945) *Sequential Analysis of Statistical Data: Application.* New York: Columbia University Press.

Wainer, H. (1978) *A Methodological Evaluation of Uniform Parole Reports: A Report to the National Institute of Law Enforcement and Criminal Justice.* Washington, DC: Bureau of Social Science Research, Inc.

Wald, A. et al. (1945) *Sequential Analysis of Statistical Data Applications.* New York: Columbia University Press.

Ward, R. H. et al (1978) *Police Patrol Operational Decision Making.* Chicago: University of Illinois at Chicago Circle Center for Research in Criminal Justice.

Zeisel, H. (1977) "The Deterrent Effect of the Death Penalty: Fact v. Faith," pp. 317-343 in P. Kurland (ed.) *The Supreme Court Review, 1976.* Chicago: University of Chicago Press.

––– (1973) "The FBI's Biased Sampling." *Bulletin of the Atomic Scientists* 39: 38-42.

––– (1971a) "The Future of Law Enforcement Statistics," pp. 525-555 in *Federal Statistics: Report of the President's Commission, Volume 2.* Washington, DC: Government Printing Office.

––– (1971b) "And Then There Were None: The Diminution of the Federal Jury." *University of Chicago Law Review* 38: 710-724.

––– (1967) "The Law," pp. 81-99 in P. Lazarfeld et al. (eds.) *The Uses of Sociology.* New York: Basic Books.

––– (1956) "The New York Expert Testimony Project: Some Reflections on Legal Experiments." *Stanford Law Review* 8: 730-749.

––– and T. Callahan (1963) "Split Trial and time-saving: A Statistical Analysis." *Harvard Law Review* 76: 1606-1625.

Zeisel, H. and S. S. Diamond (1974) "Convincing Empirical Evidence on the Six Member Jury." *University of Chicago Law Review* 41: 281-295.

––– (1977) "Search for Sentencing Equity: Sentence Review in Massachusetts and Connecticut." *American Bar Foundation Research Journal* 4: 883-940

14

Evaluating the Deterrrent Effects of Criminal Sanctions

Charles R. Tittle

Evaluating social response to illegal behavior inevitably requires confrontation of the deterrence question. Almost all legal theorists, as well as laypeople, see control of prohibited behavior as a major, if not the primary, objective of the justice process, and it is assumed that sanctions or sanction threats help to prevent undesirable conduct, mainly by making the costs of criminal behavior greater than the rewards. Therefore, the extent to which legal threats and processing actually inhibit illegal behavior that might otherwise occur must be established before reasonable assessment of the effectiveness of criminal sanctioning can be made.

But this is easier said than done. The truth is, social scientists are not presently in a position to say with confidence whether sanctions or sanction threats make any difference, much less to say how much difference they might make under various kinds of implementations. This is because there is relatively little empirical research to draw upon, it is difficult to interpret the research that has been done, and the available data neglect some of the most important questions about deterrence. The following section summarizes the situation under the four headings, sparcity of evidence, interpretive problems, methodological defects, and theoretical inadequacies.

WHY EVALUATION IS DIFFICULT

Sparcity of Evidence

The empirical basis for judging whether sanctions deter is weak, partly because social scientists have only recently come to consider the question important enough or problematic enough to warrant large-scale attention. For a long time most social scientists believed that research had already provided a definitive answer to the deterrence question, or that issues about sanctions were theoretically insignificant. After all, most sociological theories gave short shrift to force and coercion as elements in social life, emphasizing instead socialization, structural integration, or value consensus (Cohen, 1966; Goode, 1972), while economic theories took a cost-benefit model for granted (Becker, 1968). In the late 1960s interest in assessing the general effects of sanctions was stirred, perhaps by the thrust of the labeling perspective or practical concern about the apparent failure of the therapeutic model in criminal justice, or even faddish pursuit of easy publication, once the potential for using official statistics was made known by some early papers. But whatever the reason, the past decade has seen a flurry of empirical research resulting in several dozen published papers on the deterrence question. Still, there is only a smattering of the data needed for answering the complex questions that are now recognized. In fact, research has raised so many questions that were scarcely conceived even a decade ago, that it seems that the more research is compiled, the more it is needed.

Interpretive Problems

Not only does the work of the past decade show the deficiency of the data, but consideration of the sanction question has given birth to a host of interpretive issues that have rendered much of the accumulated data of questionable value. For example, there is disagreement about the most fundamental point— what *deterrence* means. Some would restrict the term to refer only to individual suppression of a deviant impulse that results directly from fear of punishment (Gibbs, 1975). Others are content to speak of deterrence as any curtailment of deviance that is brought about by sanctions or sanction threats, regardless of the mechanisms by which the curtailment results (Zimring and Hawkins, 1973). Thus, for some deterrence has occurred if potential offenders are prevented from acting because a sanction has incapacitated them, because their opportunities to misbehave are restricted as a result of the stigma from a sanction, or even if potential deviant acts are prevented because sanctions strengthen moral or normative imperatives (Tittle, 1978).

In addition, scholars disagree about the meaning of *sanction*. Some think only court disposition by sentence or fine counts as punishment. Yet, there is good reason to believe that any involvement with criminal justice processing is conceived as unpleasant by many people and could itself be thought of as a sanction, regardless of outcome. For many, arrest, questioning by the police, or even surveillance is punishment. And any form of processing involves financial and social cost for most of those who must undergo it. On the other hand, there are people for whom arrest, processing, and incarceration hold little punitive potential. Indeed, for some these may be rewarding events because they reinforce deviant self-images, enhance prestige within a subculture, or in other ways provide advantages for the recipient. Clearly, some things that one might conceptualize as punishment really are not, and some that one might think are not sanctions actually have that status for many. What, then, should be counted as a sanction in an assessment of the justice system?

Given these differences in conceptualization, it is clear that much of the extant research is problematic. For example, most research has analyzed official statistics for entire political units, but such ecological data can never provide information about general deterrence, if deterrence is taken to mean individual suppression of criminal impulses to avoid negative consequences. There is simply no way of inferring from ecological data whether individuals within political units actually perceive the sanction possibilities and act accordingly, as Gibbs (1975) so convincingly argues. Even experimental data are questionable for drawing narrow deterrent conclusions, because an experimenter can never know for sure what goes on in the minds of the subjects, where the deterrent process presumably occurs (according to the restricted conceptualization).

But even if one bypasses this technical and semantic aspect of the deterrent question and moves directly to the larger issue of whether criminal sanctions result in less crime than otherwise might occur, one still encounters conceptual difficulties. It is now recognized that sanctions may prevent future deviance by those actually punished (specific deterrence) and/or they may prevent future deviance by citizens who were not punished (general deterrence); they may prevent all deviance in a political unit or an individual (absolute deterrence) or they may reduce the frequency with which deviance occurs (restrictive or marginal deterrence); and they may change the way deviance occurs or the flagrancy of its manifestation (channeling). Yet, some maintain that deterrence is not operative unless there is absolute prevention, while others would accept marginal curtailment as evidence of deterrence. Furthermore, many generalize failures of specific deterrence and conclude that the deterrent argument, in toto, is false, while others clearly differentiate types of deterrence and interpret the evidence accordingly.

Finally, conclusions about the degree of deterrence achieved by sanctions depends upon whether deterrence is regarded as the absolute number or as the proportion of contemplated acts that are prevented. For example, one individual may contemplate an act of robbery two times in a given time period but be restrained from acting by fear of punishment, while another individual may contemplate the same act ten times in the same time period and because he or she has less fear of the consequences may actually do it five times. From one point of view, the first person has been more deterred because all contemplated crime was prevented, while only 50 percent of the contemplated criminal acts of the second individual were suppressed. But from another point of view, more deterrence has occurred in the second case, since five crimes were stopped while only two crimes were prevented in the first case.

Hence, available information may be interpreted by some as demonstrating that the criminal justice process deters effectively, while others may draw just the opposite conclusion because they begin with different concepts of deterrence and sanctions, or because they apply different standards of success. Nowhere is this more apparent than in judging whether imprisonment produces specific deterrence. Even if it could be shown unequivocally that 40 percent of those who are released from prison commit new crimes while 80 percent of them would have recidivated had they not been incarcerated (which cannot be shown, of course), some would consider that to be evidence of great success (50 percent less crime), while others would judge it to be evidence of gross inadequacy (40 percent failure).

Methodological Defects

General Deterrence. Existing data are also hard to interpret because they are rife with methodological uncertainties. Although some field and laboratory experiments have been done within the past few years and some survey data have been gathered, the vast majority of work on the question of general deterrence has been conducted using police or other official government data reported for ecological (or political) units. Such studies can never provide strong conclusions, for several reasons. First, official data do not permit good measurement of the key variables. For example, in the work that has been done, measures of sanction probability have usually consisted of estimates based on some ratio of prison admissions, arrest, or arrest clearance to offenses officially known to enforcement agencies. But it is known that most crime is hidden from enforcement agents and much of that of which they are aware is unrecorded or recorded in ways that are inconsistent with research objectives. Moreover, even if enforcement agents did know of all or most offenses, sanction ratios based on that information would still be inaccurate. Arrest rate is inadequate because most arrests are not of guilty parties (judging by clearance and conviction data). Clearance rates are weak because standards for deciding when a case has been cleared vary from one jurisdiction to another. Imprisonment rates fail because many are punished, although not imprisoned, and many who are imprisoned are convicted of crimes other than those with which they were originally charged.

While measures of the independent and dependent variables in ecological research have been weak, the most crucial defect has been inability to measure other factors which must be controlled in order to draw correct inferences about deterrent effects. Everybody recognizes, for example, that relationships between sanctions and crime may be spurious because of the influence of extraneous variables, such as moral support for the law, which could increase sanction probability at the same time that they lower crime (Erickson et al., 1977). But aggregate official data cannot provide good indicators of the moral status of laws or of a host of other essential control variables, such as community cohesion, collective perceptions of the wrongness of particular acts, or the strength of informal bonds which would permit investigators to rule out nondeterrent interpretations of statistical findings.

Moreover, limitations of aggregate data prevent good inferences about causal direction. Crime may prevent punishment rather than being prevented, or there could be a strong reciprocal relationship between crime and punishment (Blumstein et al., 1978). But sorting out such relationships requires the availability of data for a large number of units over several points in time; it requires that the critical variables not be too highly interrelated; and it requires that the investigator be able to locate a variable which presumably influences one of the simultaneous variables but not the other (solving the "identification" problem). These conditions are rarely met (Nagin, 1978).

Even when useful data are compiled routinely, they have not always been available through published sources for the various political units that might be under consideration. Clearance data are not generally published for all cities, counties, or states, and even when they are published, the reporting practices vary over time so as to make the sequential entries incomparable (see, for example, Florida Department of Law Enforcement, 1971). Prosecutorial or conviction statistics are not published at all and have not been easily accessible for any meaningful ecological units that would make effective research possible. Furthermore, many of the official data are strongly interrelated, and finding appropriate "instruments" to solve the identification problem in simultaneous equation models has proven to be exceptionally difficult (see Blumstein et al., 1978: 117-129).

Official data studies, then, do not permit strong inferences about general deterrence. And neither do existing data of other types. There are only a few case studies and experiments that have broad application, and most of them suffer from inability to rule out alternative interpretations of results. Analyses of the consequences of changes in sanction characteristics as they occur in the natural environment have rarely been made simply because such changes have been infrequent, at least where the modifications were discrete and dramatic enough to permit causal inference. As a result, there are just not enough such studies to allow meaningful conclusions, and particularly those studies which have been done do not represent enough different kinds of contexts to permit useful conditional statements to be derived (see Zimring, 1978, and Zimring and Hawkins, 1973, for descriptions of extant field experiments).

Similarly, experiments add little to our knowledge, despite their potential as sophisticated and elegant tools. There have been few opportunities to conduct field experiments (where sanction characteristics could be manipulated) and even fewer opportunities to undertake field experiments in which the characteristics of subjects could be varied (see Sigelman and Sigelman, 1976, for a clever attempt). Moreover, field experiments inevitably lack the control of extraneous variables that would make the results compelling. Laboratory work has been innovative and some of the findings have been especially exciting (Friedland et al., 1973; Thibaut et al., 1974). But in the final analysis laboratory manipulations are too artificial and removed from everyday life to satisfy serious scholars who try to judge the work of the criminal justice system.

Although the best supplemental data for drawing conclusions about general deterrence ought to be self-report surveys, they have not really fulfilled the promise (there are now about a dozen self-report data sets relevant to deterrence work; see Anderson et al., 1977a, 1977b; Bailey and Lott, 1976; Burkett and Jensen, 1975; Cohen, 1978; Erickson et al., 1977a; Erickson, 1976; Erickson and Gibbs, 1978; Grasmick and Appleton, 1977; Grasmick and McLaughlin, 1978; Grasmick and Milligan, 1976; Jensen and Erickson, 1978, Jensen et al., 1978; Kraut, 1976; Meier, 1979; Meier and Johnson, 1977; Minor, 1977, 1978; Silberman, 1976; Tcevan, 1972, 1976a, 1976b; Tittle, 1977, 1980). Some surveys have provided data about individual perceptions of sanction characteristics, personal and demographic information, and other variables of interest which were linked, on the individual level, to personal admissions of criminal conduct or willingness to engage in criminal acts, with specification of intervening or contingent conditions. And these studies have proven exceptionally useful for addressing some key questions. As yet, however, the crucial linkage between individual-level variables and ecological indicators of criminal justice activity has not been made (Gibbs, 1975; see Parker and Grasmick, 1979, for an indirect attempt). Currently available survey data cannot tell us whether there is a direct and short-range effect produced by actual official sanctioning; they can only suggest to us that perceptions (or reported perceptions) about official sanctions—perhaps incorrect perceptions—may influence conduct.

Furthermore, the self-report surveys have been of much less help than they might have been, because most have sampled only juveniles or college populations, all but one have gathered data at only one point in time (thereby making causal ordering and inferences difficult), and the samples have not corresponded to meaningful ecological units of sufficient number to permit linking of official statistics with survey results. In addition, there is good reason to regard all conclusions from survey data with much caution. There is always sampling error as well as loss of respondents who cannot be located or who refuse to be questioned, and there are response errors of unknown magnitude. Some subjects do not recall accurately, some distort answers, and some withhold information which could cast them in a bad light or even incriminate them legally. Although tests for accuracy are usually reassuring (see Hardt and Peterson-Hardt, 1977; Tittle, 1980), such tests are always limited and there is still the possibility of enormous error, the direction of which cannot be determined.

In addition, there is often considerable room for doubting whether surveyors have even asked the questions that would permit correct inferences about deterrence, assuming that the respondents answered completely and truthfully. Some investigators, for example, ask respondents to estimate probabilities of arrest in categories, while others elicit the information by agree-disagree formats; some ask about arrest for people in general and others ask about perceived probabilities for themselves; and some inquire about probabilities of arrest in a specific political unit, while others query perceptions of arrest likelihood as a free-floating probability. Similarly, reports of criminal behavior are sometimes reports of past behavior and sometimes reports of estimated future probabilities; often they concern whether the respondent ever does the thing in question, but at other times the question has to do with frequency of commission. Rarely are respondents asked about how often they contemplate the acts in question. Under these circumstances we simply do not know what is being measured nor how comparable the data are.

Finally, surveys are limited in the kind of offenses about which they can speak and in the type of potential offenders they can reach. Almost always they investigate amorphous rather than specific offenses that have direct legal analogues, and the offenses considered are rarely those of interest to one who would judge the overall deterrent effectiveness of the justice system. Hypothetically, surveys could query general samples about murder, rape, and grand larceny, but usually they do not, and if they did most readers would be skeptical of the evidence. Nobody knows to what extent data about other offenses, such as marijuana use, can be generalized to these more serious behaviors. In addition, there is reason to believe that those most likely to commit the very serious offenses of greatest concern to the justice system are precisely the ones who cannot be located or questioned in a survey.

Added to these multitudinous problems with the evidence concerning general deterrence, there is still the question of whether the presumed deterrent effects of legal sanctions can be ascertained with the time-limited data we now have or can have for the foreseeable future. Some theorists maintain that penalties are important primarily as long-range reinforcers of socialization and moral training (Andenaes, 1975; Packer, 1968; Toby, 1964; Van den Haag, 1975). If that is true, then their effects can only be observed over several generations. We do not have good data for even one generation, much less several. Hence, even if we had three times as much research to draw upon as we now have, interpretive problems as well as time limitations of the data would make confident assessment of the general deterrent impact of legal sanctioning impossible.

Specific Deterrence. Methodological concerns also make it dangerous to draw conclusions about specific deterrence. The problem of measuring the criminal behavior of those released from custody is difficult enough, but the absence of data about recidivism among those who commit crime but are not taken into custody makes reasonable conclusions about deterrence impossible. Even if we knew without question that the recidivism rate for arrested offenders was, say 50 percent, we would not know what it signified, since it is not known what the recidivism rate is among similar offenders who have escaped arrest. If the comparable recidivism rate were known to be 75 percent, then 50 percent recidivism for arrestees would demonstrate some marginal deterrence, but if that comparable rate were only 25 percent, then the data would deny the deterrent doctrine and instead would support the "secondary deviance" hypothesis. But, of course, we do not know what the general recidivism rate is for those who break the law, nor do we know what the recidivism rate is for specific groups of nonarrested offenders who would be comparable with arrested offenders (see Gold, 1970, and Klemke, 1978, for approximations with juveniles).

Still more troublesome, good estimates of the recidivism, even of those who are arrested, processed, and/or punished, cannot be generated. Although rearrest is often taken as the appropriate estimator of recidivism (indeed, the FBI treats it as synonymous with recidivism), it is woefully deficient. If self-report and victimization studies are at all reliable, it is pretty certain that most criminal acts never result in arrest. On the other hand, the probability of arrest for those who have previously been in custody is probably inflated because they are more likely to be suspected and kept under surveillance. Return-to-prison rates, which are probably more often cited than rearrest figures, are even more deficient, because they mix further criminality with parole revocation for noncriminal activity, because the probability of reconviction is greater regardless of actual criminal behavior, and because surely an even smaller proportion of criminal acts by ex-incarcerees results in imprisonment than in arrest.

Furthermore, if all this is ignored and those studies using rearrest or reimprisonment rates are taken at face value, we are still in a pitiful condition to draw meaningful conclusions about specific deterrence, because such studies are comparatively rare (see Glaser, 1964). Rearrest and reincarceration rates are not systematically compiled; to generate them for a sample of offenders requires extensive follow-up work as well as cooperation of the FBI, which has rarely been forthcoming. Not only that, but to be reasonably useful recidivism rates ought to be available for offenders who have experienced various kinds and degrees of sanction—from simple arrest to incarceration for differing lengths of time, including fine, probation, and restitution. In addition, those statistics would need to be available for enough different political units to ascertain if there is interaction between system characteristics and the presumed deterrent effect of these different kinds of sanctions. Such data just cannot be acquired.

Theoretical Inadequacies

Added to the conceptual and methodological problems already mentioned are some important theoretical weaknesses that make currently available data uninterpretable. First, most studies of general deterrence assume that effects of sanctions are at least monotonic, if not completely linear. Yet, it is plausible to imagine that thresholds must be reached before there are deterrent effects (Brown, 1978; Tittle and Rowe, 1974), and there may even be critical levels all along continua of sanction characteristics (such as severity and certainty of sanction) which might mark dramatic changes in deterrence. For instance, there could be a point of diminishing returns, and at given levels of threat particular amounts of increase or decrease may have quite different effects (Logan, 1972). Hence, there may be no difference in the effect of threats at a 75 percent and a 90 percent credibility level, while the difference between 10 percent and 25 percent may be remarkable. Moreover, within particular ranges of threat probability there may be insignificant changes in deterrence.

However, we have no theory that would direct us to an understanding of these possibilities, and as a result of this theoretical deficiency, we have scarcely any evidence about effects of sanctions within various ranges of sanction certainty and severity. Without such knowledge most of the research reported in the literature is not interpretable. For instance, what now looks like negative evidence for the deterrent proposition may actually be the result of measurement of the sanction variable within a relatively inert range; and what now looks like at least modest support for the deterrent postulate may turn out to be extremely unimpressive if we learn that in those studies certainty or severity of sanction was measured in the most potent part of the continuum.

Similar interpretive barriers grow from the absence of theory about interaction effects. Despite good ad hoc reasons for believing that the effects of sanction severity may be contingent upon the level of certainty, and vice versa, the nature of those contingencies is problematic. On one hand, it is plausible to hypothesize that severity cannot be effective unless certainty is high enough to generate credibility (Tittle and Logan, 1973); on the other hand, severe penalties may compensate for low certainty (Logan, 1972). Yet we do not have adequate theory to understand this, especially since such interactions may vary from group to group of potential offenders. Moreover, there are probably many other conditional situations involving other currently unspecified variables, especially those having to do with informal sanctions. Without refined theory, we are apt to interpret some extant research as indicating a deterrent effect, when in reality that conclusion might be untenable if the actual value of an interactive variable were taken into account. Or we might erroneously interpret some evidence as contradictory to the deterrent hypothesis because we fail to view it as a conditional phenomenon. Similarly, theoretical deficiency leaves us groping for control variables that might render a supposed deterrent relationship spurious (Gibbs, 1975).

Overall, then, theoretical and practical problems as well as neglect have left a legacy of sparce data for judging the work of the criminal justice system; and conceptual, methodological, and theoretical snags continue to undermine confident interpretation of the data that have been compiled. Therefore, a prudent person ought to be hesitant to *assert* any conclusion about the deterrent consequences of the criminal process (see Tullock, 1974, and Van den Haag, 1975, for examples of those who disagree about the confidence with which assessment can be made).

WHAT CONCLUSIONS CAN BE DRAWN?

Still, with this caveat in mind, I believe most would conclude from a review of the literature that the bulk of the evidence is consistent with a deterrent argument, although some of the research poses a serious challenge to that interpretation (Bailey and Lott, 1976; Forst, 1976; Logan, 1975; Nagin, 1978; Tittle, 1977), at least for formal sanctions. There is scarcely room here even to reference all relevant literature (references alone run to half the length of this essay), much less review it. But my conclusion from surveying that body of material (Tittle, 1980) is that the data so far have not been sufficient to prove that sanctions or sanction threats generally have causative effects in limiting criminal behavior, but at least such effects have not been ruled out, and circumstantial evidence supporting the inhibitory consequences of punishment has been powerful. Yet it is as true now as it was in 1973 that the only really safe conclusion to be drawn is that "sanctions apparently have some deterrent effect under some circumstances" (Tittle and Logan, 1973: 385). Unfortunately, we still cannot specify with any clarity the conditions under which sanctions are important influences on criminal behavior, and, in particular, we cannot at this point even show that the apparent effects of formal sanctions are not spuriously attributable to the informal sanctioning process. Hence, we seem to be justified in entertaining the notion that criminal justice processing has some deterrent effects, but that notion must be thought of as tentative while we search for more definitive evidence.

HOW TO MAKE ASSESSMENT MORE FEASIBLE

1. Specify Conditions of Deterrence

The major task before scholars now seems to be to narrow down the conditions under which deterrence probably occurs. In the effort to compile more compelling evidence and to specify our knowledge, future research efforts must not only solve the methodological problems outlined before, but they must incorporate a larger number of variables, many of which have not been measured before. Such variables include sanction characteristics, characteristics of norms that are being enforced by sanction threats, the nature and strength of motivation involved in various kinds of illegal acts, characteristics of potential law-breakers, and contextual variables that are thought to strengthen or weaken the deterrent effect.

Sanction Characteristics. Although much research has dealt with the sanction characteristics of certainty and severity of sanctions, a great deal still remains to be learned. More work needs to be done on threshold and maximum effect levels of these characteristics, rather than assuming a monotonic linear effect. In addition, the interaction of certainty and severity remains problematic both theoretically and empirically.

Moreover, other sanction characteristics have hardly been investigated at all. Most work has focused on formal sanctions, but most theory suggests greater efficacy for informal sanctions (Anderson et al., 1977a; Tittle, 1977). Also, the interaction of the two remains problematic. Further, the relative or interactive effects of objective sanction characteristics, as opposed to subjective perceptions of sanctions, must be clarified. Indeed, understanding of the relationship between the two types is essential to the interpretation of most of the deterrence research that has already been done. The untested assumption is that objective sanctions for a political unit bear some reasonable relationship to individual perceptions within that unit (Gibbs, 1975; Parker and Grasmick, 1979). Furthermore, the question of celerity has hardly been investigated (Minor, 1977).

A related issue that requires more testing concerns the effect of specific risks as opposed to aggregate risks. Perceptions of general sanction probabilities may be more closely related to objective sanctions than are perceptions of personal risk (Bailey and Lott, 1976; Jensen et al., 1977; Waldo and Chiricos, 1972), and it is reasonable to postulate that assessments of personal risk are more relevant to deterrence than assessments of general risk. Yet knowledge about the factors that cause one to assess risk for oneself differently than for others has not been developed.

Finally, an important sanction characteristic is the mode by which a threat is communicated. Theorists differ in their expectations about whether mass media, interpersonal, or diffuse cultural communication is more likely to produce deterrent effects (Erickson and Gibbs, 1975; Geerken and Gove, 1975), and there is really no direct evidence at all. Some indirect evidence suggests that one's perception of getting punished for any crime (diffuse perception) is as relevant as one's perception about being punished for a specific crime that one might be contemplating (Erickson and Gibbs, 1975; Tittle, 1980).

Type of Law. Theory suggests that the kind of norm heavily influences the likelihood of deterrence by sanction threats. It is said that some laws are obeyed whether sanctions are provided or not, and that others are disobeyed frequently, despite provisions for sanctions (Andenaes, 1975; Zimring and Hawkins, 1973). But the empirical evidence is incomplete as well as contradictory. Norms, as they are expressed in laws, do vary in how just they are perceived to be, how legitimate they are, how important they are perceived to be, and how morally imperative they are. Yet little data exist to differentiate laws on these dimensions, much less test variations in deterrability.

Motivation. Not enough evidence has been brought to bear on the kind and strength of motivations that are typically involved in various kinds of criminal acts, and hardly anybody has empirically related motivations to deterrent effectiveness. This remains true despite the early emphasis on the "utility" of deviant acts and upon contemporary theoretical statements suggesting that strength of motivation is a key factor in whether deterrence is possible (Andenaes, 1952; Chambliss, 1967; Zimring and Hawkins, 1973).

Positioning of Acts. A further neglected question concerns the deterrability of acts positioned at different points in a series of actual or potential criminal acts. It has been suggested that deterrence is more likely for an initial deviant act than for subsequent acts, after deterrence has once failed (Thorsell and Klemke, 1972), but it has also been postulated that the association between certainty of punishment and future conduct will be greater among those who have already committed the act (Geerken and Gove, 1975). Yet there has been very little empirical attention to this question (Sinha, 1967; Tittle, 1980).

Characteristics of Potential Lawbreakers. Extant research has done little more than identify possible individual characteristics which might affect how much sanction threats deter, and where more than one study has been reported, the results are contradictory (for example, see the gender findings of Sigelman and Sigelman, 1976, and Tittle and Rowe, 1973, as opposed to those of Silberman, 1976, Burkett and Jensen, 1975, and Anderson et al., 1977b). Thus the differences in deterrability by gender, age, socioeconomic status, race, and personality remains to be determined.

Conditional Variables. A number of contingent variables have been identified but incompletely investigated. Such things as the degree of moral commitment to a norm (Andenaes, 1966; Toby, 1964; Zimring and Hawkins, 1968), peer influences (Burkett and Jensen, 1975; Zimring and Hawkins, 1973), the degree of social bonds to conventional others (Hirschi, 1969; Zimring and Hawkins, 1968), or the integration of the individual into the community, have been postulated as theoretically important (Geerken and Gove, 1975).

In addition, there are some "contextual" factors that may influence the degree to which sanction threats can be effective. These include the cohesion of a community, the religiosity of a population, the ethnic or racial heterogeneity of a place, the general reputation of enforcement agents, socioeconomic level of the community, age and sex composition, distribution of wealth in a particular context, the type of occupational structure, and cultural history of the community.

Ecological Variables and Contextual Effects. Almost every variable identified so far can be conceptualized as a community as well as an individual characteristic. An individual perceives the certainty of sanction to be of a particular level, but communities can also be characterized by the average perceived probability of sanctions among its citizens, or perhaps by the proportion who perceive the sanctions to be above a particular threshold level. Moreover, communities can differ considerably in the dispersion of such perceptions, even when the averages are similar or the proportions perceiving sanctions above the threshold level are similar.

It is plausible to imagine that general perceptions of sanctions will provide the linkage between sanction threats and crime rates, but until heretofore unmeasured variables on the community level are directly brought into analysis, alternative interpretations are too easy. Sanctions may affect crime rates by other mechanisms than fear, and other conditions may determine effects. The theoretical literature suggests a wide variety of ecological-level variables that have not been explicitly hypothesized as antecedent or intervening with respect to the relationship between sanctions and deviance, but which may nevertheless account for or condition such a relationship.

Not only is there a need for measurement and analysis of a greater number of ecological-level variables in order to understand community-level relationships; there is a need as well to investigate the contextual effects of such variables on the deterrent process at the individual level. For example, a person who perceives a low probability of being caught and punished for marijuana-smoking but lives in a community where most other people perceive a high probability, may refrain from smoking because he or she is following the example of the others who are themselves conforming because of fear of the possible consequences of apprehension. Although this individual has not been directly deterred by fear of sanctions, sanctions have nevertheless indirectly influenced his behavior through their effects on the individual's social context.

Obviously there are many ways in which the deterrence-relevant variables mentioned here could conceivably affect deterrent interpretations on the ecological level and indirectly affect the deterrent process on the individual level, through contextual influences. Yet there is almost no theory, and certainly no empirical evidence, about this. Until more ecological-level variables are measured and brought into analysis, our knowledge will remain uncertain.

2. Broaden Focus of Inquiry

Successful compilation of research on which to judge the work of the criminal justice system not only requires more precise theoretical focus, but also awaits reformulation of the question. Usually scholars approach the deterrence issue as if there were only two alternatives—either sanctions deter or they do not. Actually, there are several logical possibilities. Sanctions can deter, they can have no effect, or they can cause more crime. Moreover, all three of these outcomes may occur simultaneously, depending upon what specific sanctions, subgroups, or other of the above-mentioned conditions are operative. Hence, the fundamental problem to be investigated is not whether sanctions deter, but rather *what the effects of justice-processing are under various conditions, with an open mind as to possible outcomes.* When scholars recognize this larger focus, they will develop better research designs, and they will interpret their findings more judiciously and usefully. In addition, they will be able to tap a deeper pool of theory and research in predicting and explaining results. This kind of systematic approach seems far more promising than the piecemeal struggle that is carried on now by separate and noncommunicative camps. After all, there are plausible theoretical arguments which suggest that sanctions may actually cause crime rather than deter it. At least three distinct species of work lead to that position.

Labeling. The labeling perspective maintains that sanctioning of individuals will lead them to commit more crime (secondary deviance) because processing through the justice apparatus usually involves some form of classification as a criminal, regardless of actual adjudication as guilty (see Gove, 1975). This criminal classification (label) presumably generates negative reactions by others, resulting in attribution of bad character and stereotyped expectations of behavior. These responses then restrict opportunities for the individual to participate in society in normal ways and activate a process of self-image transformation. Presumably, if others think of and respond to a person as a criminal, that person will come to think of himself or herself as a criminal. As a result, the individual is compelled to break the law to satisfy needs as well as to reinforce an emerging criminal self-image (Klemke, 1978).

Although research and thinking generated by this perspective has to a large extent been separate from deterrence work, the two perspectives are really different sides of the same coin (Tittle, 1975a). The question is, "What effect does sanctioning (or criminal processing) have on the future behavior of those sanctioned?" At this point it is impossible to say. I have already pointed out the sparcity and weakness of deterrence research, and the same problems exist with labeling research (see Tittle, 1975b). But even if there had been more and technically better research, it is unlikely that we would be any closer to deciding between deterrence and labeling theories. This is because they are not really competing theories but are explanations for different outcomes. It seems likely that under some conditions (not yet precisely known) processing will deter. But it is also obvious that under other conditions (also not yet precisely known) processing will lead to secondary deviance. Furthermore, under still other conditions (yet to be discovered) processing no doubt is irrelevant to future conduct. The point is clear: Ostensibly hostile camps need to combine forces to solve a common problem (Thorsell and Klemke, 1972).

Brutalization. A second argument suggesting that punishment may in fact enhance the production of crime concerns the general effect on a population of punishing some of those who break the law (Bowers and Pierce, 1975, King, 1978). It is said that punishment per se tends to brutalize those punished as well as those not punished so that all citizens, in turn, emulate actions of the collectivity by hurting or killing those who displease them, just as the political entity does when it punishes offenders. The collective example presumably undermines individual conscience that otherwise would inhibit violent and punitive impulses. If the political entity of which one is a member can willingly hurt somebody (even if doing so seems justified by the offender's earlier act), then it is easier for one to hurt those who in one's view "deserve to be hurt." Hence, the long-range effect of punishment, particularly severe punishment, may not be general deterrence but, instead, encouragement of crime.

As with labeling and deterrence theories, the brutalization thesis lacks firm empirical grounding, and the methodological difficulties in testing it are probably even greater since this hypothesis seemingly requires comparative designs that include a large number of similar political units with much sharper differences in punishment practices than usually exist. But again, it is unlikely that any research will help to decide between the brutalization and the general deterrence models. It is more likely that in the final analysis it will be shown that under some circumstances (not presently known) some kinds of punishment do generate crime by enticing citizens to imitate the punishers; and it will probably be shown that some conditions permit punishment to deter by strengthening moral inhibitions, creating fear in the hearts of would-be violators, or in other ways encouraging obedience to the law. The full spectrum of possibilities must be entertained, and until research is formulated in such terms, we will always be approaching a serious issue in desultory fashion.

Association. "Prisonization" theory also suggests that punishment, at least in some forms, will lead to more rather than less crime. A major theme of correctional literature is that incarceration "criminalizes" inmates by encouraging them to cultivate loyalties to each other, to form contracultural value systems, and to adopt hostile and rebellious attitudes toward prison officials and programs. Involvement in these prison subcultures is assumed to create or strengthen already existing criminal inclinations which will later lead to crime. Hence, rather than bringing about specific deterrence, imprisonment (which in theory, if not practice, is the primary sanction used in modern legal systems) may cause crime through the influence of inmates on each other.

Still, as with all these arguments, the data are weak and the conclusions ambiguous (Tittle, 1974). As noted before, we do not know what the recidivism rate is for those released from prison, much less for those who never were imprisoned, and the existing figures can be interpreted in many ways. Furthermore, there is little research which directly links prison attitudes and behavior to later conduct. In fact, much of the research on institutional living challenges the assumption of a relationship between prison behavior and general antisocial characteristics by showing that prisonization is adaptive and tenuous in character (Wheeler, 1961; Garabedian, 1963). Moreover, the idea that institutional environments create the anticorrectional characteristics that inmates manifest is now problematic (Irwin, 1962; Wellford, 1967; Thomas and Petersen, 1977). In addition, there is some reason to believe that any "criminalizing" effect of incarceration may be balanced out by an "incapacitative" effect on those who are already criminalized before they are imprisoned (Blumstein et al., 1978). Thus, the same integrative principle enunciated above is applicable here as well. Surely incarceration deters crime among some who experience it; and just as surely it engenders crime among others. The trick is to specify when one rather than the other will be likely.

Summary. The point here is that narrow and partisan theoretical orientations (or in some cases hardly any theoretical orientations at all) have hampered progress toward an understanding of sanctions and their effects as much as have methodological problems. Unless researchers attend to these theoretical issues, all the methodological tinkering that is going on now will lead nowhere.

3. Avoid Common Pitfalls

Improving our ability to assess justice-processing also requires that scholars correct some crucial errors of the past. These include ignoring the problem of causal ordering, failing to distinguish between effects at various levels, and allowing ideological commitments to rush us into rash conclusions.

Causal Ordering. Much of the extant literature assumes rather than demonstrates causal direction. As many have noted, covariation between sanction variables (perceived or actual) and crime indicators (official or self-reported) may indicate deterrence or may indicate generation of crime (Minor, 1978; Pontell, 1978). There is good reason to imagine that crime itself, which could be the independent product of many social forces, is the major impetus leading to variations in sanction characteristics. The more crime there is, the less efficiently it can be managed, given fixed resources, such as prison cells or police budgets. Likewise, the more crime one has committed and gotten away with, the more likely one is to perceive that crime can be committed with impunity. Obviously one cannot evaluate the work of the justice system until social scientists determine the extent to which sanctioning is a product of, rather than an influence on, crime.

Most current research dealing with ecological variables does recognize this necessity and does involve some attempt to establish correct causal ordering or describe the nature of reciprocal influence. But survey studies, which in my opinion represent the main hope for the future, have not yet confronted the problem of causal order. Most self-report researchers have measured the controlled association between reports of *past* crime and *present* perceptions of sanction characteristics, and have interpreted the results within a deterrent framework. Obviously, this procedure violates the entire logic of causal order. But even when investigators have tried to solve this problem by eliciting data about respondents' willingness to engage in future criminal behavior, there has still been the problem of simultaneous influence of these two perceptual properties. Clearly, survey work must move to panel designs.

Level of Effects. Those who would evaluate the effects of justice-processing have not always kept in mind the distinction between general and specific effects. The law mandates enforcement in the expectation that there will be consequences on two levels—on the level of the person who is sanctioned and on that of the general population who are not at that moment being "managed," but who are potential lawbreakers. It is entirely possible that the management of individual offenders is largely generative of further crime, but at the same time this defective management process may actually serve to deter most of the other potential offenders. Thus, even if recidivism were judged to indicate failure of correctional endeavors, it might still be true that sanctioning constituted a successful general deterrent. The problem is to ascertain effects on both levels and then to judge their net impact. Perhaps both produce a net deterrent effect, or maybe one has a net deterrent effect while the other has a net generative effect. It could even be that neither has a deterrent effect. If it is found that the two levels have opposite effects, it will then be imperative to determine if the net crime prevented on one level is greater than the net crime generated on the other level, as well as to specify the conditions under which that tradeoff is more or less likely to be positive.

Ideological Barriers. Before real progress can be made in understanding the effects (or noneffects) of sanctions, scholars must throw off some of the prejudices which have held them back. The literature is marred and deficient, partly because much research has been cast in the mold of an ideological struggle. Some true believers are out to prove or convince that sanctions deter, while others are determined to do just the opposite. Moreover, a good number of capable social scientists refuse to consider the question lest they become handmaidens of "the capitalist elite." Although no person is ever completely free of preconceptions and their biasing effects, this really is one of those questions which must be treated as problematic. It is of such immense theoretical and practical importance that we cannot afford to prejudge it. Furthermore, the truth, once it is known, will unquestionably serve many ideological masters. In the meantime, we must formulate and execute our research, and draw our conclusions, with a keen eye to the possibility of bias.

CONCLUSION

Given the meagerness of data that are actually relevant and interpretable, the complexity of the issue, and a multitude of methodological problems, it is almost impossible at the present time to draw meaningful conclusions about the deterrent effects of criminal sanctions. About all that can be said is that evidence sufficient to take seriously the deterrent hypothesis does exist. However, there is also enough data consistent with other possibilities to mandate extreme caution. More definitive statements will not be feasible until researchers focus their work on the conditions under which sanctions have various effects and enlarge the field of inquiry to encompass plausible outcomes besides deterrence. In addition, researchers and evaluators must avoid some of the mistakes that have plagued inquiry.

REFERENCES

Andenaes, J. (1975) "Deterrence and Specific Offenses: Drunken Driving," pp. 421-425 in W. J. Chambliss, *Criminal Law in Action*. Santa Barbara, CA: Hamilton.

——— (1966) "The General Preventive Effects of Punishment." University of Pennsylvania Law Review 114: 949-983.

——— (1952) "General Prevention—Illusion or Reality?" *Journal of Criminal Law, Criminology and Police Science* 43: 176-198.

Anderson, L. S., T. Chiricos, and G. P. Waldo (1977a) ' Formal and informal sanctions: a comparison of deterrent effects." Social Problems 25 (October): 103-114.

——— (1977b) "A Longitudinal Approach to the Study of Deterrence." Presented at the American Sociological Association Convention.

Bailey, W. C. and R. P. Lott (1976) "Crime, Punishment and Personality: An Examination of the Deterrence Question." *Journal of Criminal Law and Criminology* 67 (March): 99-109.

Becker, G. (1968) "Crime and Punishment: An Economic Approach." *Journal of Political Economy* 76 (March-April): 169-217.

Blumstein, A., J. Cohen, and D. Nagin [eds.] (1978) *Deterrence and Incapacitation: Estimating the Effects of Criminal Sanctions on Crime Rates*. Washington, DC: National Academy of Sciences.

Brown, D. W. (1978) "Arrest Rates and Crime Rates: When Does a Tipping Effect Occur?" *Social Forces* 57 (December): 671-682.

Bowers, W. L. and G. L. Pierce (1975) "The Illusion of Deterrence in Isaac Ehrlich's Research on Capital Punishment." *Yale Law Review* 15 (December): 187-208.

Burkett, S. R. and E. L. Jensen (1975) "Conventional Ties, Peer Influences, and the Fear of Apprehension: A Study of Adolescent Marijuana Use." *Sociological Quarterly* 16 (Autumn): 522-533.

Chambliss, W. J. (1967) "Types of Deviance and the Effectiveness of Legal Sanctions.'' *Wisconsin Law Review* (Summer): 703-719.

Cohen, A. K. (1966) *Deviance and Control*. Englewood Cliffs, NJ: Prentice-Hall.

Cohen, L. (1978) "Sanction Threats and Violation Behavior: An Inquiry into Perceptual Variation," pp. 84-99 in C. Wellford (ed.) *Quantitative Studies in Criminology*. Beverly Hills, CA: Sage Publications.

Erickson, M. L. and J. P. Gibbs (1978) "Objective and Perceptual Properties of Legal Punishment and the Deterrence Doctrine." *Social Problems* 25 (February): 253-264.

——— (1975) "Specific vs. General Properties of Legal Punishment and Deterrence." *Social Science Quarterly* 56 (December: 390-397.

——— and G. F. Jensen (1977) "The Deterrence Doctrine and the Perceived Certainty of Legal Punishments." *American Sociological Review* 42 (April): 305-317.

Erickson, P. G. (1976) "Deterrence and Deviance: The Example of Cannabis Prohibition." *Journal of Crimal Law and Criminology* 67 (June): 222-232.

Forst, Brian (1976) "Participation in Illegitimate Activities: Further Empirical Findings." *Policy Analysis* 2 (Summer): 477-492.

Friedland, N., J. Thibaut, and L. Walker (1973) "Some Determinants of the Violation of Rules." *Journal of Applied Social Psychology* 3 (April/June): 103-118.

Garabedian, P. G. (1963) "Social Roles and Processes of Socialization in the Prison Community." *Social Problems* 11 (Fall): 139-152.

Geerken, M. R. and W. R. Gove (1975) "Deterrence: Some Theoretical Considerations." *Law and Society Review* 9 (Spring): 498-513.

Gibbs, J. P. (1975) *Crime, Punishment, and Deterrence.* New York: Elsevier.

Glaser, D. (1964) *The Effectiveness of a Prison and Parole System.* Indianapolis: Bobbs-Merrill. ,

Gold, M. (1970) Delinquent Behavior in an American City, Belmont, CA: Wadsworth.

Goode, W. J. (1972) "Force in Human Society." *American Sociological Review* 37 (October): 507-519.

Gove, W. R. [ed.] (1975) *The Labelling of Deviance: Evaluating a Perspective.* New York: John Wiley.

Grasmick, H. G. and L. Appleton (1977) "Legal Punishment and Social Stigma: A Comparison of Two Deterrence Models." *Social Science Quarterly* 58 (June): 15-28.

Grasmick, H. G. and S. D. McLaughlin (1978) "Deterrence and Social Control [comment on Silberman]." *American Sociological Review* 43 (April): 272-278.

Grasmick, H. G. and H. Milligan, Jr. (1976) "Deterrence Theory Approach to Socioeconomic/Demographic Correlates of Crime." *Social Science Quarterly* 57 (December): 608-617.

Hardt, R. H. and S. Peterson-Hardt (1977) "On Determining the Quality of Delinquency Self-Report Method." *Journal of Research in Crime and Delinquency* 14 (July): 247-261.

Hirschi, T. (1969) *Causes of Delinquency.* Berkeley: University of California Press.

Irwin, J. and D. R. Cressey (1962) "Thieves, Convicts and the Inmate Culture." *Social Problems* 10 (Fall): 142-155.

Jensen, G. F. and M. L. Erickson (1978) "The Social Meaning of Sanctions," pp. 119-136 in M. D. Krohn and R. L. Akers (eds.) *Crime, Law, and Sanctions: Theoretical Perspectives.* Beverly Hills, CA: Sage Publications.

Jensen, G. F., J. P. Gibbs, and M. Erickson (1977) "Perceived Risk of Punishment and Self-Reported Delinquency." *Social Forces* 57 (September): 57-78.

King, D. R. (1978) "The Brutalization Effect: Execution Publicity and the Incidence of Homicide in South Carolina." *Social Forces* 57 (December): 683-687.

Klemke, L. K. (1978) "Does Apprehension for Shoplifting Amplify or Terminate Shoplifting Activity?" *Law and Society Review* 12 (Spring): 391-403.

Kraut, R. E. (1976) "Deterrent and Definitional Influences on Shoplifting." *Social Problems* 23 (February): 358-368.

Logan, C. H. (1975) "Arrest Rates and Deterrence." *Social Science Quarterly* 56 (December): 376-389.

——— (1972) "General Deterrent Effects of Imprisonment." *Social Forces* 51 (September): 64-73.

Meier, R. F. (1979) "Correlates of Deterrence: Problems of Theory and Method." *Journal of Criminal Justice* 7 (Spring): 11-15.

——— and W. T. Johnson (1977) "Deterrence as Social Control: The Legal and Extralegal Production of Conformity." *American Sociological Review* 42 (April): 292-304.

Minor, W. W. (1978) "Deterrence Research: Problems of Theory and Method," pp. 21-45 in J. R. Cramer (ed.) *Preventing Crime.* Beverly Hills, CA: Sage Publications.

——— (1977) "A Deterrence-Control Theory of Crime," pp. 117-137 in R. F. Meier (ed.) *Theory in Criminology: Contemporary Views.* Beverly Hills, CA: Sage Publications.

Nagin, D. (1978) "Crime Rates, Sanction Levels, and Constraints on Prison Population." *Law and Society Review* 12 (Spring): 341-366.

Packer, H. L. (1968) *The Limits of the Criminal Sanction*. Stanford: Stanford University Press.

Parker, J. and H. G. Grasmick (1979) "Linking Actual and Perceived Certainty of Punishment: An Exploratory Study of an Untested Proposition in Deterrence Theory." *Criminology* 17 (November): 366-379.

Pontell, H. (1978) "Deterrence: Theory vs. Practice." *Criminology* 16 (Spring): 3-22.

Sigelman, C. K. and L. Sigelman (1976) "Authority and Conformity: Violation of a Traffic Regulation." *Journal of Social Psychology* 100 (October): 35-43.

Silberman, M. (1976) "Toward a Theory of Criminal Deterrence." *American Sociological Review* 41 (June): 442-461.

Sinha, J.B.P. (1967) "Ethical Risk and Censure-Avoiding Behavior." *Journal of Social Psychology* 71 (April): 267-275.

Teevan, J. J. (1976a) "Deterrent Effects of Punishment: Subjective Measures Continued." *Canadian Journal of Criminology and Corrections* 18 (April): 156-159.

——— (1976b) "Subjective Perception of Deterrence [continued]." *Journal of Research in Crime and Delinquency* 13 (July): 155-164.

——— (1972) "Deterrent Effects of Punishment: Toward Subjective Measures." Presented at the Eastern Sociological Association Convention.

Thibaut, J., N. Friedland, and L. Walker (1974) "Compliance with Rules: Some Social Determinants." *Journal of Personality and Social Psychology* 30 (December): 792-801.

Thomas, C. (1970) "Toward a More Inclusive Model of the Inmate Contra-Culture." *Criminology* 8 (November): 251-262.

Thomas, C. W. and D. M. Petersen (1977) *Prison Organization and Inmate Subcultures*. Indianapolis: Bobbs-Merrill.

Thorsell, B. A. and L. W. Klemke (1972) "The Labeling Process: Reinforcement and Deterrent?" *Law and Society Review* 6 (February): 393-403.

Tittle, C. R. (1980) *Sanctions and Social Deviance: The Question of Deterrence*. New York: Praeger.

——— (1978) "Restitution and Deterrence: An Evaluation of Compatibility," pp. 33-58 in B. Galaway and J. Hudson (eds.) *Offender Restitution in Theory and Action*. Lexington, MA: D. C. Heath.

——— (1977) "Sanction Fear and the Maintenance of Social Order." *Social Forces* 55 (March): 579-596.

——— (1975a) "Deterrents or Labeling?" *Social Forces* 53 (March): 399-410.

——— (1975b) "Labelling and Crime: An Empirical Evaluation," pp. 157-159 in W. R. Gove (ed.) *The Labelling of Deviance*. New York: John Wiley.

——— (1974) "Prisons and Rehabilitation: The Inevitability of Disfavor." *Social Problems* 21 (Fall): 385-395.

——— and C. H. Logan (1973) "Sanctions and Deviance: Evidence and Remaining Questions." *Law and Society Review* 7 (Spring): 372-392.

Tittle, C. R. and A. R. Rowe (1974) "Certainty of Arrest and Crime Rates: A Further Test of the Deterrence Hypothesis." *Social Forces* 52 (June): 455-462.

——— (1973) "Moral Appeal, Sanction Threat, and Deviance: An Experimental Test." *Social Problems* 20 (Spring): 488-498.

Toby, J. (1964) "Is Punishment Necessary?" *Journal of Criminal Law, Criminology and Police Science* 55 (September): 332-337.

Tullock, G. (1974) "Does Punishment Deter Crime?" *Public Interest* 36 (Summer): 103-111.

Uniform Crime Reports, State of Florida: Crime in Florida. (1971) Florida Department of Law Enforcement, Tallahassee.

Van den Haag, E. (1975) *Punishing Criminals: Concerning a Very Old and Painful Question.* New York: Basic Books.

Waldo, G. P. and T. G. Chiricos (1972) "Perceived Panal Sanction and Self-Reported Criminality: A Neglected Approach to Deterrence Research." *Social Problems* 19 (Spring): 522-540.

Wellford, C. (1967) "Factors Associated with Adoption of the Inmate Code: A Study of Normative Socialization." *Journal of Criminal Law, Criminology and Police Science* 58 (June): 197-203.

Wheeler, S. (1961) "Role Conflict in Correctional Communities," in D. R. Cressey (ed.) *The Prison.* New York: Holt, Rinehart & Winston.

Zimring, F. E. (1978) "Policy Experiments in General Deterrence: 1970-1975," pp. 140-186 in A. Blumstein et al. (eds.) *Deterrence and Incapacitation: Estimating the Effects of Criminal Sanctions on Crime Rates.* Washington, DC: National Academy of Sciences.

——— and G. Hawkins (1973) *Deterrence: The Legal Threat in Crime Control.* Chicago: University of Chicago Press.

——— (1968) "Deterrence and Marginal Groups." *Journal of Research in Crime and Delinquency* (July): 100-114.

15

Evaluation Issues and Victimless Crimes

Gilbert Geis

"Victimless crime" is a designation for behavior that in most American jurisdictions includes acts such as consensual homosexuality, proscribed forms of gambling, prostitution, and voluntary use of illegal drugs (Schur, 1965; Geis, 1972; Schur and Bedau, 1974; Smith and Pollack, 1975; Winterscheid, 1977). The major evaluative issue in regard to such behaviors usually concerns the impact of different juridicial and enforcement arrangements for handling or ignoring the acts. Concerned constituencies include enactors of the behavior, those close to them (such as family members), legislators and law enforcement agents, special interest groups, and the general public. Unlike their concern with technical matters of criminal justice such as bail arrangements, members of the general public hold very strong convictions about things such as drug use and homosexuality. These convictions create an evaluative atmosphere that demands the most meticulous kind of work if evaluation is to have a satisfactory impact on public opinion and public policy.

The moral obloquy sometimes attached to victimless crime offenses, as well as the absence of complainants, also creates unique problems for an evaluator. We can assess changes in the amount of robbery by means of police reports and/or victimization surveys, but the means to determine whether there has been an increase or decrease in the amount of homosexual behavior or gambling activity are far less satisfactory. There are millions of episodes of homosexual behavior each year: How are we to demonstrate that a new law has led to an increase or a decrease in the amount of behavior or the number of persons participating in it? Nonetheless, these items are matters of great importance to policy makers and to the public.

It must be appreciated that since moral feelings so pervade the subject of victimless crime, evaluative findings are more apt than in other criminal justice areas merely to provide highly combustible fuel for policy debate. I will consider the general implications of this situation in the latter part of the chapter. First, I will set the stage by considering specific aspects of evaluative strategy in regard to forms of victimless crime.

A CASE STUDY: GAMBLING

It will not do for the evaluator to concentrate overlong on victimless crime as a class of behaviors, inasmuch as the category includes a wide range of acts united at best by a very slim definitional thread. It is necessary to move directly into examination of a more specific type of victimless crime in order better to detail evaluative considerations. Gambling offers a useful representative of the genre for a number of reasons. It has the advantage of being a relatively asexual behavior (unlike pornography, prostitution, and homosexuality, for instance). In this regard, there is somewhat less emotional loading attached to a review of issues associated with gambling than for most victimless crime. Nor is there the same heavy connotation of sin attached to gambling as to most of its classifactory victimless cousins, nor so horrendous a roster of alleged outcomes, such as seduction of the young, venereal disease, foetal slaughter, and other indexes of supposed depredation and degradation.

At the same time, the subject of gambling presents evaluative concerns generic to the victimless crime category (see Beale and Goldman, 1974; Commission on the Review of the National Policy Toward Gambling, 1976; Fogelberg, 1973; and especially Cornish, 1977). For one thing, its very definition seems to defy satisfactory scientific statement. In England, the Churches' Council on Gambling (Edwards, 1974), a group that probably has attended to wagering issues more assiduously over time than any other person or body in the world, finds itself in an advanced state of semantic uncertainty as it tries to fix on a definition of the subject. Its endorsement of the definitional stab by an English psychiatrist (Moran, 1970) highlights the problem. The psychiatrist suggests that gambling might be comprehended as embracing the following conditions:

(1) There is an agreement between two or more persons; the participation of others is therefore essential, although sometimes, as in football pool and slot machine gambling, this is more remote.
(2) Certain property is transferred between the persons involved so that some gain at the expense of others; this is usually referred to as the *stake*.
(3) The result is dependent on the outcome of a risky or uncertain situation; it therefore involves risk-taking.
(4) Participation can be avoided (meaning that it is a matter of personal

choice) and is typically pursued in active fashion, the motivation for this is not uniform, often being unrelated to the property staked and arising out of various psychological needs.

It does not take much skill to savage this definition in terms of its scientific integrity and usefulness. It offers no distinction between, for instance, betting on horses and the purchase of life insurance or the building of a house in an area supposedly safe from nuclear fallout; and it uses a high quotient of fudge words, terms such as "typically pursued," "although sometimes," and "usually," a tactic that renders uncertain what is and what is not to be considered gambling. Surely, life itself can be regarded as little more than a continuing game of chance, but if an evaluator is basically concerned with the use of the criminal law in the arena of gambling, amorphous definitions will impede understanding.

Indeed, the Churches' Council, finding itself in an untidy definitional position, spends a considerable number of its pamphleteering pages trying without too much success to distinguish unacceptable forms of gambling from tolerable kinds. Ultimately, the Council (Moody, 1970: 10; compare Barrow, 1969; Lesieur, 1979) focuses on the idea of gambling as compulsive behavior. Compulsive gamblers are characterized in the following terms:

> At first, they must get money to gamble. Later, they must gamble to get the money back. . . . An unusual degree of impatience makes them fretful to meet all demands *now*. . . . Debts can reach staggering proportions because a compulsive gambler can charm money out of people. . . . This remorseless wheel of activity crushes truth, consideration for others, and respect for himself.

For an evaluator, the focus on compulsivity can offer a yardstick for examination of individual or diverse forms of gambling, though Oldman (1978; compare Kusyszyn, 1978), who worked two years as a croupier in a gambling establishment, suggests that, among other things, evaluators have failed to differentiate adequately between habitual behavior and compulsive activity, and also that the rhetoric of compulsion, if employed by a gambler, may be no more than a rationalization to lull criticism by others of that gambler's participation in an activity that he or she finds pleasant.

Most fundamentally, the illustration of definitional difficulties with gambling behavior highlights the pressing need in evaluation, and particularly in such an emotionally toned area as victimless crime, to set forth the issue under review clearly, neutrally, and in a defensible way. If meretricious gambling is said to be that which engenders compulsivity in its performance, then it becomes of paramount importance to state precisely why it is that compulsivity is undesirable, and, of course, why compulsivity in regard to gambling, is (or is not) more tolerable than other kinds of driven behavior. It will not do only to attempt to measure the consequences in terms of compulsive activity of different social and legal arrangements in regard to gambling—itself a quite formidable task.

The category of gambling as victimless crime also offers some striking anomalies in regard to behaviors forbidden by law and those legally sanctioned. Betting at race tracks is permitted in most American jurisdictions, while book-making—which can involve betting on the same events outside the confines of the track—is often forbidden. Lotteries are often legal, but betting on numbers is almost uniformly prohibited. Nevada permits casino gambling (Skolnick, 1978), as well as wagers on sports events, with the latter form of betting outlawed throughout the remainder of the nation, though the laws are sedulously ignored (Tuite, 1978). The quest to establish the dimensions of an underlying principle regulating gambling, presuming one exists, will trouble the evaluator, just as it will with the other victimless offenses. It appears that gambling is more likely to be legal if it is to be done (1) under state or local option auspices and (2) by those persons who seem better able to "afford" it. A third principle also frequently appears operative: When fiscally pressed, jurisdictions are apt to turn to some form of legal gambling as a method for obtaining revenue (Brooks, 1975).

For the victimless crime evaluator, the definition and rationale bearing upon victimless crimes such as gambling are matters to be attended to closely. Why is one kind of gambling not allowed while another form, which appears quite similar, is permitted? Attention might be focused on law enforcement non-chalance about things such as "private" poker clubs and church bingo games, which offer monetary prizes, in contrast to law enforcement efforts to eradicate other forms of equally illegal gambling. Evaluators will find it essential to try to get persons concerned with or about gambling to explicate beforehand the rationale they employ to distinguish among seemingly similar behaviors. These considerations can then form a focus for a field investigation to determine whether they appear to be factually or fictively based. It may be claimed, for instance, that bingo gambling under church auspices (Hendrix, 1978) is acceptable because the proceeds are earmarked for worthy causes. If so, it then can be argued that other forms of gambling, such as lotteries, where the earnings would go to medical research efforts, should be acceptable. Pressed further, the defender of the church arrangement may now insist that it should be differentiated because it does not permit the infiltration of underworld elements into its operation. This stand might be addressed by economic analysis, such as that of Schelling (1967), who maintained that if it were operated by stockbrokers, gambling on numbers and horses could easily be kept uncontaminated by organized crime elements, such as those of the genus Mafia. There might be an experimental attempt to establish such a program, and the evaluator could try to document whether it meets criteria of success and failure.

HISTORICAL RESEARCH

Historical research also plays an important role in evaluation work in the area of victimless crime. Most of the activities that fall within the category have had long careers in the realm of public controversy. They also have been treated both socially and legally in quite divergent ways through time (for gambling, for example, see Chafetz, 1960; Breen, 1977). Generally, in the United States, their historical taproots lie deep in biblical soil. A careful review of the history of methods employed for dealing with the offenses (see, for example, Fact Research Inc., 1974; Blakely and Kurland, 1978) requires scrutiny of matters such as statutory language, legislative debates, criminal statistics, and appellate court decisions (Cornell Law School Gambling Project, 1975), as well as an ability to read between the lines of such materials. This kind of analysis is not scientific: It needs to be guided by uncommon amounts of sophisticated, interpretive skill and marked by intelligence, thoroughness, and judiciousness. For criminal justice evaluators, historical research and legal analysis can be uneasy enterprises. They are not the stuff that recommends itself to their journals, with their quantitative emphasis. But they are of preeminent importance for significant work in the area of victimless crime. Some solace might be gained from the working principle of a successful researcher I know. If it is worth bothering about for a scholarly article, he will say, then it is worth writing a book about. For books, the kind of evaluative backgrounding that has been recommended here is very much in order.

CROSS-CULTURAL INQUIRY

Detailed attention to cross-cultural material in the area of victimless crime is something of a problematic enterprise. Such material is commonly discounted thoroughly when it puts forth the merest hint that what has been done elsewhere with apparent success might be worth a try here. The resisters insist that items such as demographic structure, personality traits, or geographic features are significantly different in that other place. The Japanese are said to be law-abiding by nature (Stephens, 1977); therefore, the success of a police crackdown on amphetamine abuse, reported to have been astonishingly effective (Geis, 1978), could not work in the United States, where the population is not as placid. Other nations are more homogeneous, or less homogeneous—in any event, they are quite different.

What can be gained from cross-cultural work includes documentation that certain policies need not inevitably lead to disastrous results, and suggestions for different ways to approach what appear to be common difficulties. In some countries, banks have a monopoly on betting. In others, the sale of wagering slips is restricted to handicapped persons, with maimed war veterans having first priority. In still other places, licensed betting centers are not allowed to offer contemporaneous televising of events, such as horse races, upon which wagers have been made, on the ground that such commentary heightens emotional involvement and encourages "undesirable" attitudes and practices (see Martinez, 1977). The list of useful information that can be acquired by an evaluator willing to extend his or her inquiry into alien climes is considerable, but such an effort probably ought to constitute a secondary endeavor, not to be undertaken very extensively unless this can be done at no great risk of drawing off resources for the at-home evaluative probe.

So far, then, the stress has been on the need to pinpoint with great accuracy the parameters of the behavior under review—its precise definition. The foregoing section has recommended absorption into the research issue, that is, determination of its history, its political biography, acquisition of cross-cultural data, and similar kinds of preparatory work. With this information in place, how might an evaluator working in the area of victimless crime best proceed? Again, I will draw illustrations primarily from gambling.

A. Comparative Strategy

In criminal justice work, the quest for a comparison situation against which to match evaluative findings tends to focus on neighboring jurisdictions where the change has not taken place. Thus, a law change in Illinois is matched against conditions in Wisconsin. I believe that there probably will be a higher payoff if comparisons are drawn instead between juridical units within a state where the change is inaugurated. Given the American pattern of administration of criminal justice, it can be anticipated that the different counties in a state will have varying experiences vis-a-vis the new legislation. They will differ in terms of their general support for it, their enforcement approach, and their success or failure as such items and others mesh with conditions within the juridical area. Major features of the evaluation become a depiction and study of the methods adopted to deal with the statutory change and of the consequences of such methods. This evaluation tactic is likely to provide better insight than the much more expensive and somewhat more amorphous contrast with a nonlegislating state. Besides, such an approach will tend to overcome an occasional evaluative shortsightedness, one found in work that operates on the assumption that what is dictated is done, when in truth something may be dictated, but a great variety of very different things often are done.

B. Pre- and Postchange Designs

Some of the most significant work on victimless crime is likely to come from field studies using a pre- and postchange design to examine the consequences of statutory change (see e.g., Downes et al., 1976). In the best of all possible research worlds, the evaluator will have foreknowledge of a significant shift in the statutory definition of the behavior which is generally not widely known otherwise. It is important to determine that this shift represents more than a signification of things that already have taken place. It may be true, for instance, that nobody has been arrested for bookmaking for the past three years, and the new law merely is dignifying actual practice. The law probably will make some difference, but it is not likely to be a particularly important difference.

Quick off the mark, the evaluator can sample behavior and public attitudes on the apparent pertinent issues involved in the subject, asking, for instance:

- Do you or do you not think betting on numbers [for which a definition can be provided if required] ought to be made legal?

- If so (or if not) please indicate on the accompanying checklist the most and the least important reasons you favor (or oppose) this move.

- Do you think money from legal gambling should or should not be used to fund organizations such as Gamblers Anonymous?

- Should such funds be used only for charitable and educational purposes?

- Do you or do you not believe that you will personally engage in numbers betting if a new law is passed?

- About how much do you expect you would bet each month?

- Do you or do you not think such a law would bring about an increase in property crimes?

Subject to pretesting and rewording, and depending upon the patience of the respondent group and the funds available for such public opinion sampling, the range of important issues that can be covered is highly expansible. Obviously, one prefers questions that bear on matters likely to arise in public debates, as well as those deemed to be of central importance to a fair determination of the implications of the behavior upon public opinion. Equally obviously, the aim will be to monitor over time the movements of such attitudes as the legislative process and its products proceed. It will be necessary too to check attitudes as they develop longitudinally, both with major external occurrences (e.g., a speech by the governor, disclosure of a major wagering scandal) and with public awareness and interpretation of such occurrences.

However, public attitudes need not dictate public policy, for there often is a very uncertain relationship between principle and majority views, and under certain conditions (to my mind) principle clearly ought to prevail. Despite overwhelming public support, for instance, for a legal approach that would prohibit gambling for welfare recipients (i.e., particular ethnic minorities) but allow it for others, it may be hoped that no court would condone such an approach as meeting equal protection standards.

C. Evaluative Criteria

Once the sites for evaluative work have been established, the remainder of the evaluation strategy can be formed, though, of course, site selection and evaluative approach must be interactive, each influencing decisions about the other. There usually will be concern with gathering information about the effect of the victimless crime legislation, and/or the behavior involved, on costs, morale, crime rates, and a host of other matters. The evaluator should immerse himself or herself in the milieus under review as thoroughly as possible, to capture a surer sense of what is happening. It is as relevant for evaluation as it is for novel-writing that if you truly know a thing you will be able to represent it much more effectively than if you know less and tell it all. Persons who are involved in the situation under study should be encouraged (and paid) to keep systematic written (or tape-recorded) accounts of their experiences. Such material, sagely selected, will provide flavor and add meaning to the statistical documentation.

It seems useful in regard to victimless crime, as noted earlier, to separate areas of concern into (1) participants in the behaviors; (2) those close to the participants, such as family members; (3) officials with direct and indirect concern with the behavior, such as vice squad officers and elected or appointed political figures; (4) organizations with an interest in the phenomenon; and (5) the general public. The aim is to locate and document positions and changes, if any, in attitudes, acts, and consequences. Each of the victimless crime areas also will pose evaluative considerations characteristic of it. For prostitution, there is concern whether one or another social arrangement contributes to a decrease or increase in venereal infection. For homosexuality, persons want to know whether a particular arrangement leads to better "protection" or "exploitation" of underage persons by practicing homosexuals. Such questions have their own implicit value orientations, and they should not be responded to in a rote manner, but rather addressed in both their empirical and their philosophical dimensions.

Evaluators in the area of victimless crime also should be wary not to slip into the common fallacious view that decriminalization at best can be but a lesser of alternative evils. There always are arguments that can be alleged for and against any human activity, from spending one's time running the government to sitting on the beach, and these include gambling, prostitution, and homosexuality. It is the balance between positive and negative consequences (themselves value choices) that the evaluator seeks to establish. A British commission (Royal Commission on Betting, Lotteries and Gaming, 1951: 48-55) suggested that "many of [gambling's] forms involve some mental activity, and it has a social value as a general topic of conversation." In the United States, Zola (1963) and Drake and Cayton (1945), and in Britain, Newman (1968), have portrayed what they regard as worthwhile social functions served by illegal numbers gambling:

the hope that it offers of better things (but see Harrison, 1975), the companionship, the focus of interest—in short, the same kinds of things that can be said in favor of stamp-collecting, higher education, and a taste for grand opera. Activities such as numbers gambling might also serve a useful function in a minority community by providing a strong indigenous financial institution not dissimilar to the banks that cater to middle-class needs (Light, 1977). It is also important to appreciate that some activities, though by common definition regarded as undesirable, may be far preferable to what might occur were they not available. In the victimless crime area, for instance, the use of illegal heroin might be preventing psychotic breakdowns, and a preoccupation with gambling laws might be keeping the police from doing dirtier political work; or, because evidentiary issues are complex, gambling arrests might be impelling desirable case law advances. At the same time, it should also be kept in mind that illegality itself may be an eliciting force. Homosexuality, Oscar Wilde (1909) once noted, was to him like "feasting with panthers."

D. Cost Effectiveness

The question of cost effectiveness, particularly in connection with work on victimless crimes (see, for example, Weinstein and Deitch, 1974), is one that I found to be notably troublesome. It is impressive to be able to state that the expense connected with this or that policy is strikingly higher or stunningly lower than that of another policy, and that, therefore, in fiscal terms a particular policy is clearly to be preferred. Attempts have been made, including one of my own (Geis, 1977), to calculate with some exactness what it costs to enforce victimless crime laws, such as the gambling statutes. The amounts that enter into the final figures are apt to include some segment of law enforcement and court costs, as well as outlay and amortization funds for imprisonment or other control or treatment facilities. An amount spent on the activity itself also generally finds its way into the equations, though such a figure very often involves to a greater or lesser extent (indeed, as the others do too) a recirculation of funds rather than their "waste." Certainly, the implication that monies would be put to better use if not tied to victimless crime activity is unwarranted in logic or experience. In short, judiciousness would probably dictate that costs are best handled as longitudinal data—indicating a real rise or decrease in the amounts involved in particular activities and the implications to be drawn from such information—rather than as very firm bases for policy-relevant conclusions.

E. Ethics and Caveats

The area of victimless crime involves persons who often are understandably sensitive to scrutiny. Homosexuals still in the closet can have a great deal to lose if their sexual preferences become public knowledge. The evaluator should be notably sensitive to protection of individual identities. There is also the issue of quid pro quo. Evaluators tend to be irresponsible when it comes to aiding those who have assisted them in their work. Research subjects understandably are becoming less servile about serving as the guinea pigs for the career aspirations of academics and agency workers. Contributions of money always help; so do some part-time voluntary contributions of time, energy, and expertise as partial repayment, though such activity may have to be delayed until the end of the evaluation.

I have no ready answer when the ethical issue is one of truth against injury to subjects after the evaluation is in process. I wrestled with such a matter when reporting the activities of workers in a halfway house for narcotic addicts who used highly deceptive tactics in order to secure jobs for residents. If the whistle were blown, the project could well have lost its funding. If not, a significant aspect of the evaluation would have had to be omitted or distorted. I can only hope that other evaluators do not confront similar kinds of dilemmas.

MORE GENERAL CONSIDERATIONS

It must be appreciated that no evaluative conclusions in the area of victimless crime by themselves will be sufficient to dictate what policy *ought* to be adopted in regard to the behavior under scrutiny. Considerations such as those discussed below are apt to frustrate the categoric policy relevance of the most meticulous evaluative probe into one or another form of victimless crime.

A. The Issue of Clairvoyance

There is no unequivocal manner for determining the "ultimate" impact of any set of legal arrangements, yet such considerations are chronic aspects of public and professional debate about victimless crime, generally to a much greater extent than for other criminal justice matters. Opponents of decriminalization of some victimless acts who maintain that a loosening of legal reins will point the society toward surefire doom and damnation must go empirically unchallenged. They may argue, as Durant (1954) did, that societies are born stoic and die epicurean. An indecisive sort of adjudication of such a position might be attempted by means of an examination of a panorama of social systems, and an attempt to tie their social arrangements to their elan and life-span. But such an enterprise is so fraught with complexity—the problems of definition and cause and effect alone are staggering—that it is probably best left unattended. The most an evaluator can reasonably hope to accomplish is to suggest that malaise is a common concomitant of culture change, and that the dire forebodings rarely seem to eventuate. States that have decriminalized consensual homosexual acts, for example, do not seem to have become, as legislators opposed to the move had predicted they most surely would, meccas magnetically attracting hordes of gay persons from throughout the less indulgent portions of the nation (Geis et al., 1976).

At the same time, the doom-sayers may be correct, and it would be an irresponsible researcher who did not admit as much. The path to perdition persistently has been paved by the purest of pursuits, very often undertaken under the banner of benevolence for the downtrodden, be they gays, prostitutes, addicts, or whatever. Nations do disintegrate and disappear, and one of the prods might be a failure to curb hedonistic pursuits or sexual impulses of a certain sort and to focus energy as exclusively as possible on consensual goals. The wise evaluator will grant this point, perhaps stopping only long enough to argue (if he or she so believes) that a society not satisfactorily "free" (e.g., permissive) is not worth saving.

Similarly, evaluators cannot with total satisfaction illuminate "slippery slope" or "entering wedge" arguments, which also figure prominently in the area of victimless crime. These suggest that an initial move, however benign itself, should not be permitted because, at first perhaps only symbolically, but later actually, such a move will promote further concessions. To permit naked-breast photographs to be published in the mass media greases the slide to total nudity, which inevitably will be followed by readily available pictures of sexual intercourse and, ultimately, by brutalizing depictions of masochism and the sexual exploitation of children. Legal abortion is said to encourage licit euthanasia, and sanctioned consumption of marijuana to foreshadow an open market in heroin.

Here again the evaluator can hardly pretend to be a seer. It must be granted that opened wedges can and do expand. But the evaluator can insist that there is nothing inevitable about the process, and that there are numerous historical illustrations of dialectical, cyclical, and other kinds of developments, in addition to those which show a straight-line pattern. Fashions fade, opponents mobilize and prevail, circumstances alter. Sometimes, indeed, matters further down the slippery slope after a time do not seem quite so bad and intolerable as they once appeared to be—and, perhaps, reasonably so.

B. The Issue of Aesthetics

Like clairvoyance, aesthetics is beyond evaluator competence, though it forms an important element in debate about victimless crime, and a good evaluator must be aware of the dimensions of concern and seek to address them as well as possible. Congregating prostitutes may offend the sensibilities of some strollers who seek a "pleasing" street milieu and who are bothered by solicitations of sexual business, by scenes of homosexual hustling (Rechy, 1977), or by peephole shops peddling pornography. Others, of course, may find such conditions convenient or picturesque. Many who portray "unappetizing" and "degenerate" conditions as concomitants of victimless crime activity delineate the consequences that are said to accompany such arrangements, such as an increase in the number of muggings or a decline in the values of commercial enterprises. Such matters as these can be addressed by the evaluator, but the objections then are likely to shift to less determinable matters, such as the "tone" of a neighborhood, the long-range impact on the behavior of young children, or the moral integrity of the nation.

C. The Issue of Definition

The term *victimless crime* has been particularly useful polemically in focusing public and professional attention on an important—though by no means necessarily the most important—characteristic of a congery of behaviors that often are legally interdicted. The term carries a connotation or implication of something unjust or at least paradoxical. How can there be a crime without a victim, and how can someone reasonably be punished when he or she has inflicted no harm on others?

The issue, however, is not quite so simple. For one thing, despite some surface congruence, "victimless" is by no means the same as "harmless." A participant in a victimless crime can with some logic be held to be the victim of its performance (e.g., in the case of suicide or drug overdose) and most surely the behavior can have eddying consequences of a negative nature for others. It will be a most difficult task for an evaluator seeking definitional exactitude to spell out precisely what is meant by "victimless crime," and thereafter to designate those kinds of behavior which fit and those which do not fit the classification, and to spell out reasons for this judgment. Schur (1972) has suggested that a more precise stipulation for the category of victimless crimes is that it embraces acts that lack complaining witnesses—that is, that the immediate parties to the behaviors voluntarily engage in them. But it is not too difficult to analogize such victimless crimes to other behaviors about which there is apt to be widespread agreement that legal penalties ought to prevail. It is said, for instance, that narcotic trade duplicates standard commercial enterprise; there is a seller of a product and a willing buyer. But obviously all things cannot (and, most persons would agree, should not) be legally sold, including poisons and information regarding national defense, however voluntary may be the participation of the transacting parties. Perhaps the important point about the defense secrets is that they do not legitimately belong to their vendors. But even this is arguable. A wartime spy might have observed fleet movements while casually looking out of his or her oceanfront apartment window.

Perhaps a differentiating point could be that matters such as poison and defense secrets *could* be used to harm innocent others. Such suppositious sequelae probably underlie prosecution of drunken drivers and presumably can be extended to things such as the proscription of prostitution on the inferential ground that, unless all are checked, a certain number of innocent parties will be harmed by blackmail, muggings, or venereal infections. Some persons argue, however, that if it is these that we seek to prevent (i.e., muggings, blackmail), then only those who commit these acts ought to be prosecuted, and not the presumptive precursors of those acts.

For abortion, the semantic issues are less involved, though notably beyond science. The true victim is (or is not) the expelled foetus, with derivative victims sometimes being identified as the male fertilizer (who might object to the process), the almost-grandparents, and the society at large. The pregnant woman's "rights" are also a paramount issue.

In short, the realm of victimless crime resembles a vast definitional labyrinth, and sophisticated evaluators will safeguard their position along the semantic corridors by specifying precisely the nature of the behavior under review and not allowing it merely to be shorthanded as a "victimless crime." And within the major component categories—such as narcotics use, gambling, homosexuality, and prostitution—it must be appreciated that there exists a very considerable array of different acts and actors, so that conclusions regarding one form often will not extend reasonably to another. Thus, an evaluation of numbers gambling may offer little or no insight into betting on sports events, and a review of the consequences of licensed brothels in rural Nevada is apt to provide at best only a few glimmerings of understanding about the dynamics of the call girl business in Reno or Las Vegas—much less to have bearing on possible decriminalization of prostitution in, say, Ohio or Hawaii.

D. The Issue of Olives and Walnuts

How does an evaluator attach weight to disparate, nonequivalent kinds of considerations that bear upon decisions about the proper method for dealing with forms of victimless crime? The amalgam of data that an evaluator will accumulate cannot be weighed in a manner that totally responds to value concerns combined with empirical information. In the final analysis values and, probably more basically, power (Geis, 1973), are apt to determine the use, if any, that will be made of evaluative conclusions. No matter how exquisitely drawn their terms of inquiry (and how these are drawn is a value-laden matter), evaluators cannot resolve through research the importance that *ought* to be attached to the things that they discover. This issue may sometimes be finessed (though never resolved) by prior determination or agreement about "relevant" matters and stipulated hypotheses as precursors to policy conclusions. Thus, it can be concluded that an experimental decriminalization of prostitution will be made permanent in two years' time if: (1) there is a decrease in the forcible rape rate; (2) there is no change or there is a reduction in the amount of venereal disease coming to the attention of private doctors and health authorities; (3) there is a reduction of at least 50 percent in the number of known prostitutes under the age of 16; and (4) after the experimental period, the new arrangements receive the endorsement of two-thirds of the citizens living within three miles of the area to which prostitution will be confined by law. If all of these conditions are not met, the jurisdiction will return to its prior ban on prostitution.

Items 1 through 4, of course, are arbitrary conditions declared by one or more interest groups. For behaviors such as prostitution, it could be argued that more "fundamental" issues should prevail. Some might maintain that the views of the prostitutes ought to carry the matter, while others, such as Brownmiller (1975), would insist that prostitution must be outlawed because otherwise it denigrates the position of women by defining them as sex objects readily available to those who can rent them. Such principles are believed by their adherents to be more important than considerations such as crime statistics or popular or official viewpoints.

Another illustration might help explicate this point. It may be found by an evaluator that a policy permitting heroin to be marketed in the same fashion as cigarettes or Swiss chocolate (Geis, 1968) seems to have produced, among other things, each of the following results in an experimental site vis-à-vis a comparison jurisdiction: (1) a decrease of 25 percent in the number of drug-related deaths; (2) an increase of 17 percent in the number of persons using heroin, combined with a 25 percent decline in the amounts of heroin that they use; (3) a decrease of 13 percent in the number of burglary and other property crimes reported to the police; (4) a movement of "organized crime" elements out of the narcotics field and into cigarette-smuggling, resulting in a tax loss of about $600,000 annually; (5) a 7 percent decline in public confidence in the ability of authorities to control crime in the jurisdiction, most marked in the working-class population, combined with a 4 percent rise in endorsement of the governing party; (6) an inflow of about 2 percent in the number of persons entering the jurisdiction who participate in the new heroin sales approach; (7) a savings of $500,000 yearly in police, courts, and other criminal justice costs formerly incurred to enforce the heroin statute, combined with an outlay of $65,000 to monitor the new program. The savings do not return to the general fund, but have been used to upgrade law enforcement salaries and equipment, an approach which does not, at least for the short run, appear to have made much difference in terms of arrest rates for personal or property offenses.

It is evident that persons of goodwill and intelligence examining these conclusions can sincerely reach quite different decisions concerning proper policy. They need neither distort nor underplay nor overlook the evaluative findings in order to mount an honest defense of diametrically opposed positions. Perhaps more subtle is the fact that no preordained formula has dictated for the evaluator that all of the foregoing items are to be studied. It is perfectly possible that one evaluator might limit an inquiry to only those facets of the issue that provide ammunition for persons favoring a particular policy line. The illustration should be taken as emphasis for the point that in the area of victimless crime it is necessary to concentrate on a very wide variety of issues, and that assiduous attention to the research agenda is essential. The evaluation ought to attempt to encompass as many as possible of the matters of importance that are seen to be basic by *all* parties with an interest in the question. It is a formidable task. Left undone, it is apt to result in a skewed, lopsided data bank.

E. The Issue of Advocacy

For the "concerned" evaluator, an important question becomes the advisability of moving from a more or less objective investigative role into a position of advocacy. A particularly notable illustration of such a movement can be found in the work of Chein and his associates (1964). They recounted with some dispassion the dynamics of heroin addiction in the New York slums, and then moved to a passionate humanistic plea for what they believed to be a more decent and considerate public policy. The essence of their advocacy position lay far afield in most respects from their findings. It was based on the view that heroin addiction often is an adaptation to intolerable social conditions, and that it was cruel beyond understanding to allow such conditions to prevail and then to victimize further the addict who took one of the few possible means available to escape the tyranny of his or her social position.

The subject of the scientist-advocate was thoroughly debated as an aftermath of the unleashing of the hydrogen bomb on Japan. There is no need to repeat the discussion at any length. Suffice it to say that a major consideration for adoption of an advocacy position, as I see the issue, is that no one is apt to be so thoroughly versed in the nuances of the matter as the evaluator. On the other side lies the fact that politicians, as policy makers, have constituencies that selected them and to which they ultimately are responsible, a situation at best only minimally true of the evaluator as advocate. Equally notable is the fact that when evaluators enter the public arena to press for policy, the objectivity of their findings is apt to come under suspicion. Also, the evaluator is likely to be regarded ever after as partisan rather than impartial.

All things considered, I strongly favor evaluators forcefully taking part in public debate once they have concluded their reports. Unfortunately, however, when they do debate, evaluators often fail to exercise the excruciating care necessary to distinguish between what they have found and what they believe on less-than-unarguable evidence. Nonetheless, I regard it as a default of citizenship to sit back and allow one's findings to proceed unchaperoned into the public domain. But evaluators ought not succumb to the all-too-human tendency to believe that competence in one area is widely generalizable, in the manner that motion picture stars pontificate on foreign policy, the morality of the young, and other matters in regard to which neither acting talent nor good looks provide satisfactory expertise.

In summary, it can be noted that the fundamental point of this section—the mixture of values and evaluation—bears especially hard in the area of victimless crime. These offenses are legally proscribed because of a very considerable range of considerations: aesthetic, fiscal, moral, prejudicial, medical, social defense, public opinion, class, power, welfare, criminal law, and derivative considerations all tend to become involved in decisions about victimless crime. A thorough evaluator ought to attempt to tap as many of these dimensions as possible.

F. The Issue of Generalizability

There are a number of logical pitfalls that tend to waylay the unwary evaluator in the territory of victimless crime. Momentous issues of generalizability inevitably arise after evaluators examine naturally occurring phenomena. That homosexuality has been decriminalized in, say, Kansas, without contributing notably to predicted horrors, by no means demonstrates that the same benign consequences will recur in Montana or Illinois. Obviously, there is a need for comparable scrutiny of diverse settings, so that a plethora of equivalent findings lends greater credence to predictive statements, or diverse findings encourage the isolation of significant variables.

Nonetheless, considerable restraint must be exercised in moving beyond the particular circumstances that mark the experimental condition. I pass along in this regard the cautionary tale related some three decades ago by Thomas McCormick, my statistics instructor at the University of Wisconsin.

A farmer, the class was informed, had obtained a bumper crop of potatoes when he used 12 pounds of nitrate fertilizer. He did even better when he doubled that amount. A further increment of fertilizer, however, resulted in the total destruction of the crop. The lesson pressed home to us in the gentle southern drawl of our professor was: "Don't extrapolate beyond the data."

Problems in logic also occur if an evaluator bases a recommendation for change on what is found to have resulted from a naturally arising event. The fact that "good" results, by specified standards, ensued when jurisdiction A decriminalized possession of small amounts of marijuana does not mean that there will be similar outcomes in jurisdiction B, even if the second jurisdiction seems to be much the same as the first. The satisfactory outcome in A may have been dictated by precisely those considerations that originally led to the change in the law. The conditions that have delayed the law's change in jurisdiction B might also frustrate presumed expectations if the change is instituted on the basis of the experience of jurisdiction A. The point perhaps might more clearly be made by consideration of an evaluation that showed that a spontaneously occurring dispersion of inner-city delinquents to the suburbs was accompanied by a significant decline in their lawbreaking. This does *not* signify that a housing policy that forces dispersion will produce the same results, or, even if it does, that those results will be the consequence of similar processes. The first dispersion well might have been the consequence of parental attitudes that led to the quest for a "safer" environment for children; without such attitudes, a forced geographic exodus might not produce an equivalent outcome.

FINAL STATEMENT

The area of victimless crime shares with other segments of the criminal justice system generic evaluative problems, while at the same time presenting some unique features. In particular, through its close tie to a range of moral questions (Hart, 1963; Devlin, 1965), the area at times poses notoriously complex evaluative dilemmas. Note, for instance, that virtually all debate on capital punishment tends to focus on whether or not the punishment is an effective deterrent, despite the fact that numerous other matters clearly can be said to bear significantly on the proper employment of the death penalty. Such a concentration of concern is anything but characteristic of debates about matters such as consensual homosexuality, abortion, gambling, and prostitution.

The issues involved in the victimless crime area are diverse and provide considerable intellectual stimulation. They are of fundamental importance, touching directly on basic matters of human freedom and right. It is in these regards particularly that evaluative work in the area of victimless crime provides unusually strong challenges and offers, if well done, particularly attractive satisfactions.

REFERENCES

Barrow, L. (1969) *Compulsion: One of the Major Neuroses of Our Times.* Sydney, Australia: West.

Beale, D. and C. Goldman (1974) *Easy Money: Report of the Task Force on Legalized Gambling.* New York: Twentieth Century Fund.

Blakely, G. R. and H. A. Kurland (1978) "The Development of the Federal Law of Gambling." *Cornell Law Review* 63 (August): 923-1021.

Breen, T. H. (1977) "The Cultural Significance of Gambling Among the Gentry of Virginia." *William and Mary Quarterly* 48, 2: 239-257.

Brooks, J. (1975) "State Lotteries: Profits and Problems." *State Government* 48 (Winter): 23-31.

Brownmiller, S. (1975) *Against Our Will.* New York: Simon & Schuster.

Chafetz, H. (1960) *A History of Gambling in the United States from 1492 to 1955.* New York: Potter.

Chein, I., D. L. Gerard, R. S. Lee, and E. Rosenfeld (1964) *The Road to H: Narcotics, Delinquency, and Social Policy*. New York: Basic Books.

Commission on the Review of the National Policy Toward Gambling (1976) *Gambling in America: Final Report*. Washington, DC: Government Printing Office.

Cornell Law School Gambling Project (1975) *The Development of the Law of Gambling: Federal*. Washington, DC: Commission on the Review of the National Policy Toward Gambling.

Cornish, D. B. (1977) *Gambling: A Review of the Literature and Its Implications for Policy and Research. Home Office Research Unit Report*. London: Her Majesty's Stationary Office.

Devlin, P. (1965) *The Enforcement of Morals*. London: Oxford University Press.

Downes, E., B. P. Davies, M. E. David, and P. Stone (1976) *Gambling, Work and Leisure*. London: Routledge & Kegan Paul.

Drake, S. C. and H. R. Cayton (1945) *Black Metropolis*. New York: Harcourt Brace Jovanovich.

Durant, W. (1954) *Our Oriental Heritage*. New York: Simon & Schuster.

Edwards, D. L. (1974) "Preface," pp. 5-6 in G. Moody, *Social Control of Gambling*. London: Churches' Council on Gambling.

Fact Research Inc. (1974) *Gambling in Perspective*. Washington, DC: Commission on the Review of the National Policy Toward Gambling.

Fogelberg, C. (1973) *Legalized Numbers in Washington*. Washington, DC: Washington Lawyers' Committee.

Geis, G. (1978) "Illicit Use of Central Nervous System Stimulants in Sweden." *Journal of Drug Issues* 8 (Spring): 189-197.

——— (1977) "The Criminal Justice System Without Victimless Crimes," pp. 212-217 in P. Wickman (ed.) *Readings in Social Problems*. New York: Harper & Row.

——— (1973) "Abortion and Prostitution: A Matter of Respectability." *The Nation* 217 (September 3): 179-180.

——— (1972) *Not the Law's Business?: An Examination of Homosexuality, Abortion, Prostitution, Narcotics, and Gambling in the United States*. Washington, DC: Government Printing Office.

——— (1968) "The Fable of a Fatty." *Issues in Criminology* 3 (Spring): 211-214.

——— R. Wright, T. Garrett, and P. Wilson (1976) "Reported Consequences of Decriminalization of Consensual Adult Homosexuality in Seven American States." *Journal of Homosexuality* 1 (Summer): 419-426.

Royal Commission on Betting, Lotteries and Gaming, 1949-1951 (1951) *Report [Command 8190]*. London: His Majesty's Stationary Office.

Harrison, P. (1975) "The Gambling Class." *New Society* 31 (March 20): 720-722.

Hart, H.L.A. (1963) *Law, Liberty, and Morality*. Stanford, CA: Stanford University Press.

Hendrix, L. P. (1978) "Lotteries: Small Church Raffles or Big Time Gaming?" *Nebraska Law Review* 57, 1: 175-198.

Kusyszyn, I. (1978) " 'Compulsive' Gambling: The Problem of Definition." *International Journal of the Addictions* 13, 7: 1095-1101.

Lesieur, H. (1979) "The Compulsive Gambler's Spiral of Options and Involvement." *Psychiatry* 42 (February): 79-88.

Light, I. (1977) "Numbers Gambling Among Blacks: A Financial Institution." *American Sociological Review* 42 (December): 892-904.

Martinez, T. (1977) "Gambling, Goods, and Games." *Society* 14 (September-October): 79-81.

Moody, G. E. (1974) *Social Control of Gambling*. London: Churches' Council on Gambling.

Moran, E. (1970) "Pathological Gambling." *Journal of Hospital Medicine* 4, 1: 59-70.

Newman, O. (1968) "The Sociology of the Betting Shop." *British Journal of Sociology* 19 (March): 17-33.

Oldman, D. (1978) "Compulsive Gamblers" *Sociological Review* 26 (May): 349-371.

Rechy, J. (1977) *The Sexual Outlaw.* New York: Grove Press.

Schur, E. (1972) "Victimless Crime." New York Times (January 18): 34.

——— (1965) *Crimes Without Victims.* Englewood Cliffs, NJ: Prentice-Hall.

——— and H. Bedau (1974) *Victimless Crimes: Two Sides of a Controversy.* Englewood Cliffs, NJ: Prentice-Hall.

Schelling, T. C. (1967) "Economic Analysis of Organized Crime," pp. 114-123 in President's Commission on Law Enforcement and Administration of Justice, *Task Force Report: Organized Crime.* Washington, DC: Government Printing Office.

Skolnick, J. H. (1978) *The Legalization and Control of Casino Gambling.* Boston: Little, Brown.

Smith, A. B. and H. Pollack (1975) *Some Sins Are Not Crimes.* New York: New Viewpoints.

Stephens, T. B. (1977) "Japanese Traditional Attitudes to Law." *World Review* 16 (March): 27-36.

Tuite, J. (1978) "Would Benefits of Legalized Betting on Sports Outweigh the Drawbacks?" New York Times (December 19): 24.

Weinstein, D. and L. Deitch (1974) *The Impact of Legalized Gambling.* New York: Praeger.

Wilde, O. (1909) *De Profundis.* New York: G. P. Putnam.

Winterscheid, J. F. (1977) "Victimless Crimes: The Threshold Question and Beyond." *Notre Dame Lawyer* 52 (June): 995-1014.

Zola, I. K. (1963) "Observations on Gambling in a Lower-Class Setting." *Social Problems* 10 (Spring): 353-361.

16

Discretion and Bias: The Selection Problems in Evaluation

Don C. Gibbons

INTRODUCTION

The Problem

Who would accept the claim that participation in the Boy Scouts prevents delinquency, solely on the strength of observations that few Eagle Scouts can be found in prison? Only a very naive person would find much merit in that argument, for it is obvious that Eagle Scouts (and other Boy Scouts) are recruited from the larger category of middle-class conformists, most of whom avoid entanglement in the criminal justice system principally because their social ties "insulate" them from deviance. Scouting per se probably contributes little or nothing to the prevention of youthful misconduct.

Along this same line, most persons with even slight knowledge about probation agencies in operation would be loath to contend that those organizations are directly responsible for the very high success rates reported for persons on probation. Many observers have pointed out that various sifting and sorting processes go on in the courts, so that low-risk, prosocial, "self-correctors" end up on probation, where most of them receive little or nothing in the way of treatment services (England, 1957; Diana, 1955; Hartjen and Gibbons, 1969). These individuals show little involvement in or commitment to criminality, a considerable "stake in conformity," and supportive ties to conventional persons and law-abiding lines of activity. It is these characteristics of probationers that are responsible for their good behavior on probation or in the postprobation period, rather than supervision itself or the treatment intervention which they are supposed to receive but in fact rarely experience while on probation.

AUTHOR'S NOTE: Professor Joseph F. Jones provided a good deal of useful commentary and criticism of a draft of this chapter.

However, citizens and correctional workers have not always been so knowledgeable on these matters. Erroneous contentions about the efficacy of various correctional intervention programs, based upon spurious relationships of the sort noted above, have been widely advanced and widely accepted in the past. There has been a good deal of exuberant applause for probation, based upon the belief that probation officers deliver effective treatment to lawbreakers and that it is these intervention endeavors that account for low recidivism rates. The fact that probation agencies have dealt mainly with low-risk, "square John" individuals has not always been apparent to the proponents of probation. Others have offered parallel, naive claims about the alleged benefits of Scouting, participation in the Jaycees, and myriad other correction efforts. These commentators apparently have been unaware of the fact that these programs have been focused upon a clientele of offenders, most of whom are not in need of intensive intervention services and who would probably refrain from further lawbreaking even if they received no treatment or assistance.

A second and more important point is that problems of discretionary decision-making, sifting and sorting processes, and the like continue to operate within the criminal and juvenile justice systems in various ways which are less apparent than in the case of probation. These discretionary activities often allocate to one part of the justice machinery groups and cohorts of offenders who differ in important ways from lawbreakers who are sent off to other way stations in that social apparatus. It is these problems of discretion and bias about which the researcher and research consumer must become informed in order to make sense of program evaluation reports about specific correctional programs.

Consider the case of an apparently effective treatment institution for delinquent females, reported a few years ago (Adamek and Dager, 1968). This inquiry indicated that a Catholic-operated House of Good Shepherd located in a midwestern state succeeded in producing identification with the school and its staff on the part of many of the female wards. In turn, those young women who came to identify with the institution also showed positive changes in self-esteem and improvement in other psychological characteristics during their stay in the school. Finally, these results were brought about through a relatively repressive and spartan school regimen which included rules requiring silence on the part of the youngsters, a system of demerits, and few parental visits, leavened with some more positive institutional features.

One would be ill-advised to assume that this intervention model can be transferred with minimal difficulty to a variety of other institutional settings and that such a program would be equally effective wherever located. To begin with, it is not unlikely that this set of strategies would be unworkable in training schools for male delinquents, in that these youngsters differ in a number of important ways from female offenders. The evidence (Vinter et al., 1976; Gibbons and Griswold, 1957; Rogers, 1972; Chesney-Lind, 1973) indicates that the latter have frequently been involved in less serious delinquencies than training-school males, but that at the same time, they receive more severe dispositions from juvenile courts than do comparable male offenders. In addition, female delinquents are less involved in supportive antisocial peer groups than are males and they have experienced a pattern of sex-role socialization that sets them off from the latter. For reasons of this kind, they are probably more tractable than male wards, who would be considerably more likely to engage in rambunctious rebellion against such an institutional program.

It is not at all clear that this House of Good Shepherd structure could be successfully implemented elsewhere, even if efforts to do so were restricted to training schools for females. Wards in state-operated training schools vary in important ways from youngsters who are found in private institutions. Private agencies and schools enjoy the luxury of being able to "skim off the cream" of female delinquents because, unlike state institutions, they are able to accept or reject court referrals. As a result, these places end up with relatively-young, unsophisticated charges, while the state schools receive a disproportionate number of older, more intractable wards who have been rejected as unsuitable cases for treatment by the private agencies. For example, the institution studied by Adamek and Dager selectively admitted youths over 13 years of age who had completed at least eight years of school and who were judged by the staff to have "a potential for benefitting from the program." In the light of this "creaming" activity, one ought to be chary of generalizations about this program as an effective one for all female institutions. Parenthetically, selective acceptance of referrals by private institutions is not restricted to females. For example, Lerman (1968) noted that "Boysville," a private training school in New York, accepted only one out of every eighteen boys referred to it. Many other cases of this kind could probably be uncovered.

Another revealing example drawn from the correctional field has been reported by Duxbury (1971), who conducted a study of nine experimental youth services bureaus that were established in California communities in 1969. The rationale behind these agencies was that they would reduce the juvenile court caseloads in those communities because many youngsters would be diverted to the bureaus instead of referred to the court. Duxbury indicated that the bureaus did provide services to over 1800 youths during a nine-month period in 1970. However, she also observed (Duxbury, 1971: i) that "although it was anticipated that the bulk of referrals would be from law enforcement and probation, only about one-third of the youth served have been from these sources." Instead of operating as an alternative to the juvenile court, siphoning off referrals from the official justice machinery, these bureaus dealt primarily with self-referrals and youngsters sent by their parents or their schools, in part because of the reluctance of the police and courts to send cases to them. Other, more recent, experiences with youth services bureaus and diversion programs have turned up parallel results, in which "widening of the nets" has occurred. Many of these operations have been shown to have dealt with large numbers of referrals who would probably not have been funneled into the juvenile justice machinery in the absence of these alternative agencies. Given these observations, it would be inappropriate to argue that youth bureaus and diversion programs represent effective alternatives to juvenile court processing.

This chapter is concerned with the sifting and sorting of offenders and alleged offenders that goes on at various decision points in the juvenile and criminal justice systems. However, the focus is less upon the collation of all of the evidence on system operations and differential decision-making than it is on the implications of these processes for evaluation research activities.

The sifting and sorting processes and outcomes to be examined comprise a large body of phenomena taking a variety of forms. However, most of these can be sorted into two relatively distinctive groupings. The first involves the *routine decision-making activities of justice system employees,* through which peculiar or distinctive cohorts or groups of offenders and alleged lawbreakers become allocated to one part of the social control structure or another. The concentrations in probation caseloads of petty or casual miscreants who have engaged in transitory acts of lawbreaking and of career-oriented lawbreakers in penal institutions quickly come to mind as relevant examples of these sorting operations.

Researchers and research consumers need to be aware of these processes and outcomes if they are to make sense of program evaluation results. In particular, they must be able to specify the characteristics of the subjects or targets of the program with considerable precision, so that appropriate conclusions and inferences can be drawn regarding the results (or lack of positive evidence of treatment impact) that turn up in evaluation studies.

The second general category of sifting and sorting processes centers around *the activities of experimenters and researchers, or persons who are implicated in decisions about research study populations,* that produce distinctive or distorted research samples. For example, relatively peculiar or narrow samples of offenders have been selected for a treatment-research project, but the designers of the intervention experiment have not always been careful to specify the special nature of the study group or to limit their conclusions to that sample of offenders. Then, too, individuals have sometimes been dropped from an experimental program caseload on the grounds that they were "unsuitable," "not amenable to treatment," or in some other way inappropriate subjects for treatment. However, those persons have later been ignored in the reports of program outcomes, instead of being counted as "program failures" when the correctional effort in question has been compared with a control group program outcome.

These two rubrics subsume a number of individual forms and examples. The commentary to follow is organized around these two basic groupings and is designed to provide some guidance to researchers so that the problems of bias and distortion can be identified, addressed, and thereby minimized in evaluation research efforts.

Discretion, Discrimination, and Bias

Day-to-day *discretionary* decision-making by employees within various parts of the correctional apparatus is a vast and pervasive fact of life, as is also *discriminatory* decision-making, which is a particularly vexing form of discretionary action. Discretionary decision-making refers to such matters as differential enforcement of particular laws, as in the case of police tolerance of certain forms of gambling or prostitution, or of police policies against making arrests for speeding in cases where persons have only slightly exceeded the speed limit. Discretionary decision-making also includes such things as the placement of low-risk offenders on probation at the same time that more serious lawbreakers are sent off to prison. Discriminatory decision-making points to actions taken against offenders because of sexual, racial, or other legally irrelevant characteristics of those individuals. For example, the police in some cities enforce curfew statutes only in the case of blacks, using these laws as a device for keeping black youths within their ghetto neighborhoods. More serious and frequently encountered charges that the police employ unnecessary and gratuitous physical violence in arrests of blacks or that the death penalty has been carried out most often against lower-class and/or black offenders quickly come to mind as other illustrations of discriminatory decision-making.

Discretionary and discriminatory decision-making cannot be covered in detail in a brief chapter. Although some of the dimensions of these phenomena are dealt with below, the reader would do well to examine some of the more comprehensive discussions of these topics (Gibbons, 1976: 16-34; Gibbons, 1979: 80-84; Nettler, 1978: 87-117; Reiss, 1976).

A few additional remarks are in order concerning the use of the notion of bias in the discussion in this chapter. Discretionary decisions about offenders, made on the basis of the racial, sexual, or socioeconomic characteristics of those persons rather than in terms of legally relevant attributes of lawbreakers, come closest to the meaning of *bias* as that term is employed by laypersons. However, one can also speak of bias and biased samples insofar as the nondiscriminatory differential or discretionary decision-making of law enforcement and correctional employees leads to peculiar or distinctive groupings of offenders being collected up at particular system points, at the same time that these cohorts or groups are assumed to be representative of the broader offender population. Finally, biases can also be said to exist insofar as researchers deliberately go about manipulating one or another element of a program research design so as to produce results favorable to the treatment strategy being examined by the research. Examples of all three of these forms of bias are presented below.

SIFTING AND SORTING IN THE JUVENILE AND CRIMINAL JUSTICE SYSTEMS

"The Dark Figure of Crime"

The beginning point in this discussion is "hidden crime" and "hidden delinquency," or what many criminologists have designated as "the dark figure of crime." Many offenders do not turn up anyplace in the criminal or juvenile justice systems; hence, they do not become subject to the sifting and sorting decisions with which this chapter is concerned.

One facet of "the dark figure of crime and delinquency" is that many "garden-variety offenders," that is, persons who have committed relatively crude and unsophisticated burglaries, larcenies, robberies, assaults, and the like, do not get caught up in the justice system. The number of criminal acts committed is so large, evidence upon which to base an arrest is so skimpy, and police resources are so restricted, that most lawbreakers run a very low risk of being apprehended. Moreover, in the case of those offenders who do eventually become subjects of this social machinery, many of their acts of lawbreaking remain unknown or unsolved by the authorities. The research investigations of "hidden delinquency" and "hidden crime" have more than amply documented these conclusions (e.g., Gibbons, 1976; 16-34; Tittle and Villemez, 1977), as have also the numerous victimization studies carried on in recent years by the federal government (Bureau of the Census, 1978).

However, "the dark figure of crime" includes more than the undetected acts of garden-variety lawbreakers, for it also involves white-collar offenses carried on by corporation executives and representatives of business organizations but which are rarely recorded in standard sources of data on crime, such as the FBI Uniform Crime Reports, a tabulation that is restricted to crimes such as robbery, larceny, auto theft, rape, and homicide. Nonetheless, there is abundant evidence of other kinds which points to the ubiquity of white-collar crime in America (Gibbons, 1977). The remainder of this chapter pays little attention to white-collar crime, due to the fact that program evaluation studies are rarely concerned with corporate or business criminals, a fact which in no way diminishes the criminological, economic, or social significance of upper-world lawbreaking.

Is Garden-Variety Crime Class-Linked?

There are few, if any, informed persons who would disagree with the contention that the social control machinery begins its processing with a biased sample of all offenders, for white-collar criminals rarely are drawn into the criminal justice system. However, there is considerably less consensus on the question of the extent to which apprehended offenders represent a biased subgroup of garden-variety lawbreakers. Although many of the criminal acts of conventional offenders go unrecognized or unsolved, that fact alone does not mean that apprehended miscreants differ in significant ways from those who have not been arrested, in that the former may actually constitute a representative sample of the latter.

Examination of the social backgrounds of apprehended law violators shows that many of them are relatively young, male, black, and from lower-income backgrounds. Many criminologists contend that both apprehended and undetected garden-variety lawbreakers come most frequently from such backgrounds. According to this view, conventional crime is most common among socially disadvantaged groups. If that argument is on the mark, biases revolving around economic and ethnic characteristics are not major determinants of the composition of the sample of detected offenders.

However, other observers have argued that the characteristics exhibited by apprehended persons are not correlates of criminality; rather, they are indicators of what one criminologist called "categoric risks" (Reckless, 1950: 57), or what social labeling theorists term "background contingencies" (Gibbons and Jones, 1975)—that is, social characteristics upon which discriminatory police actions are based. In short, this argument holds that conventional delinquents and criminals are not concentrated in lower-income populations; instead, the police act differentially toward lower-class individuals, arresting them at the same time that they remain unaware of or unconcerned about the violations of middle-class offenders.

The truth probably lies somewhere between the positions sketched here. There is evidence that the police do sometimes deal more leniently with middle-class offenders than they do with comparable lower-income ones. At the same time, the thesis advanced by some (Tittle et al., 1978), that garden-variety crime and delinquency, particularly the more serious instances of this behavior, are distributed equally across social class levels, seems unconvincing. Most of the research studies that are cited in support of that claim suffer from a variety of methodological problems, including the use of truncated questionnaire scales which fail to include items from the more serious end of the range of criminal offenses, such as rape, robbery, aggravated assault, burglary, and the like (Gibbons, 1976: 16-34; Nettler, 1978: 87-117). Moreover, one recent and methodologically sophisticated survey of a national sample of juveniles turned up clear evidence of socioeconomic differentials in delinquency (Elliott and Ageton, 1978).

Nettler's position on this issue is judicious and convincing, holding that garden-variety offenders are most frequently encountered among the economically and socially disadvantaged. He noted that "confessions of delinquency, surveys of victims, test situations, direct and indirect observations, and official records point to similar social sites in both developing countries and industrialized states as producing more murderers, muggers, rapists, robbers, burglars, and heavy thieves than others" (Nettler, 1978: 117). But Nettler's view only rejects the extreme argument that garden-variety crime is wholly unrelated to social class. This conclusion does not by any means deny completely the existence of significant patterns of discretionary action taken against apprehended garden-variety offenders, nor does it reject the possibility that biases based upon social backgrounds of specific offenders enter into the dispositions made of them in the justice system. It is to these matters that attention now turns.

Discretion, Bias, and Garden Variety Criminality

What are some of the major conclusions regarding selection processes, discretionary actions, and biases in the handling of apprehended offenders? Although the following generalizations gloss over a good many of the detailed findings, they are reasonable ones drawn from the available data.

First, as the preceding commentary has already argued, the juvenile and adult justice systems most often operate selectively, scooping up a clientele of persons who have committed offenses of some degree of seriousness. For the most part, these individuals have been more involved in criminality than many of those persons who are not subjects of justice system intervention. In short, the justice systems do not operate in an entirely capricious or discriminatory manner.

Juvenile Offenders. Offense seriousness ia a major factor which determines whether an apprehended juvenile will be thrust into the juvenile justice machinery or diverted out of it by the police. But in addition, police dispositions tend to be related to demographic characteristics of offenders; thus, males, blacks, lower-income youths, and older boys are more frequently dealt with formally by court referral. These demographic characteristics enter into dispositions in part because older males, blacks, and lower-income youngsters appear to be disproportionately involved in serious, repetitive delinquencies. However, some studies (Gibbons, 1976: 38-46) have indicated that the police discriminate against blacks, sending more of them to juvenile court than they do whites involved in comparable offenses.

Juvenile females are most frequently charged with status offenses when they appear in juvenile court, and particularly with allegations centering around sexual misconduct. At the same time, there is some evidence to indicate that property offenses are not infrequent among undetected female delinquents (Chesney-Lind, 1973; Wise, 1967), giving rise to the suspicion of discrimination against female offenders. That is, some have argued that the police tend to ignore acts of theft on the part of girls and concentrate their attention upon suspected sexual misconduct.

Moving to the juvenile court and court decisions, a fourth conclusion is that dispositions such as informal probation, formal probation, or institutionalization are most frequently based upon offense seriousness and the offender's prior record; thus, those youngsters who are viewed by court workers as most intractable are most likely to be shunted off to training schools (Scarpitti and Stephenson, 1971). However, there is also evidence pointing to discrimination in dispositions against blacks and females (Chesney-Lind, 1973; Rogers, 1972). Finally, although firm data are lacking on this point, it is likely that rural juvenile courts often take harsher dispositional actions against juveniles than do urban courts.

Adult Criminals. Although apprehended and system-processed lawbreakers tend to be drawn from among the group of more serious offenders, it is also the case that they constitute a diverse collection of persons, so that much justice system sifting and sorting of these individuals takes place. In general, petty offenders and "folk criminals" (Ross, 1961; Hartjen and Gibbons, 1969) tend to be most common in probation caseloads or among those who receive fines or jail terms.

Although prison inmates generally comprise a grouping of more serious offenders, some qualifications to that contention are in order. For one thing, a goodly number of criminally unsophisticated "square John" prisoners are encountered in state and federal prisons (Schrag, 1961; Garabedian, 1964). Although criminal courts tend to send persons who have relatively extensive records of prior criminality and who have been convicted of serious offenses to prison most frequently, they also respond to cries of outrage in the press or the community and to other factors of that kind, with the result that a number of individuals who do not need to be kept in close confinement and who represent low-risk cases in terms of recidivism are nonetheless shunted off to prison. In these terms, at least, the latter represent less serious cases than do the former. Manslaughter and homicide cases stand as relevant examples. Then, too, it appears that judges in rural courts not infrequently sentence persons to prison who would not be imprisoned had they appeared in a court in a metropolitan area.

The extent of discriminatory sentencing of felons to prison and to other, less serious, dispositions is still unclear. One investigation which examined prison sentences received by convicts in three southern states (Chiricos and Waldo, 1975) concluded that sentence lengths were unrelated to socioeconomic status; hence, it did not appear that discrimination operated in sentencing. However, that study was not definitive, for it may well be that discriminatory sentencing takes place principally at the criminal court level, with blacks and relatively lower-income persons more frequently being committed to prison than higher status offenders involved in comparable offenses. Discriminatory sentencing of that kind would be masked in data dealing only with the length of prison terms for those who were incarcerated. Indeed, the authors of this study have reported findings from another investigation, in which discriminatory decisions were made at an earlier stage of justice system processing (Chiricos et al., 1972). Other investigators have also turned up evidence of discriminatory sentence-setting (Gibson, 1978).

Within penal settings, a good deal of discretionary decision-making takes place in the form of policies which send relatively petty, low-risk, "square John" offenders to minimum security facilities, work-release centers, and into prison rehabilitation programs. The more serious, career-oriented prisoners are likely to be found in maximum security settings and in prison programs where they perform routine maintenance tasks or spend much of their time in "yard out," that is, in congregate idleness in the prison compound.

A final point regarding adult offenders is that although differential decision-making is most often carried on by correctional decision makers such as judges or prison officials, processes of *self-selection* for and *self-allocation* to correctional dispositions also occur. For example, persons who opt to participate in individual therapy programs within prison are often "square Johns," persons who exhibit few of the procriminal attitudes that therapy is supposed to eradicate. Those individuals who are in educational or vocational training programs within institutions also are often inmates who are least in need of intensive assistance or treatment. Drug treatment programs that center around various verbal therapies have few if any lower-class addicts in them; instead, they attract voluble, introspective middle-class drug users. Similarly, recruits to Alcoholics Anonymous rarely come from skid row; instead, they are usually middle-class alcoholics who define themselves as in need of help and who exhibit supportive ties to spouses and friends.

Evaluation Research Implications

What are the research implications of the preceding observations? Although they may be fairly self-evident, and while the recommendations regarding them offered below are hardly profound, it would be well, nonetheless, to make these implications and recommendations quite explicit.

A few prefatory comments about program evaluation methods and strategies are in order. Discussions of program evaluation methodology and procedures have often indicated that evaluation studies come down to three interrelated assessments, that is, questions to be answered about some correctional endeavor (Gibbons et al., 1976). Put simply, the queries that are directed to the agency are: (1) Do the agency "clients" really look like you thought they would? (2) Did you do what you said you were going to do, in the way of program efforts? (3) Did what you did with the offenders have any effect upon them? In the more technical evaluation literature, these are often referred to as *effectiveness, efficiency,* and *impact* evaluations.

The first of these queries is of concern here. It must be obvious that researchers who intend to go about program evaluation efforts need to know a good deal about "people-processing" operations, that is, dispositional processes and discretionary decision-making within the criminal and juvenile justice systems which sift and sort offenders into groupings if they are to produce evaluations having real impact. Program evaluation in the justice systems, whether carried on by academic or entrepreneurial research agencies, ought to be informed by detailed knowledge about the peculiarities of the offender population and various subgroups within it. Where is that knowledge to be found? Most of it is collected in criminology and delinquency textbooks and in relevant journals, so that the researcher would do well to immerse himself or herself in that literature or, in short, to take a crash course in criminology if he or she is deficient in this area.

The preceding question about agency clients implies that correctional programs usually operate on the basis of an "image of the offender" or specification of the agency clientele that is held clearly in mind by those who manage the agency; thus, the research task is to determine whether the actual clients or wards match this image. However, a frequently encountered situation in correctional settings is that evaluation researchers are called upon to spell out the major characteristics or defining attributes of the clientele being dealt with by some program, because the program personnel are only able to offer the vaguest of hints as to who is being processed by the endeavor in question. For example, in the case of a youth employment and assistance agency with which the author has been affiliated in Portland, Oregon, the administrators of that operation indicated no clear awareness of what segment of the delinquent (and non-delinquent) population was being served by its job-finding and -counseling efforts. In this instance, a program evaluator studying this correctional effort would be faced with the tasks of identifying the offender subgroup receiving services and specifying how that group differs from other lawbreakers within the community, so that others could become aware of the characteristics of the group under study, the peculiarities of that cohort that set it off from other offender groups, and kindred matters.

In other instances, agencies are able to offer clearer indications of the client group that is supposed to be the target of treatment or intervention. Even so, the researcher-evaluator needs to be able to locate that target group within the larger population of lawbreakers and must be able to offer relatively clear indications of how it differs from other offender subgroups.

It should come as no surprise to the evaluation researcher to find that the actual targets of an agency program sometimes turn out to be different from the intended ones because of discretionary decision-making by correctional decision makers. Consider the situation in Oregon, where a statewide network of privately operated youth care facilities has developed, providing "treatment modalities" or particular programs varying from one facility to the other, directed at juveniles that have been sent to them by juvenile courts. The youth care facilities are supported by state funds under a "purchase of care" arrangement and are intended to operate as alternatives to which youngsters are sent instead of being committed to state-operated training schools. However, the data show (Vinter et al., 1975) that compared to many other states, Oregon has relatively high rates of youths in both training schools and community-based facilities. Accordingly, it is not unlikely that research would indicate that the youth care facilities have been receiving a large number of "low-risk" youngsters who differ in delinquency involvement and social backgrounds from training-school wards. At the very least, that possibility would have to be explored by the program evaluator before any conclusions could be reached about the relative effectiveness of youth care facilities compared to training schools.

The number of examples of the need for program evaluators to be able to offer detailed and informed statements about the persons who have been the targets of some correctional program could be greatly expanded, but perhaps it is sufficient to enunciate the general principle, accompanied by a few illustrative cases. At any rate, attention now turns to the second general category of sifting and sorting processes, namely those instances in which distortions are introduced into research study samples by researchers or persons directly allied with a correctional research effort.

RESEARCHER-PRODUCED OR RESEARCH-RELATED DISTINCTIVE GROUPS

Introduction

The findings from existing evaluation efforts in corrections show that there are a variety of activities at various stages of research that have produced relatively distinctive or peculiar offender cohorts and/or research findings into which various distortions have been introduced.

One of the most common of these researcher-produced distortions centers about the selection of study cohorts that are relatively narrowly defined at the same time that the impression is fostered, wittingly or unwittingly, that a much broader group of offenders has been subjected to a treatment-research experience, and that the project results have much greater generalizability than they in fact do have.

Consider the example of the Sacramento (California) County 601 Juvenile Diversion Project, which has been designated as an "exemplary project" by the Law Enforcement Assistance Administration (Baron et al., 1973). This project dealt with court referrals for Section 601 of the California Welfare and Institutions Code, which defines a collection of status offenses for which youngsters can be referred to court. In practice, this provision is most commonly used in cases of runaway, truancy, and children said to be beyond parental control.

Although the observers who have reported upon this project spoke of it as a "preventive effort," the term was a misnomer, for it dealt with court referrals rather than predelinquents. Also, while the program sought to avoid adjudication; it was not a "diversion effort" as that term is usually understood, for it involved intensive, family crisis intervention services administered *within* the Sacramento County Probation Department by a special team of probation workers.

The youngsters who had been processed through the special counseling program were compared with another sample of 601 cases given regular court handling. The results seemed encouraging, in that in the first nine months of the project over 800 referrals were dealt with successfully in the crisis intervention program; only 2.2 percent of them had petitions subsequently filed against them, while over 20 percent of the control subjects were held for formal court action. In addition, a larger proportion of those who had been subjected to regular court processing became involved in further trouble during a follow-up period than did the experimental program wards.

Closer examination of this project and the clientele served by it shows that enthusiasm for it has to be tempered somewhat. Out-of-county and out-of-state juveniles were not eligible to participate in it, nor were youngsters with another case pending in court, youths already on probation, and certain other cases. In all, about 40 percent of all 601 referrals in Sacramento County were judged by the program administrators to be ineligible for the program and were excluded from it. It is difficult to escape the conclusion that the project probably dealt with status offenders whose family and social circumstances were less disordered than was true for many other 601 cases. If so, this selectivity may have had much to do with the favorable results that turned up in it.

Parenthetically, programs in corrections have often been restricted to very narrowly defined offender samples. However, the reverse has sometimes occurred as well, as, for example, in the IT (Intensive Treatment) Project in California's San Quentin Prison a number of years ago (California Department of Corrections, 1958). In that effort, nearly all of the inmates were regarded as psychologically "sick" and therefore appropriate subjects for intensive psychiatric therapy.

Another example of research-related distortion has been provided by Lerman (1968) in his discussion of the experimental Fricot Ranch Study, carried out by the California Youth Authority at one of its state training schools. That project involved the creation of a small, experimental, therapeutic-milieu cottage program which was to be compared with institutional handling in large cottages in which control group cases were to receive the regular training-school program. The results seemed to suggest that the experimental milieu regimen retarded the rate at which youths became reinvolved in delinquency, for the experimental cases showed more favorable behavior over the first two years of parole exposure than did the control cases. However, Lerman noted that for some reason which was unclear in the research reports on the project, the experimental cottage wards also differed from the control cases in terms of social backgrounds, with the experimental boys being from more favorable backgrounds. As Lerman indicated, the differences in parole outcomes may have been a function of these variations among the two groups, rather than being attributable to the differences between the training-school programs.

Although problems of selectivity and distortion can be identified at various points in the juvenile and adult justice systems, these problems often become particularly bothersome when new program directions are introduced. Let us examine the case of diversion, a new thrust that has been widely advocated in recent years.

Diversion Programs: Selectivity and Distortion

During the past decade, as evidence which points to the ineffectiveness of correctional treatment has mounted (Greenberg, 1977; Robison and Smith, 1971; Lipton et al., 1975) and as the shortcomings and inadequacies of the juvenile court as a "child-saving" institution have become more apparent, considerable agitation has been heard for programs of "benign neglect," "judicious nonintervention," or "diversion" of adults and juveniles from the justice systems. In the case of juveniles, diversion would mean that some youngsters would be dismissed to their parents, while more serious offenders might be sent to child-serving agencies that operate entirely outside of the official justice system.

As these recommendations have been implemented in various jurisdictions, diversion has come to mean different things to different persons. Recall the Sacramento 601 project, which was identified by its architects as a diversion effort even though the status offender cases were processed *within* the probation department. It is also the case that the literature on juvenile diversion has revealed a number of unsettled questions centering around such matters as the extent to which it truly is possible to divert youngsters from the court without also subjecting them to coercive controls of one kind or another (Carter and Klein, 1976; Nejelski, 1976). However, discussion of these issues, important as they may be, would take us too far afield from a concern with selectivity and bias as confounding factors in evaluation research.

It seems clear enough that if the basic idea of diversion makes sense, there is little or no warrant for restricting diversion to petty offenders, many of whom would probably best be handled by complete diversion, that is, by being excluded entirely from any intervention in their lives. Diversion efforts might profitably zero in upon "higher-risk" cases from juvenile courts, with those youths being sent to child-serving programs outside the official justice machinery.

However, in actual practice, diversion agencies have infrequently served "high-risk" groups of delinquents. Instead, many of them have resembled the youth services bureaus analyzed by Duxbury (1971), in which "widening of the nets" has occurred and youngsters who might not have been brought into the ambit of the juvenile justice system at all, were there no diversion program, are most frequently encountered in the diversion endeavor.

Why do diversion programs turn out this way? Widening of the nets and differential selection of low-risk cases and marginal delinquents sometimes occur because diversion program personnel are loath to deal with "hard-core" cases; thus, they set up various eligibility criteria that serve to screen out youngsters regarded as "violent," "uncooperative," or in some other way unsuitable for the agency. The plain fact is that program workers often prefer to deal with "a better class of delinquents."

Police officers and court officials are also sometimes sources of difficulty in diversion programs. It is not uncommon that they are reluctant to allow youngsters they perceive to be "tough guys," "bad actors," or "hard-core delinquents" to be diverted to agencies and programs outside the official juvenile justice system. One case in point can be found in a report (Klein, 1975) of an experimental program in which youths were supposed to be assigned randomly to court referral, diversion with services, or diversion without any additional intervention services directed at them. In this instance, police officers tampered with the random assignment process in such a way that juveniles whom they perceived to be "hard-core" offenders were not sent to diversion programs. Fortunately, this tampering was discovered early enough in the project so that it could be curbed and thus did not seriously interfere with the experimental design of the endeavor.

It would be a mistake to attribute difficulties of this kind to wicked or malevolent motives on the part of the police or court workers. Rather, tampering represents an instance of well-intentioned differential decision-making by persons who work in the front lines of the social control system and who frequently come to see themselves as experts whose firsthand experiences with deviants make them considerably more knowledgeable than the rest of us about crime, delinquency, and wickedness (Skolnick, 1966).

Measuring Outcomes and Counting Cases

Research-related problems of selectivity can also be discerned at the end as well as at the beginning of correctional projects. Researchers have on more than one occasion gone about making questionable or unacknowledged modifications

in study populations, or counting program successes and failures in ways which
have seriously misled the research consumer.

Lerman (1968) has uncovered a number of instances of these practices. For
example, in a comparison between Wiltwyck School, a private institution, and a
state training school, the researchers claimed that Wiltwyck was considerably
more successful than the other facility in that it showed complete success in 43
percent of the cases and partial success in another 29 percent, for a total of 71
percent successes. The figures for the state school were 48 percent complete
success and 5 percent partial success, or a total of 53 percent successes.
However, in both schools those youngsters who were recorded as partial successes had been in court for delinquent acts following release from incarceration.
Lerman quite reasonably suggested that these juveniles would more properly be
tabulated as failures, which would mean that the private institution was not
significantly more effective than the public one.

Another example of peculiar counting procedures comes from the well-
known Highfields project in New Jersey. That program illustrated a more general
finding, noted by Lerman (1968: 58): "The literature on delinquency reveals a
curious bookkeeping habit: Boys who do not complete treatment are usually *not
counted* in evaluations of organizational effectiveness." In the Highfields project,
boys were placed in a small, therapy-oriented institution and were subsequently
compared with presumably similar boys who had been sent to Annandale
Reformatory, a conventional, large state reformatory in New Jersey. The results
of this comparison (Weeks, 1963) appeared to show that black males from
Highfields had lower parole violation rates than did black youngsters from
Annandale, while the failure rates for white youths were similar for both
institutions. However, Lerman pointed out that 18 percent of the subjects
assigned to Highfields did not complete treatment and were returned to court
for resentencing. Very few Annandale inmates failed to complete their stay
there, principally because that institution has no place to which it can send
program rejects. When Highfields boys who did not complete the program were
counted as program failures, the success rates for the two places turned out to be
quite similar.

A third case discussed by Lerman involved the massive experimental Community Treatment Project, also carried out by the California Youth Authority.
In that experiment, youngsters who would normally have been sent to state
training schools were randomly assigned either to an experimental group receiving treatment in the community or to control group placement in state training
schools. The findings initially seemed to indicate that community treatment was
more effective than institutionalization, as measured by parole violation rates.
However, Lerman observed that the lower violation rates for the experimental
cases resulted from *parole officer decisions* rather than from superior parole
performance by these youngsters. The total incidence of postrelease misconduct

appeared to be approximately equal for both groups, but the parole agents of the experimental cases revoked paroles only in cases where wards had been involved in serious delinquent acts, while the parole officers of the control cases much more frequently took action against their subjects for offenses of low or medium seriousness.

Evaluation Research Implications

Limitations of space preclude the enumeration and discussion of a long list of recipes for proper research procedures that will remedy the problems noted above. Still, a broad maxim can be offered, along with some more specific suggestions about appropriate research tactics.

The broad injunction to evaluation researchers is to avoid research "funny business" and to tell the truth. It is incumbent upon them to make every effort to: (a) specify precisely the target population of the intervention effort to be evaluated, (b) determine the extent to which the actual group of offenders matched the intended target group, and (c) report upon these matters fully and accurately. Accordingly, departures from an idealized research plan that have produced research cohorts with unanticipated peculiarities or treatment and control groups that are not closely matched should be part of the public record of an evaluation research effort. In the long run, there is little to be gained from efforts to disguise the shortcomings of specific evaluation studies. Then, too, it seems unlikely that research defects of these kinds can long remain undetected; rather, someone such as Lerman is likely to come along to point up flaws of this sort.

What about more specific measures that ought to be taken in the name of research candor? At the *program intake* end, checks upon bias and selectivity should revolve around comparisons between program targets and actual cases. Data on salient offender characteristics such as age, instant offense seriousness, and number of prior offenses must be collected so that the study group can be compared to the target population. In some cases, other measures, such as IQ level, degree of family instability, or school achievement level, would be implied in the definition of the target population. In any event, a good deal of effort must be expended on ascertaining the nature of the client group to which a program was addressed.

As an intervention program unfolds, researchers must monitor the *program process* activities in order to uncover departures from the research plan and the like. For one thing, intake practices may change once a program gets under way, with the result that the program cohort of offenders may change. For example, in a program designed for "hard-core" offenders, informal eligibility restrictions may evolve and the program may become overloaded with low-risk clients. This kind of bias would not be evident from a comparison of the inaugural group of clients with the target population.

The earlier commentary in this chapter also suggested that a good deal of attention must be paid to the systematic recording of program events in which some offender cases are dropped from a program because they have been deemed "unsuitable," "uncooperative," or "unlikely to benefit from the program." In particular, when a correctional effort that enjoys the luxury of being able to shuck vexatious clients is compared with one that is not so fortunate, the discarded subjects ought to enter into the equations measuring program success or failure. The researcher is obliged to report these jettisoned cases, rather than have them be discovered by a research critic-sleuth such as Lerman!

At the *outcome* end of evaluation, a full, accurate, and valid count of program "successes" and "failures" is called for. Researchers must "tell it like it is" with respect to measures of program outcome, rather than engage in efforts to portray program results in the most favorable light possible. Program rejects must be identified and included when successes and failures are added up, such practices as the "partial success" ploy found in the Wiltwyck School experience must be avoided, and related research standards must be observed.

The issue of valid indicators of program success or failure is much too thorny to be addressed here. Marked controversy can be generated on questions of whether parole revocation, employment stability, improved mental health, or some other variable comes closest to providing the best measure of program success. But whatever the ultimate decision that is reached regarding the form of program success or failure that is to be gauged in a specific project, one research rule is clear enough. Explicit decision rules regarding the behavioral indicators of "success" and "failure" should be formulated before a program effort gets underway, rather than being allowed to evolve in an ad hoc fashion as a project unfolds. Once enunciated, these decision rules should be strictly followed by the evaluation researcher. On this point, some of the program examples considered earlier indicate that the evaluation researcher must be alert to the possibility that program workers may either knowingly or unwittingly introduce distortions into the program results.

Honesty in evaluation research means that evaluators are obliged to pay close attention to potential problems of bias and selectivity in the projects they scrutinize. One part of that responsibility requires that they exercise a good deal of restraint when generalizing their results beyond the cohort of offenders actually studied. The evaluators ought to be the first ones to draw attention to the specific characteristics of the group that was the target of the program, and to caution research consumers against unwarranted assumptions that the program in question has application to a much broader collection of lawbreakers.

It is extremely doubtful that the problems of bias and selectivity in criminal justice research will soon disappear. But as evaluation methodology improves, some of the defective research activities noted here should become less commonplace. In the interim, the watchword for the research consumer might well be "caveat emptor."

REFERENCES

Adamek, R. and E. Dager (1968) "Social Structure, Identification, and Change in a Treatment-Oriented Institution." *American Sociological Review* 33 (December): 931-944.

Baron, R., F. Feeney, and W. Thornton (1973) "Preventing Delinquency Through Diversion: The Sacramento 601 Diversion Project." *Federal Probation* 37 (March): 13-18.

Bureau of the Census (1978) *Criminal Victimization in the United States, 1976.* Washington, DC: Author.

California Department of Corrections (1958) *Second Annual Report, Intensive Treatment Program.* Sacramento: Author.

Carter, R. and M. Klein [eds.] (1976) *Back on the Street.* Englewood Cliffs, NJ: Prentice-Hall.

Chesney-Lind, M. (1973) "Judicial Enforcement of the Female Sex Role: The Family Court and the Female Delinquent." *Issues in Criminology* 8 (Fall): 51-69.

Chiricos, T. and G. Waldo (1975) 'Socioeconomic Status and Criminal Sentencing: An Empirical Assessment of a Conflict Proposition." *American Sociological Review* 40 (December): 753-772.

Chiricos, T., P. Jackson and G. Waldo (1972) "Inequality in the Imposition of a Criminal Label." *Social Problems* 19 (Spring): 553-572.

Diana, L. (1955) "Is Casework in Probation Necessary?" *Focus* 34 (January): 1-8.

Duxbury, E. (1971) *Youth Services Bureaus in California: A Progress Report.* Sacramento, CA: Department of the Youth Authority.

England, R. (1975) "What Is Responsible for Satisfactory Probation and Parole Outcome?" *Journal of Criminal Law, Criminology and Police Science* 47 (March-April): 667-676.

Garabedian, P. (1964) "Social Roles in a Correctional Community." *Journal of Criminal Law, Criminology and Police Science* 55 (September): 338-347.

Gibbons, D. (1979) *The Criminological Enterprise.* Englewood Cliffs, NJ: Prentice-Hall.

――― (1977) *Society, Crime, and Criminal Careers.* Englewood Cliffs, NJ: Prentice-Hall.

――― (1976) *Delinquent Behavior.* Englewood Cliffs, NJ: Prentice-Hall.

――― and M. Griswold (1957) "Sex Differences Among Juvenile Court Referrals." *Sociology and Social Research* 42 (November-December): 106-110.

Gibbons, D. and J. Jones (1975) *The Study of Deviance.* Englewood Cliffs, NJ: Prentice-Hall.

Gibbons, D., B. Lebowitz, and G. Blake (1976) "Program Evaluation in Correction." *Crime and Delinquency* 22 (July): 309-321.

Gibson, J. (1978) "Race as a Determinant of Criminal Sentences: A Methodological Critique and a Case Study." *Law and Society Review* 12 (Spring): 455-478.

Greenberg, D. (1977) "The Correctional Effects of Corrections: A Survey of Evaluations," pp. 111-148 in D. Greenberg (ed.) *Corrections and Punishment.* Beverly Hills, CA: Sage Publications.

Hartjen, C. and D. Gibbons (1969) "An Empirical Investigation of a Criminal Typology." *Sociology and Social Research* 54 (October): 56-62.

Klein, M. (1975) "Alternative Dispositions for Juvenile Offenders: An Assessment of the . . . Juvenile Referral and Resource Development Program." (unpublished)

Lerman, P. (1968) "Evaluative Studies of Institutions for Delinquents: Implications for Research and Social Policy." *Social Work* 13 (July): 55-64.

Lipton, D., R. Martinson, and J. Wilks (1975) *The Effectiveness of Correctional Treatment—A Survey of Treatment Evaluation Studies.* New York: Praeger.

Nejelski, P. (1976) "Diversion: Unleashing the Hound of Heaven?" pp. 94-118 in Rosenheim, M. (ed.) *Pursuing Justice for the Child.* Chicago: University of Chicago Press.

Nettler, G. (1978) *Explaining Crime.* New York: McGraw-Hill.

Reckless, W. (1950) *The Crime Problem.* Englewood Cliffs, NJ: Prentice-Hall.

Reiss, A. (1976) "Settling the Frontiers of a Pioneer in American Criminology," pp. 64-88 in J. Short (ed.) *Delinquency, Crime, and Society.* Chicago: University of Chicago Press.

Robison, J. and G. Smith (1971) "The Effectiveness of Correctional Programs." *Crime and Delinquency* 17 (January): 67-80.

Rogers, K. (1972). " 'For Her Own Protection . . .' Conditions of Incarceration for Female Offenders in the State of Connecticut." *Law and Society Review* 7 (Winter): 223-246.

Ross, H. (1961) "Traffic Law Violation: A Folk Crime." *Social Problems* 8 (Winter): 231-241.

Scarpitti, F. and R. Stephenson (1971) "Juvenile Court Dispositions: Factors in the Decision-Making Process." *Crime and Delinquency* 17 (April): 142-151.

Schrag, C. (1961) "Some Foundations for a Theory of Correction." pp. 309-357 in D. Cressey (ed.) *The Prison.* New York: Holt, Rinehart & Winston.

Skolnick, J. (1966) *Justice Without Trial.* New York: John Wiley.

Tittle, C. and W. Villemez (1977) "Social Class and Criminality." *Social Forces* 56 (December): 474-502.

––– and D. Smith (1978) "The Myth of Social Class and Criminality: An Empirical Assessment of the Empirical Evidence." *American Sociological Review* 43 (October): 643-656.

Vinter, R., G. Downs, and J. Hall (1975) *Juvenile Corrections in the United States: Residential Programs and Deinstitutionalization.* Ann Arbor, MI: National Assessment of Juvenile Corrections, University of Michigan.

Vinter, R., T. Newcomb, and R. Kish [eds.] (1976) *Time Out: A National Study of Juvenile Correctional Programs.* Ann Arbor, MI: National Assessment of Juvenile Corrections, University of Michigan.

Weeks, A. (1963) *Youthful Offenders at Highfields.* Ann Arbor, MI: University of Michigan Press.

Wise, N. (1967) "Juvenile Delinquency Among Middle-Class Girls," pp. 179-188 in E. Vaz (ed.) *Middle-Class Juvenile Delinquency.* New York: Harper & Row.

PART IV

ON THE MEASUREMENT
OF OUTCOME

Malcolm W. Klein and Katherine S. Teilmann

We have devoted almost one fifth of the chapters in this handbook to the measurement of outcome. This is evidence, certainly, of the editors' conceptual inclinations, but also of a predominant interest in the field of evaluation research. In particular, the increasing public and political concern with accountability for the effects of social programs has increased the demand for reliable and valid measures of program outcome.

More and more, we believe the general public is demanding some proof of the "bang" for its "buck." Consequently, politicians and policy makers reflect this concern and press program funders for acceptable outcome evidence. Funders, in turn, press program directors for suitable program evaluations with "hard" data on outcome. If there is a clash of values between the various audiences of evaluation, it is probably at this point, where the policy makers and funders pass on their interest in outcome to the program directors, practitioners, and evaluators. These latter audiences, often more aware of the impracticality of outcome research, and sometimes fearful of its results, have a tendency to retreat to process variables, to be concerned only with efficiency, output (e.g., number of clients contacted), and client satisfaction with services rendered.

With the chapters in Part IV, we hope to overcome some of the resistance to participation in outcome or impact evaluations. One means of reducing this resistance is to stress the wide repertoire of outcome approaches and measures which are available. In Part IV, we look at these under four headings: (1) justice, (2) cost, (3) crime, and (4) client change.

Audiences in different positions with respect to programs will have varying degrees of interest in each type of outcome. Most would not deny the importance of any of them, but each would emphasize some over others. Correspondingly, each chapter of Part IV will find different but overlapping audiences. As noted earlier, some audiences may deny any relevance of outcome measures; usually these are práctitioners or directors of "helping" or client-advocacy programs. These are the audiences who will find little to agree with in these chapters, for clearly we take the position, through our authors, that programs and their evaluations are of little value if positive or negative outcomes are not measurable.

Perhaps the least arguable of the four types of outcome (at least in terms of value) is justice. There would also be little argument about the difficulty in measuring such a concept. It is both a pervasive and an elusive issue, and as a result has been largely ignored in criminal justice evaluations. Yet, such an important concept must receive attention. The Kobrin chapter reasserts the value of the justice criterion and suggests approaches to its measurement which may even pique the interest of "antioutcome" audiences.

Second to justice, the outcome most ignored by criminal justice evaluators is probably the cost of programs. It is not difficult to see why: Criminologists and evaluators typically have no training in economics or business. They do not have the tools or the inclination to pursue the measurement of cost outcomes. The issue remains important, but how will the gap be bridged? A reading of the chapter by Llad Phillips is not likely to render criminal justice evaluators competent in cost analysis, but it is likely to give them a basis for thinking intelligently about the issue and for dealing with those who are competent in the methods. For this reason, the Phillips chapter should be especially interesting to practicing evaluators and to students training for the field.

Most often, government agencies and program funders have crime reduction in mind when they mount new criminal justice programs. Perhaps for this reason, as well as for the reason that crime, or recidivism, is concrete enough to measure comparatively easily, the technology for crime measurement is far more sophisticated than that for many other outcomes. Two chapters, one by Hirschi, Hindelang, and Weis, and one by Rossi and Henry, describe current techniques and issues surrounding self-report measures of crime and assessing the seriousness of crimes, respectively. These chapters not only make arguments of interest to experienced evaluation researchers, but can serve as a starting point for novice evaluators and students, as well as for policy makers who wish to be knowledgeable about outcome measurement which goes beyond the usual simplistic concerns with recidivism.

Finally, while emphasis is often put on crime and its reduction as an outcome variable, there are a variety of other outcome measures of interest to audiences of programs and evaluations. For some, these concepts reflect the attempt to measure efforts at helping clients of the programs being evaluated. For others such as Elliott, they are primarily a means of making crime or recidivism outcomes meaningful. They include such concepts as alienation, self-concept, and attitudes toward law violation. For Elliott, as for us, they are important theoretical concepts without which we learn little from recidivism outcomes. Similar points are made in other parts of the *Handbook* (See Empey, Chapter 6, and Short, Chapter 11), but they bear repeating in a section on outcome measures. Further, Elliott offers an unusual compendium of reliable and valid measures which, while not exhaustive, is suggestive of the advances in outcome measurement already at hand, and provides a firm base for coordinated knowledge-building in this area.

Yet, with all the work going on in outcome measurement, we cannot rely too heavily on outcome measures to tell their own story. Acceptance and interpretation remain—and will always remain—in the control of the various audiences of the evaluations. For illustration, we cite one instance.

A few years ago, the editors evaluated a police diversion program for juvenile offenders in which clients were randomly assigned to outright release, community treatment, or court petition dispositions. Two outcome measures yielded conflicting conclusions. Self-report delinquency measures revealed that in each condition the juveniles continued to commit illegal behavior at a substantial rate, but that this rate was almost identical across all three conditions. Yet official arrest records revealed significantly lower rearrest rates for the released clients, in-between rates for community treatment clients, and significantly higher rates for petitioned clients.

Our interpretation, following discussion with many parties involved in the program, was that a form of "labeling" had taken place in that police officers on the street and juvenile officers in the station were rearresting juveniles less in relation to changes in the juveniles' behavior than in relation to their prior police dispositions (even though these had been randomly assigned). This meant for many interpreters that release was the most "successful" and petition the least "successful" disposition. But one interpretation directly opposite to this was offered by a high-ranking police official.

Starting with the fact that each of the three groups of offenders had continued to commit illegal acts, this official found the release condition to be the *least* successful and the petition condition the *most* successful. His reasoning was that a higher proportion of petitioned juveniles was getting what it deserved, detection and arrest. By contrast, the released offenders were "getting away with it" at a higher rate, a measure of program *failure*.

Both interpretations, one based on labeling premises and the other on deterrence premises, are equally valid, given the data presented. Thus, outcome measures do not necessarily lead to agreement, on program *value*. The latter is ultimately a function of the evaluation audience; the mechanics of evaluation remain tools, not solutions. Outcome, whatever its measure, has meaning only through interpretation; thus, in the end, the evaluation audience has the last say.

17

Outcome Variables in Program Evaluation:
Crime Control, Social Control, and Justice

Solomon Kobrin

In selecting program outcome variables, evaluators often neglect the distinction between the crime control and the social control objectives of the criminal justice system. The efforts of system agencies to reduce crime rates do not necessarily reinforce the legitimacy of the criminal law, and do not therefore predictably serve social control purposes. Standard outcome variables employed in program evaluation are typically those which test solely for crime control effects, despite the fact that their effects with respect to the legitimation of law are of at least equal importance. I wish to examine here the usefulness of focusing evaluation interest on the social control effects of criminal justice programs, with special reference to the problem of identifying appropriate outcome variables. A cue to their identification is provided by those features of Anglo-American law which are designed to impose procedural constraints on the potential arbitrariness of arrest and conviction. Their aim is to preserve equality of power between the state and the accused, and to disperse the state's power to administer the criminal sanction among separate and autonomous agencies. Justice in this context may be operationally defined as adherence to procedural law. The justice, or fairness, with which the criminal sanction is employed is central to the social control effect of criminal justice. In the interest of assessing these effects with respect to the evaluation of criminal justice programs, it would therefore appear to be feasible to explore their implications for the maintenance of prescribed procedural norms.

Thus, consideration of the scope of choice available in selecting outcome variables in the evaluation of criminal justice programs requires attention to the relevant features of criminal justice as a social institution. All social institutions evolve with reference to defined societal tasks or interests. For criminal justice, those tasks are conceived of as centering around the control of crime. Included are: maintaining the pressure of the threatened sanction against those who would violate the law (Zimring and Hawkins, 1973), implementing punitive sanctions with respect to those apprehended for violations, and, where possible, inducing the reformation of convicted offenders. Added to these is the frequently overriding aim of accomplishing system functions efficiently, that is, with maximum effectiveness at minimum cost.

However, at a more fundamental level, criminal justice as an insitution also functions as an instrument of social control by virtue of the manner in which it attempts to achieve its crime control objectives. Of the two modes of reaching system objectives, the first and more prominent is the use of the coercive power of the state to apprehend, convict, and incapacitate offenders. The second, and less frequently attended to, is to serve the ends of social control by deploying sanction resources in a way that supports the legitimacy of the criminal law, with the effect of reinforcing the self-regulation of conduct as the basic source of law observance.

Criminal justice programs commonly assessed by evaluators focus almost exclusively on the first of these two modes of implementing the justice system's control function. In one way or another, it is hoped, programs are designed to reduce the crime rate. They are conceived of with reference to the system's proximate objective of crime control rather than the more remote aim of social control. Policy changes and innovations in police, court, and correctional practices subjected to evaluation are typically aimed at the enhancement of the crime control effectiveness of the criminal justice system. This is the case whether program objectives concern improvement in the operational efficiency of justice agencies as a means of reducing the crime rate, or substantive changes in agency procedures that are designed directly to reduce crime. Both types of program objectives appear necessarily to dictate as outcome variables either efficiency measures or crime rates.[1]

There are, nonetheless, cogent grounds for questioning the necessity of such constraints in the choice of outcome variables. Evaluation at the level described is essentially aimed at ascertaining the crime control impact of criminal justice programs. Evaluators are thus constrained to accept the view held by functionaries of criminal justice agencies that the crime rate is in fact responsive to the efficiency with which these agencies employ the criminal sanction. Input variables in innovative programs usually concern such matters as enforcement, judicial, and correctional practices, and are assessed by evaluators in terms of their effects on crime rates, whether for selected populations or for communities or jurisdictions. Agents of criminal justice assume, perhaps uneasily, that improved effectiveness in the control of crime follows improved efficiency in the use of their sanction resources, just as day follows night. In their investigation of this common type of naive theory, evaluators find themselves obliged to accept program input variables at face value, dutifully assessing their ultimate impact on crime rates. Ignored in this process are outcome variables that have their source in program features that may well obstruct or undermine the intended effect on the crime rate.

However, the usual criminal justice programs designed to reduce existing crime rates and to bring rising crime rates under control rarely exert more than a marginal effect. Typical programs endeavor to improve the effectiveness of enforcement by devising ways to increase the ratio of arrests to crime reports, and the effectiveness of prosecution and of adjudication by methods designed to improve the ratio of convictions to charged offenses and, for confirmed recidivists, the ratio of imprisonment to convictions. While designed primarily to keep convicted offenders under secure confinement, correctional programs try also in various ways to reduce the criminalizing effect of incarceration, and therefore the recidivism rate. But for the most part, unacceptably high crime rates continue to resist these efforts. Of the hundreds of programs for the improvement of criminal justice launched in recent years with federal financial support, only a handful have been identified as "exemplary" in the sense that they have demonstrated some crime-reduction effect and therefore deserve wide adoption (Law Enforcement Assistance Administration, 1978). In 1972, the Law Enforcement Assistance Administration established an "Exemplary Projects" Review Board to identify successful innovative programs developed under its sponsorship. Twenty-nine such programs were so designated during the seven-year period, 1972-1978. Eligibility for designation as an exemplary project required that four criteria be met: reduction of crime or improvement in the quality of criminal justice, mutually substitutable; cost effectiveness; adaptability to other jurisdictions; and willingness to provide program information to other communities. With discouraging frequency, program evaluators turn up findings of no conclusively demonstrable effect on the crime rate, whether they test the outcome of enforcement, court, or correctional programs, and whether they are directed toward juvenile or adult populations (Allinson, 1979).

In the face of this record, the devotion of criminal justice agencies to their sisyphean task is less a matter of undying optimisim than it is the unhappy position in which they find themselves. They function admirably as the target of public anxiety aroused by the stubbornly irreducible level of crime. Whether or not it is uniformly warranted, the fear of criminal victimization has grown as the rising volume and incidence of crime over the past several decades has kept pace during the same period with social, demographic, and technological changes which foster crime.[2] The criminal justice system is perceived by the public as the only readily identified mechanism already in place, and charged with the task of keeping predatory behavior within acceptable limits. In brief, the justice system is expected to function dependably to reduce, if not eliminate, disorderly and predatory behavior that has escaped the influence of primary social networks, an expectation to which the justice system feels obliged to respond.

That it does not and cannot accommodate this expectation is amply evident. This is not, of course, to say that the justice system is without crime control effect.[3] On the contrary, its operations are crucial to the maintenance of public order in a complex, conflict-ridden, pluralistic society intent on the preservation of individual freedom. Both the threat and the use of punitive sanction are indispensable, above all in providing continuous reaffirmation of sentiments supportive of legal norms in a majority of the population (Kobrin and Lubeck, 1975; Kobrin, 1975; Zimring, 1971); and for the minority who do not entertain such sentiments, the incapacitating effect of the criminal sanction remains important as a means of reducing the frequency of their predatory acts.[4]

However, the fact remains that the control capacity of the criminal sanction is limited. Its limitation with respect to violation of the sumptuary laws has long been noted (Packer, 1968). It is useful to note as well the limits of the criminal sanction with respect to crimes against persons and property. Historically, the distribution of crime rates in urban areas has exhibited a stable pattern. The highest rates of both adult and juvenile crime are found in the residential enclaves that house those who are competitively disabled by poverty, depreciated status, and a consequent and relatively pronounced demoralization of family and group life (Shaw and McKay, 1942).[5] The contribution of this population to the crime rate has always been disportionate to its numbers, usually inviting a disproportionate allocation of enforcement and correctional resources in an effort to reduce the crime rate in the jurisdication. There is no evidence to suggest that in the high-crime-rate urban areas such effort succeeds in reducing the incidence of crime by more than a small increment; and whatever reduction is achieved is probably attributable to a fuller use of incapacitation (e.g., higher ratios of pretrial detention and imprisonment on conviction) in the preliminary and final stages of system processing of arrests. The reference here to the limited reach of justice system control in the crime-impacted enclaves of large cities is meant only to illustrate the process exemplified. Crime is hardly confined to these communities, although it occurs elsewhere at lower rates. But to the extent that the kind of alienation and detachment from the legal norms found among the most disadvantaged groups characterizes those who are objectively less so, there will be found a related resistance to the control efforts of criminal justice.

It is thus important to face the fact that the crime control reach of criminal justice is limited by determinants of the social control process originating outside its purview, and over which it can have little direct influence. Its agencies cannot alone reverse the impaired attachment of persons to conventional norms induced by the deprivations of poverty, shifting and uncertain social values, faulty early socialization, and similar effects of contemporary urban life in an industrial society. It is precisely the effects of such "extraneous variables" on the crime rate that figure among the difficulties faced by deterrence research (Gibbs, 1968; Blumstein et al., 1978). The inaccessibility of these factors to the influence of justice agencies also informs the growing impatience with the questionable fruits of correctional programs, giving rise currently to a renewed emphasis on the use of incapacitation and retribution (Wilson, 1975; Van den Haag, 1975).

While hardly without its critics (Gibbs, 1977), this development serves to reinforce the devotion of criminal justice agencies to programs designed to improve their efficiency in increasing the ratios of arrests, convictions, and imprisonment to crimes, charges, and sentences—particularly the latter two (Wilson, 1975: 201-204). But if, as is here argued, such hoped for increases in the operational efficiency of justice agencies does little to push the crime control competence of criminal justice beyond its present limits, and if, further, the extralegal sources of impaired social control lie beyond the influence of criminal justice, there would seem to be little to guide any quest for outcome variables that may be linked to the features of efficiency-seeking programs that may have fruitful crime control possibilities.

However, careful consideration of the relationship between the efficiency with which criminal justice is administered and the procedural constraints surrounding its administration suggests leads to such links. In another chapter of this volume, Morse has defined its adversary character as the central distinguishing feature of the American criminal justice system. It is marked in addition by the separation of enforcement, adjudication, and corrections into independent and autonomous, if interrelated, functions. The historically defined purpose of these features of the system has been to limit the power of the state arbitrarily to detain and condemn suspects charged with criminal offenses. However it may work in practice, by its extraordinary emphasis on the observance of procedural rules, and by dispersing the use of discretion and the power of decision among separate agencies, the system is designed to reduce the enormous disparity in power between the individual and the state in accusatory confrontations. Moreover, it is commonly recognized that no suspect may be justly found guilty of an act of crime without regard to the procedures through which the persons's guilt may be established. It is precisely in the procedural observances in the course of establishing guilt that in large part the public recognition of "justice" inheres. In brief, the expected "products" of the system include justice as well as crime control.

THE CASE FOR JUSTICE

To put the matter directly, the curious fact is that though crime control and justice are equally expected "system outputs" of the criminal justice system, evaluations rarely, if ever, seriously consider justice as an outcome variable. Its neglect may be justified on grounds that the concept of justice can be nominally defined only with great difficulty, and that whatever the definition, it would be virtually impossible to give it operational specificity. It may be asserted that classical utilitarianism has been less than successful in pointing the way to an acceptable definition of justice, and that the work of Rawls (1971) in recent years to reshape the utilitarian doctrine as a basis for defining justice has remained embroiled in philosophical controversy.

The answer to these objections is that the Anglo-American system of criminal law and procedure has implicitly defined justice by moving forthrightly to its operational specification. Whatever justice may be in the abstract, its requirements are operationally fulfilled to the extent, first, that equality of legal power is maintained between the state as accuser and the individual as accused and, second, that each stage between arrest and conviction remains decentralized in the hands of separate agencies, thus providing a series of reviews and checks on the decisions made at each preceding stage. In brief, the concept of justice as embodied in contemporary Western criminal law has been given operational manifestation in terms of specified procedures that may well be open to measurement.

There remains, however, another possible objection to representing justice solely in terms of its procedural components. Bendix (1962) has pointed out that in his work on the sociology of law, Max Weber regarded the development of procedural justice as entailing some sacrifice of substantive justice. Weber viewed procedural justice as linked to the advent of legal rationality in modern Western societies, of which bureaucratization in the administration of law was an inescapable feature. Substantive justice, on the other hand, he saw as an expression of traditional norms and notions of equity, which remain matters of political conflict among status and class groups. In modern bureaucratized states, the administrators of the legal system, following maxims of procedural rationality, tend to increase their control over the dispensation of justice as the control of political leaders is diluted through the necessities of compromise. As Mannheim (1949: 105) has noted, the bureaucracy exhibits a "fundamental tendency to turn all problems of politics into problems of administration." Bendix (1962: 439-440) renders Weber's view of this process in these words: "Failure to achieve [effective control] over the administrative implementation [of laws] means that the bureaucracy usurps the process of political decision-making." Whatever lawmakers may have intended in specifying the character and content of substantive justice, its assimilation to a set of procedural regulations has had, according to Weber, the effect of reducing the likelihood that substantive justice will be achieved in the individual case. Briefly, he regarded procedural and substantive justice as remaining in chronic tension with one another, with no prospect that the conflict could ever be resolved.

Despite these strictures on the subversive potential of procedural law, familiar to all observers of police, prosecution, and court operations, Weber also pointed out that the historical development of formalized and bureaucratized justice represented a quantum leap forward in the stability, predictability, and rationality of its administration. These features contrast sharply with earlier types of legal systems, dominated by patrimonial or charismatic leaders. These systems tended to be concerned almost exclusively with issues of substantive justice, but were at the same time subject to arbitrariness, unpredictability, and the unchecked influence of raw group interest. The modern shift to formal or procedural justice represents one of the more important supports for any claim that the legal norms may assert, since it is on this basis principally that the doctrine of equality before the law may be validated in practice.[6] Indeed, notwithstanding Weber's insight regarding the tradeoff relationship between substantive and procedural justice, under conditions of contemporary social organization it remains altogether likely that only through the common support accorded formal procedures for trying the culpability of suspected offenders is there any prospect that substantive justice will prevail. With respect to the administration of the criminal law, it can hardly be argued that a simple concern with substantive justice would suffice, although relatively informal procedures for the resolution of conflict have had some successes in settling criminal and civil cases (Felstiner and Drew, 1978) as well as in resolving juvenile offense cases (Vorenberg and Vorenberg, 1977: 311).

In effect, then, a case may be argued for the value as well as the feasibility of evaluating criminal justice programs in terms of their output of justice. The social utility of such evaluations is, of course, hardly confined to their potential contribution to crime control. Quite to the contrary, it is likely that any increase in providing justice, like an increase in the efficiency of agency operations, would have no more than marginal impact on crime control. In fact, for certain types of criminal cases—for example, cases of organized crime—the meticulous pursuit of procedural justice can and probably does have a short-run negative impact on crime control. The same may be said for the small proportion of criminal cases in which the defendants have sufficient resources to bear the high cost of competent and skillful private defense counsel. But for the common run of such criminal cases as burglary, assault, street robbery, and the like, in which the use of the public defender is prominent, closer attention to the provision of procedural justice can well produce some short-run marginal improvement in crime control. These are the cases that, in the interest of clearing overcrowded court dockets, invite collaboration between prosecution and defense counsel in eliciting guilty pleas and in effect determining sentences (Sudnow, 1965; Skolnick, 1966; Blumberg, 1967). It is inevitable that such "administered" justice reinforces in offenders the alienation from legal norms which may have prompted the offenses that have brought them into the hands of the law.

Thus, the gain in crime control to be realized from improvement either in administrative efficiency or in the provision of procedural justice is likely to be marginal at best. However, improvement in providing procedural justice offers promise of undergirding whatever residual affinity persons may have for legal norms. Such support can be significant for that very large number of nonprofessional offenders, who, depending on the contingencies of a disordered social life and unstable occupational career, drift in and out of crime (Glaser, 1964: 465-496; Glaser and O'Leary, 1966). Glaser's research has adduced quite convincing evidence that in the careers of such offenders there is a durable commitment to neither criminal nor conventional values. It is in this context that the criminal justice system is offered an opportunity to function as an instrument of social control by contribuing to the support of the offender's prosocial impulses. And, as suggested, the social control potential of the system is persistenly undermined by the cynicism respecting the "fairness" of justice implicit in the efficiency-oriented model of criminal justice.

That model is currently best exemplified in the movement to "optimize" justice, that is, to achieve maximum crime control at minimum cost (Blumstein and Larson, 1969; Belkin et al., 1972). Reich (1977: 64) has pointed out that such optimization of crime control effectiveness entails a concentration of power in the hands of some unspecified justice system manager. Those who build rational models of the criminal justice system neglect typically to identify which of the currently dispersed agencies of the system, each focused on separate agency goals, are to provide the management function. But however unrealistic such system modeling may be in relation to the real world of criminal justice, the effort itself lends ideological support to existing tendencies to eliminate current constraints on centralized management of the multiple competing authorities at every stage of the justice process. There appears to be little awareness that centralized management of criminal justice would require the authority to control the discretionary power now lodged in enforcement, prosecution, adjudication, and correctional agencies, and to coordinate their operating policies. Reich observes, however, that "traditional notions of justice . . . have been shaped by a distrust of centralized power and an abiding assumption that there are no 'correct' answers other than those generated by the collective judgment of voters, legislators and . . . juries."

In short, the bureaucratically "rational" approach of the system modelers to crime control moves toward the replacement of the adversarial conduct of criminal justice by a managerial solution. At its most rational, such a solution would mean that the guilt of a suspect would be determined not solely by a meticulous concern with the specific facts of the individual case, but by a merging of these facts with the personal and social characteristics of the suspect and the history of his or her past offenses in order to calculate the probability of guilt or innocence. Sentences likewise could then be set on the basis of these predictors, assuring uniformity. Such efficiency-oriented procedures can, in theory, produce substantial savings in the costs of processing offenders. Curiously enough, this kind of achievement has come to be seen as highly desirable, as is evident, for example, in the work of the Committee on Economic Development (1972). However, as Reich further notes,

> in order to assure both that power will not be abused and that the contest between state and the accused will be fair, it has been thought necessary to decentralize power, to establish countervailing checks on it, and to diffuse it among various levels of discretionary authority. But because such an allocation of power cannot be justified in any terms other than that it helps to preserve what traditionally has come to be considered as justice, it has difficulty competing successfully with an optimal allocation of power that promises to minimize all costs, including the cost of erroneous judgments of guilt.

For the evaluation researcher, concerned with the selection of program outcome variables, these comments suggest a need to assess criminal justice programs simultaneously with reference to their *social control* as well as their crime control effects. There should be an awareness that while the two functions are likely to be in conflict in the short run, the responsibility of the system for the production of a "justice" output remains incontrovertible. Although the initiative in designing criminal justice programs will continue, understandably, to remain in the hands of agency functionaries focused on a concern with crime control, evaluators' interest in the social control effects of such programs is not necessarily foreclosed. As matters now stand, this output of the criminal justice system is sporadically and tendentiously examined by civil rights advocates and minority group organizations with reference typically to prominent and celebrated cases. To compound the neglect, radical criminologists, who as social scientists might be expected to conduct systematic research on the matter, offer mainly sweeping dicta condemning the system as one of structured injustice (Taylor et al., 1973).

Systematic analysis of the justice output of the criminal justice system is not, of course, without substantial methodological problems. With reference to analytic procedures, it is possible to suggest that, as has been noted, the initial and basic step of specifying the conceptual and operational components of the justice-related features of the system have already been provided in the structure of the criminal law. It should then be possible to open all criminal justice operations to examination with respect to their effects on the maintenance and support of the institutionally established decentralization of criminal justice functions, and on the integrity and intactness of the system's adversarial design.

Measures of these effects might focus, for example, on trends in ratios of guilty pleas with respect to types of offenses and offenders, of charge reductions, and similar evidence of "bargain justice"; and, with respect to system decentralization, on shifts in the balance of influence among justice agencies as indicated by trends in ratios of police charges accepted by prosecutors, and prosecution-recommended sentences accepted by judges. Data on charge reduction, for example, is often available and, with the use of controls respecting adequacy of evidence and similar contaminants, may be used as an indicator of prosecutor-defense collaboration. Similarly, programs or policies under evaluation may increase or decrease the time involved for some types of cases in processing charges at the police level, or in bringing arraigned suspects to trial, again a possible indication of short-circuiting procedural requirements in the interest of system efficiency. The most serious problems likely to be encountered in the development of such measures are those of data availability and access, particularly respecting informal practices that leave no footprints in the sands of recorded data.

Finally, it should be noted again that issues of substantive justice remain beyond the reach of such methods. However, under conditions of modern societal organization, the legitimacy of law can have its roots only in a meticulous observance of the procedures designed to salvage equity. Such observance over the long run remains the principal avenue through which criminal justice may make its contribution to the task of social control.

NOTES

1. For a parole agency, an example of the first would be an effort to increase work output by decreeing more frequent contact between agents and parolees. The latter would be exemplified by reduction in the caseload of agents assigned to supervise the most recidivism-prone parolees.

2. Among these may be mentioned the reduction of residential segregation barriers between high- and low-crime-rate populations, increases in motorized mobility giving access to a wider range of crime targets, the unparalleled diffusion of handguns, and, until recently, the increased proportion of the crime-prone younger age groups in the population.

3. Andenaes (1966) has called attention to the eruptions of criminal activity that have accompanied police strikes and similar demobilizations of police agencies.

4. But see Greenberg (1975: 541-580), who has found the research on the crime-reduction effect of incapacitation to be inconclusive, primarily because adequate data were lacking. Estimates of the effect have ranged from a 50 percent reduction in the incidence of criminal acts attributable to imprisonment, to Greenberg's estimate of 8 percent.

5. The police department of any city of substantial size can readily identify on the basis of day-to-day experience their high-crime-rate areas. These will usually conform to this description.

6. In Weber's typology of the grounds of legitimacy, this corresponds to his category of belief in the legality of formally prescribed rules. He notes its salience in modern societies in the following passage: "Today, the most usual basis of legitimacy [of law] is the belief in legality, the readiness to conform to rules which are formally correct and have been imposed by accepted procedures" (quoted in Parsons et al., 1961: 232-233).

REFERENCES

Allinson, R. S. (1979) "LEAA's Impact on Criminal Justice: A Review of the Literature." *National Council on Crime and Delinquency, Criminal Justice Abstracts* 11: 608-648.

Andenaes, J. (1966) "The General Preventive Effects of Punishment." *University of Pennsylvania Law Review* 114: 949-983.

Belkin, J., A. Blumstein, and W. Glass (1972) "Recidivism as a Feedback Process: An Analytical Model and Empirical Validation." *Journal of Criminal Justice* 1, 7.

Bendix, R. (1962) *Max Weber: An Intellectual Portrait*. Garden City, NY: Doubleday.

Blumberg, A. S. (1967) *Criminal Justice*. Chicago: Quadrangle.

Blumstein, A. and R. Larson (1969) "Models of a Total Criminal Justice System." *Operation Research* 17: 199-232.

Blumstein, A., J. Cohen, and D. Nagin [eds.] (1978) *Deterrence and Incapacitation: Estimating the Effects of Criminal Sanctions on Crime Rates*. Washington, DC: National Academy of Sciences.

Committee on Economic Development (1972) *Reducing Crime and Assuring Justice: Report of the Research and Policy Committee*. New York: Author.

Felstiner, W.L.F. and A. B. Drew (1978) *European Alternatives to Criminal Trials and Their Applicability to the United States*. Washington, DC: Government Printing Office.

Gibbs, J. P. (1977) "Review: 'Thinking About Crime,' by James Q. Wilson." *American Journal of Sociology* 83: 247-249.

——— (1968) "Crime, Punishment, and Deterrence." *Social Science Quarterly* 48: 515-530.

Glaser, D. (1964) *Effectiveness of a Prison and Parole System*. Indianapolis: Bobbs-Merrill.

——— and V. O'Leary (1966) *Personal Characteristics and Parole Outcome*. Washington, DC: Government Printing Office.

Greenberg, D. F. (1975) "The Incapacitative Effects of Imprisonment: Some Estimates." *Law and Society Review* 9: 541-580.

Kobrin, S. (1975) "Toward a Sociology of Deterrence," in Stockholm: *General Deterrence: Conference on Current Research*. Stockholm: National Swedish Council for Crime Prevention.

——— and S. Lubeck (1975) "Problems in the Evaluation of Crime Control Policy," in K. M. Dolbeare (ed.) *Public Policy Evaluation*. Beverly Hills, CA: Sage Publications.

Law Enforcement Assistance Administration (1978) "Four Local Projects Earn 'Exemplary' Status." *Law Enforcement Assistance Aministration Newsletter* (October-November).

Mannheim, K. (1949) *Ideology and Utopia*. New York: Harcourt Brace Jovanovich.

Packer, H. L. (1968) *The Limits of the Criminal Sanction*. Stanford, CA: Stanford University Press.

Parsons, T., E. Shils, K. D. Naegele, and J. R. Pitts (1961) *Theories of Society*. New York: Free Press.

Rawls, J. (1971) *A Theory of Justice*. Cambridge, MA: Harvard University Press.

Reich, R. B. (1977) "Can Justice Be Optimized?" in S. S. Nagel (ed.) *Modeling the Criminal Justice System*. Beverly Hills, CA: Sage Publications.

Rheinstein, M. [ed.] (1954) *Max Weber on Law in Economy and Society*. Cambridge, MA: Harvard University Press.

Shaw, C. and H. D. McKay (1942) *Juvenile Delinquency and Urban Areas*. Chicago: University of Chicago Press.

Skolnick, J. H. (1966) *Justice Without Trial*. New York: John Wiley.

Sudnow, D. (1965) "Normal Crimes: Sociological Features of the Penal Code in a Public Defender Office." *Social Problems* 12: 255-276.

Taylor, I., P. Walton, and J. Young (1973) *The New Criminology*. New York: Harper & Row.

Van den Haag, E. (1975) *Punishing Criminals: Concerning a Very Old and Painful Question.*
New York: Basic Books.

Vorenberg, E. and J. Vorenberg (1977) "Early Diversion from the Criminal Justice System,"
in L. Radzinowicz and M. E. Wolfgang, *Crime and Justice, Volume II.* New York: Basic
Books.

Wilson, J. Q. (1975) *Thinking About Crime.* New York: Basic Books.

Zimring, F. E. (1971) *Perspectives on Deterrence.* Washington, D.C.: Government Printing
Office.

——— and G. J. Hawkins (1973) *Deterrence.* Chicago: University of Chicago Press.

18

Cost Analysis

Llad Phillips

I. COST ANALYSES: AN OVERVIEW

Cost analysis is an aid to administration, a tool to help decision makers to allocate resources better. The forms of cost analysis are manifold: program cost estimates, comparative cost analysis, cost-effectiveness studies, cost-benefit analysis, and cost function studies, but the nature of each of these types of procedures is determined simply by the nature of the information available to the investigator. For example, program cost estimates and comparative cost analyses are input-oriented. The information requirements are quantities of inputs used, such as staffing or workload needs, and their salaries or values. The benefit of program cost estimates to the investigator lies in the quantification of the costs and their identification with the subcomponents of the program. In the process of estimation, the cost of each of the services or activities contributing to the program is discovered. In comparative cost analysis, these cost estimates are compared among similar programs, either under the assumption that each of the programs generates the same outcome, or by standardizing on a per-unit cost basis, using caseload as a proxy for outcome or output. Comparative cost analysis lends itself to a choice between competing programs and to management by exception, that is, identifying programs with unusually low or high costs per case, an indication that further investigation of these exceptional programs may be warranted.

The limitations to these input-oriented cost analyses lie in setting aside concerns about output. For example, a program with an apparently high cost per caseload may deal with potentially high-risk cases, such as probationers highly likely to recidivate, and consequently occasion high costs, but in the process produce an observed rate of recidivism at the same level as a program with a lower cost per caseload which handles probationers with a lower potential to recidivate. In this example, the additional costs incurred by the high-cost program have produced a greater output, namely, the reduction from the potentially high recidivism rate to the observed lower rate. Favoring the program with the lower cost per case may be the wrong decision.

While better resource allocation decisions can be made if one can measure the quantity and quality of outputs or outcomes, as well as the cost of the inputs that produced them, this is usually very difficult in a public service industry such as criminal justice. As a consequence, program cost estimation and comparative cost analyses are a more frequent mode for investigation and, in contrast, cost-effectiveness studies and cost-benefit analyses tend to be limited in scope and specialized for this industry. Because the criminal justice system provides a public service, there is not a market for its outputs as is the case for privately produced goods and services. Consequently, the system's services are neither readily identified nor readily valued or priced.

It is often difficult to conceptualize what agencies of the criminal justice system produce. One of the ultimate objectives of the system as a whole is to reduce or control crime, yet various agencies such as the police, the probation department, and correctional institutions may all contribute to that objective. What does each of these agencies produce that reduces crime? One may postulate that police departments produce arrests, or high-quality arrests such as persons charged with an offense, for example, or that correctional institutions produce person-years served in captivity. But these constructs, while measurable, may provide little improvement over the caseload approach unless it is possible to link them to a decrease in crime and hence to demonstrate effectiveness. The latter requirement leads to all the difficulties associated with deterrence and incapacitation research.

In spite of, or perhaps because of, all the difficulties, it may be advisable to proceed on a stepwise basis, undertaking input-oriented cost studies first, standardizing costs on a caseload or quasi-output basis next, and then turning to the identification of outputs and their relation to cost. Available studies may demonstrate the effectiveness of the output measures chosen in achieving an objective, such as crime reduction, and in this case, criminal justice agencies such as police departments can be compared on a cost-effectiveness basis—for example, by comparing costs per arrest.

While the selection and measurement of output is a major step in providing additional useful information to the investigator in cost studies, since it controls in part for the quality of the operation, it still provides insufficient information to justify the continued operation or expansion of the agency. For this purpose, it is also necessary to value the output, so that the benefits can be weighed against the costs. For criminal justice agencies, this is often a severe informational requirement. By way of illustration, in the example used for police departments, arrests were used as an output. But arrests are a means to the objective of reducing crime. To provide dollar values for arrests, it is not only necessary to show that arrests reduce crime, but to measure how much, and also to value or price the consequent reduction in offenses to the citizens. Arrests are an intermediate output, and to value them to weigh against their cost of production, these additional information requirements are necessary. These considerations suggest why the applications of cost-benefit analysis in criminal justice are often focused on particular programs, such as the education and vocational training of offenders, where the estimation of benefits, while not without problems, may appear more feasible.

The choice of the investigator among the various types of cost analyses must be determined by balancing the information desired for decision-making against the data requirements for that type of analysis. The investigator should weigh whether the additional costs of a more complex analysis such as cost-benefit will be justified in terms of the value of a better decision. It is clear that undertaking a more complicated analysis on a shaky data base may be counterproductive.

II. INPUTS, OUTPUTS, TECHNOLOGY, AND PRICES

Cost-benefit analysis examines inputs and outputs and their values or prices but says little about the technology that determines the input-output linkages. Knowledge of the technology provides information important to decision makers. How are inputs combined to produce output? To what extent can one type of labor be substituted for another? How do costs vary with output? Are there increasing returns to the scale of operation? Over a period of years, the price of one input may rise relative to others. For example, for police departments the salaries of uniformed officers have tended to rise relative to those of civilian clerical workers and relative to the cost of police cars. To what extent is it possible to substitute clerical workers and police cars for officers and yet maintain arrests? To answer questions such as these, it is necessary to investigate the technology linking inputs and outputs. To this end, economists specify cost functions, which relate costs to the price of inputs and the quantity of outputs. In recent years, the functional forms used for specifying the technology have become more general, permitting a wider variety of properties. There have been a number of applications of this type of cost analysis to criminal justice.

This cost function approach takes advantage of the market information available for service industries, namely, the demand for each of the inputs as it varies with its own price, the price of other inputs, and the outputs. Nonetheless, this approach faces the same information difficulties as the other types of cost analysis in criminal justice, the conceptualization, measurement, and valuation of outputs. However, if the output problem can be overcome, there is an additional advantage to cost function analysis: the production of multiple or joint outputs.

The various agencies in the criminal justice system often produce a number of outputs. For example, police departments make arrests for a wide range of offenses—on the one hand, for numerous burglaries and thefts, and on the other, for less numerous but more damaging or costly murders and assaults. Furthermore, the police produce outputs in addition to arrests that also decrease crime—for example, patrols. If an investigator is conducting cost-benefit analysis and is assigning values to each type of arrest, and pricing patrols as well, these various outputs can be combined into total benefits using the common denominator of dollar value. However, if the prices of output are not available, as is often the case, the existence of various outputs for an agency may make cost-effectiveness comparisons between agencies impossible, because the mix of outputs may vary in their proportions from agency to agency. There is no common output to standardize cost comparisons. This difficulty can be handled using cost function analysis (to be described later), since it is applicable to technologies producing multiple or joint outputs.

This multiple or joint output problem is one of considerable importance and arises in different contexts. Almost all criminal justice agencies engage in a variety of activities. An additional example is the probation system, which prepares presentence investigations as a service to the courts while assessing the needs of probationers and supervising them. Analysts often attempt their cost studies at a modest level, focusing on a single activity or service. This can create problems in the estimation of cost. The inputs used to produce the activity or service of interest may also be used to produce other activities as well, and the investigator is faced with the task of attempting to proportion inputs and costs among activities. There is often little data to guide judgment. An example is afforded by police agencies where some investigators have attempted to analyze the costs of producing arrests on a crime-by-crime basis, ignoring the joint nature of police activity and simultaneously producing an array of arrests. Once again, an advantage of the cost function approach is that it is applicable to joint-output technologies. All in all, there are many tradeoffs among the various types of cost analysis, and among them, the investigator must weigh the advantages of a simpler approach against the complexities of the phenomenon he or she is studying.

III. PROGRAM COST ESTIMATION

Program cost estimation involves the valuation of inputs associated with a given program or program change. A simple example of estimating the costs of a program change is afforded in the Office of Juvenile Justice and Delinquency

Prevention (1977) report, "Responses to Angry Youth," which lists the estimated costs of deinstitutionalizing status offenders in ten states. The states were different in nature and in different stages in the process of deinstitutionalization, so that no implied choice or comparative analysis was intended between deinstitutionalization procedures. The cost estimates for each state were useful in providing the order of magnitude of the funding needed. This cross-section study of ten states showed that the costs incurred varied with the approach taken toward deinstitutionalization in each state, and depended upon the nature of the juvenile justice and youth service system in each state.

A more detailed example of program cost estimation is provided by Thalheimer's (1978) study, released by the National Institute of Law Enforcement and Criminal Justice. This report estimates the costs of a typical county probation department, and compares these to estimates for "model" county probation departments operating in compliance with correction standards. Costs are estimated for providing services to the courts, such as presentence investigations, and for providing services to probationers in terms of needs assessment and supervision. Costs are standardized by estimating on a per-case—i.e., investigation-report, or client-year, basis. There is some attempt to control for the variation of the quality of the service provided by estimating probationer service costs for variable supervision (minimum, medium, maximum) and for variable needs (low, normal, high).

Program cost studies of this nature are useful in terms of organizing and estimating the costs of various services and for providing cost norms or benchmark figures to permit management by exception. As Thalheimer indicates in a discussion of "directions for additional research," there are many questions which such a study cannot answer—for example, Are there increasing returns to scale? What is the most efficient scale of operation?—and questions on cost effectiveness, such as, How cost-effective is specialization on a unit level (e.g., with respect to separate investigation, court reporting, and supervision units)?

IV. COMPARATIVE COST ANALYSIS

Comparative cost analysis can involve a comparison of costs across time, as the organization of services are changed within a jurisdiction, as well as the comparison of costs among jurisdictions, to the extent valid. A study which does both has been prepared by Peat, Marwick, Mitchell, and Co. (1978) for the Social Science Research Institute at the University of Southern California. The report estimates the comparative cost of the deinstitutionalization of status offender programs.

In comparative cost analysis, it is necessary to make sure that jurisdictions are compared for the same time period and that cost changes over time are made comparable by deflating by the consumer price index and discounting by the interest rate. In this study, the time periods were not identical across jurisdictions but were clearly defined, and costs were adjusted for inflation.

During the preprogram period, the principal costs in each jurisdiction were accounted for by juvenile justice services, including police activity, court intake, detention, hearings, probation, and incarceration. During the program period, the majority of the costs shifted to, and were borne by, social services, including the Deinstitutionalization of Status Offender screening unit, shelter care, group, and foster homes, the multiple service center, outreach intervention, and counseling. The breakdown of costs, and their percentage mix for juvenile justice and social services, was reported for both the preprogram and program periods for each jurisdiction to account for the effect of mix on the resulting costs.

Both direct costs and indirect costs for the agencies were estimated. Direct costs consisted of salaries and benefits for service personnel, materials, and supplies, and contracts to private organizations providing services. Indirect costs included estimates of agencies providing a pro rata share of their total effort to status offenders, to facilities costs or rent user charges, and centralized agency indirect services, such as accounting, purchasing, and maintenance. The pro rata estimates and estimates of indirect service costs depend upon the availability of workloard statistics and are calculated as a proportion of salary costs. Since these workload statistics are often not available or are inaccurate, this often involves considerable judgment. The report standardizes the cost estimates by reporting unit cost calculated on a workload basis, i.e., total cost divided by total youth contacts.

V. COST-EFFECTIVENESS STUDIES

As we move to cost-effectiveness studies, the difficulty of the analysis tends to increase an order of magnitude because we are moving from input-oriented studies to considerations of output as well. Cost effectiveness can mean the lowest-cost program to achieve a given output, or the program that attains the maximum output for a given cost.

One difficulty encountered is the conceptualization and measurement of outputs in a manner consonant with the objectives of the program. This problem arises because criminal justice is a public service industry and there is no market for the services and outputs of the system that would clearly identify them, a point developed by Wayson and Monkman (1976) in their discussion of criminal justice standards for corrections. Blair et al. (1977) of the Urban Institute have suggested the development of output measures to implement their recommendations for monitoring the impacts of prison and parole services. For example, to quantify the objective of holding securely, they suggest measures such as the average number of escapes per year per inmate. They suggest a number of rehabilitation objectives, such as (1) changes in attitude, measured by the percentage of inmates showing attitude improvement on psychological tests, (2) reduction in criminal activity, measured by offenders on parole rearrested within twelve months or convicted of a criminal offense in that time period, and (3) increase in social productivity, measured by the percentage of ex-offenders employed when released from parole. Their analysis is suggestive of how to develop measures and data bases to indicate the achievement of characteristic objectives.

Another difficulty encountered in cost-effectiveness analysis is establishing the effectiveness of output measures in achieving a general goal, such as crime reduction or avoidance. For example, rehabilitation is only one goal of the correctional system. General deterrence and incapacitation effects are also desired effects of the correctional system. It is necessary to link measurable outputs of corrections, such as inmate-years served, to deterrence and incapacitation in order to demonstrate effectiveness. This is methodologically difficult, a point developed by Weimer and Friedman (1978) in their discussion of criminal rehabilitation research.

The gravity of the problem of establishing effectiveness in output-oriented studies in criminal justice is highlighted by the problems of corrections studies examining recidivism. As pointed out by Rossi and Wright (1977) after reviewing 231 studies, Martinson concluded that nothing in the area of corrections works to affect recidivism. Before embarking on cost-effectiveness and cost-benefit studies in criminal justice, the feasibility of the approach should be carefully assayed.

An interesting application of the cost-effectiveness approach is Palmer's (1974) analysis of a community treatment project. This study examines an experimental project conducted by the California Youth Authority which allowed certain kinds of juvenile offenders to remain in their home communities with intensive supervision while on parole. The control group received the traditional treatment of incarceration in a large state institution before parole. The relative effectiveness of the experimental program was assessed by calculating the rate of arrest, while on parole, for youths in the experimental program, and comparing that to the control group's rate of arrest while on parole. These rates were calculated for subgroups of youths classified by personality type. For example "neurotics" accounted for 53 percent of youths and had a probability of arrest per month while on parole of .03 for experimentals and .08 for controls. In contrast, "power-oriented" youths had a probability of arrest per month of .07 for experimentals and .06 for controls. The calculation of comparative program costs per ward indicated the traditional program was less costly than the community project, but that this difference was narrowing over time. The results suggest that the experimental program was cost-effective for "neurotic" youths and that the traditional program was cost-effective for the "power-oriented" type.

A study which illustrates many of the issues discussed in this chapter was conducted by Gray et al. (1978). They examine the relative cost effectiveness of community corrections, probation, and incarceration as alternative means of reducing recidivism. The authors develop the cost analysis in stages, first estimating input cost on a cost-per-day basis (program cost estimates), then estimating cost per case (comparative cost analysis). The authors refer to cost per case as output cost, denoted in this chapter as quasi-output cost. Last, they estimate cost per reduced arrest (cost-effectiveness analysis), designated as outcome cost in their study and referred to herein as output cost. The authors estimate the costs on several bases reflecting the time horizon of the decision maker allocating resources. Thus, very short-run costs allow only variation in direct inputs used to maintain the client, such as food and clothing. Short-run costs allow some staff or labor inputs to vary. Long-run costs allow all inputs to vary. The reduction in offenses due to treatment was calculated by extrapolating the offender's offense rate prior to treatment and subtracting the observed rate of offenses following treatment. The authors attempted to correct for the quality of outcome or final output by weighing the mix of offenses by seriousness weights. That is, they price offenses, but not with a dollar price, an analysis intermediate between cost effectiveness and cost-benefit. The authors find that for juvenile offenders who have never been institutionalized, probation appears to be more cost-effective than community-based residential treatment. Residential treatment is more cost-effective than institutionalization. The authors focus on one output or outcome, the reduction of offenses for treated offenders. This single-output focus is a limitation of cost-effectiveness analysis. The authors note that additional outputs, such as deterrence of potential offenders, also reduces the total social cost to society. Thus, the policy conclusions of the authors' study about the relative cost effectiveness of alternative programs for offenders is conditional upon the assumption that recidivism is the dominant output of concern and that inclusion of other outputs, such as general deterrence, would not alter the apparent cost effectiveness of the alternative programs.

VI. COST-BENEFIT ANALYSIS

Cost-benefit analysis has many intricacies. Not the least of these, in the case of applications to criminal justice, is the valuation or pricing of outputs. These benefits can be measured as such, i.e., positively. For example, in evaluating a pretrial manpower program, Nelson estimates the benefits from job placement. Alternatively, the benefits can be measured as reduction in costs, as Nelson (1975) did in estimating the reduction in criminal justice system court and corrections costs due to diversion and the reduction in crime damages resulting from the reduction in recidivism.

The costs and benefits of a program can occur in a single period or extend over a period of time. In the latter case, dollars in one year must be made comparable to dollars in another year by correcting for inflation and by discounting by the interest rate. A general discussion of procedures can be found in Chapman (1975), Stokey and Zeckhauser (1978), or Mishan (1972).

In evaluating a program, it may be instructive to calculate costs and benefits from a number of perspectives, differentiating these by who bears the costs and benefits. This procedure is followed by Nelson in evaluating the pretrial manpower program. He calculates the benefit-cost ratio in terms of society or the effect of the program on resources or national income. Nelson also calculates the benefit-cost ratio from the point of view of the taxpayer, including transfer payments, such as taxes paid by program participants and reduction in welfare payments to participants. These transfer payments do not add or drain resources but simply redistribute them. The investigator can also calculate the benefit-cost ratio from the point of view of the flow of funds of the governmental agency involved or from the point of view of the impact on the individual convict, i.e., the impact on the income of the convict. The advantages to calculating benefit-cost ratios from the perspective of the various individuals, agencies, or entities involved is that it provides some insight into possible differing attitudes toward the program among them.

A complicating aspect of cost-benefit analysis is the treatment of unmeasurable benefits and costs, those that can not be priced. These are referred to schematically by Nelson as "tertiary," with "primary" referring to capital and operating costs direct to the program, and "secondary" referring to indirect costs—for example, costs in the rest of the criminal justice system external to the program or agency. An example of unmeasurable benefits in a diversion program might be the value to place on the relative increase of freedom from not having to be incarcerated enjoyed by the offender. This was an aspect of the California Youth Authority Community Treatment Program not evaluated by Palmer. Of course, while freedom may be a major consideration to the offender, it may be debatable whether it should be excluded from estimations from the point of view of society as a whole, which may or may not want to consider the welfare of the offender.

This raises another difficult point. Objectives may be in conflict. The best interests of society may be served by decreasing the welfare of the offender, as they often are in practice. Even from the point of view of society, there may be apparently conflicting objectives. Programs that enhance, at least potentially, the rehabilitation of the offender may simultaneously reduce the effect of general deterrence. Lengthening time served may increase recidivism but enhance general deterrence. The costs and benefits have to be offset, provided of course that they can be estimated.

Since many of the applications of cost-benefit analysis in criminal justice have involved evaluation of training programs and rehabilitation, it is worthwhile considering Noble's (1977) critique of the limits of cost-benefit analysis in guiding general rehabilitation policy. It is clear that cost-benefit analysis is as much an art as it is a science, and involves judgment and assumptions as to the estimates of the costs and benefits, which interest rate to use for discounting, and so forth. Noble examines eighteen studies and conducts sensitivity analysis on several of them, investigating to what degree the benefit-cost ratio is sensitive to variations in the assumptions that are made. This is an advisable exercise to temper the judgment of the investigator as well as the decisions of clients who may use the study.

Notwithstanding all the limitations of analysis and the caveats, the objective of obtaining information to guide decision-making better should be kept in mind, and often much is learned and gained in the attempt to develop the information. It is perhaps ironical that in making the decision whether to proceed, the expected benefits of the information to be gained from undertaking cost analysis must be weighed against the costs of the study.

VII. COST FUNCTION STUDIES

The approach in cost function analysis is to specify the technological linkage between input and output using functional forms. The basic concept is illustrated graphically in Figure 18.1. In the lower quadrant, the relationship between labor as an input and the reduction in the number of offenses resulting from a given treatment as an output is indicated as curvilinear. As labor input increases, crime reduction increases, but less than proportionally. This presumed technological relationship can be reflected in the cost function, as illustrated in the upper quadrant. Taking a unit price of labor, W, equal to one, the cost of labor, WL, can be determined by simply reflecting (or rotating upwards) the curve in the lower quadrant around the axis into the upper quadrant, a mirror image. An increase in the price of labor would increase cost at each output, i.e., raise the curve in the upper quadrant. Thus, it is clear that cost will vary with the level of output or reduction in offenses, and the price of input.

This simple example can be captured using a particular functional form where output Q is proportionally related to input L; e.g.,

$$Q = kL^\alpha,$$

where k and α are parameters. One can invert this function, solving for labor:

$$L = k^{-1/\alpha} Q^{1/\alpha}.$$

Cost, C, is, the price of labor, W, times the input level, L, or

$$C = W \cdot L = k^{-1/\alpha} W Q^{1/\alpha}.$$

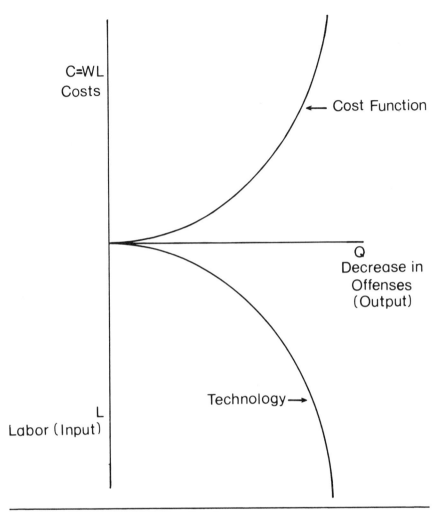

Figure 18.1: Technology and the Cost Function

Thus, cost will vary with the price of the input and output. This simple example can be generalized to include a number of inputs and input prices as well as a number of outputs. Furthermore, less restrictive or more general functional relationships can be specified.

A number of cost-function applications have been undertaken in criminal justice. Darrough and Heineke (1978) examined the behavior of police departments, defining the several outputs as arrests for each of the seven FBI index felonies as well as a proxy output of population to capture other police activities, such as traffic investigation and patrol. They estimated the parameters of the cost function and calculated the incremental or marginal cost of producing an arrest for each of the seven kinds of crime. Another result was that arrests are produced jointly, i.e., that the marginal cost of an arrest for a specific crime depends upon the level of arrests for other crimes as well. This means that the technology of police departments can not be studied on a crime-by-crime basis, but, rather, that crimes have to be considered jointly.

In an attempt to finesse the problem of defining output for police departments, Phillips (1978) specified a three-input, one-output technology, presuming there was an indexable output but not measuring it. The three inputs included in the study were police officers, civilian employees, and four-wheeled vehicles. The demand for these inputs was estimated after substituting among the demand equations to eliminate the unmeasured output variable. The results show that the demand for these three inputs is relatively price-inelastic, especially for officers—i.e., that demand decreases little with an increased salary.

Block and Ulen (1979) have estimated cost functions for correctional institutions in California. They postulate that correctional institutions jointly produce three outputs, confinement as measured by the number of inmates, hotel services, and rehabilitation. They presume the latter two outputs are constant so that costs are varying only with the number of inmates. They estimate a linear relationship between cost and the number of inmates, using seventeen years of annual data and find that the marginal cost of an additional prisoner was only $296 in 1967 prices, about one-fourth of the average cost per prisoner.

VIII. THE SERIOUSNESS OF CRIME IN DOLLARS: AN APPROACH

An objective of the criminal justice system is to limit the damages of crime through control. System activities generating deterrence, incapacitation, and rehabilitation should be increased up to the point where the incremental cost of increasing these functions just offsets the decrease in damages from the offenses they diminish. To determine these damages, it is necessary to have damage rates per offense for the various crimes.

Seriousness weights were developed for serious felony crimes by Sellin and Wolfgang (1964). The relationship between these seriousness weights and dollar damage rates is investigated for FBI index crimes by Smith et al. (1979). The procedure was to use estimates of the dollar damage rate for different felonies obtained from various sources and to examine whether there was a consistent relationship between these dollar values and the Sellin-Wolfgang scale. The damage rate for larceny was obtained from estimates in *Crime and Its Impact— An Assessment* (President's Commission on Law Enforcement and Administration of Justice, 1967). Several damage rates were available for homicide, based on estimates of the value of life reported by Jones-Lee (1976). Another source of damage rate estimates are cost function studies which can be used to calculate the marginal cost of reducing an offense. If one presumes the criminal justice system is operating properly, this opportunity cost of the resources used to reduce an offense should be equal to its damage rate. Estimates from cost function studies were available for robbery and auto theft.

The authors report that there is a log-linear relationship between the Sellin-Wolfgang seriousness score and these dollar damage rates which can be used to calibrate the Sellin-Wolfgang scores in dollars for all the appropriate offenses. However, these only include the more serious crimes. Recently, Babst et al. (1980) have extended this analysis to less serious crimes and to status offenses by applying this procedure to calibrate the Gray et al. seriousness scores. Hence, damage rates can be assigned to a wide range of crimes ranging in seriousness from murder to curfew violation. However, this involves a considerable extrapolation for the less serious offenses, and hence their estimated damage rates may be in considerable error. Nonetheless, these damage rates could facilitate the application of cost-benefit analysis in criminal justice.

IX. CONCLUSION

The application of cost analysis in criminal justice involves judgment and it is limited by data inadequacies and imprecise estimates. Great caution must be used in relying upon any single study to guide policy conclusions. Nonetheless, there is an increasing fund of cost study applications, and a discernible trend toward increasing sophistication in the design of the cost analysis and the development of the data supporting the estimates. It is probable that cost analysis will become an increasingly important tool to guide decision-making and evaluation in criminal justice.

There is an advantage to using simpler cost analysis techniques, such as program cost estimation or comparative cost analysis. These studies are input-oriented, and information on the prices and quantities of inputs is often available. Furthermore, these simpler studies avoid the difficult questions of how to conceptualize and measure output for public-sector programs that usually do not market or sell their services.

However, this input-orientation feature can also be a weakness, because it is difficult to compare the costs of alternative programs, unless they are similar in scale and structure. One can not address the issue of effectiveness or determine whether a program generates benefits commensurate with its costs.

If the latter questions are crucial to the decision maker, it becomes necessary to spend the resources to complicate the analysis, to measure the outputs, and to value them. As we accumulate more experience and knowledge in criminal justice analysis, cost function studies that describe the technology in terms of multioutputs, as well as multiinputs, will become more attractive.

REFERENCES

Babst, D. V., C. P. Smith, and L. Phillips (1980) *Costs of Crimes and Status Offenses Compared with Costs of Processing Suspects and Offenders in the Juvenile Justice System.* U.S. Office of Juvenile Justice and Delinquency Prevention, Washington, D.C., January.

Blair, L. H., H. P. Hatry, K. Bunn, L. Stevens, and K. Parker (1977) *Monitoring the Impacts of Prison and Parole Services.* Washington, DC: The Urban Institute.

Block, M. K. and T. S. Ulen (1979) "Cost Functions for Correctional Institutions," in C. M. Gray (ed.) *The Costs of Crime.* Beverly Hills, CA: Sage Publications.

Chapman, J. I. (1975) "Techniques," in *A Handbook of Cost-Benefit Techniques and Applications.* Washington, DC: American Bar Association.

Darrough, M. N. and J. M. Heineke (1978) "The Multi-Output Translog Production Cost Function: The Case of Law Enforcement Agencies," *Economic Models of Criminal Behavior,* ed., J. M. Heineke, North-Holland Publishing Co., Amsterdam (1978).

Gray, C. M., C. J. Conover, and T. M. Hennessey (1978) "Cost Effectiveness of Residential Community Corrections: An Analytical Prototype." *Evaluation Quarterly* 2, 3: 379-400.

Jones-Lee, M. W. (1976) *The Value of Life.* Chicago: University of Chicago Press.

Mishan, E. J. (1972) *Economics for Social Decisions.* New York: Praeger.

Nelson, C. (1975) "Applications," in *A Handbook of Cost-Benefit Techniques and Applications,* Washington, DC: American Bar Association.

Noble, J. H. (1977) "The Limits of Cost-Benefit Analysis as a Guide to Priority Setting in Rehabilitation." *Evaluation Quarterly* 1, 3: 347-380.

Office of Juvenile Justice and Delinquency Prevention (1977) *Responses to Angry Youth.* Washington, DC: Department of Justice.

Palmer, T. (1974) "The Youth Authority's Community Treatment Project." *Federal Probation* (March): 3-14.

Peat, Marwick, Mitchell and Co. (1978) "Comparative Cost Analysis of the Deinstitutionalization of Status Offender Programs." Social Science Research Institute, University of Southern California, Los Angeles, June.

Phillips, L. (1978) "Factor Demands in the Provision of Public Safety," in J. M. Heineke (eds.) *Economic Models of Criminal Behavior.* Amsterdam: 1

President's Commission on Law Enforcement and Administration of Justice (1967) *Task Force Report: Crime and Its Impact—An Assessment.* Washington, DC: Government Printing Office.

Rossi, P. H. and S. R. Wright (1977) "Evaluation Research: An Assessment of Theory, Practice and Politics." *Evaluation Quarterly* 1, 1: 5-52.

Sellin, T. and M. E. Wolfgang (1964) *The Measurement of Delinquency.* New York: John Wiley.

Smith, C. P., P. S. Alexander, and D. J. Thalheimer (1979) *A National Assessment of Serious Juvenile Crime and the Juvenile Justice System, Volume IV: Economic Impact.* Washington, DC: National Institute for Juvenile Justice and Delinquency Prevention.

Stokey, E. and R. Zeckhauser (1978) *A Primer for Policy Analysis.* New York: Norton.

Thalheimer, D. L. (1978) *Cost Analysis of Correctional Standards: Community Supervision, Probation, Restitution, Community Service, Vol. I.* Washington, DC: National Institute of Law Enforcement and Criminal Justice.

Wayson, B. L. and G. S. Monkman (1976) *How To Implement Criminal Justice Standards for Corrections: An Economic Analysis.* Washington, DC: American Bar Association.

Weimer, D. L. and L. S. Friedman (1978) "Efficiency Consideration in Criminal Rehabilitation Research: Costs and Consequences," in *The Rehabilitation of Criminal Offenders: Problems and Prospects,* Washington, DC: National Academy of Sciences.

19

The Status of Self-Report Measures

Travis Hirschi, Michael J. Hindelang,
and Joseph G. Weis

Following preliminary and unsystematic work by Porterfield (1946) and Wallerstein and Wyle (1947), Short and Nye (1958) introduced in the middle 1950s the self-report method of measuring delinquent behavior. Short and Nye developed a pool of 23 items (reproduced in Nye, 1958) for use in a general high school population. Comparison of the self-report scores of training school and high school boys illustrated that self-report procedures could "adequately distinguish between groups known to be different," that they could "predict the more serious and frequent delinquent behavior characteristic of institutionalized adolescents" (Nye, 1958: 15).

Short and Nye thus firmly established self-reports as a method of measuring delinquency. They were able to show that adolescents would report delinquent acts, that these reports were to some degree internally consistent, and that they were related both to "known" differences and to other differences predicted from theory and research—e.g., the quality of family relations.

Less than ten years later, the self-report technique had been sufficiently widely used to justify a conference on the topic at Syracuse University (Hardt and Bodine, 1965). The conference report summarized the procedures and results of self-report research involving 16 distinct and large-scale samples, and it included a 24-item bibliography on the self-report method. By then, both questionnaires and interviews had been used; the number of self-report items in a given instrument had ranged from 5 to 67; some effort had been devoted to the construction of typologies of delinquent behavior using subsets of relatively homogeneous items; various validation strategies had been explored; and consistent findings about the correlates of delinquency as measured by self-reports had begun to emerge (Hardt and Bodine, 1965: 7-9).

Since the Syracuse conference, work with self-reports has continued at an accelerated rate. Polygraph (Clark and Tifft, 1966) and informant (Gold, 1970) validity studies have been reported, along with various attempts to factor- (Senna et al., 1974) or cluster- (Hindelang and Weis, 1972) analyze large sets of self-report items. Perhaps most important, self-report studies have continued to produce consistent results apparently at odds with research based on official data. While official measures show strong differences by race, class, and age, self-report measures show no difference or much smaller differences in delinquency across categories of these variables. With respect to sex as well, self-report differences are typically smaller than those shown in official data.

Today, self-report procedures have replaced police and court records as the most frequently used method of measuring delinquency. These procedures have been used to develop or test theories of delinquency (Hirschi, 1969; Elliott and Voss, 1974), to assess the level of delinquency in national samples of adolescents (Gold and Reimer, 1975; Elliott, 1978), and to estimate the effectiveness of various intervention strategies (Broder et al., 1978).

The dominance of the self-report method may be traced to several sources: Self-report instruments may provide adequate variation in "delinquency" within populations that would be uniformly "nondelinquent" if official measures alone were the criterion; the content of self-report instruments is easily tailored to fit the specific requirements of particular programs or theories; self-report procedures are often relatively inexpensive compared to searches of official records. Perhaps the most important reason for the popularity of the self-report method is the widespread belief that it provides a more valid measure of delinquent behavior than do official records.

This is not to say, however, that the self-report method is without problems or critics. In fact, self-report procedures, and the results they produce, are among the most controversial topics in the field. Those who accept the traditional correlates of delinquency argue that the self-report technique does not measure serious delinquent behavior and that because of difficulties in establishing reliability and validity there is no compelling reason to reject results based on official measures (e.g., Nettler, 1978; Reiss, 1975). Reiss (1975: 214) says that "the methodological and technical foundations of these [self-report] studies do not invite confidence in the conclusions." In fact, Reiss considers the current state of self-report measurement so deplorable that he suggests that the graduate training of survey researchers in sociology be restructured to emphasize the development of valid and reliable standardized instruments.

In a nutshell, the current status of self-report measures is justifiably or deplorably high, depending upon one's point of view. Given limited cost, unusual content control, broad applicability, and presumed validity, continued wide use of the self-report method is certain. If experience in the broader field of criminological research is any guide, however, continued use of self-report techniques in their current form will only solidify the impression that they are consistently at odds with official measures. If so, debate will continue to center on the validity of the respective measures to such an extent that definitive resolution of questions of program effectiveness will be impossible.

The key to resolution of this dilemma is to be found in the phrase, "in their current form." In our view, self-report instruments and official measures have tended unnecessarily to produce *apparently* discrepant results, much to the consternation of those seeking consistent conclusions about factors in delinquency causation or treatment.

In this chapter, we provide an overview of the issues surrounding self-report procedures, and offer suggestions about their proper use. Our general stance might be summarized as follows: The self-report method is not as defective as its critics claim, nor is it as defect-free as its defenders sometimes suggest. It is, merely, a potentially useful source of information about program effects. The evaluator should use self-reports whenever they are appropriate and practical. At the same time, he or she should recognize that the value of such an all-purpose tool is dependent on the skill with which it is applied to the task at hand.

CONTENT OF SELF-REPORT INSTRUMENTS

At present, no standard self-report instrument is available. The nearest approach to a standard instrument is the *pool* of items developed by Short and Nye (1958). Subsequent users of self-reports have relied heavily on the original Short-Nye pool.[1] Nevertheless, the set of items chosen from this pool has varied from investigator to investigator, and, what with wording variations and the occasional addition of new items, use of a self-report instrument identical to an instrument employed in earlier research is extremely rare.

Failure of researchers to employ a standard instrument is of course common in social science research. With respect to self-reports of delinquent activities, the usual forces working against standardization are much intensified. Items appropriate to particular age and sex groups with a given level of expected delinquent involvement may be inappropriate to groups differing along one or more of these dimensions. Temporal and regional differences in terminology, in the value of goods, and in opportunities to commit particular delinquent acts, often seem to require change from earlier instruments.

The solution to the standardization problem at present would seem to be that suggested by the transitional experiment, where a core set of items common to earlier research is routinely included along with items unique to the needs and purposes of the instant evaluation. Given separate analysis of the common items, this compromise would be an improvement on current practice.

From their original 23 items, Short and Nye selected a subset of 7 items forming a Guttman scale, which asked respondents if they had:

(1) driven a car without a driver's license or permit;
(2) skipped school without a legitimate excuse;
(3) defied their parents' authority (to their face);
(4) taken little things (worth less than $2) that did not belong to them;
(5) bought or drank beer, wine, or liquor (including drinking at home);
(6) purposely damaged or destroyed public or private property that did not belong to them;
(7) had sexual relations with a person of the opposite sex.

As this list correctly suggests, self-report instruments have tended toward offenses unlikely to result in official action, an almost automatic result of their development for use with general population samples. Although there has been a steady drift toward inclusion of more serious offenses, instruments currently in use remain weighted in the nonserious direction (e.g., Hindelang, 1971; Gold and Reimer, 1975).[2]

There is good reason to believe that the trivial nature of the offenses measured by most self-report instruments is at least partly responsible for the discrepancy between self-report and official results with respect to such variables as age, race, sex, and social class. In any event, the assumption that a pool of self-report items reflects behavior likely to result in police or court action should be treated with great caution. It is easy to say that a self-report instrument has "face validity," that it measures such penal code offenses as "assault," "auto theft," "larceny," "robbery," and the like (e.g., Nye, 1958: 15; Hirschi, 1969: 56), but it is the rare self-report instrument that closely parallels the view of delinquency depicted by police and court data. The researcher interested in tapping the domain of delinquent behavior reflected in official records will have to pay particular attention to questions of content (and to scale construction). Few researchers have collected data illustrating the behavior their self-report items are supposed to summarize. When they have done so with general population samples, the "robberies" and "burglaries" summarized in their tables are easily seen in a less sinister light. In fact, in narrative descriptions of the behavior the respondent had in mind when he or she "confessed," it is often difficult to find acts that the police or the courts would be likely to take seriously (Gold, 1970: 30). In short, one cannot overemphasize the importance, to successful evaluation, of carefully locating the behavior "reported" by the respondent within the larger domain of delinquent or deviant acts.

One way to approach the domain problem is to recognize that sets of self-report items will never be homogeneous with respect to the seriousness of the behavior they uncover, even though they may be homogeneous by other criteria. Research shows that self-report items are weakly to moderately correlated with each other, with tendencies to cluster in such domains as "theft," "violence," and "drugs." Given these tendencies, the researcher may analyze individual items, homogeneous subsets, or global scales (scales based on all items in the set) involving all or most of the items. Although the analytical strategy to be pursued depends primarily on the nature of the item intercorrelations, our experience suggests that the evaluator would be well-advised to proceed from individual items to homogeneous subscales before attempting the use of global scales, because the global scales may obscure important variation in the correlates of delinquency. For example, the median male-to-female sex ratios for commonly used self-report items range from 1.0 for "running away" to 3.7 for "theft greater than fifty dollars" in about a dozen published studies in which these data are available. In a single data set where the sex ratios for homogeneous subscale scores range from 1.1 for "drug use" to 4.4 for "property damage," the equivalent global scale ratio is 1.2 to 1. The tendency of global scales to mask differences among demographic groups—and perhaps treatment groups—illustrated here, follows from the greater relative frequency of less serious items in self-report instruments and the tendency for traditionally nondelinquent groups to report involvement in such trivial offenses. (The same phenomenon works to a lesser extent for homogeneous subscales in relation to individual items.)

Where does this leave us with respect to construction of an ideal self-report instrument? First, the positive intercorrelation of items suggests that the inclusion of a wide variety of offenses will contribute to the common variance tapped by a global scale. While this situation makes it easy for an evaluator to find items, it is sufficiently fluid to allow obfuscation of the boundaries of the phenomenon ostensibly under investigation. For example, if the aim is to parallel official data, which may be more desirable in evaluation than in basic research, at some point the positive intercorrelation criterion will allow nonchargeable items—e.g., smoking—to creep into the pool. From an evaluation viewpoint, mechanical reliance on the positive intercorrelation criterion would allow potential intervening variables (e.g., skipping school) to become mixed in with the dependent variables; second, the positive but not strong intercorrelations mean that many individual items will tap unique variance and therefore the items included should be sufficiently interesting individually to warrant inclusion.

RELIABILITY AND VALIDITY

Contrary to the drift of criticism in the literature, self-report measures of delinquency offer nothing unusual with respect to reliability or validity. The small-to-moderate correlations among self-report items suggest that internal consistency measures of reliability will usually reach acceptable levels. In fact, split-half reliability estimates hover around .9 (Elmhorn, 1965; Kulik et al., 1968b). Test-retest reliabilities separated by periods between administrations of from one and one-half hours to several weeks yield coefficients as high as .98

(Kulik et al., 1968a; Dentler and Monroe, 1961; Belson, 1968; Clark and Tifft, 1966). When the period between administrations of the self-report instrument is as long as two years, the reliability remains surprisingly high. In fact, Farrington (1973) found a gamma of .62 under these conditions. The reliability of self-report instruments is as good as or better than that for other behavioral inventories. Thus, an evaluator using an adequate number of self-report items (say, 15 or more) and exercising care in the administration of the instrument, can be reasonably confident that acceptable reliability will be attained.

The methods for assessing validity are more problematic and controversial than those for reliability. However, in most evaluation settings, there should be abundant validational material available. The most common external validator of self-reports has been some form of official records. The idea that the self-report method is designed to circumvent the problems in official records of delinquency has prompted the view that it may be inappropriate to use that which is being circumvented to validate its replacement. Nowhere else in social science does this general objection apply. Indeed, the concept of convergent validity requires examination of this replacement relation as the first step in instrument construction (Campbell and Fiske, 1959). Once it is recognized that alternate measures of delinquency supplement rather than compete with each other, the range of potential validators expands to include not only police and court records, but also reports of friends, parents, teachers, and even of the subjects themselves about contact with the juvenile justice system. The availability of these diverse sources as validators suggests that it is unnecessary to rely exclusively on any single source.

The self-report validational literature reports correlations between self-reported delinquency and self-reported police contacts often in the .4 to .5 (Pearson's r) range (Hindelang et al., 1978). Correlations between self-report delinquency and police records of offenses range from as low as .16 (Gould, 1969) to as high as .69, with most coefficients in the upper part of this range (for coefficients in the high range, see Kulik et al., 1968b; Farrington, 1973; and Erickson, 1972). Despite the generally impressive and consistent performance of self-report measures, the fact that one study (Gould, 1969) produces very low validity coefficients emphasizes that evaluators cannot take for granted the validity of their instruments in all samples.[3] The performance of self-report measures judged by other validators, including reports of the subjects' delinquency by teachers and friends (e.g., Gold, 1970) and surreptitious observations of deviance (Erickson and Smith, 1974), is consistent with these findings.

METHODS OF ADMINISTRATION

Normally, the anonymous self-administered questionnaire is recommended for threatening questions dealing with socially unacceptable behavior (see Sudman and Bradburn, 1974: 142-43). Given the nature of most evaluation samples, however, the self-report method will usually be restricted to an interview format. Reading difficulties are so widespread among delinquent populations that the use of self-administered questionnaires is virtually ruled out. (Those unfamiliar with questionnaire methods should be reminded that completed forms are not sufficient evidence of adequate reading skill.) Although little empirical information is available on the impact of varying methods of administration on the reliability and validity of self-report results, that available suggests that the method is no more sensitive to such consideration than efforts to measure behavioral variables in general. For example, attempts to preserve the anonymity of respondents do not seem to have much of an impact on either the absolute level or the relative ranking of respondents on delinquency items (Kulik et al., 1968b). More subtle variations (e.g., interviewer characteristics) have rarely been examined, but the limited evidence now available indicates that these variations, too, have *little* effect (Krohn et al., 1975). Thus, standard interview considerations with respect to training of interviewers and matching on race and sex seem adequate to guide the use of this method in evaluation research. (Clearly, the use of treatment personnel or others in positions of programmatic authority is ill-advised.)

SCALE CONSTRUCTION

Having selected a pool of items consistent with program objectives, the evaluator has a variety of options available for scoring individuals. In delinquency research generally, this scoring decision typically comes down to a choice among a count of the number of different acts engaged in (variety), a sum of the frequency of involvement in all acts, or a seriousness weighted frequency count.

Criticisms of delinquency research have traditionally focused on the "unjustified" assumption that various delinquent acts reflect a common dimension (e.g., Gibbons, 1976). Those criticisms focusing specifically on the self-report technique commonly note the lack of seriousness in the offenses described in the typical pool of self-report items. The tendency of self-report researchers has been to parallel the official practice of dividing respondents into those who have ever and those who have never committed the act. All of these considerations suggest: (1) development of homogeneous subsets of items; (2) weighting on the basis of the seriousness of the offense, perhaps following procedures developed by Sellin and Wolfgang (1964); and (3) attempting to obtain frequency estimates for each offense, with a view toward utilizing this information for scale construction.

There can be no doubt that homogeneous subscales produce results that vary systematically with their content. For example, in Table 19.1 gammas summarizing the relation between sex and various homogeneous sets of self-report items range from .03 to .70 for variety measures, and from .08 to .67 for frequency measures; the global scale gammas in the same data sets are, however, in the .33 to .37 range. Obviously, the summary measure of delinquency, being an average of subscale scores, obscures possibly important differences in delinquency apparent in the more refined analysis. Given this line of thought, the evaluator should conduct at least an analysis of homogeneous sets of items, and perhaps of individual items, before reaching conclusions about program impact.

As is also apparent from Table 19.1, the frequency and variety scoring procedures produce comparable results, and the variability in coefficients for subscales noted above is maintained, irrespective of method used to score responses. Most delinquency researchers will continue to believe that considerations of frequency and seriousness should make a difference in the apparent effect of program variables. In principle (and according to most sociological theories), considerations of frequency and seriousness *are* important. In practice, extremely serious offenses are so rare in the general population that no practical weight can overcome their rarity. On the other hand, trivial offenses are so common that offenses after the first quickly lose their meaning. Given the difficulties of frequency counts and the serious complexities of weighting, it seems to us reasonable to suggest that, at a minimum, variety scores for homogeneous subscales should be reported.

Our findings in several independent data sets suggest that with self-report instruments currently in use, frequency measures produce correlations with standard independent variables (e.g., sex, grade point average, age) and with such "validators" as self-reported contact with the police comparable to those produced by standard variety indexes based on simple dichotomization of subjects. The evaluator aware of individual item results at one extreme and global "delinquency" scales at the other, will have captured the phenomenon at its most specific and most general levels. If, within this range, homogeneous subscales are constructed along the lines suggested in Table 1, the empirical evidence now available suggests that additional scoring refinements will not materially affect the results.

SELF-REPORTS IN EVALUATION RESEARCH

The self-report technique was designed to allow study of populations having had little or no contact with the criminal justice system. This technique permits evaluation of program results in populations having limited official contact either because of short exposure time or, as in some diversion programs activated at first contact with the police or courts, because of low levels of delinquent activity in the population. Even where official contact is relatively frequent or serious, the self-report procedure provides a versatile supplemental criterion of effectiveness which will provide insurance against the traditional bane of evaluation research—a change in official policy or practice with respect to apprehension, recording, and disposition of offenses. In most evaluation research, the respondents will be more actively involved in illegal activity than will be the general adolescent population. Hence, differences between delinquent and non-delinquent groups shown in prior research (e.g., in school performance) need to be taken into account if the self-report procedure is to be used appropriately.

Traditionally, the reference period for self-report instruments has been the preceding twelve months. In the general population, this reference period typically produces too few serious events for adequate data analysis, unless the sample is extremely large. In the selected populations with which criminal justice evaluators generally work, the restricted reference period lengths will become less problematic as the populations under study become more and more delinquent. But as delinquent activity increases in a population, the other side of the coin presents itself: Yearly volume of activity of the typical respondent in such a population may be so great that retrospective estimates of the nature, frequency, and seriousness of illegal activities may be subject to substantial memory distortions. There are two general strategies available to deal with this problem. One is to use some variant of a panel design in which subjects interviewed at regular intervals are asked to report events occurring since the last interview, say three or six months previously. The other, when panel designs are not feasible because subjects cannot be identified individually from period to period due to cost or mobility, is to use a reference period the length of which is inversely proportional to the rate of illegal activity in the population under investigation.

AN ILLUSTRATIVE SELF-REPORT INSTRUMENT

In research now in progress, we are examining the behavior of over 100 self-report items grouped into the following six categories:

(1) official contacts,
(2) delinquency,
(3) serious crime,
(4) drugs,
(5) school and family offenses, and
(6) contemptuousness.

For those interested in actually constructing a self-report instrument, we here provide illustrative items in each of the first three categories. Before doing so, we discuss two of the concrete problems facing those who would use the self-report technique: the *preamble* and the *response format.*

As far as we can determine, no special preamble is required for items covering delinquent or criminal activities. General mention of the topic in the introduc-

TABLE 19.1   Sex Ratios in Homogeneous Subscales,
Somerville and Cobleskill Data Sets, by Variety
and Frequency of Offenses

Subscale	Scoring	Somerville	Cobleskill
Drugs	Variety		
	1 or more	1.09	1.09
	8 or more	1.13	4.15
	Gamma	.03	.10
	Frequency		
	15 or more	1.35	2.26
	Gamma	.08	.12
Theft	Variety		
	1 or more	1.29	1.38
	4 or more	5.73	6.78
	Gamma	.45	.29
	Frequency		
	10 or more	6.54	4.73
	Gamma	.40	.28
Damage	Variety		
	1 or more	4.38	2.35
	3 or more	5.28	3.98
	Gamma	.69	.55
	Frequency		
	5 or more	4.14	3.10
	Gamma	.67	.51
Violence	Variety		
	1 or more	2.74	2.83
	4 or more	2.54	2.45
	Gamma	.70	.66
	Frequency		
	7 or more	4.37	2.84
	Gamma	.65	.64
Total Scales	Variety		
	1 or more	1.16	1.34
	10 or more	3.46	3.37
	Gamma	.37	.36
	Frequency		
	20 or more	2.83	2.81
	40 or more	1.80	4.0
	Gamma	.33	.37

TABLE 19.1 (Continued)

SOURCE: Secondary analysis of raw data.
NOTE: The items which comprise each of the scales are as follows:

Drugs	—gotten drunk
	—driven a car under the influence of alcohol or drugs
	—used pills to get high
	—used pot
	—sniffed glue or something else to get high
	—used LSD, methedrine, or mescaline
	—used heroin
	—sold drugs
Theft:	—stolen something worth less than $10
	—stolen something worth $10 to $50
	—stolen something worth more than $50
	—taken a car for a ride without the owner's permission
Damage:	—broken into and entered a home, a store, or a building
	—destroyed property (less than $10 damage)
	—destroyed property (more than $10 damage)
Violence:	—been in a fist fight
	—carried a weapon such as a gun or a knife
	—fought someone using a weapon
	—used force to get money or valuables from another

Variety scores were computed on the basis of the variety of acts to which each respondent admitted committing, irrespective of the number of times he indicated that he had committed any given act. Frequency scores were computed as follows: For each act, those who indicated that they had never committed the act scored zero; those who fell into the bottom third in terms of frequency of commission of the act relative to other respondents scored 1; those in the middle third, 2; those in the top third, 3. This scoring procedure has the effect of not overweighting high-frequency, low-seriousness offenses relative to more serious lower-frequency offenses (e.g., the youth who has occasionally used heroin receives a frequency score of 3, as does the regular pot user).

---

tion to the instrument or in the consent form will normally suffice to prepare the respondent for those items dealing with delinquent acts.[4] As is often the case, however, interviewers (or project directors) are likely to feel the need to announce the arrival of a sensitive topic and to reassure the respondent of the confidentiality of his or her replies. For these reasons, self-report items should follow a preamble like the following:

Young people sometimes do things that are either against the law or that would get them into trouble if they were caught. The following questions are about these kinds of acts.

Please give these questions some thought. Remember, your answers will be kept strictly *confidential*. No one other than members of our research staff will see your answers. If you don't want to answer a particular question, skip it and go to the next one.

With the exception of the "contemptuousness" items, which are attitudinal, our own *response format* is the same for all items. For example:

Have you *ever* been caught shoplifting by a clerk or owner of a store?

_____ Yes   _____ No

How many times in the *past year*? _____

Since the cost in administrative complexity and the time involved in obtaining *both* the "ever" and the "last year" information is slight (mainly because the "last year" question applies only when the "ever" question is answered in the affirmative), this format would seem to be a reasonable general solution to the reference period problem. (The length of the restricted or bounded reference period may be modified to cover the interval between administrations of the instrument, or to coincide with posttreatment or at-risk periods.)

1. OFFICIAL CONTACT INDEX

Self-reports of contact with police and court officials are strongly related to *records* of such contacts (Hindelang et al., 1978). Such reports thus provide an excellent, inexpensive measure of an important dimension of delinquency. Illustrative items include:

Have you *ever:*

(1) been reported to the police by someone in your neighborhood?
(2) been questioned as a suspect by the police about some crime?
(3) been picked up by the police?
(4) been taken to the police station?
(5) been held by the police or court until you could be released to the custody of your parents or guardian?
(6) been placed on probation by a juvenile court judge?
(7) been sentenced to a reformatory, training school, or some other institition by a judge?

Given the increasing difficulty of gaining access to official records, it is clear that the self-report method of measuring official contacts will be increasingly utilized. Fortunately, such reports have an excellent record, with several investigators noting that the self-report results have alerted them to errors in their official data (e.g., Hirschi, 1969; Farrington, 1973).

2. DELINQUENCY INDEX

The distinction between "delinquency" and "serious crime" is sufficiently important that it should receive explicit attention by those attempting to construct a self-report instrument. One way to force such attention is to construct separate pools of items for each domain. Illustrative *delinquency* items follow:

Have you *ever:*

(1) broken a car window on purpose?
(2) broken the windows of a school building?
(3) let the air out of car or truck tires?
(4) taken things you weren't supposed to take from a desk or locker at school?
(5) taken little things (worth less than $2) from a store without paying for them?
(6) helped break up chairs, tables, desks, or other furniture in a school, church, or other public building?
(7) slashed the seats in a bus, movie house, or some other place?
(8) picked a fight with someone you didn't know just for the hell of it?
(9) threatened to tell on someone unless they gave you money or something else you wanted?
(10) taken material or equipment from a construction site?
(11) driven a car when you weren't supposed to?
(12) fired a BB gun at some other person, at passing cars, or at windows of buildings?

3. SERIOUS CRIME INDEX

Illustrative items include the following:

Have you *ever:*

(1) taken a car belonging to someone you didn't know for a ride without the owner's permission?
(2) taken wheels, the battery, or some other expensive part of a car without the owner's permission?
(3) taken things worth between $10 and $50 from a store without paying for them?
(4) grabbed a purse from someone and run with it?
(5) used a club, knife, or gun to get something from an old person?
(6) used physical force (like twisting an arm or choking) to get money from another person?
(7) broken into a house, store, school or other building with the intention of stealing something?
(8) broken into a locked car to get something from it?
(9) carried a razor, switchblade, or gun with the intention of using it in a fight?

(10) used a knife or other weapon in a fight?
(11) carried tools you thought you might need to break into a car, a house, or some other building?
(12) tried to pass a check by signing someone else's name?
(13) hit a teacher or some other school official?
(14) sold illegal drugs such as heroin, marijuana, LSD, or cocaine?
(15) beat up someone so bad [he or she] probably needed a doctor?
(16) forced another person to have sex relations with you when [that person] did not want to?
(17) intentionally [set] a building on fire?
(18) taken things of large value (worth more than $50) from a store without paying for them?
(19) broken into a house, store, school, or other building with the intention of breaking things up or causing other damage?
(20) taken a bicycle belonging to someone you didn't know with no intention of returning it?

At least some "serious crime" items should be included in a self-report instrument. Lack of variation on these items would remind the researcher that the behavior of most concern to the police, and to the public, is rare in his or her sample, whatever its more general level of "delinquency."

CONCLUDING REMARKS

The flexibility of the self-report technique should remind the evaluator that he or she is not restricted to criteria of treatment effectiveness designed by others for other purposes. Treatment programs with clearly conceptualized and sharply delineated goals deserve commensurate criterion measures. Since the self-report technique allows construction of a criterion instrument derived from program goals, the failure to use a clearly relevant instrument indicates either that the program goals are not adequately specified or that the evaluator has not given sufficient attention to them. If nothing else, the technique allows active participation in the research process in a way not possible when the evaluator must rely only upon data produced by others, who may be uninterested in the program (e.g., police records) or who may be too intimately involved with the project. Unless the immediate processes through which the treatment is hypothesized to work are specified, the delinquency criterion measure will remain vaguely defined. Clear definition of the criterion variable will focus attention on the intermediate processes too long ignored by evaluation efforts that focus exclusively on some ultimate dependent variable and therefore have no way of accounting for program failure or even success. The accumulation of systematic knowledge requires more than a finding of significant or insignificant differences on the criterion available; knowing the "how" and "why" of success or failure is at least equally important.

NOTES

1. The use of the Short-Nye items in subsequent research is traced in Hindelang et al. (1978).

2. For a recent pool of more serious items, see Farrington (1973).

3. The sample on which Gould reports consisted of young (seventh-grade), primarily black males who were participants in a delinquency prevention project.

4. Respondents are rarely upset by encounters with self-report delinquency items and, as far as we know, there is no case on record in which information on delinquent activities revealed in a self-report survey has been used to the detriment of a respondent. In other words, the risk to subjects in the self-report survey has been virtually zero, thanks to the professionalism of those using this technique, not to the diligence of human subject committees.

REFERENCES

Belson, W. A. et al. (1968) "Development of a Procedure for Eliciting Information from Boys About the Nature and Extent of Their Stealing." Survey Research Centre, London School of Economics.

Broder, P. K., G. W. Peters, and J. Zimmerman (1978) "The Relationship Between Self-Reported Juvenile Delinquency and Learning Disabilities: A Preliminary Look at the Data." Presented at the NCJFCJ-NDAA Fifth National Conference on Juvenile Justice, San Francisco, California, February, and Baton Rouge, Louisiana, March.

Campbell, D. T. and D. Fiske (1959) "Converent and Discriminant Validation by the Multi-Trait-Multi-Method Matix." *Psychological Bulletin* 56: 81-105.

Clark, J. P. and L. L. Tifft (1966) "Polygraph and Interview Validation of Self-Reported Delinquent Behavior." *American Sociological Review* 31: 516-523.

Dentler, R. A. and L. J. Monroe (1961) 'Social Correlates of Early Adolescent Theft." *American Sociological Review* 26: 733-743.

Elliott, D. S. and S. S. Ageton (1978) 'The Social Correlates of Delinquent Behavior in a National Youth Panel." Annual Meetings of the American Society of Criminology, Dallas.

——— and H. L. Voss (1974) *Delinquency and Dropout*. Lexington, MA: D. C. Heath.

Elmhorn, K. (1965) "Study in Self-Reported Delinquency Among School Children in Stockholm," pp. 117-146 in *Scandinavian Studies in Criminology, Volume 1*. London: Tavistock.

Erickson, M. (1972) "The Changing Relation Between Official and Self-Reported Delinquency." *Journal of Criminal Law, Criminology, and Police Science* 63: 388-395.

——— and W. B. Smith, Jr. (1974) "On the Relation Between Self-Reported and Actual Deviance: An Empirical Test." *Humboldt Journal of Social Relations* 2: 106-113.

Farrington, P. (1973) "Self-Reports of Deviant Behavior: Predictive and Stable?" *Journal of Criminal Law and Criminology* 64: 99-110.

Gibbons, D. (1976) *Delinquent Behavior*. Englewood Cliffs, NJ: Prentice-Hall.

Gold, M. (1970) *Delinquent Behavior in an American City*. Belmont, CA: Wadsworth.

——— and J. Reimer (1975) "Changing Patterns of Delinquent Behavior Among Americans 13 Through 16 Years Old: 1967-72." *Crime and Delinquency Literature* 7, 4: 483-517.

Gould, L. C. (1969) "Who Define Delinquency: A Comparison of Self-Reported and Officially-Reported Indices of Delinquency for Three Racial Groups." *Social Problems* 16: 325-336.

Hardt, R. and G. E. Bodine "Development of Self-Report Instruments in Delinquency Research." Youth Development Center, Syracuse University.

Hindelang, M. J. (1971) "Age, Sex, and the Versatility of Self-Reported Delinquent Involvements." *Social Problems* 18: 522-535.

——— and J. Weis (1972) "The bc-try Cluster and Factor Analysis System: Personality and Self-Reported Delinquency." *Criminology* 10: 268-294.

Hindelang, M., T. Hirschi, and J. Weis (1978) "The Measurement of Delinquency by the Self-Report Method," Interim Report to Center for Studies of Crime and Delinquency, National Institute of Mental Health.

Hirschi, T. (1969) *Causes of Delinquency.* Berkeley: University of California Press.

Krohn, M., G. Waldo, and T. Chiricos (1975) "Self-Reported Delinquency: A Comparison of Structured Interviews and Self-Administered Checklists." *Journal of Criminal Law and Criminology* 65: 545-555.

Kulik, J. A., K. B. Stein, and T. R. Sarbin (1968a) 'Dimensions and Patterns of Adolescent Antisocial Behavior." *Journal of Consulting and Clinical Psychology* 32: 375-382.

——— (1968b) "Disclosure of Delinquent Behavior Under Conditions of Anonymity and Non-Anonymity." *Journal of Consulting and Clinical Psychology* 32: 506-509.

Nettler, G. (1978) *Explaining Crime.* New York: McGraw-Hill.

Nye, F. I. (1958) *Family Relationships and Delinquent Behavior.* New York: John Wiley.

Porterfield, A. (1946) *Youth in Trouble.* Forth Worth, TX: Leo Potisham Foundation.

Reiss, A. J. (1975) "Inappropriate Theories and Inadequate Methods as Policy Plagues: Self-Reported Delinquency and the Law," pp. 211-222 in N. J. Demerath, III, et al. (eds.) *Social Policy and Sociology.* New York: Academic.

Sellin, T. and M. Wolfgang (1964) *The Measurement of Delinquency.* New York: John Wiley.

Senna, J., S. Rathus, and L. Siegel (1974) "Delinquent Behavior and Academic Investment Among Suburban Youth." *Adolescence* 9: 481-494.

Short, J. F. and F. I. Nye (1958) 'Extent of Unrecorded Juvenile Delinquency: Tentative Conclusions." *Journal of Criminal Law and Criminology* 49: 296-302.

Sudman, S. and N. M. Bradburn (1974) *Response Effects in Surveys.* Chicago: AVC.

Wallerstein, J. S. and C. J. Wyle "Our Law-Abiding Law-Breakers." *Probation* 25: 107-112.

20

Seriousness:
A Measure for All Purposes?

Peter H. Rossi and J. Patrick Henry

Whether or not a given sequence of behavior is a crime is defined in the criminal statutes as a qualitative judgment. While there may be some ambiguities, it is clear that a crime is distinguished from noncriminal behavior and from other crimes on qualitative grounds. Neither is the criminality of an action a matter of degree nor are some crimes more "criminal" than others. On the manifest level, crimes are qualitative classes of behavior that do not appear to have any obvious inherent ordering among themselves.

Social science research abhors qualitative variables, a judgment that is apparent in the hierarchical ordering of levels of measurement, with ratio variables at the top and qualitative dichotomous distinctions on the bottom. Offense-specific crime rates are defensible, but overall crime rates in which every crime recorded is counted equally are not. Nor is it possible to easily describe a "criminal career," since there is no inherent way of showing change in criminal behavior except in frequency terms. For research reasons, there are strong strains toward measuring crime in quantitative terms as a variable.

But the main reason there has been so much effort to transform crimes into a higher level of measurement is that to do so is only to follow common sense. First of all, the sanctions applied in the criminal law vary from crime to crime, expressing in the severity of prescribed punishment the fact that the law recognizes that some crimes are more serious than others. Second, public reactions to criminal violations vary in intensity. Murders are relatively rare events but receive the greatest share of media and public attention, while "everyday" shoplifting is regarded relatively, with some degree of equanimity. In short, there appears to be a quality of seriousness along which crimes can be ordered. Furthermore, with luck, numbers that represent degrees of seriousness can be assigned to criminal offenses. With even greater luck, the numbers assigned would have ratio properties, i.e., a crime that is assigned the number 2X is twice as serious as the crime assigned the number X.

Of course, such seriousness scores would be maximally useful if they were robust and were not subject-, method- or time-dependent. Such robustness would make it possible to use the scores to track changes over time, contrast the criminal trends in subgroups, and serve as a general anchoring in a wide variety of research studies.

Obviously, such scores would be enormously helpful in evaluation studies. Since an important outcome measure is amount and quality of crime, it is especially important to have some handle on the mix of crimes occurring before and after an intervention in order to assess whether or not expected changes occurred in fact.

The devising of such a set of scores for criminal acts turned out to be remarkably easy. All that was necessary was somehow to get members of our society to attach numbers to crimes according to the degree of seriousness, as it appeared to them. Sellin and Wolfgang (1964), in their pioneering study undertaken in the late 1950s, used "captive" audiences of students at two Philadelphia universities and a group of judges and police to rate various sets of descriptions of criminal acts according to their seriousness. Two rating tasks were set, ratings on an eleven-point numerical scale and ratings using the ratio scale measurement approach pioneered by S. S. Stevens (1957). No great surprises appeared in the findings about which crimes were regarded as more serious and which are less serious. Perhaps the only surprise was the fact that the ordering by the two methods did not differ by very much and that the several rater groups produced ratings that were very similar.

Several excellent surveys (Wellford and Wiatrowski, 1975; Turner, 1978) of the now extensive literature that the pioneering work of Sellin and Wolfgang (1964) inspired have been published, and that task need not be repeated here. The important points brought out by the surveys are as follows:

(1) Crimes that involve physical harm to individuals are regarded as the most serious, while violations of administrative rules are regarded as least serious. The range runs from planned murder at the one extreme, to parking violations at the other.
(2) Seriousness scores can be devised that will satisfy the requirements of ratio scales.
(3) Alternative ways of measuring seriousness correlate highly. In short, the phenomenon is robust, surviving alternative measurement approaches.

(4) Remarkable degrees of consensus obtain across populations and across subgroups within populations. In short, considerable agreement on which crimes are to be considered more serious exists across cultures and within cultures among classes, educational and age groups, ethnic enclaves, and between the sexes.

(5) Dramatic changes apparently have not occurred across time; results of earliest studies agree strongly with results of later studies.

While the robustness of the seriousness measures appears to consist of features that make the scores attractive to use in a wide variety of applications, it is important to appreciate the limitations of the scores as well. First, although correlations across different measures of seriousness range above +.85, those high coefficients indicate mainly that there are no gross differences produced by alternative measures. That is to say, a change in method does not produce any gross inversions in seriousness: Murder is regarded as most serious and a parking ticket as least serious, no matter how seriousness is measured. Seen in this perspective, the robustness characteristics listed above are not as impressive. Indeed, the high correlations are compatible with considerable disagreement over the relative placement of particular offenses that are close to each other in seriousness.

Second, how serious a behavioral act legally defined as a crime may be regarded does not speak to the etiology of the criminal acts in question. Thus, the most serious crimes and the least serious crimes are not necessarily on a continuum of criminality, forming a natural progression from the entry points in criminal careers to the culmination of such careers. In short, receiving a parking ticket is not the first step on the road through larceny to murder.[1] This characteristic has important implications for the use of seriousness scores in a wide variety of applications.

Third, agreement on the relative ordering of criminal acts is compatible with considerable differences in the absolute level of seriousness attributed to any given act. Thus, there are consistent significant differences in the mean level of seriousness attributed to all criminal acts by sex, levels of education, and place of residence. Men regard all criminal acts as less serious than do women, persons living in large urban centers are more tolerant than small city and rural dwellers, and so on. Overall agreement on the relative ordering of crimes does not mean that everyone agrees on how serious any one crime may be or how serious criminal transgressions are in general.

The seriousness measures have not been received with complete acceptance in all sectors of the social science community. Many serious questions have been raised about the technical aspects of the ratings and about the substantive import of the ratings and their characteristics. The next section reviews some of the major controversies in some detail.

CONTROVERSIES OVER THE MEANING OF SERIOUSNESS

Typically, the measurement of seriousness is undertaken without specifying to subjects used precisely what is meant by *seriousness*. For example, in our own study of crime seriousness, a small (N = 200) sample of Baltimoreans were asked to sort a set of eighty cards bearing descriptions of criminal acts, into nine categories labeled "most serious" to "least serious."[2] No definition of seriousness was offered to the respondents, who were simply asked what were their "opinions about how serious . . . different crimes are." No respondent balked at the task or asked what we meant by "seriousness." Apparently, philosophers might puzzle over the meaning of seriousness, but ordinary persons experience little difficulty both in understanding the term and in making seriousness discriminations.

At least several critics of such studies have raised the question of what seriousness means. To begin with, are persons reporting what they perceive the norms of the society to be or are they reporting their own evaluations of criminal acts, a question that raises the distinction between seriousness as cognition and as evaluation. While existing studies of seriousness provide no means of deciding one way or another, the question can be raised whether the seriousness scores could be expected to vary depending on whether or not respondents were reporting perceived norms or personal opinions. Unless there were some severe differences between the two, differences in seriousness could not be expected to appear. If the norms consist of the aggregated opinions of others, on which respondents are reporting, then the aggregated opinions of respondents would be identical with the norms that respondents were reporting on. Perhaps one could expect more variance in opinions than in norms since, in the one case, individual variation around the norms is retained, while in the other case it is not; it certainly is not clear whether it would make any difference at all.[3] Furthermore, the fact that studies asking respondents their own personal opinions do not produce results that differ in any marked degree from studies that ask for perceived norms, bears out the point made above.

The ambiguity of the term *seriousness* had led some critics to take another line of attack (e.g., Needleman, 1975). Here the claim is made that without further specification of the rating task, some might respond by guessing what were typical sentences meted out to convicted offenders, others in terms of the damages typically incurred by victims, and still others in terms of the moral indignation aroused when such crimes are committed. Indeed, at least one researcher has attempted to show that there are differences in ratings that can be produced by specifying more precisely what is meant by the rating. Unfortunately, this criticism comes up against two sets of obstinate findings: First, attempts to use more specific dimensions do not produce radically different orders[4] when compared to the orders produced by seriousness. Second, the degree of similarity among subgroups in the seriousness ratings themselves indicate that if there is variation from individual to individual in interpretations of the meaning of seriousness, such variation cannot be very substantial either in extent or in outcome.

Additional attacks have been made on the seriousness scores for their claimed numerical properties. For example, Rose (1966) has questioned whether the ratio scale measurements of Sellin and Wolfgang really have their advertised attribute of additivity; e.g., is a crime in which two murders have been committed to be rated as twice as serious as one in which only one homicide has occurred?

This criticism has been countered by showing that the correlation between respondents' scores on "complex" offense acts (descriptions which include multiple offenses or more than one offender) and the sum of scores for single acts which go into the construction of complex offenses, indicates a high degree ($r = .969$) of correspondence (Wellford and Wiatrowski, 1975).

Furthermore, these criticisms have been countered as misunderstandings of the technical issues involved. Thus, additivity is not a quality that implies simple addition of components in more complex criminal events: For example, additivity is compatible with seriousness being determined completely by the most serious single component or by averaging over the component criminal acts, and so on.

Questions have also been raised (e.g., Chilton and DeAmicis, 1975) concerning whether average ratings for certain crimes in which the interindividual variance in ratings is high are meaningful representations of central tendencies. Especially for crimes in which there were no victims, individual ratings were so dispersed that central tendency measures appeared particularly unrepresentative. However, the dispersion around the central tendency of ratings for particular crimes does not necessarily invalidate such measures as the average. All that such dispersion means is that the average is not the only index to be used in describing seriousness. Indeed, variation in dispersion can be a topic in its own right and might, as Chilton and DeAmicis (1975) suggest, indicate that some criminal acts are in process of changing either to a more or to a less serious position in the future.[5]

The attacks on the crime seriousness measures are indicative of some degree of uneasiness about them and their properties. It does seem counter-intuitive that there be so strong a degree of consensus among raters as the crime seriousness researchers appear to assert. For example, in the Baltimore study (Rossi et al., 1974), it is shown that scores computed from ratings made by high school graduates, those who did not graduate, whites and blacks, males, females and the cross-classifications among these dichotomies all correlate with each other[6] on the average +.75, with a range that extends from +.93 (better educated white males with better educated white females) on the high side, to +.61

(poorly educated white females with poorly educated black males). While the sizes and signs of these coefficients indicate considerable agreement across these subgroups, it is important to examine quite carefully exactly what that agreement means.

First of all, the distributions of scores are not normal but tend to be rectangular. That is, in the usual study there are fairly large numbers of high and low seriousness crimes, with an underrepresentation of crimes in the middle range, as compared to what one would expect on the basis of normality in the distribution of crime seriousness. This rectangularity implies that the correlation coefficient primarily reflects the fact that all subgroups agree on the crimes that are most serious and the crimes that are less serious since it is these scores that contribute most to the covariance. Hence, such high correlation coefficients are quite compatible with considerable disagreement on specific crimes of middling seriousness. In short, everyone agrees that murders are heinous and parking tickets are trivial. The issues over which there may be disagreement are whether shoplifiting is as serious as small-time burglary.

It is important to distinguish between "global consensus" and "local consensus." By "global consensus" is meant the agreement that exists on the total range of seriousness; that is, on the overall ordering of crimes from murder to traffic rules. In contrast, "local consensus" refers to agreement on the ordering of crimes that are close together in seriousness. Here one would be concerned for example with whether there is agreement that thefts of a certain amount from business enterprises are as serious as comparable amounts stolen during burglaries of homes. It should be noted that research on local consensus has been almost entirely missing,[7] with almost all the studies published focused on global measures.

This lack of research on "local" consensus is an especially critical gap when it comes to considering the use of seriousness scores in evaluation. If there is less than strong consensus on crimes of middling seriousness, as, for example, most property crimes and minor assaults, that fact reduces the utility of crime seriousness scores as output measures in the evaluation of criminal justice programs. Thus, if the criterion for the success of a program of law enforcement is expressed as a reduction in the overall seriousness of crimes reported to the police, the ambiguity about the seriousness scores of the bulk of the crimes in any jurisdiction is a disability that must be countered.

Part of the problem of the crime seriousness research is that the crimes that are evaluated are not representative of the bulk of the crimes that are reported to the police. After all, murder is relatively rare, but is represented by 13 entries out of 140 crimes in Rossi et al. (1974), while property-related crimes are represented by 32 entries. Among crimes reported to the police, more than 90 percent are property-related crimes. The full richness of variation in behavioral acts that are classified as property crimes clearly cannot be captured by such a lopsided emphasis on relatively rare events, such as murder.

It should be noted that the unrepresentativeness of the crimes rated in the crime seriousness studies also contributes to the inflated estimates of consensus referred to above. Hence, it is precisely in that portion of the crime seriousness continuum where most of the crimes are located that the descriptive power of the crime seriousness scores is weakest.

SOME UNSETTLED ISSUES IN THE USE OF CRIME SERIOUSNESS

However dramatic and startling the findings of crime seriousness studies may be, it is important to approach the use of crime seriousness scores with considerable skepticism and caution. The fact that crimes can be rated consistently by the general public and by special groups of criminal justice personnel is certainly a fact of interest in and of itself. At minimum, these findings indicate that there is a normative structure that is widely diffused and cognitively appreciated by most segments of the population. Whether they have further implications for criminal justice theory and research is problematic, as we will indicate below.

CRIME SERIOUSNESS AND THEORIES OF CRIME

Competing paradigms attempting to explain crime react differently to the crime seriousness studies, when they react at all. The widespread agreement of many respondents on the relative seriousness of crimes is apparently supportive of criminal theories associated with the functional paradigm. That is, functional theories[8] assume a general value consensus from which the "moral boundaries" of unacceptable public conduct are derived and represented in the criminal law (Chambliss, 1973). A superficial consideration of the seriousness results may appear to conclude that criminal law does not represent only the values of the powerful, a conclusion that seemingly undercuts the conflict perspective. Either of these conclusions is misleadingly oversimplified.

While it would be quite damaging to the functional paradigm if there were no evidence of consensus over the seriousness of crimes, the fact of consensus is not sufficient in and of itself to validate the functional perspective. The fact that there is some considerable consensus is consistent with the idea that there is a considerable normative basis to the criminal justice system, but there is nothing in the functional viewpoint that would lead to expectations that there would be agreement across cultures. In Newman's study (1976) of comparative deviance across six countries, high degrees of cross-national consensus are found in seriousness ratings attached to the "traditional" criminal acts (e.g., "robbery," "incest," and "appropriation"). A derivative of the functional paradigm, the subculture of violence theory (Wolfgang and Ferracuti, 1967) is challenged by the similar seriousness pattern attached to traditional crimes in Sardinia, a subculture of violence, when compared to countries where no such subculture is evident.

It should also be noted that Newman (1976) finds some cross-national disagreements in seriousness ratings of "traditional deviant" acts such as homosexuality. Such findings are also evident in other crime seriousness studies (Rossi et al., 1974) and are not incompatible with the functional paradigm. Quarrels over whether homosexuality and abortion are crimes still agitate the U.S. public.

Conflict theories of crime that regard the criminal law as a social control device arising out of the conflict among social classes, between power elites and the oppressed, are only superficially challenged by the crime seriousness findings. According to conflict theorists, conflicting class interests at any one time may be latent rather than manifest. In addition, while the interests of the lower classes may be in challenging the definitions of criminality allegedly foisted on the society by the ruling elites, these interests need not necessarily manifest themselves across the total set of criminal acts. Perhaps these interests are only those that challenge, say, the property rights defined by the society. Thus, one might expect that all classes would agree that murder and assault are serious crimes, but differ on how serious pilfering or violations of workers' rights to organize into unions may be.

Consensus is also generated through control over the school systems, mass media, and churches, a pattern that means that all classes are indoctrinated in the views of the ruling elites.[9] Hence the consensus that is shown in crime seriousness merely documents the efficiency of the socializing and indoctrinating media of the society. The conflicts recognized in the conflict theories are latent ones, not necessarily always manifest in disagreements among the potentially conflicting groups of the society.

It is not at all clear whether conflict theorists should find much of interest in crime seriousness studies as they are typically formulated. Schwendinger and Schwendinger (1975) note that descriptions of criminal acts usually presented refer, at best, to the isolated behavior of individuals, ignoring the "social conditions" which give rise to the behavior. For example, if the act of purse-snatching is evaluated in absence of a description of impoverished conditions in which the offender lived, the potentially criminogenic element—poverty—has been omitted. Raters are not given the opportunities to evaluate the seriousness of inequitous social conditions, nor to direct policy attention toward regulation of those conditions, but only to judge individuals or behaviors.

While criminal acts are not necessarily motivated by conditions of inequality, there is considerable merit in the idea of considering more complete descriptions of crime. Robbery does not take place in a vacuum, and one cannot assume that the context and the persons involved in the act are completely subordinate to the act of robbery.

Certainly the labeling perspective is not contradicted by the crime seriousness studies: Indeed, if anything, the fact that persons generally react in a similar manner to "labels" describing criminal acts is supportive of the notion that it is the social construction of reality that determines criminality. Hence, it would appear that the "labeling" theory approach to crime could benefit by incorporating crime seriousness studies. Labeling studies proceed on the basis (Tittle, 1975) "that the imposition of any sanction or any official act of negative classification constitutes labeling," i.e., arrest, conviction, or institutionalization. Community reaction to such labeling predisposes an offender to commit additional deviant acts. Community reaction to the label of a deviant individual increasingly cuts off avenues of legitimate support until he or she is "forced" to return to criminal activity.

Seriousness ratings can be regarded within the framework of labeling theory as measures of how strong will be the community's negative reaction to a convicted offender. Persons convicted of serious crimes about which there is considerable consensus should be more consistently rejected. Criminal acts over which there is less consensus (and also less imputed seriousness) may be met with less or inconsistent rejection by society.

This brief and necessarily somewhat superficial review of the implications of seriousness studies for paradigms of criminal behavior indicates that the findings of such studies neither are anticipated by each of the major competing paradigms nor do they contradict any of these contending positions. This double-edged generalization points up the distressing lack of theoretical base for crime seriousness. There appears to be no particular a priori reason these findings should be as they are, nor do the findings themselves appear to fit into some overall conception of crime and its etiology.

The compatibility of the crime seriousness findings with a variety of theories about crime arises because the studies do not address themselves to the question of how these evaluations of criminal justice acts become absorbed by members of a society. Consensus may simply reflect cognitive understanding of how the criminal justice system operates,[10] how successful have been the socializing and indoctrinating institutions of the society, or reflections of the normative structure of the society. While the present authors prefer to regard the findings of crime seriousness research as reflective of the normative structures of the society, there is no convincing evidence that such is the case.[11] It should also be noted that the competing paradigms of crime theory do not make any direct predictions about crime seriousness, although each school can simultaneously produce post facto explanations for the findings.

CRIME SERIOUSNESS AS THE BASIS FOR CRIMINAL LAW

It is tempting to envisage the use of crime seriousness scores as a guide to the setting of punishment for convicted offenders.[12] In the absence of clear rationales for the setting of statutory punishments, and with some philosophers of law basing the authority for law in public opinion, one can easily imagine that legislators would find the crime seriousness approach attractive. Indeed, the Colorado State Legislature did require that a survey of crime seriousness be undertaken among the general public and among criminal justice personnel in that state in connection with the drafting of a revised criminal code based on level sentencing.

There are several reasons such a use should be approached with considerable caution if not outright skepticism. First of all, it should be noted that such a usage implicitly looks upon the criminal law primarily as retributive. If punishment is to be proportional to how serious the public regards the criminal act, then notions of criminal sanctions as deterrent or as rehabilitative tend to be subordinated.

Second, the criminal acts that have been studied in the crime seriousness studies[13] have been descriptions of behavior abstracted from the contexts in which they occurred and abstracted from the individuals involved. Any given criminal case as presented to the police, public prosecutor, judge, and jury contains a host of details concerning the circumstances of the alleged offender, the particular circumstances surrounding the crime, some information on the victim, if any, and so on. Judgments about seriousness and about the appropriate treatment that ought to be brought to bear on the case can be expected to vary with the particular details in question. Indeed, there is more than a little hint to that effect in the findings of some of the studies in which slight changes in the criminal act as described produce considerable variation in seriousness.[14]

If the sentence to be meted out to offenders is to be reflective of general public opinion, then should not the statutes also reflect this actual variation? If so, then the crime seriousness studies that would provide the appropriate information have simply not been undertaken systematically as yet.

Third, the criminal acts that have been studied are hardly representative of the full range of criminal acts that have been singled out in the statutes. The National Crime Information Center codes recognize over 400 general crime classifications, while the most any crime seriousness study has covered is 140 criminal acts that most probably are covered by only a handful, perhaps as many as 25, of the general crime classifications. Any of the better known crime seriousness studies would simply be inadequate for the purposes of matching the criminal statutes of any state.

Fourth, it is not at all clear that seriousness and punishments are monotonically related. Only a small number of studies[15] have attempted to relate crime seriousness to perceptions of appropriate punishment. Punishments may very well be qualitatively differentiated and possibly multidimensional. Hence, for example, probation, fines, and incarceration could be separate dimensions of punishment, such that, for example, some combinations of fines *and* probation might be seen as equivalent to certain terms of incarceration. In short, what is needed is research on the relationship between perceived seriousness and the appropriate punishment types and levels that correspond to levels of seriousness.

Sudnow's (1965) concept of "normal" crime illustrates the difficulties of postulating a direct relationship between crime seriousness and the workings of the criminal justice system. The administrative requirements of the courts demand that a high priority be assigned to "settling" cases (Skolnick, 1967). If the dispensation of justice required that every criminal case be brought to jury trial, the system would crack under the heavy strain. Hence, a large majority of criminal cases (60 to 80 percent) are settled by "plea-bargaining." As Sudnow points out, this process of bargaining[16] proceeds most smoothly when a given offense is typical of a normally occurring crime of that type. It is apparently not the severity of the criminal act or even the specific features of the immediate event that determine if a crime is normal. Rather, it is a combination of: the characteristics of the offender as they signal the "type who commit [this] crime" (including race, class, prior criminal record insofar as it reveals the offender's "style" and personal appearance), the regularity with which the crime is encountered by courts in a given jurisdiction, and the ecological location of the offense (suggesting that certain crimes are typical of specific areas in a community). If the crime qualifies as normal, then a routinized range of potential plea reductions will be considered in the defending attorney's negotiation with both the defendant and the prosecutor. Insofar as burglary or drunkenness or narcotics use are equally normal crimes for a given jurisdiction, the relative severity of these crimes will have little bearing on the process of settlement.[17]

It is possible that crime seriousness takes on quite a different meaning from within the criminal justice system. Crime is not an uncommon event to the court; to the contrary, "it is their business." Seriousness may not be so much a matter of social or individual harm incurred in the act of a crime, but the relative cost to efficient administration of justice agencies.

It is also instructive to note that what is normal crime in one jurisdiction may very well be abnormal in another. As crimes vary to the degree with which they come to the attention of the criminal justice system from area to area, they may also vary to the degree which they are perceived by the public. It is probably the case that the practice of criminal justice shapes the perception of crime seriousness; and further, those perceptions shape the operation of justice agencies. It is not at all clear how such relationships work. If seriousness mirrors the criminal law, reflecting however imperfectly the reactions of the criminal justice system to crimes, then adjusting the criminal law to crime seriousness simply adjusts to widespread errors of perception.

In any event, without additional knowledge about the nature of crime seriousness and clear theoretical understanding of how seriousness judgments are made, it would be hazardous to run the criminal justice system by looking to crime seriousness as a guide.

CRIME SERIOUSNESS RATINGS AS OUTCOME MEASURES IN EVALUATION STUDIES

One of the main sources of motivation for the development of crime seriousness scores was dissatisfaction with conventional ways of aggregating crime statistics. The Uniform Crime Report's use of Index Crimes, a simple summation across seven crime categories, is perhaps the most commonly used indicator of the trends of serious crimes. The index crime approach simply weights each of the seven crimes equally. Since the crime categories included ranged from homicide through larceny, acts that are clearly not comparable in seriousness have been given equal weights. A more sensitive indicator of crime trends, and hence of the crime problem, would weight crimes differentially according to how important crimes were. Indeed, the original Wolfgang and Sellin study was undertaken to make possible such weightings in a subsequent longitudinal study of a cohort of young persons in Philadelphia (Wolfgang et al., 1972).

The use of seriousness weighted crime rates as an indicator of crime trends has been disputed by Alfred Blumstein (1974), who computed seriousness weighted crime rates and compared them over time with the UCR Index Crimes. Blumstein was able to show that because the mix of crimes in the historical period used (1960-1972) remained quite steady, the correlation between the measures was so high that little would be gained by using seriousness weighted indexes as opposed to the Index Crimes. Indeed, it appeared that because offense-specific crime rates increased and decreased in concert over the period of time, change in the total amount of crime was as good an indicator as any weighted combination of crimes.

Blumstein's critique of the use of crime seriousness weights is, of course, historically conditioned.[18] A different historical period in which offense-specific rates changed differentially over time would have produced greater differences between the two indexes being compared. However, the sensitivity of seriousness weighted indexes depends also on the amounts of offense-specific crimes as well as their rate of change. Thus, even a large change in the number of murders would be unlikely to change the total seriousness weighted crime indicator by much since murders are relatively infrequent and hence even when weighted heavily cannot make that much of a difference. A shift in the proportion of property crimes between robbery and burglary, in contrast, can make more of a difference, since burglary and robbery are much more frequent.

It has also been suggested that crime seriousness scores could be used in the evaluation of criminal justice programs whenever the objectives of the program include reductions in crime. The main problem with such a use has been alluded to earlier in this chapter, but bears repeating in this context. Ranking crimes by their seriousness does not line them up on a continuum with respect to either causation or increasing involvement in criminal activities. Crimes against the person that do not involve property are clearly regarded more serious than straight property crimes and presumably are quite differently motivated. Similarly, a criminal "career" is not a simple progression from parking tickets to murder for profit. It seems likely that programs designed to reduce crime seriousness would end up being a set of offense-specific programs. In that event, the success of such subprograms would best be gauged by observing shifts in offense-specific rates.

In short, it appears that little is to be gained by the use of crime seriousness scores in the evaluation of criminal justice programs. Such scores cannot substitute for offense-specific crime rates.

THE FUTURE OF CRIME SERIOUSNESS RESEARCH

There appear to be two distinct directions in which crime seriousness research has been carried: (1) consideration of the validity and usefulness of Sellin and Wolfgang's index of offense seriousness, and (2) attempts to explain seriousness ratings in terms of respondent characteristics and broad classes of crime type. This review of findings from seriousness researches has raised more questions than answers. Consensus over seriousness rankings appears to hold, but several possible explanations of why this is the case have yet to be thoroughly explored. There is also evidence of dissensus within localized ranges of seriousness, and over so-called victimless crimes. However, analyses of respondent characteristics have not identified convincingly groups which may be responsible for dissenting opinion; thus, it is not known whether collective conflict of values over seriousness even exists.

The major difficulties with crime seriousness research stem from the relative primitiveness of the field, a condition that is concealed to a large degree by the rather startling nature of the crime seriousness findings, in particular the seeming robustness of the ratings under shifts in methods and populations studied.

Assuming for the moment that knowing about crime seriousness is worthwhile (and we believe that such is the case), then there are several directions in which research on this topic might proceed to its considerable enrichment.

First, future research should pay more attention to studying offenses which are more common.[19] For example, at least as much attention should be paid to various forms of breaking and entering as to murder. If seriousness scores are going to be useful, they have to distinguish among the more common offenses.

Second, an important line of research endeavor should go into making the criminal acts used in the rating tasks fit more closely to the real world. As mentioned earlier in this chapter, in the real world specific persons commit criminal acts to specific victims with specific outcomes in terms of damages to the victim. A program of research which would extend the early work of Berk and Rossi (1977) and Garrett and Rossi (1978) by enriching the criminal incidents being rated, would go a long way toward understanding the ways in which persons actually judge events as they occur.

Third, while there is not much evidence that better samples will yield different results, it is also the case that existing studies have used samples of convenience to an extent that is hardly justifiable. Probability samples of the public drawn from sensible universes are clearly needed in order to provide a firm, generalizable foundation beneath seriousness researches.

Finally, analyses of crime seriousness must clearly go beyond the assessment of overall agreement on the relative positions of homicide and parking tickets. The issues of interest both theoretically and practically center around disagreements about the relative ordering of offenses that are closer together in crime seriousness. The issue centers, for example, around whether stealing from a large corporation is more or less reprehensible than from a private home, or whether killing through environmental pollution is more or less reprehensible than killing through drunken driving. And to whom does it matter?

NOTES

1. For example, Wolfgang and his colleagues find that there was no detectable drift from the less serious to the most serious offenses in the delinquent careers of Philadelphia youths. (Wolfgang, Figlio, and Sellin, 1972.)

2. Actual wording was as follows: "Criminal law covers a very large number of different kinds of crime. Some are considered to be very serious acts and others are not so serious. We are interested in your opinions about how serious you think different crimes are" (Rossi et al., 1974).

3. A similar issue besets the study of occupational prestige, defined as the relative evaluation of occupations in which the question has been raised again and again whether the findings reflect normative structure or individual evaluation (see Reiss, 1961).

4. For example, Needleman (1975) finds correlations of between .8 and .9 of ratings of wrongfulness when compared to seriousness ratings of the same crime.

5. Such variation may indicate changes in an individual's perception of crime over his or her lifetime, as well as historical shifts of attitude. Many seriousness studies indicate disagreement over "crimes of morality," such as taking drugs and participating in uncommon sexual activity, thus possibly revealing changing social values. High tolerance for such acts is often associated negatively with age, suggesting that social changes in seriousness, should they be occurring, are not uniformly distributed across all groups.

6. Scores were computed over the ratings given by members of each of the eight subgroups so defined. Since the total Baltimore sample was only 200, the numbers of respondents fitting into each subgroup tended to be quite small, ranging from 9 poorly educated black females to 19 poorly educated white males. The scores computed over such small numbers of respondents are somewhat unstable; hence, these correlations are understated.

7. For example, the correlation between average seriousness scores derived from a sample in Macomb, Illinois, and Baltimore, Maryland, is .918 over the 136 comparable offenses. However, when subsets of offenses are considered, as shown below, the correlations drop considerably:

middle 100 offences	.851
middle 50 offences	.504
top 20 offences	.195
bottom 20 offences	.690

The classification used in the computations shown above were on the basis of seriousness as defined in the Rossi et al. (1974) Baltimore study. Crime scores for Macomb, Illinois were obtained from Cullen et al., 1979.

8. This discussion of the basic perspectives on crime refers to one as the "functional" or "consensus" model, and the other as the "conflict" model. Although several distinct approaches of distinct emphasis are contained within each of the two major paradigms (see, for example, Austin T. Turk, 1977 and Gwynn Nettler, 1974), for present purposes it is mainly necessary to be concerned with the basic positions of functional and conflict perspectives.

9. Such an explanation superficially suggests that consensus across seriousness rankings is indicative of "false consciousness," and thus supports conflict theory. Thomas et al. (1976) anticipated such an interpretation of the consensus they found in evaluations of "fair sentence" lengths given to 17 offenses. They suggest that one cannot have one's cake and eat it too: "The notion of a 'false consciousness' is, practically speaking, tautological: had we detected class-based differences, they would have been accepted as support for a conflict interpretation; the fact that no such differences were found cannot, therefore, also be interpreted as supportive."

10. Indeed, in a study of political elites in three states, Berk and Rossi (1977) found that the best predictors of how elites saw the way the criminal justice systems in their states operated were the crime seriousness scores of the crimes in question. Furthermore, elite members did not differentiate clearly between what they reported was the common practice in sentencing in their states from what they believed to be desirable procedures.

11. It is also quite difficult to specify what evidence would be needed to distinguish between alternative explanations of the findings.

12. Crime seriousness scores applied to cases being handled by a prosecutor's staff have been suggested as a means of guiding the allocation of time to cases. Thus, more time would be spent on cases rated as serious offenses as compared to those that are more trivial. Crime seriousness scores have been built into the PROMIS system of case management installed in

the Washington, D.C., criminal courts. Presumably, more attention paid to more serious cases would produce a criminal justice output system that would maximize public approval of the criminal justice system.

13. Exceptions can be found in the literature, e.g., Riedel (1972) and Garrett and Rossi (1978), as well as Berk and Rossi (1977). Each of these studies examines how seriousness judgments are modified by the inclusion of information on the victims, background information on offenders, and potentially extenuating circumstances.

14. For example, in Rossi et al. (1974) the seriousness scores given to forcible rape varied according to the circumstances described as follows:

	Scores (Normalized on 0-100 basis)
After breaking into a home	88.75
Of a stranger in a park	86.25
Of a neighbor	85.00
Of a former spouse	70.00

15. The most directly relevant study was by Berk and Rossi (1977), who used the crime seriousness scores generated in Rossi et al. (1974) to predict the desired treatment for hypothetical convicted offenders in interviews with the political elites of three states. Treatments ranged from probation to long-term incarceration (more than ten years) in a graduated set of categories.

16. Private, as well as public, defense attorneys engage in plea-bargaining with the prosecutor, but we do not know the degree to which different characteristics of their clients or conditions of their office affect the decision to engage in plea-bargaining. Nor are judges excluded from plea-bargaining, but their involvement is usually not directly part of the negotiating.

17. This does not imply that these crimes will result in similarly severe sanctions. Each normal crime carries a range of potentially acceptable reductions that is, to some degree, bounded by the statutory punishments prescribed for the act. It does imply that a given crime will repeatedly result in a particular type of sanction, such that if there is discontinuity between the public seriousness of a normal crime and the appropriate punishment, it will be carried on quite regularly.

18. In comparing FBI Crime Index and the Sellin-Wolfgang Index, Blumstein examined sensitivity to varying seriousness weights. He did not conduct sensitivity tests based on variation in the relative occurrence of crimes over time (Blumstein, 1974).

19. Research currently under way using the Current Population Survey, and under the direction of Marvin Wolfgang, may well fulfill the need.

REFERENCES

Berk, R. A. and P. H. Rossi (1977) *Prison Reform and State Elites.* Cambridge, MA: Ballinger.

Blumstein, A. C. (1974) "Seriousness Weights in an Index of Crime." *American Sociological Review* 39, 6: 854-864.

Chambliss, W. J. (1973) *Sociological Readings in Conflict Perspective.* Reading, MA: Addison-Wesley.

Chilton, R. and J. DeAmicis (1975) "Overcriminalization and the Measurement of Consensus." *Sociology and Social Research* 59, 4: 318-329.

Cullen, J. R., B. D. Link, and C. W. Pozanzi (1979) "The Seriousness of Crime Revisited: Are Attitudes Toward White-Collar Crime Changing." Western Illinois University (unpublished)

Garrett, K. and P. H. Rossi (1978) "Judging the Seriousness of Child Abuse," *Medical Anthropology*, 2, 1: 1-48.

Needleman, B. (1975) "Offense Intensity and Offense Wrongfulness Hierarchies," State University of New York, Oswego. (unpublished)

Nettler, G. (1974) *Explaining Crime*. New York: McGraw-Hill.

Newman, G. (1976) *Comparative Deviance: Perceptions and Law in Six Cultures*. New York: Elsevier.

Reiss, A. J. (1961) *Occupations and Social Status*. New York: Free Press.

Riedel, M. (1972) "The Perception of Crime." Ph.D. disseration, University of Pennsylvania.

Rose, G.N.G. (1966) "Concerning the Measurement of Delinquency." *British Journal of Criminology* 6 (October): 414-421.

Rossi, P. H., E. Waite, C. E. Bose, and R. A. Berk (1974) "The Seriousness of Crime: Normative Structure and Individual Differences." *American Sociological Review* 39 (April): 224-237.

Schwendinger, H. and J. Schwendinger (1975) "Defenders of Order or Guardians of Human Rights?" pp. 113-146 in I. Taylor et al. (eds.) *Critical Criminology*. London: Routledge & Kegan Paul.

Sellin, T. and M. Wolfgang (1964) *The Measurement of Delinquency*. New York: John Wiley.

Skolnick, J. H. (1967) "Social Control in the Adversary System." *Conflict Resolution* 11, 1: 52-70.

Stevens, S. S. (1957) "On the Psychophysical Law." *Psychological Review* 64: 153-181.

Sudnow, D. (1965) "Normal Crimes: Sociological Features of the Penal Code in a Public Defender Office." *Social Problems* 12: 255-275.

Thomas, C. W., R. J. Cage, and S. C. Foster (1976) "Public Opinion on Criminal Law and Legal Sanctions: An Examination of Two Conceptual Models." *Journal of Criminal Law and Criminology* 67, 1.

Tittle, C. R. (1975) "Deterrents or Labeling?" *Social Forces* 53, 3: 399-410.

Turk, A. T. (1977) "Class, Conflict, and Criminalization." *Sociological Focus* 10, 3: 209-220.

Turner, S. (1978) "Introduction to the Reprint Edition," in T. Sellin and M. E. Wolfgang, *The Measurement of Delinquency*. Montclair, NJ: Patterson Smith.

Wellford, C. F. and M. Wiatrowski (1975) "On the Measurement of Delinquency." *Journal of Criminal Law and Criminology* 66, 22: 175-188.

Wolfgang, M. E. and F. Ferracuti (1967) *The Subculture of Violence*, London: Methuen.

Wolfgang, M. E., R. Figlio, and T. Sellin (1972) *Delinquency in a Birth Cohort*. Chicago: University of Chicago Press.

21

A Repertoire of Impact Measures

Delbert S. Elliott

Treatment and rehabilitation programs have flourished in the field of crime and delinquency over the past decade. Dixon (1974) estimates that, for juveniles alone, there have been more than 6500 different delinquency prevention and treatment programs since 1965. There has also been a corresponding increase in the number of evaluations attempting to document the effectiveness of these intervention programs. Indeed, designing and conducting evaluations of crime and delinquency programs became a major enterprise in the 1970s, with considerable financial investments at the federal, state, and local levels, as well as the development of criminal justice program evaluation specializations at many colleges and universities.

Such an investment of resources should have produced a body of knowledge about the effectiveness of specific prevention/treatment strategies, and an accumulation of empirical evidence relative to the theoretical models upon which these strategies are based. Unfortunately, this is not the case. While a few evaluations have produced evidence of program success, there is no clear evidence overall to support the effectiveness of any specific treatment approach for reducing involvement in criminal behavior (Romig, 1978; Lipton et al., 1975; Bailey, 1966).[1] Further, evaluation studies to date have had little or no impact upon theory development or verification. The expected payoff for effective crime and delinquency policies has simply not occurred. The accumulation of evidence relative to both program success and theory verification remains very limited.

AUTHOR'S NOTE: I wish to express my gratitude to Judy Beth Berg-Hansen for her editorial assistance in the preparation of this chapter.

The explanation for the limited utility of program evaluation studies involves a number of factors. While most observers have focused upon the serious methodological problems in these studies, the focus of this chapter is upon another equally important factor—the lack of comparability in treatment/service program evaluations. Conceptually, the lack of comparability is the result of a nearly universal absence of any explicit theoretical rationale linking program objectives to expected outcomes (Short, 1980; Elliott, 1980; Lundman and Scarpitti, 1978). Operationally, it is the result of very few attempts to replicate earlier studies and the widespread practice of researchers to develop their own unique measures of key variables. Given these two conditions, there is virtually no comparability among evaluation studies. Without this comparability, there is simply no basis for accumulating evidence and building generalizations about treatment strategies.

ESTABLISHING COMPARABILITY

Studies are said to be comparable when their findings lend themselves to being aligned, integrated, or combined with those from other studies into generalizations. Rittenhouse (1978) identifies six problem areas for establishing comparability: (1) population definitions, (2) sampling design, (3) data collection techniques, (4) conceptualization and measurement of variables, (5) analysis techniques, and (6) reporting. While Rittenhouse notes that reporting is not conceptually as serious as problems 1 through 5, she argues that the failure to report findings in sufficient detail to allow for comparison may be "the single biggest bar to effective comparability of results" (1978: 5). Conceptually, the most critical problem involves the definition of concepts and their measurement. Comparability depends heavily upon the conceptual similarity of the variables involved and the standardization of the measures used to represent them. It is with these two issues that this chapter is concerned.

The use of replication studies and a fuller cooperation among researchers evaluating crime prevention and rehabilitation programs would certainly facilitate the comparability of evaluations. However, another and perhaps more fruitful strategy is first, to encourage the use of theoretically guided evaluations, and second, to establish a set of standardized measures for key theoretical variables. This strategy is consistent with the Social Science Research Council's effort to develop model-descriptive demographic measures (Social Science Research Council, 1975); the attempt of the International Conference on Comparability in Epidemiological Studies to develop a standardized set of concepts and measures for cross national epidemiological investigations (Acheson, 1965; Harvard Medical School, 1972); and the effort of the Task Force on Comparability in Survey Research on Drugs to develop standardized variables and item formats for use by drug researchers (Rittenhouse, 1978).

This chapter represents an initial effort in this direction for evaluations of crime and delinquency treatment programs. A greater commitment to theoretically guided evaluations is a critical first step toward achieving comparability and accumulating a body of knowledge in this area. A second step is the identification of a set of key theoretical variables which have some potential relevance for treatment and prevention programs, together with specific indexes and scales which have been developed and established as valid and reliable measures of these variables.

Conceptual Comparability: The Need for Theory-Based Evaluations

Theoretically guided evaluations contribute to the accumulation of knowledge about treatment interventions in several important ways. First, it is the theoretical paradigm which provides the logic for interpreting evaluation findings. A theoretical/experimental approach to program development and evaluation involves the following sequence:[2]

(1) a causal model or theoretical paradigm which identifies a set of variables (attributes, relationships, or circumstances) connected by some logical process to criminal behavior;

(2) the identification of a set of program activities or interventions which are designed to manipulate these causal variables;

(3) the implementation of the program with these manipulations operationalized as program objectives;

(4) information feedback during operation to determine if the program activities are, in fact, occurring and the objectives are being met (process evaluation);

(5) feedback to determine if the realization of these program objectives is having the theoretically expected effect on criminal behavior (impact evaluation); and

(6) the modification of the theoretical paradigm and/or the program activities and objectives as suggested by the process and impact evaluations, in order to increase the program's effectiveness in reducing crime.

This approach provides a logic for interpreting specific impact results, accumulating evidence relative to the validity and utility of the theoretical paradigm employed, and documenting the utility of specific program activities or interventions. If one or more of the first four of these elements is missing, the interpretation of impact evaluation results becomes problematic, there is no accumulated knowledge concerning the validity of the theoretical paradigm, and the utility of specific program activities remains unknown.

It is essential in any evaluation to determine that the immediate intervention objectives were, in fact, achieved—that is to say, that tutorial programs did improve participants' academic skills; that employment programs did find jobs for offenders; and that counseling programs did have the postulated effect with respect to changing attitudes, perceived negative labeling, levels of alienation, and so on. This part of the total evaluation is typically called the process evaluation and is considered a test of program success, as distinguished from the impact evaluation, which is considered a test of the theory's validity. But these two aspects of evaluation are interdependent.

Assuming that immediate treatment objectives are achieved (program success), it is still very difficult to interpret impact findings without the ability to specify a causal hypothesis, i.e., a series of intervening variables linking the treatment objective to a reduction in criminal behavior. Without such an a priori theoretical rationale, causal interpretations of impact findings are not warranted, regardless of the outcome of the process evaluation and the magnitude of the pre-/postchange or the experimental/control group difference observed with respect to some outcome measure (Hirschi and Selvin, 1967). A compelling causal interpretation requires a theoretical rationale.

For example, consider a tutorial program for delinquent youth. There is no explicit theoretical rationale, and the program contracts for a simple recidivism impact evaluation which finds no difference in recidivism between controls and participants after six months. What can be concluded? Can it reasonably be concluded that improving academic skills was unrelated to involvement in delinquent behavior (theory failure)? Can it be concluded that the program was unsuccessful in achieving its treatment objectives (program failure)? Neither of these conclusions is warranted. Neither are there any clear and direct implications from this evaluation for changing the program (or the theoretical model) to increase its effectiveness.

Consider a second evaluation of this tutorial program based upon a rationale derived from control theory. Specifically, improving academic skills (the immediate treatment objective) is viewed as a means for improving regular school performance, which is postulated to increase the youth's stake in conformity and his or her integration into the school (bonding variables), and thereby reduce his or her involvement in delinquent behavior and lower subsequent risk for rearrest (recidivism). The process evaluation indicates that the program did improve participants' academic skills. The impact evaluation discloses that there were (1) no changes in the participants' school performance, (2) no changes in participants' feelings of alienation from school or perceived importance of academic success, (3) no changes in self-reported levels of delinquency involvement, and (4) no difference between participants and controls in recidivism.

The outcome of this recidivism analysis is thus identical to the first evaluation example, but much more is known. The program did, in fact, achieve its initial objective of improving academic skills. In this sense, the program was successful. On the other hand, improving academic skills did not appear to impact on either delinquent behavior or rearrest as hypothesized. Thus, the impact evaluation failed to provide support for the theoretical rationale.

However, these data from the impact evaluation provide some important feedback suggesting a number of new objectives or directions for the program. Improved academic skills did not result in improved academic performance. Perhaps this was due to prior labeling by teachers which negated the actual improvement in academic skills. Perhaps the time-lag (six months) was insufficient for the improved skills to result in improved grades, and therefore a longer follow-up was needed.

Had the impact evaluation indicated an improved school performance, reduced alienation, increased value placed upon education, reduced involvement in delinquent behavior, and reduced arrests, the causal argument would be much stronger than it could possibly have been given the simple recidivism analysis in the first evaluation example. Likewise, had the second evaluation example shown positive change on all variables but recidivism, it could still be concluded that the evidence supported the theoretical rationale. In sum, evaluations based upon a theoretical rationale provide a better basis for interpreting results, the potential for more compelling causal arguments, and more useful information for program modification.

As illustrated in the above example, projects with a theoretical rationale can often identify multiple success criteria. These additional success criteria are typically intervening variables by which program activities are logically connected to a reduction in crime. The identification of such variables depends in large part upon the presence of some clear, explicit theoretical rationale. The specification of intervening variables affords a much more sensitive test of the theory underlying the intervention and, in the case of more complex theories, provides for the accumulation of empirical evidence relative to each specific linkage proposed. This allows for a more precise determination of the points at which a causal argument stands or falls.

Projects operating without a rationale have no clear conceptual basis for identifying success criteria and typically resort, by default, to recidivism as a success criterion. The appeal of recidivism is practical—the data are readily available, the cost is minimal, and there is historical precedent for using this outcome measure. Unfortunately, the theoretical link between program treatment and recidivism is often very indirect and, in such cases, there is no compelling logic to suggest that the program should have any immediate impact upon recidivism. The use of more theoretically relevant success criteria in past evaluation studies might well have resulted in more consistent, positive findings.

The specification of a theoretical rationale also provides a more abstract set of concepts through which cross-program comparisons are facilitated. A wide variety of interventions may be employed to impact upon specific causal variables identified by a particular theory. For example, employment, counseling, and vocational training/skill development may all be viewed as interventions designed to impact upon a general set of social control variables which, in turn, are tied theoretically to a reduction in criminal behavior. A comparison of program evaluations involving different interventions but employing a common set of theoretical concepts allows for several independent tests of the theoretical model. The comparison should also provide an indication of the relative success of these different intervention strategies in affecting the causal variables identified in the model.

Operational Comparability: Key Theoretical Variables and Measures

Weiss (1972: 34) argues, "It is worth a fair amount of searching to locate measures that have already proved workable, rather than to create new ones." The development of measures is a demanding, time-consuming task, often involving much trial and error. The use of established measures facilitates evaluation research by eliminating much of this work. Not only are a measure's psychometric properties often established in prior research, but its predictive validity (i.e., its over-time association with delinquent or criminal behavior or some other criterion variable) can often be assessed as well. Further, the prior research often provides comparative data, thus helping to identify the unique characteristics of the group being evaluated and the extent of their differences from other groups in similar programs. The repeated use of such measures on different groups greatly facilitates the accumulation of knowledge, with respect to both the theoretical validity of particular intervention models and the relative effectiveness of particular programs.

While this chapter clearly argues for the increased use of established measures, it is important to note that the decision to use such measures requires careful consideration. The fact that a particular measure is well established as a predictor of criminality, has known psychometric properties, and perhaps even has established national norms, is not, in and of itself, a reason for employing such a measure. The appropriateness of a measure must be judged by its logical relationship to the theoretical construct it is designed to represent. The selection of appropriate measures thus requires some a priori conceptualization of the intervention process and a face-validity judgment as to whether a given measure is a fair and reasonable operationalization of the relevant theoretical construct.

The fact that few common measures are used in impact evaluation studies is explained, in part, by the atheoretical nature of most of this research. To some extent, however, it may be due to a limited awareness of measures developed and employed by other researchers, particularly in the more basic area of theory-testing. This chapter, therefore, will identify a number of key theoretical variables and particular measures of these variables which have been used in prior crime and delinquency research. In most cases, the measures selected and described have established reliability and validity. In some cases, national norms are also available for these measures.

Several compendia of established measures have been published,[3] and the reader is encouraged to review them. Unfortunately, they are very general collections, and they contain few measures which are directly relevant to the theoretical concepts in current theories of crime and delinquency and validated relative to a measure of criminal behavior. The measures identified herein are singled out because of their particular relevance to crime and delinquency theory and their use in large-scale evaluations of crime and delinquency programs or national etiological studies of crime and delinquency. The latter studies provide a particularly rich resource for theoretically relevant measures, since they more frequently report on the reliability and validity of their measures and often provide national norms, which are particularly useful in characterizing and comparing client populations.

CRITERIA FOR THE SELECTION OF VARIABLES AND MEASURES

The following catalog of variables and measures is not intended to be comprehensive. Rather, a limited number of theoretical perspectives were identified, and a number of major variables within each of these perspectives were selected. Because this chapter is concerned primarily with evaluations of individual treatment rehabilitation programs seeking to modify the offenders' attitudes, perceptions, relationships, social roles, and behavior, theoretical perspectives are limited to those which focus upon these types of variables as intervention objectives.[4] As a result, the theories selected are primarily social psychological theories, with a central focus upon the interaction of the individual with his or her social environment. Organizational or purely structural theories (such as conflict theory, anomie, and certain aspects of labeling theory) are not included, as they have little or no direct individual treatment implications. Biological and psychiatric perspectives are also excluded because of their more limited focus upon the individual, and personality theories are represented only to the extent they overlap the social psychological theories.

Theoretical perspectives represented are opportunity theory (Cloward and Ohlin, 1960); social control theory (Nye, 1958; Hirschi, 1969); labeling theory (Schur, 1971, 1973; Lemert, 1951; Becker, 1963); and differential association/social learning theory (Sutherland, 1947; Akers, 1977). In Table 21.1, the major concepts derived from these theoretical perspectives are listed, and specific measures of each are identified and described briefly.

For each theoretical construct selected, an attempt was made to locate scales and indexes with reasonable levels of reported reliability, homogeneity, and validity. As a minimum validity requirement, only those scales with an established simultaneous or predictive relationship to a measure of criminal or delinquent behavior are included.

An extensive search of the treatment evaluation literature revealed very few measures of any of these theoretical constructs. This is not surprising, given the atheoretical nature of this body of research. In the vast majority of published impact evaluations, the only success criterion measure is a recidivism measure. The majority of measures selected come from large-scale basic research studies in crime and delinquency. Most of these studies focus upon adolescent populations rather than adults. Since measures developed for adolescent populations may not be appropriate for adults, the age range of the populations involved is reported in each case. It is unfortunate that so few of the measures located involved adult populations. It is also clear that the measures are drawn heavily from the few national surveys available, i.e., the Gold 1967 and 1972 National Surveys of Youth; the Bachman et al. Youth in Transition study; and the Elliott et al. 1976-1980 National Youth Panel.

The following information is provided for each specific scale listed in Table 21.1: one or more references; a brief description of the scale, including its general content, number of items, sample items, response sets, and administration form; a description of the study sample; reliability, homogeneity, and stability estimates; and data relative to validity.[5] In the section of the table listing alienation scales, a number of well-known measures such as Srole's Anomia scale, the Tennessee Self-Concept scale, the Coopersmith Self-Esteem Inventory, and Gough's SO scale are not listed, as they are described in considerable detail in Robinson and Shaver (1973). A section on crime and delinquency scales is also included in Table 21.1. Several of the more recent self-report scales used in studies with national probability samples are described. These measures may be particularly useful to evaluation researchers, given the availability of national norms and age, sex, race, and class gradients.

SUGGESTIONS FOR THE FUTURE

The identification of this particular set of theoretical variables and measures is not meant to suggest that any specific measure become a standardized measure. Such a suggestion is clearly premature, given the present state of knowledge and the documentation of existing measures. Rather, the intent is to provide crime and delinquency evaluation researchers with a catalog of existing measures developed in prior research which will furnish at least some basis for comparison with other studies. The suggestion that researchers use these measures is not intended to preclude the development of other measures, but there are some advantages to including these measures as well. If every researcher develops his or her own unique measures, all hope of comparability is lost. The identification of this set of theoretically relevant measures, with documented psychometric properties and validity, is designed to encourage researchers to make explicit the theoretical rationale for the intervention being evaluated, and to build in some comparability with other theoretically relevant research outcomes through the use of comparable measures.

TABLE 21.1   A Catalog of Crime and Delinquency Impact Scales

Scales	Description
I. Strain and Bonding	
A. Limited Opportunity for Goal Attainment	
1. *Awareness of Limited Opportunity* Landis et al., 1963 Landis and Scarpitti, 1965	14 items selected from a pool of 126 items using Sletto's (1936) internal consistency technique discriminating between known class groups. Based upon Cloward and Ohlin's (1960) conceptualization, items reflect perceived life chances for education, occupation, power, influence, wealth, family, and neighborhood. Sample items: "I'll never have as much opportunity to succeed as guys from other neighborhoods," and "A guy like me has a pretty good chance of going to college." Response set: 5-point continuum from "strongly agree" to "strongly disagree." Questionnaire form.
2. *Perceived Access to Legitimate Goals* Short et al., 1965	11 items, based upon Cloward and Ohlin's (1960) theory, reflecting educational orientations, abilities, and prospects. Respondents were asked to indicate whether or not these statements were true of the *area in which their group* hung out. This scale was designed to reflect boys' perceptions of opportunities for legitimate goals in their immediate neighborhoods. Sample items: "In our area it's hard for a young guy to stay in school," and "Most of the guys in the area will probably get good paying honest jobs when they grow up." Response set: true/false. Interview form.
3. *Perceived Access to Illegitimate Goals* Short et al., 1965	9 items based conceptually upon Cloward and Ohlin's work. As with the Legitimate Goals scale, the neighborhood is the reference rather than the individual respondent. Sample items: "Some of the most respected people in our area make their money illegally," and "A guy from this area has a chance of really making it big in the rackets." Response set: true/false. Interview form.

TABLE 21.1   A Catalog of Crime and Delinquency Impact Scales (Cont)

Sample	*Reliability/Homogeneity*	*Validity*
A general sample of 1030 school children in sixth and ninth grades in Columbus, Ohio. Adequate representation of class, ethnic, and sex groups. A second sample of 515 boys from an industrial school for adjudicated delinquents.	Reliability (split-half) = .84 No homogeneity reported.	Simultaneous correlations with: SO scale (Gough, 1960) = −.49 Self-Concept scale (Dinitz et al., 1958) = −.31 Significant differences in public school and industrial schoolboys' mean scores. Significant differences (Critical Ratio) between class groups and by delinquency status (i.e., in public school or industrial school).
A sample of 500 gang and nongang boys in Chicago. Age range not reported. The larger study (Short and Strodtbeck, 1965) included youth up to age 26.	No reliability or homogeneity reported.	Rank ordering of 6 race-by-class-by-gang-status groups on this scale was the same as that based upon official delinquency rates. Group scores varied by race, class, and gang status.
A sample of 500 gang and nongang boys in Chicago. Age range not reported. See Perceived Access to Legitimate Goals scale above.	No reliability or homogeneity reported.	Within racial categories the ordering of class-by-gang-status groups on this scale was the same as that based upon official delinquency rates. The correlation between the Legitimate and Illegitimate scales is negative.

TABLE 21.1   A Catalog of Crime and Delinquency Impact Scales (Cont)

Scales	Description
4. *Perceived Access to Educational Roles* Elliott et al., 1975, 1978 Brennan and Huizinga, 1975	5 items. Sample items: "How far would you like to go in school? _____. What do you think your chances are for getting this much education? Good, fair, or poor?" and "What are the chances you will drop out or be forced to quit school? Good, fair, or poor?" Response set: 3-point continuum from "good" to "poor," "most" to "none," or "better chance" to "worse chance." Both interview and questionnaire forms.
5. *Perceived Access to Occupational Roles* Elliott et al., 1975, 1978 Brennan and Huizinga, 1975	6 items. Sample items: "What kind of job would you like to have as an adult? _____. What do you think your chances are of ever getting that kind of job? Good, fair, poor?" and "How good are your chances of getting any job as an adult you felt is a good, steady, dependable one? Good, fair, or poor?" Response set: 3-point continuum as for the Educational Roles scale above. Both interview and questionnaire forms.
6. *Expectations for Academic Achievement* Jessor and Jessor, 1971	10 items. A common stem is used for all items: "How strongly do I expect." Sample item: "to be considered a bright student by my teachers." Response set: 10-segment linear scale labeled "Sure it will not happen" at one end and "Sure it will happen" at the other. Questionnaire form.

TABLE 21.1   A Catalog of Crime and Delinquency Impact Scales (Cont)

Sample	Reliability/Homogeneity	Validity
General probability samples of youth 11 to 17 in 7 U.S. cities. Total N = 8375. In some cities the samples were in-school samples; in others they were samples of dwellings. The documentation of scales was based upon a special sample of 250 cases drawn randomly from each of the 7 sites (N = 1750).	Reliability (alpha) = .531 Homogeneity = .186 Separate reliability and HR presented for each age, sex, race, class, geographical group, and adminstration form (interview or questionnaire).	Simultaneous correlations with: Self-Esteem = .42 Self-Reported Delinquency = −.33 Parental Rejection = −.37 Normlessness = −.34 Negative Labeling by Teachers = −.29 Lagged correlation with: Self-Reported Delinquency = −.25
Same sample as for the Perceived Access to Educational Roles scale described above. Age range 11 to 17.	Reliability (alpha) = .745 Homogeneity = .328 Separate reliability and HR presented for each age, sex, race, class, geographical group, and administration form (interview or questionnaire).	Simultaneous correlations with: Self-Esteem = .26 Self-Reported Delinquency = −.26 Parental Rejection = −.15 Normlessness = −.24 Negative Labeling by Teachers = −.21 Lagged correlation with: Self-Reported Delinquency = −.16
A random sample of 589 students in 3 (junior) high schools (grades 7-9) and 276 first-year college students. The (junior) high school sample was stratified by grade and sex; the college sample by sex. The (junior) high school sample was 13-15 years of age in year 1 and and 16-18 years in year 4. The college sample was 19 in year 1 and 22 in year 4.	Reliability (alpha) year 4 scales: = .92 (HS) = .90 (college) Homogeneity year 4: = .57 (HS) = .49 (college) Stability: the average interyear correlation ranged from .67 to .73	Simultaneous correlations in HS sample year 4 with: GPA = .64(M); .61(F) Deviant Behavior Index = −.28(M); −.29(F) Multiple Problem Behavior Index = −.26(M); −.26(F) Simultaneous correlations in college sample year 4 with: GPA = .63(M); .59(F) Deviant Behavior Index = −.17(M); −.05(F) Multiple Problem Behavior Index = −.10(M); −.03(F)

TABLE 21.1   A Catalog of Crime and Delinquency Impact Scales (Cont)

Scales	Description
B. *Value and Goal Orientations*	
1. *Value on Academic Achievement* Jessor and Jessor, 1977	10 items. Except for a common stem, the items are parallel to those in the Expectations for Academic Achievement scale described above. The stem reads, "How strongly do I like." Sample item: "to be considered a bright student by my teachers." Response set: 10-segment linear scale labeled "Sure it will not happen" at one end and "Sure it will happen" at the other. Questionnaire form.
2. *Value Orientation* Landis et al., 1963 Landis and Scarpitti, 1965	13 items selected from a pool of 100 items representing 6 general value dimensions described by Cohen (1955): (1) self-improvement, ambition, and achievement; (2) work, wealth, and property; (3) aggression and physical violence; (4) responsibility and control; (5) behavior norms; and (6) social institutions. Items were selected on the basis of their power to discriminate between lower- and middle-class groups. Sample items: "Good manners are for sissys," and "Most police are crooked." Response set: 5-point continuum from "strongly agree" to "strongly disagree." Questionnaire form.
3. *Religiosity* Jessor and Jessor, 1977	7 items. The items were designed to reflect the importance of involvement with religious teachings, services, prayer, and the internalization of religious values. Sample items: "Do you agree with the following statement? Religion gives me a great amount of comfort and security in life," and "When you have a serious personal problem, how often do you take religious advice or teaching into consideration?" Response set: 5 alternative responses to each item. Each response set is unique to the item. Questionnaire form.

TABLE 21.1   A Catalog of Crime and Delinquency Impact Scales (Cont)

Sample	Reliability/Homogeneity	Validity
Same sample as for the Expectations for Academic Achievement scale described above. Age range 13 to 22.	Reliability (alpha) year 4: = .90 (HS) = .91 (college) Homogeneity year 4: = .48 (HS) = .51 (college) Stability: the average interyear correlation ranged from .62 to .67	Simultaneous correlations in the HS sample year 4 with: GPA = .20(M); .19(F) Deviant Behavior Index = −.21(M); −.39(F) Multiple Problem Behavior Index = −.28(M); −.39(F) Simultaneous correlations in the college sample year 4 with: GPA = .22(M); .18(F) Deviant Behavior Index = −.10(M); −.18(F) Multiple Problem Behavior Index = −.09(M); −.07(F)
Same sample as for the Awareness of Limited Opportunity scale described above. Sixth- and ninth-grade youth.	Reliability (split-half) = .84 No homogeneity reported.	Simultaneous correlations with: SO scale (Gough, 1960) = −.52 Self-Concept scale (Dinitz et al., 1958, Scarpitti et al., 1960) = −.47 Significant differences (Critical Ratio) by race, sex, class, and delinquency status (i.e., in public school or industrial school).
This scale was administered to the (junior) high school sample as described above in the Expectations for Academic Achievement scale. Age range 13 to 18.	Reliability (alpha) year 4 = .89 Homogeneity year 4 = .55 Stability: the average interyear correlation ranged from .63 to .67	Simultaneous correlations year 4 with: Marijuana use = −.27(M); −.31(F) Church Attendance = .58(M); .48(F) Deviant Behavior Index = −.17(M); −.27(F) Multiple Problem Behavior Index = −.23(M); −.31(F)

TABLE 21.1   A Catalog of Crime and Delinquency Impact Scales (Cont)

Scales	Description
C. *Family and School Relationships*	
1. *Positive Attitudes Toward School* Bachman et al., 1978 Davidson, 1972 Bachman, 1970	15 items. Each item reflects some intrinsic value of education. Sample items: "I think school is important not only for the practical value, but because learning itself is very worthwhile," and "I like school because I am improving my ability to think and solve problems." Response set: "I feel this way: very much, pretty much, a little, not at all." Questionnaire form.
2. *Negative Attitudes Toward School* Bachman et al., 1978 Bachman, 1970	8 items. These items reflect a dissatisfaction or devaluation of school in comparison with other sources of experience. Sample items: "Instead of being in this school, I wish I were out working," and "School is very boring for me and I'm not learning what I feel is important." Response set: "I feel this way: very much, pretty much, a little, not at all." Questionnaire form.
3. *Perceived Parental Rejection* Elliott et al., 1978	5 items. Items reflect the belief that parents are not interested in youth, would not help them if they were in need, and do not see them as important persons. Sample items: "My parents would help me if I were to get into serious trouble," and "My parents blame me for all of their problems." Response set: 5-point continuum from "always" to "never." Interview form.
4. *Parental Punativeness* Bachman et al., 1978 Bachman, 1970	10 items. Sample items: "How often do your parents completely ignore you after you've done something wrong?" and "How often do your parents take away your privileges (TV, movies, dates)?" Response set: 5-point continuum from "always" to "never." Questionnaire form.

TABLE 21.1   A Catalog of Crime and Delinquency Impact Scales (Cont)

Sample	Reliability/Homogeneity	Validity

A national probability sample of 2213 tenth-grade boys. This sample served as a national youth panel, with initial data collection in 1966 and subsequent data collections in 1968, 1969, 1970, and 1974. Age range 15 to 25.	Reliability (alpha)
	    year 1 = .91
	    year 3 = .91
	Reliability (test-retest)
	    = .69
	Stability = .82 to .83
		Simultaneous correlations with:
		    SES (eta) = .10
		    Family Relations (eta)
		        = .35
		    Serious Delinquent
		        Behavior = − .27
		    Interpersonal Aggression
		        = −.31
		    Theft and Vandalism
		        = −.29

Same sample as for Positive Attitudes Toward School scale described above.	Reliability (test-retest)
	    = .67
	Stability = .83 to .84
		Simultaneous correlations with:
		    SES (eta) = −.21
		    Family Relations (eta)
		        = −.38
		    Serious Delinquent
		        Behavior = .28
		    Interpersonal Aggression
		        = .36
		    Theft and Vandalism
		        = .25

An evaluation of diversion programs in 3 cities. The sample involved 766 youth (male and female) arrested by the police between January and July, 1975. Longitudinal study with 4 data collection waves. Age range 7 to 17.	Reliability (alpha) year 4
	    = .64 to .82 (by site)
	Homogeneity year 4
	    = .27 to .47 (by site)
		Simultaneous correlations year 1 (by site) with:
		    Self-Esteem
		        = −.37 to −.38
		    Self-Reported
		        Delinquency = .26
		Lagged correlations with:
		    Self-Esteem
		        = −.25 to −.36
		    Self-Reported
		        Delinquency
		        = .16 to .23

Same sample as for Positive Attitudes Toward School scale above. This scale obtained at year 1 only.	Reliability not reported.	Simultaneous correlations with:
		    Educational Attainment
		        = −.20
		    Serious Delinquent
		        Behavior = .28
		    Interpersonal Aggression
		        = .31
		    Theft and Vandalism
		        = .25

TABLE 21.1   A Catalog of Crime and Delinquency Impact Scales (Cont)

Scales	Description
D. *Normative Orientations*	
1. *Parent Approval for Problem Behavior* Jessor and Jessor, 1977	4 items. A measure of the perceived likelihood of parental sanctions for drinking, marijuana use, sex, or activist protest. Sample items: "How do you feel about people your age drinking?" and "How do you think your parents would feel about your using marijuana?" Response set: "would approve, wouldn't care, would disapprove, would strongly disapprove." Questionnaire form.
2. *Perceived Sanctions for Deviance—Parents* Elliott et al., 1979	9 items. A measure of the perceived approval or disapproval by parents for 9 different behaviors. The stem, "How would your parents react if you," is used for all items. Sample items: "stole something worth more than $50," and "broke into a vehicle or building to steal something." Response set: 5-point continuum from strongly disapprove to strongly approve. Interview form.
3. *Perceived Sanctions for Deviance—Peers* Elliott et al., 1979	9 items. This measure is similar to the Perceived Sanctions for Deviance—Parents scale above. The stem here is "How would your *close friends* react if you." The same items and responses are used. Interview form.
4. *Attitudinal Intolerance of Deviance* Jessor and Jessor, 1977	20 items (college sample). An additional 6 items included for the high school sample. A measure of a generalized personality attribute regulating tendencies to engage in deviant acts. The stem, "How wrong is it," is used for all items. Sample items: "to take something of value from a store without paying for it," and "to cheat on an important exam." Response set: 10-point continuum from "not wrong" to "very wrong." Questionnaire form.

TABLE 21.1   A Catalog of Crime and Delinquency Impact Scales (Cont)

Sample	Reliability/Homogeneity	Validity
Same sample as for the Expectations for Academic Achievement scale described above. Age range 13 to 22.	Reliability (alpha) = .66 (HS) = .53 (college) Homogeneity = .33 (HS) = .22 (college)	Simultaneous correlations in HS sample year 4 with: Deviant Behavior Index = .19(M); .04(F) Multiple Problem Behavior Index = .37(M); .23(F) Simultaneous correlations in college sample year 4: Deviant Behavior Index = .22(M); .00(F) Multiple Problem Behavior Index = .31(M); .27(F)
A national probability sample of 1726 youth 11-17 in 1976; 4 annual data collections with this youth panel to date. Age range 11 to 20.	Reliability (alpha) year 1 = .85 Homogeneity year 1 = .39	Simultaneous correlations year 1 with: Normlessness = −.33 Negative Labeling by Parents = −.35 Self-Reported Delinquency = −.12
Same sample as for the Perceived Sanctions for Deviance–Parents scale described above. Age range 11 to 20.	Reliability (alpha) year 1 = .89 Homogeneity year 1 = .49	Simultaneous correlations year 1 with: Normlessness = −.46 Negative Labeling by Peers = −.59 Self-Reported Delinquency = −.32
Same samples as for the Expectations for Academic Achievement scale described above. Age range 13 to 22.	Reliability (alpha) year 4: = .93 (HS) = .92 (college) Homogeneity year 4: = .36 (HS) = .36 (college) Stability: the average interyear correlation ranged from .69 to .73	Simultaneous correlations in HS sample year 4 with: Church Attendance = .18(M); .22(F) Deviant Behavior Index = −.61(M); −.57(F) Multiple Problem Behavior Index = −.47(M); −.48(F) Simultaneous correlations in college sample year 4 with: Church Attendance = .12(M); .16(F) Deviant Behavior Index = −.32(M); −.33(F) Multiple Problem Behavior Index = −.12(M); −.23(F)

TABLE 21.1   A Catalog of Crime and Delinquency Impact Scales (Cont)

Scales	Description

II. *Alienation and Self-Concept*

  A. *Alienation*

    1. *Normlessness*
       Elliott et al., 1979

14 items. 3 context-specific subscales: family, school, and peer normlessness. The family and peer scales have 4 items each, and the school scale has 5 items. Items reflect the belief that one must violate the norms in order to achieve socially accepted goals. Sample items: "to stay out of trouble, it is sometimes necessary to lie to teachers" (school); "You have to be willing to break some rules if you want to be popular with your friends" (peers); and "Sometimes it's necessary to lie to your parents in order to keep their trust" (family). Response set: 5-point continuum from "strongly agree" to "strongly disagree." Interview form.

    2. *Powerlessness*
       Nowicki and Strickland, 1973
       Elliott et al., 1975, 1978
       Brennan and Huizinga, 1975

21 items. Scale developed by Nowicki and Strickland as a locus of control measure. Authors have not validated scale with crime or delinquency measures. Scale was employed by Elliott et al. in a delinquency study. Sample items: "Are you often blamed for things that just aren't your fault?" and "Most of the time, do you feel that you can change what might happen tomorrow by what you do today?" Response set: yes/no. Both interview and and questionnaire forms.

TABLE 21.1   A Catalog of Crime and Delinquency Impact Scales (Cont)

Sample	Reliability/Homogeneity	Validity

Same sample as for the Perceived Sanctions for Deviance–Parents scale described above. Age range 11 to 20.	Reliability (alpha) year 1:
	  Family scale = .66
	  School scale = .66
	  Peer scale = .62
	Homogeneity year 1:
	  Family scale = .33
	  School scale = .28
	  Peer scale = .30
		Simultaneous correlations year 1:
		Family scale with:
		  Perceived Sanctions for
		  Deviance–Parents = –.33
		  Negative Labeling –
		  Parents = .44
		  Self-Reported
		  Delinquency = .22
		School scale with:
		  Perceived Sanctions for
		  Deviance–Peers = –.46
		  Negative Labeling–
		  Parents = .41
		  Self-Reported
		  Delinquency = .22
		Peer scale with:
		  Perceived Sanctions for
		  Deviance–Peers = –.41
		  Negative Labeling–
		  Parents = .44
		  Self-Reported
		  Delinquency = .17

Nowicki and Strickland: 1017 youth in grades 3-12 in 4 different communities. Elliott et al.: same sample as for the Perceived Access to Educational Roles scale described above. Age range 8 to 18.	Nowicki and Strickland reliability (split-half) by grades:
	  3-5 = .63
	  6-8 = .68
	  9-11 = .74
	  12 = .81
	Elliott et al. reliability (alpha) by age:
	  10-12 = .73
	  13-15 = .74
	  16-18 = .79
	Elliott et al. homogeneity by age:
	  10-12 = .11
	  13-15 = .12
	  16-18 = .15
	Elliott et al. reliability (alpha) and homogeneity also available by sex, race, class, geographical area, and administration form.
		Simultaneous correlations (Elliott et al.) with:
		  Self-Esteem = –.36
		  Normlessness = .30
		  Negative Labeling by
		  Teachers = .21
		  Self-Reported
		  Delinquency = .26
		Lagged correlation with:
		  Self-Reported
		  Delinquency
		  = .07 to .14

TABLE 21.1   A Catalog of Crime and Delinquency Impact Scales (Cont)

Scales	Description
3. *Internal-External Control* Jessor and Jessor, 1977	22 items (high school sample). Scale for college sample included 18 items. Sample items: "I often feel that working for political and social change is useless, since my efforts would not make any real difference," and "I don't see much connection between how hard I study and the grades I get on tests." Response set: 5-point continuum from "strongly agree" to "strongly disagree." Questionnaire form.
4. *Societal Estrangement* Elliott et al., 1975, 1978 Brennan and Huizinga, 1975	16 items. A modified version of the McClosky and Schaar (1963) 9-item Anomie scale. Sample items: "It's hard to know who you can trust these days," and "I sometimes feel like nobody cares about me anymore." Response set: 4-point continuum from "strongly disagree" to "strongly agree." Interview and questionnaire forms.
5. *Social Isolation* Elliott et al., 1979	15 items. 3 context-specific subscales: family, school and peer isolation, each 5 items. Sample items: "I don't feel I fit in very well with my friends" (peer); "I feel close to my family" (family); and "Teachers don't call me in class, even when I raise my hand" (school). Response set: 5-point continuum from "strongly agree" to "strongly disagree." Interview form.

TABLE 21.1   A Catalog of Crime and Delinquency Impact Scales (Cont)

Sample	Reliability/Homogeneity	Validity
Same samples as for the Expectations for Academic Achievenemnt scale described above. Age range 13 to 22.	Reliability (alpha) year 4: = .77 (HS) = .76 (college) Homogeneity year 4: = .13 (HS) = .15 (college)	Simultaneous correlations in HS sample year 4 with: GPA = .19(M); .18(F) Deviant Behavior Index = −.27(M); −.12(F) Multiple Problem Behavior Index = −.21(M); −.13(F) Simultaneous correlations in college sample year 4 with: GPA = .21(M); .27(F) Deviant Behavior Index = −.11(M); .03(F) Multiple Problem Behavior Index = −.14(M); −.04(F)
Same samples as for the Perceived Access to Educational Roles scale described above. Age range 11 to 17.	Reliability (alpha) = .80 Homogeneity = .21 Both reliability and homogeneity estimates are available by age, sex, race, class, geographical area, and administration form.	Simultaneous correlations with: Self-Esteem = −.37 Normlessness = .32 Powerlessness = .44 Negative Labeling by Parents = .20 Self-Reported Delinquency = .29 Lagged correlation with: Self-Reported Delinquency = .09 to .12
Same sample as for the Perceived Sanctions for Deviance–Parents scale described above. Age range 11 to 20.	Reliability (alpha) Family scale = .74 School scale = .68 Peer scale = .69 Homogeneity year 1: Family scale = .38 School scale = .30 Peer scale = .32	Simultaneous correlations year 1: Family scale with: Normlessness = .50 Negative Labeling– Parents = .49 Self-Reported Delinquency = .18 School scale with: Normlessness = .29 Negative Labeling– Parents = .44 Self-Reported Delinquency = .11 Peer scale with: Normlessness = .27 Negative Labeling– Parents = .42 Self-Reported Delinquency = .05

TABLE 21.1   A Catalog of Crime and Delinquency Impact Scales (Cont)

Scales	Description
B. Self-Concept	
1. *Self-Esteem* Bachman et al., 1978 Bachman and O'Malley, 1977	10 items. The first 6 items are identical to those developed by Rosenberg (1965). Sample items: "I feel that I am a person of worth at least on an equal plane with others," and "I feel that I can't do anything right." Response set: 5-point continuum from "almost always" to "never." Questionnaire form.
2. *Self-Esteem* Elliott et al., 1975, 1978 Brennan and Huizinga, 1975	10 items. A modification of Rosenberg's scale (1965). Slightly different wording and format from Bachman et al. (1978) version. Sample items: "All in all, you are inclined to feel that you are a failure," and "You feel satisfied with yourself." Response set: 4-point continuum from "always" to "never." Interview and questionnaire forms.
III. *Exposure and Commitment to Criminal/Delinquent Groups* A. *Differential Association* 1. *Differential Association* Short, 1957 Voss, 1964	9 items. Scale developed by Short and used in a replication study by Voss. 2 subscales. Specific DA is composed of 4 items reflecting the frequency, duration, priority, and intensity of interaction with delinquent friends. General DA is composed of the other 5 items reflecting general knowledge of delinquent activity in the community. Sample items: "Have any of your *best* friends been juvenile delinquents while they were your best friends?" and "How well have you known criminals?" Response set: variable response sets. For the above items: "most were, several were, very few were, and none were," and "very well, fairly well, not very well, only knew their names, didn't know their names." Questionnaire form.

TABLE 21.1   A Catalog of Crime and Delinquency Impact Scales (Cont)

Sample	Reliability/Homogeneity	Validity
Same samples as for Positive Attitudes Toward School scale described above. Age range 15 to 25.	Reliabilities (alpha) = .75 to .81 (over 4 data waves) Reliability (test-retest) = .75 Stability ranged from .82 to .91	Simultaneous correlations year 1 with: Intellectual Ability = .21 Rebellious Behavior in School = −.33 Educational Attainment = .26 Serious Delinquency = .15 Interpersonal Aggression = .16 Lagged correlations (year 1 to year 2): Serious Delinquency = .14 Interpersonal Aggression = .13
Same samples as for Perceived Access to Educational Roles scale described above. Age range 11 to 17.	Reliability (alpha) = .75 Homogeneity = .23 Separate reliability and homogeneity presented for each age, sex, race, class, geographical area, and administration form.	Simultaneous correlations with: Powerlessness = −.36 Perceived Access to Educational Roles = .42 Negative Labeling− Parents = −.23 Self-Reported Delinquency = −.22 Lagged correlations with: Self-Reported Delinquency from −.04 to −.12
Short study: 176 males and females in a state training school. Age range 16 to 17. Voss study: Simple random sample of 620 seventh-grade students in Honolulu and 183 youth in Hawaii's training schools. The modal age of the school sample was 12. No age range reported.	No reliability or homogeneity reported in either study.	Simultaneous correlations (for proportions−rp) with Self-Reported Delinquency: Short study: Specific DA = .58(M); .61(F) General DA = .68(M); .39(F) Total DA = .67(M); .51(F) Voss study: seventh-grade sample Specific DA = .31(M&F) General DA = .40(M); .30(F) Voss study: training school sample Specific DA = .20(M); .40(F) General DA = .30(M); .31(F) Total DA = .40(M); .41(F)

TABLE 21.1   A Catalog of Crime and Delinquency Impact Scales (Cont)

Scales	Description
2. *Differential Association* Elliott and Voss, 1974	3 items. A modified version of Short's Specific Differential Association subscale as described above. The priority dimension was dropped, and items were reworded slightly. Sample items: "Think of the friends you have been associated with *most often*. Were any of them ever in trouble with the law?" and "Think of the friends you have known *for the longest time*. Were any of them ever in trouble with the law?" Response set: 4-point continuum from "most were" to "none were." Questionnaire form.
B. *Exposure to Criminal/Delinquent Groups* 1. *Peer Pressure for Delinquency* Elliott et al., 1975, 1978	8 items. The scale reflects perceived pressure toward delinquent behavior from one's friends. Sample items: "Getting into trouble in my group is a way of gaining respect," and "When I choose a group of friends I choose kids that are not afraid to have a little fun, even if it means breaking the law." Response set: "yes, don't know, no." Questionnaire and interview forms.
2. *Exposure to Delinquent Peers* Elliott et al., 1979	10 items. A scale measuring the involvement of one's friends. The stem, "During the last year, how many of your close friends have," is common to all items. Sample items: "cheated on school tests," and "suggested you do something that was against the law." Response set: 5-point continuum from "all of them" to "none of them." Interview form.

TABLE 21.1   A Catalog of Crime and Delinquency Impact Scales (Cont)

Sample	Reliability/Homogeneity	Validity
A purposive sample of 2617 ninth-graders in 2 west coast cities. This sample was recontacted annually in tenth, eleventh, and twelfth grades. Age range 13 to 18.	Reliability (alpha) = .84 Homogeneity = .64	Simultaneous correlations with: Total Self-Reported Delinquency = .59(M); .52(F) Serious Self-Reported Delinquency = .53(M); .36(F) Lagged correlations with: Total Self-Reported Delinquency = .27(M); .27(F) Serious Self-Reported Delinquency = .22(M); .11(F)
Same samples as for Perceived Access to Educational Roles scale described above. Age range 11 to 17.	Reliability (alpha) = .64 Homogeneity = .18 Separate reliability and homogeneity presented for each age, sex, race, class, geographical area, and administration form.	Simultaneous correlations with: Normlessness = .45 Access to Educational Roles = −.33 Negative Labeling− Parents = .35 Self-Reported Delinquency = .47 Lagged correlations with: Self-Reported Delinquency ranged from .31 to .35
Same sample as for Perceived Sanctions for Deviance−Parents scale described above. Age range from 11 to 20.	Reliability (alpha) year 1: = .83 Homogeneity year 1: = .38	Simultaneous correlations year 1 with: Negative Labeling− Parents = .39 Normlessness (school) = .45 Perceived Sanctions− Peers = −.66 Attitudes Toward Deviance = −.58 Self-Reported Delinquency = .40

TABLE 21.1   A Catalog of Crime and Delinquency Impact Scales (Cont)

Scales	Description
3. *Peer Commitment* Empey and Lubeck, 1971	13 items. 4 subscales reflecting how respondents react to peers in a variety of situations. Based upon a factor analysis and Guttman scale analysis: (1) Ratfink scale (3 items)—extent to which respondents would give information to parents, teachers, or police if their friends were in trouble; (2) Ace-in-the-hole scale (2 items)—willingness to hide friends if they ran away from home or were in trouble with the law; (3) Sociability scale (3 items)—responses to nondelinquent situations; and (4) Deviancy scale (5 items)—willingness to follow friends involved in delinqent situations. Questionnaire form.
IV. *Labeling*	
A. *Perceived Negative Labeling* Elliott et al., 1975, 1978 Brennan and Huizinga, 1975	18 items. Three 6-item semantic differential scales measuring perceived negative or antisocial categorization by significant others (parents, teachers, and peers). Sample dimensions: troublesome/cooperative, good/bad, law abiding/delinquent. Each continuum involved a 7-point scale. Both interview and questionnaire forms.

TABLE 21.1   A Catalog of Crime and Delinquency Impact Scales (Cont)

Sample	Reliability/Homogeneity	Validity

Sample of 261 youth referred to correctional institution in Los Angeles County, plus a purposive sample of 85 nondelinquents from a high school in Los Angeles County. Age range for both samples was 15 to 18.	Coefficients of Reproducibility:
	  Ratfink scale = .95
	  Ace-in-the-hole scale
	    = .97
	  Sociability scale = .95
	  Deviancy scale = .93
	No minimum marginal coefficients are presented.
		Simultaneous correlations with official delinquency:
		  Ratfink scale = .15
		  Ace-in-the-hole scale
		    = .60
		  Sociability scale = .28
		  Deviancy scale = .49

Same samples as for Perceived Access to Educational Roles described above. Age range 11 to 17.	Reliability (alpha)
	  Parent scale = .82
	  Teachers scale = .85
	  Peers scale = .72
	Homogeneity:
	  Parent scale = .43
	  Teachers scale = .50
	  Peers scale = .30
		Simultaneous correlations:
		Parent scale with:
		  Perceived Parent
		    Rejection = .46
		  Peer Pressure for
		    Delinquency = .35
		  Self-Reported
		    Delinquency = .41
		Teachers scale with:
		  Perceived Access to
		  Educational Roles
		    = −.29
		  Peer Pressure for
		    Delinquency = .38
		  Self-Reported
		    Delinquency = .50
		Peer scale with:
		  Peer Pressure for
		    Delinquency = .43
		  Self-Esteem = −.28
		  Self-Reported
		    Delinquency = .39
		Lagged correlations with Self-Reported Delinquency:
		  Parent scale = .32 to .35
		  Teacher scale
		    = .21 to .32
		  Peer scale = .30 to .32

TABLE 21.1   A Catalog of Crime and Delinquency Impact Scales (Cont)

Scales	Description

B. *Perceived Labeling*
   Klein, 1979
   Elliott et al., 1978, 1979
	24 items. A perceived labeling scale developed by Klein involving a series of descriptive phrases or labels. 3 subscales based upon a factor analysis of items: sick labels (8 items), bad labels (7 items), and good labels (9 items). A shorter version of the scale involving 4 items for each of the 3 subscales (total of 12 items) was developed by Elliott et al., based upon a scale analysis of the original items. The stem, "How much would your parents (teachers, friends) agree that you," is common to all items. Sample items: "are well liked" (good), "need help" (sick), and "do things that are against the law" (bad). Response set: 5-point continuum from "strongly agree" to "strongly disagree." Interview form.

C. *Counterlabeling* Elliott et al., 1978, 1979	12 items. This scale reflects the respondent's perception that mother, father, and friends (4 items each) would or would not stand up for him/her in the face of negative labeling by others. Sample items: "If you got into trouble at school, how often would your mother (father, close friends) defend you or stick up for you?" and "If you got in trouble and the police brought you home and told your parents you were a delinquent, how often would your father (mother, close friends) tell you that you were still a good person and not to worry?" Response set: 4-point continuum from "almost always" to "almost never." Interview form.

TABLE 21.1   A Catalog of Crime and Delinquency Impact Scales (Cont)

Sample	Reliability/Homogeneity	Validity
Elliott et al., 1979: national probability sample of 1726 youth aged 11-17 in 1976. 4 annual data collections with this youth panel to date. Age range 11 to 20. Elliott et al., 1978: sample of 766 youth arrested in 3 cities in in 1975. 4 data collection waves. Evaluation of 3 diversion programs. Age range 7 to 17.	Reliability (alpha) year 1 (1979 study): Parents: General = .84 Subscales = .63 to .81 Teachers: General = .86 Subscales = .67 to .85 Friends: General = .81 Subscales = .54 to .85 Homogeneity year 1 (1979 study): Parents: General = .31 Subscales = .31 to .58 Teachers: General = .35 Subscales = .34 to .61 Friends: General = .29 Subscales = .29 to .59	Simultaneous correlations Parent scales with: Normlessness = .35 to 51 Perceived Disapproval– Parents = −.29 to −.43 Self-Reported Delinquency = .15 to .27 Teachers scales with: Normlessness = .33 to .52 Self-Reported Delinquency = .12 to .26 Friends scales with: Normlessness = .29 to .50 Self-Reported Delinquency = .00 to .30 (The Bad subscale consistently correlated highest and the Good subscale lowest with delinquency.)
Same samples as for the Perceived Labeling scale described above. Age range 7 to 20.	Reliability (alpha) year 1 (1979 study): Counterlabeling: Mother = .72 Father = .76 Friends = .73 Homogeneity year 1 (1979 study): Counterlabeling: Mother = .40 Father = .44 Friends = .40	Simultaneous correlations Counterlabeling Mother scale with: Perceived Labeling– Parents = −.24 Perceived Sanctions– Parents = .12 Self-Reported Delinquency (Lifestyle Measure) = −.19 Counterlabeling Father scale with: Perceived Labeling– Parents = −.27 Perceived Sanctions– Parents = .11 Self-Reported Delinquency (Lifestyle Measure = −.17 Counterlabeling Friends scale with: Perceived Labeling– Peers = −.24 Self-Reported Delinquency (Lifestyle Measure) = −.14

TABLE 21.1   A Catalog of Crime and Delinquency Impact Scales (Cont)

Scales	Description

V. *Crime and Delinquency Scales*
 	
  A. *Self-Reported Delinquency*
    Gold and Reimer, 1974
    Williams and Gold, 1972
	16 items in 1967; 17 items in 1972. In Gold's 1967 and 1972 national surveys each item was listed on a Hollerith card, and respondents were asked to sort the cards into 3 piles, indicating whether they had committed each act "never," "once," or "more than once" during the previous 3 years. Sample items: "hit one of your parents," "took a car without permission of the owner, even if the car was returned," and "ran away from home." Response set: sorting procedure into "never," "once," "more than once." Interview form.

B. *Interpersonal Aggression*
    Theft and Vandalism
    Serious Delinquency
    Bachman et al., 1978
    Bachman, 1970
	These 3 scales are based upon a set of 17 items from a 26-item measure. Interpersonal Aggression involves 8 items; Theft and Vandalism, 9 items; Serious Delinquency, 10 items (3 from the Aggression scale and 7 from the Theft and Vandalism scale). Sample items: "hit an instructor or supervisor" (IA); "took something not belonging to you worth over $50" (T&V). Response set: "never, once, twice, 3 or 4 times, 5 or more times." Questionnaire form.

C. *Self-Report Questionnaire*
    Jones, 1977
    Barnes, 1977
	30 items. 15 items describe positive behaviors and 15 items describe negative behaviors, most of which are delinquent acts. 4 scales are derived from these items based upon a cluster analysis: (1) Drug-Related (6 items); (2) Non-Drug Deviant (8 items) (3) Pro-Social A (9 items); and (4) Pro-Social B (4 items). Each scale is scored 2 ways: the length of time since any of the behaviors occurred (a behavior-free measure), and a frequency count during a 3-month period prior to administration. The stem, "How long has it been since you," is common to all items. Sample items: "entered a house or building and took something," "shoplifted," and "tried to break up a fight." Response set: now, _____ days, _____weeks, _____months, _____ years, _____never. Respondent enters.

TABLE 21.1   A Catalog of Crime and Delinquency Impact Scales (Cont)

Sample	Reliability/Homogeneity	Validity
National probability samples of 847 youth in 1967 and 1395 youth in 1972. Age range in 1967 was 13-16; in 1972 it was 11-18.	No reliability data reported.	Significant differences (Mann-Whitney U test) by sex and age. No differences in frequency by class or race. Significant differences by both race and class for seriousness delinquency scores (higher scores for blacks and higher status youth). Frequency scores associated with police contacts (Tau $C = .11$)
Same sample as for the Positive Attitude Toward School scale described above. A national probability sample of 2213 youth. Age range 15 to 25.	Reliability (test-retest): estimates for these scales ranged from .50 to .55. Stability estimates ranged from .86 to .90.	Simultaneous correlations year 1 with: Education Attained = $-.25$ (IA) -12 (T&V) $-.16$ (S) SES = $-.07$ (IA) $-.02$ (T&V) $-.01$ (S) GPA = $-.17$ (IA) $-.09$ (T&B) $-.12$ (S)
A sample of 754 youth in 50 community-based residential treatment programs for delinquent and predelinquent youth across the U.S. National Teaching-Family Evaluation project. Age range 12 to 21.	Reliability (alpha): Drug-Related = .80 Non-Drug Deviant = .69 Pro-Social A = .71 Pro-Social B = .41	Lagged correlations with successful completion of program: Drug-Related = $-.14$ Non-Drug Deviant = $-.04$ Pro-Social A = .26 Pro-Social B = $-.02$ Corrected agreement coefficient between youth and staff reports on the 15 negative items = .88.

TABLE 21.1   A Catalog of Crime and Delinquency Impact Scales (Cont)

Scales	Description
C. *Self-Report Questionnaire (cont)*	the appropriate number of days, weeks, months, or years. Questionnaire form and tape administration form.
D. *Self-Reported Delinquency* Elliott et al., 1979	40 items. An extensive delinquency checklist designed to be representative of the full range of behaviors for which youth can be arrested. In the 1980 survey, the measure included 46 items. The stem, "How often in the last year have you," is common to all items. Sample items: "attacked someone with the idea of seriously hurting him/her," and "stolen (or tried to steal) something worth more than $50." Response sets: (1) an open-end frequency estimate by the respondent, and (2) categorial response set (used whenever the frequency estimate was ⩾ 10) with a 6-point continuum from once a month to 2-3 times a day. Interview form.

NOTES

1. This author takes issue with the widely held conclusion that "nothing works." Most of the evidence for this conclusion comes from nontheoretical studies using simple recidivism as the sole outcome criterion. A more appropriate conclusion is that "we don't know if any general treatment strategy works" (Elliott, 1980). That is to say, no generalizations about treatment success or failure appear warranted, given the weaknesses of evaluation programs to date (their incomparability, their serious methodological problems, their inability to distinguish between program failure and theory failure, and their use of recidivism, which is a crude outcome measure of questionable theoretical relevance to the treatment involved).

2. There are those who take exception to this experimental approach and propose substantially different approaches to evaluation. For example, see Guttentag (1973), who argues for an alternative model based upon decision theory.

3. See Bonjeau et al. (1978), Buros (1965), Chun and Miller (1964), Robinson and Shaver (1973), and Straus (1969).

4. In many cases, the intervention implications of these theoretical perspectives on the etiology of criminal behavior have not been made explicit. The basic intervention assumption is that by reversing etiological processes, eradicating criminogenic conditions in the environment, and changing criminogenic attitudes and perceptions, those already involved in crime will terminate (or at least decrease) their involvement in this type of behavior. However, the two processes (toward and away from criminal behavior and roles) need not be symmetrical, and the verification of one does not necessarily verify the other. The intervention hypotheses derived from these theories must be tested and verified directly.

TABLE 21.1 A Catalog of Crime and Delinquency Impact Scales (Cont)

Sample	Reliability/Homogeneity	Validity
Same sample as for the Perceived Labeling scales described above. Age range 11 to 20.	Reliability (alpha) year 1 = .91 Homogeneity year 1 = .24	Significant differences (t test and F ratio) by age, sex, race, class, and SMSA/ nonSMSA residence. Significant race and class interaction (ANOVA) for Predatory Crimes Against Persons subscale. Significant age and sex interactions for the total SRD scale, Predatory Crimes Against Property, and Status Offense subscales.

5. In the description of the sample, general demographic characteristics (e.g., sex, race, and class) are reported only when the sample is restricted in some way. For samples limited to males, whites, youth arrested, or the like, these limitations are noted. The age range is reported for all samples. When reliability coefficients are reported, the type of reliability measure is identified. The most frequent reliability measure reported is Cronbach's alpha (Cronbach, 1951). The homogeneity measure (when reported) is Scott's homogeneity ratio (Scott, 1968). In the validity section, correlation always refers to a Pearson's product-moment correlation, unless otherwise indicated. Simultaneous relationships refer to measures taken at the same time. Lagged relationships refer to predictive relationships between the scale being described and some subsequent measure of the criterion variable. In most cases, the time-lag between measures is a year. Stability estimates (Heise, 1969) are for a one-year follow-up.

REFERENCES

Acheson, R. M. [ed.] (1965) "Comparability in International Epidemiology: Selected Papers from the International Conference on Comparability in Epidemiological Studies." *Milbank Memorial Fund Quarterly* 43, 2.

Akers, R. L. (1977) *Deviant Behavior: A Social Learning Perspective.* Belmont, CA: Wadsworth.

Bachman, J. G. (1970) *Youth in Transition, Volume II: The Impact of Family Background and Intelligence on Tenth-Grade Boys.* Ann Arbor: Institute for Social Research, University of Michigan.

———, S. Green, and I. D. Wirtanen (1971) *Youth in Transition, Volume III: Dropping Out—Problem or Symptom?* Ann Arbor: Institute for Social Research, University of Michigan.

Bachman, J. G. and P. M. O'Malley (1977) "Self-Esteem in Young Men: A Longitudinal Analysis of the Impact of Educational and Occupational Attainment." *Journal of Personality and Social Psychology* 35, 6: 365-380.

——— and J. Johnston (1978) *Youth in Transition, Volume VI: Adolescence to Adulthood: Change and Stability in the Lives of Young Men.* Ann Arbor: Institute for Social Research, University of Michigan.

Bailey, W. C. (1966) "Correctional Outcome: An Evaluation of 100 reports." *Journal of Criminal Law, Criminology and Police Science* 57, 2: 153-160.

Barnes, B. (1977) 'Self Report Questionnaire: Teaching Family and Comparison Treatments." Evaluation Research Group, Eugene, Oregon. (unpublished)

Becker, H. S. (1963) *Outsiders.* New York: Free Press.

Bonjeau, C. M., R. J. Hill, and S. D. McLemore (1978) Sociological Measurement: An Inventory of Scales and Indices. New York: ITT.

Brennan, T. and D. Huizinga (1975) *Theory Validation and Aggregate National Data: Integration Report of OYD Research FY 1975, Volume 12.* Boulder, CO: Behavioral Research Institute. (Prepared for the Office of Youth Development, Department of Health, Education and Welfare, grant HEW-OS-74-308, September.)

Brenner, M. H. and D. Carrow (1976) "Evaluative Research with Hard Data," pp. 11-62 in *Evaluation Research in Criminal Justice: Materials and Proceedings of a Research Conference Convened in the Context of the Fifth United Nations Congress on the Prevention of Crime and Treatment of Offenders.* Rome, Italy: United Nations Social Defense Research Institute.

Buros, O. (1965) *Mental Measurement Yearbook.* Highland Park, NJ: Gryphon Press.

Chun, K. and F. C. Miller (1964) *Handbook of Research Design and Social Measurement.* New York: David McKay.

Chun, K., S. Cobb, and J. French (1975) *Measures for Psychological Assessment: A Guide to 3,000 Original Sources and Their Application.* Ann Arbor: Institute for Social Research, University of Michigan.

Cloward, R. A. and L. E. Ohlin (1960) *Delinquency and Opportunity.* New York: Free Press.

Cohen, A. K. (1955) *Delinquent Boys: The Culture of the Gang.* New York: Free Press.

Cronbach, L. J. (1951) "Alpha and the Internal Structure of Tests." *Psychometrica* 16: 297-334.

Davidson, T. N. (1972) *Youth in Transition, Volume IV: Evolution of a Strategy for Longitudinal Analysis of Survey Panel Data.* Ann Arbor: Institute for Social Research, University of Michigan.

Dinitz, S., B. A. Kay, and W. C. Reckless (1958) "Group Gradients in Delinquency Potential and Achievement Scores of Sixth Graders." *American Journal of Orthopsychiatry* 28 (July): 588-605.

Dixon, M. (1974) *Juvenile Delinquency Prevention Programs.* Washington, DC: National Science Foundation.

Elliott, D. S. (1980) "Recurring Issues in the Evaluation of Delinquency Prevention and Treatment Programs," pp. 237-261 in D. Shichor and D. Kelly (eds.) *Critical Issues in Juvenile Delinquency.* Lexington, MA: D. C. Heath.

——— and S. S. Ageton (1980) "Reconciling Race and Class Differences in Self-Reported and Official Estimates of Delinquency." *American Sociological Review* 45, 1: 45-110.

Elliott, D. S. and H. L. Voss (1974) *Delinquency and Dropout.* Lexington, MA: D. C. Heath.

Elliott, D. S., S. S. Ageton, R. J. Canter, and D. Huizinga (1979) "The Dynamics of Delinquent Behavior–A National Survey." Boulder, CO: Behavioral Research Institute. Progress report for the National Institute of Mental Health, grant MH27552, May 25.

Elliott, D. S., S. S. Ageton, M. Hunter, and B. Knowles (1975) *Research Handbook for Community Planning and Feedback Instruments, Volume I.* Boulder, CO: Behavioral Research and Evaluation Corporation. (Prepared for the Office of Youth Development. Department of Health, Education and Welfare, grant HEW-OS-74-308, September.)

Elliott, D. S., F. W. Dunford, and B. Knowles (1978) "Psychometric Properties of Social Psychological Scales." (unpublished) (To be an appendix to the final report to the National Institute of Mental Health on grant MH26 141, *Diversion–A Study of Alternative Processing Practices.* Boulder, CO: Behavioral Research Institute.)

Empey, L. T. and S. G. Lubeck (1971) *The Silverlake Experiment.* Chicago: AVC.

Gold, M. and D. J. Reimer (1974) "Changing Patterns of Delinquent Behavior Among Americans 13 to 16 Years Old: 1967-1972." Ann Arbor: Institute for Social Research, University of Michigan. (Report 1 of the National Survey of Youth, National Institute of Mental Health grant MH20575.)

Gough, H. G. (1960) "Theory and Measurement of Socialization." *Journal of Consulting Psychology* 24 (February): 23-30.

Guttentag, M. (1973) "Subjectivity and Its Use in Evaluation Research." *Evaluation* 1, 2: 60-65.

Harvard Medical School (1972) *Guidelines for Producing Uniform Data for Health Care Plans.* Washington, DC: Department of Health, Education and Welfare.

Heise, D. R. (1969) "Separating Reliability and Stability in Test-Retest Correlation." *American Sociological Review* 34, 1: 93-101.

Hirschi, T. (1969) *Causes of Delinquency.* Berkeley: University of California Press.

––– and H. C. Selvin *Delinquency Research.* New York: Free Press.

Jessor, R. and S. J. Jessor (1977) *Problem Behavior and Psychosocial Development.* New York: Academic.

Jones, R. R. (1979) "Longitudinal Assessment of Group Home Outcomes." Comprehensive Progress Report for the National Institute of Mental Health. (grant RO1MH31018)

Klein, M. W., K. S. Teilmann, S. B. Lincoln, and S. Labin (1978) *Diversion as Operationalization of Labeling Theory.* Los Angeles: Social Science Research Institute, University of Southern California. (Final report to the Center for Studies in Crime and Delinquency, National Institute of Mental Health, grant MH26147, September.)

Landis, J. R., S. Dinitz, and W. C. Reckless (1963) "Implementing Two Theories of Delinquency: Value Orientations and Awareness of Limited Opportunity." *Sociology and Social Research* 47 (July): 408-416.

Landis, J. R. and F. R. Scarpitti (1965) "Perceptions Regarding Value Orientation and Legitimate Opportunity: Delinquents and Non-Delinquents." *Social Forces* 44, 1: 83-91.

Lemert, E. M. (1951) *Social Pathology.* New York: McGraw-Hill.

Lipton, D., R. Martinson, and J. Wilks (1975) *The Effectiveness of Correctional Treatment.* New York: Praeger.

Lundman, R. J. and F. R. Scarpitti (1978) "Delinquency Prevention: Recommendations for Future Projects." *Crime and Delinquency* 24, 2: 207-220.

McClosky, H. and J. H. Schaar (1965) "Psychological Dimensions of Anomy." *American Sociological Review* 30, 1: 14-40.

Nowicki, S., Jr. and B. R. Strickland (1973) "A Locus of Control Scale for Children." *Journal of Consulting and Clinical Psychology* 40, 1: 148-154.

Nye, F. I. (1958) *Family Relationships and Delinquent Behavior.* New York: John Wiley.

Rittenhouse, J. D. [ed.] (1978) *Report of the Task Force on Comparability in Survey Research on Drugs.* Washington, DC: Government Printing Office. (Prepared for the National Institute on Drug Abuse under grant DA4R6012.)

Robinson, J. P. and P. R. Shaver (1973) *Measures of Social Psychological Attitudes.* Ann Arbor: Institute for Social Research, University of Michigan.

Romig, D. A. (1978) *Justice for Our Children: An Examination of Juvenile Delinquent Rehabilitation Programs.* Lexington, MA: D. C. Heath.

Rosenberg, M. (1965) Society and the Adolescent Self-Image. Princeton, NJ: Princeton University Press.

Scarpitti, F. R., E. Murray, S. Dinitz, and W. C. Reckless (1960) "The 'Good' Boy in a High Delinquency Area: Four Years Later." *American Sociological Review* 25, 4: 555-558.

Schur, E. M. (1973) *Radical Nonintervention.* Englewood Cliffs, NJ: Prentice-Hall.

——— (1971) *Labeling Deviant Behavior.* New York: Harper & Row.

Scott, W. A. (1968) "Attitude Measurement," pp. 204-274 in G. Lindsay and E. Aronson (eds.) *The Handbook of Social Psychology, Volume II.* Reading, MA: Addison-Wesley.

Short, J. F., Jr. (1980) "Evaluation as Knowledge Building—And Vice Versa," in M. W. Klein and K. S. Teilmann (eds.) *Handbook of Criminal Justice Evaluation.* Beverly Hills, CA: Sage Publications.

——— (1957) "Differential Association and Delinquency." *Social Problems* 4, 3: 233-239.

——— and F. L. Strodtbeck (1965) Group Processes and Gang Delinquency. Chicago: University of Chicago Press.

Short, J. F., Jr., R. Rivera, and R. A. Tennyson (1965) "Opportunities, Gang Membership, and Delinquency." *American Sociological Review* 30, 1: 56-67.

Sletto, R. F. (1936) "Construction of Personality Scales by the Criterion of Internal Consistency." Minneapolis, MN: Sociological Press.

Social Science Research Council (1975) *Basic Background Items for U.S. Household Surveys.* Washington, DC: Author.

Straus, M. (1969) *Family Measurement Techniques.* Minneapolis: University of Minnesota Press.

Sutherland, E. H. (1947) *Principles of Criminology.* Philadelphia, PA: J. B. Lippincott.

Voss, H. L. (1964) "Differential Association and Reported Delinquent Behavior: A Replication." *Social Problems* 12, 1: 78-85.

Weiss, C. H. (1972) *Evaluation Research: Methods for Assessing Program Effectiveness.* Englewood Cliffs, NJ: Prentice-Hall.

Williams, J. R. and M. Gold (1972) "From Delinquent Behavior to Official Delinquency." *Social Problems* 20, 2: 209-229.

ON SUBSTANTIVE ISSUES

Malcolm W. Klein and Katherine S. Teilmann

Throughout the first four sections of this handbook, we have been concerned primarily with the concepts of evaluation research as applied to criminal justice, with the emphasis on the former more than the latter. Conceptions of method have dominated conceptions of the substance of criminal justice, although we have attempted to highlight the method-content interaction. In Part V, we place more emphasis on content issues.

The criminal justice system, and criminology generally, are most certainly marked more by stability than by change, although it is often the latter which captures our interest. Our approaches to evaluation must be capable of responding to both the old and the new, of stabilizing our procedures with the old and modifying them to respond most effectively to the new. In Part V, we have attempted to illustrate both by commissioning chapters on specific *content* areas, with the thought that the nature of the content would draw out the pertinent evaluation issues. As the reader will readily note, these issues do indeed vary directly in response to the nature of the substantive content areas involved.

The chapters in Part V are clearly not exhaustive. They should be seen as a sample of content areas which might have been selected to illustrate both stable and emerging interests. We might, in addition, have solicited discussions in such areas as these:

(a) Politics in criminal justice evaluation: *Every* evaluator would cherish the opportunity to discourse on this topic and unburden himself or herself of the horror stories so commonly attendant upon the evaluation process in public policy areas.

(b) Ethics in evaluation: Each evaluator has had to face and make decisions on one or more ethical issues—client identification, revealing data to program directors, withholding knowledge or service from control groups, and so on.

(c) Feedback of negative findings: Negative results have been more common than positive results. The procedures are not well explicated for informing consumer audiences of negative results without seriously harming the evaluation process and while still allowing these results to have their deserved impact.

(d) Neoconservatism in criminal justice: The current wave of enthusiasm for retributive justice and the "just deserts" model is having a major impact on criminal justice policy and practice in the United States. It seems clear that comprehensive evaluations must in some way reflect this current cycle in the nation's response to crime, since most programs cannot help but be affected by it.

(e) Drug and alcohol abuse: Here is a stable facet of the entire field, yet one which continually spawns new forms of response (diversion, methadone, decriminalization, and so on) to the failures of past responses.

Readers can add their own content areas to those suggested above. The point is that each is deserving, and each requires careful consideration for its evaluative implications. The five areas we have selected have this same feature of some content-specific issues imbedded in the larger paradigms of evaluation.

The Simon and Benson chapter on female criminality, for instance, raises, among other issues, the paucity of both volume and quality of available data on female crime. Our neglect of women in the past now costs us severely. How often, it seems, we have read project reports that say, "This research will employ data on males only, since females constitute such a small portion of the problem and to include them would only make analyses more difficult."

Equally common in our past but given prominence only in the last decade is the issue of net-widening addressed by Blomberg. The appropriate generalization to be drawn from that chapter is that many programs, like the diversion projects Blomberg discusses, have side effects which seldom are considered in narrowly focused evaluation designs. As with the problem of net-widening, these side effects may be of greater importance than the main effects under study; our evaluation designs must be prepared to discern and evaluate them with some sophistication.

The Simon and Benson and the Blomberg chapters discuss old problems with emergent properties; the next two illustrate new paradigms designed to evaluate problems inadequately explored in the past. The chapter by Miller, Coates, and Ohlin grows out of the most dramatic experiment in deinstitutionalization undertaken in many decades, and presents a truly comprehensive systems approach to the evaluation of major community change programs. Such a model has not heretofore been available. Similarly, the chapter by Berk, Burstein, and Nagel pulls together for the first time an integrated view of the issues in evaluating criminal justice legislation. This is, we believe, a major "growth area" in evaluation research as scholars come to realize more fully the place of the legislative process as both precursor and codifier of social change. It is the authors' skill in specifying the probable requirements of evaluation in this emerging substantive arena that makes their chapter a good illustration of the method-content interaction.

Finally, and as an appropriate concluding chapter, we have Ross Conner's discussion of the issues in evaluating the utilization of evaluations. It is a problem area given little careful attention in the past, partly because researchers have not cared enough and partly because research consumers have not sought independent validation of their own professional opinions. Conner provides an approach to building utilization concerns into the process of evaluation so that evaluation of utilization may follow as normally as the reporting of evaluation findings. As with the preceding chapters, we hope that no evaluation consumers in the future will be able to say, "If only we had known."

22

Evaluating Changes in Female Criminality

Rita James Simon and Michael Benson

Ten years ago the topic "women in crime" did not appear as a chapter heading in any of the major criminology texts. Indeed, the only reference to women that appeared in the indexes of such volumes referred to them as victims of rape or in their role as prostitutes. Writing in 1979, we confront a dramatically different situation. The issue of women and crime has not only become a worthwhile intellectual problem for which research funds are more readily available than they are for many other issues in criminology, but it is also a favorite topic of the mass media and an important issue on the agenda of the women's movement. To what extent any or all of these changes is a function of a real increase in women's participation in crime, in the greater visibility that women have achieved in the social, political, and economic institutions of our society, or in the media's exaggeration of relatively small increases in female crime rates is difficult to sort out.

Chronologically, events seem to have occurred in the following order. The movement for women's liberation developed largely out of the social activism of the civil rights and new left movements of the 1960s. The development and expansion of the women's movement served to place the spotlight on women's aspirations, on their legal rights, and on their socioeconomic and political opportunities. With the spotlight still shining, interest in other aspects of women's lives attracted attention.

In 1973, the Crime and Delinquency section of the National Institute of Mental Health commissioned a monograph that analyzed and summarized data pertaining to women's participation in crime in the United States. Publication of that monograph occurred within months of the appearance of Freda Adler's book, *Sisters in Crime.* Together, the two works attracted attention in the print and electronic mass media at about the same time stories about women who murdered, robbed, kidnapped, or attempted to assassinate public figures appeared in the New York *Times,* the Washington *Post,* and other major newspapers. Patty Hearst and the Symbionese Liberation Army, Sara Jane Moore and Lynette Fromme, and the Baader-Meinhof terrorist group all served to remind the public that women are capable of heinous criminal acts.

The major purposes of this chapter are (1) to interpret the data that are currently available, (2) to specify the issues on which research about women in crime needs to be done, and (3) to indicate the types of data that need to be collected so that the research can move forward.

THE ARREST STAGE

Among researchers who are currently working in the area of women and crime, controversy centers around these issues: (1) Do the data support the beliefs and impressions that there has been a big increase in the amount of crime committed by women in this country over the past decade? (2) If there has been such an increase, have women concentrated on certain types of crimes, or has the increase been across the board? (3) If women favor some forms of criminal activity over others, which types of crime do they favor and why? (4) What are the demographic and socioeconomic status characteristics of the women who are committing the crimes?

Drawing upon the statistics collected by the FBI and published in the Uniform Crime Reports, Table 22.1 describes the number, rate and percentage of women arrested for all crimes reported between 1958 and 1977.

Looking at each of the columns separately, we see that there have been reasonably steady and consistent increases in female participation over the past two decades. Female participation appeared to peak in 1974; and between 1975 and 1977 there was a slight decline. However, more observations are obviously needed before we can determine whether the drop is indicative of a consistent decline.

Earlier work (Simon, 1975; Adler, 1975; Steffensmeir, 1978; Terry, 1978) has discussed whether there has been a disproportionate increase in women's involvement in serious (or Type I) offenses as opposed to all reported crime categories. We find some evidence that the increases have been disproportionate in the fact that the average rate of change between 1958 and 1977 for all crimes is 4.6, but for the Type I offenses it is 7.7.

Further probing of the data on women's arrests for serious offenses reveals that the increase has not been uniform across all Type I categories, but, rather, that female arrests for property offenses have predominated. A more detailed breakdown of the property and violent categories reveals that "larceny or theft"

TABLE 22.1   Number, Rate, and Percentage of Females
Arrested for All Crimes, 1958-1977

Year	Number	Rate/100,000	Percentage
1958	238,429	455	10.63
1960	422,704	397	10.72
1965	533,996	464	11.99
1967	618,119	478	12.57
1968	681,777	498	12.96
1969	716,032	559	13.86
1970	862,736	628	13.54
1971	951,453	683	15.05
1972	966,794	678	15.11
1973	945,915	637	15.36
1974	848,995	745	16.42
1975	1,071,747	735	16.25
1976	1,106,466	680	15.90
1977	1,374,963	729	16.07

NOTE: For the years between 1965 and 1977, the data are based
on city and rural arrests. The data for 1958 and 1960 are not
strictly comparable.

is the Type I offense for which females are most likely to be arrested. Table 22.2
describes the percentage of female arrests for all Type I crimes, and from it we
note that since 1970, the larceny-theft category has had more than twice the
representation of any of the others.

As shown by the percentages in Table 22.2 1965 marked the beginning of a
steady increase in the percentage of females arrested for larceny. The percentage
of females arrested for the other property offenses, burglary and auto theft, has
also increased; but in 1977 females accounted for only 6 and 8 percent of the
arrests in those categories. Female arrests for robbery have also increased; but
like burglary and auto theft, women still account for less than 10 percent of all
robbery arrests.

In shifting from the Type I to the Type II property offenses, we find that
women in 1977 accounted for about 30 percent of all the arrests for embezzlement, fraud, and forgery. Like the arrest percentages for larceny-theft, the
increase started in the mid-sixties and has continued steadily over the past dozen
years.

Another way of analyzing the female arrest data is by comparing male and
female profiles for different offenses over time. Table 22.3 describes the proportion of female and male arrests for each of the Type I offenses and some of the
Type II property offenses as a percentage of total male and female arrests for all
crimes reported over the past two decades.

TABLE 22.2 Females Arrested: Percentage of All Arrests for Type I Offenses, 1958-1977

Year	Criminal Homicide	Robbery	Aggravated Assault	Burglary	Larceny-theft	Auto Theft	Rate[a] Violent[b]	Property[c]	Percentage[d] Violent	Property
1958	16.4	4.5	15.7	2.4	14.3	3.2	10	37	11.97	9.26
1960	16.1	4.6	15.3	2.8	16.8	3.6	13	49	11.74	10.76
1965	16.3	5.3	14.4	3.8	23.2	4.2	12	77	11.11	14.42
1967	15.4	5.2	13.6	4.1	24.8	4.3	13	88	10.57	15.48
1968	15.4	5.5	13.1	4.1	25.2	4.9	13	92	10.17	15.54
1969	14.8	6.3	13.2	4.3	27.2	5.1	14	109	10.30	17.45
1970	14.8	6.2	13.3	4.6	29.0	5.0	16	130	10.39	18.84
1971	16.0	6.4	13.9	4.8	29.1	6.0	18	141	10.68	19.12
1972	15.6	6.6	13.9	5.1	30.8	5.7	20	146	10.79	20.27
1973	15.1	6.8	13.2	5.4	31.5	6.0	19	146	10.85	21.09
1974	14.6	6.8	13.4	5.4	30.7	6.5	24	192	10.98	21.35
1975	15.6	7.1	13.9	5.5	32.5	7.0	23	199	11.08	22.14
1976	14.5	7.2	13.3	5.4	31.7	7.2	18	181	11.34	22.68
1977	14.0	7.4	12.9	6.0	31.8	8.1	21	182	11.08	22.53
Average rate of change 1958-1977	-.8	3.7	-.5	4.0	2.6	6.8	5.8	8.1	-.05	.7

a. Rate = women arrested per 100,000 women.
b. The violent offenses include homicide, robbery, and assault. Rape has been left out because it is an offense for which practically no women are arrested.
c. The property offenses include burglary, larceny, and auto theft.
d. Percentage = percentage of females arrested out of all arrests for violent or property crimes.

TABLE 22.3   Serious Crimes: Percentage of Total Arrests of Females and Males, 1958-1977

Year	Criminal Homicide Female	Male	Robbery Female	Male	Aggravated Assault Female	Male	Burglary Female	Male	Larceny-theft Female	Male	Auto Theft Female	Male	Embezzlement and Fraud Female	Male	Forgery and Counterfeiting Female	Male
1958	0.2	0.2	0.3	0.7	1.6	1.0	0.6	2.8	6.8	4.8	0.4	1.4	1.1	0.8	0.7	0.5
1960	0.2	0.1	0.3	0.9	2.0	1.4	0.8	3.3	8.6	5.3	0.5	1.6	1.3	0.8	0.8	0.5
1965	0.2	0.1	0.4	1.0	2.0	1.6	1.1	4.0	14.5	6.6	0.7	2.2	1.6	0.8	0.8	0.5
1967	0.2	0.1	0.5	1.2	2.1	1.9	1.3	4.4	16.0	7.0	0.7	2.3	1.7	0.9	0.9	0.5
1968	0.2	0.2	0.5	1.4	1.8	1.9	1.3	4.7	16.1	7.2	0.8	2.4	1.7	0.8	0.9	0.5
1969	0.2	0.2	0.6	1.5	1.8	1.9	1.3	4.5	17.5	7.5	0.8	2.3	1.8	0.9	1.0	0.5
1970	0.2	0.2	0.6	1.5	1.7	1.9	1.3	4.6	19.3	8.1	0.7	2.1	2.0	0.9	1.0	0.5
1971	0.2	0.2	0.7	1.7	1.8	2.0	1.4	4.8	19.4	8.4	0.7	2.1	2.3	1.0	1.0	0.5
1972	0.2	0.2	0.7	1.8	2.0	2.2	1.4	4.7	20.2	8.2	0.7	1.9	2.4	1.0	1.0	0.5
1973	0.2	0.2	0.7	1.0	2.0	2.3	1.5	5.1	21.4	8.2	0.7	2.0	2.4	1.0	1.0	0.5
1974	0.2	0.2	0.8	2.1	2.0	2.5	1.7	6.1	23.9	10.2	0.7	1.9	2.7	1.1	1.1	0.5
1975	0.2	0.2	0.8	2.0	2.1	2.5	1.8	6.1	25.4	10.3	0.6	1.7	3.3	1.2	1.2	0.6
1976	0.2	0.2	0.6	1.4	2.0	2.4	1.7	5.8	24.3	9.9	0.6	1.5	4.9a	1.7	1.3	0.6
1977	0.2	0.2	0.6	1.5	2.0	2.6	1.9	5.6	22.3	9.2	0.8	1.7	5.1a	1.8	1.4	0.6

SOURCE: Federal Bureau of Investigation Uniform Crime Reports (1958-1977).
a. Of the women arrested in 1976 and 1977, .2 and .1 percent were arrested for embezzlement.

Looked at this way, the distinctive involvement of women in larceny and fraud holds up. Men, on the other hand, are much more likely to acquire property through burglary, auto theft, and robbery, than are women.

Pausing briefly to assess what we have learned thus far, we note that the answer to the question posed initially is "yes"—there has been a big increase in the proportion of females arrested over the past two decades. But the increase has not been random across all the offense categories. It has been concentrated mainly in the property categories of larceny-theft, fraud, embezzlement, and forgery.

In earlier work, Simon has argued that although the data do not allow a clear test of the hypothesis, the higher female arrest rates are likely to be related to the greater participation of women in the labor force over the same time-span. The facts that support such a relationship are that the increase in women's arrests has been primarily in the property and white-collar categories, and that among those women who are in the labor force (in 1958, 35 percent were employed full-time; in 1977, the percentage was close to 50), over 70 percent work as secretaries, clerks, bookkeepers, and salespeople. These are positions that provide the opportunities, and require the skills, to commit those criminal acts that have increased most markedly among women. But until data are collected that provide specific information about the demographic and socioeconomic characteristics of the female arrestees, it is not possible to test the validity of that hypothesis. Data are needed that describe educational level, occupational status, marital status, whether the woman is a head of household, and whether she is the mother of children dependent upon her for financial support.

The data also show that there has been no noticeable increase in the percentage of women who have been arrested for homicide and aggravated assault. Earlier studies (e.g., Ward et al., 1969) have shown that women arrested for violent acts usually direct their violence against men with whom they have been emotionally involved—most often their husbands, their lovers, sometimes their pimps. The attack by the woman is often precipitated by violence to which she has been subjected during much of her relationship with the victim. For example, wives charged with homicide have described how they endured years of physical and emotional abuse until something exploded inside them and, in a moment of rage, in self defense, or in anger, have killed their husbands. As women take on more self-sufficient roles, as they provide financial support not only for themselves but for their minor children, as they come to see themselves not as trapped and dependent, but as persons who have choices they can exercise and skills for which they can obtain financial rewards, they are less likely to find themselves victimized. Rather than endure intolerable or dehumanizing relationships, they will leave the situation before the crisis arises to which a violent response appears as the only alternative. Projecting then a few years into the future, the incidence of serious, violent acts by women are likely to decline.

To summarize briefly what we know about women's criminal activities from the arrest statistics, we have learned that there has been an increase in female arrests over the past decade and that the increase has been primarily in the property-economic offenses, such as larceny-theft, fraud, and forgery.

The questions for which we have no answers because even crude data are not available, concern the demographic and socioeconomic characteristics of the women who have contributed to the rise in female arrests over the past one and one-half decades. Are they women in the labor force who are using their employment opportunities and technical skills as clerks, secretaries, book-keepers, and the like, to steal, defraud, or embezzle? Are they women who have assumed sole or primary responsibility for supporting their families because they are husbandless mothers of young children? We would hypothesize that women property offenders are motivated by the same interests and desires that men have when they commit property crimes. If this hypothesis is correct, it implies that police and other law enforcement officers should not consider women as special cases. Rather, the existing crime prevention programs and general police operations should be altered so as to do away with any practices that are based on seeing women criminals as somehow innately different from men. Standard police operating procedures should be applied to all criminals and all crime prevention programs. Sex, in this case, becomes an insignificant variable in deciding upon police programs.

The next section focuses on women offenders in courts and considers primarily the question of whether women are treated differently from men when charged with the same types of offenses.

WOMEN OFFENDERS IN COURT

Two schools of thought prevail on how women defendants are treated in the courts. The view held by most observers is that women receive preferential treatment. In operational terms it means they are less likely to be convicted than men for the same type of offense, if convicted they are less likely to receive prison sentences, and if sentenced they are likely to receive milder or shorter terms. The factors that are believed to motivate judges toward lenient treatment of women are chivalry, naiveté (for example, judges often say that they cannot help but compare women defendants with other women they know well—namely, their mothers and wives, whom they cannot imagine behaving in the manner attributed to the defendant), and practicality (most women defendants have young children, and sending them to prison places a burden on the rest of society).

The less popular view is that judges behave more punitively toward women than they do toward men. They are more likely to throw the book at the female defendant because they believe there is a greater discrepancy between her behavior and the behavior expected of women than there is between the behavior of the male defendant and the behavior expected of men. In other words, women defendants pay for the judges' belief that it is more in man's nature to commit crimes than it is in woman's. Thus, when judges are convinced that the female defendant has committed a crime, they are more likely to overreact and punish her, not only for the specific offense, but also for transgressing against their expectations of womanly behavior.

The existence of such statutes as the indeterminate sentence for women, or the sanctioning of procedures whereby only convicted male defendants have their minimum sentences determined by a judge at an open hearing and in the presence of counsel, while the woman's minimum sentence is decided by a parole board in closed session at which she is not represented by counsel, is offered as evidence of the unfair, punitive treatment accorded women by the courts (Singer, 1973).

Unfortunately, once researchers move out of the arrest stage, the availability of data drops precipitously. For all of the grumbling and complaining that we have done about the inadequacy of the arrest statistics and the lack of information about demographic and socioeconomic characteristics of the offenders, there is at least a national data set from which it is possible to determine and compare changes in the types of offenses for which women have been arrested over the past four decades and, more recently, to compare adult and juvenile female arrest patterns. But save for the statistics compiled by the Administrative Office of the U.S. Courts, for offenders in the federal system, there is no central source where state court judicial statistics are collected and stored. Since the great majority of criminal cases are heard in state courts, it is foolish to generalize about crime trends from federal data. Federal statistics are even less useful in describing female trends, because the major offenses are ones women are least likely to be involved in: illegal immigration and auto thefts.

Since there is no uniform body of state judicial statistics in the United States, it is not possible to determine from existing data for the society as a whole how significant a factor the sex of the defendant is in determining guilt or innocence, or in the sentence that is handed down. Thus, on a national basis there are no empirically sound answers to the question, "Are women victims of negative, or recipients of positive, discrimination; or, is the sex of the defendant an insignificant factor in the courts' decision?"

On an ad hoc basis, some data have been collected in various jurisdictions that have allowed comparisons to be made between male and female defendants by types of offenses. In California, for example, between 1960 and 1972, when all of the crimes for which women have been arrested were combined, there was an increase of 31 percent from 8.3 to 10.9 in the percentage of women convicted.

A comparison of female convictions in California and Ohio for the three-year period 1969-1971, revealed that the rank order for the four most frequently committed crimes from highest to lowest conviction rates in each year was the same in both states. Forgery had the highest percentage of female convictions, followed by homicide, narcotics, and larceny-theft.

For the years 1974 and 1975, the Institute for Law and Social Research (INSLAW) in Washington, D.C., followed men and women through the District of Columbia criminal justice system from the time they were arrested through the time they were sentenced (Simon and Sharma, 1978). The judicial data collected by INSLAW permits a more in-depth analysis of how women offenders are treated by the courts than has been available previously. For example, the tables shown below describe the treatment accorded men and women by the prosecution. They describe the percentage of men and women arrested that have had the charges against them dropped at the initial screening, or before going into court, and the percentage of men and women who pleaded guilty or opted to have their case go to trial. We see (p. 558) that there are no major differences between men and women.

When the data were broken down into various types of offenses, the prosecutor appeared more inclined to drop charges for violent crimes than for other types of offenses, and seemed more prepared to do so for women than for men. Only among defendants charged with victimless offenses were women consistently less likely than men to have their cases rejected at screening. For the other offense categories, there was little difference and little consistency in the prosecutor's treatment of men and women.

Following the cases of men and women that had gone to trial (about 42 percent of the women and 46 percent of the men in 1974, and about 51 and 53 percent in 1975), we see in the data on page 558 that the courts did not appear to treat men and women differently. The courts dismissed between 6 and 12 percent of all the cases, but made no particular distinction by the sex of the defendant. Of the remaining cases, the ratio of defendants who chose to plead guilty as opposed to those who chose to stand trial was between 2.5 and 3.3 to 1. But again, the percentage of women who opted to plead guilty was not noticeably different from the percentage of men who pled guilty. Of the approximately 10 percent of defendants whose cases went to trial, at least 60 percent were found guilty.

As shown in Table 22.4, when the data were broken down by types of offenses, judges were more inclined to dismiss robbery cases than any other type of case, but they did not distinguish between men and women in doing so.

Among the men and women who were found guilty, the only consistent and noticeable difference was that the men were more likely to be found guilty for robbery and the women for victimless crimes. Among those who were found not guilty, there was no consistent and noticeable difference between men and women in any of the offense categories.

Prosecutor's Decisions (percentages)

	1974		1975	
	Women	Men	Women	Men
Reject at screening	20.3	23.1	17.4	18.9
Nolle prosequi or dismiss	37.8	30.7	31.8	28.1
Take a plea or go to trial	41.9	46.2	50.8	53.0

Percentage of Arrests Rejected at Screening

	1974		1975	
Type of offense[a]	Women	Men	Women	Men
Property	18.0	22.5	17.5	18.0
Economic	13.3	16.8	9.0	8.6
Violent	35.9	27.0	34.5	22.9
Robbery	18.3	13.8	11.7	9.3
Victimless	12.2	20.0	9.7	14.7

a. Property offenses include larceny, burglary, auto theft, and dealing in stolen property; economic offenses include fraud, embezzlement, forgery, and counterfeiting; violent offenses include murder, manslaughter, and aggravated assault; victimless offenses include gambling, drug law violations, and sex offenses, excluding rape and sexual assault.

Courts' Dispositions of Arrests (percentages)

	1974		1975	
	Women	Men	Women	Men
Court dismissed	11.9	9.6	6.0	8.5
Pled guilty	21.5	25.2	34.1	32.8
Found guilty	5.2	6.3	7.7	7.5
Found not guilty	3.4	4.0	2.6	3.5
Cases open	0.8	1.1	0.4	0.7

TABLE 22.4   Court Dismissals and Verdicts for Male and
Female Defendants: 1974 and 1975 Arrests
Accepted for Prosecution (Washington D.C.)

Type of Offense	1974		1975	
	Women	Men	Women	Men
Percentage Dismissed				
Property	5.9	9.1	5.8	8.8
Economic	3.1	8.4	7.7	8.4
Violent	8.5	9.4	6.2	11.6
Robbery	12.9	14.1	14.9	12.7
Simple Assault	11.9	10.9	5.8	7.9
Victimless	18.4	9.0	5.1	6.0
Percentage Found Guilty				
Property	4.3	6.4	6.3	7.8
Economic	5.5	3.9	2.6	5.6
Violent	4.3	7.0	10.5	9.0
Robbery	6.5	9.1	6.4	9.4
Simple Assault	14.3	10.1	7.7	9.9
Victimless	5.3	4.1	9.2	6.3
Percentage Found Not Guilty				
Property	2.1	4.3	2.7	3.3
Economic	2.3	0.8	1.3	2.2
Violent	4.0	3.7	3.9	4.7
Robbery	1.1	3.1	4.3	3.3
Simple Assault	4.8	8.0	7.7	3.6
Victimless	4.6	4.0	2.3	3.1

We see in Table 22.5 that robbery is the only category for which at least half of the defendants convicted received prison sentences. Even among those who were found guilty of violent offenses, only about one-third of the men and one-quarter of the women were sentenced to prison. Note that while the percentages found guilty among the women and men are quite similar (5.2 versus 6.3), men are much more likely to receive prison sentences than are women. Our guess is that many of these women have young children and that that fact influenced the judge's decision. But the data by themselves allow us neither to confirm nor deny that guess.

For a shorter time-span, Bernstein et al. (1978) collected data on how men and women offenders were treated in a New York State court. In the table below, we compare their New York data against the Washington, D.C., statistics.

Although the Bernstein et al. data show bigger differences between men and women than do the Washington data, they conclude that "females are no more

TABLE 22.5   Sentence by Sex and Type of Offense, 1974 (Washington, D.C.)

	Offense Categories (percentages)											
	Property		Economic		Violent		Robbery		Victimless		Combined	
Sentences[a]	Male	Female	Male	Female	Male	Female	Male	Female	Male	Female	Male	Female
Probation	63.7	78.8	71.0	90.9	63.5	70.6	39.2	55.0	72.4	69.3	65.2	74.8
Fine	2.2	5.1	5.6	0.0	2.6	2.0	1.3	0.0	18.0	20.2	6.3	10.1
6 months – 1 year	16.9	9.3	9.7	6.1	9.6	7.8	8.3	25.0	6.1	10.6	11.4	10.7
1 – 3 years	11.0	5.1	7.3	3.0	8.2	5.9	15.5	10.0	2.7	0.0	8.4	2.3
2 – 15 years[b]	6.2	1.7	6.5	0.0	14.1	13.7	35.7	10.0	0.8	0.0	8.5	2.1
20 years – life	0.0	0.0	0.0	0.0	1.9	0.0	0.0	0.0	0.0	0.0	0.2	0.0
N[c]	1128	118	124	33	425	51	375	20	753	218	2505	515

SOURCE: Simon and Sharma (using PROMIS data), 1978.

a. Only the 1974 data include sentences.
b. Although there appears to be an overlap of this category with the previous one, in fact there is none. The sentence categories were ordered in terms of the minimum sentence: All individuals in this category were given a minimum of two years in prison, while those in the previous category were given a minimum of one year in prison.
c. Those defendants assigned to youth corrections and to narcotics treatment have been excluded.

or less likely than males to have their cases dismissed, and are somewhat more likely than males to avoid a probation or prison sentence after an adjudication of guilt." They continue, "On our more global measure of court income, we find that females charged with a crime are significantly less likely than males similarly charged to spend any time behind bars." They concluded:

> We began with the competing hypotheses that women are preferentially treated or discriminated against solely because of their sex. Examining three outcomes, we find no difference between males and females in the decision to terminate or fully prosecute a defendant's criminal case. For convicted defendants, we find that being female provides some small advantage, with females being less likely to receive the more severe sentences. For all defendants, we find that being female has a substantial advantage, with females being less likely than males to spend any time imprisoned.

The Washington, D.C., data revealed that about the same percentage of men and women had their cases dropped by the prosecutor or dismissed by the judge. Among the approximately 30 percent of defendants who pleaded or were found guilty, the major difference between men and women was that a greater percentage of men were sentenced to prison. As we have seen, these findings are consistent with those reported for New York by Bernstein et al.

Concerning those women who do go to prison, closer inspection may reveal that they are ones whose criminal records do not differ in any significant way from those women whose sentences are suspended or who are acquitted. But they may be distinctive in their demographic characteristics. Most notably, they may be women who do not have young children. On the other hand, it is also plausible that those women offenders who draw prison sentences are tougher and have a longer record of arrests and/or convictions than do men charged with the same offense.

To summarize the major finding in this section: Contrary to popular impression, the treatment of women by the judiciary smacks neither of preferentialism nor of punitiveness when decisions pertaining to dismissal or determination of guilt or innocence are being made. But women defendants do appear to be the recipients of positive discrimination at the point at which sentence determinations are made. Judges, at least those in New York and Washington, D.C., are less likely to sentence women to prison for the same types of offenses than they are men.

In 1974, Simon (1975: 87) reported the results of interviews with some 30 criminal court judges in major cities in the Midwest (Chicago, St. Louis, Milwaukee, and Indianapolis). She had asked them how they responded to female defendants and reported that more than half of the judges said they treated women more leniently and more gently than they did men; that they were more inclined to recommend probation rather than imprisonment; and that if they sentenced a woman, it was usually for a shorter time than for a man. Only a small proportion of the judges said that they were less likely to convict the women. The point at which they differentiated in favor of the women was at the time of passing sentence.

These remarks are consistent with the data from the courts in New York and Washington, D.C. Altogether, they suggest that judges are not (yet) "sex-blind." Many of them may still see images of their mothers, wives, or sisters in front of them at the time they pronounce sentence against a woman embezzler, thief, forger, and so on. Judges may also not be indifferent to the practical problems created when women who are mothers of young children are sent off to prison and their children are left behind.

In the last section, we look at women offenders incarcerated in state and federal prisons.

WOMEN IN PRISON

In 1974 women comprised about 3.4 percent of the total prison population. Between 1950 and 1974 the range of women inmates compared to men was between 2.9 and 3.8 percent. The data thus offer no indication that a larger percentage of females were committed in the early seventies than were sentenced in the previous two decades.

Although compared to men the number of women inmates is small, we are nevertheless talking about several thousand people at any given time; thus it is important to consider the particular problems women inmates confront.

The two problems that importantly affect women during the period of their incarceration and after they are released are: what will happen and what has happened to their children, and what sort of education and vocational training have they received.

About 70 percent of the women inmates are mothers. In a recent study of the children of women prisoners, McGowan and Blumenthal (1978) wrote:

> Mothers face a number of special problems during their incarceration, the most critical of these being the enforced separation from their children. Visits, phone calls, and letters help, but they cannot substitute for continuous, daily contact. Although more facilities are beginning to experiment with open or "contact" family visits in recreation rooms or in the mother's own room, many facilities still permit only visits across a table or through a glass partition or a screen. Visiting hours are generally quite restricted, and transportation of children presents a major problem because distance and costs are often great. One woman in a northeastern state said that she had been unable to see her three children, aged four, seven, and eleven, for one-and-one-half years because the children lived with an elderly grandmother 300 miles away.

Because of restrictive prison policies regarding inmate communications, as well as the attitudes of many of the children's caretakers, mothers in prison frequently find they are not provided adequate information about their children's development, school problems, or health needs. This leaves them unable to participate sufficiently in planning for their children. They are likely to feel anxious and guilty about what their children may be suffering because of their conduct; they also feel unfairly excluded from meeting parental responsibilities and even from comforting their children or offering them needed support.

The pregnant prisoner faces special problems: Proper diet and gynecological care are often not available, particularly in jails; pre-natal education or counseling is unusual; abortions are rarely available. The mother must decide what she will do when the baby is born—whether she will ask relatives or friends to provide care, place the baby in foster care, or surrender him for adoption. Generally, pregnant inmates are given little assistance in exploring placement options; nor is there normally any help in coping with the emotional trauma that may result from the separation of mother and baby immediately after birth.

Many women in prison fear they will lose their children, a feeling that is somewhat justified although permanent termination of parental rights is unlikely. . . . Ignorance of their rights and the absence of legal services to help them with child-related matters, as well as general uncertainty about their futures, combine to create a constant anxiety among inmate mothers as to what they can and should do about their children.

On the second problem, that of the quality and variety of educational and vocational training programs that are available to female inmates, the Women's Bureau of the Department of Labor concluded in 1970 that 85 percent of the inmates want more job training and 80 percent want more educational opportunities than were available at those institutions (Koontz, 1971). They based their conclusions on a survey of inmates in two of the three federal prisons for women. Out of 10 respondents, 9 said that they expected to work to support themselves when they were released, and a majority also expected that they would support others who were dependent upon them.

Examination of the vocational training opportunities that were available at most women's prisons in the early seventies suggests that those responsible for the programs hold a view of the roles women ought to perform in society that is characteristic of at least a pre-World War II era. Quoting from a note in the *Yale Law Journal* (Arditi et al., 1973), Simon reported the diversity and types of vocational programs available for men and women inmates at 47 institutions for males and 15 institutions for females that in 1973 housed approximately 30 percent of the men and 50 percent of the women inmates in the country. The average number of programs in the prisons for men was 10; in the institutions for women the average number was 2.7. Whereas male prisoners had a choice of some 50 different vocational programs, the women's choices were limited to cosmetology (in some states convicted felons are forbidden by law to work in this field), clerical training, food services, serving, IBM key punching, and nurses' aides.

In a more recent national study of women's correctional institutions, Glick and Neto (1976) examined services and programs available for women in jails and prisons in fourteen states. They found that 42 percent of the inmates were enrolled in vocational programs, the most popular of which were clerical training, cosmetology, and food services. Of the women, 21 percent were enrolled in academic programs, and of these, 28 percent were in remedial education, 41 percent in high school, and 31 percent in college-level programs.

These more recent data from the Glick-Neto survey indicate that changes are being made in order to provide more vocational opportunities and more diversity for women inmates. The fact that training in cosmetology is still among the most popular of programs is disturbing, given the existence of statutes that bar women inmates from practicing. But that clerical training is available and that academic programs are opening up, suggest that changes are being instituted to meet the needs of women, once they are released, in a more realistic manner. Note also that the Glick-Neto survey found that over 40 percent of the female inmates were at least high school graduates. This finding provides some evidence that the female offenders of the 1970s are of higher socioeconomic status than were their predecessors, and that, indeed, they may well have been women who were caught with their hand in the "till" at their offices, stores, or plants.[1]

The relative paucity and lack of variety in rehabilitation programs for women may be due to society's stereotypical notions concerning the needs of women and their motivations for engaging in criminal activities. The predominance of individual-level psychological explanations of female criminality, as opposed to the social structural explanations often given for male criminality, would support this. The traditional explanation for why women engaged in crime has tended to focus on psychological deficiencies in their nature. The causes of criminal behavior among men, on the other hand, were viewed as arising either from socially structured pressures relating to their social class origin or from a natural human tendency to pursue personal gratification at the lowest possible cost.

Perhaps because of these differences in the explanation of male and female criminality, there arose a difference in the proposed treatments. Programs were designed to teach men how to achieve their ends through legitimate means (vocational training), while women were not even recognized as having those needs and were taught how to become good mothers, good "girls," or good housewives. This approach to the problem ignored the possibility that the motivations women have for committing crimes may be similar to those of men and therefore deserving of the same responses. This is especially the case if one considers the changing roles of women in society generally. What counts as a successful outcome for men in vocational training programs (i.e., learning a job skill and supporting oneself independently) may not have been considered as a legitimate and worthwhile goal by the operators of rehabilitation programs for women. But the disproportionate increase in property crimes among women would indicate that women's prime motivations are utilitarian in nature, and that programs designed to help them handle these needs would be more efficacious than other, more psychologically oriented, programs. This, of course, rests on the somewhat unfounded utilitarian assumption that property crimes are committed solely out of a desire to maximize personal gains. Such an assumption makes a great deal of intuitive sense, but the literature in criminology is divided on whether it is the best way of looking at crime. More case histories on women criminals would be extremely helpful in solving this practical and theoretical problem.

Information on the participation of women in diversion programs, halfway houses, and innovative probation programs is also needed to see if they are being funneled in at the same rate as men. Since programs of this sort are usually oriented toward making the individual self-sufficient in the community, their rate of success should be compared closely to the more traditional female prison programs.

One more issue pertinent to a discussion of the female inmate is that of segregated versus integrated facilities. In the early part of this decade, the equal rights movement made the American prison system one of its targets. Separate prisons had been established for women, beginning in the 1880s, as a reform intended to give women the benefit of rehabilitation then being sought for younger men and boys in new reformatories (Singer, 1973: 173). Advocates of the Equal Rights Amendment who directed their interests at the female offender claimed that the same reasoning that was persuasive to the Supreme Court in Brown v. Board of Education, namely, that segregation by itself denies to blacks equal opportunities and equality in their educational experiences, applies to women when separate prison systems are maintained. Schools that segregate by race and prisons that segregate by sex are basically discriminatory.

In the 1973 *Yale Law Journal* note cited earlier, Arditi et al. (1973) stated that although the Supreme Court had not as yet made the same determination concerning segregation on the basis of sex that it made for segregation on the basis of color (separate, by its nature, cannot be equal), the Equal Rights Amendment would compel such a result.

In June 1978 the National Institute of Law Enforcement and Criminal Justice of the Law Enforcement Assistance Administration published its first evaluation of co-correctional institutions. Table 22.6 lists the names of all twenty federal and state correctional institutions that housed men and women beginning in July

TABLE 22.6   Co-Correctional Institutions in the United States

Institution	Location	Implementation Date
FYC-Morgantown	Morgantown, W. Virginia	July 1971 (July 1975)[a]
FCI-Fort Worth	Fort Worth, Texas	November 1971
Muncy State Correctional Institution	Muncy, Pennsylvania	December 1971
Massachusetts Correctional Institution	Framingham, Massachusetts	March 1973
FCI-Lexington	Lexington, Kentucky	February 1974
Dwight Correctional Center	Dwight, Illinois	May 1974 (May 1977)[a]
Vienna Correctional Center	Vienna, Illinois	May 1974 (June 1977)[a]
FCI-Pleasanton	Pleasanton, California	July 1974 (January 1978)[a]
Correctional Institution for Women	Clinton, New Jersey	August 1974
Claymont Institution for Women	Claymont, Delaware	October 1974 (May 1975)
Metropolitan Training Center	Circle Pines, Minnesota	March 1975 (May 1976)
FCI-Terminal Island	Terminal Island, California	March 1975 (January 1978)[a]
Taycheedah Correctional Institution	Taycheedah, Wisconsin	July 1975
Connecticut Correctional Institution	Niantic, Connecticut	September 1975
Renz Correctional Center	Cedar City, Missouri	September 1975
Chittenden Community Correctional Center	South Burlington, Vermont	January 1976
Maine Correctional Center	South Windham, Maine	April 1976
North Idaho Correctional Institution	Cottonwood, Idaho	May 1976
Memphis Correctional Center	Memphis, Tennessee	April 1977
Westville Correctional Center	Westville, Indiana	August 1977

a. These institutions are being or will be phased out as of the date in parenthesis.

1971. According to the National Institute's report, 58 percent (997) of female and 7.5 percent (2077) of male federal prisoners, and 9.7 percent (1232 of female and .5 percent (1277) of male state prisoners, occupied coed correctional institutions. The report described future plans for co-correctional institutions as follows:

> Communications with state correctional agencies identified eight state or other jurisdictions which were planning coed institutions. Three of these appeared to be in the operational planning stage, and five considered co-corrections part of a long-range plan. Of the three institutions which were at the operational planning stage, one has recently "gone coed" by introducing its first contingent of women; a second will soon open (after several months of delay in acquiring a non-correctional facility); and a third state has cancelled plans to add males to the sole women's institution in the state, due to increases in the female offender population, which have eliminated the problem of sub-maximal space utilization. The plans in at least two of the other five jurisdictions have been affected by difficulties in obtaining sufficient funds: one state, which had originally planned to build a modern co-correctional facility to open in 1976, has "indefinitely" pushed back its target date to 1981; a second jurisdiction has, in the absence of funds for architectural modifications and program expansion, tabled its plan. Two other jurisdictions have retained co-corrections as part of a long-range plan, and one state was found to be exploring the potential impacts of pending equal rights legislation on the obligation to integrate all public institutions, including prisons.

> An emerging trend in states which have recently opened, or plan to open, coed facilities is the maintenance of single-sex placement options for females, as well as for males. One state which recently opened a coed facility is planning the construction of a second facility for women; another recently-opened state facility brought some of the women in the state "closer to home," but still allows women the choice of single-sex incarceration elsewhere in the state; a third state, soon to open its coed facility, will continue to permit women the alternative of single-sex incarceration which has generally been retained, in other jurisdications operating coed facilities, only for men.

> Despite the relatively short history of co-corrections, six co-correctional facilities have gone out of existence. The reason for termination of co-corrections mentioned in five out of six institutions was the prospect for greater space utilization through a different distribution of the inmate population. The effects of population pressure have also been cited as the primary motivation for projected program terminations.

In their conclusions and recommendations, they said:

> The underlying concepts behind coeducational corrections are relatively simple. Corresponding to the non-programmatic and programmatic pur-

poses for the integration of incarcerated men and women, are two basic concepts, neither of which is necessarily valid in all circumstances:

> Two can live as cheaply as one; and
> male and female need each other.

Derived from these basic concepts are the expectations that the presence of men and women in institutions used to capacity will serve the system economy, and that the interaction of incarcerated men and women will have a positive effect on institutional functioning, or the inmates' lives.

*   *   *

Co-corrections has been implemented amidst fears of pregnancy, sexual assault, and emotional involvement; and, as a result, heavy external controls have often been applied, in the form of surveillance and sanctions. However, even where a minimum of external controls has been applied, the co-corrections has been valued for its effects on institutional life, it has often been suggested that "it develops a normal atmosphere, but then extracts the normal consequences of that atmosphere."

*   *   *

Whenever possible, women should be afforded the same choice of single-sex or coed confinement that is offered to male offenders. The presence of a choice reconciles two arguments: on the one hand, that female offenders should have an opportunity to develop *apart* from male-influence in an essentially male-dominated correctional system; and, on the other hand, that "normal" society contains both sexes, and that co-corrections offers opportunities to adjust to two-sex society in a controlled setting. In order to provide the option of single-sex confinement to women in jurisdictions operating coed institutions, inter-jurisdictional arrangements will frequently have to be developed, ordinarily with either other states, or local institutions.

It is too early to say how important an influence the co-correctional institutions have been or are likely to be on the psychic and social well-being of the women inmates, or on how important they have been in expanding the number and types of educational and vocational opportunities for women. Additional evaluations are planned by LEAA. Further innovations in the structure and organization of co-correctional institutions are also anticipated.

To summarize, of the two big problems women inmates confront,[2] changes seem to be occurring in the state and federal prisons in the direction of meeting the vocational and educational needs of women who are expected to support themselves or contribute to their own and others' support. There are signs that more opportunities are being made available for women to obtain training and skill in vocations in which they will be able to find employment after they are released. There is also evidence that educational programs at all levels are being introduced and expanded in those institutions that house women.

On the matter of babies and children, there are practically no signs that change is in the offing. In a few countries, such as Sweden, Denmark, and West Germany, prison officials have been willing to allow experimental programs such that women inmates may keep babies born to them in prison for a few months; there are no such opportunities in the United States.[3] Neither has there been any major institutional effort that might ease the anxiety and fears that women inmates have about losing those children born to them before they entered prison whom they have left behind with relatives, friends, or in the care of welfare agencies.

The issue of integrated versus segregated facilities is at the time of writing very much "under consideration."

CONCLUDING REMARKS

We return now to the three issues mentioned in the beginning of this chapter. As we have interpreted the data in each of the sections, the pattern that has emerged is that there has been an increase in female arrests over the past decade, and the increase has been primarily in the property-economic offenses, such as larceny, fraud, and forgery. Popular impressions about women being the recipients of positive or negative discrimination by prosecutors and judges have, by and large, not been substantiated. At the time of sentencing, however, from the limited data available, it appears that judges are more reluctant to sentence convicted women defendants to prison than they are men. In addition to the usual deprivations that are associated with serving time, a large majority of the women inmates also have the "special" problem of coping with the pain that is a result of the forced separation from their children, and with their anxiety about losing custody of them. Surveys of the vocational and educational programs available for women inmates indicate that improvements are being made; however, both in terms of the amount of training and education and the types of courses and skills that are available, women inmates are still not receiving comparable opportunities.

One point that has been emphasized earlier but that can bear repeating because it is so essential, is the need for more and better data at all stages of the criminal justice system. At the arrest stage, demographic and socioeconomic status information should be collected as a matter of course.

Some of us who have been working on the issue of "women and crime" see a relationship between the growing percentage of women in the labor force, the growing percentage of women who are heads of households, and the increasing percentage of women arrested for property and economic offenses. We claim that an important explanation for the increase in women's crime rates is that women have greater opportunities and technical skills for committing crimes. Their work as bookkeepers, sales clerks, secretaries, and the like places them in positions where they have the opportunity for handling money and goods not available to unemployed, untrained, and/or uneducated women. The accuracy and validity of that hypothesis can only be borne out by the collection of data on a continuing and systematic basis. If the hypothesis is borne out, then the traditional profile of the woman offender as a passive, ineffective, immoral, almost childlike creature who can be vicious and cruel, but not rational and instrumental, will have to be redrawn.

More and better data also need to be collected at the court level. The United States is far behind almost all of the countries of Western Europe in its lack of judicial statistics that describe numbers of defendants charged, convicted, and sentenced by type of offense in courts at different levels in the judicial hierarchy. In the absence of a national data bank of state court judicial statistics, it is impossible to follow cohorts of offenders from their initial contact with the criminal justice system through imprisonment, and subsequent release or acquittal. The same types of demographic and socioeconomic status information that need to be collected at the arrest stage should also be included in the judicial statistics.

Finally, additional studies of the types of women who serve time in prison need to be made, and special attention should be paid to the vocational opportunities they receive and to the opportunities they have for maintaining contact with their children.

NOTES

1. Glick and Neto also collected data on the demographic and social characteristics of the female inmates. Of the 6466 women in their sample, 50 percent are black, 36 percent are white, 9 percent Hispanic, and the other 5 percent are Indian or "other" categories. There are 73 percent with at least one child; the mean number is 2.5. Over 40 percent are at least high school graduates and 18 percent have had some college education.

2. We do not mean to rule out other problems that some smaller groups of women may confront during their incarceration, such as sexual advances that they are unable to deter or various types of physical or emotional suffering.

3. Federal prisons have begun to experiment recently with allowing mothers to keep babies born in prison. So far, the program is limited to children born while the mother is incarcerated, and only low-risk prisoners are eligible. These programs have apparently developed out of the realization that the jailed mother and her children need more contact with each other (New York Times, April 29, 1979).

REFERENCES

Adler, F. (1975) *Sisters in Crime: The Rise of the New Female Criminal.* New York: McGraw-Hill, 1975.

Arditi, R. R., F. Goldberg, M. M. Hartle, J. H. Peters, and W. R. Phelps "The Sexual Segregation of American Prisons: Notes." *Yale Law Journal* 82 (November/May): 1229-1273.

Bernstein, I. N., W. Kelly, and P. Doyle (1977) "Societal Reaction to Deviants: The Case of Criminal Defendants." *American Sociological Review* (October).

Federal Bureau of Investigation (1958-1977) *Uniform Crime Reports.* Washington, DC: Government Printing Office.

Glick, R. M. and V. V. Neto (1976) *National Study of Women's Correctional Programs.* Sacramento: California Youth Authority.

Koontz, B. (1971) *Public Hearings on Women and Girl Offenders.* Washington, DC: D.C. Commission on the Status of Women.

McGowan, B. G. and K. L. Blumenthal (1978) *Why Punish the Children? A Study of Children of Women Prisoners.* Hackensack, NJ: National Council on Crime and Delinquency.

National Institute of Law Enforcement and Criminal Justice (1978) *Co-Educational Correctional Institutions.*

New York Times (1979) "Inmates Mother Their Babies in Prison Experiment." April 29, 1: 29.

Simon, R. J. (1975) *The Contemporary Woman and Crime.* Rockville, MD: National Institute of Mental Health.

——— and N. Sharma (1978) *The Female Defendant in Washington, D.C.: 1974 and 1975.* Washington, DC: Institute for Law and Social Research.

Singer, L. R. (1973) "Women and the Correctional Process." *American Criminal Law Review* 11: 300-318.

Steffensmeir, D. J. (1978) "Crime and the Contemporary Woman: An Analysis of Changing Levels of Female Property Crime, 1960-75." *Social Forces* 57: 566-584.

Terry, R. (1978) "Trends in Female Crime: A Comparison of Adler, Simon, and Steffensmeier." Presented at the annual meeting of The Society for the Study of Social Problems, San Francisco, California.

Ward, D. A., M. Jackson, and R. W. Ward (1969) "Crimes of Violence by Women," in D. Mulvihill, et al. (eds.) *Crimes of Violence.* Washington, DC: Governmental Printing Office.

23

Widening the Net: An Anomaly in the Evaluation of Diversion Programs

Thomas G. Blomberg

INTRODUCTION

Following the recommendations of the 1967 President's Commission on Law Enforcement and the Administration of Justice, there was a nationwide explosion of diversion programs. Diversion programs were aimed at diverting selected adult and juvenile offenders previously subject to justice system insertion into various forms of community treatment. A major conceptual rationale underlying the diversion concept was that reducing offender insertion into the justice system would avoid the danger assumed to be associated with criminal stigmatization and criminal associations, thereby reducing the likelihood of subsequent crime by the offender.[1] Stimulated by Law Enforcement Assistance Administration funding, diversion emerged as a national crime control strategy.

While the diversion concept was hailed by many proponents as a major justice policy innovation, it can be argued that the policy has early twentieth-century roots. Clearly, diversion notions were central to stated juvenile court policy and were reflected in various rationales for parole and probation at the turn of the twentieth century. Nonetheless, while the diversion orientation is not novel, the concept has flourished with largely unquestioned acceptance and continuous program proliferation.

In recent years critical concern has been focused upon diversion program accountability and has stimulated evaluation of the program's implementation

AUTHOR'S NOTE: I wish to thank Sheldon L. Messinger, Malcolm W. Klein, Jeanine Blomberg, and Theodore Chiricos for their helpful criticisms and suggested modifications on an early draft of this chapter.

efforts and results. Emerging from these evaluation efforts have been several important and alarming trends. First, and central to diversion's basic conceptual rationale, has been the documented failure of diversion programs to implement appropriate client targeting upon system-insertable clients. This failure has resulted in what is referred to as "net-widening"–namely, extending the client reach of the justice system by increasing the overall proportion of population (system-insertable and "others") subject to some form of system control. Second, diversion's net-widening has been shown to have the potential to produce a number of consequences detrimental to clients. Third, and a more subtle issue underlying the net-widening findings, is the question of how the general population may come to accept state intrusions as a matter of common course.

While there are few correctional reform examples that have been successfully implemented and evaluated, it should be possible, as Klein (1979) has contended, to implement programs which correspond to their conceptual rationales and then to evaluate the usefulness of these programs and corresponding rationales. To date, it appears that this has not occurred with diversion program implementation efforts; consequently, the efficacy of diversion and its corresponding rationales remains open to speculation. To move beyond speculation and ensure that evaluations of diversion programs are, in fact, evaluations of diversion instead of program cooptations and/or insufficient program implementations, it is necessary to alert diversion program evaluators to the net-widening potential and strategies for identifying and assessing net-widening's client effects. This chapter attempts to address this need. The primary purposes are: (1) to demonstrate through a review of diversion literature the net-widening pattern and resulting detrimental effects to clients associated with inappropriately implemented diversion programs, (2) to identify and discuss evaluation strategies for determining if net-widening is occurring and how it affects clients, and (3) to consider why net-widening occurs and if it can be avoided.

The chapter is divided into five sections. Section I provides an overview of diversion programs. Section II reviews diversion literature addressing net-widening and discusses pertinent evaluation strategies. Section III reviews diversion literature concerning the client effects resulting from diversion, particularly in relation to net-widening, and discusses pertinent evaluation strategies. Section IV considers net-widening as a trend associated not only with diversion but with a series of reforms related to corrections and reviews an organizational explanation of this trend. Section V is comprised of a summary and exploration of how the organizational stimulus facilitating net-widening may be checked.

I. OVERVIEW OF THE DIVERSION PROGRAM MOVEMENT

In considering diversion, it is important to keep in mind the broad range of adult and juvenile diversion programs.[2] Overall, both adult and juvenile diversion programs can be said to share in the attempt to replace traditional or official justice-processing with alternative processing into various community-based treatment programs. Adult diversion programs have been focused largely upon the delivery of pretrial services, but they often include delivery of services to convicted offenders as well. The Community-Based Corrections Program of Polk County, Des Moines, Iowa, for example, was judged by NILECJ to be an exemplary adult diversion project and appropriate for replication by other jurisdictions. The program provides pretrial release on own recognizance, pretrial supervised release, probation, and residence at Fort Des Moines (a correctional facility offering work and educational release) for both adult defendants and convicted offenders.[3] Although juvenile diversion programs have a broad variety of service-delivery orientations, family-centered treatment has become a dominant juvenile diversion treatment modality. For example, the 601 Juvenile Diversion Project in Sacramento, California, was designated an exemplary juvenile diversion project by NILECJ. This program provides short-term family crisis counseling as an alternative to juvenile court processing for status offenders (truants, runaways, and generally unmanageable youngsters).[4]

Participation requirements in adult and juvenile diversion programs vary from strictly voluntary to legally required. Most projects operate between the legal and the voluntary orientations (paralegal), generally gaining client participation through coercion. Typically, these paralegal diversion programs are administratively controlled by the official justice system, staffed by justice personnel (in-kind and the like), and physically based in official justice premises.[5] They have access to official justice records, grant justice personnel access to their records, and maintain a formal or informal method of reporting on client progress in cooperation with the justice system. As this form of organization suggests, paralegal diversion programs have served a supplementary rather than alternative function to the justice system (Rutherford and McDermott, 1976). Such a supplementary role suggests a net-widening potential in terms of the ultimate impact of diversion programs upon the overall administration of justice to adults and juveniles.

In the late 1960s and early 1970s the diversion literature tended to be descriptive, theoretical, and devoid of critical speculation and challenge. This includes the writings of Rosenheim (1969), Lemert (1971), and Polk (1971), who argued for the development of youth diversion alternatives on the basis of their assumed potential to produce more effective delinquency prevention and treatment. In the mid 1970s the diversion concept was subjected to critical speculation in articles by Mahoney (1974), Morris (1974), and Nejelski (1976). With regard to adult diversion, Morris (1974: 10) contended that the operation of diversion would ultimately increase the numbers under control by generating at the police level greater discretion to decide whether to arrest or to issue a notice to appear in court. The result would be fewer arrests but more individuals reaching the courts, resulting, in turn, in more pervasive but less severe control over a substantially larger number of citizens. In terms of juvenile programs, Nejelski (1976: 410) warned that "there is a danger that diversion will become a means of expanding coercive intervention in the lives of children and families without proper concern for their rights." Such critical speculation and growing interest in diversion subsequently stimulated a series of evaluation efforts concerned with the implementation and results of diversion.

II. IS DIVERSION PRODUCING NET-WIDENING?

A consistent finding that has emerged from the evaluation of diversion programs has been validation of the net-widening speculation. It has been demonstrated that both adult and juvenile diversion practices are being applied largely to clients who were previously not subject to justice system insertion. Representative of this literature are the reports of Vorenberg and Vorenberg (1973), Klein (1974, 1975, 1979); Kutchins and Kutchins (1975), Mattingly and Katkin (1975), the California Youth Authority (1976), Blomberg (1977a), Sarri (1979); and those of adult diversion by Petersen (1973), Zimring (1973), Mullen (1975), and Seitz et al. (1978).

The California Youth Authority study, for example, evaluated fifteen local juvenile diversion projects and specifically assessed the extent to which the programs did divert system-insertable clients from the juvenile system. The findings indicated that, on an average, less than 50 percent of the diversion clients were, in fact, diversion clients—namely, those who would have received imminent justice system insertion if not for the availability of diversion programs. The majority of diversion program clients were termed "prevention clients"—those youth defined as not subject to imminent justice insertion but provided diversion services to prevent their future delinquency.[6] Similarly, Mullen (1975: 24) concluded from a comparative assessment of adult pretrial diversion programs that "in the absence of diversion alternatives, few project participants would have faced jail sentence." In a case study of a juvenile diversion program, Blomberg (1977a) documented a 32 percent increase in the total number of youth receiving some form of justice or diversion service during the program's first year of operation. The significant numerical increase was attributed to the "whole" family treatment focus, in which diverted youth, their siblings, and parents were required to participate.

The net-widening finding demonstrates the lack of development of targeted client populations for diversion programs—namely, a specification of those clients who would have been inserted into the justice system previous to the availability of diversion programs. Klein (1979) argues in this regard that in the available diversion literature almost no serious attempts have been made to develop system-insertable client populations for diversion programs. In addition, the conceptual, definitional, and operational ambiguities of diversion programs have facilitated the emergence of a delinquency prevention function instead of justice system diversion function for many diversion programs. This emergence has been considerably reinforced by the commonly held assumption among various related court and probation personnel that many of the clients who were released prior to diversion programming were, nonetheless, in need of treatment that was not available before diversion.

The referral of beginning or minor offenders to treatment agencies is commonly assumed to be a professional response to these clients. Early identification and subsequent referral is felt essential for crime and delinquency prevention. Such widely held notions have substantially impeded the implementation of diversion as originally envisioned, and have contributed to the transformation of diversion programs into prevention programs, receiving the bulk of their clients from parents, schools, and welfare agencies instead of the justice system (Statsky, 1974; Dennison et al., 1975; Humphreys and Carrier, 1976; McAleenan et al., 1977; and the National Advisory Commission on Criminal Justice Standards and Goals, 1978). Further, several researchers argue that in some areas diversion clients tend to be middle-class and without prior records or serious instant offenses which would have resulted in justice system insertion. This results in diversion referral not being available to those lower-class youth with a prior record and serious instant offense who perhaps are most likely to benefit from diversion services (Hackler, 1976; Pitchess, 1976; Carter, 1978; and Klein, 1979).

It is of major importance for diversion program evaluators to be alert to diversion's net-widening potential and to be familiar with useful evaluation strategies for identifying and measuring net-widening. Any diversion program evaluation which fails to address the net-widening issue would have to be considered incomplete or superficial, given diversion's reported net-widening results. Moreover, without specific consideration of net-widening, evaluators cannot be sure whether or not they are evaluating a diversion program or various transformations of the concept.

Evaluating Diversion Programs for Net-Widening

Evaluations of diversion programs addressing net-widening have focused largely upon assessments of client characteristics and/or system processing rates. In terms of client characteristics, evaluation efforts have been aimed at determining if diversion programs are selecting clients with characteristics of clients normally inserted into the justice system. With regard to system processing rates, evaluations have been focused upon a determination of diversion's impact upon the characteristic numerical flow of clients through the justice system. Both approaches have proven useful in addressing diversion's net-widening capability.

In evaluating the extent to which juvenile diversion program clients are diversion clients normally inserted into the justice system, evaluators have considered such client characteristics as age, sex, prior offense history, and instant offense seriousness. Klein (1979) specifies several client characteristics indicative of justice system insertion for juvenile offenders—namely, that justice system-insertable youth should be older (15 to 17), predominately male (with the male-female ratio 5 to 1 or greater), generally with a prior record and instant offenses of medium seriousness, and infrequently status offenders. Several of these juvenile diversion client characteristics are relevant to adult diversion clients as well. Specifically, adult diversion clients would probably be male with a prior record and instant offenses of medium seriousness. However, jurisdictions are subject to variations concerning both adult and juvenile client characteristics which indicate imminent justice system insertion. As a result, diversion program evaluators should attempt to review with appropriate justice system personnel those system-insertable client characteristics to be used in their evaluations (court intake officers and related probation staff, district attorney staff, defense attorney staff, and judges) to ensure jurisdiction-specific relevance.[7]

In the assessment of diversion's impact upon the characteristic numerical flow of clients through the justice system, considerable emphasis has been given to the use of system processing rates.[8] Essentially, this approach involves generating system processing rates to compute numerical indicators for measuring a diversion program's impact upon the insertion of clients into the justice system. Specifically, the rates can be used to compute expected or estimated numbers of youths to be inserted into the justice system, without consideration of the anticipated diversion program's impact. Subsequent comparison of the expected or estimated numbers to be inserted with the actual numbers, provides a numerical indication of diversion's impact upon characteristic justice system client insertion. In addition, consideration of the number of diversion program clients enables evaluators to assess a diversion program's overall impact in terms of justice system diversion or net-widening.

The processing rates used to compute the expected or estimated numbers of clients to be subject to justice system insertion should be based upon the proportion of the jurisdiction's year-to-year youth or adult population figures.[9] However, in those instances where population data are not available or reliable, rates can be derived from proportion of arrests inserted into the justice system. The rates used to generate the expected or estimated numbers should be based upon data covering several years. It is important to note that use of such procedures involves reliance on official aggregate data. While these data are often all that are available, they are, nonetheless, subject to state and local jurisdiction idiosyncrasies and fluctuations. Thus, the usefulness of this approach is dependent upon consistent data collection and reporting over time. *Ideally, evaluators should use both client characteristics and numerical justice system approaches in their evaluation of diversion's net-widening potential.*

III. IS DIVERSION'S WIDENING OF THE NET HARMFUL TO CLIENTS?

Studies which have addressed the client effects of diversion have generally not differentiated between the effects on intended diversion clients and unintended clients drawn into diversion as a result of net-widening. For the most part, research related to this question has been focused upon diversion programs' abilities to change their clients, as measured by officially recorded recidivism. For example, in a study drawn from a five-year cohort of youth processed through diversion programs and the juvenile courts in Australia, Sarri (1979) reports that diverted and court-processed youth had similar rates of court reappearance. In the national evaluation of the five site replications of the Des Moines Exemplary Adult Diversion Project, Seitz et al. (1978) report similar findings. The five-site comparative evaluation indicated that, operation of the various pretrial diversion components had little impact in reducing recidivism among diverted, compared to nondiverted, offenders.

Paternoster et al. (1979) explored the extent to which juveniles discriminate between formal court processing resulting in incarceration and informal diversion processing with reference to perceptions of accrued liabilities or stigma. The youth's perception of stigma was measured in terms of: (1) parental relationships, (2) school performance, (3) relationships with peers, (4) desired employment, and (5) future involvement with the law. The findings indicated that only in the area of peer relationships was there a significant difference between the perceptions of diverted and incarcerated youths. These results remained constant when control was made for the effects of prior social liabilities, such as race and social class. The authors concluded that to the extent perceptions of stigma have implications for subsequent behavior, it makes little difference whether youths receive diversion or formally imposed incarceration. The type of treatment received appears not to be significant in shaping self-perceptions.

Klein (1979), in a general review of studies reporting on client changes resulting from juvenile diversion programs, reports that three studies cite positive findings (less delinquency), two studies cite findings of worsening effects (more delinquency), and eight studies cite equivocal findings.[10] Klein points out that, with one exception, these studies did not employ random assignment of youth to diversion and nondiversion alternatives. The study that did utilize random assignment, Lincoln et al. (1977), found substantially lower rates of recidivism for diverted youth as compared to youth who received juvenile court petitions.

However, those youth released outright, without any form of services, had even lower recidivism rates. This finding concerning youth released outright has important implications regarding the potentially detrimental client effects of diversion, particularly for those clients who would have been released if not for diversion's client net-widening. However, since the diversion studies have not generally differentiated between system-insertable diversion clients and clients normally released before diversion, it remains unclear whether diversion is or is not reducing subsequent behavior difficulties or influencing perceptions for *intended* diversion clients.

In assessing the effects on clients subject to diversion because of net-widening, there are a limited number of studies which have suggested diversion's potential to accelerate client jeopardy, system penetration, and subsequent behavior difficulties. In the earlier-cited comparative study of adult diversion by Mullen (1975: 26), for example, it was documented that clients referred to diversion programs who were unable to meet the program's requirements were likely to be subjected to informal double jeopardy—returned for prosecution on their original charge, prosecuted vigorously, convicted, and placed on probation supervision. Mullen further suggests that most of the clients handled in this manner would not have been subject to formal justice-processing if not for the client net-widening accompanying diversion program operations. Similar findings in a juvenile diversion program have been provided in relation to youth whose families were not amenable to diversion's whole-family intervention methods. Specifically, Blomberg (1977a: 277-280) indicates that when families were unable or unwilling to cooperate with diversion's family treatment process, the children were frequently referred to the juvenile court for suitable out-of-home placement. This resulted in accelerated court penetration of the siblings of diversion's targeted clients, who would not have come to the attention of the justice system if not for diversion's family focus.

The potential, related to diversion's net-widening, to create or intensify subsequent behavior difficulties related to justice system contact and subsequent increased visibility, is supported by Klein (1975) in his study of the relationship between rearrest and alternative dispositions for young offenders. Among the reported results related to various referrals, Klein indicates that providing diversion services to those youth who might otherwise have been released outright may well have increased their subsequent rearrest rates, because of their increased visibility to their "treaters" and the police, rather than increased rate of misconduct.[11]

On the basis of these results, therefore, it appears that in some client instances, because of the potentially detrimental effect accompanying diversion's widening of the client net, doing nothing (outright release without referral or nonintervention) is preferable than doing something in the name of diversion. Nonintervention, however, is neither likely nor preferable for those clients who may well benefit and/or need some form of diversion service. Yet, because of net-widening, it is unclear whether or not diversion can or does produce beneficial client results for justice system-insertable clients. Consequently, it is essential that diversion program evaluators determine the various client effects resulting from diversion program efforts, and differentiate the effects on system-insertable clients from those effects on net-widening clients.

Evaluating Client Effects Associated with Diversion's Net-Widening

It is important for evaluators to realize that demonstration of net-widening's occurrence, as a result of poor diversion program implementation, will not necessarily surprise or alter system agents' notions of their legitimate clientele. However, if evaluators can demonstrate that net-widening does produce detrimental client consequences, then clear evidence for mandating appropriate diversion client target-hardening would be provided. In the absence of such evaluation evidence, it is likely that system agents' perceptions of appropriate clients will continue to expand.

In attempting to determine the client effects associated with diversion's net-widening, evaluators must first differentiate diversion clients (system-insertable) from net-widening clients (nonsystem-insertable). This differentiation can be accomplished by following the earlier-reviewed client characteristic assessments necessary to identify net-widening. Once differentiation is made between diversion and net-widening clients, a number of evaluation approaches should be considered. Ultimately, in determining a particular evaluation approach, evaluators must consider the suitability of the approach to the evaluation's questions as well as the workability of the approach within a given project setting. Often evaluators must decide not to pursue a "preferred" evaluation orientation because of feasibility issues related to cost, legality, political volatility, and so on. Consequently, it is essential for evaluators to be informed of various evaluation approaches if their efforts to fit the approach to the evaluation questions and project setting are to be successful in this area of net-widening evaluation.

In the review of previous evaluations of diversion's client effects, it was pointed out that, with few exceptions, the evaluations did not employ random assignment of matched clients into diversion programs and the justice system. Consequently, meaningful assessments of the comparative client effects resulting from these two forms of processing could not be made. To overcome this inadequacy, and working with a population subject to diversion processing only because of net-widening, evaluators could randomly assign the clients either to diversion programs or to outright release. Subsequent tracking and follow-up of these two groups of clients in terms of official recidivism indicators (rearrest, court referral or intake, petition-filing or petition reappearance, and subsequent

sentence or disposition) and related self-report indicators (frequency of undetected misconduct, perception and attitudinal changes) would enable evaluators
to assess comparatively the beneficial or the detrimental effects resulting from
net-widening. Specifically, if diversion processing compared to outright release
was shown to result in increased rearrests, double jeopardy in terms of return to
court and vigorous prosecution for adults, or accelerated justice system penetration for juveniles, convincing documentation would be provided concerning the
detrimental client effects resulting from net-widening.

It is likely that evaluators will find, however, that control and experimental
approaches are not often workable in diversion project settings. In these
instances evaluators can focus their evaluation effort upon documenting specific
client effect indicators associated with diversion's net-widening. For example,
evaluators can track the progress of net-widening clients through diversion
programs to describe their experiences and determine any subsequent consequences particularly relevant to potential double jeopardy and accelerated justice system insertion. Official indicators of these potential consequences could
be found in diversion program intake records, type of program service recommendations, case-worker recommendations, other justice agency referrals, and
subsequent dispositions or sentences. In addition, self-report information could
be gathered regarding instances of undetected misconduct, and of clients' perceptions and attitudes reflecting the effects of their diversion program experiences. A major concern here is to collect various items of information which
together enable the evaluator to describe accurately the experiences and consequences of these experiences for net-widening clients.[12]

Since many juvenile diversion programs are focusing increasingly upon whole
families, evaluators should develop evaluation capacities in this area. Again,
various self-report measures can be used to explore family members' perceptions
of their family treatment experiences. In addition, the official indicators previously identified can be used in combination with the self-report information to
describe program experiences and consequences occurring as a result of those
experiences. However, it is essential here for evaluators to differentiate not only
between initial diversion referrals, to determine if the referrals are of system-
insertable diversion clients or net-widening clients, but also, in their client
follow-ups and assessments between the siblings of these initial referrals. Evaluators should be alert to the capacity of family intervention to produce net-widening in this double sense: first, with initial referrals, and second, with siblings.
Further, evaluators need to determine if, in fact, initial referrals and their
siblings are being accelerated into the justice system when their families are
found not amenable to diversion's family intervention methods.

Ultimately, in the evaluation of both diversion's net-widening and associated
client effects, evaluators must be imaginative. There is no specific checklist to be
followed in conducting responsible diversion program evaluations. In all likeli-

hood, such an evaluation checklist would not be equally relevant in all jurisdictions, given the variation in diversion program orientations, personnel, available data, political and jurisdiction conditions, and so on. However, as the preceding review indicates, there are a number of salient evaluation issues and means of addressing these issues in order to carry out responsible program evaluations that produce compelling results. Without such compelling results, not only will net-widening probably continue or accelerate, but diversion will remain an untested correctional concept.

IV. CORRECTIONAL REFORM AND WIDENING OF THE SOCIAL CONTROL NET: AN ORGANIZATIONAL INTERPRETATION

The net-widening phenomenon extends considerably beyond diversion to include a series of correctional reform efforts. During the 1950s and 1960s, for example, California experienced substantial population increases in its state prisons and youth reformatories. In subsequent attempts to reduce local commitments to state facilities, subsidies for the development of local institution and intensive probation supervision alternatives to state institutions were provided.[13] Studies of the impact of California's effort to decrease state institutional confinement have determined that while reductions in state commitments were achieved, overall (combined state and county) increases in the total number of persons controlled resulted.[14]

Similarly, in their national assessment of the deinstitutionalization of juvenile offenders into community-based alternatives, Vinter et al. (1975: 77) report that the ten most deinstitutionalized states had a higher combined rate of assignment (state institutions and community-based programs) than the fifty-state average. Current research is further demonstrating net-widening in association with the present national effort to deinstitutionalize status offenders.[15]

Moreover, the net-widening trend can be associated with a number of turn-of-the-century correctional reforms, including parole, probation, and the juvenile court. Specifically, since the early nineteenth-century development of prison-based corrections in the United States, there have been a series of reforms generally considered as alternatives to imprisonment. However, as Messinger (1977) argues, these reforms can perhaps be better understood as alternatives to doing nothing with individuals, or almost nothing—like reprimanding a suspect or discharging a convicted person. Thus, it is not surprising that the history of U.S. correctional reform has consistently resulted in net-widening whereby an increasing proportion of the population has become subject to some form of institution- or community-based control.

While there appears to be little doubt concerning the net-widening results that have been produced from various correctional reform efforts, there has been considerable debate as to whether or not net-widening has been intentional or unintentional. A number of writers have argued that the history of social control reform can best be understood as an intentional and persistent effort by a privileged and powerful few to increase the network of social control and the population subject to control, in order to strengthen or ensure the status quo (Gusfield, 1963; Erikson, 1966; and Platt, 1969). This critical historical orientation is often contrasted with the liberal or "march of progress" interpretation, in which credence is given to the stated reform rhetoric and humanitarian motives of the reformers (Reith, 1952; Handler, 1965; Fox, 1970; and McKelvey, 1977). Undoubtedly, both approaches have explanatory merit, as evidenced in recent historical studies combining both approaches (Rothman, 1971; Schlossman, 1977; and Scull, 1977). However, if the consistent occurrence of correctional net-widening is to be interpreted, there are a number of questions that must be addressed beyond reformer motives.

Beginning primarily in the 1960s, there emerged critical research interest in the organizational characteristics of justice agencies. This represented a significant departure from the major focus of previous research. Prior studies had been primarily concerned with the causes of crime, emphasizing the importance of the individual, the group, the environment, or some combination of these factors in creating crime. It was assumed that justice agencies were guided by their formal goals, defined rules, and a sense of disinterested professionalism. This assumption was increasingly questioned with the emergence of the labeling perspective, which stimulated critical interest and study of justice agencies. This includes the studies of Newman (1962), Sudnow (1965), Skolnick (1966), Blumberg (1967), and Packer (1968). In a review of the organizational perspective emerging from these studies, Feeley (1970: 413) summarizes:

> They all tend to view the organization of the administration of criminal justice as a system of action based primarily upon *cooperation, exchange,* and *adaptation,* and emphasize these considerations over adherence to formal rules and defined "roles" in searching for and developing explanations of behavior and discussing organizational effectiveness. Rather than being the primary focus of attention, formal "rules" and "disinterested professionalism" are viewed as only one set of the many factors shaping and controlling individuals' decisions, and perhaps not the most important ones.

This organizational orientation has been referred to as the "functional-systems approach" because of its view that justice agency goals, structure, and processes are functions of technological and environmental forces rather than static elements existing in a vacuum, to be manipulated by management (Mohr, 1976). With respect to the courts, the connection between environment, technology, structure, and process is clear. Courts can vary considerably across jurisdictions with regard to available dispositions or sentencing alternatives. Further, disposition and sentencing alternatives change over time, influenced as they are by broader economic and cultural developments. Such variations have direct implications for court structure and process in terms of how offenders are viewed and ultimately processed. Thus, patterns of court decision-making are not timeless but are affected by the specific organizational arrangements and context in which they take place and to which they have relevance. The court's organizational context provides a framework of constraining court service alternatives which influence offender insertion into the court, and subsequently structure patterns of court decision-making relative to those offenders.

It has been argued in functional-systems studies of diversion innovations that, because justice agencies are characterized by operational and technological instability, externally funded program innovations such as diversion will be perceived as compatible with the functional necessities, goals, and practices of these agencies.[16] Further, perceptions of continued instability predispose the agencies to implement innovations as *supplements* to previous practice (formal or informal), rather than as significant *alternatives* to previous practice; this partially explains the net-widening finding. As the court organization's disposition or sentence alternatives expand as a result of diversion, there is initiated a modification of client insertion and processing patterns whereby clients previously viewed as unsuitable for justice system insertion and processing are judged, within a less constrained context of alternatives, as suitable for diversion.

The net-widening brought on by diversion's "discovery" of new clients is further influenced by the fact that justice agency funding is based upon numbers of client contacts or workload units. Static or declining client loads result in corresponding static or declining budgets. Throughout this century the trend has been consistently upward in numbers of justice clients and corresponding justice budgets. However, with the present concern over ineffective public policies and spiraling government spending, a new demand for accountability is being voiced loudly throughout the country. The historically consistent pattern of public agency growth and ever-increasing fiscal support appears to be unsuited to the times. As a result, change in the characteristic growth of the justice system could be anticipated. The question is, how will justice policy emerge in the wake of accelerated conditions of environmental scarcity and social-political demands for performance accountability?

V. SUMMARY AND DISCUSSION

The major purposes of this chapter have been to demonstrate diversion's net-widening potential and resulting detrimental client effects, and to identify strategies for evaluating net-widening in diversion programs. In considering the literature addressing diversion's overall impact, net-widening was consistently documented. In effect, diversion programs produced net-widening by selecting the major proportion of their clientele from a population previously not subjected to justice system insertion. With regard to net-widening's effect on clients, a number of detrimental consequences were identified, including double prosecution jeopardy, increased rearrest rates, family intrusions, and accelerated justice system insertion. Relevant evaluation strategies concerning diversion's net-widening and client effects were identified and reviewed to alert evaluators to various means of discovering and assessing these diversion program capabilities.

The documentation of diversion's net-widening and related detrimental client effects could be used as arguments for terminating diversion practice. As Dunford (1977) speculates, diversion may be rejected in practice, not because it did not fulfill its promise, but because it was not given the opportunity to do so. Certainly the net-widening results associated with diversion programs do not demonstrate failure of the diversion concept, but demonstrate instead failure in the implementation of diversion programs. As a result, diversion cannot as of yet be considered a failure or a success.

A significant implication that can be drawn from the overall net-widening that is occurring (in relation to diversion and other deinstitutionalization and community-based treatment efforts) is the need to check the continuing sprawl of the correctional system. A catchphrase now often heard concerning various public agencies is the need for quality instead of quantity. Education, welfare, government, justice, and correctional agencies are becoming increasingly subject to scrutiny with regard to cost-effective accountability. Certainly, the increasing emphasis upon justice and correctional evaluation has not emerged out of a social vacuum but fundamentally reflects a growing awareness of basic conditions of scarcity in which ineffectual practice must be reduced. The provision of support for various programs without documented accountability is clearly declining.[17]

In Florida, effort, stimulated by the legislature, is being made to develop an alternative funding formula for correctional agencies. Traditionally, correctional funding in Florida, as in most states, has been based upon a workload unit formula in which numbers of clients served provided the essential basis for funding allocations, thus encouraging net-widening client selection practices. Florida's alternate funding proposal would, for example, convert the workload unit system to school-age enrollment funding. Specifically, the current number of professional staff within juvenile probation will be divided into the total number of school children aged 10 to 17, producing a ratio of professionals to children "at risk" of delinquency or related behavioral difficulties. Since the school enrollment in this age bracket has not been subject to growth in Florida, the juvenile probation budget would reflect a no-growth allocation. Further, if this age bracket declines, so would the budget allocation to juvenile probation, reflecting a downward trend in the "population at risk" ratio.[18]

In the absence of compelling results concerning various correctional strategies to guide policy makers, and in view of the negative trends associated with previous correctional system reforms and proliferation, there is a need for serious consideration of such funding alternatives. Perhaps determinant funding formulas for correctional agencies could thwart traditional organizational impediments to appropriate implementation of innovative program strategies and stir a corresponding commitment to the evaluation of these strategies. Certainly, the integral role of evaluators in shaping subsequent correctional policy decision-making is becoming increasingly apparent.

NOTES

1. Diversion's major conceptual rationale reflects labeling and differential association theories. For summary statements and critiques of labeling theory, see Kitsuse (1963), Gibbs (1966), Mahoney (1974), and Wellford (1975). For a similar review of differential association theory, see Cressey (1960), Burgess and Akers (1966), and DeFleur and Quinney (1966). For identification and discussion of additional rationales underlying diversion, see Public Systems Inc. (1974).

2. For general elaboration upon the organization and treatment variations reflected in diversion programs, see Biel (1974), Rovner-Pieczenik (1974), O'Brien and Marcus (1976), and Rutherford and McDermott (1976). For a specific review of juvenile diversion programs, see Kobetz and Bosarge (1973), Sarri and Isenstadt (1973), Klapmuts (1974), and Crime and Delinquency (1976).

3. For further description of the Des Moines Community-Based Corrections Program, see National Institute of Law Enforcement and Criminal Justice (1975, 1976a, 1976b).

4. Further description of the Sacramento Family Counseling Diversion Project is provided in Baron and Feeney (1976).

5. For example, a recent survey by Bellassai (1978) documented that of 148 pretrial diversion programs compiled by the ABA Pre-trial Intervention Service Center in 1976, only 17 percent were administered by independent agencies. In contrast, 11 percent were court-affiliated, 16 percent prosecutor-affiliated, and 36 percent were under the control of county probation departments.

6. See California Youth Authority (1975a, 1975b, 1976).

7. For elaboration on client characteristics assessments in diversion program evaluations, see Behavioral Research Institute (1977).

8. Several researchers have relied upon versions of system processing rates for measuring diversion's justice system impact, and have termed the approach differently. See Elliott (1974), Elliott et al. (1976), Klein (1975), and Blomberg (1977a, 1978a).

9. For further specification of procedures, computations, and applications of system processing rates in assessing net-widening, see Blomberg (1978a: 43-49, 66-70, 87-90).

10. The studies reviewed by Klein which cited positive effect findings were Baron et al. (1973), Klein (1974), and Ku and Blew (1977). The studies which cited negative effect findings were Lincoln (1976) and Elliott (1978). The studies which cited equivocal findings

were Carter and Gilbert (1973), Binder et al. (1976), Forward et al. (1974), Klein (1974), Stratton (1975), Berger et al. (1977), Lincoln et al. (1977), and Elliott (1978).

11. For additional discussion of the potential of increased client visibility, resulting from diversion program contact, to increase the likelihood of rearrest, see Tittle's 1979 review of Fishman's (1977) study of adult and juvenile diversion programs in New York City.

12. For an example of diversion research which has combined official rearrest data with self-report data, see Klein (1975). For an example of diversion research aimed at assessing perceptions through interviewing techniques, see Pasternoster et al. (1979).

13. For a detailed account of California's local institution and intensive probation alternatives to state institutions, see California Probation, Parole, and Correctional Association (1963) and Smith (1971).

14. See Lerman (1975) and Blomberg (1978a).

15. See, for example, Rutherford and McDermott (1976), Young and Pappenfort (1977), Schneider et al. (1978a, 1978b), and Klein (1979).

16. See Blomberg (1977a, 1978a, 1978b).

17. California's Proposition 13 and similar legislative considerations reflect a growing mood that will no doubt considerably influence justice system funding and operations. LEAA's current nationwide effort to train various federal, state, and local criminal justice personnel in project-monitoring and evaluation, together with offering evaluation technical assistance, reflects the trend toward increased accountability.

18. This information was gained through interviews with administrative personnel of Florida's Department of Health and Rehabilitative Services, and through review of related departmental and legislative budget documents.

REFERENCES

Baron, R. and F. Feeney (1976) *Juvenile Diversion Through Family Counseling.* Washington, DC: Government Printing Office.

——— and W. Thornton (1973) "Preventing Delinquency Through Diversion." *Federal Probation* 37, 1: 13-18.

Behavioral Research Institute (1977) *Work Plan National Evaluation of Diversion Programming.* Boulder, CO: Author.

Bellassai, J. (1978) "Pretrial Diversion: The First Decade in Retrospect," pp. 13-16 in American Bar Association, *Pretrial Services Annual Journal.*

Berg, D. and D. Shichor (1977) "Methodology and Theoretical Issues in Juvenile Diversion: Implications for Evaluation." Presented at the National Conference on Criminal Justice Evaluation, Washington, D.C. (mimeo)

Berger, D., M. Lipsey, L. Dennison, and J. Lange (1977) "The Effectiveness of the Sheriff's Department's Juvenile Diversion Projects in Southeast Los Angeles County." Claremont Graduate School, Claremont, California. (mimeo)

Biel, M. (1974) "Legal Issues and Characteristics of Pretrial Intervention Programs." Pretrial Intervention Service Center, American Bar Association.

Binder, A. (1976) "Diversion and the Justice System: Evaluating the Results." University of California, Irvine, California. (mimeo)

———, J. Monahan, and M. Newkirk (1976) "Diversion from the Juvenile Justice System and the Prevention of Delinquency," in J. Monahan (ed.) *Community Mental Health and the Criminal Justice System.* New York: Pergamon.

Blomberg, T. (1978a) *Social Control and the Proliferation of Juvenile Court Services*. San Francisco, CA: R and E Research Associates, Inc.

―――― (1978b) "Diversion from Juvenile Court: A Review of the Evidence," in F. Faust and P. Brantingham (eds.) *Juvenile Justice Philosophy*. St. Paul, MN: West.

―――― (1977a) "Diversion and Accelerated Social Control." *Journal of Criminal Law and Criminology* 68, 2: 274-282.

―――― (1977b) "The Juvenile Court as an Organization and Decision-Making System." *International Journal of Comparative and Applied Criminal Justice* 1, 2: 135-145.

―――― and M. Miller (1979) "Converting Existing Juvenile Justice Transaction-Based Reported Information to Offender-Based Retrieval Information." Tallahassee: School of Criminology, Florida State University. (mimeo)

Blumberg, A. (1967) *Criminal Justice*. Chicago: Quadrangle.

Bohnstedt, M. et al. (1975) *The Evaluation of Juvenile Diversion*. Sacramento, CA: California Youth Authority.

Burgess, R. and R. Akers (1966) "A Differential Association―Reinforcement Theory of Criminal Behavior." *Social Problems* 14: 128-147.

California Probation, Parole, and Correctional Association (1963) *Probation Camp in California*. Sacramento, CA: Author.

California Youth Authority (1976) *The Evaluation of Juvenile Diversion Programs: Second Annual Report*. Sacramento, CA: Author.

―――― (1975a) *The Evaluation of Juvenile Diversion Programs: Survey of Diversion Programs*. Sacramento, CA: Author.

―――― (1975b) *The Evaluation of Juvenile Diversion Programs: First Annual Report*. Sacramento, CA: Author.

Carter, G. and G. Gilbert (1973) *An Evaluation Progress Report of the Alternative Routes Project*. Los Angeles: University of Southern California Regional Research Institute in Social Welfare.

Carter, R. (1978a) "The Diversion of Offenders," in G. G. Killinger and P. F. Cromwell, Jr. (eds.) *Corrections in the Community: Alternatives To Imprisonment―Selected Readings*. St. Paul, MN: West.

―――― (1978b) *Evaluation of the Deinstitutionalization of Status Offenders Project Through the System Rates Methodology*. Los Angeles: Social Science Research Institute, University of Southern California.

―――― and M. W. Klein (1976) *Back on the Street: The Diversion of Juvenile Offenders*. Englewood Cliffs, NJ: Prentice-Hall.

Cressey, D. R. (1960) "Epidemiology and Individual Conduct: A Case from Criminology." *Pacific Sociological Review* 3: 47-58.

―――― and R. A. McDermott (1973) *Diversion from the Juvenile Justice System*. Ann Arbor: National Assessment of Juvenile Corrections, University of Michigan.

Crime and Delinquency (1976) "Diversion in the Juvenile Justice System: A Symposium" 22, 4.

DeFleur, M. and R. Quinney (1966) "A Reformulation of Sutherland's Differential Association Theory and a Strategy for Empirical Verification," *Journal of Research in Crime and Delinquency* 3: 1-22.

Dennison, L., L. Humphreys, and D. Wilson (1975) "A Comparison: Organization and Impact in Two Diversion Projects." Presented at the meeting of the Pacific Sociological Association, Victoria, British Columbia.

Dunford, F. W. (1977) "Police Diversion: An Illusion?" *Criminology* 15, 3: 335-352.

Elliott, D. S. (1978) *Diversion: A Study of Alternative Processing Practices*. Boulder, CO: Behavioral Research Institute.

——— (1974) *Evaluation of Youth Service Systems: FY 1973*. Boulder, CO: Behavioral Research Evaluation Corporation.

———, F. Blanchard, and F. Dunford (1976) *The Long and Short Term Impact of Diversion Programs*. Boulder, CO: Behavioral Research Evaluation Corporation.

Empey, L. T. (1973) "Juvenile Justice Reform: Diversion, Due Process, and Deinstitutionalization," in L. E. Ohlin (ed.) *Prisoners in America*. Englewood Cliffs, NJ: Prentice-Hall.

——— (1967) *Alternatives to Incarceration*. Washington, DC: Government Printing Office.

Erikson, K. (1966) *Wayward Puritans: A Study in the Sociology of Deviance*. New York: John Wiley.

Ewing, B. (1979) "Responding to the Policymaker's Need for Research," in P. Brantingham and T. Blomberg (eds.) *Courts and Diversion: Policy and Operation Studies*. Beverly Hills, CA: Sage Publications.

——— (1978) "Change and Continuity in Criminal Justice Research: A Perspective from NILECJ." *Journal of Research in Crime and Delinquency* 15, 2: 266-278.

Feeley, M. (1973) "Two Models of the Criminal Justice System: An Organizational Perspective," *Law and Society Review* 7: 407-414.

Fishman, R. (1977) *Criminal Recidivism in New York City: An Evaluation of the Impact of Rehabilitation and Diversion Services*. New York: Praeger.

Forward, J. R., M. Kirby, and K. Wilson (1974) *Volunteer Intervention with Court-Diverted Juveniles*. Boulder: University of Colorado.

Fox, S. (1970) "Juvenile Justice Reform: An Historical Perspective." *Stanford Law Review* 22: 1187-1239.

Gibbons, D. C. and G. F. Blake (1976) "Evaluating the Impact of Juvenile Diversion Programs," *Crime and Delinquency*, 22, 4: 411-420.

Gibbs, J. P. (1966) "Conceptions of Deviant Behavior: The Old And the New." *Pacific Sociological Review* 9: 9-14.

Gusfield, J. R. (1963) *Symbolic Crusade: Status Politics and the American Temperance Movement*. Urbana: University of Illinois Press.

Hackler, J. (1976) "Logical Reasoning Versus Unanticipated Consequences: Diversion Programs as an Illustration." *Ottowa Law Review* 8, 2: 285-289.

Handler, J. F. (1965) "The Juvenile Court and the Adversary System: Problems of Function and Form." *Wisconsin Law Review:* 7-51.

Humphreys, L. and J. M. Carrier (1976) *Second Annual Evaluation Report: Pomona Valley Juvenile Diversion Project*. Claremont, CA: Pitzer College.

Kitsuse, J. I. (1963) "Societal Reactions to Deviant Behavior: Problems of Theory and Methods." *Social Problems* 9: 247-256.

Klapmuts, N. (1974) *Diversion from the Juvenile Justice System*. Washington, DC: National Council on Crime and Delinquency.

Klein, M. W. (1979) "Deinstitutionalization and Diversion of Juvenile Offenders: A Litany of Impediments," in N. Morris and M. Tonry (eds.) *Crime and Justice*. Chicago: University of Chicago Press.

——— (1976a) "On the Front End of the Juvenile Justice System," in R. M. Carter and M. W. Klein (eds.) *Back on the Street: The Diversion of Juvenile Offenders*. Englewood Cliffs, NJ: Prentice-Hall.

——— (1976b) "Issues and Realities in Police Diversion Programs." *Crime and Delinquency* 22, 4: 421-427.

——— (1974) "Labeling, Deterrence, and Recidivism: A Study of Police Disposition of Juvenile Offenders." *Social Problems* 22, 2: 292-303.

——— (1975) *Alternative Dispositions for Juvenile Offenders*. Los Angeles: University of Southern California.

——— and K. S. Teilmann (1976) *Pivotal Ingredients of Police Juvenile Diversion Programs.* Washington, DC: National Institute for Juvenile Justice and Delinquency Prevention.

Kobetz, R. and B. Bosarge (1973) "Diversion of Juvenile Offenders: An Overview," in National Association of Chiefs of Police, *Juvenile Justice Administration.*

Ku, R. and C. H. Blew (1977) *A University's Approach to Delinquency Prevention: The Adolescent Diversion Project.* Washington, DC: Government Printing Office.

Kutchins, H. and S. Kutchins (1975) "Pretrial Diversionary Programs: New Expansion of Law Enforcement Activity Camouflaged as Rehabilitation." Presented at the Pacific Sociological Association meetings, Hawaii. (mimeo)

Lemert, E. (1971) *Instead of Court: Diversion in Juvenile Justice.* Washington, DC: Government Printing Office.

Lerman, P. (1975) *Community Treatment and Social Control: A Critical Analysis of Juvenile Correctional Policy.* Chicago: University of Chicago Press.

Lincoln, S. B. (1976) "Juvenile Referrals and Recidivism," in R. M. Carter and M. W. Klein (eds.) *Back on the Street: The Diversion of Juvenile Offenders.* Englewood Cliffs, NJ: Prentice-Hall.

——— et al (1977) "Recidivism Rates of Diverted Juvenile Offenders." Presented at the National Conference on Criminal Justice Evaluation, Washington, D.C. (mimeo)

Mahoney, A. R. (1974) "The Effect of Labeling Upon Youths in the Juvenile Justice System: A Review of the Evidence." *Law and Society Review* 8: 583-614.

Mattingly, J. and D. Katkin (1975) "The Youth Service Bureau: A Re-Invented Wheel?" Presented at the Society for the Study of Social Problems meeting, San Francisco. (mimeo)

McAleenan, M. et al. (1977) *Final Evaluation Report. The West San Gabriel Valley Juvenile Diversion Project.* Los Angeles: Occidental College.

McKelvey, B. (1977) *American Prisons: A History of Good Intentions.* Montclair, NJ: Patterson Smith.

Messinger, S. L. (1977) "The Future of Punishment," pp. 43-44 in *Crime and Justice in America.* Del Mar, CA: Publishers, Inc.

Mohr, L. (1976) "Organizations, Decisions, and Courts." *Law and Society Review* 10: 621-642.

Morris, N. (1974) *The Future of Imprisonment.* Chicago: University of Chicago Press.

Mullen, J. (1975) *The Dilemma of Diversion: Resource Materials on Adult Pre-trial Intervention Programs.* Washington, DC: Government Printing Office.

Myer, M. et al. (1978) *Environments and Organizations.* San Francisco: Jossey-Bass.

National Advisory Commission on Criminal Justice Standards and Goals (1978) *Corrections.* Washington, DC: Government Printing Office.

National Institute of Law Enforcement and Criminal Justice (1979) *Program Plan Fiscal Year 1979.* Washington, DC: Government Printing Office.

——— (1978) *Criminal Justice Research Solicitation: Methodology Development Program.* Washington, DC: Government Printing Office.

——— (1976a) *Community Based Corrections in Des Moines: An Exemplary Project.* Washington, DC: Government Printing Office.

——— (1976b) *Program Announcement: Diversion of Youth from the Juvenile Justice System.* Washington, DC: Government Printing Office.

——— (1975) *A Handbook on Community Corrections in Des Moines: An Exemplary Project.* Washington, DC: Government Printing Office.

National Pretrial Intervention Service Center (1974) "Baltimore Pretrial Intervention Program," in *Portfolio of Descriptive Profiles on Selected Pretrial Criminal Justice Intervention Programs.* Washington, DC: American Bar Association.

Nejelski, P. (1976) "Diversion: The Promise and the Danger." *Crime and Delinquency* 22, 4: 393-410.

Newman, D. J. (1962) *The Decision as to Guilt or Innocence.* Chicago: American Bar Foundation.

O'Brien, K. E. and M. Marcus (1976) *Juvenile Diversion: A Selected Bibliography.* Washington, DC: Government Printing Office.

Packer, H. (1968) *The Limits of the Criminal Sanction.* Stanford, CA: Stanford University Press.

Paternsoter, R., G. Waldo, T. Chiricos, and L. Anderson (1979) "The Stigma of Diversion: Labeling in the Juvenile Justice System," in P. Brantingham and T. Blomberg (eds.) *Courts and Diversion: Policy and Operation Studies.* Beverly Hills, CA: Sage Publications.

Peterson, T. K. (1973) "The Dade County Pretrial Intervention Project: Formalization of the Diversion Function and Its Impact upon the Criminal Justice System." *University of Miami Law Review* 28: 86-114.

Pitchess, P. (1976) "Law Enforcement Screening for Diversion," pp. 221-233 in R. Carter and M. W. Klein (eds.) *Back on the Streets: The Diversion of Juvenile Offenders.* Englewood Cliffs, NJ: Prentice-Hall.

Platt, T. (1969) *The Child Savers.* Chicago: University of Chicago Press.

Polk, K. (1971) "Delinquency Prevention and the Youth Service Bureau." *Criminal Law Bulletin* 7: 490-529.

President's Commission on Law Enforcement and Administration of Justice (1967) *The Challenge of Crime in a Free Society and Task Force Report: Juvenile Delinquency.* Washington, DC: Government Printing Office.

Public Systems Inc. (1974) *California Correctional System Intake Study.* Sunnyvale, CA: Author.

Reith, C. (1952) *The Police Idea: Its History and Evolution in England in the Eighteenth Century and After.* London: Oxford University Press.

Rojek, D. G. (1978) "Evaluation of Status Offender Project, Pima County, Arizona." Quarterly Progress Report submitted to the National Institute of Juvenile Justice and Delinquency Prevention, Office of Juvenile Justice and Delinquency Prevention, Law Enforcement Assistance Administration.

Rosenheim, M. (1969) "Youth Service Bureaus: A Concept in Search of Definition." *Juvenile Court Judges Journal* 20: 69-74.

Rothman, D. (1971) *The Discovery of the Asylum.* Boston: Little, Brown.

Rovner-Pieczenik, R. A. (1974) *Pretrial Intervention Strategies: An Evaluation of Policy-Related Research and Policymaker Perceptions.* Washington, DC: American Bar Association Commission on Correction Facilities and Services, National Pretrial Intervention Center.

Rutherford, A. and O. Bengur (1976) *Community-Based Alternatives to Juvenile Incarceration.* Washington, DC: Government Printing Office.

Rutherford, A. and R. McDermott (1976) *Juvenile Diversion.* Washington, DC: Government Printing Office.

Sarri, R. (1979) "Juvenile Aid Panels: An Alternative to Juvenile Court Processing," in P. Brantingham and T. Blomberg (eds.) *Courts and Diversion: Policy and Operation Studies.* Beverly Hills, CA: Sage Publications.

––– and P. Isenstadt (1973) *Remarks, Presented at the Hearings of the House of Representatives Select Committee on Crime, April 18, 1973.* Ann Arbor: NAJC, University of Michigan.

Sarri, R. et al. (1976) "Justice for Whom? Varieties of Juvenile Correctional Approaches," in M. W. Klein (ed.) *The Juvenile Justice System.* Beverly Hills, CA: Sage Publications.

Schlossman, S. (1977) *Love and the American Delinquent: The Theory and Practice of "Progressive" Juvenile Justice, 1825-1920.* Chicago: University of Chicago Press.

Schneider, A. L., C. M. Cleary, and P. D. Reiter (1978a) *The Clark County, Washington, Deinstitutionalization of Status Offenders Evaluation Reports.* Eugene, Oregon: Institute of Policy Analysis.

——— (1978b) *Evaluation Report on the Spokane Project to Deinstitutionalize Status Offenders.* Eugene, OR: Institute of Policy Analysis.

Scull, A. T. (1977) *Decarceration: Community Treatment and the Deviant—A Radical View.* Englewood Cliffs, NJ: Prentice-Hall.

Seitz, S., W. Rhodes, and T. Blomberg (1978) "The Des Moines Exemplary Project." Final Report submitted to the Law Enforcement Assistance Administration. (Grant 77-NI-0020)

Skolnick, J. (1966) *Justice Without Trial.* New York: John Wiley.

Smith, R. (1971) *"A Quiet Revolution: Probation Subsidy."* DHEW Publication (SRS) 72-26011, Department of Health, Education and Welfare.

Statsky, W. P. (1974) "Community Courts: Decentralizing Juvenile Jurisprudence." *Capital University Law Review* 3, 1: 1-31.

Stratton, J. G. (1975) "Effects of Crisis Intervention Counseling on Predelinquent and Misdemeanor Juvenile Offenders." *Juvenile Justice* 26: 7-18.

Sudnow, D. (1965) "Normal Crimes: Sociological Features of the Penal Code in a Public Defender Office." *Social Problems* 12: 255-275.

Tittle, C. R. (1979) "Book Review of R. Fishman (1977) *Criminal Recidivism in New York City: An Evaluation of the Impact of Rehabilitation and Diversion Services."* *Contemporary Sociology* 8, 3: 403-404.

Vinter, R. D., G. Downs, and J. Hall (1975) *Juvenile Corrections in the States: Residential Programs and Deinstitutionalization: A Preliminary Report.* Ann Arbor: National Assessment of Juvenile Corrections, University of Michigan.

Vorenberg, E. W. and J. Vorenberg (1973) "Early Diversion from the Criminal Justice System: Practice in Search of a Theory," in L. E. Ohlin (ed.) *Prisoners in America.* Englewood Cliffs, NJ: Prentice-Hall.

Wellford, C. (1975) "Labelling Theory and Criminology: An Assessment." *Social Problems* 22: 332-345.

White, S. and S. Krislow [eds.] (1977) *Understanding Crime: An Evaluation of the National Institute of Law Enforcement and Criminal Justice.* Washington, DC: National Academy of Sciences.

Wolfgang, M. E., R. M. Figlio, and T. Sellin (1972) *Delinquency in a Birth Cohort.* Chicago: University of Chicago Press.

Young, R. M. and D. M. Pappenfort (1977) *Secure Detention of Juveniles and Alternatives to Its Use.* Washington, DC: Government Printing Office.

Zimring, F. E. (1974) "Measuring the Impact of Pretrial Diversion from the Criminal Justice System." *University of Chicago Law Review* 41: 224-241.

——— (1973) "The Court Employment Project." Report to the New York City Human Resources Administration. (unpublished)

24

Evaluating Correctional Systems Under Normalcy and Change

Alden D. Miller, Robert B. Coates,
and Lloyd E. Ohlin

In this chapter we will propose a system model of evaluation that is appropriate for studying, evaluating, and guiding policy formation for a correctional system, whether or not that system is undergoing major change. Since we advocate a system model of evaluation, we will introduce a set of working dimensions that can be used to define a system in correctional research. Some of these dimensions will describe the substance of programs, and some of them will describe the programs' political viability. Finally, we will show how the dimensions can be fitted together in a compact scheme for organizing data collection, and how such a scheme can be used for substantive analysis that is relevant to both theory and policy. Such a system must be compact, comprehensive, and capable of exposing the pressure points for promoting or hindering change.

In criminal justice systems and in human service systems in general, the occasional appearance of stability is misleading. Internal and external pressures for change are always at work, as are forces resisting change. Thus, both the occurrence of major change and the continuation of relative stability require explanation as the result of a field of competing forces. In our own research on change in Massachusetts youth corrections, we found that changes which appeared sudden actually were the culmination of struggles stretching back many years. We also found that these changes set in motion new struggles that went on for many years and finally culminated in further changes, which also appeared to be sudden to the casual observer. These constant struggles were thus a central aspect of the evaluation of correctional programs, since at any given

AUTHORS' NOTE: This chapter was originally prepared under a grant from the National Institute of Juvenile Justice, Law Enforcement Assistance Administration, Department of Justice. Points of view or opinions stated herein do not necessarily represent the official position or policies of the funding agency.

time one program might be more viable politically than another. The policy maker had to understand not only the substantive logic of programs but also how to compete in the political arena, and what sort of goals were reasonable at particular times. Decision makers need to understand strategy and tactics as well as correctional theory in order to make policy choices and carry them out (Miller et al., 1977).

The chapter will be addressed specifically to correctional research. However, the argument for the system model can be generalized directly to other criminal justice evaluation. It would be possible, for example, to adapt the model presented here for use in evaluating police and court programs. Actually, all the substantive considerations we discuss concern relationships that have analogues in any human service system.

I. THE INSTITUTIONALIZATION-NORMALIZATION CONTINUUM

A. The Overall Continuum

In our seven-year study of the reforms of the Massachusetts youth correctional system, one of the strongest findings on the determinants of recidivism concerned the networks of relationships in which youth were involved. The need for networks extending beyond the traditional participation in work, school, and community programs was manifested in the importance of supportive, day-to-day relationships with family, friends, and people met on the street. Without the latter, good work and school relationships seemed insufficient to prevent recidivism (Coates et al., 1978).

We have found it useful to think about these relationships in terms of an institutionalization-normalization continuum. With this continuum we describe the relationship among people in a specific setting. We define and measure it as an integrated average of three constitutive dimensions: social climate, extent of community contact, and quality of community contact. Social climate reflects the nature of direct relationships among the persons within the setting of a particular program. Extent and quality of community contact describe key features of the relationship of the youth in that setting to the larger, surrounding community (Coates et al., 1978: 5-20).

In the correctional literature, the term *institution* is frequently used to refer to prison facilities isolated from the surrounding community by high walls, distance, or other physical barriers. As the community-based corrections movement has progressed, however, it has become increasingly recognized that group homes and other community programs can share with prisons the isolation characteristic of such institutions, even without the physical barriers. In general, the physical plant becomes less critical in identifying institution-like relationships among people when we observe that throughout society the exclusion of people from self-development resources potentially available to them in other relationship networks or systems constantly recurs. Such exclusion may or may not depend upon coercion or the threat of force. Instead, it may arise from the application of such labels as "hard-core delinquent," "intractable," "slow learner," and restrictive "tracking" actions taken in response to those labels.

While the maximum security prison remains the archetype of an institutional setting, other examples would be a family that has turned inward to keep a retarded child isolated at home, a monastery, or a theocracy or utopian movement which is very isolated, depending on tight controls and the exclusion of disturbing outside influences in order to maintain the strong communal commitment necessary for the survival of the movement. Today, examples of the latter would include the Hare Krishna movement and Synanon.

Examples at a slightly less obvious level would include tracking systems within a school system. Students who are not expected to accomplish much may be isolated in their own classes, with their own separate lunch hours and recesses, and less access to organized sports. Similarly, a family that discourages a child from attending school, severely restricts the child's social contacts, and grossly neglects care for his or her health would be a good example. A child in such a setting will rapidly exhibit the effects of isolation from opportunities for social and physical development available to others.

The characteristics of a more normalized setting are somewhat easier to identify. The archetype is the family setting, where youth are respected within the family and allowed open access to the larger community with supportive controls. Caring relationships within a normalized family are expected to extend concern well beyond the boundaries of the family. For example, if a youth is having problems at school, a parent in such a family would be expected to become involved, helping to work out the problem between the child and the teacher, or other school officials. Similarly, a normalized school setting would allow for easy flow into and out of specialized programs without labeling for various types of students, and would actively seek involvement of parents and other community people.

Clearly, a normalized correctional setting will be much like such a family or school. The children will be treated with respect and will be allowed the freedom to develop different talents. They will have access to a variety of correctional services, and will be aided in securing and maintaining extensive and qualitatively helpful access to the resources of the community at large.

In general, it would be expected that a community-based correctional system would have a large proportion of normalized settings, since normalization appears to be a key to success in the community after the correctional experience. However, because youth differ in relation to needs, problems, and stages of development, we would not expect such a youth correctional system to be made up exclusively of normalized settings. Rather, a range of settings should exist across the institutionalization-normalization continuum to meet the needs of both youth and society. We would also expect to see the more institutional settings used sparingly or as a last resort, while youths are allowed to move progressively before release into more normalized settings, where they may acquire more adequate support for their return to the community.

The conception of an institutionalization-normalization continuum can be applied to immediate, short-run, and long-run consequences of programs. Immediate consequences are experiences of the youth while they are in the program, including both the social climate within the program and the extent and quality of linkages to the community. Short-run consequences are frequently specific skills or new self-images with which youth leave the program. These are meant to supply a new element in the relationship or linkage of the youth with the larger community. Long-run consequences are the ensuing actual relationship between the youth and the community—the bottom line on extent and quality of linkages to the community.

B. Extent and Quality of Community Linkages

Extent of community linkages is simply the frequency and duration of contact with the community. We hypothesize that more frequent and durable contacts with the community lead to more stable adjustments (Coates et al., 1978: 18). The standard for what is frequent or what is durable will vary with the nature of the contact. For example, help with special problems in a work setting might not have to occur as frequently as general emotional support and encouragement, if problems at work are not a recurring source of difficulty.

Quality of community linkages can be specified by such indicators as:

(1) the nature of the communication process between the youth and people in the community;
(2) the youth's participation in decision-making in the larger community;
(3) the manner in which the community at large seeks to control the youth's behavior;
(4) the youth's perception of the fairness with which the larger community treats him or her; and
(5) the youth's overall access to the resources of the larger community (Coates et al., 1978: 18).

There are a variety of ways to measure extent and quality of community linkages. We can devise measurements of each of the attributes we have mentioned: extent, duration, communication, decision-making, control, fairness, and access. Or we can devise more summary measures of overall effect and overall strategy. For example, we could measure effect by inquiring as to whether the youth we are concerned with are treated like other youth in the community, or like suspected criminals or dangerous persons. We could measure strategy in a correctional system by asking:

(1) whether the system relies on institutional tactics, such as having volunteers provide services in the institutions or arrange field trips to the outside community; or

(2) whether the system attempts to provide more direct support through advocacy services to get youth into school, jobs, community programs, and the like, and to keep them there—or even whether the system intervenes in more formal day-to-day relationships between the youth and his or her family, friends, and people he or she meets on the street.

We can also ask how often all these things happen.

Finally, a third alternative is to use a summary measure such as recidivism. Recidivism is a complicated measure to use, especially by itself, because it is so difficult to interpret. The difficulty is that it confounds the effects of many different influences and events in addition to the correctional program itself. Furthermore, in our research on the Massachusetts system we discovered that recidivism results varied considerably when based on self-report data, court appearance, or court disposition. Self-report measures seemed to reflect more directly various social determinants of the youth's behavior, such as linkages to various social networks in the community, while court reappearance was related more to variables in decision-making by the police, such as criminal behavior and social class, and court disposition was more related to the judge's knowledge of such matters as the youth's prior encounters with the court (Coates et al., 1978: 157-172). Both court reappearance and court disposition obviously reflect idiosyncratic tendencies in decision-making by police departments and courts. It seems that while recidivism is indeed an important measure, it is essential to have other kinds of data, such as those we have been describing above, for evaluating what is happening in the correctional process.

C. Social Climate

Social climate reflects the relationships among youth, among staff, and between youth and staff within the correctional program. It can be thought of as made up of communication patterns (Do the youth feel informed?), decision-making patterns (Do the youth exercise some control over what happens to them?), nature of control (How are youth rewarded or punished for their behavior?), and fairness (What are the youth's assessments of the justice of relationships within the setting? See Coates et al., 1978: 15-18; Sykes, 1958; Clemmer, 1958; Lofland, 1969; Lerman, 1975, 1968; Martinson, 1974: 22-54; American Friends Service Committee, 1971; Fogel, 1975).

Two major strategies immediately suggest themselves for measuring social climate. One is to measure directly the dimensions of communication, decision-making, control, and fairness, and add them up. The other is to consider empirically and theoretically how the four dimensions cluster, and thus produce types. We have found in working with several sets of data that three basic types generally emerge. One is the simple custody type, where: (1) communication is severely restricted; (2) staff do the decision-making; (3) control is by punishment and illicit reward; and (4) fairness requires all to be treated alike in the continuing conflict between inmates and staff. The second is the therapy type, as in therapeutic communities, where: (1) communication is intense; (2) youth are encouraged to share in decision-making; (3) control relies more on reward than on punishment; and (4) fairness is judged differently by youth who have accepted the therapeutic subculture with its particularistic emphasis, as compared to newcomers who still equate universalism with fairness. The third type is in-between. It shares the sense of equality that one finds in the therapy type, but is not so intense. It is more like normal society than either the custody or therapy types, since its social climate appears most compatible with strong community linkages. Both types, extreme custody and therapy, tend to isolate the youth from the surrounding community. The in-between type does not. It might be called, therefore, the open type. If we choose to do our measurement by direct reference to these types, we may wish to do it twice, once in terms of the correctional strategies used to produce these types of social climate, and again in terms of the results of those strategies—the actual emerging pattern of responsibility, power, and reward.

II. THE POLITICS OF THE SYSTEM

A. Interest Groups: The Six Sides of a Correctional Issue

The politics of a correctional system impinge on everything in the system. The institutionalization-normalization continuum we have been discussing identifies the central issue to which other features of the system are adapted. But this is not to say that the institutionalization-normalization continuum is capable of describing all of the goals of different groups that affect the correctional system. Indeed, one of the major distinctions among interest groups concerns whether their primary interest is substantive—i.e., has more to do with achieving and maintaining a correctional system of a certain type, as defined by the institutionalization-normalization continuum and its three dimensions—or procedural—i.e., has more to do with the group's power in the decision-making process. The latter group may acquire considerable importance as a decisive ally in conflicts between more program-oriented groups. Thus, we may broadly distinguish three general types of interest: the first in favor of more therapy and/or linkages, the second in favor of more security and control and/or punishment, and the third in favor of making sure the right people's prerogatives are respected in the decision-making process, regardless of the outcome of the decisions.

We also find it helpful to divide each of the three broad groups into two factions, giving us six basic interest groups (Miller et al., 1977: 28-31). The delineation of factions is based on observation in Massachusetts and other states and differs for the three basic groups as follows: The first two subgroups will be in favor of therapy and/or community linkages. However, one will include people inside or outside the system who favor new programs of this sort immediately, without much consideration for the orderliness of the process of implementation. The second will consist of people, inside or outside the system, more concerned with having therapy and/or community linkages within an orderly system, and less willing to tolerate disorder in the process of reform.

The second two subgroups will be in favor of security and control and/or punishment. The first of these will consist of people inside the correctional system and the second those outside the correctional system holding this view. The second group may include persons from the courts, police, other branches of government, or the general public.

The final two subgroups will be people inside or outside the system in favor of particular ways of making decisions about such things as correctional policy, contracts and budgets, pay and promotions, and hiring and firing—or in more general terms, those interested in whose prerogatives are respected. The first subgroup will be interested in more therapy and/or community linkages as a way of achieving this interest in power, whereas the second will be more interested in fostering security and control and/or punishment as a way of furthering this interest in power. Members of these last two groups may therefore also be considered members of one of the other groups favoring particular types of programs, in addition to their concern with decision-making power and procedures; some, however, will not be.

In measuring these interests, we find it useful to find out who is active in each of the six interest groups and, also, what is the relative power of each of the six subgroups.

B. Political Action To Affect Relative Power of the Interest Groups and To Affect the Institutionalization-Normalization Continuum

These six subgroups represent basic interests that must be taken into account if program evaluation is to assess desirability, practicality, and ability to survive. Desirability has no clear meaning unless we know who desires what. Practicality and ability to survive are related not only to the goals and organization of the program, as described in the institutionalization-normalization continuum, but also to the power of the interests that surround it and the actions taken by people holding those interests.

The possible actions of any one interest group are, of course, legion. Here we are interested in noting two criteria for assessing the actions of all six interest groups taken together.

The first is the effect of the actions, or tactics, of the interest groups on the political positions of the interest groups themselves. Taking the actions of all six groups together, we want to know how they interact to affect the relative power of each of the groups (Miller et al., 1977: 31-32). We might also want to know how these interactions affect the responsibilities and rewards of each group, but the gain or loss of power seems to be the central issue.

The second variable concerns the effect of the actions of all the interest groups taken together on the correctional system as described by the institutionalization-normalization continuum (Miller et al., 1977: 31). Do the competing, conflicting, and cooperative actions of all six groups add up to reforming the correctional system, a more drastic replacement of the system with largely new personnel and facilities, or a consolidation of the system as it is? Is the direction of movement toward therapy and/or community linkages or toward security and control and/or punishment? Perhaps instead the system is being brought to a standstill by the investigation and exposure to public scrutiny of undesirable practices or conditions. This latter possibility amounts to the creation of a crisis for the system and demands for change. The system is like an assembly line until it is turned off by a crisis. While running, it demands simply to be fed and is very difficult to change. Investigation and critical exposure is the switch that turns the system off, a prerequisite, often, to reform, though it is not in itself reform. That must follow, or the system will resume as before.

III. A SYSTEM MODEL FOR RESEARCH IN CORRECTIONAL SYSTEMS

A. An Interview and Observation Guide

In the two preceding sections, we have introduced program and political variables that are crucial for theoretical and policy-relevant evaluation of correctional programs. Here we are concerned to utilize these dimensions in a compact but comprehensive system model that exposes and describes the key pressure points for promoting or hindering change. We will describe how data can be organized and collected, and indicate briefly some of the key features of a system analysis using such data.

As we have suggested in earlier sections, one way to set about measuring our concepts would be to assess actions and consequences in relation to the extent and quality of community linkages and the social climate of programs. Then we could measure interest group power and aspects of political action which affect this power structure and/or the design of the correctional system. This approach to evaluation can be stated more formally with the help of Table 24.1.

In the columns of this table, we distinguish the people-processing relationship (or the system of correctional programs contained in the institutionalization-normalization continuum) from the relationship among interest groups, which encompasses the political considerations. Each column thus describes one of these two social relationships. The people-processing relationship is between staff and youth, with the youth-community relationship a key concern in the environment of the relationship. The relationship among interest groups describes connections among interest groups that take the people-processing relationship as a central concern. Each can be described by four variables, which form the rows of the table. Focal properties of the environment include those concerns or conditions outside each of the relationships which the members seek to influence or control. Actions affecting focal properties of the environment are what they do to exert this influence or control. Internal distributions of responsibility, power, and reward constitute the internal structure of each relationship. Actions affecting the internal distributions are what the members do to maintain or change those structures. The cells of Table 24.1 are keyed by shorthand labels and numbers to Table 24.2's list of questions or issues about correctional reform which the evaluation process must cover.

This list of questions can be used either as an interview schedule or as a scheme for organizing data from multiple sources. Hence, it can serve as a tool for systematic triangulation permitting the combination of data from different perspectives to construct a multidimensional view. This allows us to verify patterns by checking consistency among different data sources. The triangulation can be done quite simply by answering the questions on the basis of one data source (e.g., interviews), and then on the basis of another (e.g., observation), and then by comparing the results for consistency. We can then consider the possibility of additional insights to be obtained by combining the two sets of results.

We can derive from the definitions of the variables the notions that in each relationship focal properties and actions affecting them can affect each other, internal distributions and actions affecting them can affect each other, focal properties and internal distributions can affect each other, and the same concrete action can contribute to both actions affecting focal properties and actions affecting internal distributions (which means that these two variables may be related to each other; see Miller et al., 1977: 191-193). We can further note that any variable in one time period may affect itself in the next time period. Then we can develop Table 24.3 which shows the possible relationships we need to investigate among these variables. All predictor variables are measured in the time period preceding the period in which the dependent variables are measured. An X in Table 24.3 means a logically possible relationship; a blank means no relationship.

TABLE 24.1 'Basic Concepts, of Which the Questions Are Indicators

	People-Processing Relationship	Relationship among Interest Groups
Focal Properties of the Environment	1 youth-community relationship	1, 2, 3, 4 people-processing relationship
Actions Affecting Focal Properties of the Environment	2 action affecting youth-community	7 action affecting corrections
Internal Distributions of Responsibility, Power, and Reward	3 staff-youth power	5 interest group power
Actions Affecting Internal Distributions of Responsibility, Power, and Reward	4 action affecting staff-youth	6 action affecting interest groups

LOGICAL PRINCIPLES:
1. The same concrete action can contribute to both actions affecting internal distributions and actions affecting the focal properties of the environment; hence, the two may be related and action begun in one may spill over into the other.
2. Focal properties of the environment and actions affecting them may mutually influence each other.
3. Internal distributions and actions affecting them may mutually influence each other.
4. Focal properties and internal distributions may mutually influence each other.
5. A variable in one time period may influence itself in the next time period.

C. Some Hypotheses that Form a System

In our research on the Massachusetts reforms, we developed and tested through qualitative data analysis five empirical principles that take us beyond Table 24.3's display of possibilities to the articulation of empirical hypotheses which may be explored and verified in other correctional systems. The five principles were used in the construction of a mathematical simulation involving sixteen variables, including the seven we have introduced above and nine others describing the individual interest groups. The simulation demonstrated that the principles can shape, in conjuction with the conceptual scheme, a coherent account of the political process and the development of a program (Miller et al., 1977: 181-226).

Sequencing. It is usually difficult to promote change in a relationship network, such as the people-processing relationship or the relationship among interest groups, unless one begins by moving simultaneously to change both actions affecting the focal properties of the environment and actions affecting the internal distributions. Internal distributions and focal properties affect each other, and if attention is directed to only one, the other may neutralize the

TABLE 24.2   Issues in a Correctional System

1. *Youth-Community Relationship*. What is the relationship of the youth to the community during and after the program? What percentage of the youth returning to the community are:

   _____ 1. treated like other youth in the community?
   _____ 2. treated like suspected or criminals or potentially dangerous persons?

2. *Action Affecting Youth-Community*. What does the correctional program do to affect the reintegration of the youth into the community in the near future? What percentage of the youth returning to the community are:

   (PROBE: How many days a week is a youth exposed to each?)

Days	Percentage	
_____	_____	1. allowed to find their own way in the community which some supervision by staff, to protect the community?
_____	_____	2. exposed, before release, to people from the community coming into the facility to visit the youth and provide them with extra resources?
_____	_____	3. taken on regular field trips before release to see movies, visit museums, go on picnics, and so on?
_____	_____	4. given strong emotional support before and after release to try to "make it," with staff trying to give youth a sense of confidence that they can make it?
_____	_____	5. provided help in finding jobs and keeping them, getting into school and staying there, or getting services from local community?
_____	_____	6. affected by strong interventions by staff into the day-to-day relationships between the youth and his/her family, friends, and the people he/she meets in the street?

3. *Staff-Youth Power*. What are the relationships among youth and staff within the correctional system? What percentage of the youth returning to the community have experienced each of the following since their last court appearance?

   (PROBE: What type of program is involved in each case — nonresidential, foster home, forestry, group home, boarding school, secure care, or adult facility?)

Types	Percentage	
_____	_____	1. programs where youth and staff share power and youth feel responsibility to make each other confront personal problems
_____	_____	2. programs where youth and staff share power but youth do not feel responsibility to make each other confront personal problems
_____	_____	3. programs where power is concentrated in the staff and the responsibility of the youth is to be obedient.

TABLE 24.2   Issues in a Correctional System (Cont)

4. *Action Affecting Staff-Youth.* What does the correctional system do to affect the relationship between youth and staff in the near future? What percentage of the youth returning to the community have experienced each of the following since their last court appearance?

_____ 1. programs where staff pay a lot of attention to individual relationships among youth and emphasize rewards in supervised, verbal confrontation.

_____ 2. programs where staff pay a lot of attention to individual relationships among youth and emphasize general nonconfrontive support and rewards for doing well

_____ 3. programs where staff rely on punishment and physical restraint to ensure conformity to rules

_____ 4. programs that consist mostly of physical restraint on youth—temporary warehousing

5. *Interest Group Power.* Who is in each of the following groups or categories?

_____ 1. people giving highest priority to therapy and/or linkages with the community who want new programs and do not want to wait to develop an orderly, step-at-a-time process of implementation

_____ 2. people giving highest priority to therapy and/or linkages to the community who want to maintain or develop an orderly system of liberal programs

_____ 3. people within the correctional system who give highest priority to security and control and/or punishment

_____ 4. people outside the correctional system who give highest priority to security and control and/or punishment

_____ 5. people who advocate particular ways of making decisions about such things as correctional policy, contracts, budgets, pay and promotions, hiring and firing, and who favor the advocates of therapy and/or linkages to the community

_____ 6. People who advocate particular ways of making decisions about such things as correctional policy, contracts, budgets, pay and promotions, hiring and firing, and who favor the advocates of security and control and/or punishment

_____ 7. Other: _____

_____

_____

Please rate each of the groups on a scale of 1 to 10, with 10 being the most powerful.

TABLE 24.2   Issues in a Correctional System (Cont)

6.   *Action Affecting Interest Groups*. How are the efforts of all six groups, taken together currently shaping up to affect which of the groups will be most powerful in the near future? Please rate each of the groups on a scale of 1 to 10, with 10 being object of the most action, supporting greater power in the near future.

 _____   1. advocates of therapy and/or linkages to the community who want new programs

 _____   2. advocates of therapy and/or linkages to the community who want an orderly system

 _____   3. advocates of security and control and/or punishment who are within the correctional system

 _____   4. advocates of security and control and/or punishment who are outside of the correctional system

 _____   5. advocates of particular ways of making decisions who favor the advocates of therapy and/or linkages to the community

 _____   6. advocates of particular ways of making decisions who favor the advocates of security and control and/or punishment

 _____   7. Other: _____

7.   *Action Affecting Corrections*. How are the efforts of these six groups taken together currently shaping up to affect juvenile corrections programs in the near future? (Circle one answer.)

 1. to reform them in the direction of therapy and/or community linkages

 2. to replace them with new therapy and/or linkage programs with largely new staff and facilities

 3. to consolidate therapy and/or linkage programs

 4. to reform them in the direction of security and control and/or punishment

 5. to replace them with new security and control and/or punishment programs with largely new staff and facilities

 6. to consolidate security and control and/or punishment programs

 7. to investigate and expose to public scrutiny the day-to-day functioning of individual programs

intended changes. Thus, for maximum effect, changes promoted by interest groups should start simultaneously with action affecting corrections (question 7) and action affecting interest groups (question 6), and lead to simultaneous changes in action affecting youth-community (question 2) and action affecting staff-youth (question 4). Significant change for an individual youth must involve both action affecting youth-community and action affecting staff-youth, which is to say both linkages and social climate in the institutionalization-

TABLE 24.3 Possible Relationships

Dependent Variables	Predictor Variables						
	Youth-Community Relationship 1	Action Affecting Youth-Community 2	Staff-Youth Power 3	Action Affecting Staff-Youth 4	Interest Group Power 5	Action Affecting Interest Groups 6	Action Affecting Corrections 7
1. Youth-Community Relationship	X	X	X		X		
2. Action Affecting Youth-Community	X	X		X	X		X
3. Staff-Youth Power	X		X	X	X		
4. Action Affecting Staff-Youth		X	X	X	X		X
5. Interest Group Power	X	X	X	X	X	X	
6. Action Affecting Interest Groups					X	X	X
7. Action Affecting Corrections	X	X	X	X		X	X

normalization continuum (Miller et al., 1977: 89-144; Coser, 1956; Thompson, 1967; Etzioni, 1963: 407-421). For example, when Massachusetts closed its training schools, it bargained with the employees union and actually hired the union spokesperson as personnel director to deal with the training school staff (action affecting interest groups). At the same time, it moved to place the youth in community programs (action affecting corrections). In the new programs, staff spent a lot of time advocating for the youths' interests in local community services (action affecting youth community) at the same time that they worked directly with youth to create humane social conditions within programs (action affecting staff-youth).

The Inertia of the People-Processing Relationship. The people-processing relationship, constituting the focal properties of the environment of the relationship among interest groups, carries a great weight, or inertia. It strongly influences (a) the internal distributions in the relationship among interest groups (question 5) and (b) the actions affecting the focal properties of the environment of that relationship (question 7), and, hence, makes it particularly difficult to change either of these two variables. Yet, such change is essential to produce change, by interest group action, in the people-processing relationship itself. However, the people-processing relationship and its self-protective influence over the other variables in the relationship among interest groups are susceptible to being weakened by public investigation and scrutiny at the individual program level (category 7 of question 7; Miller et al., 1977: 145-164; Blumer, 1951: 167-222; Turner and Killian, 1957). Thus, in Massachusetts the explosive scandals over brutality in the training schools and the discrediting of the division head served to challenge the system's credibility sufficiently for radical change to be seriously considered.

The Formal Decision-Making Group as a Swing Power. The groups advocating the protection of political prerogatives are essential allies for the advocates of either therapy or punishment. They are not primarily influenced by the characteristics of the people-processing relationship, since their interest is largely in the prerogatives of the decision-making process and less in the substantive outcomes of that process as they affect youth (Miller et al., 1977: 165-169; Dahrendorf, 1959). Thus, the Massachusetts Legislature, looking for alliances within which its decision-making prerogatives would be respected, swung back and forth between liberals and conservatives. If it found that it was not being listened to, it would mount an investigation of the established regime and swing its support to the coalition of critics.

Responsiveness of the Other Groups to the People-Processing Relationship. The four other groups, advocates either of therapy and/or community linkages or of security and control and/or punishment, are both affected by the people-processing relationship per se, since both are interested in substance. When they are in danger of losing control or cannot quite change that relationship as they want when they do have control, both are likely to use extreme tactics (showing up in question 7, action affecting corrections, as one of the replacement categories, and in question 6, action affecting interest groups, as action favoring one of these four groups and lowering the power of its ally among the formal decision makers). When they get what they want, both tend to stop pushing (showing up in question 7, action affecting corrections, as consolidate), and in so doing become more vulnerable to attack (Miller et al., 1977: 169-176; Smelser, 1963). In Massachusetts the reformers worked very carefully with powerful people in the legislature until it became apparent that the reforms were not drastic enough really to change the fundamental character of the youth correctional system. Then they adopted the more extreme tactic of closing the training schools altogether. They circumvented the legislature in the process by announcing the decision to close the schools and completing the operation while the legislature was out of session. In addition, the reformers tried to ignore and rebuff a legislator who raised questions. Later, with the new programs barely in place, many of the reformers left the state to fight new battles elsewhere. The task of consolidating the reforms passed to administrators less concerned with generating pressure for further reform.

Short- and Long-Run Effects of Extreme Tactics. Extreme tactics of the four substantively oriented groups that push aside their allies among the formal decision-making groups, alienate the formal decision makers as a whole by shifting power to the decision-making group favoring the other side (visible in action affecting interest groups and interest group power, questions 6 and 5). Though these tactics may achieve their immediate objectives, they risk long-run defeat (Miller et al., 1977: 176-180; Gamson, 1961: 373-382). Thus, as noted above, the closing of the training schools, while ignoring the legislature in Massachusetts, caused many legislators to abandon the reformers and swing support over to the conservatives. However, the development of this "backlash" took long enough that, before its effects were fully felt, many of the new reform programs were already in place. Some of the reformers felt they had succeeded and wondered why severe challenges and problems developed later.

Of these five principles, the first, the sequencing principle, is the most basic. It is the bedrock of political strategy to effect corrections. Perhaps even more important, it is the bedrock of effective correctional programs themselves. The community-based corrections movement is implementing this principle in correctional programs today far more aggressively and realistically than has been the norm in recent decades. The hallmark of the movement is the addition of aggressive action affecting youth-community (question 2) along with action affecting staff-youth (question 4).

D. The System Model as a Tool for Research and Advocacy

Evaluation research is implicitly linked to advocacy. It usually throws some cold water on any incipient euphoria of success and yet provides a basis for trying again. Good evaluation research should thus be prescriptive as well as accountive.

Our system model has been designed for this dual purpose. It can be used to develop a dramatic snapshot of a correctional system at a single point in time. It will show where the system lies on the various dimensions of the institutionalization-normalization continuum with a realism that can be disheartening, but it can also show strengths in the system that one might otherwise miss. It will show the degree of consistency between the social climate of the system and its efforts to promote community linkages; and it will show the system's liabilities and assets for effective programming in the surrounding political field. All of this works most powerfully when the model is used to synthesize data of several kinds. Such a synthesis could draw upon interview data derived from using the model itself as an interview guide, informal interviewing and observation, and both cross-sectional and longitudinal interviewing of individual youth about their experiences as they pass through the correctional system.

This use of the model to diagnose the state of the system in a particular time period can be useful for the development of better programs and policies. For more analytical research purposes, the aim should be to improve conceptualization and theory. This improvement may be important for understanding and for the planning of practical advocacy, either within the correctional system as one advocates for specific children, or in the larger political arena as one advocates for a better correctional system. In such a situation one needs to apply the model itself to events and conditions over time. Thus, one needs to construct a series of snapshots, rather than stopping with only one. We have found that a six-month interval between snapshots seems to be about right. Each snapshot can be built up by using the model as described above for diagnostic purposes. Then the snapshots can be put together and analyzed from a longer time perspective, again using the model. Both the cross-sectional approach for diagnostic purposes and the longitudinal approach for analytical purposes can be pursued as projects in themselves. They may also be used to provide the background or context for more focused studies of specific features of the system, such as secure care, a most difficult problem for a community-based system.[1] The model then provides a sounder basis for continuity in policy development as well as research.

NOTE

1. We are currently doing this sort of contextual analysis as part of a two-year study of decision-making about youth in secure care in Massachusetts, and, to a lesser extent, in several other states.

REFERENCES

American Friends Service Committee (1971) *Struggle for Justice.* New York: Hill & Wang.

Blumer, H. (1951) "Collective Behavior," pp. 167-222 in A. M. Lee (ed.) *Principles of Sociology.* New York: Free Press.

Clemmer, D. (1958) The Prison Community. New York: Holt, Rinehart & Winston.

Coates, R. B., A. Miller and L. E. Ohlin (1978) Diversity in a Youth Correctional System: Handling Delinquents in Massachusetts. Cambridge, MA: Ballinger.

Coser, L. (1956) The Functions of Social Conflict. New York: Free Press.

Dahrendorf, R. (1959) *Class and Class Conflict in Industrial Society.* Stanford, CA: Stanford University Press.

Etzioni, A. (1963) "The Epigenesis of Political Communities at the International Level." *American Journal of Sociology* 68, 1: 407-421.

Fogel, D. (1975) . . . We are the living proof. Cincinnati, OH: Anderson.

Gamson, W. (1961) "A Theory of Coalition Formation." *American Sociological Review* 26, 6: 373-382.

Lerman, P. (1968) "Evaluative Studies of Institutions for Delinquents." *Social Work* 13, 12.

Lerman, P. (1975) *Community Treatment and Social Control: An Analysis of Juvenile Correctional Policy.* Chicago: University of Chicago Press.

Lofland, J. (1969) *Deviance and Identity.* Englewood Cliffs, NJ: Prentice-Hall.

Martinson, R. (1974) "What Works?—Questions and Answers About Prison Reform." *Public Interest* 35 (Spring): 22-54.

Miller, A., L. E. Ohlin, and R. B. Coates (1977) *A Theory of Social Reform: Correctional Reform in Two States.* Cambridge, MA: Ballinger.

Smelser, N. (1963) *Theory of Collective Behavior.* New York: Free Press.

Sykes, G. (1958) The Prison Community. New York: Holt, Rinehart & Winston.

Thompson, J. D. (1967) *Organizations in Action.* New York: McGraw-Hill.

Turner, R. and L. M. Killian (1957) *Collective Behavior.* Englewood Cliffs, NJ: Prentice-Hall.

25

Evaluating Criminal Justice Legislation

Richard A. Berk, Paul Burstein,
and Ilene Nagel

INTRODUCTION

It should come as no surprise that methods for evaluating the impact of criminal justice legislation have much in common with methods for evaluating the impact of criminal justice programs. Both criminal justice legislation and criminal justice programs typically reflect a conscious, systematic response to some "social problem": an initial recognition that all is not well, a vision of alternative futures, a "theory" of how change might be brought about, and a mechanism through which to deliver the remedy. In addition, both criminal justice legislation and criminal justice programs are in principle subject to close scrutiny from elected and appointed public officials, interest groups, and taxpayers. In short, there exists a common set of methodological concerns that are well documented at various levels of complexity (see Rossi et al., 1979; Cook and Campbell, 1979; Riecken and Boruch, 1974).

Yet, beneath the many similarities in evaluation research methods, there are also some differences, at least in emphasis. First, evaluations of the impact of criminal justice programs may begin with the program itself: its goals, its implementation, and its content. Evaluations of the impact of criminal justice legislation must start at least one step farther back, analyzing the text and intent of the relevant statutes as well as the new programs or institutional alterations to which they lead. Second, one must find ways to measure the legislative "treatment." This requires not only one or more metrics for literal statutory content, but metrics for statutory intent coupled with ways to assess *changes* in content and intent over time. Third, difficulties in properly inferring causation are significantly complicated by exogenous forces affecting the legislation, actions of the criminal justice system, and outcomes of interest. In other words, by having to move back one step farther in the causal chain, internal validity (Cook and Campbell, 1979: 50-58) becomes especially problematic. This in turn may well require more sophisticated theory and method than when one begins with a criminal justice program. Finally, since the legislative process is necessarily imbedded in a host of ongoing social phenomena, it is extremely difficult to implement evaluation research designs that alter business as usual. Legislators, public officials, and lobbyists, even if they fully acknowledge the importance of controlled experiments, are extremely unlikely to alter the usual legislative parameters in service of more powerful research designs. And their reluctance is well founded if a preferred research design produces genuine inequities. For example, any experimental alteration in the penal code that subjects some convicted offenders to one set of penalties (i.e., an experimental group) and another group of similar convicted offenders to an alternative set of penalties (i.e., a comparison group) violates a variety of ethical standards. Consequently, the options for powerful research designs are severely constrained, making effective evaluations more difficult to undertake.

In this context, there are two aspects of the evaluation research enterprise that warrant special consideration when legislative impact is at issue: properly characterizing true causal process and properly characterizing the legislative "treatment." While these are always evaluation research problematics, evaluations of the impact of criminal justice legislation (or any kind of legislation) raise special complications with important implications for how one proceeds. We begin, then, with issues of internal validity.

ISSUES IN ESTABLISHING INTERNAL VALIDITY

Figure 25.1 provides the beginnings of a causal model for evaluating the impact of a piece of criminal justice legislation. We use the term *causal* because (a) we have singled out certain phenomena that are presumably associated with one another, (b) we have specified a temporal sequence among the phenomena in question, and (c) we have indicated where causal relationships should exist and where they should not exist by implicitly constraining some causal links to zero. In other words, we have addressed the existence of associations, temporal order, and spuriousness in the best evaluation research traditions (Cook and Campbell, 1979: 30-36). We use the term *model* in the sense that Figure 25.1 represents a simplified abstraction of the underlying causal mechanisms through which the relevant empirical phenomena are generated. Thus, we are following closely in the footsteps of econometric perspectives (Berk and Brewer, 1978: 202-206). Finally, we use the term *beginnings* because there are a number of specification issues we have ignored. For example, we have neglected the functional forms relating the causal factors to one another and have ignored the

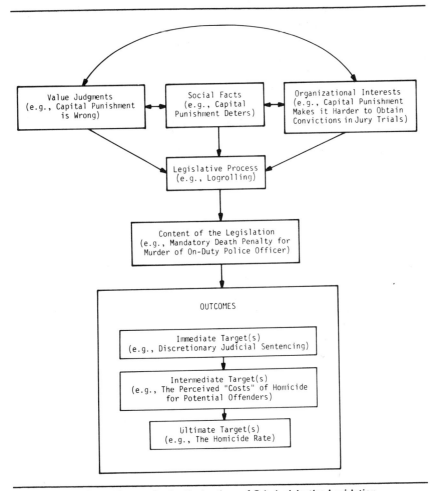

Figure 25.1: A Causal Perspective for Evaluations of Criminal Justice Legislation

role of stochastic processes. On the other hand, there is some evidence that Figure 25.1 is not totally unrelated to reality (e.g., Platt, 1969; Roby, 1969; Heinz et al., 1969; Berk et al., 1977; Teilmann and Klein, 1980).

We begin at the top of Figure 25.1 with three causal factors which for present purposes are treated as fully exogenous. These are the givens in the model. "Value judgments" refers to salient beliefs with normative implications among the significant actors and groups involved in the legislative process. If one took capital punishment as an example, value judgments would include such things as whether the state has the right to take human life or whether retribution should be a consideration in the criminal law. "Social facts" speaks to understandings about the empirical world that have some consensual foundation. That is, ultimate truth is less important than the body of opinion that a particular claim is true. Again, using the example of capital punishment, social facts might include the belief that the death penalty deters would-be murderers and that the marginal impact is felt over and above the prospect of life imprisonment. "Organizational interests" addresses the concerns of actors within relevant institutions with respect to the survival, evolution, and performance of these institutions. In the case of capital punishment, prosecutors might worry that a mandatory death penalty for certain crimes will make convictions more difficult to obtain, or prison guards might support the death penalty as a deterrent against attacks from prisoners who otherwise might have little to lose. Note that while all three of these initial causal factors may well be associated with one another, no statements are made about causal priority.

The second step in the causal model addresses the legislative process. Value judgments, social facts, and organizational interests converge on the legislative arena, and penal code sections are rewritten. Thus, police organizations claiming that the death penalty deters might actively lobby for capital punishment, while the governor might threaten to veto solely on moral grounds (as was the case recently in California). Meanwhile, legislative liberals might try to bottle up the legislation in committee and avoid having to vote publicly on the issues. As a result of these and many other contending forces, the penal code revisions take shape, often in a form that bears little resemblance to the original proposals for legislative change (Berk et al., 1977).

The legislative process is further complicated by political considerations that may or may not be directly relevant to the proposed statutory alterations. There is far more than the immediate substantive issues at stake: The exchange of political favors, the enhancement of political careers, the implications for state expenditures, and the like. Consequently, legislative reforms are often seriously compromised soon after they surface in committee. There is no guarantee that the intent of the original reforms will materialize in the legislation, and no guarantee that the final product will correspond to mandates or resources of agencies responsible for implementation. As we have observed elsewhere (Berk et al., 1977: 276),

> criminal justice proposals became law in the broader environment of state politics; and these concerns, which were at best marginally related to criminal justice, were often the principal determining factors. One is reminded of the aphorism that a camel is a horse made by committee.

Because the legislative process is extremely complex, the content of legislation is no simple function of legislators' motivations. The content and meaning of the revised statutes, therefore, must be the focus of the next step in our causal model. Moreover, it is presumably the statutory text from which concrete actions will follow. In short, since the legislation is in essence the "treatment" whose effects are to be evaluated, there is absolutely no substitute for thoroughly documenting the treatment characteristics. We will have more to say about this later.

With the treatment in place, attention may be directed at outcomes. Here it is critical to distinguish between the immediate targets of the legislation, ultimate targets of the legislation, and targets in-between. For example, the immediate target of a mandatory death penalty for certain crimes may be judicial discretion; the goal is to limit this discretion. Yet, reduced judicial discretion is unlikely to be the ultimate goal. The ultimate goal is to reduce the homicide rate. Finally, in order to get from reduced discretion to a reduction in the homicide rate, the *perceived* "costs" to potential offenders must be raised. In other words, the death penalty will not deter (in principle) unless knowledge of the new law is widely disseminated. This might imply getting public officials to make newsworthy statements to the effect that a crackdown is under way. It is important to distinguish among these different outcomes in order to avoid focusing solely on intervening consequences that may in fact be unrelated to the problem for which the legislation was designed. At the same time, exclusive focus on ultimate outcomes will at least leave unspecified the mechanisms through which the impact occurs, and may also introduce problems of spurious causal interpretations. For example, if, in fact, considerable discretion remains in the application of the death penalty because of plea-bargaining, the inference that a mandatory death penalty for certain kinds of offenses deters may be inaccurate.

With Figure 25.1 now in hand, we can turn to several important implications for the internal validity of evaluations. First, it is often of utmost importance to obtain measures of all causal factors described. Thus, hardening public sentiment about the legitimacy and deterrent value of the death penalty may have a chilling effect (again, in principle) on at least the more rationally motivated sorts of homicides. Another example is drug-related offenses. Changing value judgments and social facts probably have a substantial impact on the use of virtually all sorts of drugs. If these are ignored, one may be seriously misled when the causal effects of antidrug legislation are assessed. More generally, and frequently, the factors which lead to the passage of new legislation are likely to have both direct and indirect effects on the outcomes of interest—direct, through the impact of public opinion, officials' interpretations of their mandate, and the like, and indirect, through the changes in legislation. Consequently, what one attributes to the formal legislation may in fact stem from other sources. Put a bit more formally, some of the causal relationships that are constrained to zero in Figure 25.1 may not really be zero, and this possibility should be considered seriously whenever the impact of changes in criminal justice legislation is assessed.

Second, by documenting in Figure 25.1 a number of important causal factors, we have been assuming *implicitly* that all other causal factors cancel out in the aggregate. In statistical terms, the expected values of excluded causal factors at each step are zero. But for any particular application, this may be totally unreasonable. Perhaps the most common instance is in longitudinal studies with aggregate data where the changing age mix of the target population is neglected. Since crimes are primarily an activity of the young, crime rates are heavily dependent on the proportion of young people in the target population. In the case of homicide, a second critical factor in such studies is the availability of weapons (Zimring, 1972). In addition, we have been assuming that outcomes have no effect on the legislative process, social facts, and the like. In the short run, this may be a reasonable assumption, but in the long run it is not. The accumulation of convincing evidence that capital punishment does not deter, for example, might provide opponents with the social facts they need to abolish it. In short, there is no substitute for a causal understanding of the relevant processes and an effort to include a range of confounding factors.

Third, our concern with spurious causal interpretations has been premised on the low probability that powerful research designs will be feasible in most evaluations for criminal justice legislation. Yet, design considerations are hardly irrelevant, and some approaches may add considerably to internal validity. To begin, it is best to avoid working with highly aggregated data. Ehrlich's (1975) controversial work on the death penalty, for instance, has been thoroughly critiqued, in part for using the overall homicide rate in the United States from 1933 to 1969 as the outcome variable (see, for example, Blumstein et al., 1978). This obscures whether executions in one state affect homicides in another, and treats one kind of homicide (e.g., one spouse killing another) the same as any other (e.g., homicide during a robbery). Similarly, Ehrlich's work on capital punishment assumes that the overall conditional probability of execution (i.e., for the United States as a whole) accurately taps the risks faced by potential offenders in individual states. More generally, aggregate data always risk the well-known ecological fallacy. For instance, if one finds that deinstitutionalization of young offenders precedes an increase in the crime rate, one must be very careful not to assume automatically that it is the deinstitutionalized youths who are committing the crimes.

In addition, the importance of obtaining extensive qualitative data cannot be overstated. For example, we have suggested that criminal justice reforms are often jeopardized during the legislative process through the myriad compromises that are almost inevitable. That is, the intended treatment is not the treatment that materializes in the law. It is precisely for these sorts of processes that qualitative data may be especially instructive; one may learn about the mismatch between original intent and actual reform and come to understand why a reform was perhaps doomed to failure *even before implementation.*

Qualitative data can also be critical in examining the legislative proposals once they become law. For instance, in Figure 25.1 we suggest that the death penalty legislation may reduce sentencing discretion. Field observation would play a significant role in determining such things as whether reference to the new legislation was made by prosecutors, defense counsel, and judges, and whether awareness of the legislation figured significantly in plea-bargaining and sentencing. In other words, qualitative data would help establish whether there was any visible response to the legislation and, if so, the nature of that response. If no evidence of reactions to the legislation could be found, assertions that the legislation ultimately affected the homicide rate must rest on different causal mechanisms or be subject to considerable skepticism.

Qualitative data can be further used to establish the temporal sequences related to the legislative reforms. And since temporal order is one essential ingredient in causal inference, qualitative data involve more than "mere" description. Thus, one would certainly want to establish that judicial discretion changed *after* the relevant legislation was passed. If judicial discretion changed before, one might claim that it was the legislative process and the feelings this revealed that altered the behavior of judges and that the statute itself was irrelevant. That is, judges were responding to implicit political pressures and the tenor of the times. Alternatively, one might seek causal forces entirely outside the legislative arena.

Finally, qualitative data will often convey rich insights about the mechanisms by which the legislation affects or does not affect outcomes of interest. In other words, qualitative data may allow one to step inside the proverbial black box and discover why the outcome phenomena proceed as they do. Besides the more general interest in such matters, one may learn a great deal about the limits of legislative change and/or how more effective legislation may be designed in the future. Thus, it would be important to document why juries were less likely to convict when conviction carried a mandatory death penalty.

In addition to a call for disaggregated data and the use of qualitative techniques, concerns for internal validity will often require the use of rather sophisticated formal research designs and statistical procedures. For example, considerable success has been achieved of late with time-series data and interrupted time-series designs (Deutsch and Alt, 1977; Ross, 1973), where the idea is to consider critical outcome variables arrayed over time. For example, one might examine the rate of homicides associated with property crimes month by month for a period of ten years. Presumably, at some point in the interval a law is passed with possible implications for the time series of interest. For a time series of homicide rates associated with property crimes, the law may place a number of restrictions on the purchase and possession of handguns (see Deutsch and Alt, 1977). Then the question is whether the pattern of longitudinal observations after the law was passed differs from the pattern before. If the law "works," the homicide rate should decline after the legislation, relative to the rate before. While in these broad terms the logic is simple enough, there are a number of complications involving such things as controlling for certain kinds of spurious causal conclusions, modeling the precise manner in which change occurs, and taking patterns of correlation among the random errors into account (Box and Tiao, 1975).

Time-series approaches can be considerably enhanced when additional time series can be introduced as control variables much as in the case of multiple regression. While there are nontrivial technical complications that are still being sorted out (Granger and Newbold, 1977; Nerlove et al., 1979), one is able to capitalize on the combined strengths of multivariate procedures and time-series procedures together.[1] Alternatively, time-series designs may be strengthened when one can in essence carry out parallel time-series analysis in several different settings (e.g., in different states). Basically, one pools the data into one large data set in which one can compare the effects of legislative change both over time and in locales with and without the relevant legislation (Kmenta, 1971; Berk et al., 1979).

To summarize, for a number of reasons internal validity will be especially problematic in evaluations of criminal justice legislation. This requires that one develop a tentative formal model of relevant processes *before* empirical work is begun, in order to guide the development of appropriate research designs and data collection. Typically, one will find that the tentative model implies a host of nontrivial complications requiring the best evaluation research procedures available. Evaluating the impact of criminal justice legislation may be among the most difficult of the evaluation research enterprises.

MEASURING THE CONTENT OF CRIMINAL JUSTICE LEGISLATION

If one wishes to gauge the impact of legislative change with any precision, the treatment must be characterized. Basically, two standard ways of quantifying legislative action have been commonly used in the past. The first employs a yes-no dummy variable to indicate whether a legal provision (capital punishment, for example) is part of the penal code. The second uses expenditures or other obvious measures of resources, such as number of personnel, to gauge government activity in an area. Both approaches have severe shortcomings. The dummy variable approach can be used to analyze a very small number of changes in the law, but because a different variable is needed for each change in the law, the approach quickly becomes unwieldy when there are many changes in the law to analyze. In addition, a dummy variable is hardly an informative description of altered legislative content. The expenditures approach is useful for dealing with budgetary aspects of law enforcement, but is virtually useless for dealing with many kinds of legislation–changes in procedure or in the definition of criminal activity, for example.

Fortunately, considerable progress has been made in the ability to measure the content of legislation. There are major problems in measuring legislation that have not been solved; we do not yet have a single, agreed-upon, "best" way to measure legislation. Nevertheless, enough is known to provide a framework for analyzing the content of criminal justice legislation.[2]

At least four central issues must be faced in any attempt to measure criminal justice legislation: defining what domain of law is to be measured; deciding what dimensions best describe the legislative domain; giving each item of legislation a quantitative score on each dimension; and determining how to deal with large numbers of legislative changes over time (see Burstein, 1978).

Domain of Legislation

The first issue is what domain of legislation to measure. Past concerns have ranged from the very narrow–a single provision, such as capital punishment–to the very broad–the content of an entire penal code (see Ehrlich, 1975; Berk et al., 1977). The domain of concern will generally fall between these two extremes.

The main determinant of what laws to consider will be the aim of the evaluation, of course. Yet, even when the legislative motivation is clear, deciding precisely what changes in the law to analyze may be difficult. One approach, the most common in past work, is to keep the focus as narrow as possible, considering only those provisions most clearly and directly relevant to the research question. Those interested in capital punishment, for example, might consider only the presence or absence of provisions permitting capital punishment, and ignore the rest of the penal code.

The advantage of a narrow focus is clear; the smaller the number of revisions to deal with, the easier the task. Keeping the focus narrow also has a significant disadvantage, however. The behavior of people potentially involved in the criminal justice system may be affected by numerous aspects of criminal justice legislation. An individual thinking of robbing a liquor store, for example, may be affected not only by his or her notions of the sentence meted out to those convicted of robbery, but also by knowing the number of police likely to be in the vicinity, the resources available to the prosecutor, special penalties for repeated offenders, and the like. The individual's behavior might be affected by changes in any relevant aspect of the law. If research were to focus on changes in sentencing while ignoring other relevant changes in the law taking place simultaneously, changes in the incidence of robbery might be erroneously attributed to changes in sentencing, rather than to another, more effective cause.[3]

Ideally, therefore, it is desirable to analyze change in all laws potentially relevant to one's concerns. Doing so, however, will greatly increase the magnitude and complexity of the analysis, and may make it unmanageable. There is, unfortunately, no theory that can tell us in advance which laws should be considered in any particular analysis. At this point, therefore, common sense refined by experience must be the guide. Based upon our experience, the best advice would be to include any statutory alterations that intuitively seem likely to have a strong effect on the central object of concern. This will typically mean considering a significant range of revisions, including, possibly, some not in the penal code,[4] drawing on insights from prior research, personal experience, theory, or the advice of practitioners.

To summarize, while there may be a single legislative treatment, a large number of related revisions may actually be involved. Moreover, it is not uncommon to find other revisions, ostensibly addressing other issues, whose possible impact on the outcomes of interest cannot be ignored. Such complexities require a careful a priori consideration of what legislative changes need to be measured.

Dimensions of Legislation

After defining the domain of laws to be analyzed, the next step is to determine how to describe many items of legislation in terms of a relatively small number of dimensions. How this is done depends essentially upon the researcher's aims and his or her confidence in the a priori knowledge of the legislation being examined.

In the simplest case, the researcher will be concerned with an obvious dimension and will be confident that other dimensions need not be considered (e.g., a concern solely with lengths of sentences).

In more complex cases, which are also more common, the scope of the research will be broader and the degree of certainty about how to describe the legislation will be lower. When confronted with such a situation, the researcher has a choice between two approaches used in past work.

The first approach is content analysis, used by Berk et al. (1977) and by Ratner (forthcoming). The dimensions are defined by the researcher on the basis of past research, common sense, and expert knowledge of the legislation, guided by theory where any is relevant. Berk et al. (1977) decided that all changes in the California Penal Code (more than 700 significant changes during the period they studied) could be characterized as changes along no more than 55 dimensions which described functionaries within the criminal justice system, potential and convicted offenders, types of criminalization, and severity of penalties. Ultimately they found that the 55 dimensions could be reduced to 12 for most practical purposes. It was this reduction of over 700 changes in the law to changes along 12 dimensions that made possible the systematic, statistical analysis of change in the California Penal Code.

This approach has several advantages. Although it may be laborious to develop coding rules and to train coders, the procedures are relatively easy to understand. The approach allows the researchers to use their prior knowledge of the legislation when they develop the coding procedures. And the results will typically be easily communicated to less sophisticated audiences.

There are potential disadvantages, however, which stem from the fact that the researcher may not interpret the legislation in the same way as the legislators who voted on it. The researcher may misinterpret the legislators' intentions, and consequently use different dimensions than the legislators, or may include too many dimensions in the coding scheme, or too few. In addition, the researcher may inadvertently ignore basic shifts in the ways legislators view important aspects of criminal justice legislation (when, for example, changed perceptions alter legislators' notions about the kinds of measures likely to be effective in a particular area; see Ulmer, 1974).

The second approach, which might be called the voting analysis approach, derives the dimensions of legislation from statistical analyses of legislators' votes on proposed changes in the law. With this strategy, it is the legislators themselves, rather than the researcher, who interpret the laws and make their interpretations known through their voting behavior (Burstein, 1978).

In essence, one employs multidimensional scaling to reduce a large number of motions (legislative proposals) voted on by legislators to a small number of dimensions, and to give each proposal a score on each dimension. Each proposal is treated as a variable, with legislators' votes scored 1 for yea and 0 for nay, or 2 for yea, 1 for abstain, and 0 for nay. When legislators interpret various proposals as having similar meaning, they will vote the same way on each, it is presumed, so the variables representing these proposals will be relatively strongly correlated. Highly intercorrelated sets of variables form the basis for dimensions, much as in factor analysis. It may also be possible to array the variables along each dimension, with the most highly correlated within a dimension being close together and the relatively weakly correlated farther apart. The result can be similar to a Guttman scale, with "weak" items at one end and "strong" items at the other. Thus, the approach may enable one to discover that, for example, a "severity of punishment" dimension exists in the eyes of legislators and that proposals can be given scores representing a range from "mild punishment" to "severe punishment" (see Burstein, 1978).

The voting analysis approach has three advantages. The dimensions are based upon the actions of those actually responsible for the legislation, not upon outsiders' interpretations. The number of dimensions needed to describe legislation is likely to be small, so the description of legislative content will be simpler than when content analysis is used. Finally, because the approach does not rely so much on the perspectives of the researcher, it is more likely than content analysis to detect less-than-obvious aspects of legislation and to lead to a deeper understanding of legislative change.

There are three disadvantages to the approach as well. First, the statistical techniques (various forms of multidimensional scaling) are fairly complicated, and probably require more specialized training than content analysis. Second, in those situations wherein the legislators have no clear overall picture of the changes they are making, the results of the analysis, like the legislators' actions, may be confused and difficult to interpret. In essence, one undertakes a kind of indirect content analysis in which legislators interpret the content of proposed laws and then the researcher analyzes the behavior of legislators. From the voting patterns one is able to determine which code revisions are treated alike and which are treated differently and, from this, a set of underlying dimensions may be extracted. Finally, much as in the case of factor analysis and cluster analysis, there is no guarantee that all the dimensions that surface will have any straightforward substantive meaning. A subset of code revisions may be treated alike by legislators for a host of reasons that may covary empirically but defy any simple summary.

Given the advantages and disadvantages of each approach, the most practical advice would probably be the following: If the researcher has the necessary resources, the voting analysis approach is likely to be the more fruitful when the researcher is exploring a new area, looking for unexpected findings, trying to understand the legislator's viewpoint, or lacking in confidence in past work.

Yet, under most circumstances it is probably more practical to use content analysis. The specific dimensions most useful for describing any particular set of laws will vary with the purpose of the research and the historical context. Much of what is important in criminal justice legislation, however, may fit within five general "targets" of such legislation. Using these targets as a kind of outline should help analyze almost any body of criminal justice legislation; more specific targets will probably fit within the broader targets (see Berk et al., 1977):

(1) functionaries within the criminal justice system (for example, law enforcement, personnel, prosecutors);
(2) potential and convicted offenders (for example, suspects, defendants, prisoners);
(3) victims—how they are dealt with by the criminal justice system (for example, treatment of rape victims, restitution for victims of property crimes);
(4) types of criminalization—laws affecting the types of behavior labeled illegal (for example, crimes against persons or property); and
(5) severity of penalty—changes in the fines and/or periods of incarceration for given offenses.

Scoring Legislation on the Dimensions

Once the dimensional structure of a legislative domain has been decided upon or discovered, the next task is to quantify precisely the kind, direction, and magnitude of legislative change on each dimension—that is, to place each item of legislation on the relevant dimensions.

The first, simplest, and best method involves using a metric inherent in the definition of a dimension: expenditures of money, length of sentences, number of staff, and so on (see Ratner, forthcoming). There is little conceptual difficulty in at least roughly locating items of legislation on such dimensions; the actual content of the law translates almost automatically into a place on a dimension, and the meaning of the placement will be clear to everyone.

Unfortunately, most dimensions of legislation do not have obvious metrics, so methods that are more complex and less direct normally must be used to quantify the magnitude and direction of change in the content of legislation. One such method is part of content analysis and another is part of voting analysis.

Using content analysis, Berk et al. (1977), for example, gauged the direction and magnitude of change in legislation along their dimensions in terms of some general properties of criminal justice systems. For the actors in the system, the metric was the amount of "legal rights and resources" available to the role in question. Thus, a change in the law that was seen as greatly increasing the power of the police would get a high positive score along the "police" dimension; a large decrease in police rights and resources would get a high negative score. In this way, the many kinds of legislative changes that might affect the police (changes affecting search and seizure, the questioning of suspects, the use of weapons, and the like) would all be reduced to a single dimension, "legal rights and resources." Similarly, where criminalization was the issue, the scores pertained to the amount of behavior criminalized. Where severity of sentence was the issue, the score referred to the length and/or type of sentence and/or amount of fine. Appropriately trained coders proved able to agree consistently on their judgments about the magnitude of change made by each item of legislation on each dimension. Content analysis made it possible to reduce over 700 changes in the law to readily interpretable quantitative measures along a relatively small number of dimensions.

While the metrics used by Berk et al. proved useful in their research, other metrics within a content analysis framework are certainly possible. For example, in their work on changes in juvenile court law in California, Teilmann and Klein (1980) suggest rather different metrics, including the clarity of the message implied by the legislation (the clarity of the "signal"), the degree to which the legislation is but a codification of ongoing trends, and the degree to which discretion is increased or decreased.

The second way to score items of legislation is associated with the voting analysis approach. The statistical procedures which derive dimensions of legislation from legislators' voting patterns also give each item of legislation a score on each dimension. As with content analysis, a large number of changes in legislation can be described in terms of scores on a relatively small number of dimensions.

Both methods of scoring items enable one to describe the content of legislation quantitatively, even when there is no inherent metric associated with the dimensions. Both methods make it possible, therefore, to analyze the causes and consequences of legislative change with a rigor that was not possible previously.

Both approaches share a serious flaw, unfortunately. Intuitively, the most appealing measure of the content of legislation is one in which the actual words of a law translate directly into a quantitative measure which would have an obvious meaning to everyone; an example would be a "severity of punishment" measure for which it would be perfectly plain that a law specifying a ten-year prison term for a crime was more severe than a law specifying a five-year term. The results of both content analysis and voting analysis are more difficult to interpret, however, because they typically lump all kinds of laws (every law affecting resources available to the police, for example) into a single category and measure changes in the law along dimensions that are abstractly defined in the course of carrying out the procedure. The measures of the content of legislation do not, therefore, flow directly from the actual words of the law. No way has yet been discovered to solve this problem. This means that the methods have considerable practical utility, but the researcher must always keep in mind the degree of abstraction involved in the measurement process when interpreting the results.

CHANGE OVER TIME

Dealing with change in legislation over time, especially fairly long periods (more than a couple of four-year electoral cycles, for example), is one of the most difficult problems confronting those trying to measure legislation and legislative change. When the dimensions and metric are clear, there is not likely to be a problem. But when the dimensions or the scoring systems are fairly abstract and based on either content analysis by the researchers or analyses of legislators' voting, serious problems may arise because of changes in the social, political, and legal context. The content analysis by Berk et al. (1977) for example, depended upon coders reaching agreement about the direction and magnitude of changes in legislation as they affected, for instance, the resources available to certain roles in the system. If the political context changed, or new theories of how to treat criminals became popular, or the time period analyzed was 75 years rather than 17, changes that seemed large in the context of the California Penal Code circa 1970 might come to seem small or insignificant, and there would be no way of easily reconciling the scores derived by Berk et al. with the scores in a new study, because there would be no comparable metric.

Similarly, voting analyses are time-bound as well. If legislators change their notions about the relevance of particular dimensions over time, or reconceptualize the relationships they see between particular provisions of the penal code, laws that are identical in manifest content might receive different scores at different times.

Past works employ ad hoc procedures to avoid these problems in specific research contexts; unfortunately, no satisfactory general way to overcome these problems has been devised. The best advice is therefore probably a cautionary note: the extant methods of measuring the content of legislation can probably be relied upon when the basic structure of the legislation being analyzed does not change fundamentally during the time period under consideration. As the magnitude of change being analyzed increases, as the time period under consideration lengthens, and as perceptions of the legislative domain change, the reliability and validity of any set of measures probably decreases proportionately.

To summarize, unless the legislative treatment is a very simple alteration unconfounded with other statutory revisions, it will be necessary to characterize the changes in some detail. Two quantitative approaches have proved useful in the past, although they are hardly trouble-free. In addition, qualitative data (when feasible) can be enormously helpful in both guiding and interpreting one's scaling procedures. Indeed, the study by Berk et al. (1977) makes extensive use of a wide range of historical materials (e.g., committee reports, newspaper articles, retrospective interviews). Similarly, Teilmann and Klein (1980) rely heavily on qualitative approaches in characterizing the nature of legislative change. In short, our earlier admonitions about the importance of such approaches are clearly relevant here.

SUMMARY AND CONCLUSIONS

Changes in criminal justice codes come in all manner of forms, directed at an enormous variety of problems and implemented through a wide range of mechanisms. Consequently, there is no single set of issues and certainly no single way in which to undertake evaluations. In order to provide a thorough account of options in the evaluation of criminal justice legislation, we would have had to reproduce any of several fine texts and in addition discuss how one might deal with problems that are of special importance. All we could do here is suggest in rather general terms what that supplemental material might include: an examination of the particular difficulties associated with internal validity and properly characterizing the treatment. Stepping back even further, however, it seems to us that there are three basic questions that an effective legislative evaluation must answer.

First, what is the fit between what legislators were trying to accomplish and the content of the legislation? Presumably, criminal justice legislation is goal-directed, but the aims of legislators (and those they represent) may be thwarted initially because the legislation is poorly conceived or sloppily drafted. In more common evaluation research terms, the first question is whether the "treatment" is consistent with the underlying premises and aims of its designers. That is, the underlying premises and aims comprise the "theory" (or theories) being implemented, and one wants to know if the treatment is consistent with the theory. Later, if the legislation does not bring about the desired changes, it may be possible to afix blame on the failure effectively to translate the legislative theory into statutory content.

For example, let us suppose that there is a legislative consensus that the incidence of family violence is far too high and that if the chances that offenders would be severely punished were significantly increased, the rate of violence would decline.[5] However let us also suppose that in drafting the legislation, attention was directed exclusively at making penalties more severe; the probability of *applying* the more severe penalties was neglected. Then it is apparent that the legislative theory was not properly captured in the code revisions and that if a decrease in spousal battery fails to occur, fault may well lie in the poor fit between the theory and the content of the revision. For instance, prosecutors fearing a decline in convictions as a result of seemingly draconian punishments might choose to prosecute only their very strongest cases. The net effect might be actually to *lower* the probability of severe sanctions; the failure may be attributed in part to initial errors in how the legislation was drafted.

Second, one must determine if the legislation was implemented properly. The analogous question in the evaluation of criminal justice programs is whether the actual program reflects the goals of its designers (or indeed, whether there is any program at all). Clearly, a legislative revision may fail in the translation from legislative intent to actual practice.

Consider legislative efforts to ease the economic hardships faced by ex-offenders in the first few months after release from prison. Legislators might believe that if a bit of support were provided for those ex-offenders unable to find jobs within a short time after release, there would be less motivation to commit new crimes, especially those motivated by financial need. As a mechanism for delivering such support, unemployment benefits (for which ex-offenders are rarely eligible) might be extended to newly released individuals. (For an evaluation of a recent effort to experiment with just such a program, see Rossi et al., 1980.) That is, ex-offenders unable to find work would be immediately eligible for a modest level of transfer payments. However, suppose that despite the best intentions of all of the parties involved, bureaucratic procedures make it impossible to process the unemployment claims of ex-offenders in less than a minimum of four weeks. Clearly, if the aim was to provide modest support soon after release, the legislation was not implemented properly and a failure to affect recidivism might well result.

Finally, one must determine what sort of impact (if any) the legislation had on the outcomes of interest. This is, of course, the usual goal of all evaluation research, and perhaps the main message here is that internal validity and characterizing the treatment may well require special efforts. One will need to dig deeply into the evaluation research bag of tricks in order to complete a compelling evaluation successfully.

NOTES

1. We are implicitly assuming here that one is using single-equation models. This is not a necessary restriction; indeed, some of the most exciting work in time-series procedures involves multiple-equation nonrecursive models.

2. The most important works are Berk et al., 1977; Burstein, 1978; Ratner, forthcoming. The latter two, in particular, have extensive bibliographies.

3. Technically, a narrow focus is likely to lead to specification error in the statistical analysis, and consequently to bias in estimates of the impact of legislation.

4. As a practical matter, this advice implies considering a wider range of laws than is usual in evaluation research, but a narrower range than is usual in statistical studies of legislative behavior (see Burstein, 1978).

5. One could determine this through a range of data (e.g., reports from committee hearings, interviews with key political actors) using quantitative and qualitative procedures.

REFERENCES

Berk, R. A. and M. Brewer (1978) "Feet of Clay in Hobnail Boots: An Assessment of Statistical Inference in Applied Research," in T. D. Cook (ed.) *Evaluation Studies Review Annual.* Beverly Hills, CA: Sage Publications.

Berk, R. A., H. Brackman, and S. Lesser (1977) *A Measure of Justice: An Empirical Study of Changes in the California Penal Code, 1955-1977.* New York: Academic Press.

Berk, R. A., D. M. Hoffman, J. E. Maki, D. Rauma, and H. Wong (1979) "Estimation Procedures for Pooled Cross-Sectional and Time Series Data." *Evaluation Quarterly* 3, 3: 385-410.

Blumstein, A., J. Cohen, and D. Nagin [eds.] (1978) *Deterrence and Incapacitation: Estimating the Effects of Criminal Sanctions on Crime Rates.* Washington, DC: National Academy of Sciences.

Box, G.E.P. and G. C. Tiao (1975) "Intervention Analysis with Applications to Economic and Environmental Problems." *Journal of the American Statistical Association* 70, 349: 70-79.

Burstein, P. (1978) "A New Method for Measuring Legislative Content and Change." *Sociological Methods and Research* 6 (February): 337-364.

Cook, T. D. and D. T. Campbell (1979) *Quasi-Experimentation: Design and Analysis Issues for Field Settings.* Skokie, IL: Rand McNally.

Deutsch, S. J. and F. B. Alt (1977) "The Effect of the Massachusetts' Gun Control Law on Gun-Related Crimes in the City of Boston." *Evaluation Quarterly* 1, 4: 543-568.

Ehrlich, I. (1975) "The Deterrent Effect of Capital Punishment." *American Economic Review* 65 (June): 397-417.

Granger, C.W.J. and P. Newbold (1977) *Forecasting Economic Time Series.* New York: Academic Press.

Heinz, J. P., R. W. Gettleman, and M. A. Seeskin (1969) "Legislative Politics and the Criminal Law." *Northwestern University Law Review* 64: 277-312.

Kmenta, J. (1971) *Elements of Econometrics.* New York: MacMillan.

Mallar, C. D. and C.V.D. Thornton (1978) "Transitional Aid Among Released Prisoners: Evidence from the LIFE Experiment." *Journal of Human Resources* 13, 2: 208-236.

Nerlove, M., D. M. Grether, and J. L. Carvalho (1979) *Analysis of Economic Time Series.* New York: Academic Press.

Platt, A. M. (1969) *The Child Savers: The Invention of Delinquency.* Chicago: University of Chicago Press.

Ratner, R. S. (forthcoming) *A Modest Magna Charta: The Rise and Growth of Wage and Hour Standards Laws in the United States.* New Brunswick, NJ: Rutgers University Press.

Riecken, H. W. and R. F. Boruch [eds.] (1974) *Social Experimentation: A Method for Planning and Evaluating Social Intervention.* New York: Academic Press.

Roby, P. A. (1969) "Politics and Criminal Law: Revision of the New York State Law on Prostitution." *Social Problems* 17: 83-108.

Ross, H. L. (1975) "The Scandinavian Myth: The Effectiveness of Drinking-and-Driving Legislation in Sweden and Norway." *Journal of Legal Studies* 4, 2: 285-310.

——— (1973) "Law, Science, and Accidents: The British Road Safety Act of 1967." *Journal of Legal Studies* 2, 1: 1-78.

Rossi, P. H., R. A. Berk, and K. Lenihan (1980) *Money, Work and Crime.* New York: Academic Press.

Rossi, P. H., H. E. Freeman, and S. R. Wright (1979) *Evaluation: A Systematic Approach.* Beverly Hills, CA: Sage Publications.

Teilman, K. S. and M. W. Klein (1980) "Juvenile Justice Legislation: A Framework for Evaluation," in D. Shichor and D. H. Kelly (eds.) *Critical Issues in Juvenile Delinquency.* Lexington.

Ulmer, S. S. (1974) "Dimensionality and Change in Judicial Behavior," pp. 40-67 in J. Herndon and J. Bernd (eds.) *Mathematical Applications in Political Science, VII.* Charlottesville, VA: University of Virginia Press.

Zimring, F. E. (1972) "The Medium is the Message: Firearm Caliber as a Determinant of Death from Assault." *Journal of Legal Studies* 1, 1: 97-123.

26

The Evaluation of
Research Utilization

Ross F. Conner

The primary rationale for applied research is that its products will be useful in guiding future policies and practices. The Law Enforcement Assistance Administration (LEAA) supports studies of police behavior, for example, because they are expected to increase our understanding of current police practices and to result in improved practices in the future. Likewise, studies of innovative demonstration programs, such as a new rape/sexual assault crisis center, are funded because they can aid policy makers by documenting program activities and evaluating program effects. The assumption exists, then, that research findings from these types of studies will be used by policy makers, either as primary or secondary sources of information.

This common belief in the utilization of research results seems to be based more on faith than on fact. In the late 1960s, four national commissions and committees investigated the use of social research in policy-making and concluded that the degree of utilization was low (United States House of Representatives, Committee on Governmental Operations, 1967; National Academy of Sciences, 1968; Special Commission on the Social Sciences, National Science Foundation, 1968; Social Science Research Council, 1969). The results of these and more recent studies (e.g., Wholey et al., 1971; Goodwin, 1975; Hargrove, 1975; Deitchman, 1976) have demonstrated the importance and necessity of studying the utilization process. A small number of government agencies have started to investigate the dissemination and utilization of their research knowl-

AUTHOR'S NOTE: The author gratefully acknowledges the help of Gilbert Geis and especially Donald C. Pelz in reviewing drafts of this chapter.

edge (see Emrick and Peterson, 1978, for a discussion of recent utilization efforts in the National Institute of Education; and Beck, 1978, for those in the National Institute of Law Enforcement and Criminal Justice). In addition, a small but growing group of researchers has begun to conduct studies of utilization, particularly that in the evaluation research field (Caplan et al., 1975; Knorr, 1977; Rich, 1977; Patton et al., 1977; Weeks, 1979; Weiss and Bucuvalas, 1977). As Weiss (1977: 19) has noted, however, "large-scale studies on research use are a relatively new enterprise."

The literature in the criminal justice area on the use of research knowledge is particularly limited. As Yin reports (1976: 7), "until recently, most of the major works in criminal justice have failed to discuss the utilization or implementation process at all."[1] In view of this deficit in criminal justice research, a conceptualization of the utilization process is necessary to guide the discussion of research utilization and to suggest useful ways to evaluate utilization. This chapter addresses basic questions about the research utilization process: How does utilization occur, and how can the kind and degree of utilization be evaluated? Factors which increase or decrease utilization and techniques to increase utilization will not be a primary focus, since these topics have been well covered by others (e.g., Argyris, 1965; Bennis et al., 1976; Bernstein and Freeman, 1975; Caplan et al., 1975; Chester and Flanders, 1967; Coe and Bernhill, 1967; Davis and Salasin, 1975; Fairweather, 1967; Fairweather et al., 1974; Glaser and Taylor, 1973; Havelock, 1969, 1976; Human Interaction Research Institute and National Institute of Mental Health, 1976; Weiss, 1972, 1977). Instead, this chapter will focus on a description and analysis of different aspects of the utilization process and on a discussion of a general model for evaluating the effects of research utilization with particular attention to the criminal justice system.

THE UTILIZATION PROCESS

One of the most salient, as well as frustrating, aspects of utilization is its complexity: "Research utilization is an extraordinarily complicated phenomenon" (Weiss, 1977: 11). The definition of research use requires specification of what is used, who uses it, and when and how it is used. Has "use" occurred if one (or ten or one hundred) police chiefs read a news brief (or an "executive summary" or a complete "final report") on an effective innovative patrolling system? Does "use" mean that these chiefs must institute part (or all) of the same new system, or is it sufficient that they simply begin to think about police patrol in a new way?

In the criminal justice area, the definition of research utilization is particularly difficult because of the large number of actors (e.g., judges, police, juveniles), organizations (e.g., public, private) and levels (e.g., local, county, state, federal) potentially involved in usage. Yin (1976) states that the absence of utilization in the criminal justice area is attributable to the simplistic view of the utilization process held by the public and by practitioners. Because of this inaccurate view, the traditional techniques which have been used in the criminal justice area to achieve research utilization (e.g., disseminating information to potential users, promoting exemplary projects for others to model) have not been successful.

Before we can develop a model for evaluating the effects of the research utilization process, we need to understand the process well, just as we would need a thorough understanding of a new criminal justice reform project before we could develop an evaluation plan for such a project. There are eight characteristics of the utilization process which will be discussed here. These characteristics were developed after reviewing a number of discussions of knowledge and research utilization (cited in the sections which follow). These aspects are those most characteristic of the utilization process as it usually occurs in disseminating and utilizing criminal justice or other human service research. The eight aspects are: the quality and importance of the research results which are to be utilized; the pattern, type, rationale, and timing of the utilization process; the level of the utilization target; and the state of the utilizers, including their previous experiences with research and the reward contingencies which affect their behavior.

1. The Quality of Research Results

The utilization process is affected by the quality of the research results or findings which are at the center of utilization attempts. *Quality* in this context refers to the validity and reliability of findings. Consider, for example, the results of a study of a group of five specially chosen inmates involved in a work-release project. Because of the small number and the special selection of the inmates, the validity and reliability of the research findings, no matter how positive, would be problematic at best. Any attempts by the researchers to disseminate these results and urge replication would probably be met with understandable resistance, particularly from other researchers. In this case, practitioners, who often are unable fully to understand methodological disputes among researchers, will be confronted with two differing recommendations for utilization. If this happens frequently, as it tends to do because of the difficulty of conducting flawless social research, practitioners may become prone to discount research results as a matter of course, following the lead of the many research critics they have observed. This type of practitioner or policy maker bias will stop or impede any dissemination-utilization effort. To avoid this, only research of high quality should be disseminated.

The evidence that exists suggests that methodological quality is a necessary but not a sufficient condition for utilization. Weiss and Bucuvalas (1977), in a study of local, state, and national mental health decision makers, found that a factor they called "research quality" emerged as quite important in these decision makers' ratings of the usefulness of 50 actual mental health studies. "Technical quality" was the rating with the highest loading on this factor. The sample of studies, however, was biased toward those of higher quality; consequently, decision makers' judgments of the importance for utilization of high-quality research, when contrasted with low-quality research, is unclear. Technical quality, while important to these decision makers, was only one component of the "research quality" factor. Two other aspects not strictly related to methodology were important: "lack of [personal] bias" and "recommendations supported by data."

In another study, Patton et al. (1977) found that methodological quality was not among the most important factors noted by decision makers in explaining utilization of results from studies of large-scale health projects. The large majority of these studies, however, had been rated by these same decision makers as "high" or "medium" in quality, so quality may have been high enough to remove this as a primary consideration in their judgments and to permit other considerations to surface.

2. The Importance of the Research Results

The importance of research results refers to the social, as contrasted with the statistical, significance of the findings, as well as to their generalizability. Social significance pertains to the practical consequences of research findings and their importance for policy-making. A research study may show, validly and reliably, that an intensive training program for prisoners raises their reading ability by several points. Practitioners, however, probably would question whether it is worth conducting such a training program in their institution if the sole result for participants would be such a small increase in ability. Generalizability, the other aspect of the importance of research results, refers to the exportability of research findings from one setting to another. In the inmate reading program example, even if the increase in ability was 20 or 30 points and, so, socially as well as statistically significant, practitioners might question whether the same results would occur in their own institutions, where the population consists of prisoners who are different (e.g., have lower ability, have committed different offenses) from those in the experimental program.

The Weiss and Bucuvalas study (1977) provides support for the role of the importance of research results in utilization. The "research quality" factor in the judgments of utilization contains the characteristics, "generalizable to equivalent populations" and "comprehensive set of explanatory variables." Both were important for utilization. Another factor identified by Weiss and Bucuvalas, "action orientation," provides additional evidence of the importance of socially and practically significant results. Studies were judged to be more utilizable if they had examined the results of manipulable variables and added to practical knowledge. (Interestingly, the characteristic, "inexpensive to implement," was not part of this "action orientation" factor, nor was it part of any of the other three factors Weiss and Bucuvalas identified.)

Research reports, then, will have importance to potential utilizers if the results reveal socially meaningful changes. In addition, the replication of the results in different settings at different times and under different circumstances will increase the importance of results to practitioners. It should be noted that the level of importance of the research results, like many of the factors we will be considering, affects the course of the utilization process in combination with other factors. High quality plus low importance of findings, for example, will result in less utilization than high quality and high importance.

3. The Pattern of the Utilization Process

This factor relates to the sequencing of activities in the utilization process, from the compilation of research results to the adoption of the results into new policies or practices. The simplest sequence would involve only a few steps between the starting and ending points: the results are given to the relevant policy maker who reads, understands, and accepts the results, then institutes new policies based on the research. This simple, linear sequence rarely occurs, however. Instead, the sequence of events is likely to be quite complex and labyrinthine.

The reason for this complicated sequence relates to the general amorphousness of the policy decision-making process. Weiss (1977: 11) describes this situation well: "Options are somehow progressively narrowed by a series of almost imperceptible choices. A variegated group of persons, uncoordinated, takes minor steps. Almost without conscious decision, a decision accretes." Emrick and Peterson (1978), in their analysis of five studies in educational dissemination and change, consistently find that change is a process, not an event.

In undertaking a utilization attempt, then, it may be unclear as to which policy maker is the most relevant target for utilization attempts. In other cases, several policy makers may appear to be potential targets, or no particular policy maker may be the best target. Once one or a few policy makers are selected, the approach to them may be direct or indirect (e.g., through aides or other staff), through formal channels or informal ones (e.g., via friends or personal advisors of a policy maker who are able to lobby). Once the target is reached, the process of winning acceptance of the recommendations based on the findings can be difficult, since the policy maker usually has many factors which he or she must consider in adopting changes. These other factors may be present overtly or covertly; only in the former case can their relationship to the research findings be known. A research utilization project now under way at the University of Michigan School of Nursing is exploring some of the many factors which are part of the pattern of the utilization process (Horsley et al., 1978).

The pattern of utilization for any particular set of research findings will vary greatly. One sure generalization, however, is that the pattern will be complex and will be characterized by many dead ends, detours, and wrong turns. The utilization of research on a number of criminal justice topics could illustrate this point. Consider a hypothetical case where data on deinstitutionalization and diversion of juvenile offenders is disseminated to state lawmakers and local policy makers. The utilization of these data in the creation of legislation is likely to be very difficult to follow and even more difficult to see in the final version of the legislation, which probably will reflect an artful compromise of many interests and a general but carefully worded statement of intent. Local interpretations and implementations of the bill are likely to be quite varied—even contradictory, perhaps—further obscuring the link between the research findings and the eventual individual utilizations of those findings. Klein (1979) provides numerous examples of variations in implementation in the areas of deinstitutionalization and diversion.

4. The Type of Utilization Process

The type of utilization refers to the kind and degree of use which occurs. Various writers have presented different conceptualizations of type of utilization (Caplan et al., 1975; Knorr, 1977; Rich, 1977; Weiss, 1977). Pelz (1978) presents a framework which combines these different viewpoints. He distinguishes two types of knowledge: soft and hard. Soft knowledge is characterized as nonresearch-based, qualitative and stated in everyday terms; hard knowledge is research-based, quantitative, and stated in scientific terms. These two types of knowledge are combined with three modes of utilization: instrumental, conceptual, and symbolic. The instrumental mode is direct, documentable use for decision-making. The conceptual mode is indirect, intellectual use of research findings for the general enlightenment of decision makers. Rich (1977) has characterized these two modes as "knowledge for action" and "knowledge for understanding." The third mode, "symbolic," will be considered below, under "rationale for the utilization process."

Consider an evaluation of a prison legal services clinic, containing both quantitative findings (hard data) and qualitative statements (soft data). Both types of data indicate that the legal services generally were needed and effective in solving inmates' legal problems; particular types of problems (e.g., appeals of convictions), however, were less effectively dealt with than were others. A decision by the clinic director to discontinue work on appeals would be an example of instrumental utilization of these results; a decision by the director to rethink the best use of clinic resources for legal service provision would constitute conceptual utilization.

The utilization processes associated with these two types of utilization are quite different. In the case of instrumental utilization, the targets are easy to identify and the recommended changes are concrete and specific. In the case of conceptual utilization, on the other hand, the general subject of the recommendations is clear, but the targets are diffuse and specific changes cannot be suggested. Because the underlying processes are different, these two types of utilization are independent of each other; research findings can result in (a) no instrumental utilization but wide conceptual utilization, or vice versa, (b) neither instrumental nor conceptual utilization, or (c) both instrumental and conceptual utilization.

5. The Rationale for the Utilization Process

Research results can be promoted and used because of the implications the results have for improved policy-making. In addition, results can be promoted and used because they can substitute for decision-making, legitimate a predetermined decision, discredit an unpopular policy, and the like. These latter rationales for utilization have been termed "symbolic" (Knorr, 1977; Pelz, 1978). A symbolic rationale is not necessarily undesirable. As Weiss (1977: 15) says about the use of social research findings for legitimation:

> It seems to me neither an unimportant nor an improper use. Only distortion deserves reproof. . . . If the issue is still in doubt, what research can do is add strength to the side that the evidence supports.

In the case of the prison legal service clinic, a decision by the director to disseminate only the positive findings would be symbolic conceptual use (i.e., designed to enlighten other policy makers, albeit only with positive enlightenment). Symbolic instrumental use also may be involved if the director intends the positive findings to cause a positive refunding decision for the program.

Knorr (1977) addressed the issue of the rationale for the utilization process in her study of 70 middle-level decision makers employed in Austrian federal and municipal government agencies. These people, who were recipients and users of social research, were questioned about the rationale for the use of social research, as well as about other aspects of the research process (see Knorr, 1977: 180 n 2). In about 23 percent of the projects discussed, a symbolic or legitimative rationale was identified as the primary reason for use. One respondent (Knorr, 1977: 172) describes this rationale well:

> There is a kind of fiction in the whole thing which we all play, that policy is becoming "scientific" through research, that arguments and results from

social science studies influence legislation. In reality this is not the case. . . . You've got the argument, then you look for somebody to prove it for you. Then you stand up and say: Study XY shows, too . . . exactly as you think things are, etc.

6. The Timing of the Utilization Process

Utilization of research results occurs in different time frames. Occasionally the time frame from production of results to the implementation of changes based on them is very short. A study of police practices in a particular department, for example, may indicate various alterations which should be made in daily routines. Once informed of these results, the police chief may institute new procedures immediately. More likely is a long-term time frame. Research results are produced and disseminated; then begins the process of identifying the best target and level, making contact with the target, arranging for consideration of the research findings, waiting for a response, arguing for and securing a commitment for action, then waiting for the action to occur. In some cases utilization requires years or decades, including dormant periods, until either the political climate or the reform trend is such that certain practices can be adopted. In the criminal justice area, the use of capital punishment offers a good example of the latter case. The longer the period of time involved in the utilization process, the more complex the process is apt to become, as main actors and issues change and as new considerations arise. The study by Emrick and Peterson (1978) on educational change supports these ideas on the relevance of the time frame.

7. The Level of the Utilization Target

By level of the target, we are referring to the organizational level of the person or persons who are potential utilizers. Dissemination-utilization efforts can be directed at any or all of these levels: the project level, the program level (i.e., a more general unit), the agency or department level, the legislative level, the executive level, or the academic level. Results from a new halfway house project, for example, can be disseminated to the project director, to the program administrator in charge of this project and several others, to the agency staff, to state or national legislators, to state or national executive officials (e.g., the Attorney General) and to criminal justice researchers or theoreticians.

Depending on the level of the utilization target, the mode and method of dissemination-utilization efforts vary. As an example, consider two potential target levels for dissemination-utilization efforts based on results of a special juvenile diversion project. If the project director is the target selected for an instrumental effort, the mode of dissemination-utilization activities could be a memo or a report focusing on the particular aspects of the project which are satisfactory and those which need improvement. The method associated with this could involve direct and ongoing discussion with the project director and project staff. If, on the other hand, the target were the U.S. Attorney General's office and the goal were instrumental utilization (i.e., the establishment of these projects across the country), the mode and method of dissemination-utilization activities would be quite different. The mode could not be a brief memo but instead would have to be a complete report, detailing the history, goals, activities, outcomes, and costs of the project. The method of dissemination-utilization efforts could not be direct, ongoing discussions but would, rather, involve limited formal and informal contacts with those near the Attorney General, via telephone, letter, and, to a much lesser degree, personal meeting.

Typically, two or more levels are involved in a dissemination-utilization effort. Consequently, dissemination-utilization activities must be tailored to each level. This may entail multiple modes and methods if the effort is to succeed at all levels. A study in the field of education by Emrick and Peterson (1978) concludes that successful utilization should involve at least two levels: the potential utilizers and those just above them in the hieararchy. In this study, Emrick and Peterson analyzed studies of five large programs designed to facilitate the dissemination and utilization of educational improvements. One of their conclusions was that school administrators, though not the target of these dissemination-utilization efforts, "occupy a crucial role in establishing change orientation, in creating incentives for participation, and in supporting implementation efforts by appropriate staff [i.e., teachers]" (1978: 91). Consequently, dissemination-utilization activities need to involve the potential utilizers as well as their superiors. As Emrick and Peterson (1978: 91) state: "Overall, utilization occurs most effectively when involved staff perceive such utilization to be in their own interests as well as in the interests of relevant leadership and authority figures."

8. The State of the Utilizers

The last factor to be considered here relates to the people who will be the targets of attempts at utilization. Although projects, units, or departments are the structural elements in undertaking implementation of research results, the actual implementers are individuals. These individuals play a central role in the utilization process. Changes in policies and procedures can be facilitated or hindered by cooperative or recalcitrant individuals who actually carry out the changes. Although their behavior can be affected by many factors, two of direct relevance in this context are their past experience with research and the reward contingencies which control their professional behaviors.

Caplan et al. (1975), in a study on the use of social science knowledge in policy decisions at the national level, documented the importance of this factor. In his discussion of the findings, Caplan (1977) lists the information-processing style of the policy maker as the most important determinant of use. He found three predominant styles: clinical (i.e., unbiased diagnosis of the problem weighed against political and social factors), academic (i.e., major attention to internal logic of policy issue), and advocacy (i.e., primary attention to political and social factors). The clinic type was the most active user of scientific information; the academic type was a moderate user; and the advocacy types was a limited user, usually only for symbolic purposes.

Caplan (1977: 187) also identified another important state or attitude of the utilizer, the ethical-scientific value:

> An important characteristic of the more frequent users of social research is a quality of mind or what might be called a "social perspective," which, put simply, involves a sensitivity to contemporary social events and a desire for social reform: they react as if what is happening in the larger society were undistinguishable from what is happening within themselves.

Traditional criminal justice utilization strategies have not been particularly relevant to the people who are potential utilizers. Police officers, for example, derive little reward from reading research reports. By contrast, police officers derive great rewards (such as certification and promotions) by learning the methods and techniques taught to them at training school. Yin (1976) proposes that this type of natural entry point into the system be used to educate officers about new practices. By doing this, important reward contingencies in police officers' professional lives facilitate learning and adoption of new policies and practices.

These eight aspects of the utilization process are important determinants of its form and direction. The factors are sometimes independent, but more often they combine with each other to produce differential consequences. The quality of the findings, the importance of the findings, and the level of the target, for example, interact in different ways, depending on the value of each factor. At the academic level, the quality of the findings must be quite high, regardless of the importance of the findings, if utilization is to occur. At the project level, importance of the findings is more likely to propel the utilization process than is the quality of the findings (which project staff may be unable to assess). The same interactive situation occurs for the other factors. The important conclusion is that the utilization process is not a simple, linear, semiautomatic event which follows the publication of a research report. Just like any other aspect of research, the utilization of research requires careful planning and constant attention to many factors under the control of the disseminator, as well as to other factors beyond his or her control. Like research, utilization can involve different methods and different behaviors, some of which are fixed by the context of the process and others of which are set at the discretion of the disseminator. The dissemination-utilization process, then, is complex and non-linear—qualities which present difficult problems in evaluating utilization.

THE EVALUATION OF UTILIZATION

In the discussion of evaluation which follows, we will focus on two types of research utilization: planned and unplanned. Primary attention will be given to planned utilization because this type of utilization has the greater chance for success. A planned research utilization effort is one in which either (a) utilization is envisioned as one of the primary goals at the outset of the research project on which the utilization effort is to be based, or (b) utilization becomes a primary goal as the research project concludes and significant results emerge which can be disseminated. In both instances, the dissemination-utilization targets are selected and appropriate strategies are planned and then implemented. Planned efforts of this sort are similar to other social action programs, where goals are established, clients are selected, and appropriate interventions are instituted to achieve the goals. Consequently, techniques used to evaluate social programs can be applied to the evaluation of research utilization.

Systematic evaluation requires a program which is consciously planned and conscientiously implemented, onto which an evaluation plan can be overlaid (Rossi et al., 1979). Even if consciously planned, a dissemination-utilization project is difficult to implement, due to the factors discussed in the previous section of this chapter. An evaluation design for such a project, therefore, must involve a careful monitoring of the dissemination process as well as an assessment of the type and extent of utilization. These evaluation components will be discussed in more detail below.

An unplanned research utilization effort is one in which utilization goals are not specifically established, dissemination targets are not carefully selected, and dissemination and utilization strategies are not systematically developed. This is the less preferred but more common type of utilization effort. It is exemplified by the research director who decides he or she has some "interesting findings," sends copies of the final research report to "a few people who might be interested," prepares a journal article and a conference presentation on the findings, then assumes that utilization somehow will occur.

Evaluating a planned dissemination-utilization project, no matter how complex and convoluted, is an easier task than evaluating an unplanned effort. This is so because the evaluation researchers cannot, in the unplanned case, use certain scientific techniques which are appropriate if the evaluation plan is developed in conjunction with the dissemination-utilization plan (e.g., using control or comparison groups; pretest, baseline measures; systematic variation of dissemination strategies). An evaluation of unplanned dissemination and utilization, particularly if conducted after the fact, precludes the use of these techniques and, so, must make use of less rigorous methods which do not permit definitive conclusions about causes and effects. Because attention to research utilization in the criminal justice area has been so limited and because many dissemination-utilization efforts are likely to be of the unplanned variety, some less rigorous evaluation methods will be presented which can be used to give a limited assessment of the effectiveness of unplanned dissemination-utilization efforts.

PLANNED DISSEMINATION-UTILIZATION

The evaluation of planned utilization can be conceptualized in the same manner as evaluation for a more conventional program. In developing an evaluation plan for a program such as a new police patrol project or an experimental pretrial release procedure, four general aspects of these programs are important for the evaluator to consider: goals, inputs, processes, and outcomes. The goals of the program address the primary and secondary ends to which the program is directed. The inputs refer to the human and physical resources required to undertake program activities. The program processes are the specific activities that operationalize the concepts of the new program; these processes are the means whereby changes are effected. Finally, there are the outcomes—the changes which actually occur due to the program processes. Outcomes include those which are intended as well as those which are unintended or unexpected.

An illustration of these four general aspects is provided by an innovative paralegal training program for prison inmates (Conner et al., 1978; Conner and Huff, 1979). The primary goals of the program were to train inmates to deliver paralegal services in the prison's legal aid clinic and, upon release, to work successfully as regular paralegals. Secondary goals included changing inmate-trainee attitudes. The inputs into the project were a group of inmate-trainees, a director of paralegal training, a group of volunteer attorney-instructors, and a set of legal materials. The processes of the project involved classroom sessions several times a week for about six months, during which the inmate-trainees were instructed in many aspects of state and federal law. In addition, trainees prepared case materials and served an apprenticeship in the prison legal aid clinic. The outcomes of the project included a significant improvement in legal knowledge among trainees but no attitude changes, and general success by the paralegals, following their release, in obtaining and keeping paralegal jobs (conclusions on this latter goal are tentative, because few trainees have been released). One unintended outcome of the project was resistance from local prison "jailhouse lawyers" (i.e., self-taught inmates who give legal advice).[2]

The four general aspects of evaluation can be applied to a dissemination-utilization project, with the eight characteristics of the utilization process discussed in the previous section constituting special contingencies which need to be considered in defining the model for the case of research utilization. Each aspect has particular relevance to one of the four main components of evaluation. In Figure 26.1, the conceptual model of evaluation is diagrammed, and each of the eight aspects of the utilization process is listed under one of the four evaluation components. In the sections below, the four evaluation components will be applied to the research utilization case, with particular attention to the associated subset of characteristics of the utilization process.

Goals

None of the aspects of the utilization process as it usually occurs relates to the first component of evaluation. In view of this fact, it is not surprising that the amount of research utilization in policy-making has been limited, and that the amount of research on utilization has also been insignificant. When goals are undefined or ill-defined, it is impossible to know what constitutes research utilization. Without knowing the goals of a research utilization effort, the person attempting to effect utilization or the person attempting to evaluate that attempt cannot define the relevant inputs, processes, and outcomes.

To understand the futility of the evaluation effort in this situation, consider this analogy. Someone tells us that he wants to travel. He does not know where he wants to go, how he will get there, or when he will depart or arrive; he simply wants to "travel." Given this limited definition of his goal, we have no way of assessing whether or not he has traveled. Does "travel" mean leaving town or does a walk across the street (or the room) constitute travel? We have no way of knowing, except to let the traveler himself decide when he has accomplished his goal. Unfortunately, many attempts at utilization are as ill-defined as this traveler's "trip." Those hoping for research utilization rarely consider questions such as: How will the results be disseminated? How will we know if the dissemination has been successful? What do we want potential utilizers to do with our results? Who will direct the potential utilizers in their efforts? What criteria will be used to assess the degree of utilization?

To evaluate utilization we need to work from the outset alongside those who are promoting utilization. Consider the case of a new juvenile diversion program. If dissemination and utilization of results are key goals of the program, utilization-planning ought to begin as the program begins, not as the program nears completion. The reason for this is that we need to know who will be the primary target of the utilization efforts, and any secondary targets as well. If the results of the juvenile diversion program are to be disseminated to police officers, then several officers or their representatives need to be consulted at the outset of the program (1) to be sure that the new diversion procedure, if successful, could be a realistic new option for the officers, and (2) if so, to learn what data would be

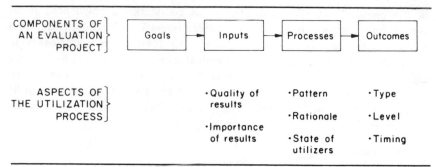

Figure 26.1: A Conceptual Model of an Evaluation Project Related to Aspects of the Research Utilization Process

required to convince officers to use the new practice. Once the targets of the utilization effort are determined, then the utilization can be formulated.

Goal-setting often is a difficult step. This is particularly true for a utilization program because of the interdependence of the utilization program and the research program. It is advisable to establish goals for the utilization program at the outset of the research program, long before the utilization program begins in earnest. The initial utilization goals should be thought of as tentative goals, however, which can be regularly reevaluated and updated as the research program unfolds. In the juvenile diversion program, for example, dissemination of results to local police officers may be the initial primary utilization goal. In the course of the research, however, this utilization goal could change to the dissemination of results to state legislators and policy makers, who come to be viewed as more appropriate change agents.

Changes in utilization goals should be recorded and documented, since these changes will later become one source of data to evaluate utilization. These changes may provide an instructive and fascinating log of the ways in which the central issues and questions change over the course of study. The process of doing social research in the criminal justice area or any other human service area usually affects the way the topic or question is viewed. Typically, we begin with one question of particular relevance to one group of policy makers or practitioners, then reformulate or refine the question; in the process, the most relevant group of policy makers or practitioners may change. In other instances, we maintain our original question but uncover answers which suggest that future changes be directed at groups we had not thought of at the outset, as in the case above, concerning state legislators and policy makers.

In sum, preliminary planning for research utilization (i.e., the selection of the targets for the utilization program and the description of the kind of results which these targets will require) needs to be undertaken, ideally, at the outset of the research program, or near the conclusion of the research program but prior to any dissemination. Such planning should be as detailed as possible but should not be viewed as immutable. It serves as an initial focus for utilization and a standard against which to assess changes in utilization goals.

Inputs

Once the research results are complete, the utilization program can begin. The general goals of the utilization program will have been formulated (and perhaps revised during the course of the research), so attention now can shift to the program inputs. In a utilization effort, the primary inputs are the research findings. The quality and importance of the findings need to be assessed before dissemination and utilization begin. The researcher should consider first whether the data have sufficiently high validity and reliability to warrant a utilization effort. Following his or her own assessment, the researcher should consult several other researchers to verify that conclusion. In some cases, a replication in a similar setting may be necessary to assure high validity and reliability.

If the results are of high quality, then the question of importance should be addressed. Do these results have socially significant implications for changes in current policies and practices? Do the recommendations which follow from the data make clear, unambiguous statements and suggestions which policy makers and practitioners can understand? The answers to these questions should be positive if a dissemination-utilization program is to be undertaken; however, the degree to which these conditions need to be met will depend on the changes which are to be advocated. If major changes are suggested, practitioners and policy makers will demand findings of great importance before they will be willing to institute significant changes.

Outsiders should be involved in the assessment of the importance of the findings. Not only should other researchers make these ratings, but potential utilizers also should rate the degree of importance. There are two reasons for this: These outside judgments will serve as reliability checks on the researcher's own assessments and, if positive, as endorsements of the findings to be used in the dissemination-utilization effort.

The research findings are the most important input in a utilization effort. There are, however, other inputs which may exist: the materials to be disseminated and the people who will direct the utilization program. The materials should be assessed for their appeal and clarity and their appropriateness for the targets selected. Consider a dissemination-utilization program on a successful juvenile diversion project directed at local police chiefs. If the program relies on the dissemination of copies of the complete final research report, there probably will be little if any utilization, not because the results are unconvincing, but because the form of presentation was inappropriate. Instead, a brief, attractively prepared research summary, highlighting findings and clearly specifying recommendations and actions, would be more appropriate and more effective (Cohen, 1977). Pilot tests of the materials with potential utilizers could provide instructive assessments of clarity, appeal, and appropriateness (made, for example, on seven-point scales, anchored with very positive ratings at one end and very negative ratings at the other).

There is one additional input into some dissemination-utilization efforts: the people who will direct and implement the effort. The utilization evaluator should verify that these people have the skills and temperament to conduct the effort. This is an important point, but one that is often ignored. The skills required of a good dissemination-utilization project director probably are closer to those of a public relations expert than those of a research scientist. Many researchers feel uncomfortable promoting their findings and so should not take a central role in a dissemination-utilization effort beyond the type of "promotion" that occurs at professional meetings. The utilization evaluator's assessment of the appropriateness of the staff and their roles need not be extensive; a review of staff resumes and functions, plus some interviews focusing on staff assessments of their own abilities, probably would provide sufficient evidence to assess this aspect of the dissemination-utilization program.

Processes

This third component of evaluation is particularly important for an assessment of utilization efforts. Because research on utilization is at an elementary stage, we need to know much more about the many paths that lead to utilization. A primary task, then, in evaluating research utilization is to monitor and document the course of dissemination and utilization efforts. In any social reform effort, there are many differences between what is planned and what is actually implemented (see Geis, 1975, for a discussion focused on the criminal justice area). In some cases, the actual program is so different from the planned program that an evaluation which ignores the implementation process will result in misleading conclusions. For this reason, evaluation researchers have stressed the importance of process-monitoring to identify the components of a program as it actually is delivered (e.g., Rossi et al., 1979). In the criminal justice area, Lewis and Greene (1978) have argued for a variation of process-monitoring, which they call "implementation evaluation," and Krisberg, in Chapter 8 of this volume, discusses the importance of process evaluation in crime and delinquency programs.

The type of process-monitoring which should occur will vary, depending on the kind of dissemination-utilization program. Frequently, the distribution of the summary report of research findings is the extent of a dissemination-utilization program. In this case, a record should be kept of who received the report, why they received it (i.e., was it requested or was it sent automatically?), and what their reactions and subsequent actions were. The best approach to assessing reactions and actions would be to sample a representative group of those who received the report, then obtain their opinions about the findings and their judgments of the degree of subsequent utilization and the reason for it. Supplementary interviews with a sample of those who indicate some degree of utilization would be useful to document thoroughly the extent and type of use. In addition, interviews with a sample of nonutilizers would be needed to differentiate the amount of nonuse due to doubt and lack of acceptance of the research results, acceptance of the results but inability to convince others, acceptance by all parties but lack of funds, and so on. Reasons for nonuse may be more instructive than those for use. A less satisfactory way to obtain this information would be to enclose a questionnaire with the report and ask that it be completed and returned. Because of the significant problems of self-selection, this latter approach is not recommended.

The content of the interview or questionnaire should include assessments of those aspects of the utilization process which are particularly relevant to this stage of the utilization project (see Figure 26.1): the pattern and rationale, both overt and covert, for the process, and the state of the utilizers. These aspects will vary greatly and will interact in different ways. Structured questions which tap these aspects could be developed following a review of relevant utilization literature (e.g., Caplan et al., 1975; Weiss, 1979). This type of question, however, would need to be supplemented by open-ended questions or, preferably, loosely structured interviews which permit the researcher to uncover unexpected patterns, infer covert rationales, understand the idiosyncratic organizational arrangement of the utilizer unit, and identify the personal state and situation of people in the unit.

Other strategies may be employed in addition to or in place of the dissemination of a final summary report. Meetings of relevant policy makers, practitioners, legislators, academics, or other groups may be convened. The utilization evaluator would need to attend these meetings, interview participants, then follow up with participants to track the patterns of use and nonuse and to explore the reasons for these patterns. Although not an easy task, this type of intensive analysis will be useful not only to those interested in the course of the utilization for particular criminal justice findings, but also to those interested generally in the evaluation of research utilization. Out of these studies could come preliminary models of the utilization process which could be empirically tested.

Outcomes

Now we come to the central question of the evaluation process: Were the results, in fact, utilized? To answer this question, the evaluator must assess the type, level, and timing of the utilization process. Has instrumental or conceptual usage occurred, or have both occurred? The answer to this question will be determined in part by analyzing who has used the information (i.e., the level of utilization) and how it was used. These tasks are complicated by the various time frames, modes, and methods which can characterize dissemination-utilization activities at different levels.

The outcomes of a dissemination-utilization program can be assessed in two primary ways: utilizing an actual-targets focus or a potential-targets focus. The "actual-targets" approach involves questioning (via interviews or questionnaires) people who have been the targets of utilization efforts (e.g., recipients of a research report, participants in a dissemination workshop). LEAA's National Institute of Law Enforcement and Criminal Justice (NILECJ) has used this approach in some of its attempts to disseminate criminal justice knowledge (Beck, 1978). NILECJ, acknowledging that utilization does not occur automatically, has instituted a series of utilization packages to encourage use of criminal justice research. These packages include the exemplary projects program, the model project program, the Executive Training Program, and several others. Some of these packages have an evaluation component (e.g., a tear-out questionnaire at the back of an exemplary project description booklet) which requests feedback from utilization targets.

One common problem with this "actual-targets" approach to outcome evaluation of dissemination-utilization programs is the self-selection of respondents which typically is involved. Because of this, the representativeness of the outcome findings cannot be known. The NILECJ tear-out questionnaires have this problem. This shortcoming can be alleviated by contacting a representative sample of utilization targets for interviews or questionnaire responses, rather than allowing respondents to select themselves.

There is an additional problem with the "actual-targets" outcome evaluation focus which is not as easily solved: What if the utilization targets were the wrong targets? The solution to this problem requires a different approach: the "potential-targets" focus. In this case, the evaluation researcher first determines the individuals and groups who are most relevant for utilization of the findings. Then, these individuals and groups are contacted to learn whether they received the summary report, for example, or participated in the dissemination workshop and, if so, what type and degree of utilization occurred. (See Berg et al., 1978, for an example of this approach in a study of the utilization of technology assessment reports.) A more ambitious solution would be to use representative samples from the outset to test experimentally the outcome of a dissemination-utilization program. Some groups would be selected randomly as utilization targets; others would be selected randomly as controls or (more appropriately in this case) as utilization targets for a different type of dissemination-utilization approach. In this way, the relative effectiveness of two approaches could be assessed.

A thorough evaluation of a research dissemination-utilization program will involve descriptions and assessments of goals, inputs, processes, and outcomes, as well as a discussion and analysis of the interrelationships among these four components. It might be asked why a utilization evaluator is required to undertake all of these difficult, time-consuming, costly tasks. Can we not simply wait for some reasonable amount of time, then check all potential utilizer units for implementation? There are several problems with this approach. First, we have no guides to use in setting a "reasonable" time limit. Second, recommendations will rarely, if ever, be instituted just as designed. If the outcomes to be effected are minor ones, we may not be able to detect any effects if we have not followed the process of adoption and "translation" of the recommendations to fit the local situation. If the outcomes are major ones, we have a different problem with a post hoc assessment. Our evaluation of the degree of utilization is likely to be very conservative and could miss the many potential utilizer units which technically fail to adopt the new practice but, in the course of considering it, make many minor but important adjustments in their practices. This post hoc approach is analogous to the case of unplanned dissemination-utilization, which will be considered next.

UNPLANNED DISSEMINATION-UTILIZATION

In evaluating an unplanned effort, the utilization researcher still must assess goals, inputs, processes, and outcomes. This task is not simple in the case of a planned dissemination-utilization program and, for an unplanned effort, which typically is completed by the time the evaluator enters the scene, the task becomes even more difficult. Because goals never were explicitly formulated, it is difficult or impossible to specify the aim of the dissemination. Inputs can be specified retrospectively, but there will be the problem of inaccurate and distorted reporting. Processes are particularly difficult to identify accurately, because reports of the process will be colored by the type of utilization which subsequently occurred. Finally, major outcomes can be tracked but minor ones will be more difficult to identify and assess, particularly instances of nonutilization or partial utilization.

In the sections which follow, suggestions will be given for the "trapped utilization evaluator" (see Campbell, 1969) who finds him- or herself confronted with the task of assessing the degree of utilization in a post hoc manner. The approach becomes a more qualitative one (Patton, 1978) than that for a planned effort, with some methods drawn from quasi-experimental and goal-free evaluation techniques (Cook and Campbell, 1979; Scriven, 1974). It should be emphasized, however, that evaluations of unplanned efforts will result, at best, in qualified, tentative assessments. Evaluations of planned efforts can be more accurate, detailed, and conclusive because the utilization researcher can follow the planning, implementation, and outcomes of a dissemination-utilization effort while these events are occurring.

Goals

Because of the nature of an unplanned effort, statements of dissemination-utilization goals will be nonexistent or so general as to be useless as evaluation guides. Consider, for example, this hypothetical statement from the research proposal for a halfway house for released inmates: "Our final goal will be to disseminate the findings from this research to interested practitioners and researchers in the criminal justice area." This type of statement, which probably could be found in many criminal justice research proposals, provides no guidance to the utilization evaluator.

A better approach in this instance would be to adopt, in part, the attitude of a goal-free evaluator (Scriven, 1974). That is, the evaluator observes what has and has not occurred and, from this, deduces the goals and objectives. If, for instance, summary reports on a study of halfway houses were received by many state correctional officials but by few judges, the utilization evaluator could infer that certain officials rather than others were explicitly or implicitly the primary dissemination targets. The evaluator should be cautious in drawing these kinds of conclusions, however. Perhaps the state correctional officials received the report and the judges did not, because the former officials routinely receive research summaries from this particular funder, whereas the latter do not. This findings says more about the funder's general dissemination-utilization goals than about the goals for this particular dissemination-utilization effort.

To supplement a goal-free approach, the evaluator could set out specific goals which a particular dissemination-utilization program, in his or her opinion, should have had. These goals would be developed after an extensive study of the topic or the area to learn about the relevant targets and the important issues. The goals derived in this way might or might not correspond to those in official documents and those revealed by a goal-free analysis; the extent of overlap would provide some convergent validation of the accuracy of the evaluator's goal statement.

Inputs

The major tangible inputs into a dissemination-utilization effort usually are identifiable after the effort is completed. Summary reports, workshops, and conferences are capable of being documented. The challenging task is identifying the more minor and less tangible inputs (e.g., the quality of presentations at the workshop, the types of interactions at the conference).

Repeated interviews with recipients and participants is one method which can be used to uncover some of these latter inputs. A conference on diversion research sponsored by NILECJ, for example, will have an official program which the utilization researcher can obtain. With luck, copies of papers and perhaps tapes of presentations will be available. The tenor of the conference, however, will have to be reconstructed and verified by participants. This method will not necessarily provide a complete listing of relevant inputs, so, again, the utilization evaluator will have to use caution in making inferences.

Processes

This component of unplanned dissemination-utilization efforts is particularly difficult to assess. Process is dynamic and, therefore, is best observed while it occurs. Individual reconstructions, while potentially useful, are subject to serious problems of distortion and bias. Because reactions to process are subjective, it will be virtually impossible for the utilization researcher to verify individual reports.

Some information on process, however limited, is better than none at all. At least in broad outline, participant reports will give some indication of the kinds of events which occurred. In soliciting these reports, the utilization evaluator should ask general questions and let the respondents structure the answers. This more open-ended format will increase the chance that important aspects of the process will be identified.

Outcomes

The evaluation of the effectiveness of any type of program, if conducted after the program is completed, cannot provide definitive cause-and-effect conclusions. Rival explanations as to the cause of observed effects (i.e., threats to internal validity; see Cook and Campbell, 1979) cannot easily be ruled out. If, for instance, a city has instituted a juvenile diversion program similar to one promoted as an exemplary project, we cannot be sure of the main factor which caused the new program to be initiated (e.g., the disseminated material, a new police chief, a panel of juvenile court judges, the efforts of a reformer). In evaluating a *planned* effort, the researcher follows the process closely as it occurs and so is in a better position to differentiate primary and secondary causal factors. In addition, different dissemination-utilization strategies can sometimes be experimentally tested, permitting more definitive causal statements.

Unplanned efforts do not provide these opportunities. What the researcher can do is to find approximations to these opportunities. Reports of the rationale, type, timing, and pattern of utilizations provided by people in utilizer units will approximate the firsthand researcher observations. Several reports will be necessary for each utilization case, however, to provide reliability checks on the information. Comparisons may even be possible between similar units which did or did not utilize the research. Actual and potential targets could be contacted to determine the type and extent of utilization. Together, these sources of information will provide some evidence, albeit limited, on the outcomes of the unplanned effort.

CONCLUSION

This review of approaches for assessing planned and unplanned dissemination-utilization efforts demonstrates that meaningful, conclusive evaluation is not an easy undertaking. Even if the utilization package can be easily described (e.g., as a 25-page "executive summary" research report), the dissemination-utilization goals, inputs, processes, and outcomes associated with this package can be complex. As many evaluation researchers have documented for a variety of social reform program evaluations (and utilization can be considered a special subset of these reform programs), systematic evaluation requires creativity and ingenuity for meaningful, successful implementation.

Why, it might be asked, should we devote all this effort to so complex a task? There are five potential benefits which can be cited to justify the effort and expense required to evaluate research utilization. First, utilization efforts, like other social reform efforts, must be subjected to critical review. If the effectiveness of these activities cannot be demonstrated, support for them from agencies like LEAA will cease. Second, the evaluation of research utilization will cause increased recognition by researchers and policy makers of the fact that dissemination-utilization is an important activity in its own right, not a perfunctory last step in a research project.

A third benefit of utilization evaluation, related to the second, is the increased attention to utilization goals and objectives which will occur, with consequent improvement in the selection of appropriate targets and relevant dissemination procedures. Fourth, attempts to evaluate utilization, even if less than successful, will provide more data on the processes which appear to facilitate and hinder research utilization in the criminal justice area and in other areas as well. These data will aid in developing conceptual models of the utilization process which can be subjected to empirical testing. Finally, the evaluation of research utilization will increase the amount of interchange between researchers and practitioners by providing a means of communicating ideas and concerns via a neutral party. If these two groups are very separate communities, as some have argued (Caplan, 1979), the utilization evaluator may serve an important linking function and help to bridge, if not close, the gap between research and subsequent practice.

NOTES

1. This fact is also noted in a request for proposal, from LEAA's National Institute of Law Enforcement and Criminal Justice, for a study of knowledge utilization in criminal justice (Beck, 1978).

2. The curious reader will be pleased to learn that there was a happy ending to the dispute with the jailhouse lawyers. An agreement was reached whereby certain jailhouse lawyers became paralegal instructors and certain potential clients of the prison legal clinic were referred to jailhouse lawyers.

REFERENCES

Argyris, C. (1965) *Organization and Innovation*. Homewood, IL: Irwin.

Beck, M. A. (1978) "Effecting the Research to Action Linkage: The Research Utilization Program of NILECJ." Washington, DC: National Institute of Law Enforcement and Criminal Justice.

Bennis, W. G., K. D. Benne, R. Chin, and K. E. Corey [eds.] (1976) *The Planning of Change*. New York: Holt, Rinehart & Winston.

Berg, M. R., J. L. Brudney, T. D. Fuller, D. N. Michael, and B. K. Roth (1978) *Factors Affecting the Utilization of Technology Assessment Studies in Public Policy-Making*. Ann Arbor: University of Michigan Center for Research on Utilization of Scientific Knowledge.

Bernstein, I. and H. E. Freeman (1975) *Academic and Entrepreneurial Research: Consequences of Diversity in Federal Evaluation Studies*. New York: Russell Sage.

Campbell, D. T. (1969) "Reforms as Experiments." *American Psychologist* 24: 409-429.

Caplan, N., A. Morrison, and R. J. Stambaugh (1975) *The Use of Social Science Knowledge in Policy Decisions at the National Level*. Ann Arbor: University of Michigan Center for Research on Utilization of Scientific Knowledge.

Caplan, N. (1979) "The Two-Communities Theory and Knowledge Utilization." *American Behavioral Scientists* 22: 459-470.

——— (1977) "A Minimum Set of Conditions Necessary for the Utilization of Social Science Knowledge in Policy Formulation at the National Level," pp. 183-197 in C. H. Weiss (ed.) *Using Social Research in Public Policy Making*. Lexington, MA: D. C. Heath.

Chester, M. and M. Flanders (1967) "Resistance to Research and Research Utilization: The Death and Life of a Feedback Attempt." *Journal of Applied Behavioral Science* 3: 469-487.

Coe, R. M. and E. A. Bernhill (1967) "Social Dimensions of Failure in Innovation." *Human Organization* 26: 149-156.

Cohen, L. H. (1977) "Factors Affecting the Utilization of Mental Health Evaluation Research Findings." *Professional Psychology* 8: 526-534.

Conner, R. F. and C. R. Huff (1979) *Attorneys as Activists: Evaluating the American Bar Association's BASICS Program*. Beverly Hills, CA: Sage Publications.

Conner, R. F., J. Emshoff, and W. Davidson (1978) *Legal Aid and Legal Education for Prisoners: An Evaluation of the State Bar of Michigan's Prison Project*. Chicago: American Bar Association.

Cook, T. D. and D. T. Campbell (1979) *Quasi-Experimentation: Design and Analysis Issues for Field Settings*. Skokie, IL: Rand McNally.

Deitchman, S. (1976) *The Best-Laid Schemes: A Tale of Social Research and Bureaucracy.* Cambridge, MA: MIT Press.

Emrick, J. A. and S. M. Peterson (1978). A Synthesis of Findings Across Five Recent Studies in Educational Dissemination and Change. San Francisco: Far West Laboratory.

Davis, H. E. and S. Salasin (1975) "The Utilization of Evaluation," pp. 621-666 in E. L. Struening and M. Guttentag (eds.) *Handbook of Evaluation Research, Volume 1.* Beverly Hills, CA: Sage Publications.

Fairweather, G. W. (1967) *Methods for Experimental Social Innovation.* New York: John Wiley.

――― D. H. Sanders, and L. G. Tornatzky (1974) *Creating Change in Mental Health Organizations.* Elmsford, NY: Pergamon.

Geis, G. (1975) "Program Descriptions in Criminal Justice Evaluations," pp. 87-96 in E. Viano (ed.) *Criminal Justice Research.* Lexington, MA: D. C. Heath.

Glaser, E. M. and S. Taylor (1973) "Factors Influencing the Success of Applied Research." *American Psychologist* 28: 140-146.

Goodwin, L. (1975) *Can Social Science Help Resolve National Problems?* New York: Free Press.

Hargrove, E. C. (1975) "The Missing Link: The Study of the Implementation of Social Policy." Washington, DC: Urban Institute.

Havelock, R. G. (1976) "Research on Utilization of Knowledge," in M. Kochen (ed.) *Information for Action: Reorganizing Knowledge for Wisdom.* New York: Academic.

――― (1969) *Planning for Innovation Through Dissemination and Utilization of Knowledge.* Ann Arbor: University of Michigan Center for Research on Utilization of Scientific Knowledge.

Horsley, J. A., J. Crane, and J. D. Bingle (1978) "Research Utilization as an Organizational Process." *Journal of Nursing Administration* 8: 4-6.

Human Interaction Research Institute and National Institute of Mental Health (1976) Putting Knowledge to Use: A Distillation of the Literature Regarding Knowledge Transfer and Change. Los Angeles: Human Interaction Research Institute.

Klein, M. W. (1979) "Deinstitutionalization and Diversion of Juvenile Offenders: A Litany of Impediments," in N. Morris and M. Tonry (eds.) *Crime and Justice—1979.* Chicago: University of Chicago Press.

Knorr, K. D. (1977) "Policymakers' Use of Social Science Knowledge: Symbolic or Instrumental?" pp. 165-182 in C. H. Weiss (ed.) *Using Social Research in Public Policy Making.* Lexington, MA: D. C. Heath.

Lewis, R. G. and J. R. Greene (1978) "Implementation Evaluation: A Future Direction in Project Evaluation." *Journal of Criminal Justice* 6: 167-176.

National Academy of Sciences (1968) *The Behavioral Sciences and the Federal Government.* Washington, DC: Government Printing Office.

Patton, M. Q. (1978) *Utilization-Focused Evaluation.* Beverly Hills, CA: Sage Publications.

――― P. S. Grimes, K. M. Guthrie, N. J. Brennan, B. D. French, and D. A. Blyth (1977) "In Search of Impact: An Analysis of the Utilization of Federal Health Evaluation Research." pp. 141-163 in C. H. Weiss (ed.) *Using Social Research in Public Policy Making.* Lexington, MA: D. C. Heath.

Pelz, D. C. (1978) "Some Expanded Perspectives on Use of Social Science in Public Policy." pp. 346-359 in J. M. Yinger and S. J. Cutler (eds.) *Major Social Issues: A Multidisciplinary View.* New York: Free Press.

Rich, R. F. (1977) "Uses of Social Science Information by Federal Bureaucrats: Knowledge for Action Versus Knowledge for Understanding." pp. 199-211 in C. H. Weiss (ed.) *Using Social Research in Public Policy Making.* Lexington, MA: D. C. Heath.

Rossi, P. H., H. E. Freeman, and S. R. Wright (1979) *Evaluation: A Systematic Approach.* Beverly Hills, CA: Sage Publications.

Scriven, N. (1974) "Evaluation Perspectives and Procedures." pp. 1-93 in W. J. Popham (ed.) *Evaluation in Education.* Berkeley, CA: McCutchan.

Social Science Research Council (1969) *The Behavioral and Social Sciences: Outlook and Need.* Englewood Cliffs, NJ: Prentice-Hall.

Special Commission on the Social Sciences, National Science Foundation (1968) *Knowledge into Action: Improving the Nation's Use of the Social Sciences.* Washington, DC: Government Printing Office.

United States House of Representatives, Committee on Governmental Operations (1967) *The Use of Social Research in Federal Domestic Programs.* Washington, DC: Government Printing Office.

Weeks, E. C. (1979) "Factors Affecting the Utilization of Evaluation Findings in Administrative Decision-Making." Ph.D. dissertation, University of California, Irvine.

Weiss, C. H. [ed.] (1977) *Using Social Research in Public Policy Making.* Lexington, MA: D. C. Heath.

——— (1972) "Evaluating Educational and Social Action Programs: A Treeful of Owls." pp. 3-27 in C. H. Weiss (ed.) *Evaluating Action Programs.* Boston: Allyn & Bacon.

——— and M. J. Bucuvalas (1977) "The Challenge of Social Research to Decision Making." pp. 213-233 in C. H. Weiss (ed.) *Using Social Research in Public Policy Making.* Lexington, MA: D. C. Heath.

Weiss, J. A. (1979) "Access to Influence: Some Effects of Policy Sector on the Use of Social Science." *American Behavioral Scientist* 22: 437-458.

Wholey, J. S., J. W. Scanlon, H. G. Duffy, J. S. Fikumoto, and L. M. Vogt (1971) *Federal Evaluation Policy.* Washington, DC: Urban Institute.

Yin, R. K. (1976) *R & D Utilization by Local Services: Problems and Proposals for Further Research.* Santa Monica, CA: Rand Corporation.

ABOUT THE AUTHORS AND EDITORS

MALCOLM W. KLEIN is Chairman of the Sociology Department at the University of Southern California, where he also teaches courses in social psychology, group dynamics, role analysis, delinquency, and criminology. In 1972 he initiated the establishment of the Social Science Research Institute at USC, and he continues as a Senior Research Associate there. In addition to various articles in professional journals, he is the author or editor of *Juvenile Gangs in Context* (1967), *Street Gangs and Street Workers* (1971), *Back on the Streets: The Diversion of Juvenile Offenders* (1975, with Robert M. Carter), and *The Juvenile Justice System* (1976). He has served on technical advisory committees for almost a dozen major evaluation projects, has directed evaluation and basic research projects dealing with juvenile gangs, and has served on proposal review panels for the National Institute of Mental Health and the National Institute of Law Enforcement and Criminal Justice. From 1969 on, his research has centered around comprehensive criminal justice planning, especially in the juvenile area, the diversion of juveniles from the justice system, evaluation of deinstitutionalization programs, and assessment of legislative impacts.

KATHERINE S. TEILMANN is a native southern Californian, born in Burbank, California, in 1943. Her early career was in long-range planning and advertising in the oil tool industry. Following a decision to make a substantial career change, she received a Ph.D. in sociology from the University of Southern California. Between 1974 and 1980 Dr. Teilmann played central roles in five criminal justice evaluation projects of local, state, and national scope, and has consulted on others. These projects involved data collection and interviewing in all levels of the system, including police, probation, courts, district attorneys, public defenders, prisons, county camps, and juvenile halls. Her most recent involvement is as Principal Investigator and Project Director for a major study of juvenile court reform in California and its impact on the justice system.

MICHAEL BENSON is a graduate student in sociology at the University of Illinois, Urbana-Champaign. He is currently doing dissertation research in Chicago on white-collar offenders in the federal judicial system.

RICHARD A. BERK is Professor of Sociology at the University of California. He has published widely in the fields of evaluation research methods and, more generally, criminal justice. Some of his more relevant works include *A Measure of Justice* (Academic Press, 1977), *Prison Reform and State Elites* (Ballinger Press, 1977) and *Crime as Play: Delinquency in a Middle Class Suburb* (Ballinger Press, 1979).

THOMAS G. BLOMBERG is Associate Professor of Criminology at Florida State University. His research interests include the history of U.S. social control, the evaluation of criminal justice reforms, and organizational theory and criminal justice decision-making. He is author of *Social Control and the Proliferation of Juvenile Court Services* (1978), *Images of Crime and Strategies of Control: Past, Present, and Future* (forthcoming), and coeditor of *Courts and Diversion: Policy and Operations Studies* (1979).

ALFRED BLUMSTEIN is J. Erik Jonsson Professor of Urban Systems and Operations Research and the Director of the Urban Systems Institute in the School of Urban and Public Affairs of Carnegie-Mellon University. He has had extensive experience in research on the criminal justice system. He served the President's Commission on Law Enforcement and Administration of Justice as Director of its Task Force on Science and Technology, and he is currently on the Advisory Committee of the National Institute of Law Enforcement and Criminal Justice. He also served as Chairman of the Panel on Research on Deterrent and Incapacitative Effects of the National Academy of Sciences. He is currently Chairman of the Pennsylvania Commission on Crime and Delinquency. He received the degrees of Bachelor of Engineering Physics and the Ph.D. in operations research from Cornell University, and he served as President of the Operations Research Society of America in 1977-1978.

PAUL BURSTEIN has taught at Yale University in the Department of Sociology. His major interests are in political sociology, social stratification, and social policy. His publications include "Equal Employment Opportunity Legislation and the Incomes of Women and Nonwhites" in the June 1979 issue of *American Sociological Review,* and he is now completing a book on the causes and consequences of the passage of equal employment opportunity legislation.

ROBERT B. COATES is Assistant Professor in the School of Social Service Administration at the University of Chicago. From 1971 to 1978 he was engaged in research and publication on the Massachusetts youth correctional system. He earned his doctorate in sociology and taught community-based corrections at the University of Maryland.

ROSS F. CONNER is Associate Professor in the Program in Social Ecology and

Research Psychologist in the Public Policy Research Organization, both at the University of California, Irvine. He received his bachelor's degree from the Johns Hopkins University, and his master's and doctoral degrees in social psychology from Northwestern University. He is the coauthor of *Sesame Street Revisited* and *Attorneys as Activists: Evaluating the American Bar Association's BASICS Program,* and the author of a number of papers on evaluation research. His current work focuses on the ethics of using control group research designs in evaluation projects, participants' reactions to randomization in evaluation research programs, and the evaluation of research utilization.

WARD EDWARDS is Professor of Psychology and of Industrial and Systems Engineering and Director of the Social Science Research Institute at the University of Southern California. A psychologist by training, his personal research interests are mostly concerned with the methods and applications of decision analysis and with behavioral decision theory. He helped introduce Bayesian ideas into psychological research, primarily from the perspective that sees Bayes's Theorem as a model of human inference processes. His current research is concerned with the characteristics of multiattribute utility models, with elicitation methods appropriate to their use, and with their application to social program evaluations. His research has always attempted to blend abstractions with applications; most of it is set in or relevant to solution of some real-world decision problem.

DELBERT S. ELLIOTT is Director of the Behavioral Research Institute and Professor of Sociology at the University of Colorado in Boulder, Colorado. He is the senior author of *Delinquency and Dropout* (D. C. Heath, 1974), the coauthor of *The Social Psychology of Runaways* (D. C. Heath, 1978), and has contributed numerous articles to professional journals and books. He was the principal investigator for the national evaluation of delinquency prevention programs funded by the Office of Youth Development (under HEW) in 1973 and 1974; the Project Director for the national evaluation of the Law Enforcement Assistance Administration's diversion programs, 1977-1980; and currently is the principal investigator on the National Youth Panel, an eight-year longitudinal study funded by the National Institute of Mental Health.

LaMAR T. EMPEY, Professor of Sociology at the University of Southern California, was formerly Chairman of the Sociology Department and Director of the Youth Studies Center at USC. His chapter on Field Experimentation in Criminal Justice is the result of over a decade of experience in the conduct of *The Silverlake Experiment* (1971, with Steven G. Lubeck) and *The Provo Experiment* (1972, with Maynard L. Erickson). Among his other published works are: *Explaining Delinquency* (1971, with Steven G. Lubeck), *American Delinquency: Its Meaning and Construction* (1978), *Juvenile Justice: The Pro-*

gressive Legacy and Current Reforms (as editor, 1979), *The Future of Childhood and Juvenile Justice* (as editor, 1980).

GILBERT GEIS is a professor with the Program in Social Ecology at the University of California, Irvine. He has held visiting appointments at the Harvard Law School, the Institute of Criminology of Cambridge University, the School of Criminal Justice at the State University of New York, Albany, and the Sydney Law School in Australia. His work is largely in the areas of white-collar crime, victimless crime, and forcible rape.

DON C. GIBBONS is Professor of Sociology and Urban Studies at Portland State University. He has written widely in criminology and criminal justice. He has authored or coauthored seven books dealing with criminology, juvenile delinquency, correctional treatment, and criminal justice planning. His most recent book is *The Criminological Enterprise.*

DANIEL GLASER is Professor of Sociology at the University of Southern California and President of the American Society of Criminology, as well as a past chairman of the criminology sections of the American Sociological Association and the Society for the Study of Social Problems. He is the author of well over a hundred publications, including *Crime in Our Changing Society* (1978) and *The Effectiveness of a Prison and Parole System* (1964, 1969).

DON M. GOTTFREDSON is Dean of the School of Criminal Justice at Rutgers University. He received his M.A. and Ph.D. degrees in psychology from the Claremont Graduate School, has taught psychology at the California State Universities at Fresno and Sacramento and the University of Hawaii, and has worked as a Supervising Correctional Counselor in the California Department of Corrections, where he later helped to establish the Research Division of that agency. Since 1976 he has been Vice President of the American Society of Criminology, and he is a member of numerous law enforcement and justice organizations, including the Advisory Council of the National Institute of Law Enforcement and Criminal Justice, the National Center for Juvenile Justice, and several committees and task forces on criminal and juvenile justice. He has been the executive editor of the *Journal of Research in Crime and Delinquency,* editorial adviser for various other professional journals, and author or coauthor of seventy-six papers, articles, reports, monographs, and books. His most recent work includes *Decision-Making in the Criminal Justice System,* and, with others, *Classification for Parole Decision Policy, Probation on Trial, Sentencing Guidelines: Structuring Judicial Discretion,* and *Guidelines for Parole and Sentencing: A Policy Control Method.*

MICHAEL R. GOTTFREDSON teaches in the School of Criminal Justice at the State University of New York at Albany. Formerly he was the Director of the Criminal Justice Research Center in Albany, New York. He has coauthored (with Michael Hindelang and James Garofalo) *Victims of Personal Crime: An Empirical Foundation for a Theory of Personal Victimization* (Cambridge, MA: Ballinger, 1978) and is coeditor of the annual *Sourcebook of Criminal Justice Statistics* (Washington, DC: Government Printing Office). He has been engaged in research projects involving victimization surveys, parole decision-making, and pretrial release decision-making. His present research project is a feasibility study of bail decision guidelines. Currently he is an Associate Editor of the *Journal of Research in Crime and Delinquency.*

GLORIA A. GRIZZLE is Associate Professor of Public Administration at Florida State University. She does research and teaching in evaluation, budgeting, and policy development and implementation. Her evaluation research includes experimental, quasi-experimental, and cost-effectiveness designs applied to drug-abuse prevention and law enforcement programs. She is currently working on performance measurement theory for corrections programs, a cost-effectiveness measurement system for state social programs, and alternative policy-making strategies.

J. PATRICK HENRY is a Ph.D. candidate in sociology at the University of Massachusetts in Amherst. His current research is concerned with the impact of job transition and the quality of employment on the postrelease adjustment of ex-felons. Criminal justice, criminal recidivism, and the sociology of work are at the forefront of his substantive interests and professional curiosity.

MICHAEL J. HINDELANG received his doctorate in criminology from the University of California, Berkeley, and is currently Professor of Criminal Justice at the State University of New York, Albany. His research interests include criminal justice statistics and juvenile delinquency. He is the author of *Criminal Victimization in Eight American Cities,* coauthor of *Victims of Personal Crime: Toward a Theory of Personal Victimization,* and coeditor of the annual *Sourcebook of Criminal Justice Statistics.* His current research projects involve studying methodology of self-reported delinquency techniques, the utilization of criminal justice statistics, and various aspects of criminal victimization.

TRAVIS HIRSCHI is Professor of Criminal Justice at the State University of New York at Albany. He received his doctorate in sociology from the University of California, Berkeley, and has taught at the University of Washington and the University of California, Davis. His publications include *Causes of Delinquency,*

Delinquency Research, and, most recently with his coauthors of the chapter in this volume, "Correlates of Delinquency: The Illusion of Discrepancy Between Self-Report and Official Measures of Delinquency" in *American Sociological Review* (1979).

SOLOMON KOBRIN is Emeritus Professor in the Sociology Department, and Senior Research Associate at the Social Science Research Institute, of the University of Southern California. His research interests have centered around various aspects of the criminal and juvenile justice systems and on matters of theoretical perspective in the investigation of the causes of crime. His more recent work has focused on problems of program evaluation in the delinquency field.

BARRY KRISBERG is Research Director with the National Council on Crime and Delinquency and Director of the National Evaluation of Delinquency Prevention of the Office of Juvenile Justice and Delinquency Prevention. He received his Ph.D. in sociology from the University of Pennsylvania, has taught at the University of California at Berkeley, and has acted as project director of, or consultant to, several organizations concerned with criminal and juvenile justice, including the National Institute of Corrections, the California Youth Authority, and the National Institute of Standards and Goals for the Office of Juvenile Justice and Delinquency Prevention. His publications include *Pioneering in Delinquency Prevention: The California Experience* (1978, with Carolyn McCall and Judy Munson), *The Children of Ishmael: Critical Perspectives on Juvenile Justice* (1978, with James Austin), *Crime and Privilege* (1975), and *The Gang and the Community* (1975).

ALDEN D. MILLER is Associate Director of the Harvard Center for Criminal Justice and has been engaged in research and publication on the Massachusetts youth correctional system since 1970. He has taught sociology at Boston University and Indiana University. His doctorate in sociology is from the University of North Carolina at Chapel Hill.

STEPHEN J. MORSE is Professor of Law and Psychiatry at the University of Southern California Law Center, and Professor of Psychiatry and Behavioral Sciences at the USC School of Medicine. He received both the J.D. and the Ph.D. (in personality and developmental studies) from Harvard University. He specializes and has written extensively in the areas of criminal law and procedure, mental health law, and family law.

ILENE NAGEL is Associate Professor of Law at the Indiana University School of Law. Professor Nagel is the coauthor of *Academic and Entrepreneurial*

Research: The Consequences of Diversity in Federal Evaluation Studies and the editor of *Validity Issues in Evaluative Research.* Along with her several articles on evaluation methodology, she has published articles on sentencing, plea-bargaining and bail decisions in metropolitan, state, and Federal District Courts. Her current research (with John Hagan) is a study of bail, plea and sentencing decisions for defendants prosecuted in Federal District Courts.

LLOYD E. OHLIN is Roscoe Pound Professor of Criminology at Harvard Law School, and Research Director at Harvard Center for Criminal Justice. He has directed the Center's research on Massachusetts youth corrections. With Richard Cloward, he is author of *Delinquency and Opportunity.* He has served as Special Assistant on Delinquency to the Secretary of the Department of Health, Education and Welfare (1961-1962), and as Associate Director of the President's Commission on Law Enforcement and Administration of Justice (1966-1967).

LLAD PHILLIPS is Professor of Economics and Chairman of the Economics Department at the University of California at Santa Barbara. He received his Ph.D. from Harvard University. His research interests are in the economics of criminal justice, econometrics, and population economics. He is coeditor of and a contributing author to *Economic Analysis of Pressing Social Problems.* His recent work includes "Factor Demands in the Provision of Public Safety" in *Economic Models of Criminal Behavior,* and "Some Aspects of the Social Pathological Behavior Effects of Unemployment Among Young People" in *Legal Minimum Wages.*

ALBERT J. REISS, Jr., is the William Graham Sumner Professor of Sociology at the Institute for Social Policy Studies at Yale University. He also is a Lecturer at Yale Law School. He has served as a consultant to several U.S. commissions and, under presidential appointment, as a member of the National Advisory Commission on Juvenile Justice and Delinquency Prevention (1975-1978). The author of numerous scholarly publications, he is perhaps best known for his books, *The Police and the Public* and *Studies in Crime and Law Enforcement in Major Metropolitan Areas.* His work in *Social Characteristics of Urban and Rural Communities* and *Occupations and Social Status* reflects his broad range of interests in community and society.

PETER H. ROSSI is currently Professor of Sociology and Director of the Social and Demographic Research Center at the University of Massachusetts—Amherst. He has been on the faculties of Harvard University, Johns Hopkins University, and the University of Chicago, where he also served as Director of the National Opinion Research Center. He has been a consultant on research methods and evaluation to (among others) the National Science Foundation, National Institute of Mental Health, the Federal Trade Commission, and the Russell Sage Foundation. His research has largely been concerned with the application of social research methods to social issues and he is currently engaged in research on natural disasters and criminal justice. His most recent works include *Evaluation: A Systematic Approach (with W. Williams)*, Reforming Public Welfare *(with* K. Lyall), and *Prison Reform and State Elites* (with R. A. Berk). Professor Rossi is currently coeditor of *Social Science Research.* He is serving as President of the American Sociological Association for 1979-1980.

JAMES F. SHORT, Jr., is Director of the Social Research Center and Professor of Sociology at Washington State University, where he also served as Dean of the Graduate School from 1964 to 1968. He was an at-large member of the Council of the American Sociological Association from 1968 to 1970, and from 1978 to 1980 served as Secretary of that organization. He was Codirector of Research for the National Commission on the Causes and Prevention of Violence, and has been a member of review committees and a consultant to numerous governmental agencies. He was editor of the *American Sociological Review* and has served on the editorial boards of numerous other professional publications. His honors include fellowships from the Center for Advanced Study in the Behavioral Sciences, the John Simon Guggenheim Memorial Foundation, the Institute of Criminology and Kings College at Cambridge University, an honorary degree from Denison University, the Paul W. Tappan Award of the Western Society of Criminology, and the Edwin H. Sutherland Award of the American Society of Criminology, as well as numerous visiting professorships. He is widely published in the professional literature.

GEORGE SILBERMAN is a social scientist at the National Institute of Justice of the Department of Justice. In that capacity he has managed the Methodology Development Program for the last three years. Prior to coming to NIJ, he taught research methods courses at Brooklyn College and worked on several funded research projects, including a study investigating the impact of the decriminalization of public inebriation and an evaluation of a teacher training program. His training is in political science at the City University of New York, where he is currently a Ph.D. candidate.

RITA JAMES SIMON is Professor of Sociology, Communications Research, and Law, and Director of the Program in Law and Society, at the University of Illinois, Urbana-Champaign. She is the author or editor of seven books, including *Women and Crime, The Jury System* (editor), *Transracial Adoption,* and *Continuity and Change: A Study of Two Ethnic Communities in Israel.* She has also been editor of the *American Sociological Review* from 1977 to 1980.

CHARLES R. TITTLE completed his Ph.D. in sociology in 1965 at the University of Texas, Austin. From 1965 to 1970 he served on the faculty of Indiana University in Bloomington. Since 1970 he has been affiliated with Florida Atlantic University, where he is currently Professor and Chairman of the Department of Sociology and Social Psychology. His interest in deviance and social control is reflected in his numerous articles in the sociological and criminological literature and in his authorship of two books, *Society of Subordinates* (Indiana University Press, 1972) and *Sanctions and Social Deviance* (Praeger, 1980).

JOSEPH G. WEIS is Director of the Center for Law and Justice and Associate Professor of Sociology at the University of Washington. He is currently a coprincipal investigator with Michael Hindelang and Travis Hirschi on a project, funded by the National Institute of Mental Health, on the measurement of delinquency, which is described in the forthcoming book, *The Measurement of Delinquency by the Self-Report Method*. In addition, he is Director of the National Center for the Assessment of Delinquent Behavior and Its Prevention, funded by the Office of Juvenile Justice and Delinquency Prevention. His research interests include the measurement of crime, the role of adolescent social arrangements and peer influence on delinquency, projections of crime rates, and the relationship between criminological theory and research and criminal justice policy, planning, and programs.

ANN D. WITTE is Associate Professor of Economics at the University of North Carolina at Chapel Hill. Her research and teaching have concentrated in the areas of applied microeconomic theory and applied econometrics. Substantively, her research has been concentrated in the area of law enforcement and the administration of justice, land use, and housing. She has completed criminal justice evaluations using quasi-experimental designs, statistical designs and benefit-cost analysis. Her other work in the criminal justice area ranges from management consulting work and multivariate statistical modeling to work with various congressional committees and membership of the National Academy of Sciences' Committee on Law Enforcement and the Administration of Justice.

MARVIN E. WOLFGANG is Professor of Sociology and Law and Director of the Center for Studies in Criminology and Criminal Law at the University of Pennsylvania. He is a member of Phi Beta Kappa, received his Ph.D. at the University of Pennsylvania in 1955, is an elected member of the American Philosophical Society, and is President of the American Academy of Political and Social Science. He is a member of the Board of Directors of the International Society of Criminology, a Fellow of Churchill College, Cambridge University, England, and, most recently, the Lady Davis Visiting Professor of the Faculty of Law at Hebrew University, Jerusalem.

AUTHOR INDEX

SUBJECT INDEX

Abortion, 107, 413, 415, 419, 496
Accountability, 11, 12, 16, 53, 145, 147, 443, 583, 584
Acquittal, 243
Addington v. Texas, 339, 351
Addivity, 493
Adjudication, 435
Adlerian therapy, 131
Administrative Office of the U.S. Courts, 115, 371
Adversary system, 327, 331, 332, 334, 336, 337, 338, 340, 341, 342, 345, 346, 347, 349
Advocacy, 417
Age, 83, 100, 103, 106, 124, 128, 129, 155, 439, 474, 475, 476
Aggregate utility, 188
Aggregation, 182, 200, 201, 281, 282
Alcohol, 25, 27, 39, 277, 432, 546; see also drunk driving
Alcohol, Tobacco and Firearms Division (U.S. Department of the Treasury), 275, 277
Aliases, 101, 102
Alienation, 160, 445, 453
Allegheny County Regional Planning Council, 250
Amenability, 133, 134, 426
American Bar Association Commission on Correctional Standards, 252
American Correctional Association, 110
American Institute of Research, 263
American Justice Institute, 130
Amphetamines, 407
Analysis, bivariate, 48; cluster, 57, 622; cohort, 111; comparative cost, 459, 463; content, 33, 620-624; cost, 306, 444, 459, 460, 471; cost-benefit, 459, 461, 466, 468; cost-effectiveness, 282, 291; cost function, 462, 468; decision, 178, 179, 183, 202; discriminant, 265, 266; discriminant function, 69; economic, 406; experimental, 153; factor, 83, 622; frontier cost, 59; legal, 407; multiattribute, 181; multiattribute utility, 260, 282, 290-293; multiple regression, 66; multivariate, 107, 130; network, 58; ordinary least squares, 265-269; path, 33, 78; predictive attribute, 265; process, 292; regression, 65, 75; scientific, 407; structural equation, 85; substantive, 593; systems, 250, 327, 600; time-series, 240, 260, 273-278, 291; Tobit, 266; voting, 621, 622, 625
Analytical evaluation, 253, 260, 282-285, 287, 288, 290-293
Andresen v. Maryland, 349, 351
Annandale Reformatory, 438
Anomie, 25, 26, 514
Anonymity, 479
Anthropology, 138, 165
Applied science, 15, 123, 135, 137
Apprehension, 481
Argersinger, v. Hamlin, 350, 351
Arrest, 83, 84, 90, 91, 94, 98, 99, 101, 102, 103, 111, 112, 113, 114, 124, 168, 196, 224, 225, 242, 248, 249, 254, 374, 384, 416, 462, 497
Arson, 101
Assaults, 99, 101, 103, 107, 277, 428, 429, 476, 494, 496
Asylums, 150

Autocorrelations, 275
Automated Criminal Justice Information System Directory, 110